C0-AZQ-825

Contemporary Authors
Autobiography Series

ISSN 0748-0636

Contemporary

Authors

Autobiography Series

Adele Sarkissian

Editor

volume **6**

GALE RESEARCH COMPANY • BOOK TOWER • DETROIT, MICHIGAN 48226

EDITORIAL STAFF

Copyright © 1988 by Gale Research Company

Library of Congress Catalog Card Number 84-647879
ISBN 0-8103-4505-6
ISSN-0748-0636

Contents

Preface

Each volume in the *Contemporary Authors Autobiography Series (CAAS)* presents an original collection of autobiographical essays written especially for the series by noted writers. *CAAS* has grown out of the aggregate of the Gale Research Company's long-standing interest in author biography, bibliography, and criticism, as well as its successful publications in those areas, like the *Dictionary of Literary Biography, Contemporary Literary Criticism, Something about the Author, Author Biographies Master Index,* and particularly the bio-bibliographical series *Contemporary Authors (CA),* to which this *Autobiography Series* is a companion.

As a result of their ongoing communication with authors in compiling *CA* and other books, Gale editors recognized that these wordsmiths frequently had more to say—willingly, even eagerly—than the format of existing Gale publications could accommodate. Personal comments from authors in the "Sidelights" section of *CA* entries, for example, often indicated the intriguing tip of an iceberg. Inviting authors to write about themselves at essay-length was the almost-inexorable next step. Added to that was the fact that the collected autobiographies of current writers were virtually nonexistent. Like metal to magnet, Gale customarily responds to an information gap—and met this one with *CAAS.*

Purpose

This series is designed to be a congenial meeting place for writers and readers—a place where writers can present themselves, on their own terms, to their audience; and a place where general readers, students of contemporary literature, teachers and librarians, even aspiring writers can become better acquainted with familiar authors and make the first acquaintance of others. Here is an opportunity for writers who may never write a full-length autobiography (and some shudder at the thought) to let their readers know how they see themselves and their work, what carefully laid plans or turns of luck brought them to this time and place, what objects of their passion and pity arouse them enough to tell us. Even for those authors who have already published full-length autobiographies there is the opportunity in *CAAS* to bring their readers "up to date" or perhaps to take a different approach in the essay format. At the very least, these essays can help quench a reader's inevitable curiosity about the people who speak to their imagination and seem themselves to inhabit a plane somewhere between reality and fiction. But the essays in this series have a further potential: singly, they can illuminate the reader's understanding of a writer's work; collectively, they are lessons in the creative process and in the discovery of its roots.

CAAS makes no attempt to give an observer's-eye view of authors and their works. That outlook is already well represented in biographies, reviews, and critiques published in a wide variety of sources, including *Contemporary Authors, Contemporary Literary Criticism,* and the *Dictionary of Literary Biography.* Instead, *CAAS* complements that perspective and presents what no other source does: the view of contemporary writers that is reflected in their own mirrors, shaped by their own choice of materials and their own manner of storytelling.

CAAS is still in its youth, but its major accomplishments may already be projected. The series fills a significant information gap—in itself a sufficient test of a worthy reference work. And thanks to the exceptional talents of its contributors, each volume in this series is a unique anthology of some of the best and most varied contemporary writing.

Scope

Like its parent series, *Contemporary Authors,* the *CA Autobiography Series* aims to be broad-based. It sets out to meet the needs and interests of the full spectrum of readers by providing in each volume twenty to thirty essays by writers in all genres whose work is being read today. We deem it a minor publishing event that more than twenty busy authors are able to interrupt their existing writing, teaching, speaking, traveling, and other schedules to converge on a given deadline for any one volume. So it is not always possible that all genres can be equally and uniformly represented from volume to volume. Of the sixteen writers in Volume 6, about half are novelists and half are poets. Like most categories, these oversimplify. Only a few writers specialize in a single area. The range of writings by authors in this volume also includes books of nonfiction as well as work for movies, television, radio, newspapers, and journals.

Format

Authors who contribute to *CAAS* are invited to write a "mini-autobiography" of approximately 10,000 words. In order to give the writer's imagination free rein, we suggest no guidelines or pattern for the essay. The only injunction is that each writer tell his or her own story in the manner and to the extent that each finds most natural and appropriate. In addition, writers are asked to supply a selection of personal photographs, showing themselves at various ages, as well as important people and special moments in their lives. Barring unfortunate circumstances like the loss or destruction of early photographs, our contributors have responded graciously and generously, sharing with us some of their most treasured mementoes, as this volume readily attests. This special wedding of text and photographs makes *CAAS* the kind of reference book that even browsers will find seductive.

A bibliography appears at the end of each essay, listing the author's book-length works in chronological order of publication. If more than one book has been published in a given year, the titles are listed in alphabetic order. Each entry in the bibliography includes the publication information for the book's first printing in the United States and Great Britain. Generally, the bibliography does not include later reprintings, new editions, or foreign translations. Also omitted from this bibliography are articles, reviews, and other contributions to magazines and journals. The bibliographies in this volume were compiled by members of the *CAAS* editorial staff from their research and the lists of writings provided by many of the authors. Each of the bibliographies has been submitted to the author for review. When the list of primary works is extensive, the author may prefer to present a "Selected Bibliography." Readers may consult the author's entry in *CA* for a more complete list of writings in these cases.

Each volume of *CAAS* includes a cumulative index that cites all the essayists in the series as well as the subjects presented in the essays: personal names, titles of works, geographical names, schools of writings, etc. The index format is designed to make these cumulating references as helpful and easy to use as possible. For every reference that appears *in more than one essay,* the name of the essayist is given before the volume and page number(s). For example, W.H. Auden is mentioned by several essayists in the series. The index format allows the user to identify the essay writers by name:

Auden, W.H.
 Abse **1:**24, 31   Bowles **1:**86
 Allen **6:**18, 24   Burroway **6:**90
 Ashby **6:**36, 39, 43   Grumbach **2:**208
 Belitt **4:**60, 65   Howes **3:**143
 Bourjaily **1:**68   Jennings **5:**104, 110

For references that appear *in only one essay,* the volume and page number(s) are given but the name of the essayist is omitted. For example:

Stieglitz, Alfred **1:**98, 99, 104, 109, 110

CAAS is something more than the sum of its individual essays. At many points the essays touch common ground, and from these intersections emerge new mosaics of information and impressions. *CAAS* therefore becomes an expanding chronicle of the last half-century—an already useful research tool that can only increase in usefulness as the series grows. And the index here, for all its pedestrian appearance, is an increasingly important guide to the interconnections of this chronicle.

Looking Ahead

All of the writers in this volume begin with a common goal—telling the tale of their lives. Yet each of these essays has a special character and point of view that set it apart from its companions. Perhaps a small sampler of anecdotes and musings from the essays ahead can hint at the unique flavor of these life stories.

Dee Brown, describing his first meeting with Sherwood Anderson: "Over the years I read everything I could find that Sherwood Anderson published, and while I was living in Washington, D.C., during the 1930s, I finally met him . . . at one of those numerous little gatherings that were always being held for some burning cause or other in those yeasty days of the New Deal. . . . He had recently acquired two weekly newspapers . . . and when I found an opportunity to talk alone with him I said that my lifelong dream was to own a country weekly . . . . Alas, he had no magic formula for me to follow his example, but he invited me to visit his printing shop in Marion, and I later did so."

Nikki Giovanni, recalling the turbulent sixties: "When I enrolled in Fisk University . . . one of the things I most looked forward to was sitting-in. There was a sort of style to it. Assuming you weren't actually molested, it was cool. You sat on the stool and watched the white people panic. Dick Gregory has the best story. When he stopped at a diner the waitress said, 'We don't serve niggers'—to which Gregory replied, 'I don't eat them.' You always hoped someone would say something to you to let you be cool. Mostly you were scared."

Nat Hentoff, reflecting on his early infatuation with jazz: "When I was very young, I would slip into Sunday jam sessions and then into jazz clubs at night. At Boston Latin School, I hid *Down Beat* in my geography book; at Northeastern University, we talked of jazz, James Joyce, and Trotsky between classes; and at Harvard, I abandoned a scholarship in the graduate school because I realized one night, in Widener Library, that I was not going to be a professor . . . . There was a lot I liked in the academy—especially that library—but I didn't feel the academy had much joy in it or rage or intimate lyricism. It was all so well-mannered."

M.L. Rosenthal, ruminating on poetry and criticism: "Self-education has always been my instinctive critical purpose. It is inseparable from an almost helpless participation in any poem I read, as though I had merged with its author and were in some sense thinking my way into it once more. From one perspective, every poem is a draft that might have gone beyond its present point and might have been altered in some interesting way or other; and so we cannot respond fully to its quality, or respect its elastic integrity, without understanding the tentative nature of even the most accomplished writing."

Karl Shapiro, obliquely recounting his experience as a GI in World War II: "The poet wrote what was to be his most anthologized poem in afteryears, an elegy for a soldier who was killed, who died while he was watching, whose funeral he took part in. He was not a battle casualty, but the poet left that up in the air; he was an accidental death, maybe even a suicide. The soldier was cleaning his M-1 and it fired and struck him in the chest. Accident, suicide, battle casualty, it was neither here nor there; the poet saw his first dying, first death, first funeral—at the age of thirty . . . . It was not a flag-waving poem and it was not an anti-flag-waving poem, a hard balance which the poet always tried for, slipping from one side to the other while his balancing pole wavered."

These brief examples can only suggest what lies ahead in this volume. The essays will speak differently to different readers; but they are certain to speak best, and most eloquently, for themselves.

Acknowledgments

A special word of thanks to all the writers whose essays appear in this volume. They have given as generously of their enthusiasm and good humor as of their talent. We are indebted.

Authors Forthcoming in *CAAS*

Mulk Raj Anand (novelist, short-story writer, nonfiction writer, and critic)—As an eminent guide to the culture and life of India, Anand has increased the world's understanding of the great Asian subcontinent through such powerful books as *Untouchable* and *Confession of a Lover.*

R.H.W. Dillard (novelist, poet, critic, editor, educator)—Using techniques which have been termed "cinematic," Dillard presents a darkly comic picture of humanity in such unconventional works as *The Book of Changes* and *News of the Nile: A Book of Poems.*

Philip Jose Farmer (science fiction novelist and short-story writer)—A three-time winner of the Hugo award, Farmer introduced innovative themes and techniques to the sci-fi genre in works like his "Riverworld" and "World of Tiers" series.

Leslie Fiedler (critic, novelist, poet, editor)—Fiedler is one of today's most distinguished, and often controversial, literary critics. His well-known writings include *Love and Death in the American Novel* and *The Last Jew in America.*

Andrew Greeley (novelist, educator, editor)—A writer of numerous scholarly and popular articles, Greeley is a sociologist and a Roman Catholic priest whose views on sexuality, church leadership, and the role of religion in modern life have stirred controversy. He is also the author of best-selling novels like *The Cardinal Sins* and *Thy Brother's Wife.*

Donald Hall (poet, essayist, editor)—Praised for his skillful management of a wide range of poetic forms in verse collections like *Exiles and Marriages* and *Kicking the Leaves,* Hall has also written the engaging prose works *Ox-Cart Man* and *Fathers Playing Catch with Sons.*

W.P. Kinsella (short-story writer, novelist, educator)—Kinsella, who calls himself "an old-fashioned storyteller," is best known for his entertaining short-story collections *Dance Me Outside* and *Born Indian,* as well as his novels of the national pastime, *The Iowa Baseball Confederacy* and *Shoeless Joe.*

Harry Mark Petrakis (novelist, short-story writer, screenwriter, educator)—In such novels as *Nick the Greek, A Dream of Kings,* and the award-winning *Odyssey of Kostas Volakis,* Petrakis combines an enthusiasm for life with elements of classical tragedy in exploring the lives of Greek immigrants in America.

Rene Wellek (critic, translator, editor, educator)—A leading figure in contemporary literary criticism, Wellek believes that the study of literature should focus on the work itself and the world it creates. *Theory of Literature* and *A History of Modern Criticism* are among his most influential works.

11

Contemporary Authors

Autobiography Series

Walter Allen

1911-

Robin Adler

Walter Allen, 1960

During the past ten years, years in which I have been an invalid and therefore leading a secluded life, it has become clear to me that not only have my interests been predominantly literary but that my values are as well; and this regardless of what literary merit my works may have, which in the nature of things can only be minimal. It is common form to think that literature refers to life. I believe this myself, but I see that from childhood I have acted as though literature is more important and that life refers just as much to literature as otherwise. More exactly, though I have known others—factory life, newspaper life, academic life—life for me has always meant primarily the literary life, even in the days when I had no firsthand knowledge of it.

I can see how this came about. When I was seven or eight I was given *Robinson Crusoe* as a Christmas or birthday present, not, as I know from readings of Defoe's text, a too damnably abridged or bowdlerised version. Its effect on me was immediate. I became drunk on it. More accurately, it became my ambition to write *Robinson Crusoe*, and I wrote what seemed to me thousands of words in an exercise book in imitation of it. *Robinson Crusoe* still seems to me one of the seminal masterpieces of imaginative writing. More important in the present context, it showed me that when I grew up I must be a writer. I could conceive of no other destiny, even though my notions of what writers did or what they wrote was vague in the extreme.

There was nothing in my immediate family circle or in the environment which was its setting to suggest that writing was a natural activity. In fact, it was most unnatural. Living as we were in Birmingham, we were of the working class of the industrial West Midlands, traditionally workers in metal. I say traditionally, but the tradition didn't go back far. According to my father, my great-grandfather, earlier than whom there was no one to our knowledge, was born in a Black Country workhouse and put to work in the coalpits as a child. How he got to Birmingham I don't know, but my grandfather, who died before I was born, was a worker in metal there and by family legend a remarkably fine one, for he did things with aluminium, a metal only recently isolated, that had never been done until then. An outstanding craftsman, but with it illiterate; by the end of his life, apparently, he had managed to spell out the headlines in the local newspaper. All the same, with his skill at his trade, he should have been comfortably off as artisans went, but there were too many children in the family; I forget the precise number, but it was certainly more than a dozen. Moreover, weekends were a drunken orgy. My poor grandmother couldn't have got by without the Monday morning visit to the pawnshop.

There can't have been any books in Great-grandfather Allen's house; in ours, by the standards of the time, there were many, even though they were not such as to interest me. I remember several primers of algebra, geometry and trigonometry, some Ruskin, the first volume of *Capital,* books on economics and Plato's *Republic,* and as my father grew older the number of books on philosophy increased. He had had a year or perhaps eighteen months at a grammar school, the equivalent of an American high school. He became a diesinker, engraver and designer, and a craftsman famous in what was a local trade. His interests were bewilderingly wide; he plainly had too many for his own good. Some were related to his daily work, some to his zest for knowledge, and some, I fancy, to his sense of social obligation. Others, perhaps, were pursued just for the hell of it. There was his boxing, about which I can only speculate. As quite a young man, he had taken up youth work in the Birmingham slums. You must picture a very small man, not more than five-feet-two-inches high, mild in his disposition and visibly earnest, ripe, one might reasonably have assumed, for ragging, persecution. But Father knew something. He had learnt at his boxing club that no matter how small you are, if you know how to box you can hold your own with anyone who doesn't, however much bigger he may be. It was Father's practice to produce gloves and invite delinquent youths to have three rounds with him. One may imagine the glee with which they accepted the challenge, only to find out that they couldn't hit him and that he could make them appear clodhoppers, make them look foolish in the eyes of their fellows.

Then there was his conjuring. He was pretty good at it and much in demand at Sunday-school children's parties and the like. It was a hobby he indulged himself in with more and more reluctance as the years passed. I remember the occasions he went conjuring as times when one had to beware. They were times of bad temper, and one was likely to get cuffed if one got in his way.

But these were not serious pursuits, as his violin-playing was. He took lessons and practised assiduously all his life. He had a wistful—I can only think of it as a naive—dream of one day earning his living as a violinist. It was a dream not realised, which I can only think was merciful, for he didn't aspire to more than a place in one of the string quartets that dispensed music to go with cream buns in restaurants. After he retired he applied himself ardently to the craft of lens-grinding, which demands relentless patience. It was plainly a substitute for daily work, and it was an offshoot of his lifelong interest in astronomy. He had craved bigger and better telescopes than he could afford and in his retirement he planned to learn how to make one to his own requirements. He turned out dozens. All the neighbors' children brandished telescopes made by Father, and I remember how he turned the blitzes on Birmingham into a blessing for him. After raids, he went hunting for pieces of glass of a suitable size and thickness for grinding.

Lens-grinding was connected with another favourite pursuit of Father's. He had been an ardent student at evening classes of the university extension movement in Birmingham. First he had gone to economics classes to argue with the lecturer about Marx, and then a growing interest in philosophy took over. This became dominant as he grew older. Of all philosophers Spinoza was the one he found most sympathetic, and Spinoza, of course, had made a livelihood of lens-grinding.

I have said nothing of his watercolour sketches or of his photography. Nor have I mentioned his ceaseless quest for a religious belief that would satisfy him intellectually; he had begun as a Congregationalist, flirted for a time with High Anglicanism—for those were the days of Christian Socialism, which was invariably High Church—then with the Baptists, while in the end he settled uneasily for the Society of Friends, uneasily because so many Quakers are highly successful capitalists. Nor have I said anything about his passion for walking and for mountains; he celebrated his seventieth birthday with a final climb of Snowdon, Wales's highest and most formidable peak.

It isn't to be wondered at that my father was the greatest single influence on me, despite the fact that he showed no interest in literature as such. There were no novels in our house, and the only poetry was a copy of Burns bound in imitation red morocco, which I later found out was something almost obligatory in left-wing working-class households of those days. I don't remember him ever referring to or quoting from Burns, whose morals he would have found deplorable. I now have the feeling that imaginative writing was something he hadn't dared venture into lest it should take too great a hold on him, and I suspect he mistrusted fiction on good Puritan grounds. To my knowledge, he had never been to the theatre, and his visits to the cinema could have been counted on the fingers of one hand. Films, he once told me, he found "too real"; they disturbed him, I suspect, because of their rendering of sexual passion. Yet when I in my adolescence announced my intention of being a writer he did nothing to discourage me and took my statement seriously, as a being who recognised writing as a serious activity worthy of man's following.

There is another thing too. As a very young man, nineteen or so, he had gone to the United States, for the oldest of all reasons, to better himself. He had gone to Philadelphia, for that city too was a centre of the silversmith's craft. He didn't make his fortune, for he had discovered when he got there that the United States was in a period of intense industrial depression. Within eighteen months he was back in Birmingham. But his trip to America was the great adventure of his life. He never tired of talking about it, and he dreamed of seeing the United States again before he died. He didn't, but his adventure impelled me to see America for myself as soon as I could. Philadelphia wasn't my goal, though; for me, the great romantic places were Kansas City and Omaha, Nebraska.

When I was eleven I won a free place at the grammar school. For my first three years, I was constantly towards the bottom of the form. Then, by the school's standards, I was seen as brilliant in English. I was good enough in Latin and French and History and still among the bottom half-dozen in Mathematics, Physics, and Chemistry—out of sheer lack of interest as it seems to me now, because I wasn't stupid. From fourteen on, I led a sort of double life, that of a normal schoolboy and that, by analogy with a secret drinker, of a fiercely secret reader. My earliest literary heroes were Wells and Bennett, with Shaw, who seemed to me the wisest as well as the wittiest of men, following a little later. In two years I managed to see most of his plays from the galleries of local theatres. A year or so later, I discovered more closely contemporary authors, Hux-

The author as a young man

ley and Lawrence, the Sitwells and Graves, and Eliot. I was much too wary to let on about my private reading to my schoolmasters. I had heard one or two of them make snide remarks in class about the Sitwells and scoff at what they called Huxley's "cleverness": hearing them, I would smirk to myself, knowing that I knew better. I had begun writing myself; I was fifteen when I first appeared in print in a popular literary weekly. It was the great age of "appreciation," gossip about great men, the eccentric, the pathetic, the fallers-by-the-wayside. I found myself well equipped to deal with such, and within the next few months I had managed to sell half-a-dozen short articles of the kind and earned enough money to buy myself a secondhand portable typewriter; it lasted for years. Then I dropped writing these pieces; they were too easy, merely a trick of devising a formula and writing to it; though later, when I was trying to live on my writing, to my consternation I found I had lost the knack altogether.

Besides, most of my free time now was spent writing poetry, that together with an interminable introspective journal in which I tried to chart the course of my inner life. It took me years to realise the futility of introspection as aid to self-knowledge.

These journals were written in notebooks which disappeared many years ago. I am tempted to say "Thank goodness," though I regret the loss of the detailed lists of the books I was reading.

It is the index of my naivety and of my remoteness from spheres where writing was considered serious work for serious people that I believed all writers, irrespective of what they wrote, must have begun as newspaper reporters; I simply thought that newspaper reporting, on local weeklies especially, was the apprenticeship all writers had to serve. Accordingly, I applied to editors of the local papers in the district seeking a job. I didn't get one, but they all replied saying that the essential thing was to have good shorthand. I had no wish to learn shorthand and was saved from that fate when I was eighteen by being awarded a scholarship to Birmingham University. It tickles me to recall that I took it up almost *faute de mieux;* I thought of it merely as an extension of school; it would mean I would have to put off being a writer for another three or four years. I consoled myself with the reflection that I'd have to read Wordsworth and the English classics; I had nothing against them but I knew that left to my own devices I would have read nothing but contemporary stuff.

Of course, before the first day was out, I knew that university was nothing like school and university lecturers nothing like schoolmasters. I enjoyed my years at the university greatly. It was freedom; I made friends, wrote much bad verse for which the university magazine found space, and fell in love time and again, favouring girls who were in distant places in vacations and to whom I could write long letters reminiscent of the journals I had abandoned, letters in which one could boast without risk of having the bluff called.

I went down in 1932 with a pretty good degree in English and promptly set up my stall as a writer. It was another sign of my naivety. I had no conception of what I was letting myself in for; if I had had, I might well have been appalled and defeated by my own temerity. I knew no one, could bring to bear no influence on my behalf; Birmingham University was not Oxford or Cambridge, it was no springboard into writing. I had no private income, I had to make a living from my writing straightaway. This fact, as I see now, may well have been my salvation, and I did manage, which in retrospect seems rather remarkable, to keep myself by writing articles for the Birmingham papers, of which there were then at least half a dozen, and from children's stories which I sold and broadcast from the local BBC station. When I learnt that I was rather a good broadcaster I became more ambitious; I proposed a talk on young Midland writers and it was commissioned. I dealt with Auden and Day Lewis and the novelists Henry Green and John Hampson. All I knew of Green was that he was the son of someone who owned a foundry in Birmingham and that he had worked his way through it, and I knew that Green was not his real name. I admired *Living,* which still seems to me the best novel of factory life by an Englishman. Hampson I knew lived near Birmingham, and that was all.

In successive weeks I met Auden and Hampson, having sent them the script I was to broadcast. Auden was my hero; I admired him as I did Yeats and Eliot, and the marvellous thing was that he was only four years older than I was. He was teaching at a prep school in Herefordshire and invited me to meet him. His very position as the most famous young poet to have arrived since Rupert Brooke made him intimidating, and he must have found me naive to a degree. He questioned me, and I told him what I was doing and how it was my intention to review regularly for what were then called the sixpenny weeklies. He told me that was exactly what he wanted to do himself; I was chagrined: here he was, this brilliant poet who was revolutionising poetry, and not even he had achieved what I was dreaming of doing. What chance was there for me? I had spoken in innocence but I felt he must have found me pretentious. If he did he didn't say so. I told him of the novel I was writing. He said the only novels he enjoyed were novels that were light in tone; he could see that William Faulkner was a genius but could not read him. I left the Downs School, Colwall, with an assortment of books he lent me: *Ulysses,* which was still banned and I knew only by repute; Pound's *Cantos*—I was trying to write a study of Pound, which I had to drop because the *Cantos* defeated me; the latest volume of Graves; and the holograph manuscript of *The Memorial,* by his friend Christopher Isherwood, a name new to me and whose novel proved a seminal work as far as I am concerned, one of those one can use as a touchstone to gauge other men's works.

A week later, I met Hampson, whose first novel, *Saturday Night at the Greyhound,* had had a *succès d'estime* when it had appeared two or three seasons before from Leonard and Virginia Woolf's Hogarth Press, and whose second novel, *O Providence,* had recently been published. He had invited me over to dinner and arranged to meet my train. I had seen no photograph of him and was ignorant of his background and circumstances. When I got to the station I saw waiting on the platform a tiny figure with an underslung Hapsburg jaw and sitting on a bench behind him, a boy, or so I supposed, who should have been beautiful but was now grown fat and in a state of what I can only call deliquescence; he was making noises to himself. He was the half-wit Hampson looked after and in fact a year or two older than John, who was ten years older than I. We walked slowly the mile or so to the house that John's employers had retired to when they discovered their child was an idiot, John and I talking, Ronald, whom it was difficult not to think of as a child, frisking clumsily about us, mooing to himself and occasionally uttering "Cuckoo." We turned into a narrow, winding drive at the end of which was a half-timbered Elizabethan cottage of the sort Warwickshire is rich in; we were not, I suppose, a dozen miles from Stratford-upon-Avon, and one felt Birmingham was a long way off. John's employer was a Birmingham businessman, and he and his wife received me warmly; if one hadn't known otherwise, one might have thought that John was the much-indulged eldest son and not the male nurse of their son. The Wilsons were of nonconformist stock, dedicated, one would have guessed, to plain living and cautious thinking, but John's presence had made itself felt. While he was in their employ, they had seen him blossom into a distinguished author whose friends, men of the calibre of E.M. Forster and William Plomer, would come up from London to spend weekends with them. John had expanded their horizons, as was evident both in the books that were everywhere and in the meal we ate that evening.

After dinner, Mr. Wilson returned to the gardening which was his joy; Ronald the idiot youth was put to bed, and I joined John in his bedroom, a long narrow room which he was already converting into a kind of shrine to himself. He dominated the room: a portrait painting of him hung on one of the walls; there was a framed newspaper cartoon depicting him at a publisher's party with an outré figure who must have been Una, Lady Troubridge; on the chest of drawers were perched snapshots of John with the Woolfs, with Forster, with Plomer, with various Bloomsbury characters. And as soon as I saw the contents of his bookshelves I knew that this was the finest collection of contemporary novels I had encountered.

We were instantly friends and soon very close ones. John was of a well-known Birmingham family, which in his childhood had suddenly lost its money; this, and the fact that he was a sickly boy, meant that he had had little schooling; he was indeed largely an autodidact, and he was a man of strong idiosyncrasy: there were certain words he pronounced or mispronounced according to a system of his own—deliberately I am sure—and he always wrote in brown ink. During the war, at sixteen or so, he had run away from home and worked as a kitchen-hand in big

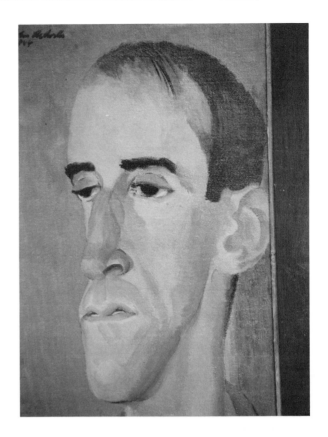

John Hampson (from a painting)

London hotels and as a billiard-marker in billiard saloons. For a time—and in its way this was appropriate, for I have never known a man to whom books meant more—he was a book thief. He was caught, brought up before a magistrate and served a term in jail. After this, he sought refuge in the provinces, was a barman in the remote Derbyshire inn which is the scene of *Saturday Night at the Greyhound,* and then became a waiter and later a chef in various hotels in the Midlands. How he came to the Wilsons I do not know, but it must have seemed to him an ideal job. Nor do I know how he came to writing, though by the time I met him one could say of him, in Henry James's words, that he was one of those who "was born a novelist, breathing, feeling, thinking, speaking, performing every action of his life, only as that votary." He was the first kind of the tribe I had met, and it should be noted that not all novelists, perhaps indeed few, are to be described in James's terms. I doubt if I was one myself though I thought I was and I found John's absorption in the novelist's art exemplary.

In 1935, the earliest of my ambitions was realised. I went to the United States, having been invited to lecture in the summer session of the University of Iowa by the Director of the School of Letters, Norman Foerster, who came to know of me through a friend. I was in Iowa City for three months, and my general condition can best be conveyed by a remark alleged to have been made about me by the novelist Vardis Fisher, who was on the campus. Fisher, a sardonic observer of the human scene, was reported to have said: "He's as happy as a kid in a candy store." I felt humiliated when this was told me, but looking back now it seems to me just. I was intoxicated by the novelty of it all, of Iowa, of summer schools, which were unknown in Britain. I was, literally, in a New World, more expansive, franker, less inhibited than the old one I had left. I didn't know that the atmosphere of summer sessions is invariably heady. I made friends, young men who were graduate assistants or assistant professors in the university or from other universities, in residence because they were taking credits in the summer school. I discovered creative-writing classes, conducted by a kindly old gentleman named Edwin Ford Piper and known as the "cowboy poet," where I read my stories. In that creative-writing class I met a woman with whom I fell in love, and what made it more romantic and thrilling was that she was married. I was living life but also fiction.

When the session ended I spent two weeks in Kansas City as the guest of a friend who had been in one of my classes. He had invited me the second morning the class met, something I still think could only happen in the United States. I went back to Iowa City to an apartment I had been lent till the new session began, and it was there I started to write the novel which was published later as *Innocence Is Drowned*. I was hoping for an appointment for the regular session, but it was not to be. By Greyhound bus I went to New York by way of Chicago, where I spent a week trying to get a job in broadcasting; in those days, English accents were not wanted. After five weeks in New York incipient poverty forced me back home. I crossed the Atlantic by freighter, which at that time was an incredibly cheap way of travelling, and arrived back in Birmingham with the equivalent of a dollar in my pocket.

I intended to go back to my free-lancing but within a week I had a job and a regular salary. In my university days, I had met a few newspaper men, one of whom, H.S. Cater, became a friend. He had abandoned his subeditor's job on a Birmingham paper in order to launch his own news agency and by this time had five or six young reporters working for him. He was a restless entrepreneur and when I got back from the States he suggested I should join him

as a feature writer. I was with him for eighteen months. When we shut up shop at five-thirty I stayed on in the office for an hour or two writing the novel I had begun in Iowa City. I finished it and dedicated it to Hampson. It wandered around the publishers for about a year until it found one willing to make an offer for it. This was Michael Joseph, who had just started his own firm. I gave up my job to go up to London to lead the literary life. I had already begun a new novel and was looking for reviewing. I got a little, though not enough to live on. I did get regular work of a sort. Edward J. O'Brien, an American expatriate who lived in London, where he edited an annual anthology of the year's best short stories, had recently been appointed story editor of Metro-Goldwyn-Mayer British Studios and he invited me to become one of his readers. It was miserably paid but enabled many young writers, Olivia Manning and Leslie Halward among them, to get by. The smallness of the fees we were paid was no fault of Edward's. I had met him two years earlier when he was running a magazine called *New Stories* to which I contributed. He was a generous man and went out of his way to help me. He had been in New York at the time I was there, and I had seen a lot of him; he had had me made a temporary member of the Harvard Club of New York, and in London he introduced me to people he thought would be useful and gave me lunch at the Cafe Royal once a month.

I saw a lot of MacNeice, who had taught me Latin at Birmingham University and who was now lecturing in London University, and of course a lot of Hampson when he was in London. It was through John that I met Graham Greene. I admired his novels with reservations, but the man himself I found the most intriguing person I had met. Today, he seems to me the best English novelist among my contemporaries. I greatly enjoyed the London ambiance, the sense one had of being at the heart of things. I had lodgings in Bloomsbury, and it pleased me to know that when I got off the last tube train at night I might run into E.M. Forster, who got off at the same stop since he lived in a square very close to mine. And I thought nothing of seeing T.S. Eliot, though I didn't know him—in pubs, post offices, at theatres, and on escalators at underground stations.

Innocence Is Drowned was published in 1938, had good reviews from people I respected, and sold negligibly. War broke out a year later, and I decided to write a third novel before I was called up, which I anticipated to be in May 1940. I don't think I was being melodramatic, for many of my generation thought similarly, but I took it as axiomatic that I should not survive; we had been brought up on tales of the mass slaughter in the trench warfare of the First World War. I finished the novel, which was called *Living Space,* a catchpenny title. It was not good; it was written in a hurry and to a formula that was none the better for being of my own devising. It was published in the autumn of 1940, by which time I'd thought I'd be in the army but instead was working to my great surprise in an aircraft factory near Bristol. I think I did a useful job but I can't say I enjoyed it much; though I had friends, I was out of my element and had, besides, the uncomfortable feeling that I was living in one of my own novels. That was a tribute, perhaps, to the accuracy of my imagination, for though I had had no experience of factory life I hadn't hesitated in setting scenes of factories in my novels. I know now how useful the time was, for I got from it knowledge I was able to draw upon in later work; it prevented my later fiction from being merely literary in the perjorative sense and set it in the context of common life.

Part of the dissatisfaction I felt came from finding myself unable to write. It wasn't for want of trying, but I was always defeated by the sense that there were more important things to do; as indeed there were. It took time to learn that life in wartime is a constant improvisation. Things became better when I moved my lodgings into central Bristol. I was thought daft, because Bristol was suffering what we thought was heavy bombing, but I wanted to be in action. I joined the Civil Defence Service as an air-raid warden, and writing could now be only an intermittent luxury, for most nights I was on duty for many hours. I was never in any great danger, though I was once blasted off the telephone switchboard by the explosion of a German bomb falling perhaps a hundred yards away. And, as an intermittent luxury, writing once again became possible and purposive, for John Lehmann invited me to write critical pieces for the magazine he had just begun, *Penguin New Writing.* I did not realise till much later that he'd sent my career off on a new, unexpected track.

In 1943 a man I had known slightly at Birmingham University, a highly qualified metallurgist who was now director of a research establishment in the field of aluminium alloys, invited me to join him; he was looking for someone who could turn technical accounts of the working of alloys into copy that could be read by workers in the aircraft industry on the factory floor. So I went back to Birmingham and wrote little books on such matters as the casting, forging, and fabrication of the aluminium alloys. They were, of course, anonymous. Whenever I could, I went to London, and I now had good reasons to go,

Walter Allen, 1960

Robin Adler

apart from the pursuit of pleasure. Some time before I had left Bristol, Louis MacNeice, who had become a features producer for the BBC, had recruited me as a writer of propaganda scripts.

It was on one of these weekend visits to London that I met the girl I married. She came from a background very different from mine, for she was a Wiltshire farmer's daughter. When we met she was a physiotherapist on embarkation leave before going abroad with the Red Cross Service. We were married three weeks after, and within days she was on her way to North Africa. She was abroad for the best part of a year.

Things were becoming easier; the Allies were plainly winning the war and Birmingham, where I was again an air-raid warden, was no longer being bombed. Though one was scarcely aware of it, normality, a peacetime life, was slowly taking over. And I now had reviewing, as much as I could cope with, for my critical articles in *Penguin New Writing* had been seen by literary editors who actually urged me to review for them. And I had taken up my old contacts with the BBC in Birmingham and was broadcasting again. Moreover, I was writing a new novel, which was published in 1946 as *Rogue Elephant,* not a good novel but valuable all the same because it was a break from the kind of fiction I had previously produced.

Peggy, my wife, came back from Italy and took a job in a Birmingham hospital. As soon as it was possible, we resigned our respective jobs and went back to London. Housing was very difficult to come by, but Michael Joseph lent me a flat above his trade department in Bloomsbury. This was in a five-storey Georgian house which had been badly shaken by bombs; the ground floor, which housed Joseph's trade department, had been repaired, and so had the flat, which was at the top of the building, no doubt at one time the servants' quarters. All the windows were out in the rooms between us and the ground floor, and the wind whistled through them, causing our carpet to ripple like a field of corn. It was one of the most bitterly cold winters of the century, and the flat was never really warm. I recall that one early evening our door bell rang and I descended to street level wondering who it might be because we had few visitors. It was an American naval officer, who had been a colleague at Iowa City. He had seen a review of mine in the *Spectator* and had tracked me down through the good offices of the paper. We asked him to have dinner with us—I remember that by a lucky chance, lucky because fish wasn't rationed, Peggy had bought some plaice. We ate huddled over the one-bar electric fire which was our only source of heat, our guest in his heavy service greatcoat. But he had come armed with a bottle of bourbon, which was a godsend, for hard liquor was almost impossible to obtain.

It was not the most comfortable of apartments, for among other things it was invaded by black rats, which though pretty, are never welcome because they are the plague-bearing variety. During the war years there had been a concentrated onslaught on the sewer rat in the interests of preserving food supplies; but when the sewer rat is driven out the black rat invariably takes its place. After a few months, again through Michael Joseph's kindness, we were able to move into a small modern flat in a mews off Gower Street, behind Bedford Square. It was ideal for two people, within walking distance of most of the theatres and of Soho and not two hundred yards away in one direction from the office of the *Spectator,* for which I was reviewing regularly, and in the other from Michael Joseph Ltd., whose literary adviser I became at about this time. *Rogue Elephant* was published in 1946, and with it I first acquired American publication. Around the same time, too, appeared a critical biography of Arnold Bennett and a short book

on the Black Country, which Peggy and I had walked over while staying with John Hampson.

London was exciting at this time. Bomb-scarred as it was, there was a sense of life burgeoning. Old friends were coming back from the services, new careers were under way on all sides. To me now, this sense of new life was especially evident in the theatre, for it was then that the most memorable season in modern theatrical history was mounted; one saw in succession the Royal Shakespeare Company, with its stars Gielgud, Richardson, Olivier, and Guiness, all in their prime, put on productions of both parts of *Henry IV, King Lear, Oedipus Rex,* and *Uncle Vanya.*

Our first child, a boy, was born, and then the flat was too small. We decided to move into the country, on the grounds that cities were not the places in which children should be brought up. But where could we move to? Everybody told us that houses for rent were impossible to find in the country, and we couldn't afford to buy. The luck I have always had with accommodation was with me, and we found a small Georgian house on the main street of Lydd, a little town in Romney Marsh, on the border between Kent and Sussex. At that time it was Lydd's distinction to be the smallest borough in England; it was one of the ancient Cinque Ports or, more accurately, a limb of one of them, New Romney. Four or five centuries ago, it had actually been on the sea, which had now receded. But until the eighteenth century it had been a great place for smugglers; there was said to be an underground passage from our garden to the shore, though if there was we didn't find it.

Romney Marsh was unlike any part of England that either of us knew. It was very flat, a country of great vistas and great skies, beyond the London commuters' belt and yet not more than seventy miles from the capital; I could be in Bloomsbury in three hours: James, Conrad, Ford Madox Hueffer, Stephen Crane, and Wells had all lived on it or near it, and so, more recently, had Richard Aldington and Elizabeth Bowen, for this was the territory of the Heccombs in *Death of the Heart.* As I walked along the shore east from Dungeness I liked to think that at any moment I might see coming down into the sea off the hotel at Greatstone the balloon of the first men in the moon coming back to earth. And particularly, when I looked out of the window of my front room on to Lydd High Street, I could not help but recall an anecdote Wells relates in his *Experiment in Autobiography* of how looking out of *his* window in New Romney he had seen approaching Henry James and Edmund Gosse, mounted on bicycles, coming to spy out the land and ascertain whether he needed help from the Royal Literary Fund; he didn't, for as he tells, he was making more than a thousand a year, which wasn't bad for an author around thirty in the early eighteen-nineties. I had worked it out that James and Gosse might well have used the road that passed my house on their way to New Romney for that memorable visit of inspection.

I had the best of two worlds, for I was in London often, sometimes for as many as three days in the week. For three months, during a period of internal change, I acted as assistant literary editor of the *New Statesman* and I was also in the BBC's weekly discussion programme called "The Critics," in which half-a-dozen people who had read a new book, listened to a new piece on radio, and seen a new play, a new film, and a new art exhibition, gave their views on them. It was stimulating to take part in, and I was in the programme for spells of six weeks at a time for nearly twenty years, dropping out for a year when in 1952 I was invited to review books on the air every Sunday afternoon. The programme was called "Talking of Books," which defines what I was asked to do. I was not ordered necessarily to review new books; I had *carte blanche* to talk about well nigh anything that appealed to me in the way of books. For someone like

myself it was an ideal assignment, one I consciously used to propagate my own tastes and discoveries.

It brought me into contact with one of the most remarkable men of the century, Wyndham Lewis. I thought him as original a master of English prose as any in the language and knew, if no one else spotted it, he had affected my use of it. What especially intrigued me was the way he seemed to transform human beings into mechanisms; this is most apparent in his earlier works and is the verbal counterpart of his vorticist paintings and drawings, for he was as distinguished in the graphic arts as he was as a writer. But his fascination for me was not only literary; it was the fascination held by someone at extreme odds to oneself. My social and political beliefs were liberal and social democratic, his authoritarian and dogmatic; he was commonly called a fascist. If he was a fascist he was one of great intellectual power and wide range of reading, which made him the most formidable critic of everything I stood for. It happened that a new edition of his novel *Revenge for Love* had just appeared, together with a new polemical work, *The Writer and the Absolute*. It would have been cowardice not to have tackled them, and it seemed to me their appearance gave me the perfect opportunity to come to terms with the puzzled fascination he exercised on

Interviewing Aldous Huxley for the BBC program "London Echo," 1961

me.

What follows was something I hadn't dreamed of: it was a letter from Lewis forwarded by the BBC thanking me for what I had said about him and urging me to come to his studio one Sunday evening after broadcasting and have a drink.

When I met him, Lewis was already almost blind. He sat in his wooden armchair like a sightless Buddha. Still, I could not fail to be reminded of Kerr-Orr's description of himself in *A Soldier of Humour:*

> I am a large blond clown, ever so vaguely reminiscent (in person) of William Blake, and some great American boxer whose name I forget. I have large strong teeth which I gnash and flash when I laugh. . . . My body is large, white and savage. . . . It still looks like a visigothic fighting-machine, but it is really a laughing machine. . . . Everywhere where formerly I would fly at throats, I now howl with laughter.

There follows the highly significant

> This forked, strange-scented blond-skinned gutbag, with its two bright rolling marbles with which it sees, bull's-eyes full of mockery and madness, is my stalking-horse. I hang somewhere in his midst operating it with detachment.

The passage is not only a splendid example of Lewis's prose but a statement of how he saw himself.

I went to meet him not knowing what to expect, for I knew no one who knew him. I was prepared to be terrified, for legends had accreted about him. He was said to be paranoid. He was acerbic, but he had a mellowness I hadn't anticipated. He struck me as a very formal man, and he treated me with old-fashioned courtesy. Though the prodigality of his talents had always been recognised, his career both as writer and draughtsman had been attended by rebuffs and disasters. Part of his difficulties, it seems to me, stemmed from his origins. What was he? He had been born on a yacht in the Bay of Fundy, off the coast of Nova Scotia, the son of a professional soldier of Canadian stock who had fought on both sides in turn in the American Civil War. Lewis himself had been brought to England as a child and educated at Rugby and the Slade without, it seems to me, ever having been wholly assimilated into the English upper-middle class. After the Slade, he had been an art student in Paris and in Germany, and the tenor of his mind and his ways of thinking were derived from the French; he felt impatience with English habits of mind, English intellectual rigour (or lack of it),

English distrust of extremes, English faith in compromise as a virtue.

It was at a dinner I had with him some weeks later that what he had in mind became clear. It was that I should write a book on him. I realised that I had been caught up in what I can only call the Lewis machine. I doubt whether he had heard of me before my broadcast, and he counted the *New Statesman* as one of the foremost of his persecutors, but he seemed to trust my good faith to the point, I couldn't help thinking, of credulity. I was flattered by his seemingly unreserved acceptance of me. I warned him I wouldn't be able to start the book for two years at least, for I was already at work on *The English Novel,* which had to take priority over everything else. I signed a contract for the book with Lewis's publisher, but the book was never written, for after his death, it was to be a biography, which was fatal. I saw it asked for more time and effort than I could afford, for it would involve me in major research, while at the same time I knew I would be working against the grain, for I had to realise that Lewis's mode of thinking was so foreign to my nature that in the end there would be no way of reconciling myself with it.

I am glad to have met him, for he was one of the two unquestionable men of genius I have known, the other being Wystan Auden. There was little intellectual sympathy between them, but each admired the genius of the other.

These immediate postwar years were rich in events for me. In 1950 the British Council invited me to undertake a lecture tour of Czechoslovakia. It was my first visit behind the Iron Curtain and deeply shaking. I remember Prague as the most beautiful city I have been in and can only wish that I had known it in happier times. During these years, our family increased; first a girl and then a boy were born. For health reasons we moved from Romney Marsh to Devon, though I was in London as often as before. My fifth novel, *Dead Man over All,* appeared in 1950; it still seems to me one of the best novels about factory life in the British part of the English language. Four years later, *The English Novel* was published, and it was like a dead weight being lifted off me, for it had been seven years in the making. I was reading for it as I was writing it, which accounts, I think, for the freshness of judgement people tell me still marks the work, for I was writing as though the books I was treating were new to me, fresh from the press, as indeed many were. It has remained in print ever since publication, which is gratifying though surprising, for I know how dated, how much of their times, the views expressed must be. In these days, I am staggered at the amount of work I managed to get done, for besides this monstrous book I was reviewing and broadcasting regularly. But the novels I'd always assumed I would write went to the wall. My enthusiasm for the form had landed me in the position of being regarded not primarily as a writer of novels but as a critic of them. A poor exchange.

In 1955, I was invited to be visiting professor for a year at Coe College, Cedar Rapids, Iowa. That I happened to be returning to Iowa and to a place less than twenty miles from Iowa City, was accidental. My name had been suggested to the college by an Americanist who thought well of my reviews. I had visited the place in 1934 once or twice from Iowa City; they were connected, I remembered, by an interurban railroad, a tramcar in British English. By 1954 that had long gone, the permanent way, and the tracks pulled up. Cedar Rapids had become different from how I recalled it, much bigger, with a population of more than seventy thousand and its economy no longer geared to local agricultural products and needs, for it had become a centre of the new projectiles industry. Everything in Iowa City in my time had been dependent on the university; Iowa City was as much a university town as Cambridge and much more so than Oxford. By contrast, Coe College, with its student body of rather less than a thousand, had to exist in a nonacademic environment. Most of my colleagues, I think, felt themselves beleaguered, however much they sought to identify themselves with the city, whether through work with the Community Chest, membership of Rotary, the Kiwanis, the Elks and the Lions, or through their churches, for affiliation with a religious body was all but obligatory. As for me, the tone of the United States was much less pleasant and congenial than it had been in 1935, when depression ruled and poverty was incipient. Senator McCarthy had only recently lost power, and his spirit, repressive, vindictive, little-minded, still lingered. I found this when teaching American literature. One of the texts I was discussing was Thoreau on civil disobedience. There was no student who sympathised with Thoreau. He was obviously a Commie bastard who got no more than he deserved. I made it clear that I found that unworthy of a nation born of a revolution and believing, in the words of the Founding Fathers, that all men are endowed by their creator with certain unalienable rights, among them life, liberty, and the pursuit of happiness. I don't know whether any of them took to the point; most likely they thought I was a Commie bastard too.

Still, I enjoyed my year at Coe College, liked my colleagues, with some of whom I remain in touch, and found teaching pleasurable. And I was enabled to do

myself personal favours by discovering American poetry from Frost onwards and sketching out the novel published in 1959 as *All in a Lifetime*.

Back home I resumed my work with the *New Statesman*, Michael Joseph, and the BBC. I was also—obviously I had learned nothing from writing *The English Novel*—launched on a new project, a book on the course of the novel since 1914. I felt it couldn't be an arduous task, since I had been reviewing new fiction continually since 1945; it hadn't dawned on me that a reviewer who reviews novels only once a month, as I did, sees only a quarter of his possible material, which meant I had a great deal of reading to make up. The book had also to take in the contemporary American novel, which I knew less well than the English.

I hoped, when I joined the *New Statesman* as literary editor in 1959, to have more time for the book. I had achieved another ambition, one I had had since adolescence; besides, it was supposed to be a part-time job. I discovered that no job which is engrossing and to be taken seriously can ever be part-time. I lasted for four years. By then, the book, *Tradition and Dream*, was with the publisher.

In 1963, an American friend, W.K. Rose, who taught at Vassar College in New York State, suggested that I should take his place while he took a sabbatical year. I did so, and it was a most enjoyable experience. I found the whole emotional climate of America changed; the days of McCarthy were long over, and we were in the period when the major political issue was the campaign for civil rights. And then Poughkeepsie, where Vassar is located, is only sixty miles from New York City, whither I repaired most weekends, to the Players on Gramercy Park, a part of the city I grew especially fond of, with its literary associations with Washington Irving and one of the best restaurants in New York, Luchow's, just round the corner on Fourteenth Street. I liked my students, who were all talented young women, and had firm friends who are still friends on the Vassar faculty. While at Vassar I wrote for the *New Republic*, the *New York Times Book Review*, and the newly founded *New York Review of Books*, and I had time to travel in the States, to revisit Cedar Rapids, and give lectures at the Universities of Illinois and of Kansas.

Three years later, I went out to Kansas for a semester as a visiting professor, and this time my wife and youngest child were with me. The little girl had the time of her life. She settled in at the local school, pledged allegiance to the flag each morning and within a week had an authentic Middle-West accent, which she lost in a similar time when she returned to England. My wife and I, though, both felt we were a

Mark Gerson

The author in 1965

very long way from home and found orientation difficult. Kansas University is good, but I have to admit I found the state of Kansas itself a nowhere state, identityless; my colleagues too for the most part didn't seem to know where they were. Some adopted Eastern Seaboard values, others were geared to San Francisco. They were tugged in both directions, but judging from the poets visiting the campus, and there was one almost every week, California, the Beats, and the Black Mountain prevailed.

It was quite otherwise in the State of Washington, where I went after Kansas to teach in the summer session at the university at Seattle. I could feel I was in a region vibrant with a sense of its own life, its own identity. I knew that, in American terms, California wasn't far away, but I found no influence of San Francisco, except perhaps in the presence of the flower children who occupied one corner of the campus; rather, there was strong opposition to California and San Francisco, which was Seattle's great rival as a port. I had the strongest feeling that the next state, the nearest state, was Alaska, where it seemed that everyone in Seattle had been, and the next country Japan.

It was while I was in Seattle that I had a letter, forwarded from home, from the vice-chancellor of the New University of Ulster asking if I was interested in being considered for the Chair of English there. It was a university I had not heard of; in fact, it was a university in process of becoming. I decided I was interested; for some time, I had been weary of living on my wits, which is what every free lance must do, weary of the incessant grind to deliver copy on time, weary of the incessant struggle to find new ideas. The notion of living in Ulster had no great appeal to me, but I reflected that the province couldn't be further from London than Kansas was.

I was appointed. I can't say I was enamoured of Ulster, and often I felt as far away from London as I had done in Kansas. Very early on, I picked up the evening paper and read the letters to the editor with a feeling of *déjà vu;* I might have been back in Kansas, with the difference that there the letters to the editor would have been about the iniquities of Communists while here they were about the wickedness of Roman Catholics.

That was in 1968, the university was to open its doors to the first intake of students in the autumn. I had to devise a syllabus against that time; my life as a writer was ended, or at least writing had to take a poor second place. I had done nothing like compiling syllabuses before and found I had definite ideas of how English should be taught. I acquired a staff that was happy to humour me. When teaching began, the air of exhilaration was infectious; there was a sense of us all being freshmen together, undergraduates and faculty alike. Those early years were good years; and then the Troubles got worse. Students were unwilling to come from England; the university building was liable at any moment to be evacuated because of bomb threats. Nevertheless, I believe we did good work.

I was a professor at Ulster for five years, not quite in a solid block of time, because I was granted a session's leave of absence in 1970 because I had been invited to be Berg Professor of English for the year at New York University. My association with NYU began in my Vassar days when the English faculty at New York entertained me to lunch, and I gave a lecture to the graduate students. I had found a firm friend in the poet and scholar M.L. Rosenthal, who was responsible for my being invited to the Berg Chair. An apartment in Greenwich Village went with the chair, and Peggy and I spent a very happy nine months there, exploring Manhattan and entertaining friends and being entertained by them. When my stint at NYU ended I went up to Toronto University for the summer session. Again I had good students, and the time passed very agreeably. What surprised me was the difference in life between Canada and the United States; in Toronto one was conscious of the nearness not of England but of Scotland.

By 1973 my itchy feet prevailed again, and I resigned my chair at Ulster; five years are quite long enough in any job. I took up a visiting professorship at Dalhousie University, Halifax, Nova Scotia, where again I was conscious of a bedrock of Scotland beneath my feet and also of strong links with the British royal family. This surprised me until I learned that Queen Victoria's father had been commander-in-chief there and that the Queen had given the city gifts of land. And Halifax lived up to its royal past, a notably handsome city with the Citadel, a fine eighteenth-century fort, towering above it.

From Halifax, I went on to be C.P. Miles Professor at Virginia Polytechnic Institute and State University at Blacksburg. Again it was a new scene for me, as the American South was unknown to me, and the feel of life was different from anything I had come across in the States before, even though Blacksburg was not in patrician Virginia of the Tidewater but in the Appalachians close to the West Virginia line. Life seemed more relaxed than elsewhere, and speech slower; the flag of the Confederacy was visible everywhere; and the Mecca we turned to was not New York, perish the thought, but Atlanta, Georgia.

I was curious to know something about the C.P. Miles whom my chair was named for. I discovered that he had been professor of German but had first arrived at Blacksburg as football coach. It amused me to think I might reverse the process and when I was no longer professor become a football coach.

It was not to be. On the eve of the new session of 1975 I was struck down. Peggy had to fly out to get me back to London. It was the end of my active life but not my writing. Since the visitation I have published three more books, *The Short Story in English;* my literary memoirs, *As I Walked Down New Grub Street;* and *Get out Early,* the first novel I have written for seventeen years. At the time of writing, it is just out, and I do not know how informed opinion regards it. I am pretty satisfied with it at the moment, though if it came my way for review I could write a pretty hostile notice of it.

But I found it great fun to do. That, I admit, is irrelevant; fun could quite easily be tantamount to self-indulgence. *Get out Early* could, I think, be described as Arnold Bennett mediated through Christopher Isherwood. What especially fascinated me in the writing was to see how much my idea of the novel as a form had changed. I realised how utterly, when writing of it, I had failed to take into account

The author today

the part played in it by the romance. I had seen the novel and the romance as antithetical, the triumph of either being death to the other. I know now I was wrong. The romance is a necessary element in any novel, no matter how realistic. Indeed, any successful novel, I think, can be reduced to the fairy tale that it enshrines.

Which means that the novel is a poetic form, making use of all resources of poetry except metre, and like poetry it is always ambiguous, Janus-faced, showing the impossibility of any one fixed interpretation of experience. It is concerned with emotional truth, the supreme aim of its being.

But I am much too old to profit by these new insights into fiction, for I am unlikely now to write another novel.

BIBLIOGRAPHY

Fiction:

Innocence Is Drowned. London: M. Joseph, 1938.

Blind Man's Ditch. London: M. Joseph, 1939.

Living Space. London: M. Joseph, 1940.

Rogue Elephant. London: M. Joseph, 1946; New York: Morrow, 1946.

The Festive Baked-Potato Cart and Other Stories (for children). London: Muller, 1948.

Dead Man over All. London: M. Joseph, 1950; also published as *Square Peg.* New York: Morrow, 1951.

All in a Lifetime. London: M. Joseph, 1959; also published as *Threescore and Ten.* New York: Morrow, 1959.

Get out Early. London: Robert Hale, 1986.

Nonfiction:

The Black Country. London: Elek, 1947.

Arnold Bennett. London: Home & Van Thal, 1948; Denver: A. Swallow, 1949.

Reading a Novel. London: Phoenix House, 1949; Denver: A. Swallow, 1949.

Joyce Cary. London and New York: Longmans, Green, 1953.

The English Novel: A Short Critical History. London: Phoenix House, 1954; New York: Dutton, 1955.

The Novel Today. London: Longmans, Green, 1955.

Six Great Novelists: Defoe, Fielding, Scott, Dickens, Stevenson, Conrad. London: Hamish Hamilton, 1955; Belfast, Me.: Bern Porter, 1985.

George Eliot. New York: Macmillan, 1964; London: Weidenfeld & Nicolson, 1965.

Tradition and Dream: The English and American Novel from the Twenties to Our Time. London: Phoenix House, 1964; also published as *The Modern Novel in Britain and the United States.* New York: Dutton, 1964.

The Urgent West: An Introduction to the Idea of the United States. London: J. Baker, 1969; also published as *The Urgent West: The American Dream and Modern Man.* New York: Dutton, 1969.

The Short Story in English. Oxford, England: Clarendon Press, 1981; New York: Oxford University Press, 1981.

As I Walked down New Grub Street: Memories of a Writing Life. London: Heinemann, 1981; Chicago: University of Chicago Press, 1982.

Editor of:

Writers on Writing. London: Phoenix House, 1948; also published as *The Writer on His Art.* New York: McGraw, 1949.

Transatlantic Crossing: American Visitors to Britain and British Visitors to America in the Nineteenth Century. London: Heinemann, 1971; New York: Morrow, 1971.

The Roaring Queen, by Wyndham Lewis. London: Secker & Warburg, 1973; New York: Liveright, 1973.

Cliff Ashby

1919-

Cliff Ashby at Heckmondwike, 1986

I suppose I am impeccably working class. My paternal grandfather was a cobbler, although he preferred to be called a shoemaker, for had he not served an apprenticeship at his trade! It didn't make the pay any better but it made for a more comfortable poverty. My memory of Grandma and Grandad begins with their caretaking at a Primitive Methodist chapel in Harrogate, their home town. Their end was my beginning, for it was the last employment they held before retiring.

They always seemed reasonably comfortable, food was always sufficient. Surrounded by their bits and pieces of furniture, the family, or some of them, living in the same street, they retired fairly pleased with themselves and their lot. They were the crude, nonconformist side of my antecedents; given to the amusing fart, delighting in my unbuttoned fly, and the possibility of "my horse" coming out of its stable. They were not very disciplined themselves, and their attempts to temper my exuberance were mainly in the form of "policemen coming round the corner" or "a blackman waiting on the stairs." Warm-hearted people: who knows what private dreams of a more delicate society washed around in their sleep? Certainly they were ambitious for the family, especially the boys, and their dreams were probably fulfilled by them to some degree.

Uncle Willy and my father were recruited into the ranks of the lay preachers when they were little more than boys. Indeed, Uncle Willy was billed as "the boy preacher" in the Harrogate area, a little like a performing seal. He was a modest man, shy and self-effacing. In contrast my father was vain and outgoing. Dad had this fine opinion of himself, but it didn't go very deep, and it was necessary for it to be reinforced from week to week. A "splendid sermon, Mr. Ashby," assured us of a peaceful and well-digested lunch. Eventually, though he never went through theological college, he became a fully fledged Primitive Methodist minister, and this was more than most barber's assistants and telegraph boys could reasonably have expected. It was an uneasy, and somewhat unhappy realisation of his ambitions, for it took him away from his working-class roots into an area of mild refinement that he was uncomfortable in. Being the youngest child, and spoilt, meant that he was not used to being polite when he didn't feel like it. He had not very much experience of the way of compromise, and if he didn't get his own way he could become petulant and inclined to rudeness. But perhaps the most difficult problem he faced was the constant demand on his brains. Writing sermons demanded he closeted himself in the study, or some area of the sitting room set aside for composition, and punished his brains. It also denied him the admiration of his cronies, the garage hand and the shop assistant.

When I was a young man, my heart was not touched by his childishness, and early loss of ambition. Not until his last days did I really love and respect him, for he squandered his gifts without seeming to be aware that he had any, or foolishly thought they could be kept alive without any effort on his part.

My maternal grandfather died when he was about forty. He was a farm labourer originally, but he

Young John Clifford Ashby, about 1923

suffered from asthma so severely, he had to leave the land, and moved into the north of England where he became a signalman on the railway. My mother was born near Stockton-on-Tees. Her memory of Grandad was very limited, so details of his character and presence were not passed down to me, or if they were I was not attentive to them. She had three sisters and a brother, and Grandma brought them all up in a boarding house in Harrogate, where they lived in respectable poverty. In one of the rooms was a portrait of Grandad looking down at the family with some solemnity. He was a gentle man, and certainly his eyes confirmed this. His face was covered with a fairly fierce beard, the sort of accoutrement weak men tend to wear to disguise their weakness, but I only guess this from my own.

There was certainly nothing weak about Grandma. She had an immense, moral presence that quite terrified me, as I suspect it did even the most innocent. There was little, if any, trace of a northern accent in her speech. She had a refinement, which she passed on to her children, that was absent from the Ashbys. While they displayed the crudity of nonconformity, she had some of the grace of the Book of Common Prayer, being a member of the Church of England, and never succumbing to the unhealthy

passions that drew her children to more unorthodox sects! This confused me as a child, for as far as I know she came from a working-class background. Certainly she suffered from the grinding poverty and cultural death that most of the working class of that time had to bear. She seemed content to suffer these things, her eyes fixed on a Heavenly mansion. She belonged to the teeming millions I identify myself with, often, it must be said, without a great deal of pleasure. The masses, who willingly die for their betters when asked to. Who down the ages have been robbed of their homes and their imagination; driven from the land into the dreadful cities to create wealth for their superiors. Ancestors who lie in unmarked graves; anonymous men and women whose bodies fertilise this beautiful land of England. The landowners, even if they can't take it with them, at least ensure it remains in the family, a mark of their continuing existence on the face of time.

Obviously my mother had a complex background. She rarely talked of her childhood. Now, when I sit down to write something about her early days, I find I know little. Was she happy as a child? I don't know. At that time they didn't so easily assume that one had a right to happiness. Like everyone else, she accepted the life that appeared before her from day to day, and that had to be lived. Was she good at school? Nothing she ever said leads me to believe she had a high opinion of herself as a scholar. Her greatest pride seemed to be in working her way from a junior assistant, at the Scotch Wool and Hosiery Store, to the position of manageress. This triumph, and the pleasure her success brought her, was retailed to me time and time again. Perhaps the high spot of her employment was the holiday her employers gave her in Scotland, her only excursion out of England that was purely for leisure, and what she used to believe was the reward for service. Being wanted was an enormous boost to her confidence. Marriage didn't give her this; on the contrary her independence was forfeited and her personal ambition destroyed. I doubt if she really wanted to be a clergyman's wife. She was shy, awkward in the presence of chapel folk, though in her later years she managed a little better. She was one who stood at the back, or was in the kitchen making sandwiches. Watching her over the years, one was forced to the unhappy conclusion that neither her husband nor her children compensated her for the loss of a career. What a small fire the wool shop was to warm her through all the awfulness of living.

I started my schooling at Brudenall Road School, Leeds, in the West Riding of Yorkshire. It was a

Brother, Norman Ashby; Grandad John Ashby;
Grandma Sarah Ashby; John Clifford Ashby

monstrous, red-brick building surrounded by what seemed like acres of concrete playground. This in turn was enclosed by mean back-to-back houses. Yet, on a spring Monday morning, with the sun shining, and a breeze stirring the filthy city air, the washing made a brave and beautiful show stretched across the cobbled back streets.

At that time school didn't intimidate me very much. As the teachers treated me kindly, I must assume that they were satisfied with my work and behaviour. I graduated from the chalk and board to pen and paper, with no more blemishes than anybody else. My form mistress was a Miss Pickering; she had soft eyes, and I thought her beautiful. Of course, I fell in love with her, so I must have been a fairly normal little boy at that time. As always, there was some bullying. Boys with fleet feet chased me home, while I laboured under the disadvantage of leaden boots. I had two recurring nightmares. One found the world expanding, the walls and buildings growing larger and farther away while I grew smaller and more fearful. The other found me in a dark tunnel, the

womb, perhaps, which was contracting and squeezing me with its muscular walls. The night-light was little comfort when one was confronted by these two monsters.

Life was by no means unhappy. I became very friendly with a policeman's son; he lived in a house that smelt of linoleum, polish, and malt extract. Outside the moral constraints of the house, I discovered that girls were of a different physical structure from myself. This in an old Victorian wardrobe, with the stuffy smell of furs, tweeds, dust, and the sweaty smell of young lust.

Obviously I was not observing my parents very carefully. One day, coming into the house from play, I saw Dad threatening Mother with a carving knife. I remember it was a lovely summer day, and the carnations were out in the front garden. Quietly closing the door, I wandered in a panic, back into the sunny street and my civilised scooter. This sad tale is probably part of most children's childhood in some degree. Pushed away into a corner of the mind it emerges in adult life making one wonder if it was true, or merely another nightmare.

Not surprisingly, we were soon on the move again, this time to the Isle of Man. Our destination was a tiny fishing village on the west coast of the island, Peel, another name for paradise. If peace of mind was something you were really interested in, nowhere could you stand a better chance of finding it than in Peel. In the neck of the Irish Sea, between Scotland, Ireland, and England, warmed by the Gulf Stream, able to sustain palm trees, it was a boys' heaven.

My new school seemed to have the sound of poverty built into its name, the Peel Clothworkers School, and not the sign of a clothworker in sight. The headmaster was a bulky man who wore steel-rimmed glasses and an air of menace. His navy serge suit shone with age and morality. His black shoes had round, stubby toes. One could not really imagine that he cared for children all that much, and perhaps the fearful stories of his disciplinary methods were true. If we felt any affection for him it was due to his rumoured brutality.

"Comeovers," as we who moved from the mainland to the island were called, were generally, and perhaps intellectually and morally, inferior to the standing incumbents. Just as to the Englishman the Scot is mean, the Irish simple, and the Welsh crafty, the Manxman too had these insular misconceptions. So it should have been no surprise when my new teacher on discovering that I could not do "joined up" writing, spoilt my first morning by milking this fact for all he was worth. And there you are, I was told to get on as best I could, and left to my own devices. Even to this day I can't write decently.

By this time I was enjoying the literary excitements of the *Rainbow* and *Tiger Tim.* Hey: just a minute, hang on there. Just a cotton-picking minute! Here I am revelling in the delights of the written word, and nothing has been said about the tedium of learning to read it. Well, it does strike me as odd, but I don't remember anything of the "learning to read" process; neither does Ann, nor do any of my children. By what process it became part of our intellectual equipment I have no idea; like manna, it appears to have dropped from heaven. I do remember doing some lines of strange scribble across a virgin page and offering it to my mother for inspection. She asked me what it was, and I was infuriated to the point of saying "what is the use of me writing you a letter if you can't read it."

Nothing I learnt at the Clothworkers School can be recalled, nothing I remember about my time there concerns education. Sitting upright, and looking intelligent was important, I realised that. As to learning anything else, alas, what went in was understood for an instant, but it wasn't retained. By the time the teacher had finished talking to us, I had forgotten all he had said, so hard was I trying to look intelligent. But then, the rest of the class didn't seem any better, so I can only assume we were all as thick as one another.

My brother and my father had reached an impasse in their war. In our usual style we tried to solve it by running away from it, returning to the mainland in 1929. I suppose that Chester was my last opportunity to acquire an education, though I didn't realise this at the time. Education wasn't considered very important by Mother and Father, being good was the real aim in life, not being clever. I was aware that in the scholastic stakes not a lot was expected of me, their hopes were pinned on my cleverer brother. But thanks to Peel, I experienced a freedom that would never have come my way in the industrial areas of northern England. My first money was earned rowing holidaymakers across the bay and back for sixpence. I learnt how to get cigarettes on Mother's grocery account. I discovered, from experience, that honesty was the best policy, being caught nicking sweets from the counter of the local shop. The threat of public humiliation set me on a path of honesty from which, if I strayed, I knew the punishment and the act equally dishonoured me.

We arrived back at Liverpool docks in even greater disarray than when we had left two years earlier. Father had made a romantic attachment which he pursued, on and off, with a schoolboy's

Father, Harold Ashby; Mother, Hilda Ashby; Norman Ashby; 1950s

enthusiasm. Mother seemed to have lost her desire to achieve anything, and had taken to going to bed with a sick headache at the first sign of trouble. Norman was consumed by a violence over which he had no control, and I was frightened of shadows.

Chester was a very beautiful town. The Roman walls, fine Elizabethan buildings, and the antique shops made excursions into the city an exciting experience. Like most boys, I longed to own a pistol: a sword or some piece of armour would have done, but I never had any money and nobody else in the family showed any interest in such things. My pocket money was only twopence a week, and this left little scope for enterprise, so I contented myself with a catapult, and a throwing stick. God help, I thought, any rabbit foolish enough to come within six feet of me!

I was ten; in four years time I had to present myself to the world, "it is I, Ashby, here to claim my dues." But of course, although time seemed to stretch into an ever-expanding future, and taking thought could be left until tomorrow, the reality of the situation was that I had already attended, and been taken away from, the local elementary school. Violence at home I might just have been able to cope with, but violence at school as well, that was too much. There seemed no respite from the flying chalk, the rap of the pointer on stretched knuckles. No let-up in the thrown plates, the silly token fighting on the sitting-room floor. The tension in bed as one waited for the foolish word that would provoke the harsh tongue. Cricket in the park gave me more pleasure than my home. The escape into the wireless with its dance music and popular song was a greater comfort than the statement that God loved me. And my absorption with the written word found me with a mind that seemed only able to tackle the thrillers of that time, and these increased my fears.

My distress must have been noticed, for casting around for another school found Mr. Grimes, a retired Anglican clergyman and Greek scholar, on the end of the line. He, and his son, Mr. Tommy, as I had to learn to call him, ran a private school at Upton, on the outskirts of Chester. Mr. Grimes's wife acted as matron and caterer, looking after the needs of the one or two boys who boarded there. The fee asked must have been very small, matching Dad's salary. It was, so he told me, "one clergyman's response to the difficulties of another." It would appear that I was the difficulty!

Mr. Grimes was a large man, but not intimidating. His voice was a half-choked gobble that nobody could mimic. Even so, when he read matins on my first morning, he might have been an angel. I had never seen, let alone read, from the Book of Common Prayer, and its beautiful and elegant language jolted me into tears.

> Almighty and most merciful Father; We have erred and strayed from thy ways like lost sheep. We have followed too much the devices and desires of our own hearts. We have offended against thy holy laws. We have left undone those things which we ought to have done; And we have done those things which we ought not to have done; And there is no health in us. But thou, O Lord, have mercy upon us, miserable offenders. Spare thou them, O God, which confess their faults. Restore thou them that are penitent; According to thy promises declared unto mankind In Christ Jesu our Lord. And grant, O most merciful Father, for his sake; That we may hereafter live a godly, righteous, and sober life, To the glory of thy holy Name. Amen.

I enjoyed the year I spent at Stanton House under Mr. Grimes. He was strict, but just. Should he punish a boy, the beaten wretch felt the justice of his aching behind. He had no need to remonstrate with me; I

was very happy learning my French and Latin, and I added the long southern A to my speech! But after a year Mr. Grimes decided to leave Chester, and move the school into the Midlands. He called round to discuss the move with Dad, and offered to take me on "special terms" but we hadn't the money. Perhaps more to the point the will wasn't there. Why should Dad beggar himself to give an education to one with such dubious talents? I could always become a barber or a shop assistant, which Dad himself had been—so the opportunity was lost.

Holly Bank was the name of my last school. The name alone should have been a warning to an astute parent. It was an establishment that catered for the difficult sons and daughters of farmers and tradesmen. The fee asked was very small, and all that was required of the proprietors was for them to keep me quiet until my fourteenth birthday. Two or three of the pupils were quite clever, all girls if my memory serves me right, and being primed for exams. The rest of us volunteered nothing, and hoped that we wouldn't be noticed as we sat out the afternoon and left with undignified haste. The two ladies who ran the school were thought to be rather vulgar, dissolute perhaps, for they smoked in public, and talked of "gaspers." All this sort of thing was unusual in 1931. At that time my grandma King would not allow anyone access to any literature on the Sabbath except the Bible, and the *Joyful News.* The only cooking was the ritual boiling of the sacred potato. Toys and all entertainments were locked away on Saturday night until Monday morning. We would sit in my aunty's bedroom—she was an invalid, in fact I had never seen her out of bed at that time—unrolling tiny scrolls of paper that we picked from a cardboard box. These bore such quotations as "Jesus saves" or "He lifted me" on them, and that was enough excitement for one day.

Around Saturday lunchtime I generally discovered a pain. The severity of this pain I couldn't describe for it was in a place that was indefinable, but very near, "Oh, there!" But it had gone—until a time later in the day, when it was resuscitated sufficiently to keep Mother aware of my affliction, but not to completely spoil the rest of the weekend for me, or make Father remark "he would be better in bed." Sometimes I would be off school for three weeks or a month, then return for another stretch of abject fear and anxiety. For I was ill with a disease that had only been accepted in the world of the fashionable, or those with artistic tendencies. The working class, if they showed extreme sensitivity, were generally regarded as mentally unstable.

My time at home was spent reading. Edgar

Wallace, W.W. Jacobs, Plutarch, *Gem* and *Magnet* were given equal importance, and they gave me equal pleasure. At mealtimes, the labels on jam jars or sauce bottles came under my scrutiny. When I was attending school, my friend Frank Littler, and myself, used up a lot of time listening to his brother's jazz records. We were puzzled by what seemed to be Louis Armstrong's ability to sing the lyric and accompany himself on trumpet. Of course, it was Henry Allen playing, and sounding uncannily like the Master. Being born in 1919, I was in at the beginning of recorded jazz, and much excited by it from an early age.

By the summer of 1933, I was educated to the standard of a twelve year old, and perhaps that is not being flattering to that age group. Around June, we moved to Leeds again, and Dad decided that as I was fourteen in the November, it wasn't worth my going back to school for the last few months. There was nothing to be gained subjecting anybody to the misery of trying to educate me, so I spent the months until I was allowed to be gainfully employed playing snooker at the youth club attached to the chapel.

Ungrateful though it must have seemed in those days of very high unemployment, the three jobs on offer far from pleased me: behind the bacon slicer at the Thrift Stores, a junior at the Fifty Shilling Tailors, or a limp-wristed windowdresser. In the end, I settled for the windowdressing job and a two-year apprenticeship at a very good wage for those days. Here I was, starting work in the same city I had started school in, and cautiously optimistic that things were going to take a turn for the better.

I have a general preference for the company of women. My first six years in employment kept me preponderantly in contact with girls who bought and sold Ladies' Fashion, and I got a lot of pleasure in my relationships with them. Also, having a family of four daughters I have found women to be less aggressive and more civilised in their conduct than men. But at fourteen I spent my time off work playing cricket with the boys. In public parks, on grit, stones, grass, or concrete, we practised our skills in that most beautiful of games, cricket. Nature I loved, too, and it was seeing the Wharfe Valley from the vantage point of Otley Chevin that made me acutely aware of the link between joy, sorrow, and beauty. For looking at such a lovely scene from a threat of war somehow brought out its full sadness. This was also true of music to a degree that upset me. Tears seemed too eager to rush down my cheeks when I listened to an orchestra or a soloist. At five, "Liebesträum" never failed to fill me with sadness. The whole thing was too much for me and my face became convulsed with sorrow. Nobody else I knew was affected in this way, and I felt myself to be abnormal. As I grew into my teens, I attempted to distance myself from these disturbing emotions.

> All very well, but what about that shameful
>   thing?
> What shameful thing, what are you talking
>   about?
> You know what I'm talking about, shameful
>   things.
> Will you be quiet, sir, be quiet I say.
> Shameful things, that come back in the middle
>   of the night when frightened of the dark
>   you lie in bed disturbed by Shameful Things.
> Everybody has these memories. I was only a
>   boy. Boys are in a learning. . .
> Who kicked the panel out of the shithouse
>   door?
> Oh, go away, I'm busy.
> And let Barnett take the blame!
> I would prefer not to discuss. . .
> Shameful things.

Cliff Ashby, Rothwell, 1939

In my early teens I was intensely patriotic. Nothing sent me into a rage more quickly than the denigration of England. There was a lot of disillusionment about in the thirties; the Great War was so recently over, and one was aware, in that area that refused the accepted lie, that another war was going to *purge* the nation very soon. I had my own brand of conservatism. I despised the Conservative Party, but believed passionately in the right of the individual to carve out his own niche in the world. He should be allowed to make his own decisions and mistakes, make his own profit and not be overly oppressed by the state. My ambition was to retire at the age of thirty-five—a millionaire! As the thirties took their course, it became apparent that capitalism was unable to do anything about the world's rapid decline into barbarism. Energy and confidence were lacking in the democracies. When I was called upon to register for National Service, in 1939, the decision was far from a simple one for me. The young boy's patriotism had been shocked by six years' observation of the dishonesty of man: his cruelty towards those he was responsible for, the adroit way that capital and the big families trimmed their sails to meet any wind that might buffet them. There seemed to be no answer to Europe's dilemma other than surgery. The knife was already pricking our flesh in Spain.

The dark still frightened me. Nineteen, and still afraid of the dark! Frightened to go to the toilet after the sun had gone down. Petrified by what might be on the landing. Up the stairs two at a time, then a wild, breathless dash across the landing and a dive into the bathroom. The door slammed and locked with me leaning weakly against it. Secure—for the moment, but the return. . .

Shameful secrets.

Get out.

Shameful secrets.

The knife that I sensed poised over Europe's neck was one that I knew I couldn't wield myself. And after drifting with the decade, when the time came for me to take thought I found I could no longer float in its unhealthy waters. Unfortunately for me, thought was the one thing I wasn't practised in; well, not the one thing, but certainly it was not what I did in the morning when I woke up and viewed the louring sky. Everything was instinctual; the primitive man's method of survival and understanding was, and still is, all I seemed to have to enable me to deal with my days. Which is a pity, because mental attitudinising has won the day hands down. Anyway, by a process of feeling and whatever thought I could muster, the conclusion was arrived at that I must register as a conscientious objector. I was overwhelmed with horror at the idea

of killing a man, and my dreams were drenched in blood. Also, I felt that history was on my side, and that the scourge of war could never be eradicated by the practise of it. Neither then, nor now, do I consider that the doctrine of the true church permits or condones the actions that are considered necessary for the pursuit of war. The end of 1939 found me practising the skills of the wheelbarrow, and the turnip knife. The former I persisted in loading as high as the men around me, and then, when I attempted to lift the thing and push it, invariably it tipped over and dropped the load in the position I had started at! The latter I cut my knuckles with as I attempted to carry on a conversation as I worked.

That being said, farming came relatively easily to me. Soon I was settled into the fairly thoughtless routines that were the duties of the labourer. Perhaps coming from a line of agricultural workers helped, I seemed to feel the work in my blood, especially the understanding and management of animals. At the beginning of the forties I was idly listening to the radio when, among the light music and the comedy shows, John Middleton Murry was heard. He was giving a series of talks about community, and suddenly there I was, listening to a complete stranger mouthing the words and ideas that vaguely occupied my mind at midnight. It was an enormous tribute to the British that a pacifist could be given freedom of the air in time of war, and I was very proud that Murry, although opposed to the general feeling of the nation, made no attempt to subvert or undermine the will of the people. What he said made me realise that if life was to be in any way tolerable over the next few years, somewhere must be found where I could live without the pressures I was encountering in a small West Riding village. People were refusing to speak to me, and sometimes when I was introduced to people who were complete strangers to me, they refused to shake hands. Others crossed over the road when they saw me coming, and going out became unpleasant, and put me under great strain.

The idea came to me that Murry might know of some agricultural community where I would find some fellowship with other young men who thought as I did; so I wrote to him. This was more difficult than you may imagine, as I could not spell, had no knowledge of grammar, and very little confidence in myself. Somehow a letter was concocted, and despatched, in which I put my position to Mr. Murry as clearly as I knew how. After some weeks my stamped addressed envelope was returned with a short note asking me to rewrite, and state my business. It turned out that the Special Branch had raided his house and taken all his correspondence, so although he was left with my address, he had no idea of what I had written to him about. The upshot was a recommendation to write to Max Plowman of the Adelphi Community, in Langham, Essex, and after some correspondence with Frank Lea, the secretary, it was agreed that I should go down there and work with them. All this gave my confidence a needed boost, but Dad was very much opposed to the move. Did the police ever disturb the peace of honest, upright, and decent citizens? Respectable nonconformists never held views that laid them open to such suspicions, it would be a corrupting influence—no good would come of it!

And in a way he was right, for I entered a world inhabited by men of whose existence I had been completely unaware. Young men who spoke beautifully, and were at ease with music, and literature. The music and literature of our shared country, but which we, the majority of the working class, knew nothing about. How could we be expected to inherit a culture when we didn't know it existed? I was completely out of my depth in this world where young men read Spengler with their breakfast, propping *The Decline of the West* up against the milk jug. Seemingly highly respectable, sensible young men wrote poetry, and put their ideas down in nicely handprinted pamphlets. The tunes that I whistled, and Mozart was not unknown to me, they knew the title and the number of. It was all a bit too much for me, and after about seven months I left, emotionally and mentally exhausted. Not that I was without my own gifts. So sensitive was I to the surroundings, I could tell what people were thinking. Listening to a conversation, I could guess with a frightening accuracy what people were going to say. Looking at a face, I knew the thoughts that were in the mind, and all this added to my apprehension and anxiety. My difficulty was that my mind was untrained, it lacked the discipline of an education. In too many ways I was an ignorant man.

I left Langham with a greater sense of my inadequacy than the one I had ignobly borne when I arrived. It didn't seem to me that poetry, and its attendant disciplines, were a lot of use in the kit bag one carried around in this merciless world. It didn't stop people killing one another, and it didn't appear to me to have much to say about the true nature of love. Talking about poetry, and being clever were not, mainly because I could do neither, of much use to a man in 1941. Or so I thought with envy and malice, and I was not entirely right—as usual.

From Easter, until the spring of 1942, I worked for short periods on farms in Warwickshire, Shropshire, and Lincolnshire, mainly to help people out of labour difficulties. It opened my eyes to the true beauty of England, and for the first time, I fell in love

with a countryside different from the Yorkshire dales. Standing on Clee Hill, a spot not far from Ludlow, one could see the mountains rolling back into Wales with a view I had never seen before. The sheer magnificence took my breath away. Looking the other way took one into the Malvern Hills, where Piers Plowman wandered and wrote. Such gentle hills, and so soothing to the spirits.

Spending a rare day off in Stratford-upon-Avon, and dreaming and browsing around the local bookshop, I came across an anthology of poetry by, and here I have to confess I am not sure to whom I owe this debt of gratitude. I think it was edited by someone called Flowers, and for some reason I have the idea that the publishers were Cassells. Probably Flowers remains in my mind because the local brewery was called that, but this little book altered my whole life and I shall always be grateful to the unknown editor. In it, for the first time, I read Auden, Yeats, Browning and Eliot, Lawrence, Arnold and Lovelace. Oh, a host of poets delighted me, and for the first time I read and understood poetry and its particular pleasures. About the same time I came into possession of *A History of English Literature* by Legouis, and found there this exquisite piece by Richard Rolle of Hampole.

> Therefore Jesu es thy name. A! A! that wondyrful name! A! that delittabyll name! This es the name that is abown all names. . . I yede abowte be coveytise of reches and I fand noght Jesu. I ran to the wantonness of flesche and I fand noght Jesu. I satt in companyes of worldly myrthe and I fand not Jesu. . . Therefore I turned by another waye, and I ran abowt be poverte, and I fand Jesu, pure in the worlde, laid in a cryb and lappit in clathis.

It was time for me to try the Adelphi Community again, see if this terrible loneliness could be dulled.

Back in Langham, things seemed hardly to have changed. There was an air of self-righteousness, not entirely peculiar to the young pacifist, which comes, I suppose, from an enormous ignorance. I didn't work on the community farm, but I lodged at the big house. My farm work was paid employment on a farm managed by an unlikely pacifist. Early on my return, sitting down to the evening meal with a friend, my eyes caught those of a woman sitting on the opposite side of the table. Her face glowed with what I saw as untapped love, which in turn was masked by an awful loneliness. Later, I asked about her, and discovered her name was Ann Smith, and that she worked at the big house doing whatever duties came to hand. Her

Ann at Temple Newsam

husband I had met on my first visit to The Oaks. He, I remembered, was a small, shortsighted man, who spent most of his time with the refugees from London who were billeted at the community. Poor man, though he tried desperately to be friends with everybody, and certainly offended nobody, eventually he was a crushing bore and, if possible, avoided. Ann had followed her husband down to Langham, but arrived after he had returned to London. To say that I was fascinated by this young woman would be a gross understatement. Overcoming my own shyness, and Ann's, was more than a little difficult, but flying in the face of the moral code of the time was something else. Yet it never entered my head that I had any other option but to start a relationship with Ann. So I found myself manoeuvring things so that I was in her company. Plying her with the currency of the time, cigarettes, laying on what charm I could muster. Soon we were listening to Beethoven's Seventh on a tinny portable gramophone, in the meadow that lead down to S.L. Bensusan's house. Not only that, but we compounded this foolishness by reading poetry to one another in any quiet corner we could find!

Ann's pleasure in all things was so childlike and complete. Nothing gave me greater pleasure than watching delight light up her face. A Disney film or a Suffolk landscape, the intensity of her joy seemed so much more natural and unself-conscious than mine.

Morning found me cycling off to work whistling bits from Mozart's Haffner Symphony into the splendid East Anglian air, happy in the knowledge that the notes were floating into her delightful ears. Night would find us moving from room to room, and ultimately driven outside, as we searched for that solitude that two people in love so desperately require. It seemed to become more and more difficult, and people were getting fed up with the embarrassment of continually finding us in each other's arms. Finally, we were obliged to take rooms with a woman in a local village. Her husband was in the navy, and to ease her loss she had a "living in" companion whom her children euphemistically called "uncle." "Uncle" disappeared from time to time as her husband returned home on leave.

Dorothy Plowman, a friendly, loving woman, wished us well and some of the evacuees raised a somewhat muted cheer as we drove away to our first home. The donkey was refused us as a luggage carrier however, the idea seeming to be that in some way it might become entangled in our immoral and unsocial attitudes. All around, poetry was waving and dancing, singing songs and lyrics I had never heard before, and for the first time in my life I felt utterly happy. If I had been aware of how intractable love could be, my love would have been more restrained, setting a little aside for hard times. A farmworker's wages at that

Cliff and Ann with their daughters, 1952

Ashby's parents and children, 1952

time was around two pounds a week, and the rent for our rooms was twenty-eight shillings leaving us only twelve shillings for all our other commitments. By the midsummer of 1942, Ann was pregnant, and not a little frightened. The tensions that arose revealed the desperately sad side of Ann. How I tried and longed to console her, change the nature of life to ease her distress and depression. It was hard, living like monks while we were overflowing with affection.

Eventually, we moved into our first tied cottage. Inside, the plaster was crumbling from the wall; in moments of crisis we would sit and look at the peeling wallpaper. The outside lavatory had a door, but it had no hinges. Our possessions were basic. We had a table, a couple of chairs, a wardrobe, and a single bed to pander to our lusts. This was all that remained of Ann's first marriage! Fortunately between us we owned a violin and a decent pen, neither of much use to us, so we pawned them and bought something more practical, cooking utensils. By working hard at singling sugar beet, and the extra money earned by piecework, we began slowly to set a little aside.

Hill Farm, where I worked, was a very interesting farm, of around some three hundred acres. The owner was a physically delicate old gentleman who,

for reasons best known to himself, ran the arable side of the farm entirely without the aid of an internal combustion engine, though the cowman had a milking machine. We, however, farmed with traditional techniques and customs. While the rest of the country became more and more reliant on the tractor and a huge array of implements, we went quietly about our business with the horse. Though the work was physically demanding, it was silent, without the noise and stress of mechanical farming. The men retained the pace of the centuries, and generally thought of themselves as craftsmen. They were proud of their horses, their skills with the handtools that they used. A poor piece of work was an eyesore they could hardly bare to live with. I was on one of the only farms in England to retain these old ways, and I felt very privileged to have spent nine months working there. But with the baby coming, it seemed sensible to go to London where the housing, and the amenities were so much better.

Foolishly, on hindsight (nothing I've ever done doesn't look foolish on reflection, or so I think in certain moods), we went to live with a young man who owned a house in what was then called Enfield West, in the north London area. He was very generously prepared to give us shelter if Ann would act as his housekeeper. Under normal circumstances, we could have given him satisfactory service, but Ann, carrying a child, was in no condition to look after anyone but herself. I worked in the greenhouses out at Crews Hill which was some way away. What with the travelling, and fire watching two nights in every five, sometimes, leaving early on a Monday morning, I didn't return until the Tuesday evening. Really, I saw very little of Ann; she was left at home all day with nobody she knew to talk to. So, large with child, and very bored with herself, somehow she managed to clear the larder of the large stock of baked beans carefully sought and bought by the previous house-keeper. The householder was a mild man, very slow to anger, but the sight of those empty shelves infuriated him. Come the Armageddon, there he was, without the consolation of a tin of beans. Quite sensibly he felt that he could be better served, and phoned up his late housekeeper to come round and tell us so!

Spring of 1943 found Ann staying with her

Cliff, Ann, and daughter Jane, Harrogate, 1960

parents just outside Croydon, while I lived in digs with an elderly couple in Enfield. My eldest daughter, Jane, was born in the April at Lord Brocket's mansion in Hertfordshire. At that time it was being used as the maternity wing of the City of London Hospital. Ann seemed to be in labour for ever, and after a difficult confinement she was imaginatively put in a bedroom slept in by von Ribbentrop when he visited the noble lord. It was a blue, melancholy room, large in proportion and decorated with peacocks. Every time I visited her she was in tears, due to an attack of acute depression. Nobody had told me that this also was the nature of love. On Ann's discharge, after six weeks in hospital, we went to stay with my parents in Didcot, where they were now living. There we lived out the days in anger and acrimony as my parents came to terms with my daughter and her mother.

In the summer I spent a day in Oxford. The real purpose was to have my eyes tested at the Ratcliffe Infirmary, so it was a tremendous bonus to pick up *Another Time,* by Auden, and on opening it find:

> Every Eye must weep alone
> Till I will be overthrown. . .

in the dedication. *Another Time* was by far the best book of verse I had read, better than my anthology, better than Lawrence, the only other books of poetry I owned. I turned over page after page in stunned silence. An uneducated labourer in communication with the sophisticated mind of an Oxford man. For over a week I walked about a man in a dream. What talent, and how easy Auden made it all seem.

> O plunge your hands in water,
>   Plunge them up to the wrist;
> Stare, stare in the basin
>   And wonder what you've missed.

And the more I read, the more I realised what I had missed.

As far as I could I kept my reading going, though some of the farms were too far from any libraries to make this possible. For some reason, farming and poetry never seemed to mix for me. I couldn't read it, and it never occurred to me to write it. Usually my nose was in some run-of-the-mill novel. The sort of stuff that one got from a newsagent who had a few books tucked away in a corner, and called it a library. But they often did me proud, coming up with Joyce Cary's *Mister Johnson,* and *A Portrait of the Artist as a Young Man,* so a fairly representative amount of current modern literature presented itself to me. But for thirteen years I read no poetry at all, and as long as I engaged in farm work I never felt the need to.

The war finally ended. It had been going on for so long, it seemed that normality was a state of war. With the huge volume of men returning from the services, industry totally geared to arms production, and a general lack of energy, finding alternative employment was not easy. When I approached employers for work, they very properly told me that the first people to be found employment were the men returning from the services. They were, in the main, very sympathetic, but that buttered no parsnips as far as I was concerned, and it became apparent that if I wanted to keep a roof over the family, I should have to continue farming. The trouble was that not enough money could be made as a labourer to live in any comfort. The answer seemed to be to change direction within the industry, so I became a cowman, and found dealing with stock was something I seemed to have an instinct for. During the next ten years I spent my time on farms in the West Midlands, where I specialised in the management of Jersey cattle. Cows were very profitable at this time, and the herdsman was considered one of the key men on the farm. I was delighted to have more authority, and more money, for this enabled me to provide a better standard of living for the family. Not that anybody had much in the way of comforts, for a number of essential goods were still rationed, and we were to find that the transition from war to peace was going to take us as long as the war had lasted. I like to think that I was a good farm labourer. Certainly I gave it the bulk of my time and energy, and found caring for stock a

Daughter Sarah, 1983

particularly rewarding job, but physically I was not built for this manual work. Although over six feet tall, I only weighed just over ten stones (140 pounds) and wasn't blessed with a robust constitution. As the years passed, a back complaint that had dogged me since my entry into agriculture became so severe that I was told I must find work outside the industry.

Though still an invalid, I had to find somewhere to live very quickly, as the farmer wanted my cottage for his new cowman. The housing authorities were not very helpful, but then, in 1956 there was a chronic housing shortage. In Boreham Wood, where my local council was located, they told me they had a waiting list of ten thousand, and another ten thousand were waiting to get onto the waiting list! We all came under a lot of stress, for a court order was being sought, to enable the farmer to regain possession of his cottage, and have us put out onto the street. The local welfare officer seemed to think that we could be accommodated in hostels when things finally came to a head. Ann and the children in one home and myself in another, as it was not policy, at that time, to let families stay together. A monstrous, and impossible, situation. There seemed nothing for it but to see if my family in Harrogate, where my parents had retired to, could, or would, do anything to help us.

Two aunties, my mother's sisters, very kindly

At Merriscourt, 1950

agreed to put us up until we could rent some accommodation, or found work that would provide it. My aunties were, in their own way, deeply Christian. Aunty Mina had taken to her bed in the early twenties, and didn't get up again until her mother died in the forties. Both she, and her sister, my Aunty Winnie, were fragile and twisted in body, while Winnie had a simplicity that bordered on the simple. Neither of them ever had the outside world impinging on them. Relatives and social workers did everything for them, though they bravely kept the house in some disorder. When the world, in the shape of my family, blew into their lives, it was a hurricane and they had soon had enough of it. After a couple of months, Mina told my mother that we must move; I think the persistent sound of children was too much for them, and with the best will in the world they would be glad to see the back of us. And Mina being a shrewd woman, probably knew that this would encourage my father to help us in a tangible way. Fortunately, my father-in-law seemed to become aware of our difficulties, and came up with a hundred pounds which Dad matched, and soon we were looking for a run-down house which our two hundred pounds would be a deposit for. Dad also guaranteed the mortgage, and in the February of 1957 we moved into a house of our own—unemployed, but hopeful.

Cliff and Ann with the Aussie connection: daughter June, Sonali, Stephen, and Michael; Heckmondwike, Yorkshire, 1986

Getting a job proved more difficult than I had imagined it would. I was still attending the hospital for treatment on my back, and was now registered as "a disabled person," but this seemed more of a hindrance than a help. Grocers turned me down because they thought I was *too good* for packing parcels and delivering them. Warehouses thought my back too problematical. The post office found me unsuitable for their telephone exchanges, and overskilled for cleaning out the kiosks. Ringtons, the door-to-door tea sellers, thought me incapable of this onerous job, and gave it to a man I thought was only fifteen pence in the pound! Coming back from a fruitless interview for a porter's job at Harrogate Ladies College, I came across a ten shilling note laid on the pavement. What a moral dilemma this placed me in! All my background said "take it to the police station" but Yorkshire shrewdness told me to "put it in thee pocket" and I did. To be poor and moral is a terrible burden, this happened thirty years ago, but the guilt remains to this day.

In the April, after eight months out of work, I presented myself to the personnel officer of a firm of structural engineers located in a suburb of Harrogate. Clad in my steel-ribbed corsets, and Co-op suit, if I didn't look very ambitious, at least I was upright. I was started at the princely wage of six pounds and ten shillings as a printman, taking copies of drawings for

Grandson Patrick, 1984

Bob and Jane Elstree, Ann (in back); Stephen, Michael, Lawrence, Betty, Sonali, Sarah; and Thomas (in front); Brandenston, Suffolk, 1986

the draughtsmen and designers. Though it was less than half the wage I earned as a cowman, I was grateful to whatever gods had me under their wing that bright, sunny spring morning. Anxiety was lifted off my shoulders like a tangible weight. Before long I had progressed from taking prints to writing out work orders, and apart from an occasion when I had some stanchions manufactured two feet short, didn't do too badly in a job I was supremely disinterested in. Five years later, when I left, I was working in the estimating department, a respectable, clerical worker and houseowner. One thing's for sure, nobody wants you when you're down and out!

Things began getting better for me financially, but probably because the work was so boring, I found myself down at the library, looking at the poetry section again. It didn't seem to me, as I dipped into the poetry of the fifties, that there was much interesting stuff being written, certainly not on the evidence of a provincial library. I liked James Kirkup very much, especially a poem set in the unlikely setting of a gents' lavatory. It was the shared experience, the brotherhood of observers who saw in the everyday scene the material for a poem. Had I not stood in the stalls relieving myself, an ear on the squirt of water being flushed out of the pipes, and an eye on the

movement of birds outside the window or over the wall? So the idea of birds being squirted out of trees was a very happy invention to me. Philip Larkin was another poet I liked very much, perhaps because his raw material was so unexceptional. It lit a small hope in me that I might be able to do something myself, for the lack of outstanding poetry was, strangely enough, very encouraging. Walking about Harrogate, one was aware of poems in every shop, and on all the street corners. Certainly I could see the stuff of poetry all around me, and though in my head I seemed able to come up with good lines, I had not the technique to enable me to put it down on the page. Returning to Larkin, I saw that his poetry was based on a skill that enabled him to conceal the midnight oil that I felt was in his work. What generally came out of his verse was his goodness, and romanticism. His weakness, to me, was in his recourse to "fucking" and "shitting" about the place. It underlined his respectability, his lack of knowledge of the real world. He was a sad, middle-class man, in the world but not really of it. Of course there were other poets around, and one of my favourites was William Plomer, who had a delightful sense of humour. A little later, I came across George Barker, and was enormously impressed by his work. Especially *The True Confessions of George Barker,* surely

Daughter Betty with Tony (right), Lawrence, and Rachel, Upper Holton, Suffolk, 1986

one of the best long poems of this century. He was not, as far as I can remember, one of the names bandied about by the critics in the Sundays; Hughes and Gunn seemed to excite them. In the main, poets of my age, and younger, didn't seem to be saying much that Auden and Lester Young hadn't said in the thirties.

After a time I found myself jotting down lines of verse, sometimes even managing a whole stanza! Mostly I did this at work, when the boredom of having a spare moment was greater than the work itself. The idea of cold-bloodedly sitting down at home, and deliberately trying to write verse was too daunting for me to tackle. It seemed such a pretentious thing to do. Words and ideas came into my head as I walked about the town, but when I sat down to write, nothing happened, and I couldn't remember what had been in my mind. The paper was there, the pen was poised, but out of this great expectancy, nothing. Bits of paper with lines of verse began to litter up the whole house, and part of my table at work. Draughtsmen came in for a print, and while they waited, rummaged among my bits and pieces, mystified in the main as to what the hell I was at. Christmas, 1959, in my fortieth year, found me looking at the *Sunday Times* Poetry Competition. It was for a poem about Pasternak, a writer I had never heard of, apart from reading in the tabloids about his Nobel prize, and the difficulties this caused for him. In the nature of ignorance, it didn't stop me from sending off an entry. The ensuing wait for some information about this was my introduction to the pains of publication. I had this silly, yet positive feeling that what I had sent, though not very profound, could not be overlooked as trivial. The phrase, "his bowels were turned to water," accurately described my condition over the next few weeks. But it was all made worthwhile when I opened the *Sunday Times,* and saw I had been mentioned in despatches. The adjudicator remarked, "J.C. Ashby, devastatingly described the fundamentals of the Pasternak dilemma," and quoted:

> Wiser perhaps to live a life of
>   self-effacement
> Retired to some dingy, Moscow
>   basement,
> Than tour the world, the current,
>   literary lion,
> With nothing but a hotel bed to cry on.

Sometimes things happen to you that are so amazing, they are unbelievable. I sat and looked at this damned paragraph thinking, "This has been done by someone

A visit to the publisher: Cliff and Ann with Michael Schmidt and his daughter Isabel (Manchester Cathedral can be seen through the window.)

else, not me the totally unsure man lacking all belief in himself." But it had. Naturally, I thought my father would be pleased by this small triumph, but he wasn't. He had this idea of me as "grocer's assistant" material, and he was too old to start adjusting his ideas of the family; he grunted, and turned back to his paper, more concerned with the racing page and his favourite, Lester Piggott. I can understand this now, though at the time I felt rather hurt. Changing your way of thinking about those close to you is very hard, and disturbing. It makes you doubt your judgement, wipes out all the confidence in your opinions, those precious things you have carried around in your baggage for years without questioning. For me, who has allowed the world to alter my opinions all my life, the result is that I am unsure of nearly everything, believe nothing, never continue in one stay; but this is preferable to being stunted by a dogma in which the truth has been lost.

A year or two after this competition, I found another piece in the *Sunday Times* that altered the course of my life. Cyril Connolly, writing about a new magazine called *X,* remarked that it was the only magazine available that gave room to the unknown

"View over my town"

writer, and as nobody was more unknown than me, I was interested. The editor, a poet I hadn't heard of at that time, David Wright, was contacted and by extraordinary good luck I managed to get a handful of poems in the magazine's last two issues. *X* was a beautiful magazine, but in the nature of things it was almost impossible to find capital to keep it going. If the Arts Council had existed at that time, its fortunes might have been very different.

David Wright was always more than an editor. He wrote me long letters, "pooh-poohing" my lack of education, the fragility of my grammar and punctuation. Over the years he managed to insert a little iron into my spine. And the friendships I made during this period have stood the test of twenty-six years. Martin Seymour Smith, Charles Sisson, and David Wright have nurtured me over this period with a rareness of affection. Almost they have persuaded me that I am a poet, but I still feel uncomfortable with the designation. My background doesn't seem to be seeded with the stuff of poetry, and that it should grow in such infertile soil is beyond belief. I look at what I have written, and cannot associate myself with what I see; I am only the physical presence used to articulate it.

Whatever virtue it holds has little to do with me. I try, to the best of my ability, not to spoil it.

> O fragile happiness
> That shatters at the impact of a shadow,
> Making me tread with unaccustomed care
> Around the fragmants of a harsh experience.

BIBLIOGRAPHY

Poetry:

In the Vulgar Tongue. London: Hodder & Stoughton, 1968.

The Dogs of Dewsbury. Manchester, England: Carcanet, 1976.

Lies and Dreams. Manchester, England: Carcanet, 1980.

Plain Song: Collected Poems, 1960-1985. Manchester, England: Carcanet, 1985.

Fiction:

The Old Old Story. London: Hodder & Stoughton, 1969.

Howe and Why. London: Hodder & Stoughton, 1969.

Dee Brown

1908-

My birthplace was a Louisiana sawmill town, Alberta, near Red River, but after my father was killed, my mother moved across the line into Arkansas to be near relatives. While she worked in a dry-goods store in the town of Stephens, one of my grandmothers looked after me and my younger sister, neither of us being old enough for school.

This grandmother, Elizabeth Cranford, had been a schoolteacher most of her life, and on the top shelf of a cabinet in her bedroom she kept a small collection of McGuffey's readers and Blue Back spellers that she had used in her profession. One afternoon when I was four or five years old, she sat me down in her lap and opened a first-grade primer to a drawing of a running dog. Beneath the illustration were some little black marks that I had previously observed below or above pictures in books and magazines. My grandmother pointed to the little black marks in the primer. "The dog ran," she said slowly, tapping each of the printed three-letter words with a finger. And the mystic marks gradually became words: *The Dog Ran.*

I must have thought: What magic is this? What wonder is this? To me, the event was the discovery of a hidden secret that for some reason had been kept from me by conspiring adults. It was the most startling event of my childhood. Had that incident not been momentous I would not have remembered it all the rest of my days—the setting, in a room beside a window with a blooming apple tree outside, the picture of the running dog before me in the book, the mystery of reading suddenly unlocked.

From that moment I was an addict of the printed word, and addicts of the printed word, I eventually discovered, are almost certain to become compulsive writers, hooked on pencils and pens, and typewriters, and nowadays marvelous contrivances called word processors.

My mother also was a reading addict, and she saw to it that plenty of good books were put in my way. By the time I started into the first grade I was devouring Robert Louis Stevenson and had access to Mark Twain and some of the great British authors of the nineteenth century—although I do not recall reading the latter until I was in school. Two of my

Dee Brown, 1985

aunts who lived nearby were subscribers to numerous magazines, and in that period when radio was just beginning, movies were silent, and television had not been invented, the national periodicals were quite superior to the species seen nowadays on newsstands. Several of the better book publishers issued quality monthlies in which their forthcoming books often appeared in instalments.

Up the street from where we lived, just on the edge of the town's business section, was a printing plant from which came the weekly newspaper. Several times each day I passed this building's wide open door, from which flowed the sweet perfume of printing ink and the sound of clanking presses. At last, one day I summoned the courage to venture inside. It was a father-and-son enterprise, both always busy, but the son spared the time to lift me upon a typesetter's high stool. He put a composing stick into my hand and showed me how to set and read type, metal letters that were backward and upside down. That was a milestone day, but Charles Parker and Son had not the faintest idea what they had done for me.

The house we lived in until my teenage years was of considerable size with a long hallway dividing it in half, and with large porches front and back. The spare bedrooms were in use much of the time, as we had many visitors, mostly relatives from Louisiana and Texas, and in those days, before automobiles replaced trains for travel, visits usually extended for a month or more. Consequently I grew up with the belief that half brothers and sisters—as well as numerous aunts, uncles, and cousins—were a normal state of family life.

Because of the wide differences between the Louisiana relatives and the west Texas relatives, I was never quite certain whether I was growing up in the South or Southwest. The west Texans spoke in different cadences from our own; they were always sunburned, and wore rougher clothing than the Louisianans. Because they were different, I strove to emulate the Texans when they were visiting. I became

quite envious of one of the Texas cousins because his horsemanship was so superior to mine. I forgave him when he told me he was going to become a cowboy as soon as he finished high school and would find a place for me on the same ranch. But he was later to disappoint me by becoming an undertaker.

When I was about thirteen, our sleepy little village with its cotton gin and sawmill turned overnight into an oil boom town. The world rushed in upon us—oil drillers and roustabouts from all over the Southwest, wildcatters, geologists and oil scouts, promoters and confidence men, lease hounds, and several exotic female office workers with bobbed hair under tam-o'-shanters, rouged cheeks, low-cut shirtwaists, and rolled white stockings.

Dee Brown with Grandmother Elizabeth Cranford; Mother, Lula Brown; and sister, Corinne; about 1920

Father, Daniel Alexander Brown, about 1907

At about this same time, my mother was appointed postmistress only to be almost overwhelmed by a sudden upsurge in the volume of mail because of the oil boom. I was pressed into service to carry special-delivery letters to strangers with no address except the town itself. Each morning and late afternoon I weaved my way through a tent city along the railroad track, or into the only hotel, which had cots lined up on its porches and in its hallways, and then if unsuccessful I went from house to house where rooms were posted for rent. For each letter delivered

I received ten cents, and sometimes was given another dime as a tip from the more generous recipients.

Until the boom receded and the oil men departed for richer strikes, I was blessed with a constantly renewable pocketful of dimes, many of which went for books and magazines that were purchased either from train vendors or from the town's first newsstand that was established to supply demands of the transients. In addition to "foreign" newspapers from such distant cities as Houston and Dallas and Tulsa, the previously unknown world of pulp magazines suddenly was unveiled. Sea stories, adventure stories, western stories, mystery stories, war stories; I'd had no idea such garish riches existed. Being a compulsive reader, I acquired samples of all of them. Two of my favorite pulps were *Argosy* and *Blue Book,* the latter being the first magazine to publish one of my short stories, done while in high school.

The high school I attended was in Little Rock— not the Central High of the much later notorious 1957 desegregation conflict, but an ancient structure on the east side of the city. One of my mother's sisters lived in Little Rock, and it was decided that we should move there for better schooling.

I do not know whether the schooling was any better or not, but downtown there was a splendid public library that in those more literate times was warmly supported by a majority of the citizens and their elected officials. The library became almost a second home. Far more reading was done from the library's collections than in school, perhaps because I did the choosing.

On one occasion, however, a school librarian pointed me to a three-volume set of books that started me upon a course that I was to follow into my career as a writer. For this I have always been most grateful to her. The title of the set was *History of the Expedition under the Command of Captains Lewis and Clark.*

It has been said that the most enduring works of literature are stories of journeys in which the chief interest of the narrative centers around the adventures of the hero or heroine. If this be true, there is no greater adventure story in American history than the expedition of Meriwether Lewis and William Clark, a journey filled with danger, mystery, romance, and grueling suspense. Instead of one hero it contains several, and one sterling heroine, the Shoshone woman, Sacajawea, without whose aid they might not have reached their destination.

The school librarian, who was also a teacher in those days, loaned the three volumes to me one at a time. There began my first real interest in the American West, and the history of my country.

By chance, during my high-school years, I discovered two writers of my own time who were to influence my view of American life and literature. It came about in this way. To reach the school, which was two miles from where we lived, we either walked or rode a trolley car. The fare was five cents, but if the weather was good most of the boys in my neighborhood walked in order to save the nickels for candy bars or movie tickets. On the walking mornings I began to notice a plump little man hurrying in the opposite direction, toward the nearest trolley-car stop. One day he was reading a book as he approached, balancing it on his slight paunch, and occasionally glancing briefly over the top of his glasses to make certain of his footing.

Next morning he was still reading the same book, and my curiosity was aroused as to what could be so absorbing that he was compelled to read while walking to the trolley stop. On the third morning I saw that he was near the last pages of the book. If I was to know its title, I must follow him. Deciding to sacrifice my five cents, I followed him aboard the streetcar. While he was paying his fare, I caught a glimpse of the book's title: *Winesburg, Ohio,* by Sherwood Anderson. Furthermore, the sticker on the volume's spine told me it was a library book.

Dee and Corinne at Hot Springs National Park, 1920

Within the week, *Winesburg, Ohio* was in my hands, and I soon understood why the rotund stranger could not wait to reach his seat on the trolley to continue his reading. I do not know if he was from a small town, as I was, but I suspect he was. Although Anderson's Ohio was foreign to me, most of the characters in his book were as familiar as if they had been flesh and blood. Yet, being a boy, I knew only the surfaces of the parallel characters in my small town. Anderson told me the secrets of their lives—the meanness and goodness of small-town America. I identified with his main character, George Willard, who was really Anderson himself.

Over the years I read everything I could find that Sherwood Anderson published, and while I was living in Washington, D.C., during the 1930s, I finally met him—in somebody's apartment, at one of those numerous little gatherings that were always being held for some burning cause or other in those yeasty days of the New Deal.

Anderson was the guest of honor, of course, writers being highly esteemed by the Roosevelt administration (but shunned by all others since, except the brief reign of Kennedy). He said a few words to the group, something about Washington being the only place in America where everybody was important, therefore nobody there was important. He had recently acquired two weekly newspapers in Marion, Virginia—one Democratic, the other Republican—and when I found an opportunity to talk alone with him I said that my lifelong dream was to own a country weekly. That had been an early dream for him, also, he said, but he had been unable to achieve it until he received a little money for a novel that had done better than most of his books. Alas, he had no magic formula for me to follow his example, but he invited me to visit his printing shop in Marion, and I later did so.

John Dos Passos, I discovered in the public library shortly after I reluctantly returned the copy of *Winesburg, Ohio.* The first book was *Manhattan Transfer,* a realistic treatment of New York and its area. I was fascinated by the introductory passages to the chapters, a technique that he later brought to perfection in the "newsreel" and "camera eye" sections of his *U.S.A.* trilogy. I did not shift my allegiance from Anderson to Dos Passos, however, until that trilogy was published, the first two appearing while I was in college, each striking me with the effect of lightning bolts, so that I read and reread them until I knew parts of them by heart.

Later of course there was Faulkner, and then Joseph Conrad, to form the quartet of authors who influenced me most, I think, in attitude. Writers do not spring full-grown from the forehead of Zeus. They are the products of family members, friends, teachers, and other writers. These human forces were all a part of the process that moved my pen across the pages of manuscript after I found my own subject niche in the nineteenth-century American frontier.

Although I was fortunate to stumble upon some of the better contemporary writers while in high school, I was still reading my favorite pulp magazines—especially during the long summers. In an issue of *Blue Book* I noticed an announcement that the editor would pay a hundred dollars for 2,000-word stories of real adventure. A hundred dollars then was equal to a thousand dollars now, and I immediately set about concocting a story of "real adventure."

We lived only two blocks from the Arkansas Travelers ballpark, and baseball was then the most real adventure I knew about. Creating a story around an actual scene I had witnessed in front of the home team's dugout, I told it from the viewpoint of a shortstop who was supposed to be me. The plot involved a rookie pitcher, a conceited sportswriter, the sportswriter's girlfriend, and her dog. A few weeks after mailing it to *Blue Book,* I received a check for one hundred dollars. Being only seventeen, I was absolutely certain that I had it made for life. Disillusionment was not long in coming, however. Rejection slips soon taught me that no writer ever has it made for life. In fact, I learned that writing and baseball have much in common. Every time one goes to bat, it's a new ballgame. A home-run hitter will strike out or pop out more often than he will slam one over the fence or into the stands, whether it be a baseball or a manuscript.

Yet during the next two years I did sell two more stories of "real adventure" to *Blue Book,* slightly changing my name each time, although I doubt if that fooled the editor, Donald Kennicott, who seemed to be genuinely interested in beginning writers.

Baseball was the outdoor mania of the teenaged boys of my neighborhood. When the Travelers were on the road, we usually played every afternoon on a vacant lot near the ballpark. There were no "little leagues" in those times, no adults to supervise us, but someone was usually available to umpire and keep our batting averages, a record we considered very important.

For summer jobs, most of us sought morning employment so that we would be free for baseball by midafternoon. Night baseball had not yet been inflicted upon the fans. During two summers I worked as an iceman's helper. Electric refrigerators had been introduced, but the early models were expensive and not very efficient, and only a few families had them. The

Dee getting a man out at first base,
Beltsville Research Center, Maryland, 1940

housewives posted cards in their street windows, indicating the number of pounds of ice they wanted each day. Twenty-five pounds was easy to carry, but I hated the fifty-pound loads. Each day we started out at dawn and were usually finished by noon.

Getting into a seat in the ballpark required strategy and fast footwork. Whether we had money in our pockets or not, none of us ever wasted it buying a ticket. The Travelers had a long-standing rule that any baseball knocked over the fence in batting practice or during the game could be presented at the gate as admission to the bleachers. Because of its short outfield and low board fence, quite a few balls went out of that park. Consequently, an hour before game time, a group of eager youths was always gathered outside the very short left-field fence.

Luck played a large part in the retrieval of those fly balls, but skill at catching them increased one's chances. Most of us brought along our gloves, yet even so on many days luck deserted us and we had to retreat up the slope to climb a tree from which we could see only about half the ball field.

Our fortunes improved considerably the summer that Moses Yellowhorse joined the Travelers. Yellowhorse was an Indian, Osage as I recall, a pitcher who had played for one of the big-league teams. He could fire a ball like a rifle shot, but had a tendency to walk too many batters, which is probably the reason he was sent down to the Southern Association. Yellowhorse spent much of his time in the bullpen, warming up to relieve the other pitchers.

Instead of the eight-foot board fence that surrounded most of the ballpark, a close-meshed wire fence ran along part of the bullpen. Because of a bleachers-supporting wall, the playing field could not be seen from outside the wire fence, but if we had not been lucky enough to catch a ball and get inside, we would stand near the wire and watch the pitchers warm up. They had a small roofed shed to sit in, and sometimes they would talk to us.

From the very first time I saw him, Moses Yellowhorse fascinated me. During the oil boom at Stephens, several Indians had come from Oklahoma to work on the rigs, and a Creek boy was one of my closest friends in school. After his family returned to Oklahoma, I visited him in Muskogee one summer. He liked to say that his people belonged to one of the "five civilized tribes," and that he was not a "wild" Indian. Yellowhorse was a "wild" Indian, with a chiseled nose in a noble face. If he was not warming up, he liked to watch us try for those fly balls over the fence, gravely applauding when one of us made a good catch.

One day, after the game had started and I was lingering in hopes that a high foul might come floating over the fence, I noticed Yellowhorse watching me. He was sitting alone in the shelter, idly flipping a ball up and down. He got up and walked close to the wire fence. "Hey, kid," he said softly, and tossed the ball over the fence. I caught it easily, and stared at him in astonishment. He winked and grinned. "Take the ball in, kid. See the game."

I have told all this about baseball and Moses Yellowhorse because knowing him, even so slightly, made a difference in my life. All through that last summer before graduating from high school, I and a few other boys favored by the Indian pitcher often obtained seats in the bleachers, thanks to his kindness. His actions lost the Travelers no money or balls. Yellowhorse delighted in our joy, and we delighted in his frequent Indian "giveaways." From that time, I scorned all the blood-and-thunder tales of frontier Indian savagery, and when I went to the Western movies on Saturday afternoons, I cheered the warriors who were always cast as villains.

I did not find Little Rock High School very interesting until I discovered that it offered courses in printing. At the earliest opportunity I enrolled in one of Mr. John Nolan's classes, eventually going through the whole lot of them. Sometimes I was irked by Mr. Nolan's unrelenting insistence that everything had to be as perfect as I could make it—the adjustment of space in the design of display ads, the proper choices of type faces, the setting of intricate material on that now extinct machine, the linotype, the impressions of inked type upon paper—not too heavy, not too light.

I suppose the only persons from whom I learned anything worthwhile as a youth were those who believed in excellence. They insisted that if you could not excel, at least you could try to excel. And so, John Nolan made me into a fair printer, ready upon graduation from high school to enter the trade as an apprentice.

Finding jobs in those days was no easier than it is now; probably it was more difficult. As there were no jobs locally for an eighteen-year-old printer, I wrote to several small-town newspapers around the state. Miraculously an angel responded. When I left Little Rock to go up into the heart of the Ozarks to report for my first full-time job, I was Sherwood Anderson's George Willard leaving Winesburg, Ohio.

My angel was Mr. Tom Newman of the Harrison *Daily Times* in Boone County. He employed me during the pre-Christmas season to imprint names upon Christmas cards on one of the job presses. And after the Christmas season ended, his brother John employed me as a linotype operator on the newspaper.

My transition from full-time printer to part-time printer and part-time news reporter was the result of one of those chance events that sometimes change the course of one's life. On a springtime evening I was in the courthouse square where the teenagers of Harrison usually gathered between suppertime and bedtime. Suddenly a truck wheeled up from a side street, the driver calling for volunteers to go to the town of Green Forest to help rescue victims of a tornado. Earlier that evening we had noticed wild flashes of lightning off to the west, and someone had remarked that a bad storm must be in progress.

We all volunteered, of course, a dozen boys piling onto the bed of the trunk, and we soon reached the dark and devastated town. We found that a number of victims had already been brought to the two churches that had been spared by the tornado. One church was used as a morgue, the other as a hospital.

We were quickly organized into a search party by a man with a lantern who led us into an area on the outer edge of Green Forest. Along the way we passed piles of debris that had once been buildings, tree trunks with all their limbs torn away, and then a row of houses whose front walls had vanished, the furniture undisturbed in the rooms facing the street so that they resembled shadowy stage sets. We met other parties with lanterns and flashlights returning with injured or dead victims of the storm.

Beneath a sheet of galvanized roofing we found a little girl crying softly. The man with the lantern decided that four of us should carry her back to the church that was being used as a hospital. I was chosen as one of the four. Using the galvanized sheeting as a stretcher, we carried the little girl to the hospital church. Doctors and nurses were beginning to arrive from surrounding towns, and were trying to bring order out of the chaos of injured lying on the floor or on church benches. Odors of carbolic acid and other antiseptics soon filled the church.

We spent the remaining hours until well past sunrise searching in ever widening arcs, but found only a few badly frightened people, and some injured animals. At the railroad station where I was given a sandwich and a cup of coffee, I suddenly realized that I was overdue at my linotype machine in Harrison. The truck that had brought me to Green Forest, I soon discovered, had already returned. My only means of transport was the passenger train on the Missouri and North Arkansas Railroad. Running an hour late as usual, it brought me into Harrison shortly before press time.

Without pausing to wash up or change out of my soiled clothing, I rushed to the *Daily Times* building. Both Newman brothers gave me reproving looks. John had been working frantically to set enough straight matter to fill the paper, but he had no firm news at all on the Green Forest tornado. "You were there," he said gruffly. "Write it." I turned toward the typewriter in the front office. "No time for that," John growled. "Write it while you set it on the linotype. Enough to fill a whole column."

I did the best I could, describing the devastated town as I had seen it at night, the sounds and smells, the anxious faces of the people milling in and out of the two dimly lit churches, the grim scenes at dawn. When I finished I carried the linotype slugs to the proof press, but again John stopped me, saying there was no time for correcting errors. He had already handset a black banner headline, and he handed my linotyped composition to the make-up man to fit beneath it. The typographical errors were numerous, but at least we had beat out the Associated Press which sent us a story too late to use until the next day.

Neither of the Newman brothers ever said whether or not they liked what I had done, but a few days later they sent me to report an automobile accident, followed by a shooting in the hill country, and then a progression of other violent incidents. I discovered that the local reporter for the *Times,* an earnest young lady, disliked violence, and there seemed to be a considerable amount of that in Boone County. Soon I was spending half my time writing news stories that were frequently composed directly on the linotype.

Occasionally one or the other of the Newman brothers would point out to me a better way to tell a news story, and from them I gradually learned about clarity and conciseness. When I left their employment to go to college, they probably soon forgot me, but I have never forgotten Tom and John Newman for the parts they played in helping me learn the skills I would use the remainder of my days.

The reason I went to college was the gradual realization that I did not know enough about the world and its institutions, its languages, literatures, its history, and all the other elements of learning that I sensed were swarming somewhere outside my uninformed boundaries. A local boy named Eugene Wilson came to work one summer at the *Times*. He had spent a year in college and was looking forward to returning in the autumn if he could save enough money. His knowledge of the world, his vocabulary, and most of all, his sophistication, convinced me that I should follow his example. Wilson and I became lifelong friends. He helped lead me to college; later on, I helped lead him to become a librarian, one of the outstanding members of that profession.

And so I left the Ozarks for the Arkansas River valley to enroll in the Arkansas State Teachers College at Conway. I was not certain that I wanted to be a teacher, but the tuition fees were modest, and part-time jobs were available to pay expenses. By some miracle, during the three years I was there, the small college was blessed with several young professors just starting their careers in the humanities. They had come from good universities around the country, had not yet become bored with academia, and were eager to prove themselves. My favorite was Dean D. McBrien, fresh from the University of Nebraska, an enthusiastic student of Western American history. Years later he became a college president.

Dean McBrien, more than any other mentor, set me upon the course I took as a writer. He probably did not care very much for the historical novels I published during his lifetime. But he must have liked my documented histories because I borrowed, or stole, the methods he used in his classes to charm his students into attentive listeners.

McBrien's view of history was that the past consisted of stories, fascinating incidents, woven around incisive biographies of the persons involved in the happenings. He liked little dashes of scandal—if they could be documented, and he insisted firmly that everything had to be authenticated from the available sources. He loved the history of the Ameri-

With Dean McBrien, Arizona, 1930

can West. Before I met him, I was interested in the American West, but he converted me into a fanatic like himself.

Almost every summer during those years, he traveled across the West, usually with two students as companions. On two of these expeditions I was privileged to be invited. McBrien preferred to travel in a Model T Ford. Although the Model A had replaced the Model T by the 1930s, the latter was still available for a few dollars in various used conditions. Before I was twenty-one I owned or shared ownership in four different rattletrap Model Ts. A ten-year-old could learn to drive and repair that remarkable vehicle.

McBrien expected his invited students to drive, fix flat tires, and take care of necessary repairs while he kept busy with observing and notetaking. He said he liked Model Ts because they moved slowly, were open to the sun and wind, afforded a perfect view of the landscape, and they could be easily and cheaply repaired. He never forced upon us his knowledge of events that had occurred in the places where we traveled in the West, but if we gave him an opening— and we usually did—he would respond with one of his delightful little incidents, accompanied perhaps by an incisive biography, all laid out for us right where it had happened. When I hear that old adage about a good teacher needing only a simple bench with the teacher at one end and the student at the other, I want to amend it to the front seat of a Model T Ford with the student at the wheel and the teacher at his side, unlocking the past and relating it to present and future.

These journeys and others that crisscrossed the West formed a basis for most of the books I would later write. That was half a century ago, in a time not too distant from the years of cattle drives and the last Indian wars. We traveled mainly over unpaved roads, across landscapes little different from those of the nineteenth century. We had many small adventures, meeting inhabitants of little towns and Indians on reservations who remembered the great events of that earlier time.

Two other college activities were important to my future, although I did not realize this at the time. One was being editor of the student newspaper, a position that afforded frequent opportunities to experiment with words in print. Student newspapers don't have to show a profit, and their editors are usually excused for youthful peccadillos. The other campus activity was employment in the library. Virtually every student in the college worked part-time, and because of my fascination with books, I obtained a student assistantship in the library. During my last semester, I changed my mind about becoming a teacher, and resolved to become a librarian.

By graduation time, I had applied to various universities where library science was taught, and had narrowed my choice down to two. In the world outside of the sheltered college campus, the greatest economic depression of our times waited for us like a treacherous quagmire. We were aware that jobs were hard to find, and I knew I must earn my way through graduate school. Shall I go to the University of Illinois in the small town of Urbana, or George Washington University in Washington, D.C.? I took this quandary to my college mentor, Dean McBrien. Go to the nation's capital, he advised immediately. A year in Washington would be an education in itself; it was a prosperous city; part-time employment should be easy to find. Fifteen years later I finally reached the University of Illinois, but I followed McBrien's advice and went first to Washington. He was right about the city being an education in itself, and its prosperity, but he was wrong about good jobs being easy to find.

By the time I arrived there, even the nation's capital was engulfed in the Great Depression. From all across the country, college graduates by the hundreds, and aging veterans of World War I, were pouring into the city seeking employment or military bonuses. I found a place to sleep in a basement room with seven other college graduates, our cots pushed together in a solid line. One man boasted a Ph.D., and appropriately he had the best job of the lot of us; he drove a taxicab.

George Washington University's library school, being a victim of World War II, no longer exists, but in the 1930s its small faculty was supplemented by dozens of visiting professional librarians from government agencies and other institutions in the capital. By working as a part-time elevator operator, janitor, tire repairman, and filling-station jockey, I managed to pay for one or two night courses each semester in the university. After I went to work nights for Willard Marriott, I had to switch to day classes.

Marriott opened the first drive-in barbecue stands in Washington, one near the baseball park, where the old Senators team played, the other on the edge of the District of Columbia near Chevy Chase, Maryland. Marriott called them Hot Shoppes, and developed a system for serving customers at no expense to himself. The pretty girls he employed took orders from customers in their automobiles, then rushed into the Hot Shoppe, purchased the sandwiches and drinks, and delivered them on a tray attached to the car doors. Tips were their only income, and if the girls were busy with several customers, and one drove off without paying, the girls were out-of-pocket for whatever they had paid for the food and drinks.

To prevent such thefts and to remove trays from cars ready to leave, as well as to stop quarrels over territorial rights among the girls, Marriott employed a male known as a curbmaster. That was the job that I endured for several months. The salary was small, but after midnight the girls departed and a curbmaster could pick up a few tips serving trays to night owls. During the midwinter months, however, business was so slow that almost all of us were laid off until spring. Fortunately during that dark period, my younger sister, who had come to Washington to work for the Patent Office, took me in out of the cold and let me sleep on a divan in her apartment.

That winter was the very depth of the Great Depression, the last weeks of President Hoover, and the first days of President Roosevelt who brought his New Deal to Washington and changed it from a somnolent Southern town into an exciting and glittering city.

From the time of my arrival in Washington I had

At Romany Marie's in Greenwich Village, late 1930s:
from left, Grace Lumpkin, unidentified man,
Bruce Crawford, Sally Brown, Dee Brown, Myra Page

taken every civil service examination that I felt qualified for, and suddenly a very minor library position in the Food and Drug Administration was offered me.

I remember Willard Marriott's reaction when I told him I was leaving to work for the government. He promised that if I would stick with him he would make me a manager of one of his new Hot Shoppes. If I left him for the government, I was a fool. He was probably right. How could I know that his Hot Shoppes would grow into a billion-dollar food and hotel and theme-park industry? But he drove his employees and himself at a hard pace. He might have made me rich, but I probably would not have lived to enjoy it.

After reporting for duty at the Food and Drug Administration library, I reentered night classes at George Washington University. While I was completing work for a library degree, I was fortunate enough to persuade Sally Stroud to marry me. I had known her during college days. Along with an army of other young Americans she had come to Washington to work for the New Deal.

As I have already noted, those were exhilarating times. President Roosevelt surrounded himself with several brilliant men and women of good intentions, as well as a few eccentrics who made life interesting. During this same period, the voters out in the states were electing congressmen several notches above the old-line politicians who had let the country slide into economic stagnation and despair. Most of these lively newcomers to the federal government made themselves available in frequent meetings large and small, so that everyone in Washington had a sense of

participation in the various New Deal programs that we seriously believed were keeping the nation from collapsing.

One enterprise that especially appealed to me was the Federal Writers Project. If I had not been fortunate enough to receive promotions and transfers into better jobs within the Department of Agriculture library system, I would have made an earnest effort to join the Writers Project which eventually created a considerable body of badly needed American source materials, including those wonderful WPA guidebooks to the states. After almost half a century these books are so esteemed that most of them are kept constantly in print.

Several friends worked in the Writers Project, so that I was often invited to their Sunday gatherings and occasional weekend jaunts and hikes into the Blue Ridge Mountains. Best remembered are Ben Botkin, the folklorist; Jack Conroy, the proletarian author and editor; Jerre Mangione, who eventually wrote the project's history; John Cheever, before he became famous; and Vardis Fisher, who often came in from Idaho.

Dee Brown (center) with Jack Conroy and Nick Ray,
Washington, D.C., 1938

I admired these people, and it was largely through knowing them that I began submitting manuscripts to the numerous "little magazines" that were springing up to set the world to right. A short story I wrote that was based upon experiences at the drive-in barbecue was published in one of them, and was noticed by a New York literary agent, Mavis McIntosh. An inquiry from her as to whether I might have a novel in progress inspired me to start one immediately. I decided to try a satire on the burgeoning bureaucracy of New Deal Washington. Compared to our present governmental bureaucracy—which would be impossible to satirize—the New Deal's was a fairly lighthearted state of confusion rather than total bedlam. The phenomenon was new to almost everybody, and I thought it had its amusing aspects. And so I pummeled the government in a broad way.

To my surprise, Mavis McIntosh placed the manuscript rather quickly with a small publisher in Philadelphia—Macrae-Smith. My editor was Edward Shenton, who was also an artist and had done illustrations for some of Marjorie Kinnan Rawlings' books about Florida. Shenton evidently liked my satirical novel. He suggested only a few changes, and had it copy edited for the printer during the last week of November 1941.

On December 8, the day after Pearl Harbor, I received a call from Shenton, a brief statement that he was coming down to Washington the next day on government business and would like to meet me in the bar of the old Willard Hotel. At the agreed hour I met him, and after a few preliminary remarks about the shock of war that had come with such suddenness upon us, he told me that his company could not publish my book. In wartime, especially when the nation seemed to be so disorganized, any criticism of the government, no matter how mild, would be considered unpatriotic. "You must have some plan for a second novel," he said. "Perhaps something patriotic?"

I had nothing particular in mind, but I told him I did. Stung by the loss of my ill-starred contemporary novel, I resolved to retreat into the nineteenth century, where I have remained ever since. During my boyhood, one of my grandmothers told me stories about Davy Crockett who, she said, had hunted bears with her father along the Duck River in Tennessee. I wanted to write Crockett's biography, but I sensed there would be no time for the research and so I made his life story into a historical novel. In three months I had the manuscript ready, and in about the same length of time Macrae-Smith published my first book, *Wave High the Banner,* a title that my wife plucked out of an obscure poem by Shelley.

Six months later I was in the army doing basic training with the Eightieth Infantry division in Tennessee. Almost everybody who served in the military during World War II has stories to tell of inexplicable foul-ups and plain lunacies, and I had more than my fair share.

In retrospect I look upon the continuous muddling as being the result of an army of untrained

*End of basic training at Camp Forrest, Tennessee, 1942:
the author (right) with friend*

civilians placed in uniforms with varying degrees of command authority that few of the bearers understood how to apply. After completing basic training we left our barracks for maneuvers along the same Duck River in Tennessee where my great-grandfather had hunted bears with Davy Crockett. During the maneuvers, one of my feet was injured in a truck accident that put me on limited service and assignment to a jeep as assistant to a sergeant in charge of the battalion's situation maps. With the onset of cold rainy weather we moved northward with another division to re-enact the Civil War's Battle of Stones River in the same area where it had been fought eighty years or so before.

For this exercise, the jeep, the maps, the sergeant, and I were assigned to an intelligence company commanded by Major James Warner Bellah, who was as much an amateur as the rest of us. Because he spent considerable time examining the battle maps, we saw Major Bellah frequently and soon learned that he was a student of American Indian guerrilla warfare. Somewhat like the heroes of the movie scripts he later wrote for John Ford and John Wayne, Bellah took daring risks. He led us behind the "enemy" lines where most of us were captured and imprisoned in the opposing division's stockade. Some of the men were amused by Major Bellah, but I thought he had style.

Before we won or lost the Battle of Stones River, one of those inexplicable orders from on high transferred me to a special-training program at Auburn University in Alabama, where with thirty or

Linda and Mitchell Brown, 1950s

was then the army. I wound up at the Army Ground Forces Headquarters in Washington.

For the first time I was assigned duties similar to those I had performed in civilian life. Although the war was nearing its end, and I had not fired a shot in my country's defense, I found the AGF headquarters schedule quite absorbing. A procession of colorful military officers came and went, including the peripatetic Major Bellah who had been invalided home from Southeast Asia.

Sally and Mitchell Brown, 1968

so other puzzled enlisted men I was subjected to numerous tests. One morning without warning we were hurried aboard a Pullman car bound for Philadelphia, our commander a master sergeant who carried all our records in a large military folder. Our destination, he told us, was the University of Pennsylvania. Upon arrival in Philadelphia, we discovered that the University of Pennsylvania had never heard of us. As the master sergeant put it, all of us could have gone over the hill to home.

We were quartered in a dormitory where we lived for several weeks, awaiting clarification of our status and spending most of our waking hours under the command of a football coach who kept us running up and down the banks of the Schuylkill River. Other details of this bizarre period are too lengthy to relate, but eventually the military machine informed us that the University of Iowa should have been our destination and that we would be traveling there immediately.

At Iowa City, Iowa, the first uniformed army officer we had seen in some time told us that we had been selected to devise tests for various military specialties. At the end of our training period, he assured us, we would be commissioned and assigned to appropriate posts. We went into the project with some enthusiasm, but I think few of us were surprised several weeks later when the mysterious powers above decided to abandon the entire enterprise and distribute us to other duties in the vast machine that

It was my good fortune to meet Martin Schmitt there. We worked together on several assignments, and after the war ended, leaving us with much idle time until we were eligible for discharges, we set out upon a project of our own—collecting photographs for a pictorial history of the Indian wars.

Getting the book into print was a long and arduous process. The cost of printing collections of photographs at that time was relatively much more expensive than at present. Macmillan was quite interested at first, but decided they could not risk the investment. The University of Oklahoma Press attempted to obtain a special grant to cover expenses, but failed to do so, and after many months returned the photographs in rather poor condition. Not long after that, a historian at the university published a history of the Indian wars, using as illustrations a number of the photographs we had collected.

At U.S. Senate hearings with Senator Jim Abourezk and Alvin Josephy, 1976

By this time Schmitt and I were out of the army and back into civilian life. When Schmitt came east on vacation from his post on the West Coast, we decided to replace the damaged photographs and try to interest Charles Scribner's Sons, resolving that this would be our last effort to find a publisher. We knew that Scribner had recently published a selection of Civil War photographs without going bankrupt.

Scribner was enthusiastic from the beginning; Charles Scribner II wrote us a personal letter. Because I was in the East while Schmitt was in the West, I had the pleasure of working closely with a pair of splendid editors, R. V. Coleman and Joe Hopkins. The only time of doubt about the book's fate was on the day I was summoned to New York for a final meeting that was to include a consultation with the famous Maxwell Perkins, who at that time made the final approval on every book published by Scribner. I had never met or seen him.

Before I was sent to Perkins's office, Coleman and Hopkins both warned me that he often turned off his hearing aid during conversations, but that I should answer all his questions to the point, and make no comments about anything unless asked.

Perkins's office was a long room with several windows that had very wide sills. Along the windowsills and then around the edges of a large table, Perkins had placed in sequence the 270 eight-by-ten photographs, their typed captions beneath. With Perkins leading the way, we walked along the lines of photographs, he occasionally pointing down at one and asking a question. Three or four times he shifted the order of arrangement, glancing at me as if to demand my approval and saying something about a slight alteration of captions being necessary with the change of sequence.

At the very end, he stood erect and looked me straight in the eyes. "Where are the Navajos?" he demanded.

Somewhat lamely I explained that we had been unable to find enough Navajo photographs to fit the period and theme of our picture narrative. (Some years later the very photographs we had wanted suddenly appeared from some lost hiding place.)

Perkins looked unhappy over my reply. "The Navajos are my favorite tribe," he said. Then he shrugged, waved me out of his office, and turned toward his desk. "We'll make a fine book," he called after me. "Tell Coleman it's all right." That was my only meeting with Maxwell Perkins.

Before the book was published by Scribner under the title *Fighting Indians of the West,* I returned to my library position at the Department of Agriculture. An offer of a better post at the Aberdeen Proving Ground in Maryland took me back to the military as a civilian employee.

In 1948 the University of Illinois gave me a chance to return to my preferred subject field by appointing me agriculture librarian. I had long dreamed of working on a campus, with access to a great library, and Illinois has one of the great collections.

By this time I was the father of a son, Mitchell, and a daughter, Linda. Life in a small university-town in the 1950s proved to be quite stimulating. Martin Schmitt had gone to the University of Oregon as an archivist, but we managed to meet and correspond often enough to put together two more books of historical photographs that told in narrative form the story of the early cattle industry (*Trail Driving Days*) and of frontier settlement (*The Settler's West*). Both were published with some success by Scribner, and the trilogy has been reprinted many times, once even in reduced size paperback.

Using sources that fell into my hands almost serendipitously, I wrote *Grierson's Raid,* my first Civil War history. It was published by the University of Illinois Press in 1954. Honors and prestige may result from university-press books, but they seldom repay more than the research costs. In those pre-Sputnik years, university salaries were low, and I needed a new automobile. One of Harold Matson Company's agents, James Street, Jr., assured me he could sell a western novel I outlined for him, for enough money to buy a car. And so was published my first western, *Yellowhorse,* at Houghton Mifflin.

At this period in my life I thought I knew the different kinds of books I could write, and those I wanted to write. Yet writing was still an avocation, something I did partly for pleasure, especially the pleasure of research. With full-time librarianship, which required time-consuming tasks both delightful and onerous, I was a part-time writer. By the end of the 1950s, however, I had published nine books, three fiction and six nonfiction. Among the latter were *The Gentle Tamers,* a study of women in the Old West, and a second Civil War history, *The Bold Cavaliers,* the story of Morgan's Kentucky cavalry raiders.

During the 1960s I completed eight more, including *The Galvanized Yankees* which required the most painstaking research of any of my books, and *The Year of the Century: 1876* which is my favorite

With grandson Nicolas, 1962

because the research was so enjoyable.

By this time I did not know it, but I was ready to write *Bury My Heart at Wounded Knee.* An editor, Lee Schryver of McKay, suggested that I write a book for juveniles about the Indian wars. For several years, while doing research for works on the American West, I had been collecting speeches and statements made by American Indians, with some expectation that I might eventually fit them into a book. I prepared an outline for a short volume meant for young people, told from the viewpoint of a young Indian, but when I sent it to my agent, Peter Matson, he reacted with an enthusiastic suggestion that I enlarge the scope of the book so that it would no longer be a short work for juvenile readers. When the final outline was ready, Matson obtained a much larger offer from John Dodds at Holt, Rinehart and Winston than Schryver's company was willing to meet. During the two years that followed, the text and title went through several changes, and the manuscript was guided by two editors, Alan Rinzler and Tom Wallace.

The success of *Bury My Heart* surprised the publishers and me. It moved into the best-seller lists early in 1971 and remained at the top most weeks until the end of the year. The resulting travel and television requirements I managed to handle, but the flood of letters overwhelmed me. At first I tried to answer every letter, but by midsummer I simply gave up until the mail subsided. Within a year or so, the paperback and foreign-language editions started the torrent all over again.

For about a year these unfamiliar distractions kept me away from my writing. When I returned to the typewriter, I completed two books for young

Nicolas and Dee at Pinnacle Mountain, 1983

people that I had been working on before I started *Bury My Heart.* Then Holt, Rinehart and Winston proposed a big illustrated book about the West to be published jointly with George Rainbird and Michael Joseph in London. I decided that I did not want to assemble a mere album with running captions around a clutter of pictures. Instead I selected a gallery of representative Westerners and did a serious treatment of their reasons for venturing into the American frontier. While I was still writing the chapters, the Rainbird editors began collecting illustrations. They manufactured a beautiful book filled with drawings, photographs, and paintings that fit the text remarkably well. Although it has been referred to as my "coffee-table" book, I like to think that *The Westerners* is more than that. The publishers invited me to London to celebrate its publication and several foreign-language editions followed.

After the *The Westerners* I tackled a difficult research effort in hopes of writing a new version of the history of western railroads—the chicanery as well as the romance. *Hear That Lonesome Whistle Blow* was published in 1977. After that, for a change of pace, I selected some of my favorite Indian tales (*Teepee Tales*) and retold them for modern young readers. Before this book was published, I was already at work on *Creek Mary's Blood,* a long historical novel that began in Georgia in the eighteenth century and ended in Montana early in the twentieth century. Before writing *Creek Mary's Blood,* I had read many novels about white families moving westward and I thought it was time for a story about an Indian family following the frontier into the West. It was published in 1980.

Killdeer Mountain (1983) and *Conspiracy of Knaves* (1987) are both historical novels, the first set in the West, the second during the last year of the Civil War. Like almost all the fiction I have written, they are based upon actual events and real people.

Nicolas, Linda, and Dee, 1984

And what of the future? Because far too many books are published, we writers should give more deliberation to what we are about to create. Is it entertaining, is it informative, is it unique? Can the world get along without it? I prefer nonfiction, which can be entertaining as well as informative, but I have not yet written that picaresque novel I've long dreamed of doing. Perhaps I shall get to it after I finish the nonfiction work that is still in the slow stages of planning and research, and which I hope will contain at least some small kernel that the world is in need of.

BIBLIOGRAPHY

Fiction:

Wave High the Banner. Philadelphia: Macrae-Smith, 1942.

Yellowhorse. Boston: Houghton, 1956.

Cavalry Scout. New York: Permabooks, 1958.

They Went Thataway. New York: Putnam, 1960; also published as *Pardon My Pandemonium.* Little Rock, Ark.: August House, 1984.

The Girl from Fort Wicked. Garden City, N.Y.: Doubleday, 1964.

Action at Beecher Island. Garden City, N.Y.: Doubleday, 1967.

Teepee Tales of the American Indians (retold by the author; illustrated by Louis Mofsie; for children). New York: Holt, 1979.

Creek Mary's Blood. New York: Holt, 1980.

Killdeer Mountain. New York: Holt, 1983; London: Hutchinson, 1983.

A Conspiracy of Knaves. New York: Holt, 1987.

Nonfiction:

Fighting Indians of the West, with Martin F. Schmitt. New York and London: Scribner, 1948.

Trail Driving Days, with M.F. Schmitt. New York and London: Scribner, 1952.

Grierson's Raid. Urbana, Ill.: University of Illinois Press, 1954.

The Settlers' West, with M.F. Schmitt. New York and London: Scribner, 1955.

The Gentle Tamers: Women of the Old Wild West. New York: Putnam, 1958; London: Barrie & Jenkins, 1973.

The Bold Cavaliers: Morgan's Second Kentucky Cavalry Raiders. Philadelphia: Lippincott, 1959.

Fort Phil Kearny: An American Saga. New York: Putnam, 1962; also published as *The Fetterman Massacre.* London: Barrie & Jenkins, 1972.

The Galvanized Yankees. Urbana, Ill.: University of Illinois Press, 1963.

Showdown at Little Big Horn (for young people). New York: Putnam, 1964.

The Year of the Century: 1876. New York: Scribner, 1966.

Bury My Heart at Wounded Knee: An Indian History of the American West. New York: Holt, 1970; London: Barrie & Jenkins, 1971.

Andrew Jackson and the Battle of New Orleans. New York: Putnam, 1972.

Tales of the Warrior Ants (for young people). New York: Putnam, 1973.

The Westerners. New York: Holt, 1974; London: M. Joseph, 1974.

Hear That Lonesome Whistle Blow: Railroads in the West. New York: Holt, 1977; London: Chatto & Windus, 1977.

The American Spa: Hot Springs, Arkansas. Little Rock, Ark.: Rose Publishing, 1982.

Editor of:

Pawnee, Blackfoot, and Cheyenne, by George B. Grinnell. New York: Scribner, 1961.

Rural America Series. Wilmington, Del.: Scholarly Resources, 1973.

Dee Brown in caricature

George Fisher

George Mackay Brown

1921-

The author outside his door, 1981

I

Look at the globe: Orkney is a small cluster of islands to the north of Scotland, with the North Sea on one side and the Atlantic on the other—a few bits of clay discarded from the continents' making.

Orkney is of small consequence in the geopolitics of today.

But when Europe was the main world-stage, in the Middle Ages, the earldom of Orkney was of consequence in the counsels of Europe. Earl Thorfinn in the eleventh century was as powerful at least

as the King of Scotland. Orkney lay midway on the great sea routes between Norway and Scotland and Ireland. Kinsmen of Thorfinn were the Dukes of Normandy, one of whom became William the Conqueror of England. The same Thorfinn, by intermarriage with the ruling house of Scotland, was a cousin of Macbeth.

The medieval Earls of Orkney lived in considerable style in their halls at Orphir, Birsay, and Kirkwall. They played their parts stylishly enough on the political chessboard of Europe. They fostered poets in their little courts. When Earl Rognvald II in mid-twelfth century pilgrimed in fifteen ships to Jerusalem and Byzantium and Rome he had a company of poets with him to celebrate the voyage, and he himself was as good a poet as any of them.

Rognvald's uncle, Earl Magnus, is the most astonishing figure in all that rich history. He was born to political dominance; he chose (or was chosen) instead to fulfil his days beside a barren stone in Egilsay island, waiting for the bite of the executioner's axe into his head. So, he seemed to be "out of the story," as the saga-men described a death. For Magnus the end was the beginning. He was called a saint first by the common people; then the bishop of Orkney and all the Western church cried "laudate" and "amen." A cathedral of Saint Magnus in red stone was soon rising in Kirkwall, at the centre of Orkney.

The history of the earls and vikings and chief men of Orkney over three centuries is written in a magnificent narrative called *Orkneyinga Saga*. Without that source-book, I would be a very different kind of writer; I acknowledge the debt.

The secular glory did not last. Orkney passed from the Norwegian into the Scottish orbit. Long centuries of darkness, poverty, oppression followed. The Norse lawbook was thrown out. The free farmers of Orkney suddenly found themselves serfs. Their language slowly gave way to Scots, which is a fine language in its own right; but when an alien tongue is forced on a people, a whole tradition is corrupted and brought down. From those dark centuries only a few ballads and song-fragments and bits of oral tradition survive.

The modern Orcadians are a mixture of Scandinavians, Scots, and Picts (those early Celts who tilled and defended the islands, not unworthily, until the Vikings fell on them suddenly from the east). Orcadians remember the great story, but in a romantic way, claiming to be "sons of the Vikings," though most genealogies peter out a few generations back. For the most part, the twenty thousand modern Orcadians are moderately prosperous farmers—the islands are fertile—and men knowledgeable about the sea: sailors and fishermen abound through the generations, and there is a wealth of traditional stories about their kind. The pirate Gow, an eighteenth-century Stromness man, troubled the North Atlantic for a winter. A midshipman, George Stewart, sailed on the *Bounty* and joined the mutineers. John Rae, an Arctic explorer, came on the few tragic relics of the Franklin expedition that set out to find the northwest passage a century and a half ago. . . . There was an outflurry and flame of witches in the seventeenth century. Here and there, in his manse, a minister sat beside his winter candle over books and papers and quill: learned men whose natural-science observations are still admired.

Year by year, except in times of famine and tempest, there was the golden harvest of corn and the silver torrents of fish.

Shipwreck, smuggling, the press-gang: the annals of Orkney are starred with the stuff of narrative and poetry. There is no escaping it. That richness was there, waiting for me, when I began to write.

There is the capital town, Kirkwall, with its cathedral and merchants and administrators, and its recent wealth of scholars and men of talent—Laing, Hossack, Mooney, Hugh Marwick, Robert Rendall, D.J. Robertson, Ernest Marwick.

Stromness, in the southwest, is a younger town, and with its closes and piers more beautiful, like a salt-sea ballad in stone. There I was born, in 1921.

I can't go back further in ancestry than my father's father, who was a shoemaker in Stromness. Brown is a common name in the southwest part of Orkney: Stromness and Sandwick. I think the original Browns must have come out of Scotland sometime in the seventeenth century, in the wake of all the Scots who flooded the islands after the sinister-royal Stuart earls, Robert and Patrick. I think, by my grandfather's time, the Browns had come down a little; some earlier Browns had been fairly prosperous farmers and merchants.

My mother first saw Stromness when she was sixteen. She was one of a family of nine, Gaelic-speaking children of a crofter-fisherman in Strathy, Sutherlandshire. When she went to school, aged five, she could say only "yes" and "no" in English.

I have been told that a famous Mackay poet flourished in that part of the Highlands. I know nothing about him, but I am aware of a Celtic element in my writing—the numinous mystical strand—which can only have come to me through my mother.

A small croft couldn't keep such a large family. A distant relative had prospered in the hotel trade. To his new hotel in Stromness my mother came to be a waitress. She was pretty, with black hair and blue eyes and altogether pleasant in her nature. Having been brought up in the extreme Calvinism of the Free Presbyterian Church, she was horrified when she was told that she must work in the hotel on Sundays as well as on other days. I think she spent a few sleepless nights. In the end she decided to stay, for a time at least, in this little Babylon, Stromness. She stayed, as it turned out, for the rest of her life, except for a brief holiday now and then in the midst of a hardworking cheerful life.

I think she met my father at a local dance. She thought him very forward when he asked for a goodnight kiss, and determined not to see him again. But she must have. They were married in Strathy, Sutherland, in midsummer 1910. A tribe of passing tinkers joined in the wedding dance.

My father and mother settled down in a house a stone's throw from where I'm writing this.

John Brown was a tailor, but there was little work for tailors in those early days of ready-made clothes, and so he became a postman, and sat only occasionally on the tailor's bench.

Six children were born of the marriage, of whom I was the youngest. That was in another house, nearer to the big pier that was the hub of the town.

II

About fifty boys and girls, clustered around the age of five, we sat at our desks. It was our first day at school. Miss Matheson, a dark severe kind lady, stood at that magical thing, the blackboard, and made shapes on it with coloured chalks.

The desks were magical too. I had never been in such a huge high room before. I had not seen so many boys and girls together. We sat at the desks, two by two, with slates in frames slotted into them.

Most of the boys wore jerseys with glass buttons at the neck, and short trousers, and stockings pulled up to the knees. We each had a little satchel, to carry our reading books.

But first there was the business of learning to read. Miss Matheson chalked an *a* on the blackboard. "This is the school cat!" said she, "and it says 'aah!'. . . ." Every letter of the alphabet was a crea-

"The pier of G.M. Brown's childhood"

ture and it made its own sound. *S* was a snake and it hissed, "ssss! . . ."

I forget how Miss Matheson managed with letters like *g* and *x*. But the signs and the sounds were magical too.

We were lured into literacy by such cajolery.

There were threats too, if we went astray: a conical dunce's cap to wear, exiled and ashamed, in a corner of the classroom. If we swore, or told a lie, there was a bar of soap to wash our tongues. But the punishments were never put into effect, that I remember.

The reading book we were given had pictures in it. The very first page read, "A fat cat sat on a mat."

There were counting frames to learn numbers. So, with coloured beads, we were initiated into the mystery of mathematics.

Outside, on the stone steps, a bell rang. It was the dismissal.

Hundreds of boys and girls aged from five to twelve swirled, shouting, through the school gates, like a flock of birds.

I can't remember this: but my mother said I came home from school that first morning, and threw my new satchel in the corner, and said, "I'm never going back to that place again."

III

My sister was ten years older than I. She told me stories, she recited ballads. They were mostly about forlorn and tragic love. Many of the heroines in the stories "died of a broken heart." I couldn't imagine what it might be to die of a broken heart. Death to a six-year-old, like birth or love, is an unimaginable state. Yet a child accepts it. To "die of a broken heart"—as the bell tolled in my sister's mouth—was a marvellous if melancholy resolution. There is a Scottish ballad, "Willie Drowned in Yarrow," in which the hero is drowned going to the love tryst with his sweetheart. For many days an image lingered in my mind: a brimming stream, and a straw hat (Willie's) floating on it. It was a sad yet beautiful image.

My father sometimes sang Edwardian music-hall songs, or evangelical hymns, especially round about New Year: "I'll Stick to the Ship, Lads" or "It Was Only a Beautiful Picture in a Beautiful Golden Frame" or "While London Sleeps" or "The Bible at Home." He sang with style and gusto and true theatricality. He might have been a good actor, given the chance.

What I cherished most about my father was his

quick satirical wit. He hated any kind of hypocrisy or false sentiment: especially certain women bewailing about the doors some local tragedy, like a cat gone missing or some local magnate laid aside with rheumatics or a flu. He had no respect, as many of the islanders did, for professional people or idle well-to-do people. "Poor boys who had got on in the world"—ah, but they were to be admired. A crofter's son called John Gunn—a poor country lad who had walked to school in Stromness every morning, maybe barefooted, certainly with a peat under his arm to keep the classroom fire going—my father had an enormous respect for him. John Gunn had gone on to Edinburgh University, and got a doctorate there, and become a director in a famous publishing firm, and had edited serious works and written adventure stories for boys.

For the useless sons of privileged people my father kept a biting satirical tongue.

For the poor and outcasts of the earth he had a deep genuine sympathy. Among his favourite books were *The People of the Abyss* by Jack London, *The Ragged-Trousered Philanthropists* by Robert Tressall, *The Rat-Pit* by Patrick MacGill: all books that celebrate the downtrodden and the oppressed. Socialism moved his heart rather than his head.

His greatest hero was General William Booth, founder of the Salvation Army. He had, as a young man, heard Booth preach twice in one day in Glasgow. He mentioned as a strange coincidence that on both occasions, in that huge crowded hall, he had found himself sitting next to the same stranger.

Many of my father's attitudes towards hypocrisy and social pretention rubbed off on to me; and they still quicken in me at the least provocation.

"Whatever happens to you in your lives, remain humble," he was forever telling his children. (He didn't mean "humble" in the Uriah Heep sense, but in the theological sense of dust having to return to dust.)

Meantime, all day and every day, my mother went singing wordlessly about her baking and sweeping and washing. She had no ear for music at all, but her mouth-music was to me, always, a very happy and reassuring sound. There may have been some remnants of ancient Celtic chant in it.

IV

We boys devoted all our passion and latent aggressiveness to playing football. Football put excitement and pattern into our childhood. So long as there was a ball, we played football, and if there was no ball, we would kick an empty tin. And we played

George (holding a football book) with Mother, Mary Jane Mackay Brown, about 1930

anywhere, in the school playground, or in a field, or on the street (wary always of the two policemen who went back and fore, back and fore, all day long, two tall blue dreaded guardians). Stromness being a little town, we divided it into a "north-end" and a "south-end," and regularly we played football against each other—sometimes in a high field near the summit of Brinkie's Brae, sometimes in a field with an old well in it. On those famous occasions we had a real football (boys' size) owned by a boy from one of the richer families. For years I loved football more than anything else in life. Our town had its adult football team that played regularly against one or other of the Kirkwall teams. We watched our heroes in action every week or so at the Market Green, and Greeks and Trojans never had more thrilled spectators at their battles. (Stromness Athletic was a good team in those days, and won famous victories.)

South of Orkney was the great nation of Scotland, and the Scottish towns and cities had professional teams that did battle every Saturday afternoon. We read newspaper reports of those games as if the hackneyed metaphors were epic poetry. Glasgow housed the two most famous teams, Rangers and Celtic. Quite arbitrarily, I chose Celtic to give all my allegiance to. In view of some things that happened later, it is interesting that Celtic was then the team of the powerful Catholic faction in the west of Scotland. (Rangers to this day is strictly Protestant, and has never had a Catholic player or director or groundsman.) One of the great tragedies of my childhood was the death of the young Celtic goalkeeper, John Thomson; going down to save a certain goal by the Rangers' centre-forward Sam English, he was accidentally kicked on the head and died that same night.

Radio (or "the wireless") was just beginning in Orkney in the early thirties. Our household was too poor to have a wireless then. In the families that did have it, the reception was thin and fluctuating. One great Saturday fell each April, the international football match between Scotland and England. With what cunning, or brazenness, we boys contrived to get into houses that had wirelesses! We were just too young to remember the greatest Scottish team there has ever been, that defeated England by five goals to one in London in 1928. But we were always hoping for a repeat of that most glorious of victories. There were victories, of course, but more often than not we went home heavy-hearted, for the English seemed to be getting harder to beat as the years passed.

Football set one part of my imagination free. At home, in front of the fire or in the bedroom I shared with my three elder brothers, I invented imaginary football teams—a score of them, maybe, in a first league and a second league, and I had them playing against each other in the wildly excited arena of my mind. The throwing of dice, I think, decided the result of each game—a win, a loss, a draw. Hours and months I spent in this fantasy world, and for me at the age of ten it had all the excitement and delight that later I got from writing stories and poems. Literature too is a lonely trade, in which the author and some unknown protagonist ("the collective unconscious" perhaps) dice with each other for control of the masks and the dance. It is a liberation into a world uncluttered by the trash and trivialities of everyday life.

About the same time I edited a magazine called, of course, *The Celt.* The single handwritten copy, of which I was sole contributor of stories, crossword puzzles, jokes, and letters, had a circulation of five or six; all the readers were classmates and supporters of Glasgow Celtic.

If any adult asked me what I was going to be when I grew up, I answered promptly, "A football reporter." Surely no job on earth could be so satisfying and exciting: the shifting coloured patterns, the lyrical interplay of passes, the epic surge of a forward-line on the goal, the chorus of triumph, the elegiac cry of defeat—I could compass them all with my reporter's pencil.

But what are those ball games, really? A ritualis-tic masque, a dance of opposites, winter and summer contending for the life-giver, the sun. Perhaps, to find the source, we have to back much further than the first Greek chorus and "goat-song."

V

I remember quite clearly writing my first poem. I was sitting alone in a field between the Temperance Hall and a big house—now a hotel—called The Braes, and I wrote the poem in pencil on a scrap of paper. What could I have been sitting alone in a field for, on a Saturday morning? It must be that my friends hadn't turned up for a kick or two at the ball.

The poem is lost, but I remember it was written in ballad-type quatrains, and that it was in praise of my native town, Stromness.

I must have thought well of the poem, because I took it home and showed it to my parents, and they read it and were very pleased (though in general neither of them cared very much for verse).

I don't think, after that first fine careless rapture, that I wrote another poem for five years at least. Then, in adolescence, they came in a spate, and they were altogether different in tone, sombre and morbid, for I was going through a rough time.

VI

A child does not know that he has a gift, for he exercises it naturally and joyfully, as he runs or swims. I did not know that I had any particular way with words, until we had to write a weekly essay, or composition, in class. Every week the teacher would say, "George Brown has written the best essay this week again. . . ." Why, I asked myself, should that be? Why should the pupils at the desks around me be grunting and fretting to get a few more words on to the page, and the essay had flowed out of me, easy and graceful from beginning to end?

I could not account for it. At the other school subjects I had average ability only. History touched my imagination. Arithmetic and music were unendurably dull. I think I was among the very worst at art.

"George writes good essays," said our teacher, "because he reads good books."

In fact I didn't read the books considered good at all: Robert Louis Stevenson, Dickens and Scott, Bulwer Lytton and Ballantyne. The literature we boys devoured was disapproved of by parents and teachers—they were the "twopenny dreadfuls," five of which every week issued from a press in Dundee, Scotland. We couldn't afford to buy them all—*Wizard, Adventure, Rover, Hotspur, Skipper*—but we managed to get hands on most of them by some complex form of barter. *Hotspur* I liked best for it was mostly about English public schools. Why this kind of aggressively all-male fiction should have cast such a spell I still can't explain: it may have been an early instinctive revolt against the mysterious perilous feminine principle, without which life is barren and unfulfilled; and yet the growing boy dreads the intimations of that mystery. Most of the women I knew were gentle good people, except for a few schoolteachers and neighbors going with whispered gossip between the doors. Girls were strange creatures to be avoided as best one could. . . . I have learned since that life in those English public schools was often a hideous torment for sensitive boys. To me, then, they were like medieval fortresses of adventure and enchantment and dragon-slaying. Best of all the boys' papers were the weekly *Gem* and *Magnet*—one of which was about Grayfriars School and a fat gluttonish cowardly boy called Billy Bunter, whom the other boys tormented mercilessly. Bunter was a kind of juvenile Falstaff, without Falstaff's poetry and humour. . . . Two novels of school life, *The Fifth Form at St. Dominic's,* and *St. Winifred's; or, The World of School* reduced me to secret lyrical tears.

As for the excluded women of that genre: of course when I started to write seriously I had to give them entrance into the world of my imagination. "The feminine principle" was a good leaven. It set free those elements of courage, compassion, wisdom, mystery, serenity, steadfastness that are different in quality, and on the whole more to be admired, than the equivalent virtues in men. . . .

The unfolding imagination must feed on what it finds nourishing—never on what it is told must be good for it. I still can't read Scott or Dickens with any joy; school, in early adolescence, destroyed them for me.

VII

Suddenly, in mid-teens, the boy becomes the man. It can be a metamorphosis very dreadful and devastating. As I am concerned here merely with the craft of literature as I have come to practice it, I will say nothing about my experiences crossing the border into the iron-gray country of adulthood. There was intense loneliness and suffering, that seemed to last for years, but may have occupied only a few winter months. At that dreadful time, literature was a drug and an anodyne; the Romantic poets, especially Shelley and Keats, were my priests and doctors. As heroin addicts inject brief tastes of heaven into themselves, perhaps at that time I could not have lived

George with his mother, late 1960s

without daily shots of "Adonais," "Ode to a Nightingale," "Christabel," "To a Skylark," "The Garden of Proserpine," "The Lady of Shalott," "Lines Written Among the Eugenian Hills. . . ." It was the words and the sound and rhythms that made me drunk. I never stopped to ask what the poets meant; the music and the dance of words were the whole meaning. All this delight I absorbed in secret, like a drug-taker.

I began to write poems, very gloomy and sepulchral: a figure lies on a bed, lamplight shining on the still face—that is the only image that remains out of the morbid welter. . . . But perhaps those bad verses, like dim lanterns, helped me to endure the black winter that raged all around.

Apart from poetry, I had discovered the solace of cigarettes. I would almost have sold my soul to get twopence to buy five of the cheapest cigarettes, "Woodbines." I know that I sometimes stole and cheated, when I was desperate for "a fag." Slowly they began to rot my lungs.

Something had to give under the strain; in my late teens I developed lung tuberculosis. In the early forties, that was like being sentenced to death, for the miracle cures didn't come for another decade. I received the doctor's verdict calmly, and almost gladly, after a first qualm of dread. How better to die than to take the road that Keats, Francis Thomson, Emily Brontë, had taken; and, like them, soon rather than late?

I know very well that there is a wisdom, a patternmaker, that shapes our lives, and operates in a fuller richer sphere than the lateral conscious mind. I did not die, nor was I entirely cured, but for years I lived in a limbo-land beyond the normal round of "getting and spending" that I hated and feared so much. In poverty, almost pauperdom, I read and wrote occasional stories and verses. My mother kept me from rags and crusts. It was the time of the Second World War. In our house was billeted an army officer, who was a well-known contemporary poet called Francis Scarfe, a peace-time lecturer in French Literature at Glasgow University. We sat at night under the gaslight at the table writing poems in our council house. Scarfe's were not the first words of encouragement I got; the Classics master at Stromness Academy had read sheafs of my verse and had told me I would be "a well-known writer at the age of forty"—a prophecy which, though it thrilled me, I flatly declined to believe. I never for a moment thought of my scribbled words as being actually printed in a book; those things happened in a different world. . . . But now Francis Scarfe added his conviction that my verse was good enough to be published. I did nothing about it, of course.

The editor of a local paper, the *Orkney Herald,* asked me to be his Stromness correspondent. He was short of reporters—all ablebodied men were in the services—and besides local news (often delivered more out of imagination than fact, whereby I incurred a certain amount of trouble), I did book reviews for the *Orkney Herald,* and a column called "Island Diary" full of reflections, bits of island history, and reminiscence. One week I had dried up. I sat on a bench at the back of the town and wrote a short story to fill the space, called *Tam.* It flowed easily, joyously, and required little correction. I didn't know it, but that summer day it was as if a key had been put into my hand. I was given the freedom of narrative. (But still I was convinced my writing would never appear between covers.)

Writing is a gift one is born with: that is a platitude, but true. It can never be taught. The born writer waits for the rhythms and the patterns that have always been there since words began, the loom of language; then his work can begin; though a lifetime of strict discipline is necessary too. Unconsciously I had absorbed rhythm and pattern in the classroom, at an early age, when the teacher read to us the great biblical stories—Noah, Abraham and Isaac, Joseph and his brothers, Samson and Saul and David. The Border ballads provided rich nourishment, and classical stories like Ulysses and the siege of Troy. Rhythm and pattern: these are the graces that a writer needs. Professors of literature, however brilliant and trenchant and penetrating their under-

standing of texts, don't have the key to "the workshop of the looms." It may be given to any passing scoundrel or vagrant.

The years seemed to stretch away, in poverty and poor health, and reading, without a break. I got great pleasure from discovering the novels of Eric Linklater and the poetry of Edwin Muir; there was an added zest in the knowledge that those well-known authors were Orkneymen.

I had for some time been aware that Orkney was not what it seemed to be, an unimportant cluster of islands between the North Sea and the Atlantic Ocean, inhabited by farmers and fishermen and merchants. For three centuries and more Orkney had been one of the great earldoms of medieval Europe; the Viking longships harried, to begin with; then brought farmers and settlers, and the Earls of Orkney, nominally lieges of the King of Norway, were great rulers in their own right, with territories extending deep into Scotland, and were lords of the seaways between Scandinavia and the Hebrides and Ireland. This was no dry piece of history. The lives of those earls, and their friends and enemies, were chronicled in a magnificent piece of literature, *The Orkneyinga Saga.* The bareness of the narrative, interspersed with elaborate poetical "kennings," has taught me a great deal about how a story ought to be constructed: at least to a writer with my temperament. Such episodes as the martyrdom of Saint Magnus, and Earl Rognvald Kolson's pilgrimage to Rome, Jerusalem, and Byzantium, in the twelfth century, have given me endless delight and wonder. I am amazed that they are not more widely known. . . . Extracts from the Dasent translation of the *Saga* I remember first reading, lying against pillows in bed on a winter afternoon. I felt a bit like Keats when he first opened Chapman's Homer. A whole new world lay before me. I have exploited it to the full.

VIII

One Sunday, soon after the end of the war, I sailed with a group of friends to the island of Hoy (in Norse, "the high island"). We drove in a lorry between the hills, dark as "the valley of the shadow." The road opened suddenly on to a green valley that sloped down to the sea, called Rackwick ("the bay of wreckage"). Rackwick is enclosed on both sides by enormous red sea-cliffs. I had never seen a place so beautiful. But a melancholy air moved upon the pastoral loveliness; most of the little crofts, or farms, had fallen into decay, or were tenantless. Lacking a fire on the hearth, a house quickly dies. It had once been a populous valley; now most of the inhabitants were ageing, or beyond work. The once fertile floor of the valley was reverting to rushes. Most of the fishing boats had gone from the magnificent beach. A lyrical burn, where the valley women had washed their clothes and brought the water home in buckets, gathered to a deep dark silent pool, then rushed among huge coloured stone spheroids to the sea, where the Pentland Firth meshes with the open Atlantic. This place entered deeply into my imagination during those few summer hours, and hardened at last into a symbol, like "the island valley of Avilion" to the medieval writers and to Tennyson, or the village Auburn to Oliver Goldsmith. It stood for the vanished Orkney that was everywhere in retreat before the irresistible forces of Progress: machines, money, the necessary erosions of language, custom, and courtesy. I wrote the first of many poems about Rackwick.

Let no tongue idly whisper here.
Between those strong red cliffs,
Under that great mild sky
Lies Orkney's last enchantment,
The hidden valley of light.

Sweetness from the clouds pouring,
Songs from the surging sea.
Fenceless fields, fishermen with ploughs
And old heroes, endlessly sleeping
In Rackwick's compassionate hills.

Twenty-five years later, I published a long verse sequence about Rackwick, taking as title a phrase from that first inept heart-felt poem—*Fishermen with Ploughs.*

IX

Stromness voted itself "wet" again in 1947, after a quarter-century of prohibition. A bar—first of a few—and a serviceman's club were opened, and I made another joyous discovery: beer. Sitting talking to a friend in that austere pub one afternoon, I thought, "If only I could have two pints of strong beer every day, I could stand up to all the ills of life," rather like the luckless lads in Housman's poetry. I discovered soon enough that alcohol makes as much wretchedness as merriment, and I have spent more alcoholic pain-racked mind-wrung weekends than I

"In a Stromness pub, 1979"

care to think about. It still remains a wonder to me that a fermentation of corn can rouse the leaden soul to laughter and joy, in spite of all. There are deeper soul-stirrings—love, literature (when the muse is whispering in your ear the words that *must* be written). But I look always on cornfields with delight. (The cornstalk and the fish are recurring images in my writing—and for even the poorest islander they are everywhere: the daily nurture, that can also harden into symbols of great richness.) I am thrilled always by the five loaves and the two fishes of the scriptural miracle.

X

I used to while away a winter by attending, idly, a few evening classes. After a class one night, the Director of Adult Education asked me if I would like to study for a year at Newbattle Abbey College, a nonvocational establishment set up in the thirties where young working men and women who had a taste for such things could go for a year and read what interested them at leisure, under the guidance of tutors. I doubt if I would have turned my face in that direction, but that a new Warden had been appointed the previous year: Edwin Muir, the Orkney-born poet and critic. For his work, especially his later poetry, I had come to have a great admiration. He had written an autobiography: the chapter on his childhood on the island of Wyre had a radiance hardly known in literature since Vaughan and Traherne in the seventeenth century. I applied, and was accepted.

I have written many times about Edwin Muir and Newbattle (most recently in *Selected Prose of Edwin Muir* [1987] which I edited for the publisher John Murray in celebration of Muir's centenary). The Newbattle year 1951–52 remains the happiest of my life. Newbattle is built on the remains of a pre-Reformation abbey; it is beautifully situated eight miles from Edinburgh, on the banks of the Esk, with trees all round (a new and beautiful offering of nature to a student from the bare windswept Orkneys). I found myself, for the first time, among a group of contemporaries whose interests were much the same as my own; but literature was the lodestone that drew us together. After beer in the Justinlees Inn on a Saturday evening, we would read our favourite poems to each other beside the fire in the crypt. And we wrote poems and stories that we were selfish and arrogant and hopeful enough to show to the Warden (in the guise of "essays" that we were meant to submit once a month or so). I was amazed and delighted that Edwin Muir seemed to like my poems

Newbattle Abbey College

*The poet Edwin Muir at
Newbattle Abbey College, 1951*

so much—he went so far as to submit a few of them to the *New Statesman* and the *Listener.* Joy unbounded—the *New Statesman* accepted one called *The Exile!* . . . A year or two later, greatly daring, I gathered a sheaf of my verses and had them printed in a small book by the *Orkney Herald.* Edwin Muir contributed a generous introduction. Copies of *The Storm and Other Poems* are now rare and rather expensive: and greatly to be shunned.

"Dr. Muir is a saint," one of the Indian students at Newbattle said. We felt a goodness and a radiance in the college when "wee Edwin" (as the Lowland Scots students called him affectionately) was around. The equal kindness of his wife, Willa, had a much more robust and earthy quality. The Muirs seemed to conspire to make my writing known. I would never have approached an established publisher myself—Edwin sent a selection of my poems to The Hogarth Press in London, and a letter from Norah Smallwood—first of many—confirmed the acceptance of *Loaves and Fishes* in 1959.

The Muirs left Newbattle for America; Edwin had been invited to give the Charles Eliot Norton lectures at Harvard in 1955, later published as *The Estate of Poetry.* In America too he showed my poems to editors. *Harper's Bazaar* accepted a few, and paid me a staggering sum of dollars! But for Edwin Muir, I would not be writing these words now. He opened the door to the marketplace for me, where I could sell the tapestries I had woven, and begin to be independent and sure of myself.

XI

But years were to pass before I could make a living by my pen. After Newbattle, what then? It would be impossible to return to my former round in Orkney, reading and beer-drinking and living on social security. One way of escape suggested itself: a university course. I was accepted as a mature student of English Language and Literature at Edinburgh. After a few uncertain weeks, I came to love that beautiful city: especially in late spring when foliage and blossom seemed to be everywhere suddenly, and the citizens and the students shared gladly in the light and colour. Of the hundreds of lectures and seminars, I remember little, but there must have been an enrichment. The course I had dreaded—Old English—gave me the greatest rewards, after I had got the key to the difficult grammar. To trace everyday words back to their source was a constant delight: to understand, for example, that "lord" means "keeper of the bread" and "lady" means "baker of the bread." This is to dignify the humblest toil; this is to "scatter the proud in the imagination of their hearts." There were profound spiritual undertones: but all rooted in the four elements and the five senses.

But at Edinburgh University, as at Newbattle, friendship was more rewarding than books. Laughter with ale leavened the dullest darg of texts, essay-writing, exams. In certain taverns along Rose Street—a dark narrow rather sinister street in those days that runs parallel to Princes Street with its gardens and fountains and statues—the poets and artists of Scotland foregathered at weekends (MacDiarmid, McCaig, Scott, Senior, Garioch, Campbell Hay, Goodsir Smith). I was quickly welcomed among them. Often, after closing-time, the drinking and the talk and the poetry went on in this or that hospitable house till early next morning—sometimes till breakfast time. The fountain of the muses spilled over, night after night. Except for occasional hangovers, it was unsullied delight.

Once, friendship deepened into a state precious and delicate. The girl was one of those radiant creatures who are naturally at home with the arts and artists, and who give in the way of inspiration and delight far more than they ever receive. Other poets than myself were touched by her good enchantments. *"Sunt lachrymae rerum"*—such graces and virtues as that beautiful young woman had in full measure cannot, it seems, last in the mortal air we breathe. The more delicate and pure the gift, the more open it is to hurt and to loss. Blake's lyric on the rose might

"The girl Charles Senior, poet, called 'The Muse of Rose Street,'" Edinburgh

experience in one classroom convinced me that teaching was not my vocation.

I spent two more post-graduate years, pleasantly enough, trying to work out Gerard Manley Hopkins's theories of prosody. In the end, I think it is not all that important that people should understand them; the marvellous anvil-ringing poetry is what matters.

There seemed nothing for it but to return to the islands, to beer and social security and random words on paper. Poems and stories were being published here and there, and broadcast, but the fees would hardly have kept a cat.

Norah Smallwood, having published a second book of my poems, *The Year of the Whale,* looked at some short stories I had written over the years. *A Calendar of Love* (stories) came out in 1967. I was quite overwhelmed by the good reception that book got in most of the reviews. I hadn't really set much store by them. Mostly they were written quickly—impromptus—and required little in the way of correction or alteration. One undervalues what comes easily: especially perhaps Scotsmen, who have convinced themselves over the centuries that anything worthwhile must come out of sweat and blood and tears. I agree with Keats now—"Poetry ought to come as naturally as leaves to the tree." I am sure that my best work has always come easily and joyously. "Work ought to be fun," said D.H. Lawrence. "If it isn't fun, don't do it. . . ." Lawrence was, again, quite right.

A second book of short stories, *A Time to Keep,* came out in 1969, and got an even better reception than *A Calendar of Love.* Three stories from *A Time to*

have been written for her. She is dead now. No history of Scottish poetry in the fifties and sixties can do without her; the mere fact that she existed accounted for some of the literary richness of the period. There remain memories—laughter and sealight at Cramond; music and flowers at Juniper Green; murmurs of verse among the smoke and trembling yellow circles of The Abbotsford bar:

> Not every woman so
> Can turn again
> And draw such pure delight
> Out of such pain
> The way a star shines through
> Ruins of rain.

I studied sufficiently hard to get a degree in English after four years. *"What then?* sang Plato's ghost, *What then. . . ."* For most arts graduates, the door opens into teaching. I passed through that door; and came back out again almost as quickly, for a bitter

With Irish poet Seamus Heaney, 1982

*With an Indian friend, Parameswaran,
at Frenich, Scotland, 1985*

Keep were made into television films, that were not much liked in Orkney, as alcohol ran like a lurid constant thread through them; and also Orcadians, who like to think of themselves as being as progressive in all ways as city dwellers, objected to being screened against the more timeless setting of oil lamps, scythes, and plain deal coffins. . . .

I had worked for years very hard at a play called *A Spell for Green Corn*, which is in essence a long fertility ritual, based on the Orkney folktale of a fiddler lured underground by the trows (or trolls). He agrees to play them a reel, and is set free again after—it seems to him—half-an-hour or so. Actually he has been out of the land of the living for twenty years, or fifty years. The tale seemed to me a good foundation for building some theories about the "timelessness" of art, and the use of the arts in society, and that special kind of suffering which art seems to bestow in order that something rich and strange may be made of it. I have never worked so hard at any poem or story. It was produced on BBC radio, and got one or two stage productions; and then it sank without trace. Nothing is ever wholly lost, and I think I learned much about the craft of writing from my hard work on *A Spell for Green Corn*. I could use the loom I had been given to its fullest capacity.

By this time I was earning enough to live on,

unaided by the state; instead I began to bolster the state by paying Income Tax.

It was Norah Smallwood who suggested that I ought to try my hand at a novel. I began, without much conviction; thinking of a small island with its farms and village and fishermen. The image of such a place begins, for the kind of writer I am, to pulse with the rhythms of sea and land, fish and cornstalk. But an ordinary community: literature is full of those affectionate portrayals, that tend too often to lapse into sentimentality, and provoke, in the next generation of writers, a satirical savage reaction—as *The House with the Green Shuttters* came back, like a chilling echo, from the couthiness of the Scottish "Kaleyard school." It is convenient, for the writer, to set the life and ethos of a community in a frame of time, e.g., the seven days that make a week. As I wrote, I began to see this pastoral community as being threatened by an alien way of life—not the mild "progress" represented by motorcars and radio, but by some vast anonymous alien corporate force out of the future. The novel had hardly been published when oil was discovered in the North Sea, and various parts of Orkney were being probed for uranium ore, and we became a member of the EEC.

That novel, *Greenvoe,* was moderately successful. It was followed a year later by a historical novel, *Magnus*—based on the life of the twelfth-century earl and saint—which seems to me to be a superior work of art and imagination to *Greenvoe.* But it was, relatively, a failure. (For a writer, however, his "failures" may be more precious in some ways than his "successes.") I have never had a high opinion of book reviewers; and so what they say in the way of praise or blame doesn't touch me.

I never strayed far from my first love, poetry. Books of verse appeared at fairly regular intervals, and several poems from those books appear often enough in anthologies and school textbooks. It must happen with many writers that they throw a collection of poems together haphazardly, the good with the bad and the indifferent, to make a book. Only after ten years or so is the wheat separated from the chaff. Those bad poems are, ever afterwards, a constant reproach, especially when they are praised in the writer's presence.

Poetry has strayed, perhaps dangerously, into my stories. "Poetic prose" does not stand up well in English; though I think there is room for the prose-poem. My imagination nourishes itself chiefly on narrative—on events in time—and, according as a true rhythm is found and maintained, these narratives may be compacted into poems; and a poem may be so handled that it bears with ease and grace the very

*Poet Edwin Morgan, G.M. Brown, and composer
Peter Maxwell Davies, 1985*

different balances and tensions of a story. But if there *is* any sense of strain, or broken frontiers, either the story or the poem is an unsuccessful hybrid.

It is astonishing, the number of people who have, at one time or another, tried their hand at verse. It is to fall in love with the language, though the infatuation rarely lasts. Like most writers, I get much unsolicited literature in manuscript sent to me—mainly verse. It is very rare to find anything worthwhile. Most young writers are content to pour out opinions and emotions on to the page, with small regard to form or pattern or logical sequence of images. The good poets have always been willing to subject themselves to time-proven disciplines. Once the techniques of English verse are mastered, the poet has perfect freedom to reach the high zenith of imagination (as high as his special talents can reach). Obscurity, too, is often the last refuge of a poetaster. There *can* be obscurity in verse—a reaching deep under the normal currents of meaning—a kind of verse that moves us in a way we don't understand. But only the greatest poets can use it: those who breathe the pure serene of the realms of gold.

There is no easy way of getting to the palace of poetry. Even if one gets to the gate, and knocks, there are severe and grave questions to be answered. Only the princes of verse know the mysterious password. Now, late in life, I know I am still at the gate, trying to find the answer to a few riddles; but content to have got as far as this. There's honest work to be done in the weavers' shed outside. I will not get to the inner sanctum where the crown jewels are; but the journey to the place has been good.

XII

I became a Catholic in 1961, not on sudden impulse; I had thought about it for a long time. The Presbyterianism I had been brought up with had never touched my heart or imagination; except for those Old Testament stories from the King James Bible, and certain passages from Job and Ecclesiastes and the Psalms, and the parables from the Gospels, and the tremendous drama of The Passion above all; the imagination of Dante, Shakespeare, Sophocles doesn't scale such heights. (Of course, those scriptures are older than Presbyterianism or the seventeenth-century translators. The Catholic church preserved them for us through the Dark Ages.)

There were no Catholics in Stromness when I was a boy but the tinkers and an Irish barber and an Italian ice-cream man: all well-liked in the community. But Rome cast a kind of sinister aura: purgatory, confession, rosary beads, incense, crucifixes, inquisition—we all felt it, without knowing why. To be Presbyterian boys and girls, and members of the British Empire whose great splashes of red—India, Australia, Canada, Africa—covered the classroom map: that was to be on the very crest of progress and enlightenment; no matter how poor one was.

Promptings and urgings may come from centuries back. All of Europe was Catholic once. At the heart of Orkney is the Cathedral of Saint Magnus, who had Mass sung for him just before his martyrdom on Egilsay. I was moved by documents from eighteenth-century Orkney—angry outcries because poor and sick people were still going to the ruined "Romish" chapels to pray and leave their offerings. The lovely ceremonies of Shetland peasants in midwinter, remnants of Catholicism, impressed me deeply. These very poor people still had a richness in their lives that had been lost about the time of the Reformation. Nothing remained now but a grave and gentle courtesy that was to be seen more in the country districts than in the towns, where "getting and spending" was, increasingly, all that mattered.

Lytton Strachey's essay on Manning, very anti-Catholic, fascinated me, but in quite the opposite way that Strachey intended. I was soon deep in some of the richness of Catholic literature, from the medieval carols to Newman and Francis Thomson and Hopkins, by way of certain marvellous passages of Dante ("In His will is our peace") and Chaucer ("Within the cloistre blisful of thy sydis / Took mannes shap the eternal love and pees.")

At Dalkeith and Edinburgh I began to go to Mass occasionally; it was at the time, soon to end, when the

Mass was still clothed in the majesty and beauty of Latin, and punctuated by marvellous silences. The whole history of man—what is to come as well as what has been—seems to be caught up in that brief ceremony at the altar. The arts seem to be but echoes and shadows.

"In principio erat verbum:" the last syllable, at the end of time, will round out the meaning. Meantime we content ourselves with hints and guesses.

For an artist, of whatever kind, Catholicism is a rich inexhaustible storehouse. My own writing would be much poorer, lacking those treasures of symbol and image.

XIII

I am writing this on a midwinter afternoon, with a weak sun shining in on the kitchen table where I work. There is a stillness in the air outside that bodes snow—the snow that is a delight to children, and a summoner of old men to the chimney corner.

One knows that one is growing older; but for a decade or so in middle age, time—that was a treasury to be squandered ignorantly in youth—is still no burden. Body and mind and spirit are still in accord. Then, quite suddenly, in the space of a year or so, one becomes aware of mortality. There are minor malfunctions here and there in the body. Sleep is brief and not so sweet as once it was. One confuses word and phrase, reading a book; the eyesight is failing. Pain travels like a pauper from joint to joint. There is a certain lack of relish in food and drink.

The mind becomes impoverished too, slowly. Why are there no writers nowadays like Thomas Mann, Yeats, Eliot, Bertolt Brecht, E.M. Forster? . . . That is one sign of a threadbare mind, to see little good in the vivid things of the present. Where are the never-to-be-forgotten friends that I drank with twenty years ago? I go into a pub nowadays and sit alone over my beer.

The spirit too loses its fervour. Fears, unknown a decade ago, haunt the appalled soul. "Do not let me hear / Of the wisdom of old men, but rather of their folly, / Their fear of fear and frenzy. . . . Of belonging to another, or to others, or to God. . . ." T.S. Eliot, as nearly always, was right. The gifts reserved for age are small and not to be desired.

I cling to the hope that perhaps, on the whole, I write better now than I have done. (But even here, reading certain passages of *Greenvoe* and especially *Magnus*, I can't be sure.) I think of the marvels, beauties, and joys of the world that have passed me by and that now I can never celebrate; and the pen shrivels in my hand. So little has been achieved.

Stromness Harbour ("Hamnavoe") from Brown's window

One of the most moving allegories of our century is Lawrence's *Ship of Death*. A man, all his life, is building the ship that must bear him out on the darkling death-flood. Every good word, action, intention, planes a board, drives in a nail, caulks a seam here or there. "O build your ship of death, for you will need it. . . . Already the dark waters of the end. . . ."

It is such a moving image because it has always been there, since men first arrived at the sea shore, amazed. The little churches and churchyards of Orkney always stood at the water's edge, for the ocean signified eternity. The dead Norse king was laid in his ship with all his treasure, and set adrift. There is a journey still to go. Only let the ship be worthily built and rigged.

XIV

We live in dangerous times. Increasingly, people turn from "the word" and give all their allegiance to "the number"—has not science done great things for the nations, and promises greater things to come? In the past century, most of our creative energies have gone into technology, and the arts are seen as increasingly irrelevant. No wonder people are dazzled by the prospect of ever-increasing leisure and wealth, and never pause to wonder whether we might not have entered into a Faust-compact, with some ice-

George Mackay Brown with poet Christopher Rush, inside 3 Mayburn Court, 1985

and-fire reckoning late or soon, at the end of the transaction. If that is the scenario, there was never greater need than now for the saving power of the imagination; it is the imagination that preserves the traditional sanctities, and sings the song of the earth. Poetry and music and art may yet, if the worst comes, carry a few survivors out of our time's ruin.

BIBLIOGRAPHY

Poetry:

The Storm. Kirkwall, Scotland: Orkney Press, 1954.

Loaves and Fishes. London: Hogarth Press, 1959.

The Year of the Whale. London: Hogarth Press, 1965.

The Five Voyages of Arnor. Falkland, Scotland: K.D. Duval, 1966.

Twelve Poems. Belfast, Ireland: Belfast Festival Publications, 1968.

Fishermen with Ploughs: A Poem Cycle. London: Hogarth Press, 1971.

Lifeboat and Other Poems. Crediton, England: Gilbertson, 1971.

Poems New and Selected. London: Hogarth Press, 1971; New York: Harcourt, 1973.

Penguin Modern Poets 21, with Iain Crichton Smith and Norman MacCaig. Harmondsworth, England: Penguin, 1972.

Winterfold. London: Hogarth Press, 1976.

Selected Poems. London: Hogarth Press, 1977.

Voyages. London: Hogarth Press, 1983.

Christmas Poems. Oxford: Perpetua Press, 1984.

Fiction:

A Calendar of Love, and Other Stories. London: Hogarth Press, 1967; New York: Harcourt, 1968.

A Time to Keep, and Other Stories. London: Hogarth Press, 1969; New York: Harcourt, 1970.

Greenvoe. London: Hogarth Press, 1972; New York: Harcourt, 1972.

Magnus. London: Hogarth Press, 1973.

Hawkfall, and Other Stories. London: Hogarth Press, 1974.

The Sun's Net: Stories. London: Hogarth Press, 1976.

Andrina, and Other Stories. London: Hogarth Press, 1983.

Time in a Red Coat. London: Chatto & Windus, 1984; New York: Vanguard Press, 1984.

The Golden Bird. London: J. Murray, 1987.

Juvenile fiction:

The Two Fiddlers: Tales from Orkney (illustrated by Ian MacInnes). London: Chatto & Windus, 1974.

Pictures in the Cave (illustrated by I. MacInnes). London: Chatto & Windus, 1977.

Six Lives of Fankle the Cat (illustrated by I. MacInnes). London: Chatto & Windus, 1980.

Nonfiction:

An Orkney Tapestry. London: Gollancz, 1969.

Edwin Muir: A Brief Memoir. West Linton, Scotland: Castlelaw Press, 1975.

Letters from Hamnavoe (articles). Edinburgh, Scotland: G. Wright, 1975.

Under Brinkie's Brae (articles). Edinburgh, Scotland: G. Wright, 1979.

Portrait of Orkney (photographs by Werner Forman). London: Hogarth Press, 1981.

Plays:

Witch, produced in Edinburgh, Scotland, 1969; published in *A Calendar of Love, and Other Stories.* London: Hogarth Press, 1967; New York: Harcourt, 1968.

A Spell for Green Corn, radio broadcast, 1967; produced in Edinburgh, Scotland, 1970. London: Hogarth Press, 1970.

Loom of Light, produced in Kirkwall, Scotland, 1972; published in *Three Plays.* London: Chatto & Windus, 1984; also published as *Loom of Light.* Nairn, Scotland: Balnain Books, 1984.

The Storm Watchers, produced in Edinburgh, Scotland, 1976.

The Martyrdom of Saint Magnus, music by Peter Maxwell Davies; adapted from the novel *Magnus;* produced in Kirkwall, Scotland and London, 1977; Sante Fe, 1979. London: Boosey & Hawkes, 1977.

The Two Fiddlers, music by P.M. Davies; adapted from the story *The Two Fiddlers;* produced in London, 1978. London: Boosey & Hawkes, 1978.

Three Plays (includes *The Loom of Light, The Well,* and *The Voyage of Saint Brandon*). London: Chatto & Windus, 1984.

A Celebration for Magnus. Nairn, Scotland: Balnain Books, 1987.

Television plays:

Orkney. BBC-TV, 1971; published in *A Time to Keep, and Other Stories.* London: Hogarth Press, 1969; New York: Harcourt, 1970.

Miss Barraclough. BBC-TV, 1977; published in *A Time to Keep, and Other Stories.* London: Hogarth Press, 1969; New York: Harcourt, 1970.

Four Orkney Plays for Schools. BBC-TV, 1978; published in *A Time to Keep, and Other Stories.* London: Hogarth Press, 1969; New York: Harcourt, 1970.

Andrina, BBC-TV, 1981.

Editor of:

Selected Prose of Edwin Muir. London: J. Murray, 1987.

Janet Burroway

1936-

This is the first thing I know about myself: My mother said, "When she was born, I was horrified to see she had coal-black hair an inch long that stuck out all over her head like an Indian." I must have heard this several hundred times; it was the opening sentence of the anecdote about the seventy-odd temporary "permanents" I had before I left home for college.

If it were the first sentence of a novel, I would set an exam on it. What expectations for female children are indicated? What attitude toward nonwhite races is implied? What does the choice of language tell us about the character of the mother? Which of the daughter's later problems and concerns can be traced back to the attitudes here exhibited?

Once when I came home from England, dandling a cherub on my knee, a wife, a published novelist, a university lecturer, a fashionable resident of the cultured country of my choice—a model candidate therefore for "seeing my mother as a person"—I said to her, breezily, "It must have been hard on you to have a stocky, straight-haired daughter."

"Oh," my mother said. "It was *terrible. Terrible.*"

If I had four hundred pages instead of forty to spend at the typewriter, I might give full space to the Samson story, the fight against the cutting of my hair. I might tell the story of the ugly duckling, the stories of my coming to understand the power of bigotry, of the unwilling feminist, the addictive personality in a temperance family, the story of the search for home—all of which figure in my fiction as subject matter. But this is a "literary autobiography," so I will concentrate on the portions of those stories that suggest a writing life.

My perfectly adequate but problematic body came into the world on September 21, 1936, in Tucson, Arizona, and was transported at some time before my memory begins to be raised in Phoenix.

My parents were both ex-Ohioans, of whom there were a plethora in the desert in those days. My mother had come about 1909, *her* father having been diagnosed as consumptive and having therefore left the bank in Lorain to take on the managership of a remote marble quarry in the mountains above Bowie. After a few years the quarry went broke—but not before my mother had learned the loneliness of being the only white child in Marble Camp, sitting on a rock watching the games of Mexican children with whom she was not allowed to play.

My father's father was a fishmonger and factory foreman in Canton, Ohio, and when my dad was six his mother died giving birth to his younger sister Jessie—after which my grandfather married his former wife's best friend.

The two households, rustic in Arizona and working class in Canton, were I believe models of Methodist moral rectitude, but my mother's mother had a flash of giggling madness in her that made for both more merriment and more angst. My mother herself was "frail," diagnosed at eighteen as having an ulcer. When she was of marriageable age it became obvious that Bowie, Arizona, offered her no match, and she went to Ohio to visit relatives, returning with my father as prize.

They were married in 1924 in the Little Church Around the Corner in New York, this being one of the titillating facts of their romance, since they had to travel from Ohio to New York unchaperoned before they faced the preacher. Their first house in Bowie was a barber shop, converted by railway-tramp laborers at a dollar a day during the Great Depression. In 1932 my brother Stanley was born in Tucson.

After my birth we moved to Phoenix, and my first three years were spent in "the house on Twenty-fourth Place." There I learned to "read," probably when I was two, because the occasion of it was my brother's difficulty learning in first grade (a manifestation of his resistance to being turned into a performer—truly another story). My mother therefore made flashcards, and since there was nothing in particular to do with me while Stanley practiced them, I was set on the couch beside him. I remember only two of the cards—a "Mexico" with a sombrero set askew on the *M,* and a "look" of which the two *o*'s were long-lashed eyes—and it's perfectly possible that these are the only two cards I then recognized, but all the same I was trotted out for company and presented as precocious. Why my brother didn't murder me I don't know; it was years later that he

Father, Paul Burroway, 1923

Mother, Alma Milner, 1923

broke my finger, and then for some lesser transgression.

I remember being freshly dressed for Sunday School, holding my father's hand and looking up to see beyond him the fronds of an awesomely tall palm tree, and beyond that the searing blue Arizona sky. In my first novel I gave this memory a more specific character, but really it is an image of religious awe.

Shortly after my third birthday we moved into an L-shaped stucco bungalow of my father's own design and making at 322 E. Alvarado Street. My father was a *moral* builder (I have tended to understand, and to render in print, true-caulked joints as the touchstone of good men) and the house still announces its modest solidity while many later jerry-buildings are desert dust. But the trouble with it in 1939 was that the street was newly scratched out of the sand, mostly bare lots, grudging to grass or a new hedge.

Arizona was too spare and barren for me. The real seemed bald. On our street there were few trees and small; behind us was a vast vacant lot (later a baseball field) powdery most of the time and slimy with mud in the rare rains. The farthest I could walk

on my own was to the MacAlpine Drug Store across Seventh Street for a nickel ice cream cone that melted as I ate it. My bare feet got horn-hard on the hot dirt while I dreamed of being a ballerina. I seemed to have an instinctive distaste for western music and rodeo gear. Later I understood these attitudes as snobbery, and felt abashed before writers like Tom McGuane and Tom Robbins, who had the strength of spirit to celebrate American folk rubbish—but how did I conceive such a snobbery in the first place? By the time I was eight I had an entrenched conviction that the real world was elsewhere than Arizona, and I have never entirely changed my mind.

The significant legacy of those early judgments was not that I should find my home elsewhere but that I should never entirely find my home. It is the sense of *no, not here* that is my familiar. When my five-year-old son, transplanted to America, vowed that he would return to live in England where he was born, I never doubted him. I envied him rather, that such a passion, so early conceived, should be a longing rather than a rejection.

In the meantime the things that seemed "real" to

me were the things that I would now describe as heightened, striking, technicolor. Christmas, for instance. My family had a true hedonistic talent for Christmas—a heritage I have tried to pass on, rigorously defending it against all charges of consumerism and commercialism.

Movies especially represented the world as it ought to be, and this passion was shared by all the family. We went perhaps twice a week to the Deco-decorated Fox or to the Orpheum with its Spanish courtyard and clouds moving across the plaster sky. I must have been aware even in the earliest days that the point of my mother's curling and steaming and twisting-round-her-finger of my hair, was that I should look as much as possible like Shirley Temple—which was also my heart's desire.

I was allowed dance lessons from the age of four or so, ballet and tap, later adagio, acrobatic, and—finally!—toe. I got to be measured for the tiny tutus or tap ruffles of Mr. Scholl's recitals. I watched, backstage, the annual painting for the same recital of the lady who went nude except for her leaf of gilt. It perplexed and dazzled me that this and only this particular public nudity seemed to be allowed.

More thrilling still was the Phoenix Little Theatre production of *Guest in the House* for which I understudied and, once, performed the youngest role. Whenever I see mothers defend, and toddlers mouth their enthusiasm for, public performance and beauty contests, my knee-jerk reaction is that the kids are being used, but my memory tells me I was stagestruck of my own accord, and a stage mother was the mother I most wanted.

Most thrilling, held out like a promise of every year's completion, was the trip to California, to eat in the green-lit plaster grottos of the Waldorf Cafeteria, to buy a winter coat and a storybook doll at the May Company, to ride the merry-go-round and later the bumper cars at the greasy glorious Pike, and to be tumbled in the cold and terrifying wonderful Pacific surf.

Jumping, jumping in the surf; the water jumps so I jump, with every wave. It is a jumping competition. The sea smacks me in the face, upends me, drags on whatever part of me is nearest the ocean floor. I am towed under. I fight, right myself, stand and face the next wave, jump. Salt surges backward through my nose into my throat; coughing makes the membranes above my palate sting. I don't want to get out, I never want to get out. I ignore my parents' calling. Only exhaustion will finally shove me shoreward, dump me on the sand, because even if I feel "in my element," there is something I don't have in common with the ocean, that it goes on tireless, never pulls a muscle,

heaves for breath, dizzies with churning head over gritty heels in the salt wet.

California also magically contained an extended family, a score of people one way or another connected to my grandmother, Gamie. With these people we had wonderful beach reunions. The most interesting family was that headed by my mother's cousin Walter Pierce, whose daughter Martha Anne lived in a beruffled attic bedroom in their Riverside house. Surf and trees were exotic enough, but stairs in a private house seemed like something out of books, and dormer windows. . . ! I envied Martha Anne for most of my childhood.

The Pierces were connected to Louisa May Alcott by a route I could never trace. My grandmother claimed to be Louisa May's second cousin, and one of the Pierce sisters was named Premilia, supposedly after a Premelia Alcott—but Uncle Walter and I have searched in vain for corroboration. The real connection doesn't matter, of course; the important thing is that the family believed it, and had no difficulty crediting anybody's literary ambitions—indeed, always had an eye out for them. Gamie's brother, Uncle Ernie, was the author of a "privately published" book of poems called *Infiniverse*. Uncle Ernie was considered to be "a little cracked," and in later life no doubt he was—though I never felt as certain as my mother that I would be harmed by listening to his theories about the moon and the menstrual cycle. And I liked his explanation of his book's title: "One evening I was sitting around the dinner table with my sons, and one of them mentioned the universe. I thought, Why universe?! Doesn't it go on forever? Why not *Infiniverse?*" This idea thrilled me almost as much as it seemed to thrill Uncle Ernie—I particularly liked the throwaway part, "mentioned the universe"—but I don't know whether he felt any particular affinity for his great-niece poet.

California was also "real" of course because it was where the movies were made, and my parents were as excited as I to step in the cement feet at Grauman's Chinese, collect autographs on Hollywood and Vine, get free tickets to the broadcasts of "Stella Dallas" or "Amos 'n' Andy," and expensive ones to live shows. Once we saw a striptease by mistake, and once by more profound mistake my parents took me to a performance of *A Streetcar Named Desire*, which disturbed me in a way I could articulate to no one.

Much later I noted this irony: My mother had wanted to be an actress, and had been prevented from it "by her health," which dictated that she could not leave Arizona for the Emerson School of Oratory in Boston. I always knew that her own parents were

*Janet Burroway (lower right), five years old,
dressed for dance recital*

somewhat relieved not to have to make a decision against the theatre on moral grounds, but they felt, and my mother passed on to me, a conviction that actresses were wicked. They were wicked for three clearly delineated reasons: they smoked, they drank, and they had a lot of husbands. In my late forties, when I sat to contemplate the shape of my life, I realized that my adolescent rebellion had taken some very obvious forms; I had then already given up a couple of husbands, and now I undertook to give up the drink and the cigarettes. As a friend had pointed out to me, there are two ways to let your parents rule your life: by doing as they say, and by doing the opposite.

I suppose everyone has a first memory of being able to write. What characterizes my memory is a sense of fraud. I remember being at a little table looking onto the quarter-circle of backyard from my room in the house on Alvarado Street. I had not yet started to school, but I knew my alphabet and could make all the letters. I could already form *Janet,* and didn't consider this being able to write; it was like being able to make a cat out of two circles with ears and tail; mere *drawing.* I practiced these letters on cheap slick

manila paper with turquoise lines. Then I called to my mother asking her how to spell *Burroway,* and as she slowly called out the letters from another room, I formed them. I copied them several times, then demanded that she look and see if I had it right. She must have praised me, but I don't remember. I remember writing the letters over and over again with a sense of breathless power. And then suddenly I was self-suspicious. *I* had not really done anything. Mom had spelled the name. I had only copied down letters I already knew. I was somehow taking credit for something not my own.

This odd sense dogged me. When as a teenager I won a dress-designing competition I was thrust into a desparing sense of fraud, confessed to my mother that I had taken a sleeve style from one dress, neckline from another, skirt shape from a third; the only original thing I had done was to add the applique of the fish and bubbles. Mom laughed. What did I think designing *was?* I caught the sense in the character of Miguel in my first novel, *Descend Again.* Miguel translates a Spanish lullaby, not understanding that translation is something different from plagiarism. But writing about it did not exorcize the tendency, which plagues me in the classroom: These students think I have done something for them, but it's only a fraction of what they could get from reading the books I've read.

I have learned to tell my writing students that in the world as we know it nothing is made or destroyed, only rearranged; and that the process of creation is selection and arrangement. I know this to be true. But somewhere the stubborn enemy in me does not believe it.

My mother liked to make stories of her children's accomplishments, and would assure anyone who would listen that I wrote my first poem at the age of five. Consequently, I seem to remember doing so, bringing my headful of lines out to my mother on the little red concrete front porch where purple verbena grew in a huge turquoise pottery vase, and I do remember the poem.

> There once lived a man on the street.
> He was sixty years old at that time,
> And before he was ninety-nine
> He prayed to the Lord: Lord, do not let me die
> For I am the shepherd of your sheep.
> Then he went outside, and a rope hanging from the sky.
> He took hold of it, and up and up he went
> Until he was in the sky.

Then he knew who he was.

He was Jesus, God's shepherd.

I've written worse. I still rather like the idea of Jesus not knowing who he was even though he declared it with conviction. But I also think that this effort could be duplicated by most of the first graders in a Poets in the Schools program, and that my mother's assigning it a prophetic character may in fact have been a *cause* of my later poetry.

No more poems were caused, however, until about the seventh grade, and I probably cared less about the first one than about my mother's praise. A slightly later memory marks for me the urgent connection I feel to language.

In this memory I seem very young and small, but it is crucial that I was able to write a letter, so I will put it at the summer between first and second grades.

I had been left to spend a week with my grandparents in Wilcox. At Gamie's house—it was never spoken of as my grandfather's, Gakie's; I suppose the bank was his place and the home hers—as in California, things were in sharper focus than at home, and in sharper color: the huge black and white squares of the checkerboard kitchen floor, the drawer filled with shining, miniature but real, pots and pans; Weedy the golden Pekingese who spent his waking hours padding across the checkerboard after my grandmother. The grass in the ample backyard was of some vivid apple green that we could not achieve in Phoenix. A black china cat slept on the hearth and a glass-fronted cupboard displayed a whole set of *black* dishes! The ceilings of the bedrooms were plastered in ochre over blue, and the blue shapes could be read as clouds can be, but they did not change, and became familiar: the hatted lady, the pig, the coolie hat. Over my iron bedstead in the guest room Gramma Pierce, Gamie's mother, stared stern and life-sized out of an oval frame, over the window seat and out the window, into the garden at the weeping willow—and I never hear the expression "piercing gaze," without remembering this private etymology.

Every day I walked the half-dozen blocks to the Valley National Bank where my grandfather was manager (it was my first experience of that heady female pleasure, Prestige by Association), and Gakie gave me a shiny dime, which I was then allowed to take to the Vandercamp Emporium and spend at once. Fifteen cents a week was my standard allowance; a dime a day was wealth. No one told me to save a part of it or to spend it wisely. I could buy a little frame, a book of paper dolls, a ball and jacks— anything! Back at Gamie's house I could go next door to the vacant lot and dance on a slab of concrete

*"Gakie and Gamie," Dana T. and
Maud Pierce Milner, mid-1950s*

unaccountably laid as if for my private stage. Or I could poke into the old tool shed, sniff in the musty smell that I never otherwise encountered in my childhoood, Arizona being so dry. As I recount this it seems to me a memory of longer ago than the 1940s, and I realize that part of the magic of Gamie's house was that even then, compared to the flat harsh light of home and its boxy houses, Wilcox had the feel of more graceful "olden times."

I loved the place. But one afternoon when I had been there for several days I was standing at the window seat in "my" bedroom sifting through a box of old Christmas cards. I looked up from the cards, out the window like Gramma Pierce, at the gently tossing ribbons of green willow—and I was struck a blow in the stomach of physical and yet not-physical pain. It was at once empty and lead-heavy, as if emptiness had been made lead-heavy in me. I had never felt anything like it and I could not take in the force of it. I gaped out the window, astonished, immobilized. I stood for a moment trying to breathe, and when I caught my breath I began to cry—not merely from the eyes or nose, but with desperate expulsions as if I could send the thing away, extrude it from my stomach with my breath.

Gamie came to me. "What is it, Dolly!"

I said, gasping astonishment, "I don't *know. . . !*"

She put her arms around me. "Oh, Dolly, you're homesick."

I believe that my need for words, my anxious and largely misplaced trust in definition, stems from that moment. The pain still choked me but its name had put it in the world. My grandmother knew what it was. It had been before.

My memory does a "cut to" here, to the fold-down writing desk beside the bed. "Dear Mom," I wrote, "I am . . ." I asked Gamie to spell the word and I painstakingly wrote it out. ". . . *homesick."* I was impressed at the length of it. It still sounded alien to my ears. My letters were blurry with tears, and now that I knew the pain was connected with the thought of home, the thought of home brought on the pain. But I knew what it was called and I could write it down. I could define myself by it. I was homesick. It was a mortally grown-up thing to be.

Let me not distort the meaning of this memory to me. The void is very large and the pride is scarcely a pebble. When I have lost a mother, child, marriage, lover, home—"homesick" is how I feel it. When I hurt, it is with that pain I hurt, and thousands of words must be thrown into the void before it begins to contract around them. I have been able to understand the concept of "black hole" only in emotional terms. But if my particular sort of pain took its form in that moment, so did the puny power to face it off.

M om gave "elocution" lessons, and had striking success correcting the speech defects of stammerers, split palates, and at least one girl with Down's syndrome. Most of her pupils, however, learned to "say pieces."

All through grammar school I took lessons from Mom, but she tended to be impatient with me; so I invented a game in which I left the house, toured the block, rang the doorbell, and presented myself as "Brenda." My mother approved this ruse, and on the whole she was successful in pretending that she must treat me with the politeness due a stranger's child.

I learned to recite "My Darling Little Goldfish" with appropriate inflections, and I advanced to prose, to monologue and dialogue situations in which a mother tried to telephone the grocer while keeping three small children out of trouble, or the salesgirl lost track of how much lace she was measuring as she

complained about her job. There were relaxation exercises that I have since learned are yoga, and which I still use.

The goal then was that I should stand up, at intervals of perhaps two months, at Friday night socials of the Central Methodist Church, and bring glory on myself, my mother, Methodism, and the American Way of Life.

Understand that I fully concurred in this desire. Nevertheless I sweated and wished to die. From four o'clock on the relevant Fridays I sank into a stupor of dread and prayed that the cross should be lifted from me. I sweated. After supper I dressed—in yokes with Peter Pan collars, dirndles with ruffles, pinafores with rickrack trim, in peplums, puffed sleeves, peasant blouses, scallops—and sweated.

In the church basement I sat and watched while Mrs. Logan rendered "Mighty Like a Rose" and the Robinson twins did their tap routine. I smiled and applauded, my heart banging without rhythm against my breastless fat. I strode forward with the appearance of nonchalance through the metal-backed folding chairs, paused, faced the crowd, gulped a breath, and spoke.

Afterward, four flower-hatted women and, if I was lucky, a middle-aged man, would tell me how talented I was, how charming, how to be proud of!

Do not suppose that I suspected some imbalance between the effort and the praise. I learned the lesson of my life. Praise and relief! Praise and to be done with it! Even now, when many thousand facings of a lecture hall have dimmed the anxiety, when I am free of the Peter Pan collars and my heart no longer pounds—even now, every time I speak I feel the atavistic pattern: dread, discipline, praise, relief.

On the knickknack shelf in the living room was a trophy that Stanley had won at the age of four or five in a KOY radio station competition, reciting "Moo Cow Moo" or "Nice Mr. Carrot." Shortly thereafter, however, he retired from public life and never to my knowledge acquired, desired, or competed for a trophy until, at the age of thirty-eight, as he left the *Oakland Tribune* for the *Los Angeles Times,* he was offered a slug from the press etched with the signatures of his fellow newsmen.

At the age of ten or twelve he decided to become a writer. He asked for a typewriter for Christmas and installed a lock on his door. He began to write for the *Emerson Herald,* the newsletter of our grammar school, and in the eighth grade became its editor. He went to North Phoenix High School with the intention of becoming editor of the *Mustang Roundup,* which he duly did. With two friends, he founded, wrote, and

*With brother Stanley, 1938; "the first of an
unconscionable number of studio portraits"*

These brotherly attentions were confined mostly
to vacations, though, and when Stan was with his
high-school friends I became the younger-sibling
persona non grata. I suffered accordingly. I sat outside
the door where the mysteries of *Fadical Tower* were
being plotted, invented excuses to wander through,
tried with singular lack of success to invent the sort of
joke that would make Stan, Wes, and Fred laugh the
way they did over their cartoons.

I don't know whether this forlorn adoration had
anything to do with my eventually becoming a
writer—certainly I wavered and moiled over my
choice of profession, a far cry from Stan's early and
absolute commitment. I do know that it had something for good and ill to do with my conception of
love, both the clarity of the feeling in myself, and the
anxiously low expectation of return. Having said that,
I should also say that as adults my brother and I have
become easy good friends, and we still carry on a
bantering rivalry, begun when he was in high school
and I in grammar school. When *Material Goods* came
out in 1980, he sent me a poem that ended:

Awed by slim volumes, what am I to say?
(My headlines growing cold, type going gray);
Just this: *Three million readers, kid, TODAY!*

drew cartoons for the *Fadical Tower,* a sort of early
Arizona cross between the *Village Voice* and the April
Fools' issue of a campus rag.

My relationship with my brother went through
the usual sibling changes, but I think it was quite early
for a younger sister that I began, mostly secretly, to
idolize him. A few of our California summers were
spent in a trailer on the shore at Seal Beach, and
when the hours got long, the swimming and the
Monopoly grew old, Stan used to beguile the time
with stories of stunning invention. A favorite series
was called "A Penny for Luck," in which a sequence
of characters down, out, desperate, or dying for lack
of money briefly and ignorantly held in their hands a
priceless collectors'-item penny, which at the end of
the story each would spend for something tragically
insignificant. I begged for these stories so often that
Stan finally tired of them and had one of the
characters flip the penny into a river. Once when I
marvelled at his skill Stan invented a spur to my own
invention: he asked me to name any three objects and
then he wove them into a plot; then he named three
and I had to make up the story about them. It was a
literary version of our favorite drawing game, in
which one person drew a quick scribble and the other
had to turn it into a face.

About the seventh grade I began to write poems
again. I was by this time thick of torso, my straight
hair hidden under a frizz of home perm, my feet like
my nose too large, my despair constant that I could
never expect to look like Adena Wolf nor be the
beloved of beautiful Vernon Godbehere—and in such
self-dissatisfaction I took the path more travelled by
and became the teacher's pet.

Our literature teacher was a Mr. Allsworth,
blandly aging, slightly slow, with a head full of
beautiful white hair. He was inclined to praise my
efforts with a mild, not altogether satisfactory, benig-
nity. One day we read a story about a defenseless wild
animal—I think it was a rabbit—who defended her
young against a vicious lone dog, and succeeded in
some dramatic way that left the dog dead. I thought it
peculiarly one-sided. How could we be so sure that
the dog was a villain? (I think I was predisposed to
like dogs better than underdogs at the time.) I
therefore concocted my first experiment in point of
view—with no notion that is what I was doing—and
brought Mr. Allsworth a new version of the story in
which the dog was trying to save his injured master by
feeding him until help could arrive. In my version the
dog also died (so did the master), but tragically,
hearing in his doggy brain a voice from the heavens

pronouncing that his was a job well done. A little more satisfactorily than usual, Mr. Allsworth appeared to be startled.

Then I made a wonderful discovery. In our family there had always been two capitalized *I*'s besides the ego's name. My father was in favor of anything that could be called an Idea. My mother had a mystical affection for Inspiration. I now discovered the value of the latter, for although bedtimes were considered absolute, and if I were caught under the covers with a Sylvia Seaman mystery and a flashlight I would be sharply reprimanded, it turned out that in my mother's opinion Inspiration was not subject to schedule but would come will-you nil-you, early or late, and there was nothing that a mortal could do about it. My muse suddenly declared herself to be of the midnight variety. In the space of a few months I wrote a couple of dozen after-hours poems, which made their way into the hands of Mr. Allsworth.

Now Mr. Allsworth did a much more satisfactory thing: he kept me after school on Thursday afternoons for a whole semester teaching me prosody. Dimeter. Rich rhyme. Spondee. Caesura. *Envoi.* (Every once in a while, when my job as a teacher seems routine and fruitless to me, I remember how profoundly those Thursday sessions have affected my life, how the iamb miraculously mirrored the rhythm of blood beat, how those Arabs folded their tents and in irregular anapests silently stole away.)

This was my first "workshop." I knew its purpose was to make me a better writer, not ever suspecting it was also a way to make a living. Later, lecturing on prosody to two or three hundred students at the University of Sussex, I observed (and have had no reason since to revise the observation) that grammar and high-school teachers somehow always seem to think you'll get the poetic feet later, and college teachers to assume you've had them, and unless somebody takes the effort to make sure, you'll miss a fundamental pleasure of poetry.

Mr. Allsworth reviewed my weekly efforts and made the following pronouncement: "I think the world may have found in you another Margaret Fishback." I have never learned who this lady was.

One of the poems I wrote, called "A Bundle for Britain," celebrated the birth of Bonnie Prince Charlie, and at Mr. A's urging I sent it to Buckingham Palace. I received in return a typed letter under the seal of the palace, signed by a lady-in-waiting to Her Majesty Princess Elizabeth. I was briefly famous. The letter was later stolen out of a collection of my poems at the Emerson Grammar School Hobbies Fair, and I always suspected Adena Wolf. I don't know why, unless it represents some sort of ineffable logic that

the girl I so envied for her beauty should return my envy for the one thing I had.

By the eighth grade I had entered pubescent misery and more or less forgot about poetry. Much later I tried to track Mr. Allsworth down to thank him, but I was unable to do so. Many of my regrets concern not what I've done, but the failure to let people know how much they mattered to me.

I wrote one last sentimental parting poem for the *Emerson Herald*, then a valedictory address of equal and largely unfelt nostalgia. I was anxious to get on to high school where things had to get better.

They did and didn't. There was a lot more of the same—starring in English class and standing on the sidelines at the basketball dance—and I may have been so busy doing what was then called "discovering boys" that I failed to notice I was also discovering friendship and kinds of competence.

Marilyn Lane was lanky, limber, and had a faulty muscle in one eyelid that produced an involuntary wink—usually when she was about to say something witty. I had never known a witty girl before. It was the myth of our friendship that we had begun as enemies, each finding the other conceited, which I believe was the only flaw that anybody was ever accused of. But I don't remember disliking her, only that we had a wonderful time assuring everyone that such dislike had occurred. Marilyn's parents were divorced, and she lived with her father and was good pals with her stepmother, all of which was vaguely shocking. Worse, she had a homosexual uncle she liked a lot. In my family such things were never admitted to.

"Mere" and I were both "good at English" and competed for grades and assignments on the *Round-up*, eventually in our senior year sharing its editorship, one semester each. The competition was real—neither of us ever pulled punches—but it also went along without in the least damaging our affection. I knew what the phrase "friendly rivalry" was all about (from both Stan and Mere) and later when I heard about the famous competition among females I thought what a fine thing it was.

Mere and I shaved our legs, ignoring my mother's admonitions about how we would regret it (we never did), jointly owned (this being a way to stretch our allowances) the largest collection of outsized earrings at North High, shopped for fabrics together, pored over dress designs, and taught each other to alter commercial patterns to our pleasure. Once Mere cleaned out the Baptist library and discovered a book of sex advice for Sunday schoolers. We learned horrific things from this book, and were both eager to assure each other of the truth, that we'd never *heard* of self-abuse. We figured out what it was. The close of one chapter admonished us to "Remember to take Jesus Christ with you in your sex life," and this became our secret greeting. "Remember. . . ." When, in my junior year, my brother introduced me to his college roommate and friend Bob Pirtle, and Bob and I started dating, Bob introduced me to his brother Dave, I introduced Dave to Marilyn, and we made up a foursome. All the others in this daisy chain are far-flung, but Dave and Marilyn have been married for thirty years.

Through these years I wasn't sure that I wanted to write; both dress design and acting looked more glamorous to me, and although I spent more time in the journalism room, I enjoyed drawing and silk screening, oratory and acting much more. The drama coach suggested that I become a theatre critic, but that seemed dull to me.

By my junior year I felt myself to be in a crisis of indecision over my life's work. I clerked summers and weekends for a dress shop, also designing felt skirts for them which my mother made (sequins one by one on sea horses, hundreds of tiny hand stitches on the surrey with the fringe on top). I was cast as one of the sisters in *Uncle Harry* (a middle-aged dowager; just what I thought of myself and obviously what everybody else thought of me). But as a senior I failed to be cast as the Shrew for the taming thereof, and had to settle for designing the set—a bitter second best.

The *Shrew*, however, was to be directed by my English teacher Dee Filson, and I was in love with him. He was tall, graying, horn-rimmed, and intense. His classes left me breathless. It was my first experience of the connection between eroticism and the intellect. Mr. Filson insisted that we think of ourselves as adults. When we discussed family relations we were to "relate" to our potential children rather than our soon-to-be-abandoned parents. One day when one of the students used the word "Communist" in a sneering tone, Mr. Filson said: "Hey, whoa! Would you like to define Communism for us?" (This was still the early fifties.) He then spent the rest of the hour on Marx, comparing ideological communism to the practice of the Soviet government and also to various forms of Western democracy. He concluded, "When you look at it this way, Jesus Christ was the first Communist. And *tomorrow* . . . one of your mothers is going to call the principal to tell him I said so."

Rapt, I raced home to impart to my Republican parents, who had surely somehow missed all this inspiring information and explication, what Mr. Filson had said. My mother called the principal.

Now Mr. Filson somewhat took the sting out of

"With my folks, on Fisherman's Wharf, 1954"

my failure by deploring the practice of student committee casting, saying that if it was up to him I would have had the part of Kate. I set to designing (with no experience and no training), and came up with an elaborate and barely adequate series of castle rooms for the cumbrous turntable we were using. But for the road to Padua I was inspired, and adorned it with a single tree in the form of a variegated pink cloud impaled on a black prong. Dee Filson later told me that this tree was used, repainted, in North High Players productions for the next ten or fifteen years.

By this time I was involved in public speaking, though I was too self-conscious to be good at impromptu debate, and made the best showing where I could write and memorize my lines. The Knights of Pythias Oratorical Contest (do they still have that?) was just the ticket. The subject: *Motoring Courtesy and How to Promote It.* My gimmick: pretending to forget my lines and grinning foolishly at the audience to elicit a return grin, thereby proving that friendliness was contagious. Arrgh.

But I won in the city, in the state at Globe (occasion of my first television appearance: I bored my eyes into the screen during evening news, deciding that after all I didn't look that bad), and then went to Nogales for the regional contest. Dee Filson drove, the debate coach, Mr. Harvey, sat up front with him, my mother and I sat in the back; I won, we drove back, and when we arrived home my mother lashed out at me, shocked and shouting, outraged, scandalized, that married Mr. Filson and I had been flirting the whole way.

She was, I now realize, in pain. And she was right. I may then have scoffed at her, but I have since seen a dozen marriages founder on such attraction, and have myself married a student. It is always serious. The erotic bond between teacher and student is a kind of sanctioned incest.

For the opening night of *The Taming of the Shrew* I designed and made a dress in variegated pinks to match the tree, and Mr. Filson told me that I was beautiful. It seems to have been the first time I'd been told that, and certainly the first time I believed it. The next year when I was a freshman at the University of Arizona Dee came to see me two or three times, took me to lunch and for long walks in the mountains, told me that he was divorcing, and asked me to marry him. I was too terrified even to give it serious consideration. I can't think that there is anyone alive who would mind my recording this, but I don't underestimate the seriousness of the offer, to him or me. Years later I realized the sensitivity and restraint he had shown toward a virginal Methodist adolescent; and the gift he offered, which was the first dim sense that my intellect and my femininity were not each other's enemies.

When Gakie retired from the little bank in Wilcox, Daddy had built him and Gamie a home only a few doors away from ours. Now as I finished high school Gakie was finishing his life. It suddenly occurred to me that I took him very much for granted. Two memories from his dying time stay with me. In one I am sitting on the floor beside the living-room couch watching the first television set to make its way into our lives. Gakie lies on the couch and we are holding hands. I know that what I'm about to say is dangerous because it acknowledges his dying. But the urge is strong, and I have never shied from drama. I say, "I wish I had got to know you better." He squeezes my hand, pats it. He says, "It's all right. It's all right."

Some days later I had a phone call saying that I had won an Elks or Rotary scholarship, and my mother and grandmother did a dance of distress, agitatedly asking each other whether they dared tell Gakie—he'd be so excited it might give him another heart attack! It was perfectly clear they were going to tell him, and eventually they did. I stood across the room from where gaunt white-haired Gakie was propped in bed while Mom bore the dangerous tidings. Gakie listened, grinned at me. He said, calmly, "It's starting, Sissy." My grandfather's name was Dana T. Milner, and he was known as Dana T. Remember that; it comes up later.

My brother had transferred to Stanford School of Journalism in his senior year and was now on his way to being a newspaperman. Stanford was the college generally considered coolest among my peers, and it was really the only one that interested me, but to go there I would have to get a serious Stanford scholarship. Once my grandfather had owned Sunnyslope Mountain north of Phoenix; he'd bought it for $500, but sold it soon after, with a princely profit, for $2000. Dad's home designs were being used to build 500 tract houses at a time, but because he had no architect's license they belonged to the architect whose stamp they bore, and Dad made nothing from them. Besides, he has confided in me since, he thinks it builds character to put yourself through college.

I didn't get the Stanford scholarship. Wait-listed meant that I would have to go to the University of Arizona at Tucson. I had so wanted, for so long, to leave Arizona. My brother's friend Fred Mendelsohn, who went to Harvard (when asked he would only say "I go to school in the East"—a measure of sophistication that the East imparted), urged me to try to get into Radcliffe or Barnard, but like Dee Filson's proposal, this seemed to me to require a leap into the void.

Having lived nearly all my life in the same place, with the same people—and for a dozen years with a room of my own—it was hard to share a dorm cubicle with a stranger, a bouncy, horsey, good-natured blond Hawaiian who collected snake skins and mynah bird feathers. It was hard for a night person to make it to a 6:40 class five days a week, to be barked at by a grizzled prof: "*Papa va aller à Amiens!*" It was hard to face up to how much history had already occurred, and how many names and numbers there were attached to it. At the University of Arizona I was homesick a lot of the time, and ashamed of being homesick because I had made such a production of wanting to leave home.

I "rushed," pledged Kappa Kappa Gamma, got the lead in a play, dated beer-tasting boys on frat excursions to nearby mountains, got ceremonially pinned to a Phi Gam majoring in Range Grasses; and about all of this felt anxiously grateful but slightly askew to my center—something for which it took me many years to find a name: inauthentic.

But there were also moments that prefigured deeper excitement. University of Arizona had a surprising, superior faculty, some of them asthmatics held in the desert for health's sake. In spite of myself I began to care about history (Luther was dethroned from sainthood for me in one brilliant half-hour lecture), and then—science!

One morning I exited from a botany class, my notebook page covered with fresh diagrams of vascular bundles (a term of which I had lived in happy ignorance until that morning), broke a leaf off a magnolia tree, turned it stem-end-up—and saw the organic double of my diagram. It was the first time it had occurred to me that science had anything to do with my world. I performed the only sort of homage I knew how, and hotfooted it after an A in the course. Later, in *Raw Silk*, I gave Virginia Marbelestier the same sort of rudimentary love of that single science. I gave her the vascular bundles, too.

Mademoiselle magazine, Patrick McCarthy, and Helen McCann got me out of Arizona. I was actively pursuing the *Mademoiselle* College Board Contest, doing assignments from each month's issue of the magazine, now in writing, now in design, now in merchandising, trying to impress the editors with my nouveau Renaissance quality, hoping to get brought back to New York for the month of June, all expenses paid *and* salaried.

I was spurred on by my English teacher Pat McCarthy, one of the trapped asthmatics, a Columbia graduate, an energetic teacher for all the breath it cost him; a brilliant good guy. I wrote a piece for him about the excessive thinness of the theatre types, of which he said, "If I didn't know better, I would assume that this were written by a fat person." So far as I know this is the only time anyone ever managed to salve my secret wound while praising my writing. In one of his classes I demanded, "Doesn't it (writing) get easier?" to which he replied, "It doesn't get easier. It gets *better*." It was also in one of his classes that I disgraced myself over Keats's urn. McCarthy asked, "Why does he say 'O Attic shape'?" and I replied, "Where else would you find a Grecian urn except in an attic?" He thought this witty, but I was too slow, too drearily trained in Methodist honesty, not to admit I'd meant it. I was too dashed to open my mouth for a few weeks after that, and only realized in graduate school that I'd had a couple of genuine perceptions about the urn.

McCarthy urged me to start with Plato and read, read; I'd never heard of Plato. He gave me *Catcher in the Rye* and I thought it was a test—a dirty book; would I dare tell him it was trash? He urged me to apply to Columbia; I thought he meant Stevens College in Columbia, Missouri (very high prestige among the sorority sisters).

But one day I happened to notice an article in the local paper that a Miss Helen McCann, Registrar of Barnard College, was in the area recruiting from private girls' schools. There were only half-a-dozen hotels in town, so I called them until I found her. She came out to the university and bought me lunch. I have no memory at all of what I said to make her champion my cause at Barnard. But I do remember that she said to me, "It's not easy to be poor in New

York, but everything in the city is at the end of a ten-cent subway fare."

I applied for admission and an alumni scholarship at Barnard. I wrote an article on bigotry called "Color Blind" for the *Mademoiselle* contest. It won the prize for that month's entries, which meant that I was going to New York as a contest winner, which meant that I could be at Barnard for the crucial interview.

New York, June 1959. I didn't know that my arrival was a classic. I followed from the airport, carefully mimicking, a trim and confident young beauty with a chic hatbox on which I saw, as she descended from the bus at Grand Central, an Ames, Iowa, address. I stood on the curb there waiting for the cabdriver to come around and open the door for me. When his irritation had passed he recognized a rube, and on the way to the Barbizon told me, Bronx accent, "New Yawk is like a gigantic ice cream sundae. Y'eat it all at once y'get sick to y'stomach. Y'spoon it up a little bit at a time, kid, y'never get enough."

It was the year after Sylvia Plath's spot on the *Mademoiselle* College Board junket, though of course none of us would so have dated anything then. Twenty college girls—some greener than others and I the greenest; also the only freshman—gathered in a room whose walls were partly mirrored, partly papered in Victorian newspaper clippings full of bustles and parasols. Joan Didion was one of the twenty, so was Gael Greene (of *Blue Skies, No Candy*), Adri Steckling who now designs under her own label; and Jane Truslow—laid-back, compassionate, the one I felt closest to and would most have liked to know, though our paths only once crossed again. Betsy Talbot Blackwell, with a cigarette holder that *seems* in my memory to have been a foot long and rhinestone studded, in any case certainly announced, "We believe in pink this year."

I was assigned to advertising, taken out of it to do the editorial, sent to an afternoon or two on an article about Sylvia Plath, who had just won the Mount Holyoke Intercollegiate Poetry Competition ("Guest Editor Makes Good"), taken off of that, photographed in my frizzy curls, sent to fashion shows and cocktail parties and home to the Barbizon Hotel.

One of the perks of the contest was that each of us was to be allowed to interview for the August issue the celebrity of our choice. As a recent convert, I had given as my three choices, "J.D. Salinger, J.D. Salinger, and J.D. Salinger." The editors knew about J.D.'s reclusiveness, and as I was the only one of us who showed a particular interest in the theatre, had decided that I would interview the Swedish actress

Viveca Lindfors, then starring in *Anastasia* on Broadway. I'd never heard of her. The only info I'd been able to find on her in Arizona was in the *New Yorker* blurb about the play. *Mademoiselle* required an advance list of questions I was going to ask her so, jaded, I went to the box office, picked up a playbill, and turned the "Who's Who in the Cast" notes into questions.

It happened that mine was to be the first interview. I had not seen *Anastasia* and my editor had not suggested I do so—probably because an excursion to that play was planned for the College Board the following week.

I was squeamish about the whole business, not less so when I realized that I was to be accompanied by a sinewy little photographer with a fast mouth, and a gum-chewing secretary who would take notes for me and therefore effectively remove my one device for hiding angst. I wore a blue linen suit I had made myself, a little white pique hat with a veil. Miss Lindfors' agent had forgotten to tell her about the interview, and when she nevertheless graciously let us into her cramped dressing room, she was in full fur-and-wool costume from the matinee, exhausted, sweating furrows in her greasepaint, and monumentally, breathtakingly beautiful. The secretary sat on her dressing table, chewing, swinging a leg. The photographer kept shoving my chair closer to Lindfors, my knees into hers, saying, "Cheat to the camera, baby; cheat to the camera."

Embarrassment, irritation, jadedness, angst—suddenly transformed themselves to a fist around my throat. I could scarcely squeak out my first banal question. I couldn't hear the answer at all. I sweated in the bank of dressing lights. I thought I would vomit, faint. The secretary saw that I had blanked and (chewing gum, swinging leg) prompted, "Janet!" Her panic deepened mine.

"Cheat to the camera, baby."

After perhaps the third question Viveca Lindfors handed me a copy of the playbill and said, "I think you will find all the answers to your questions in here." At perhaps the fourth she turned a dark appraising eye on me and said (with perfect justice), "You don't listen, do you?"

Chew, chew, swing. "Janet?"

"Cheat to the camera, baby."

Now I would not vomit or faint but would die. Nevertheless, somehow, perhaps to assuage her own boredom by saying something interesting, Viveca Lindfors began to talk. I could hear little, remember less, but I remember her saying, "You Americans are all so concerned with happiness. Happiness is not the most important thing. The most important thing is

the work." This, no doubt, is the one thing I remember because it was so outrageous an idea. I could hear my mother saying, "All I want is your happiness, honey," which certainly meant that I was falling from virtue somehow and would pay for it, but beyond that certainly assumed (I assumed, Americans assumed, doesn't everybody assume?) that happiness, its pursuit, *was* the main thing, the *summum bonum.* At the moment, my personal pursuit was in disarray.

Outside the stage door, the photographer took me by the shoulders and shook me hard—he was so short that he had to reach up to do it. "If the others ask you, it went fine, hear? It went fine!"

The next week, though, things did go better. My editorial was accepted. At the ball on the roof of the St. Regis I met a young poet who kissed me in a hansom cab. I recovered somewhat. Who was Viveca to me or I to Viveca? I wrote her a thank-you note in which I shamelessly played on my own naivete (first trip to New York, first trip backstage, etc.).

But then we went to see *Anastasia.* Lindfors blew me away. She was dazzling, superb, powerful. When, in the second act, Eugenie Leontovich acknowledged Anastasia as her granddaughter, I experienced for the first time what is meant by a "recognition scene." I began to cry—for Anastasia, but also that *I* had not been recognized—and I continued off and on through the third act, to the quizzical embarrassment of my peers.

I couldn't let it go. When the show was over I left the others and shouldered my way to the entrance at the side of the stage. A hoarse-voiced, horse-faced woman blocked my passage, but when I blubbered out my story she opened the door a crack and whispered, "I didn't see you, hear?"

Lindfors had her maid and her little boy with her. She sent them away.

"When I got your letter I thought I had been hard on you," she said.

My words tumbled. "I told myself it didn't matter, but I hadn't seen you act. You're a *great* actress. I couldn't let you think all that of me. It isn't true I want to be an actress. I want to write. They had me say that. I'm sorry. . ." and so forth. I began to cry again, and Viveca Lindfors, statuesque in velvet and fur, began to cry with me! Then we sat and talked, and I could listen, and when I left she said, "You go out and write with all the sincerity you feel now, and you will be a *greeeat* writer, and I will buy your books!"

Eyes streaming, I sailed from the backstage door and hailed a cab. All the way to the Barbizon I cried while the driver clucked his tongue and suffered for me: "Broadway's tough, kid; Broadway's a heartbreaker."

The young poet asked me out again. His parents invited me to dinner. After a couple of weeks they invited me to vacation with them in the Adirondacks. I got my scholarship to Barnard and gave the pin back to my Arizona aggie.

I had no sense whatever of myself as representative of a historically experimental generation, no sense of myself as having a Hollywood-distorted view of romance and love. I certainly saw myself as engaged in a search for the right man to marry, and assumed that eventually to find such a person was my inalienable right. I had no sense that this particular holy grail required certain tests and qualities in the seeker's self, nor that I was, however virginally, embarking on a life of serial monogamy.

I did know that there was a painful discrepancy between what I felt and what I felt I ought to feel. After the somehow trying glamour of the Adirondack vacation, when my poet had gone off to England in a Fulbright batch with Sylvia Plath, I felt trapped and frightened. I had discovered the Philip Larkin poem that begins:

> No, I have never found
> The place where I could say:
> This is my proper ground,
> Here I will stay,
> Nor met that special one
> Who has an instant claim
> On everything I own
> Down to my name. . .

In the days before the Barnard dorm opened I lay in a hotel room monotonously reciting it, unable to make myself go out.

But my three years at Barnard were a watershed. As soon as I arrived I went to Rosalie Colie, the Milton scholar on the Barnard faculty and a friend of my University of Arizona English teacher, told her that I was horrifically uneducated, and asked her to make a reading list for me. She began by assuring me that I overestimated my ignorance, ended by being amazed at it. Barnard students were mainly New Yorkers and it would not have been possible to grow up in New York as innocent of great works as I was. Armed with my list I went to library and bookstore, thence to the Cloisters, where—in suitable setting, I thought—I sat slogging through the *Dialogues*, then Aristotle, Sophocles, Aeschylus. I signed up for a masterpieces course, and began to get a little direction from S. Palmer Bovie, whose combination of erudition and irreverence helped ease me into my place in the world of books. (Bovie was, is, a fearsome fearless punner: years later when I wrote him from a Florida apartment on Pensacola Street he shot back: *Is that the drink that makes you think?* Bovie also taught me that the true goal of a pun is not a laugh but a groan.)

I lived with graduate and other transfer students in Johnson Hall, and in those days we walked freely along Morningside Drive and sat in Morningside Park to study. I could take a subway safely back from a party in the Village in the middle of the night. The racking homesickness passed after a few weeks or months, and I found another witty woman for friend in Judy Kaye, with whom I learned the routine and irreplaceable pleasure of the six-hour dorm talk.

I joined the Columbia Players, failed once more to get a part, but since my backward background had netted me the unusual ability to sew, I made myself indispensable by designing costumes. In the Players I made friends with Bruce Moody, who for introduction bit my knee, surely a paradigm of Bohemian behavior. (Once my grandmother came to New York. On the bus downtown to hear Norman Vincent Peale I spotted a bearded man with an earring and a woman in high heels and pedal pushers. "Look, Gamie!" I said. "Bohemians." "Oh, yes," she replied. "Or maybe Serbians.") Bruce also, when I protested that I couldn't go to a theatre party because I didn't drink, came to pick me up carrying a quart of milk and a two-quart brandy snifter.

Early in my first, sophomore, year at Barnard, something happened that had the feeling of portent as it occurred. I was one evening shoulder-deep in the tub in the dank dorm bathroom, spacey with having read a whole volume of Ogden Nash at a sitting, and an idea for a poem occurred to me. I hadn't written a poem for at least four years. "Dear Reader, I have no complaint, / As Long as you peruse my verse, / Concerning what you are or ain't. . ." It was a silly piece of Nashian verse, but my heart was racing in iambs, the rhymes kept leaping up into place, I could see the outline of the whole three-part thing and hung onto it round the edges of my mind while I filled in the center like strokes of a crayon in a coloring book, going back over and back over the lines from the beginning because I didn't have a pencil and didn't dare jar it out of my head by getting out of the now tepid water and going to my room before it was all filled in. Flinging on my robe, I went. I had enough of it memorized to be able to finish the rest, dogged, soggy, slogging. The funny thing about this verse was that, as the point of it was that the reader should *not* read a whole volume of me at one sitting, it only made sense if I went on to write at least a volume's worth of poems. I was excited in a way that has since become familiar. First cousin to my mother's old *Inspiration-capital-I,* this is the moment an idea demands to become a thing.

My alumni scholarship paid tuition, room and board, and my folks were sending me thirty dollars a month for books and spending money. It wasn't going to be enough. I went to the Young Men's Hebrew Association and applied there to be part-time secretary to John Kolodney, who ran the Poetry Center. I lied about having shorthand, but anyway Kolodney interviewed by the original expedient of having me write a letter to Edwin Arlington Robinson inviting him, in spite of his deceased condition, to read at the Center.

Thereafter for two or three afternoons a week, for seventy-five cents an hour, I bused from class to Ninety-second and Lexington, made sketchy notes of Kolodney's dictation, and invented the letters I thought he intended to write. We got along fine.

One of the duties of my job was to make the coffee and the onion dip for the Young Poets' Reading Series, so I got to meet a dozen of these enviable creatures. Once when the recent Lamont winner Donald Hall was scheduled to read, I raced in before onion-dip time to the Doubleday's on Fifth Avenue and demanded a copy of *Exiles and Marriages.* "Say again?" the slow clerk asked, whereupon a personable young man behind him held up a copy of the book. "It looks like this."

"Where'd you get that?" I said. "Will you sell it?"

"I wish I could, but I'm afraid I have to read from it tonight. I'm Donald Hall.

"And," he added, "I can't tell you how often I've dreamed of walking into a bookstore and hearing a lovely young coed ask for my poetry."

Another of my jobs was the first screening of the Center's new contest, which was to result in publication by Harper and Row. I found this task grim and long; I was not daunted by the *bad* poetry, but the floor-to-ceiling piles of the mediocre threatened me. It was clear from the most amateur and superficial reading that the best manuscript by far was *The Hawk in the Rain* by a young Englishman, Ted Hughes—so clear that I was only glancingly pleased that the final judges agreed with me.

Contests and readings were in those days extremely rare, and the Center may have much to answer for. Also relatively rare was the practice of offering writing workshops, which both Barnard and the Center, however, did. I was gluttonous for workshops, and over the three years I spent in New York I sampled nearly a dozen teaching styles, learning something (*usually* about writing) from each. I studied with George Plimpton, Hortense Calisher, Walker Gibson, Louise Bogan. Marianne Moore was a fellow classmate in one workshop. The worst teacher was W.H. Auden, who, often drunk, always bored, sat reminiscing about the *tramontana* or reciting Dante in Italian, swinging a loafer on the end of his argyled toe. The best was Rolfe Humphries, who, inventive with exercises in rhyme scheme, vowel length, consonant clusters, and stanza form, ensured that we tune our ears by forbidding us to make sense for the first half of the semester.

In my senior year I took a playwrighting workshop with Howard Teichmann at Barnard, and he helped me to get a production of my play *Garden Party,* directed by Dolph Sweet, with Barnard women and (out-of-work) professional men. The play featured a God wearing Dacron (modern miracle) and a Satan who turned Eden into a subdivision called Paradise Lots. I described it as "a rewrite of Milton from a woman's point of view," though I had not heard of feminism, and my irritation at Milton's misogyny seemed unconnected to anything in my own life.

The experience of play production was excruciating. The actors *would* not get the lines right. The second act was crushingly dull. The director had no notion what I was up to. The longer they rehearsed, the more puerile the whole thing seemed. But on opening night I sat listening to lit humans talk words I had written, surrounded in the dark by others who responded, laughed, sighed. There's nothing like it. Fan letters for a novel are remote by comparison, posthumous praise of a creature long dead to me. I thought then, and I think now, that writing for the theatre would suit me best. Unfortunately, my best ideas have come as novels and would not yield their form.

As a result of this play, I got an agent at MCA. I also got a poem in the *Atlantic,* a summer as a junior assistant at the *New Yorker,* the Elizabeth Janeway Prize at Barnard, and the Intercollegiate at Mount Holyoke. I also got deflowered, drunk, entangled with a married man, and mononucleosis. I won a Marshall Scholarship to Cambridge, but, exhausted, I wandered into Palmer Bovie's office one afternoon feeling that I didn't feel what I ought to feel, and wailed (I had started reading Henry James), "I'm not sure I *want* to go to England."

"Life is a question of alternatives," Palmer reasonably pointed out.

In England, 1965

By the time I left New York I could not imagine why anyone would want to live anywhere else. Culture shock hit me again in England. I spent the first year at Cambridge always cold, often irrationally frightened, and sometimes suicidal. This is true even though I was active and excited by the beauty and the intellectual richness around me.

I had first seen Sylvia Plath at a Fulbright reception my first fall in New York. I had worked on an article about her poetry for *Mademoiselle,* I had later pretended jealousy of her to my poet at Oxford, and he flirted back by mail that her name was really Plass, but she had a lisp; later he'd written that she was engaged to Ted Hughes, whose manuscript I'd read for the Poetry Center. Now I found that I was to live in the same room she'd inhabited at Cambridge, in the Whitstead House annex to Newnham College—a room occupied in the interim by poet Lynne Lawner, and which therefore had a tradition to keep up.

On the Marshall Scholarship application I had been asked why Cambridge was my first choice of

British university. I had no real reason. Of course I was going to choose Oxford or Cambridge, and I'd been told that Cambridge was prettier. Besides, the poet had gone to Oxford, and that love affair had not worked out. The only thing approaching an intellectual justification was that I admired David Daiches's literary criticism. I put down that I wanted to study with Daiches, assuming, however, that he would not supervise a student outside his own college. Now I was told that Daiches had agreed to take me on, and I went to his tutorial rooms at Jesus College once a week, at the civilized sherry hour, to study the English Moralists ("From Plato to Sartre" as this course was unofficially known). The following term he taught me the period 1880–1910; after that Tragedy, and the second year the Moralists again; I shared supervisions this time with Margaret Drabble, of whom I was intellectually in awe.

I was and am convinced that the accidental pattern of my studies—the American format, with fifteen class hours a week, constant assignments and frequent exams; followed by the English tradition, a week of constant reading culminating in a paper and a single hour of class—was an ideal way to cure my Arizona academic innocence. The freedom at Cambridge certainly added to my terror, but it also stretched me. I remember that one day Daiches said, "I think Forster this week. Yes, read E.M. Forster."

"What of Forster's?"

"Oh, there isn't much of Forster."

I wasn't one to defy authority. That week I read *all* of Forster. Another week I read seven novels of Henry James, huddled over a shilling-meter gas fire so close that the fingers outside my book turned red while my thumbs on the inside were still numb with cold.

The lectures at Cambridge, attendance voluntary, ran the gamut from sublime to bathetic, and I attended my share, but it is also true that most of the learning was not done in the classroom. In New York the social unit had been the couple. Men and women were not allowed in each other's rooms, so there had to be somewhere to go and a reason to go there—a "date." At Cambridge the social unit was the group, and there was always a group to join, for morning coffee, afternoon tea, evening wine, Sunday sherry. It was 1959, and the debate raged over C.P. Snow's *Two Cultures and the Scientific Revolution.* Opera, for some reason, was also a hot topic. So was Spain. I felt myself flourish, and then suddenly I would feel myself a fraud, a cowgirl in sheep's wool.

Once more I acted, designed costumes, wrote poetry and fiction for the literary magazine *Granta,* which was edited by the American triumvirate of

Richard Gooder (still at Cambridge), Andre Schiffrin, and Roger Donald (now editors at Pantheon and Little, Brown, respectively). In theatre and writing there was so much talent that I believed the British were inherently superior, never mind their superior school system. I was convinced of this for all the six years until I came back to live in England, by which time it was both news and common knowledge, that my particular years at Cambridge were phenomenal for talent. My colleagues in the theatre and literary groups, for instance, were Jonathan Miller, Dudley Moore, Peter Cook, Corin Redgrave, Ian McKellen, Derek Jacobi, Eleanor Bron, Margaret Stimpson, Margaret Drabble, Clive Swift, Bamber Gascoigne, Andrew Sinclair, Simon Gray, A.C.H. Smith, Jonathan Spence. . . . David Frost was given the editorship of *Granta* as I was leaving, but was generally recognized as an entrepreneurial, second-rate mind.

For spring vac that year Andre Schiffrin, Lena de la Iglesia, Roger Donald, and I drove down to La Napoule on the French Mediterranean and rented a yellow stucco house overlooking the sea, eighty dollars for the month. I had begun my first novel in my senior year at Barnard, and had believed I would make it my first priority at Cambridge. But I'd made no headway. Now I threatened to spoil the vacation for myself, sitting in the courtyard in the sun, my typewriter on the paving stones, blocked, hating every word that managed to transfer itself to the page. I remember feeling that, having found writing a solace, I now found it the very cause of the depression it was meant to relieve.

Nevertheless, I managed to write a scene or two of *Descend Again.* Lena—full name Maria Elena de la Iglesia—one afternoon trilled, "Oh, put my name in your novel!" so I obliged by naming an Arizona Mexican schoolgirl after her. I think it helped me write the scene. Lena was delighted—"Oh, put my name in *all* your novels!" I have done so, freely translating her into Mary Helen Church, Lena Fromkirk, Ellen Chiesa, and so forth. Lena and I see each other once a year at most, but the private joke is a powerful bond.

That summer Roger, his mother, and I did the American race through Europe—approximately one country, seven cathedrals, and twenty thousand calories a week—too rich for my budget, as was the running-water sort of hotel we chose—so that by the time they left me in Paris and flew for home, I was flat broke. I had not yet learned or decided that the middle class never starves, and I spent a worried week until I was taken on as a temporary secretary by UNICEF's office at Neuilly—which later became the setting of my second novel.

Meantime I had got my European sea legs, and this two months alone in Paris, renting a room from a kind, motherly *petit bourgeois* woman in the eighteenth *arrondissement* (so that I was playing house, not touristing) passed in a kind of exalted energy. I contracted the myth that I could *write* in Paris, and although I now had a full time job, I began to write lunch hours, evenings, and weekends—managing all the same to see plenty of the Seine and the Left Bank. I wrote all but a couple of chapters of *Descend Again,* and finished those as soon as I returned to Cambridge. When I had a letter from Charles Monteith at Faber and Faber that he would publish it, I literally fell, hard on the left kneecap, on the stone kitchen floor.

I went down to London to meet Monteith in the old Faber offices in Russell Square. In my mind's eye I see myself wearing the same white pique hat and veil with which I had confronted Viveca Lindfors, but that is hardly possible; it must have less to do with sartorial fact than with the quality of the apprehension. Monteith had told me he wanted to discuss a few changes, and I was convinced he would say, "The male hero doesn't live. Make him live." I *knew* about that, and knew nothing to do about it.

However, Monteith's suggestions were minimal, practical, and possible. He himself sat monumental in a swivel chair, shining of dome and fob (twenty years later he looked not a day older to me), and said, "Miss Burroway, I don't think *either* of us is going to make a fortune—or indeed a living—out of this book."

I had been in England for over a year by then, and I neatly translated how positive a remark this was. If he proposed to print a book with which he expected to make no money, it meant he wanted to buy into my future.

Monteith was editor to both Hughes and Plath, and through Faber I finally met them. Anthony Smith at Cambridge had introduced me to the Indian poet Zulfikar Ghose, who was going to publish a slim—emaciated—volume of my poems at the University of Keele; and Zulfi and I went to dinner with the Hugheses at their flat just behind the London Zoo aviary.

Sylvia and I acknowledged how oddly our lives had touched without our having met before. But what I mainly remember of the evening is Sylvia's hassled handling of the few-months-old baby while she cooked. I awkwardly offered to help but she refused; I recognized the anxious inability to discommode a guest. Finally she came out to the living room and handed the baby to Ted, who held the bundle in a simian crook of arm, his body in alien relationship to the swinging bundle as he described how he lay awake at night and listened to the animals in the zoo.

That second year in Cambridge I lived with three other women in a little terrace house, mine the attic bedroom with the four-poster bed. I acted less, wrote more, had a gentle romance, and in general a gentler time than the first frenetic year. In the final term I managed to "gear up" for the tripos, had some serious luck in the exam questions (this is not modesty; on the night before I sat the exam for the English Moralists I noticed quite by chance that Plato used "love" as a verb, Paul as a noun. The exam next day asked, "Compare the concept of love in Plato and Paul")—and I sailed back to America with a First in my fist.

It was through Charles Monteith also that I had met Curtis Canfield, dean of the Yale School of Drama, and now I had the NBC-RCA Fellowship in Playwrighting—a one-year award, unrenewable, which meant that I had come to the end of Grant Road. Next year I would have to earn my living.

Bruce Moody drove me up to New Haven from New York with the books and sewing machine he had stored for me while I was at Cambridge, and we painted my second attic apartment. Always a nester, I made what was by then the half-dozenth set of curtains and bedspread for a college room.

Yale was a disappointment after Cambridge, a regression from the self-discipline of the tutorial system, and my seventh year of college was my poorest and least (though I think we didn't use the word yet) "motivated." I could not seem to make myself memorize dates and proper nouns for Theatre History. John Gassner, who taught the playwrighting course, was a brilliant critic, a vast repository of knowledge about American realism, and a warm, sweet person; but he'd been left behind by the Absurd and had no way of dealing with the plays his most interesting students were writing then. I was trying to be "experimental" myself, and was very bad at it, and Gassner could not help me.

So it was not a profitable year for me as a writer. What unexpectedly opened up was the world of costume design. It was the rule at the drama school that everyone must take a turn at every aspect of production. I was a seamstress (I had been given a naked doll at five, and a hank of calico; by high school I made all my clothes) and an experienced amateur costume designer, so I was more useful than Frank Bevans's crews expected of a playwright.

They put me to work, got me excused from stage shifting and prop crews, gave me the most intricate pleating and pintucking to oversee, taught me to make wigs, strand by strand of polyester glued on

buckram head forms. By the end of the year I had barely passed four courses and had written a consummately mediocre play, but I knew how to run a costume room from sketch to strike. As with Mr. Allsworth's prosody, I loved the learning and never supposed it was a possible profession.

But the profession of wife had meanwhile presented itself as an alternative to going back to New York next year as a secretary. John Gassner's assistant was Walter Eysselinck, a Fulbright scholar from Belgium, a director as well as a playwright, a graduate in Germanic philology from the University of Ghent (native language Flemish but equally at home in French and English), a wine connoisseur, and gourmet cook.

I think we were ready to marry—he on the verge of his Ph.D. and I facing the employment void. I also think we had so many genuine interests in common that it masked the fact we differed in some basic values. My friend Julia Kling years later observed that Walter and I would have made a fine *arranged* marriage—if only we hadn't had to believe we were in love. I remember asking Walter one day in New

"Dad on the beach at Alligator Point, Florida, 1983"

Haven if he was "glad" that I was American. What I meant was that I was glad he was European; it seemed to expand my own scope (Prestige by Association). Walter, no doubt understanding exactly what I meant, angrily said, "Not at all!" However, he was glad I was American.

It was a nervous business, telling my parents I was marrying a foreigner, but made easier by the accident of his name. There were Walters all up and down the ranks of the cousins Pierce. If I had been marrying his brother Hans, it would have seemed more foreign altogether.

More serious was the issue of my parents' fanatical anti-tobacco/alcohol stance. I had been smoking and drinking for five years, but I now thought that if I didn't say so, my parents would later blame these mortal sins on my new husband. I think this was a sound impulse, but my mother accused me (not, to my shame, altogether inaccurately) of wanting champagne at my wedding rather than *her*—and she and dad decided not to come. On the eve of my wedding day I received from my father a forty-eight-page closely handwritten letter on the evils of smoke and drink, connecting these two habits to every known sin from uncleanliness to prostitution. I felt immensely righteous on the receipt of this letter (the second I had ever received from him)—and worldly, and sorry for my father that he was such a hick. I don't know why I carried the letter around the world for twenty years after that, unearthing it in my mid-forties to discover that it was full of sense, and love, and impeccable advice.

Walter and I were married by William Sloane Coffin at the Yale chapel. I was "given away" by John Gassner, our reception was held at the Canfields' home, and in a car borrowed from a generous former boyfriend (and in which, God help me, I taught Walter to drive on our honeymoon) we traveled to Vermont where we spent a week not alone but in the excellent company of Walter's Bennington friends the Gils and the Mamises.

The following summer we bought a two-year-old Dodge, all chrome and fins, and took off on a 9,000-mile camping trip. We had a flawless attitude toward camping. We carried no tent, only blankets and blow-up mattresses. If it rained we had to go to a motel. With a shower and a mattress-night's sleep, by this expedient, every three or four days, we made our way across the Northern states, down the West Coast, and back across the South, visiting my relatives all along the way. My parents turned out to like Walter a lot, though my father did warn me that it would be "hard to live with a European" in ways that I "didn't yet

understand." Again I pitied his provinciality.

We spent three weeks in New Orleans recording and photographing Walter's octogenarian jazz musician friends and holding the kitty at Preservation Hall; then we headed north to New York and Walter's first job on the theatre faculty of Harpur College, SUNY Binghamton.

We spent two years in Binghamton, one in the third floor apartment of a molding clapboard house (Salvation Army furniture and Sears pots), the second in a plastic and polyester dorm apartment as counselors. I began to learn something about the petty politics of university life. Nesting in earnest now, I also began to learn how easy it was, without any academic pressure or expectation, to dawdle through the day's minimal housework and fail to make it to my typewriter at all.

I took a job in the continuing education department at Harpur, teaching the masterpieces course to secretaries and tool and die workers from Ansco, IBM, and Endicott shoes. I liked the students and the classroom, but I hardly felt I had a career; it had always been clear to me that I didn't want to *teach.*

I also costumed for Walter, mounting one show in which two assistants and I produced fifty-six costumes and twenty-three wigs. I had immediate pleasure of any day spent in the costume room, but paid for it in guilt that my second novel was not progressing.

Toward the end of the first year Walter was warned that he would be deported under Public Law 555, which decreed that Fulbright Scholars could not trade their student visas for resident status until they had spent two years in their country of origin. Under this particular statute his marriage to an American made no difference, and in fact the customs officials several times tried to trick him into saying he had married me for citizenship. The law made a general kind of sense, since Fulbrights were often given to law and medical students from third world countries. But Flanders was not hurting for another playwright/director.

My mother, who had only reluctantly transferred her Republican loyalties from Taft, now wrote Barry Goldwater in the U.S. Senate, and Goldwater introduced a bill "For the Relief of Walter Eysselinck." This bill had not a hope of passing, and the deportation orders continued to arrive every month, but as long as the bill was pending, the orders did not have to be obeyed.

We moved into the dorm to save money, and I went to work for Young Audiences, Inc., a non-profit organization that provided chamber-music ensembles to rural schools throughout the state. I was hired for this job by Sue Winston, a woman with a silver upsweep and a golden soul. When I explained (that Arizona honesty) the tenuousness of our situation, Sue pulled her glasses down on her nose and peered over them. "My dear. Do you really think you can go through life beholden to Barry Goldwater?"

Probably not, and after half a year of it, it became obvious that we didn't want to go through life under deportation orders either. Walter began applying for Belgian jobs. In the late spring he was hired as a director by the Flemish division of Belgian National Television. I was two months pregnant when we left for Ghent.

If the lack of academic structure had been bad for my writing, depriving me of the English language was good for it. Walter and I spoke English at home on Vaderlaanstrasse, and friends, relatives, and waiters were always anxious to practice their English on me, but the topics were pretty well confined to food, tourism, and my Expectation. I became fluent in French on these three topics with my mother-in-law, and I began a rudimentary Flemish vocabulary with the shopkeepers and wives. But the theatrical conversations that interested me were in fast Flemish, and exclusively conducted by males. I had no one with whom to talk literature. The bookstores stocked almost no English fiction. The local library had all of Hemingway, Faulkner, and Jane Austen; I read or reread those. And I wrote. In the two years we spent in Belgium I finished my second novel and wrote the third.

We lived in the striking grey stone *bas haus* that Walter's architect father had designed in the thirties. Under the contrasting tutelage of Walter (more butter, more spice!) and his mother (more subtle, more vitamins!) I got to be a pretty fair gourmet cook, although a first pregnancy is not the best time to acquire this skill.

On the other hand, Ghent was a wonderful place to have a baby. "Natural" childbirth was in full vogue, and I took a tram weekly to classes in "kinesthetic training," monthly to an extraordinary clinic staffed by nuns and lorded over by a mammoth doctor who had no "second," never took a vacation, never got sick, delivered two or three dozen babies a week with hands each as big as a newborn. When Timothy Alan was born I was attended by this doctor, my familiar kinesthetician, my husband, and several nuns; and Tim was brought to me in a white lawn smock I had designed and made—fifteen minutes old in a button-down collar. I shared a semiprivate with a young woman who translated my Flemish into gutteral Ghentenaar for her mother, and with a parade of visitors to both of us, bearing azaleas and candied violets, whom the nuns offered beer and champagne.

Adjustments, I may have mentioned, come hard for me. For the first few months after Tim's birth I fought postpartum depression. Tethered to a hawk's cry by a small metal ring in the pit of my gut, I walked my diminished round. I had pushed myself hard to finish *The Dancer from the Dance* before Tim was born, and Faber was to publish it, but *Descend Again* had never found an American publisher, and now my New York agent Phyllis Jackson reported little success with this one. By the time Tim was five months old it became alarmingly apparent that he was going to walk early. I felt that I had lost any identity outside of "Tim's mom," and that if I didn't write a novel before he walked, I would never write another. I had an outline for a tight twenty-four-hour story, so I set a schedule and went at it, piling the desk with playpen toys that I handed down one after the other through the morning. *Eyes* was finished in five months, and accepted together with *Dancer* by Al Hart at Little, Brown.

Meanwhile Walter and I had left Tim behind with "Gramma Belgium" for a short Irish vacation, and on the way had visited my old tutor David Daiches in his new job as director of the School of English and American Studies at the University of Sussex. Daiches had banteringly offered me a teaching job, which I refused on the grounds that I had a husband. "Well," he said, "we're looking for a director for the arts centre. . ."

Whenever I am introduced in a lecture hall by someone reading through my *curriculum vita,* I have the impulse to point out that, as I die by drowning, this is *not* the life that will pass before my eyes. At fifty, I find that I am mainly interested in my childhood and, of adulthood, what's going to happen in the next year or so. I'm also conscious that many authors have written their autobiographies only up to the point that they began to write other books: *A Childhood: One Writer's Beginnings.* Childhood contains all our mystery; adulthood only secrets.

As I lived the events of 1965 to 1971 in England, life's changes seemed most marked by the acquisition of a house, the birth of a second son, the loss of a third baby, domestic violence, the decision to leave the marriage. Work was what happened every day. If I was lucky some of the work was at the typewriter. I had come firmly to identify myself by the activity of writing, but a mother/teacher/writer inevitably deals with the claims of those professions in that order: the baby's cry/the class preparation/the chapter.

Nevertheless, as I look back on it, it was the

commitment to writing that steadily deepened and changed its nature in those years. My first novel had come out in England to the kind of clattering acclaim that makes promises to the writer it dubs promising. *The Dancer from the Dance* had a cool reception, *Eyes* was praised but without any exclamation points attached. In America, both of these novels fell into the critical void. When Walter produced two of my short plays, *The Fantasy Level* and *The Beauty Operators,* for the Brighton Festival, one London paper treated me to the experience of rapier attack.

I had always known that I did not write for money—that was easy. Now between the publication of my first novel and my fourth, a total of ten years, I came to understand that, my childhood lessons notwithstanding, I did not write for praise. Writing is very hard for me, I'm very slow, and a lot of the time I simply hate doing it. Nevertheless that labor and the love of that labor are who I am. The work is the reward.

The Gardner Centre for the Arts was lavishly conceived and, in the years we were there, ambitiously pursued. Walter oversaw the construction of a theatre designed by Sean Kenny, cleverly transformable from an intimate round to a full proscenium, with several sorts of stage between. The building also had artists' studios, a scene shop, and a costume room.

Walter Eysselinck (left) with Bernie Hopkins, at the Gardner Centre, 1970

It seems very odd to me now that I organized this room, equipped it, found crews, and designed the first couple of shows, without its ever occurring to me that this was the sort of work one should get paid for. I did not think of myself as a professional costumer, and it would be true to say that at the time I costumed mainly in the capacity of the director's wife. Later I got a small fee for shows at the Gardner, of which I costumed eight or ten, and also at the National Theatre of Belgium, where Walter continued to direct from time to time.

There are advantages to not being a professional, though. I always felt detached from the work, which meant that I could take an easy and immediate pleasure in it. I would be incapable of saying, "Isn't my new novel wonderful?" But I could perfectly well rush backstage with an armful of brocade or patched leather and demand, "Isn't this terrific? Didn't this turn out great? *Look* at this!"

I spent long hours in the costume room at the Gardner Centre, including many long nights, and some of my well-wishers deplored the loss of my writing time. But, unlike teaching, costuming exercises mainly the hand and eye, which is both a relief from the typewriter and an important teacher of sense detail. The costume crew offered me the richest camaraderie of my life, too—a relief from the solitude of writing. And then, one never knows where a novel is going to come from. Most of the plot and setting, and all of the professional detail, of my most recent novel, *Opening Nights,* came out of the hacking, tacking, binding, blind-hemming, and breaking-down of those days in the Gardner Centre basement.

The first year Walter, Tim, and I lived in a drearily modern rented bungalow, but the second year, with immense trepidation, we borrowed twelve thousand pounds for a brick box surrounded with two acres of garden under the Sussex Downs at Westmeston near Ditchling. This house was called "Green Hedges," which seemed both boring and untrue (in winter the hedges were brown, in spring leaf red), and for Walter's love of jazz we renamed it "Louisiana," which made us very unpopular with the neighbors.

We could not see the neighbors, however: roses, daffodils, orchards, and vegetable beds surrounded us; sheep fields and downs stretched to the horizon on every side. The house had been built in 1939 for the farm bailiff of the local manor. It had an entrance hall eighteen feet square with a manorial fireplace and a skylight thirty feet overhead. It had a living room twenty by thirty, a scullery, butler's pantry, wine cupboard, "box room" (I never did find out what that was; I kept boxes in it)—as well as seven bedrooms of

"Tim with 'Gramma Belgium' in the garden of 'Louisiana'—
with the Downs in the background," Westmeston, Sussex

which two comprised the "staff flat." The house had been lived in since the Second World War by two aging women who had retreated to one downstairs corner of it. Nothing had been painted in that time. The spiders and mice had flourished. There were a hundred and eight broken window panes. I was seven months pregnant when we moved in.

If Belgium was a good place to have a first baby, Sussex was a magical place to have a second. The British assumption is that, after a normal first pregnancy, the second child will be born at home. I was therefore scheduled on the regular rounds of the district midwife, who instructed me in filling biscuit tins with cotton wool and baking them at rice pudding temperature, and so forth. She was, however, appalled at the condition of the house, which had one temporary electrical source and no heat, and suggested that I might want after all to consider hospital. I argued her down, feeling more like a pioneer than I ever had in Arizona.

I picked the smallest bedroom, gave it yellow eyelet curtains and a two-bar electric fire, and my second boy was born in a storm on Guy Fawkes Day with the celebratory fireworks bursting over Lewes six miles to our east. The midwife cheered me on, Walter mopped my brow with cologne; five minutes before the birth our four-month Irish setter *Eh La-Bas*

wandered in and jumped on the bed.

"On the whole," said staid Dr. Rutherford, "I don't think we want that dog in here." He ushered the puppy out and washed his hands again. The midwife said, "Just pick a spot on the picture rail, aim the head for that, and *push*." Dr. Rutherford positioned his hands to receive the baby that I, of my labor alone, joyfully delivered. (Like the vascular bundles, I later gave this experience in slightly altered form to Virginia Marbalestier of *Raw Silk*.)

But I had expected a girl. "Ah," I gasped. "We'll have to have another," to which Dr. Rutherford replied that he couldn't recall ever hearing the suggestion *quite* so soon before.

For two days this creature of the unexpected gender had no name. I am by profession a namer of things, and this was very painful for me. When Tim was born, I had tried to sell Walter on the idea of "Dana" as a name, after my grandfather, for either a girl or a boy, either first or middle. He would have none of it. Now I tried again to convince him, but Walter simply didn't care for the sound. Finally we agreed that we both liked "Toby," but not "Tobias." The *Oxford Etymological Dictionary of Names* yielded "Tobyn," and we concurred in the choice of Tobyn Alexander Eysselinck.

I telegraphed my parents in relief that the

decision had been made. A week later I had a letter from my mother. How odd, she said. Did I remember that Gakie was always called Dana T.? The T. stood for Tobin, which was his mother's maiden name. But he had always hated the Tobins, and had pretended that it stood for Timothy.

I have slim patience for astrology and related pseudosciences. But I do believe that much of what we call ESP is simply memory and intuition imperfectly understood, and that telepathy probably has less in common with magic than with radio waves. The naming of my sons is one of half-a-dozen striking instances in my life of my having made a connection I am not quite willing to attribute to coincidence. Or, as I put it in the mouth of Galcher in *The Buzzards,* the novel I was then about to write, "coincidence comes from God."

While Toby and the Gardner Centre were being born, I started teaching at Sussex, sometimes full-time, sometimes half. Even half-time teaching allowed me to hire a nanny, to repaint a few walls, and replace a few window panes. Earning my own nanny was important to me—I knew that it was necessary for me to "waste" innumerable hours at the typewriter, and that I could not be beholden to Walter for the time that, as W.H. Auden observed, you don't know "whether you are procrastinating or must wait for it to come." I also wanted to teach for the experience itself, and for the comradeship of the faculty. I taught the basic courses on a modified tutorial system—usually two students at a time, occasionally small seminars—and, as at Harpur College, I enjoyed both the students and the sense that the dormant actress in me was getting exercised. But I cared less about it than about house, boys, theatre. Until I came to Tallahassee, teaching presented itself to me as a job, not a *metier.*

Occasionally I gave a university-wide lecture, and these always filled me with the terror of the early elocution student, so that I prepared heavily and long for them. The very first of these lectures was to be on Aeschylus' *Oresteia,* which had been a work of signal importance to me since the days of Palmer Bovie's great-books course.

We had begun the refurbishing of our ramshackle house with the "staff flat"—in order to rent it, in order to pay the gardener; and our first tenants were two male American graduate students. One of these—I'll call him R.—had until a few months before been engaged to Valerie Percy, daughter of the senator from Illinois. It was not long after he moved into our house that Valerie Percy was stabbed in her bed in a house full of sleeping family members. R.

With Tim and Toby, at "Lousiana," 1970

went home to the funeral.

When he returned he needed to talk, frequently and often late into the night. He was particularly haunted by the realization that now, at Sussex, he was *popular* because of the murder. His connection to celebrity-tragedy meant he could date any girl he wanted. He had not much liked Senator Percy, but he now identified grimly with the sense that Percy, who was up for reelection and would certainly win, would never know whether his victory resulted from the murder of his daughter.

So there I was, in the evening solacing this troubled student, in the daytime writing a lecture about a king who must have his daughter killed in order to make war on Troy. The plot fell on me: an American politician who must risk his daughter for his career. I had never seen myself writing a political novel, and I was afraid of the size of it; but Goldwater had run for the presidency by then, and at the distance of four thousand miles from Arizona I had often felt that the people I grew up with were peculiar aliens. This plot was one I needed to explore, in order to make some connections between the cowgirl and the lady of the English manor.

For more than a year, though, I costumed, mothered, and taught, only daydreaming this book as I drove over the downs each day to the university.

My American editor at Little, Brown helped me by sending me dozens of press handouts of speeches from Percy, Goldwater, Rockefeller, and Robert Kennedy, until I got the feel of the rhetoric. I was determined that, although there was a reference to the *Oresteia* on virtually every page, the story would be coherent to someone who had never heard of any Greek but Spiro Agnew. (I succeeded all too well, and no one—agent, editor, critic, scholar—has noticed my arduous theft until I point it out.)

The Buzzards came out in 1970 in both London and Boston, and although it was nominated for a Pulitzer in America, its real success was in England. I think I had been away from home for long enough that the perspective I had of America was detached. I don't mean by this that it was untrue; on the contrary. My journalist brother, when he first read the novel, responded that I didn't realize how dirty American politics were. When he read it again ten years later, he told me that I had "invented Jimmy Carter."

Meanwhile, the rapier attack notwithstanding, *The Beauty Operators* had been produced by Thames Television, and I had written a television play (which ended up with the dreadful title of *Hoddinott Veiling*) that was taken to the Monte Carlo Festival as British Independent Television's entry.

I could now make, if not a living, at least my nanny's living writing television plays, and I quit the university. I had also written a children's book, *The Truck on the Track,* and after a long search for an illustrator I more or less literally stumbled (he and I being stumblers both, of the amiable sort) into John Vernon Lord. John's painstaking detail and sharp colors reflected two of my own work methods (his wife describes it as "knitting"), and his vivid pictures helped sell the book to Jonathan Cape, afterwards to Bobbs-Merrill. In the last year in England I set John Vernon Lord's story *The Giant Jam Sandwich* into verse. After the publication of *The Buzzards,* I reviewed fiction regularly for *New Statesman* magazine. Once a month a stack of thirty books would arrive; I'd skim them, read eight or ten, pick four or five to review. I could get in bed at nine at night, curl up with a novel and call it work—my kind of job!—except that it was no living wage either.

The vogue in my early-mothering years was for natural childbirth and permissiveness. In the same period in my mother's life it had been for a germfree environment—with the consequence that I hadn't had the usual complement of childhood diseases. During the costuming of *A Doll's House* at the Gardner Centre I got the mumps. I remember sitting in bed miserably hemming a skirt with fourteen yards of ruffle, wondering why I had *ever* put so much energy into such an endeavor. Now, when Toby was about a year-and-a-half old, I lost a third pregnancy to rubella.

The Gardner also hit rough times. A British

Burroway with Julia Kling, at home in Tallahassee

recession strapped the university for funds, and the arts appeared among the expendable expenses. Walter ran afoul of the students, who resented the Centre's professional orientation. The fine English actor Patrick Wymark, then dying of alcoholism although we didn't know it, failed to learn his lines and put the audience through an excruciating opening night. He fully redeemed himself by his performance the following season in Eduardo Manet's *Nuns* (and by bringing into my life his friend Bernie Hopkins, who later sustained me and the children through difficult months)—but that production, the happiest I ever took part in, was a harbinger of disaster for all its participants. Wymark and the theatre designer died of heart attacks, another actor hanged himself, a third was institutionalized for a breakdown, the set designer died of leukemia—all within a year.

Walter and I separated. One way of describing this is that I started to write a comic novel about a couple impossibly at odds; and as I wrote, it became less funny.

The novel began as *Warp,* was eventually published as *Raw Silk.* I had chosen the textile industry as background because I figured that I knew enough about cloth to have a head start on the research. I had no intention of writing an academic novel, and in any case it is my practice to write from autobiographical *feelings,* housing them in fictional characters and events. (In the case of *Raw Silk* this turned out to be no favor to Walter; readers accurately picked up on the feelings and inaccurately assigned Oliver Marbalestier's rape and assault to him.)

I had by that time noticed that several themes, unchosen, had chosen me; each of my novels contained a parent in some way abandoning his or her children (a thing I could never do), a suicide or attempted suicide, and a strong older man/younger woman relationship. I resolved this time to choose the unchosen, and to face these themes head on. "This morning I abandoned my only child. . ." the book began.

There was another thing that I wanted very much to accomplish. Richmond Lattimore, in his introduction to the *Oresteia,* had opened up for me the secret of Aeschylus' use of interconnected image patterns. In *The Buzzards,* which drew heavily on the *Oresteia,* I had taught myself how to do this by building on the *same* symbol complex—the net, the web, wild birds and animals, their eggs and young, etc.—that Aeschylus had used. In the new book I wanted to create a complex of original symbols, "interweaving" images of cloth, water, travel, plant life, and balance.

The research for the novel took me into East Anglia, to textile mills in country I hadn't seen since I was a student at Cambridge; and then to Japan, the first time I had been on my own since before my marriage. Japan would not have been my choice of a new country to explore—the novel plot dictated it—so the intensity of my pleasure took me by suprise. I was humbled by my illiteracy and proud of nevertheless being able to manoeuver, from Tokyo to Nikko, Takayama, Osaka. I felt clarified by the clarity of Japanese sounds and colors, calmed by the patterns of gardens, temples, paintings, cloth. And, surprised by how much at home I felt, I was also startled at how much I loved being alone.

Years before in Binghamton, Walter and I had made friends with Blair and Julia Kling, and it had turned out to be a friendship that could survive transatlantic separation. We had all met again in Ghent, London, Sussex—and Julia and I discovered that we could take up a conversation mid-sentence after a three-year hiatus. Blair taught history at the University of Illinois, and Julia had in the interim become a family counselor there.

In December of 1971 I brought the children and returned to America. Tim was then eight, Toby five. Though I left England in manic spirits, high on freedom, it must in some dim corner of my brain have been clear to me that I was going to need my best friend and a family counselor, and so we went to Illinois.

First, though, I took the children home to Phoenix for Christmas, arriving with mystical appropriateness four hours after the death of my grandmother, so that I was able to arrange the funeral while my mother took care of the boys. Mom had for years now been subject to heart failure, and lived with an oxygen tank beside the bed while Dad cared for her and learned to give her the life-saving mercury shots. It is another of the coincidences I cannot explain, that while I arranged for the burial of her mother, and was myself unknowingly on the verge of miscarriage, I was able to offer Mom the happy distraction of Tim and Toby, their suitcase of Christmas presents to wrap. She was not, however, fooled by my blow-softening version of our surprise visit. "You've left him, haven't you?"

The next eight months in Illinois were traumatic in every way that I have since come to understand as normal, but which felt at the time as if I had invented some entirely new form and depth of pain. Luckily, I was totally ignorant of the sad state of American academic budgets, and I presented myself so persistently to the University of Illinois that they actually found me a job.

I was to teach freshman composition in a Special Opportunities Education program to students from "disadvantaged Chicago high schools." The pay was barely livable, but we got a bargain in a beautiful rental on a lake, and for as long as my freedom-high lasted, it seemed to me the best possible way to come home to America.

When classes began, I learned that the black students did not want to be taught white literature and did not want to be taught black literature by me. The two Chicanos wanted Lorca. The militants were articulate, quick, and ashamed of being at the University of Illinois at all; the moderates were cowed and quiet. Many of the students wrote well, a couple of them brilliantly, in a hip style it was my duty to destroy in order that they could produce term papers for history. They knew all this. I walked into the situation believing I would teach them Yeats. I am not sure to this day what was learned on either side.

My own emotional state so deteriorated that I could no longer write—or even cook and sew. In paralytic lassitude I tried to choose a pattern or operate a pair of scissors. I had a hundred and fifty pages of the novel done, but the only thing I could write was a journal that seemed to me to say nothing but "Help! Help!" (Actually it's not so bad, and has taught me how much of competence operates on automatic pilot, how much we misperceive our own performance or effect.) I relied heavily on Julia, both of us aware that the imbalance in this new relationship threatened our friendship. And I relied heavily on Gail Godwin, who was teaching at Illinois that year on leave from Iowa, and who lent me her house and her tough understanding when I needed them.

I knew I had to have a real job. The only

Tim Eysselinck, 1986

would have to give them up to their father, but she was no help. She said, "Did they have breakfast this morning? Did they catch the school bus? Did they have lunch money? You're coping." I told a colleague in Illinois that I was going to have to commit myself, but he was no help. He said, "How many hours a day do you think there are in a mental institution?" I decided that I would give up and go back to the marriage, but I thought that perhaps it would be better to try teaching at Florida State first, to prove that I couldn't do it; otherwise I might always wonder if I could have.

I have elsewhere written of my arrival in Tallahassee, my conviction that it was a possible place to die but not to live, my abortive search for an apartment with a gas stove, my slow reemergence as a functional self. Though I have now been here fifteen years, longer than any other place except the place where I was raised, the Tallahassee episode is ongoing, and seems to have been brief, and I can't clearly tell which are its most significant passages.

In my first year here, my mother died in Arizona. For two years I made no progress on *Raw Silk*. I had conceived it as a comedy; now it seemed both tragic

appropriate opening in the graduate office listings was an associate professorship in creative writing at Florida State University in Tallahassee. I didn't know much about my future at that point, but I knew for sure I wasn't going to *Florida.*

I had bought a rattletrap station wagon. In the spring break I loaded Tim, Toby, and three students who would pay the gas, and went back to New York to seek help from the Barnard employment office. Tim had chicken pox on the way to New York (Toby on the way back). We ran out of gas in the middle of the night in the middle of Pennsylvania. When I left England, I had left everything of my own behind except one suitcase of my favorite clothes and jewelry. We'd been in New York a half hour or so when the car was broken into and this suitcase stolen. I went to Barnard in the jeans and sweater that were now the only clothes I owned. I felt as if, having left most of myself behind by choice in Sussex, the rest had been snatched away. There was no job to be had, and there was no me.

I did not see how I could live in *northern Florida,* a regression and in any case a contradiction in terms; and after I'd got the job I could see it even less. I told Julia that I was failing to cope with the children and

Toby (now Alex) Eysselinck, 1986

and melodramatic. When I was able to see it as both funny and painful, I wrote again.

But I wrote looking out onto an asphalt parking lot. At best, Tallahassee seemed no better than a stopgap, and the stages of my reconciliation came slowly one by one.

First I discovered it was a wonderful place for raising children. Mine, having had earaches and adenoidal infections from October to March in England, now lived all year outdoors and never got sick. Then it dawned on me that Florida State was an extraordinarily congenial place to work, my colleagues supportive and disinclined to politicking, my students as badly educated, and as eager, as I had been at their age. For the first few years I felt trapped in a corner of America ("You can get to hell from here, but you have to change in Atlanta"), but after the publication of *Raw Silk* I began to be asked to speak in places far and near, large and small, by people who sent me tickets to get there. I got a dog and bought a house, and then a bigger dog, and a bigger house.

I taught narrative techniques until I figured out how to do it, and then wrote a textbook, *Writing Fiction*. The British production of *The Nuns* continued to haunt me until I found a way to wrench it around into a plot, and wrote *Opening Nights*. I began to think about my mother's childhood in the marble quarry, and am at work on a first historical novel, *Cutting Stone*.

For four years from 1978 I was married to Bill Humphries, a.k.a. Lazlo Freen or, to his friends, The Freen; a painter, a gentle person, a former student of mine, eighteen years my junior. I have also told that story elsewhere, and will tell it again. Though the marriage ended, I came out of it warmly in favor of the older-woman–younger-man liaison; Freen and I came out of it the best of friends. This is a phenomenon I would not believe if I hadn't lived it, so I'll leave it to later fiction to try to be convincing.

My boys have grown up here, so different from each other that it seems impossible they were raised under the same effort of Spock and spaghetti. Tim is twenty-three, Episcopalian, Republican, polite, a sharp dresser, a gourmet, and a second lieutenant in the U.S. Army. Toby is twenty, a radical feminist, a left-wing anarchist, and an actor, busking around Piccadilly Circus in a mohawk and shredded jeans.

But he no longer goes by that name. Like his great-grandfather before him he rejected the Tobyn. He was eight, straight-haired and stocky, inclined to suffer in the shadow of his older brother, and to believe that anyone who praised his blue eyes meant

that he was fat. He came to me and said, "Toby is a round name, isn't it?"

"Why yes," I said. "That's very clever."

"Tim is a straight-up-and-down name."

A couple of days later he announced that he had taken his middle name, and every time I got it wrong for the next two years—*every* time—he said, "My name is *Alex*."

We have traveled, together and separately, the boys to Belgium, Pittsburgh, Bavaria; I to France, Italy, India; and all of us to England, where Alex at seventeen made good his promise to take up residence. Florida State University has a London program on which I teach from time to time, so that I have been able to put back into my life the friends I left behind in Cambridge and Sussex in the total of ten years there.

Of the dozens of stories about people under the illusion that they are short-term sojourners (*Magic Mountain* comes to mind, and *It's A Wonderful Life*), my favorite is about the boy Krishna traveling with the godhead. He leaves his companion resting under a tree while he crosses the field to fetch the god a ladle of water from the farmhouse on the opposite side. The ladle is brought by a young woman with water-blue eyes that remind him of the eyes of the god. He forgets why he came. He marries the woman with the waterblue eyes, brings the farm to fruit, nurtures the animals, and fathers many children. When the woman dies he is an old man. He remembers his errand, fills the ladle, and carries it across the field. The god sits under the tree. He drinks. "Thank you," he says.

Ten years ago I moved, smack in the middle of the capital city of Florida, into a patently English house. It is white brick with forest green shutters, climbing ivy, a picket fence. The only thing that I added to the garden at Sussex was a magnolia tree; here my acre wears magnolias as its natural right; I have added the roses and the daffodils.

Spring and fall I often borrow a cottage on the beach at Alligator Point an hour away. I take a typewriter and my dogs Shirley and Pushkin. I sit and write looking out over the dunes, the sea oats, and the sand, to the Gulf of Mexico. The water doesn't jump or tumble here; it is not a competition. I am at peace, of a piece with the sand, grass, sea. I have never found the place where I could say: This is my proper ground. But I can look out at the waterblue gulf and up through the fronds of a palm tree at the searing sky, and it reminds me quite a lot of having a home.

With "Pushkin," in the back yard in Tallahassee

BIBLIOGRAPHY

Poetry:

But to the Season. Weston-super-Mare, England: Universities' Poetry, 1961.

Material Goods. Tallahassee, Fla.: University Presses of Florida, 1980.

Fiction:

Descend Again. London: Faber, 1960.

The Dancer from the Dance. London: Faber, 1965; Boston: Little, Brown, 1968.

Eyes. London: Faber, 1966; Boston: Little, Brown, 1966.

The Buzzards. Boston: Little, Brown, 1969; London: Faber, 1970.

The Truck on the Track (for children; illustrated by John Vernon Lord). London: J. Cape, 1970; Indianapolis: Bobbs-Merrill, 1971.

The Giant Jam Sandwich, with John Vernon Lord (for children; verse). London: J. Cape, 1972; Boston: Houghton, 1973.

Raw Silk. Boston: Little, Brown, 1977; London: Gollancz, 1977; New York: Pocket Books, 1979; New York: Bantam, 1986.

Opening Nights. New York: Atheneum, 1985; London: Gollancz, 1985; New York: Bantam, 1986.

Nonfiction:

Writing Fiction: A Guide to Narrative Craft. Boston: Little, Brown, 1982. Second edition. Boston: Little, Brown, 1986.

Plays:

Garden Party, first produced at Barnard College, New York City, 1955.

The Fantasy Level, first produced at the Yale School of Drama, New Haven, Conn., 1963.

The Beauty Operators, first produced at the Garden Center for the Arts, Brighton, England, 1968.

Hoddinott Veiling, first produced by ATV Network Television, London, 1970.

Due Care and Attention, first produced by ATV Network Television, London, 1973.

Translator of:

Poenulus, or The Little Carthaginian. Published in *Five Roman Comedies,* edited by Palmer Bovie. New York: Dutton, 1970.

George Dennison

1925-

George Dennison, a Sunday painter for many years, framing one of his own paintings

I f one were up to it, and were to write the history of one's feelings, and were to take feelings seriously as little constructions of self and world, and of past and present, the resulting document would manifest a time and place, people and events in otherwise unattainable substantiality—and it would run to seven volumes, as Proust's "history" did. And so I shall take only a quick look at those closest of close things, and concentrate on the facts of my life and brief descriptions of the people who have meant much to me.

I was born in Ashburn, a small country town in Georgia, where my grandfather owned a general store, and a house large enough for his ten children, of whom my mother had been fourth. She was twenty-two when she married my father, who was just twenty. We moved north after a year, to the first of several homes near Pittsburgh, Pennsylvania. Soon I had a sister and a brother, and then the Great Depression was underway—difficult years for my parents. When I think of my own character at the age of twenty or twenty-four, I marvel at the responsibilities taken on by my father, and I feel again the admiration of his courage I have felt at other times. After their first few years together my parents were not happy, but a great deal was going on, and the family held together.

My mother was an active woman, generous, compassionate, and outgoing. She was the only woman in the neighborhood who dealt in a kindly way with certain of my harum-scarum friends. She made her own dresses and hats, painted occasionally, and performed in amateur theatricals. She practiced a few country crafts, which she must have learned at home, though they were also the typical arts of the Depression: she gardened and put up food in mason jars, made delicious conserves of our own grapes and cherries, made laundry soap, braided rugs, cut her children's hair, and covered their chests with mustard plasters when they came down with coughs. She had many friends and they were devoted to her. She was good looking and walked with a posture that might have been stately if it were not so natural and unaffected. Everything in our home that was attractive, simple, and welcoming came from her. She painted walls, hung wallpaper, and made slipcovers for the easy chairs. My friends were fond of her, and were made welcome, as were my brother's and sister's friends.

All this was tempered, though not entirely contradicted, by my father's way of doing things. Two very different lives were running along side by side. His could be glimpsed simply by opening the door of his closet. Six or seven expensive and well-tailored suits would be hanging there, and a rack of silk ties, and a row of handsome shoes. His topcoats were elegant. He wore a paisley scarf, a homburg at times, or a fedora. Yet he didn't own a car, and was often in debt because of his gambling. He could walk to the

Joseph Raedle

105

trolley, five minutes away, and be in downtown Pittsburgh in half an hour. His offices were in one of the first of the Pittsburgh skyscrapers, not tall by present standards, but impressive, with a high-ceilinged lobby, dark marble walls, and bronze fittings on the elevators and mail chute. His work was semipublic. He was general manager of the Better Business Bureau, which to some extent he had helped create. Frauds of all kinds were numerous during the Depression, and the function of the Bureau was to protect both the public and the business community. Often my father's staff turned over their cases to the district attorney. In his person, my father modelled himself on some ideal business executive, speaking in measured phrases which even in private had the quality of public presentation, and at times were pompous. He carried himself with a certain importance, yet was courteous and considerate, and was capable of a teasing wit and charm. He read books on self-improvement, on salesmanship, public speaking, management of personnel. Politically he was conservative, or thought of himself that way. There was a streak of the reactionary in him. He had dropped out of college in his first year, and many of these traits must have been the insecurity and self-guidance of an untrained young man making his way in the business world without connections of family or friends. He was unshakably honest, was inventive and hardworking, and was successful. There was something about him, however, quite unlike the businessmen he tried so hard to emulate. His *presence* was powerful, and was somewhat ambiguous, with more than a hint of wayward energies. He was strikingly handsome, and there was a darkened sensual glow to him that one didn't often encounter. He seemed unfinished. One sensed a quality of naive aspiration in him, or naive hopefulness, much at odds with his sense of himself as a skeptical worldling. He was confident, and was physically brave; at the same time he was insecure and was mortally afraid of embarrassment. He was an incurable womanizer, and my mother was forced to put up with a great deal. We children were unaware of this, at least until our teens. We knew they weren't happy. Often the house was silent when he was home, and there were weekends when it was positively oppressive. Some of my worst memories are of him lying on the sofa of a Sunday listening to the ranting, hateful voice of Father Coughlin on the radio. I would rush out of the house, put on my skates and skate all day. Several times, simply to avoid the family gathering, I went home too late for supper and was punished, never physically, but by the withholding of privileges or of money for the movies. My mother, however, was put in charge of enforcement, which

Dennison with his father, George, around 1927...

meant that as she handed me the small coins for the Saturday afternoon movie, she would say, "Don't tell your father." There wasn't much risk in this. During the week he rarely came home for supper, but stayed in town drinking and playing poker at the hotel rooms of a man who promoted boxing and wrestling bouts, dealt in Due-Bills, published racing forms, and seemed always to have a crew of salesmen drifting around town. He was a large, slope-shouldered, rather fat, kindly, generous, courtly Jew. One looked at him and trusted his kindliness immediately; one sensed immediately too, that his life was not entirely within the law. He and my father had met because my father had investigated him, and had forced him to suspend certain of his activities. Some form of that was repeated in later years; it was a feature of their friendship. Aside from poker, they gambled at the "wildcat" racetracks in West Virginia and Ohio. My father lost enough to keep him almost continually in debt, and earned enough to keep clearing the debts. This pattern changed during his middle middle age, and he gradually grew more staid, but for years it was an odd life he led. He belonged to several civic organizations, was in demand as a speaker, had a public service radio program—and in the evenings

...and with his mother, Gladys, née Bass, in Quantico Bay

did as he pleased. One day in later years I remarked on my mother's forbearance and said that I had never seen her lose her temper. "You're lucky," he said, and he told me of a party they had held at the house when they were younger. She was wearing a new dress and was looking attractive, but he spent his time flirting with one of her friends. She withdrew into the kitchen and was sitting there alone when he came in and began to upbraid her for not joining the party. She screamed, picked up a fifty pound block of ice from the sink and threw it at him. "I've been threatened by gangsters," he said, "but that was the most frightening moment in my life."

For many years few things in my life were more important than the conflicts I experienced with my father. These at times were bitter. They were always painful. Once I almost struck him, and the shock of finding myself at that extremity was profoundly distressing. He was unbelievably critical, opinionated, and domineering. I was the only one who fought back. But I also made repeated efforts, over a period of two decades, to establish some kind of rapport with him. He seemed to welcome these efforts, but sooner or later—so it seems to this combatant—he would turn on me and try to assert his dominance. Perhaps

there really was a pathology at work. His egotism was dreadful, partly because it was strong, and partly because it was compensatory, desperate, and blind. He was at peace with me only when my own life reflected back to him exactly the kind of credit he wanted, as when in my senior year in high school I played football on a championship team and my pretty girlfriend called at the house in her Buick convertible; or as when, much later in my life, having refused for five years to have any contact with him, I invited him to come see us when my mother came, chiefly so that he could meet his granddaughters and they him, and he was able to say to me with pleasure that he had seen me on the "Today Show," and had read reviews in *Time* and *Newsweek* of my first book, which had become a best-seller. It would have meant so much to me to have had his good wishes even when our lives diverged, so unimaginably much! But I'm grateful that we did finally become friends. I went down to Florida and stayed for a month when my mother was dying, and then two years later stayed with him again as he himself neared death. I am too old now to feel the pain of resentment and loss that I once felt, but there are times when the ghosts of those feelings do stir in me. The other residual feelings are indicated in this passage from the novel *Luisa Domic*. It was taken verbatim from my journal.

I had been stalking partridges just two days ago in the shaggy hilltop fields beyond the woods above us, and had flushed several out of the half-dead apple trees at the woods' edge. But I hadn't fired. It was midafternoon. The stillness and the sun were irresistible. I unloaded the shotgun and lay down by a stone wall that made me think of loaves from an oven, and was pulled under instantly. I slept for a long time, and then didn't awaken all at once, but passed into a dream that was almost a waking dream, in which I imagined that I was coming into the entranceway of our present house, stamping my feet, and my father— who had visited here only once—leaned around through the inside doorway angrily. He was talking on the phone. He covered the mouthpiece and began to upbraid me, but I made some gestures of apology. I noticed, in my dream, that I hadn't respond- ed with false pride, or with anger of my own, which on occasions in the past had been severe. I felt a stirring of hope that excited me. A radiance and buoyancy came into the dream, and everything took on a quality of revelation. I put my arm around him and kissed his forehead, and he blushed, and smiled happily. I was happy, too. The excitement I felt now was the distinctive excitement that comes with new understanding, and with liberation from error. The dream changed into something like a chain of thought, or insight, and these insights stirred me as deeply as had the images. I understood that *touching*, affectionate touching, would ease our relationship of its angers, and would please him far more than had the tokens of esteem he so often demanded. I thought of times he had responded to affection with just this melting surprise, blushing and smiling. But something was wrong. Something was terribly askew. All that radiance and hope vanished abruptly, and a sour, strange anxiety took their place. I became aware that I was not awake, and promptly sat up in the cooling shadows of the wall, and remembered that my father was dead, and had been dead for several years. The ground was cold. The sun was low and the sky was white with clouds. I could see my parents' faces, younger by far than I was now, lively and good-looking. And I could see the grassy back yard and the homely, pleasant porch I had enjoyed so much and had used in so many ways, with its three broad steps and the lattice at one end thatched densely with the leaves, vines, and blossoms of honeysuckle. It was as if a curtain had been pulled aside from a window, and there were all those things. I looked at them sorrowfully, not with joy at all, yet they were bathed in a golden light and seemed utterly desirable. Then they dwindled and faded. I could feel the process beginning, the strangest of all physical sensations, an uncontrollable *otherness* within the self, that was like pain, except that it was painless. I tried to slow the process, and then tried to bring back at least an image of my parents' faces, but I couldn't, and my helplessness was so extreme that it passed beyond any feeling of frustration to a kind of creaturely humbling, as by death. I picked up the gun and started back through the woods, which very rapidly were turning cold.

Europeans, traveling in this country during the Great Depression, commented frequently on the

George (left), with sister, Adele, and brother, Dick, 1933

generosity and goodwill of Americans. Leaving aside the terrible suffering of certain regions, and of the poor in general, the crisis of the Depression brought out many good things in the American character. For the young of the middle class it was a fortunate time to grow up. It's appalling to compare the world of my childhood—especially the world of which I was aware, the world accessible to a child—with the monstrosity my children know. Sky, ocean—those vast, glorious entities no longer exist. Nature itself has vanished into a custodial enterprise called Environment. And perhaps, really, there can't be a nature at all when humankind as a whole can be destroyed by the diseased egotism of a handful of men.

Certainly there were hardships in all lives then as now, but we enjoyed certain luxuries that today are unknown: a wonderful sense of space around the self, and of human creaturely security in the natural world (of which no one can be aware until it is threatened or destroyed).

There was so much time back then! so much space! Government seemed far away, not right up close. As for the young—there was no Recreation Department in our town, no Little League, yet never a sunny day went by without a game of ball, often two, preceded by a morning of hammering on shacks in the woods, or swinging from trees on long ropes. Our town was a square mile of one-family houses with yards in front and back, the whole surrounded by extensive woods and fields. Other playgrounds were to be found in vacant lots, large cemeteries, unused schoolyards, and the borough park. Those were the days of "movie palaces," wonderful, convivial places with large lobbies downstairs and up, connected by wide, thickly carpeted double stairways. There were upholstered sofas and chairs, and wall lamps with shades of tinted glass. If you wanted to watch the movie, you sat downstairs with the adults, if you wanted to neck, you sat in the balcony. Saturday afternoon was a time unto itself, noisy and hilarious, with feats of mischief and invention, often athletic. There were ways of sneaking in, and between the ages of ten and thirteen we utilized them frequently. Many of our games were inspired by movies. There was a whole summer of Robin Hood because of the Errol Flynn extravaganza. We cut down a tree in the woods and laid it across a high-banked stream, balanced on it, and duelled with sapling quarter-staves. We made swords and longbows, built tree houses, and hung ropes from strategic branches. Johnny Weismuller's Tarzan overlapped here, and of course we practiced that marvelous yell, not knowing it was spliced together from half-a-dozen animal calls. We were excited one year by a circus film, and all that summer two trapezes dangled from the huge cherry tree at the end of my yard, just beyond the wall tent my brother and I slept in most of the summer, sometimes together, but usually alternately with friends. That same year we made an underground hideaway by digging connected trenches in the side of a hill and covering the trenches with boards and strips of sod. On the same hill we made a roller coaster by nailing a one-board track on a series of sawhorses. Down the center of the track we nailed a single rail of lath. The car one sat on, then, was a short board mounted on roller skates that straddled the central rail. There weren't any brakes; we simply piled some straw at the bottom of the hill.

As we grew older these wide-ranging games and enterprises gave way to the usual sports, softball, baseball, football, and running. We made dumbbells of cement, using flower pots for molds; and we climbed rope, hand over hand. (I could do one-handed chins in those days, and Chinese push-ups.) My best friend in high school was our football star and fastest runner; he and I and a third friend, a distance runner, went off several times on running hikes, and would run at a loping gait, with a pause for lunch, all day long. And then—quite abruptly it seemed—I found myself in love with a girl from the neighboring town. I have no sweeter memories than those of walking with her, hand in hand, on summer nights, under the large, almost continuous trees of our streets.

Some sense of the town is in this passage from the novella *On Being a Son*. The character, O'Brien, is fictional, but the town is real. O'Brien is twenty-seven. He walks at night up the familiar streets and alleys.

He went on, crossing the main street of the town, and plunged into another quarter, this one magnetized by three girls, but especially by Wanda French, who had initiated him sexually when he was fifteen. She had been three years older than he. He had probably loved her, but had been so giddy with lust and gratification that the thought of love had never occurred to him. Her fiance had finished college and come home, and she had broken with O'Brien, who had been her secret. He looked at her house with fascination. He could see an elderly man and woman reading newspapers in stuffed chairs, and they were indeed Wanda's parents. He had seen them many times, but never once had they seen him. They were close to death, those two. He walked on, circling gradually to the left, and in fifteen minutes entered a little park that he had used to love and of which, in recent years, he had dreamed. Enormous elms, maples, sycamores, and poplars were scattered on terraces down a long hill, at the foot of which lay the borough swimming pool. Midway on the hill, on the broadest terrace, there was a playground for children, and facing it across an open space with a drinking fountain was a large octagonal pavilion with a bandstand. He had attended dances there for years, looking on as an excited boy, and finally dancing himself. The usual music had been a juke box, but on special occasions a band had played. He heard voices as he walked, voices softened by the foliage of the trees, and he encountered strolling couples, their arms round each other's waists, or holding hands. An excited gang of boys hurried past him. He went up the terraces on small dirt paths he knew by heart, up a flight of wooden steps, through the open gate of a hurricane fence . . . and there lay the hard-packed, grassless football field, with simple bleachers on both sides, a black cinder track encircling it, and the red-brick high school just fifty yards away. The faces of teammates came back to him and he remembered the arduous routines he and Clatty had gone through in their training. He remembered the Friday night dances at roadhouses, victory cigars, and the late sweet hours in the car when Carole had made love with abandon. He walked the full length of the field, savoring the sky and the mellow night. Evidently there had been a baseball game that evening; groups of friends and family groups had remained in the bleachers and were talking. Several young boys, ten and eleven years old, awake, one would think, long past their bedtime, were running short sprints in the darkness on the cinder track, their heads down and their arms pumping. Two mongrel dogs chased each other among the boys.

When I think of the past, I find myself dwelling on the kinds of things I have mentioned here, and not at all on things I have written.

The first writing I can remember was a set of lengthy essays on various aspects of citizenship. These were assigned to me by my father as punishment for having set the all-time record for demerits in the fifth grade at school. I don't know what I was up to that year. At the same time that I was misbehaving I was writing and printing (on the mimeograph) the class newspaper; and I was getting good marks. I produced a newspaper again in the eighth grade, and also wrote a number of detective stories inspired by Sherlock Holmes, Sam Spade, Hercule Poirot, Ellery Queen, and Poe's "Gold Bug." I was a fan of P.G. Wodehouse and I remember reading a book of his in the hospital after a tonsillectomy. Every time I laughed, my face closed up in pain. The old gentleman in the bed next to mine—I was in a ward—watched me with real curiosity. I would turn a page and buckle with agony, read a paragraph and clutch my throat.

In high school I wrote regularly for the student paper, a news and humor column. I also wrote and directed a great many skits or little vaudevilles, which were used in our weekly assemblies. We had acquired a recording machine at home that cut discs with a stylus, and we made a number of records modeled on Fred Allen's radio show. (We also recorded all of Joe Louis's fights. I wish I had those now.) I wrote and directed several of those skits. Everybody in the family took parts, and often friends did as well. I think

of those things fondly. In my senior year I edited and helped write the yearbook of our graduating class, and wrote and directed the variety show that the seniors traditionally performed for the rest of the students. Graduation, however, was a muted affair. The war was under way, and we had all enlisted or had been called up in one or another of the armed services. I had been offered a football scholarship to a local college, as had most of our team, but not one of us could accept. We went our different ways into the Marines, the Air Force, the Army, and—for me—the Navy. I had qualified for an officer's training program—engineers were needed—and I took a full B.S. curriculum on campuses administered by the Navy. I was longest at Columbia, almost two years. This was a dim and miserable period for me. I read poetry and fiction under the covers at night by flashlight, wrote several stories and poems, but otherwise struggled with courses for which I felt extreme distaste. But I remember my first real discovery of literary form in prose. It was a Saturday afternoon. I was waiting to go out on liberty. I started reading a small paperback novel that belonged to a roommate, and I sat there after the bell had rung, and finished it all in one gulp. The arc of the plot was like a shape in the air, and there was a proportion, a scale between the individual details and the size of the book as a whole that was delightful and that seemed to constitute movement and voice. The name of the author meant nothing to me. It was F. Scott Fitzgerald, and the book was *The Great Gatsby.* I've read it several times since then. It's a strange, adolescent work—I'm not an admirer of Fitzgerald—but the poetics I have described do authentically belong to it, and they were enchanting to me at the time.

I went home after the war with the hope of reading the books I had been yearning to read, and trying my hand at writing. As a veteran I drew twenty dollars a week unemployment compensation, and that took care of my expenses. I bought books with my severance pay and put my plan into action. I fell in love, too. Perhaps that was the final straw. My father would leave for work in the morning and see me sprawled on the porch settee, reading. He laid eyes a few times on the young woman I was seeing now every night. Within three months we had a dreadful scene, and I left for New York, where I had neither friends nor family. I was lonely and confused, but the city itself was exciting and was far more humane than it is today. I went back to school on the GI Bill, made a few friends, discovered politics, art, etc., and repudiated much too much of my past, as converts do. I earned a living, in the meantime (and

"High-school pleasures: Dennison carrying the football...

...and running on the cinder track...

...then home on leave with high-school sweetheart. World War II was under way."

did for years), at blue-collar jobs. I liked the people I encountered in that work, but in fact I had no choice: the decorum and subservience of white-collar jobs were intolerable to me. And I kept going to school.

I remember the elderly, short, broad, impassive Italian who, with the gestures of a mime (he didn't speak English), showed me how to use a pick and shovel and wheelbarrow. And I remember powerful Joe Moody, the black laborer who lived in Harlem, and who on another job took me aside and said, "They goin' fire you 'less you shape up. Now you look here . . ." and showed me how to use the jackhammer, the star drill and sledgehammer, how to mix cement, how to carry a hundred-and-twenty-eight pounds of bricks with two tongs, how to walk so that shoulder loads and dangling loads wouldn't lame my back.

After a term at Columbia, I transferred to the New School for Social Research, then a tiny, quite remarkable place, with many refugee faculty and veteran students, and there I encountered two unforgettable teachers, William Troy and Meyer Schapiro.

The New Criticism, in those years, had passed its zenith, but its attitudes were everywhere, as were the attitudes of Eliot. *Partisan Review* was in its ascendancy.

Troy was not a New Critic. He was too modest to compete with his authors, too respectful of the spirit of form, too discursive and aware of history. Without being in the least hieratical, he was impressed by the recurrence of archetypal myth in works of art; and he was skeptical of the utility of psychoanalysis as a tool of criticism.

Twice he showed me kindnesses that meant much to me. Both were letters praising papers I had written for him. The second was in response to a paper on Dylan Thomas, who as yet had not been dealt with at any length (scarcely at all) in American publications. I handed in the paper so late that Troy was obliged to take it with him on vacation. There came a letter that not only forbore to reprove me as I deserved, but included the names of editors for me to contact, and his own note of recommendation. I was working by then with a gang of masons and steamfitters in the basement of a huge apartment building in Brooklyn. It was a sweltering day. I was mixing cement in the courtyard, and to my astonishment was summoned to the nearby candy store by one of the neighborhood kids who had learned my first name. My wife (long since divorced) had somehow located that number. She was elated, and in a moment so was I, since what she read to me on the phone was the generous and wholly unexpected letter from William Troy.

We exchanged brief letters over the next few years. When Paul Goodman's *Empire City* was published, I sent a copy to Troy, who in one of his lectures had mentioned very favorably an early story of Paul's. I had hoped that he would like the book and perhaps review it, and we corresponded again on this occasion. Not long afterward I received a letter from the New School. They were contacting former students of Troy's. He had undergone surgery for cancer. Blood donors were needed. I went with several others to replace blood that he had used . . . and was appalled to learn that the operation had been a laryngectomy and that Troy was mute. A year or so later we learned that he had died.

In 1948 I attended Meyer Schapiro's evening lectures in the history of modern art. This was the year of de Kooning's first one-man show, and of Arshile Gorky's tragic suicide.

It would be presumptuous of me to attempt to praise learning and genius of the order of Schapiro's. But I can indicate, at least sketchily, the kind of excitement he stirred in us during those lectures. He was not like a man who has amassed knowledge and opinion and then imparts them, but like a great traveler who has seen wonders and tells of them with an utterly winning animation. I learned in time that every artist of consequence in the city had sought him out; and I believe that it was this quality of delight, of delighted engagement, that drew them to him.

The lights would go down; a bolt of color would flash through the darkness; we would recognize one or another painting on the projection screen . . . and Schapiro's extraordinary voice would begin its high-speed arias of scholarship and creative discernment, in which one heard continually (and miraculously) the happy babbling of a child.

It was this last that set him apart in his genius, and that allowed him (so I believe) to escape the abstract formulations that are the usual penalties of the analytical process; allowed him, I should say, to handle analysis with the descriptive elan of a poet-naturalist.

The delight one heard in Schapiro's voice had the qualities and the status of moral virtue, like the patience of Freud, or the modesty of Proust. It seemed unaware of itself. It seemed to be commanded by the phenomena, and in that respect seemed quite egoless. In all these ways it was harmonious with fundamental qualities of the masterworks hovering up there in the darkness. We used to emerge from those lectures uplifted and touched lightly by gaiety, as if we were coming not from a classroom, but from some masterwork of public art: drama, dance, opera,

concert. It dawned on us finally that this evanescent spoken form—The Schapiro Lecture—was an artifact of high art. I do not mean that because of excellence, superior organization, etc., these lectures resembled art. I mean that they possessed the attributes, the kinds and quantities and proportions, the subordinations and eminences, that one finds in works of art. And they seemed to many of us to be masterpieces.

The New York painters in those days were still venturing toward unprecedented things. Schapiro only rarely lent his authority to any contemporary work, yet his presence in the city, the irradiation of the city by his own dazzling art, seemed to be endlessly encouraging to artists. There were always painters at his lectures. Many followed him for years.

A mere handful of galleries then were exhibiting the new art. Betty Parsons' was one. By chance I came to know some of the artists there. Charles Egan's gallery was another. In the spring of '48, Egan mounted the first one-man show of the work of Willem de Kooning. . . .

The immediate postwar years were a time of grim discoveries. The true extent of the Holocaust was becoming known. (We began to see it as a wound to mankind as a whole.) New revelations of Nazism, Fascism, and Stalinism deepened our sense of human monstrousness. So, too, did our perception (it was gradual) of the atomic bombing of Hiroshima and Nagasaki . . . and the firebombing of Dresden . . . and the destructive hypocrisy of the Nuremberg Trials. . . . The list might go on and on. Anxiety and doubt were not unreasonable states.

At the same time, energy (and pent-up energy) had been released. One felt it especially in the arts. A complex revolution had been under way for years, and now entered a period of great success.

It was in this year, at the show of de Kooning at the Egan gallery, that the abiding great pleasure of painting came into my own life; more than a pleasure—an affinity and a second language, a tonic and support.

These were de Kooning's black-and-white paintings which since then, of course, have become well known. I sat in front of them all day long, absolutely amazed. Amazed, moved, spellbound, mystified, exhilarated. They did truly speak *to* me and speak *for* me in ways that I sensed and trusted, but that were inexplicable, and that I never had encountered before. Some need, some intellectual/spiritual hunger or incompletion, was being met and answered for the first time. This is the kind of thing that happens probably only in one's early maturity, and that only the art of one's own time can bring about. From the emotions I felt, I derived a certain aesthetic. The paintings did provoke that effort (in many people). They were mysterious. They had been stripped utterly of recognizable forms, yet did not seem arbitrary, or merely decorative, or "poetic." On the contrary, they were powerfully objective, immediate, and, as it were, *factual*.

I asked permission to write my term paper on this show at the Egan, though it lay outside the purview of Schapiro's course. A mutual acquaintance spoke to de Kooning (who didn't have a phone), and relayed back to me a direct quotation: "Sure. Tell him to come on over." Things were that simple then.

His studio was a small loft in an old building on Fourth Avenue, in Booksellers Row, one flight up, with grimy large windows overlooking the street. I remember the large kerosene heater in the back.

It was the simplest sort of workshop, cared for but decrepit, with no amenities of any kind beyond a hot plate for coffee, chipped cups, and sugar in a blue Maxwell House can. On the other hand, by the windows up front (and in strong colors now) there was the great luxury-of-the-eye/luxury-of-the-spirit that seems attainable only to plastic artists. I mean the work itself, the work in progress, with all its attendant studies on paper.

De Kooning's paintings had not yet become beautiful; they were still taming untamed things, and were at their maximum activity in relation to the observer. A decade later, having established themselves not as events in our psyches but as psyche itself, the same works would begin to appear beautiful. What one felt in 1948 was power . . . that is, immediacy, demand, great impress of mind. It was dazzling to me to sit there and listen to de Kooning, in his wonderfully outgoing, forthright, *goodly* way, say things about Cézanne and Picasso that (it seemed to me) only a fellow artist could see and say; and it was wonderful to glance aside continually at the large painting on the work wall—that unfinished living thing that seemed to be making its way in time as authentically as we ourselves.

Something in my response to his work pleased him, as I suppose it must be pleasing to an artist when the intuitive aspects of his own work prove themselves in the responses of another person, especially when that person comes from a milieu outside the artist's own, and is of a different generation. For the next two or three years I visited de Kooning occasionally in his studio and saw the development of paintings that since then have become famous. Whatever understanding I have of art and artists began in those years. And that I should have commenced my own experience of these things as a beneficiary of

Meyer Schapiro and Willem de Kooning I count among the lucky chances of my life.

Most of the painters whom I knew at that time—especially those I met through the sculptor Herbert Ferber—were showing their work at Betty Parsons' gallery, then one of three or four in the city handling the new art. Mark Rothko was there, and Jackson Pollock; so were Bradley Tomlin, Barney Newman, Theodoros Stamos, Richard Pousette-Dart. I remember a gathering one night at Ferber's Riverside Drive penthouse when several of these painters, and a couple of others, sat around trying to think of a name for their common enterprise. They didn't like the term *abstract art*; their painting was more concrete, more confrontational and immediate than the representational work they were displacing. The conversation was intense, but often humorous. Barney Newman, who was an ebullient and warmhearted man, was the most articulate of the speakers. Pollock wasn't there, and I never did meet him, though I owned a painting of his for a while, a large gouache I bought for $250, on installments of $50 a month. Aside from de Kooning, the painter I knew best was Rothko. I wrote a paper on his work, visited his studio frequently, and later sublet the place through the whole of one summer. He showed me paintings at that time—early figurative works—that few people knew existed. I saw them again, after his death, at the Guggenheim Museum's big Retrospective.

Through these contacts, and others at the Artists' Club on Eighth Street, of which de Kooning was the first president, and also because I was an assiduous gallery goer, I acquired an intimate knowledge of the development of the New York School. For four years in the fifties, and then again in the early sixties, I was an associate editor at *Arts* magazine, for which I wrote both feature articles and hundreds of short reviews.

In my single semester at Columbia, before I transferred to the New School for Social Research, I took two writing classes and wrote several stories. These were well received, in fact were singled out by students and teachers both. I had written them with a physical enjoyment and a hopeful and warm projection of feeling that I wasn't to experience again for decades. The more I learned of social injustice, and the more I read of, especially, *Partisan Review*, with its stifling and profoundly mistaken critic's view of art, the more I repudiated my own experience. But this tendency was already well established in me. I was terribly resentful of American life, was impatient and frequently distraught, and was filled with an anger I could scarcely control, much less transmute into art. After I married my first wife and transferred to the

New School for Social Research, I didn't write fiction again for years.

My wife was a fellow student at Columbia. She was an intelligent, acutely perceptive, but terribly shy young woman my own age, and was perhaps as disaffected as I. When we came home from intellectual gatherings she would recapitulate almost everything that had been said, and would insert the opinions she had been too shy to express. These were well worth listening to, as were her penetrating observations of character. These conversations were a great feature of our marriage, which lasted four years.

In the late forties, through a mutual acquaintance at the New School, I met Paul Goodman, whose stories and novels I had admired for a couple of years. His work was brilliant, but there were qualities in it more important than brilliance, especially the interweaving of aesthetics, practical philosophy, and ethics. These presences—extremely rare in contemporary fiction—gave a moral resonance to his work, and a sense of historical dilemma and life-commitment. I found these things stirring and admirable. I met Goodman at a gathering of intellectuals. His talk was dazzling. There was no one present capable of withstanding it, or of modifying it, or even of interrupting it. I soon learned that this was very nearly an invariable situation. What Goodman did was talk. There was a demon at work. His speech was like his writing: quick and spontaneous, yet highly structured, and fully equipped with commas, colons, periods, and paragraphs. He was broadly knowledgeable, original, bold, acutely perceptive. The accuracy and finesse of his distinctions often took one's breath away. We became friendly. His daughter Susan from his first marriage was living with him. He and Sally were already raising Matthew, their own child, then just a toddler. Gradually this family became my second family, my family of choice. Paul was like an elder brother to me, at times like a father. Sally's sweetness and kindness meant a great deal to me. She was terribly overborne by Paul, and suffered from it, yet remained spirited and active. She had a lofty, austere intelligence, and at times could be oddly pedantic, and then a schoolgirl charm would break out that was utterly winning and natural. Her courage was a match for Paul's own, and perhaps exceeded it. She sustained him in many many ways. Both were paying a heavy price for Paul's principled life. He had turned his back on a ready-made academic career—certainly a correct choice for him—and was living as an independent man of letters. He was a Pacifist and an Anarchist, and was an activist through and

through, incapable of thinking something and not pursuing it in his daily life, which he would have deemed ignoble. He was a follower of Freud, a champion of Reich, an adorer of Kant, a self-interested theorist of sex, and a Harpo Marx of compulsive homosexuality, a tremendous nuisance. Paul's character has never ceased to amaze me. In certain ways he was the most admirable of men (his intellectual genius and tremendous energy of mind; his moral courage and ethical accountability; his basic kindliness, his loyalty to meaning, truth, and high principles; the vein of poetry in him that may have produced his most enduring work), and in other ways he was exasperating beyond belief and was even treacherous (his appalling arrogance, his physical cowardice, his relentless assault on other *selves*; his graceless self-centeredness and endless self-congratulation; his inability to stop talking; his compulsive efforts to convert a cerebral sexuality into a physical one). (Between writing the previous sentence and the present one, I've listened to tapes of Paul's talk at the 1967 International Conference on Liberation, in London, and I see that I haven't done justice to the qualities that made him so splendid and compelling. No doubt I'll miss again, but those qualities certainly had a great deal to do with his engagement in the problems and the hopes that bedevil and animate most of mankind. He was local and immediate, yet he lived in the milieu of the world as a whole, and was continually at grips with it. Many people were inspired by him, and many saw him as an ally and source of strength. One listened to him with what might be called altruistic self-interest. It was not that he had made a career of such things, or exercised any special dedication—it was how he *was*, or perhaps, rather, how he had become. He was like Camus in this. He lacked Camus's warm fellow-feeling and sense of an offered comradeship, but his understanding of what truly mattered in life was superior, and intellectually he was far more brilliant.)

Paul was the first American to write in praise and defense of Wilhelm Reich. When Frederick Perls came to this country needing help with a manuscript, he was directed immediately to Paul, perhaps because Perls' own analyst in Vienna had been Reich himself. Goodman had already had some Reichean therapy, and for years had studied the literature of psychoanalysis. For years, too, drawing on his training in philosophy, he had dispensed political, moral, psychological, and literary advice to distressed young men. He went to work on Perls' manuscript, and decided at the same time to formalize his own role as advisor to the young by becoming a lay therapist. I was his first patient. It was a terrible disaster for me—

and a great blessing. Intellectually it was wondrously interesting. The manuscript became the book *Gestalt Therapy*, the better part of which became entirely Paul's own. He deepened it considerably because of his knowledge of philosophy—something Perls did not possess—and maximized its debt to Reich. As my own therapy progressed, Paul came to feel—and I did, too—that I was gifted for this work. Our sessions became didactic, and for several years our friendship was dominated by the apprentice-master relation. (He introduced me once as his "disciple." I was struck by it. It was his first overt commitment to a public role. I attended seminars and workshops at the New York Institute for Gestalt Therapy, not only those conducted by Paul, but Fritz's, too, and Lore Perls'. The founders of the Institute were impressive people. Lore was a deeply cultivated woman, with training in philosophy as well as psychology. She was not as bold or as inventive as Fritz, but was more intelligent and subtle. The remarkable Elliot Schapiro was a member of the Institute, as was Paul Weiczs, who died in early middle age. (The later history of this movement has been disappointing. Perls himself bowdlerized his own work, and the younger therapists have been careerist in the most conventional way.)

After several years of apprenticeship I began to conduct group therapy with some of Paul's private patients, and then with those of another therapist as well. I took on several private patients, too, and in the mid-fifties began to work intensively with severely disturbed children, so-called "juvenile schizophrenics." I pursued this work for three years. The facility was a parent cooperative in New Jersey called The Forum School. Because the parents themselves were the governing board, the "students" were able to live at home and avoid the institutional treatment which in fact would have consisted of little more than custodial restraint. This was important work to me. It was extraordinarily demanding and was so exhausting that in order to go out in the evening I was obliged to sleep for several hours in the late afternoon. But nothing I had ever done was so rewarding. I was really salvaging a small number of doomed lives. The conditions of work were ideal; the director—Louise Emery—was wonderfully perceptive, bold, and supportive. I was able to give twenty-five hours a week to just two children a year, and the results were of a kind not considered possible at that time. I came to see that the prevailing sense of the scope of treatment, and, really, of the maladies themselves, was not based on anything scientific or philosophic, but on the fact that no practitioner was willing to give his life in large amounts to an individual patient. This is only human,

Karl Bissinger

In New York City, just before The Lives of Children *appeared*

obviously. At present there are some significant exceptions to what I have just said. They are significant precisely because their results have been so dramatic as to almost constitute cures—at least from the point of view of prevailing norms. My own results, as I have said, were spectacular. After two years—to mention the most successful—of twenty-five-hours-a-week attention, one boy, who had been diagnosed dozens of times as being without any but an institutional future (would never read, never be able to care for himself even in primitive ways, etc.) not only went to public school, but later attended a community college, and then became a department manager in a large store. People have said, "Perhaps he was misdiagnosed." Yes, he was. Many such people are misdiagnosed—and to find the error one need only look at the apartments and houses and second houses, the travel and clothing and gadgets, the cars, the second cars, and third cars of psychologists, psychiatrists, psychotherapists, and psychoanalysts, for whom it seems to have been ordained in heaven that they work for one hour a week, or two hours, with a large number of high-paying patients. I must say bluntly that I feel an abiding contempt for the profession as a whole, though I have encountered in its ranks some truly wonderful people pursuing authentically the vocation of healing.

During this period I married a young woman with whom I was much in love, an accomplished (concert solos) modern dancer. Our love did not lend itself terribly well to marriage, only to love. We lived together in the stormiest way for less than a year—and then kept seeing each other for nearly a decade.

Of special interest to me during this period, or rather from the early fifties on, were the events and people connected with the Living Theater, especially its founder/directors, Julian Beck and Judith Malina. I met them at Paul's before they started the theater. Their first season was at the Cherry Lane theater in Greenwich Village. They did some modernist classics and some contemporary works, including a play of Goodman's. It was an avant-garde, richly bohemian enterprise. At a later date I acted in a play of theirs and saw a great deal of them, since I was keeping company with a young woman who was a long-time member of their troupe. I took a hand, as did many of their friends, in the construction of their new theater on Fourteenth Street. And, as were many of their friends, I was both pleased and disappointed by the great success of their play *The Connection*. Pleased because the Becks deserved ten times over the attention they were getting; disappointed because the play ran for two years and thus deprived us of the most interesting theater group in the city (except, I should say, for their splendid Monday night programs, which included avant-garde composers and musicians like Cage, Hovannes, and Tudor, the delightful plays of Kenneth Koch and Frank O'Hara, and a staging of Samuel Beckett's marvelous radio play *All That Fall*). The Becks were Anarchists, and from the very beginning were political activists. In their later period of great fame, when they returned from Europe at the end of the sixties, they were doing plays of their own composition and had developed unusual ways of unifying art and activism. Julian died in 1985. The last time I saw him (that same year) he was performing a one-man play of Beckett's at Joe Papp's Public Theater. I took my twenty-year-old daughter backstage to meet him, and we had a chance to reminisce. I hadn't seen him for several years. His cancer was in remission. The knowledge that he might not live long made this meeting a poignant one.

In the middle fifties—again, because of my friendship with Goodman—I encountered two of the great leaders of the antiwar movement, A.J. Muste

and David Dellinger. I didn't know either one at that time, but attended their lectures and read their opinions in *Liberation* magazine, which published several things of my own. I was not interested in politics, found it repugnant, actually, yet I couldn't help but admire these two men, and I followed their work more or less regularly. Paul considered Muste a great man and an exemplar of the grand style. He was strongly placed in a strong tradition, lived his ideals with enormous courage, spoke from the heart, combined morality with political analysis, was superbly well informed, and embellished his talks with illustrative and well-chosen quotations from poetry and philosophy.

I did become stirred to political action by events in the Civil Rights Movement of the early sixties, and that engagement—its attitudes and subjects—lasted for nearly a decade. I took part in the great March on Washington and was profoundly affected by it. A year later I joined a small local enterprise that was to have a wide effect and that changed my own life drastically. This was the First Street School, which was created from scratch by Mabel Chrystie, who became my third and present wife.

Before going on, I should say that I haven't done justice to the torment and confusion in my life, the wasted days, and the berserk wandering—up to the time, anyway, of my working with the juvenile schizo-

"Mabel Chrystie, at the age of fourteen or so. This girl is still a living presence after all these years, and is what I love in her."

phrenics, which was when I began to settle down. On the one hand, things *were* happening, I was not inert, but there are sixteen waking hours in every day, and I tended to squander them. For one thing, I was continually looking for the woman I might love and who might love me, and I couldn't bear to shut down hope and sit in the apartment alone, writing or reading. People who have matured since the sexual revolution of the sixties find it hard to imagine the mores of an earlier time, or to imagine the situation outside the mainstream of American life, where an attractive woman was a rarity in the first place, and where, at that time, few women had dug in their heels and were fighting the conventions they had grown up with. I didn't like bohemians very much, and I looked down (not without compassion) on the wastrels in the bars, though I couldn't deny that I was one of them. I knocked around . . . and knocked around . . . in Key West, Mexico, California, Nevada—I was writing a bit, and I was having adventures, but I was living largely without much purpose at all.

In the early sixties I found an apartment near Tompkins Square Park in what had come to be called The East Village. It was a remarkable neighborhood in those days: working-class Ukrainian and Italian, with newly ensconced Puerto Ricans, and farther east, blacks. Many writers and painters lived there, as did some *lumpen* Beats, and some Hippies, who were new to the scene. I was acquainted with the people who had started the Poets Theater at the Judson Memorial Church, which became for a while the forward curl of the new wave in Off-Broadway Theater. I wrote four one-act plays, and all were directed there by my friend Lawrence Kornfeld, who had worked with Julian Beck at the Living Theater, and who later became well known as an Off-Broadway director. One of my plays was produced extensively in other cities.

The Judson was a social center for people interested in theater and dance. Perhaps the best of its early playwrights was Robert Nichols, who became a close friend and who, shortly after we met, married Grace Paley. She had just published the first of her marvelous books, *The Little Disturbances of Man*. When those two weren't quarreling, nothing pleased me more than to stroll with them up and down the streets of the Village, east and west, stopping here and there for coffee or beer. Bob, in those days, was a great lover of the city, and an extremely knowledgeable one, and wrote a number of plays to be performed in the streets. Grace acted in one of them, in the role of Mayor Lindsay. The largest of these outdoor plays, *The Expressway*, was, quite simply, a masterpiece of political theater and an absolute delight to watch. It was performed three or four times by well-established

"Robert Nichols and Grace Paley, at Bob's place in Vermont. He had just finished his four-part utopian novel, Daily Lives in Nghsi Altai, *published by New Directions."*

actors working for the pleasure of it . . . and it hasn't been heard of since. Masterworks of this kind were created during the Renaissance, things done on paper for fetes and balls, widely praised . . . and never seen again. I think of such things with sadness and pride. They are pure spirit, or become so, like the dazzling conversations of gifted people, remembered as long as memory lasts, but really gone, gone immediately . . .

Mabel was with me one night in '65 when I first encountered the work of Peter Schumann at his tiny loft theater on Delancey Street. The Vietnam War was in progress, and the antiwar movement, in which I was active for several years, was gathering strength, though it was still very small. Schumann's play *Fire* was not in the least propagandistic, yet it was an antiwar play and referred specifically to Vietnam. Writing now more than twenty years later, I can still say that it is the most powerful antiwar play I have ever seen. "Play" is a deceptive word here. There was no dialogue. The actors wore masks—face masks and hand masks. It was nightmarish, as if *Guernica* had come to life; and at times it was hauntingly poignant. I wrote an essay on the play that was published in the *Village Voice* and later in *Scripts* magazine, and that has been widely anthologized.

At this period Mabel and our not-yet-walking Susan, and Jules and Helen Rabin and *their* not-yet-walking Susan met at—and constituted the entirety of—a weekly antiwar demonstration in Washington

"Peter Schumann's annual Bread and Puppet Circus in Glover, Vermont, 1985. Peter is dancing on the tall stilts. Mabel, Becky, Michael, and Susan are out there somewhere. They have taken part in this for many years, helping first (for a month) with the preparation, and then performing. It's a gathering of the clans. We meet old friends from the Movement days, and keep in touch with acquaintances."

Square Park. We became acquainted also with the Schumanns, whose fifth child, Maria, had just been born. These friendships, still thriving in 1987, have amounted to an extended family for all of us, but especially for the children, whose lives have been enormously enriched not only by each other but by, especially, their participation in the workshops and performances of Peter's Bread and Puppet Theater, at first in New York, then briefly in Maine, and then for many years in northern Vermont.

Schumann is not widely known in mainstream America, but in the avant-garde/dissident community as a whole, not only here but in Europe, he is a man of considerable fame, the subject of several books in French and German, and of half-a-dozen doctoral theses in the United States. Peter's annual two-day free circus near the tiny village of Glover, Vermont, now draws crowds of ten to fifteen thousand people a day. Many writers on theater consider him to be—as do I—among the important theater creators of the century, of the stature of Brecht, O'Neill, and Genet, from all of whom he differs enormously, especially in his relation to folk art and to medieval theater. I should explain that Peter's puppets have nothing to do with marionettes. Many of his figures are eighteen feet tall and require four or five attendants (working

in full view); other "puppets" are actors in masks. My own three children have grown up as participants in this work, and nothing could have been luckier. The foreign tours, especially, have been grand experiences, hard, hard work combined with the excitement of many performances and the camaraderie of the puppeteers. Those who have seen only recent circuses in Vermont have no way of guessing what has gone before: the stylistic variety and the great number of splendid and powerful plays. The most recent tours have been to Nicaragua, where morale-raising work has been done with the embattled peasants. Susan took part in one of these.

Another friend whose work has meant a great deal to me is Hayden Carruth. I encountered both the poems and the poet in the early seventies. The ethical affinities were already in place, and I found in the poems, from the beginning, qualities of mind and feeling (ranging from elegiac introspection to powerful passions of several kinds), together with an acute sense of aesthetic form that seemed to me rare in contemporary work, and that have constituted, for me, the most rewarding *oeuvre* of any American poet. One exciting aspect of Carruth's poetry has been its access of power, both gradual and by leaps. Two of his later works, *Brothers, I Loved You All,* and *The*

"Good friends Ruth Perry and Taylor Stoehr, literary historians, at one of the Bread and Puppet Circuses"

Sleeping Beauty rank in my own mind as the strongest of recent American production. His music, that uncanny amalgam of voice, subject, and technique, has been an abiding pleasure in my life. We have exchanged many letters, visits, and manuscripts over the years—and I should add, considering the hazards of the last-named exchanges, a certain quantity of forgiveness.

Friendship has been important in my life, and at some point came to constitute, quite consciously, a family of the spirit. I would say this especially of my long friendships with literary historians Taylor Stoehr and Ruth Perry, and with scientist-author Ivan Tolstoy, people of rare and beautiful character as well as intellectual gifts. Other friends, too, seem like family to me: Sally Goodman, Geoffrey Gardner, and Diana Liben, the widow of fiction writer Meyer Liben, who also had been a friend. In a special category is my relationship with the poet Ted Enslin. Our differences are extreme and on several occasions have been so violent that we have gone through withdrawals that have seemed permanent . . . except that they have healed, though not without scars. This has been going on for twenty-two years. Our music marathons have been memorable. We would equip ourselves with a couple of gallons of wine and some barbecued chickens, and then would listen to all of Beethoven's sonatas in chronological order, or all of Mahler's symphonies, or Mozart's quintets. No one can absorb that much music in one sitting (the longest were eighteen to twenty hours), but some-

thing else happens: the music becomes a medium, a geography, a weather. These were choice events, as were—after Ted moved from Temple, where we were neighbors, to the Maine coast—our clam digging and mussel gathering expeditions, which were followed, naturally, by wonderful feasts.

But the family at the heart of my life has been Susan, who is now twenty-one, Rebecca, seventeen, and Michael, twelve; together with their mother, Mabel, who began all this when she started the First Street School, perhaps the first urban Free School in the country, back in 1964, since it was in that relationship of work that I got to know her. I was invited to join the staff because of my experience with disturbed children. None of the students at the First Street School fell into that category, but the boys, ranging in age from nine to thirteen, were unstable in many ways, some of them violent. They were my special charges. I kept a journal of my work there, and published an article in *Liberation.* This came to the attention of Jason Epstein, who commissioned a book for Random House. This—*The Lives of Children*—became a best-seller and was published in ten countries. For almost two years I traveled widely, lecturing on the theory and practice of the free school and the relation of learning to growth, as exemplified not

"Good friend Ivan Tolstoy, author, geophysicist, mountain climber, 1977"

"Early September on the front porch in Maine. Some garden chore is underway (Mabel's hands behind the golden retriever). Shem and Sashka are smiling for the camera, restrained by Susie (center) and Becky (right). Michael is readjusting the angles of Shem's tail."

"Family life in Maine: Mabel and the kids, around 1976"

"Mabel, Becky, Michael, and Susan taking part in our local Founder's Day Parade, about 1981"

"Becky, Susie, Michael ... on the reading sofa, about 1979"

last of Genet's novels were in some essential structural way my models, a costly error). I broke my connections with the alternate education movement (except for my friendship with John Holt, who spent a week with us two years ago when he was dying of cancer), and I managed to reduce the appalling amounts of time demanded by rural chores. Several of my stories were published by Ted Solotaroff (who had been my editor when I was writing reviews for *Commentary* in the early sixties) in his serviceable and really valuable *American Review*. My allegiance—it amounted to adoration, really—swung finally and permanently to Tolstoy and Proust, but especially the former, since novelistic technique is so important in his work. Random House published a collection of my stories, *Oilers and Sweepers*, and also a book for children, *And Then a Harvest Feast*. Following the example of Thomas Mann, I wrote a novella about my dog, or rather all my dogs, assembled, as it were, into one single character; and I used the dog to explore and tie together a number of people and places of my life in Maine. The most gratifying thing about the publication of this book (*Shawno*, Schocken Books, 1984) was the fact that so many of my neighbors and acquaintances, several of them lumberjacks, enjoyed and praised it, and recognized unerringly every person, house, and stream I had made use of. This book allowed me to write realistically, but from an attitude of praise, which introduced certain aspects of the idyll. I used the same combination later in the

Michael, Becky, Susie, Thanksgiving Day, 1985

only by our own experience but by, especially, the remarkable school that Leo Tolstoy had conceived and operated for the peasant children of his own estate, and, of course, by Summerhill, the pioneering school of A.S. Neill. Susan had been born and we had been spending our summers in Maine. Soon we were spending summers, falls, and winters there, and ten days after Rebecca's birth (she followed Susan by four years) we moved permanently to Maine. All of this, but especially the children, constituted an enormous change in my life. I was intoxicated by the woods and streams, by gardening, and snowshoeing, and cross-country skiing . . . and by the chores and pleasures of fatherhood, especially by what came to be my greatest pleasure: reading to the kids on the big sofa at night. I have read through all of Laura Ingalls Wilder seven times (and I take her seriously as an important writer), and through *Huckleberry Finn* six or seven times, and *Tom Sawyer*, and a lot of Leskov, Chekhov, Tolstoy, etc., etc. Our marriage has undergone some very painful stresses, as is to be expected, no doubt, from an alliance of headstrong and perhaps eccentric people, but it has survived for a good long while.

After *The Lives of Children* I wanted to go back to writing fiction, though most of my efforts in that line had failed, chiefly, I think, because the modernist attitudes I espoused simply didn't fit me (the first and

"Dennison home in central Maine. Forty below is not uncommon. The house is heated by a woodburning furnace, around fourteen cords a year."

novel *Luisa Domic* (Harper and Row—and once again I had the pleasure of working with Ted Solotaroff), the idyll this time deriving not only from the attitude of praise applied to a real place, but from the temporal setting in the brief few days of early Indian Summer, when the air is so quiet that nothing seems to move, and the colors of the autumn leaves are at their most intense. All of that, and the deeper pleasures and loves of family life, I put into contrast with the extreme suffering of a woman refugee from Chile, who after the murder of Allende, passes through Maine in her flight from Pinochet's torturers.

This book was followed by a collection of stories and novellas, some new and some appearing again. The title of the new book is *A Tale of Pierrot* (Harper and Row, 1987). At the present writing, this is my most recent work.

BIBLIOGRAPHY

Nonfiction:

The Lives of Children: The Story of the First Street School. New York: Random House, 1969; Harmondsworth, England: Penguin, 1972.

Fiction:

And Then a Harvest Feast (for children). New York: Random House, 1972; London: Faber, 1975.

Oilers and Sweepers and Other Stories. New York: Random House, 1979.

Shawno. New York: Schocken, 1984.

Luisa Domic. New York: Harper, 1985.

A Tale of Pierrot (short stories and novellas). New York: Harper, 1987.

Clayton Eshleman

1935-

INDIANA AVENUE

I

I was born at 10:50 A.M., Saturday, June 1, 1935, in the Methodist Hospital, in Indianapolis, Indiana. I was named Ira Clayton Eshleman, Jr., after my father, Ira Clayton Eshleman, and my grandfather Ira Joseph Eshleman. My mother, born in 1898, in Wabash, Indiana, was named Gladys Maine Spencer, her middle name having been chosen because the U.S. battleship *Maine* was blown up in the Havana Harbor several months before she was born. She was, until her later years, a devoted mother and housewife who sang in the church choir and introduced me to piano lessons when I was six years old. My father, born in 1895, in Wakarusa, Indiana, graduated from Purdue University with a degree in mechanical engineering in 1918. During the years that I knew him, until retirement he was in charge of time-and-motion study at Kingan and Company, a slaughterhouse and meat-packer in downtown Indianapolis. His job, as I later understood it, was to determine the number of black men needed, along with their various tasks ("Knock, Shackle & Hoist Cattle, Saw Breast & Raise Weasand, Rip Tails & Tie Bungs," etc.) for the most efficient "kill per hour." He wore a long white smock when he visited the killing-floor, and when he came home from work, the smock often had raspberry-colored bloodstains on the part that hung below his knees.

It seems that my parents had tried to conceive a child for a long time before I was born, and, given

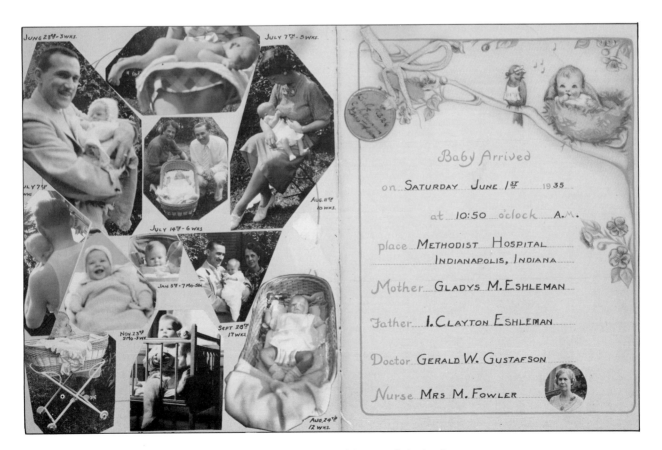

Pages from Clayton Eshleman's baby book

their ages, decided that I was it. At one point there was talk about adopting "a little sister" for me, an idea that I wholeheartedly supported, but nothing ever came of it. My mother kept a diary for the first three years of my life. Her June 1, 1935, entry concludes: "Get much medication and our little boy is born this day at 10:50 A.M. His Daddy seeing him enter this old world. A Little Clayton Jr. Our dream at last realized & our prayers answered. Thank God for it all." Before I was born, I was referred to as "little squidger" or "little sicker." As a baby, possibly because they thought I was going to be a redhead, I was "Sonny." My father kept a meticulous daily record of my infancy, in a small *Baby's Book of Events,* which had page headings like Baby's Weight, Congratulations, Gifts, Baby's First Tooth, Baby's First Shoes, First Outing, Our Baby's First Word (mine apparently was "dad-da," at ten months, three weeks, followed by "dite," "chur," "cal," "wow-wow," "cock," "wa-wa," "bot," "cacker," and "chup-chup"). On the inside front cover of this amazing record is the rose my father gave my mother after I was born. Faded russet, it is taped, under cellophane, to a photograph of the hospital, with my mother's room Xed below the windowsill. The book ends with my third birthday, as did a good deal of my father's fascination with me. On one level, he seems to always have regarded me as an infant: his last words to me, when he was dying, in 1971, as he played with a button on my shirt, were "kitchi-kitchi-coo."

To a certain extent, my mother picked up the record keeping where my father left off. I still have three large packed scrapbooks that begin with my letter to Santa Claus when I was five, and end with a photograph of my Phi Delta Theta "pledge" class, when I was eighteen. She clipped every reference to me that appeared in the daily high-school newspaper, carefully pasted in invitations to parties and dances, as well as many of my cartoons, my newspaper route record book, and my twenty-seven Boy Scout merit-badge cards. She was wildly in love with me, and whatever confidence and belief in myself that I have come up with I owe to her. As she lay dying of spinal cancer (in the same hospital where I had been born), she told me: "the most important thing in my life has been to be your mother." While her words moved me more than I can say, they also saddened me, because she had hardly any sense of a life of her own. I was, indeed, her "dream," and like many women of her generation, I imagine, her life was so centered on her only-child son, that she did virtually nothing for herself on her own.

I seldom dream these days of my father. I often dream of my mother who is usually sick in bed

Oliver Showalter

Engagement photo of Eshleman's parents, Ira Clayton Eshleman and Gladys Maine Spencer, Wabash, Indiana, 1922

someplace needing my care. Such dreams are so potent that I awake convinced that my mother *is* still alive. These dreams lead me to believe that the infant part of me knows nothing of death and as long as it is active in my dreaming will envision its mother forever living.

*

In my nightly prayer, kneeled before my bed, my wrists against the bed edge, pressed palms pointing up like a grotesque fin, I offered my sleep body to a "Lord" who was to possess and possibly keep my "soul." A "Lord" who in turn offered me nothing— no dream maps, no notions of what animals did in their sleep, no night jungle gyms for my nine-year-old mind to exercise on during the day in preparation for this nightly transfer of powers. "Soul," likewise undefined by story or image, was even more baffling than the word "Lord." Was it my "day life" that was being loaned out as I lay me down? But the I that might die before I woke up, that was my day life too!

For the I that might die in the night (HOW?), wasn't it the same I that might wake up? And if I died before I woke up, would that mean that some of me would still wake up in spite of the fact of having died?

Certainly one effect of my repeated and much mulled-over prayer was to make the night faceless and deep. It was during this time in my life that I created my own little response to the prayer and the consequent crawling in under the covers. I got completely under the covers, head and all, bunched up on my elbows and knees, and crawled around, in place, in a circle, very fast, until I got so dizzy I thought I was going to pass out. Then I stopped and took great pleasure in trying to figure out in which direction my head was pointing. After guessing all the possible room-oriented directions (north toward the Woodrings, west toward the Wardlaws, east toward Sparky's pen, south toward where Negroes lived), I would peep out for the thrill of seeing just how wrong I could be! Always, wrong or right, I was pleased with my "performance," and would then crawl back into sleep position and doze off.

It occurs to me that I may have been unfair to my prayer in the way I just discussed it: for it could be read as the kind Lord keeping watch over my "soul," and not letting it disappear if something happened to me during the night. Regardless, the weight of the prayer was that night is much different than day, and so different, that *anything* can happen to you while it is dark. Meaning that "anything" cannot, or probably will not, happen to you during the day. By this logic I reasoned that the scary-looking very poor people downtown across from the place where my father drove me to sell my old newspapers would stay put, or on their porches, during the day—but at night? Might they be the very people the "Lord" was protecting me from during the night? But the prayer said that I might die, that the Lord might not be successful in protecting me? After all, I was *alone* in bed, not with my mother or father (nor, since I was an only child, with brothers or sisters).

As I got older, the night increasingly became an emptiness to fill, or inhabit, the fearful boundary that if crossed might hurt me—and/or tell me something about "Lord" and "soul." Night became that danger-ous place where you might meet people you would not want to meet during the day, or in my case, could not meet during the day. As I grew bigger and stronger, the menacing-looking poor people sitting on their porches watching my middle-class father and me invade their surroundings (if only for fifteen minutes, the time it took the guy to weigh my stacks of newspaper and pay me), these people began to draw me, make me wonder about them. They got

Clayton at age twelve, Indianapolis

mixed up in my mind with "south toward where Negroes lived," not only because the poor parts of Indianapolis then all seemed to be south of us but because without any coherent counterinstruction I had begun to build a web out of the following associations:

> night was different and dangerous
>> but I might learn something from it that I was not learning from my parents in our sunny house—
> night was poor and Negro, it had different rules, or maybe no rules; our house, 4705, was like a toy train (even if I "derailed," I was merely whipped and put back "on track")

*

When I was around fifteen, several things hap-pened overnight: I started collecting records of "romantic" orchestra music (since it was what you danced to with dates), and discovered the record store near Shortridge High School (in a lower mid-dle-class semi-Black neighborhood), where someone was listening to "Jazz at the Philharmonic" records and *Down Beat* magazine was sold. I went to my first "Jazz at the Phil" concert, started wearing pegged pants, subscribed to *Down Beat,* and ordered, sight unseen, two 45 rpm records, one by Lennie Tristano and another by Bud Powell. What I heard on the Powell record now escapes me, but I still clearly recall Tristano's ghostly version of "I Surrender Dear." When I tried to figure out what was special about this music, it dawned on me that they were not playing the same thing over and over. While I didn't know what Tristano and Billy Bauer *were* doing, I could tell that they were doing something that made no sense in between the beginning and the ending when they played the melody. They played the melody, then got lost, and then they played the melody again. I am sure that I did not think of the "lost part" as the night part of the record, but maybe I did—my way of associating in those days was very naive but also highly irrational, and I am sure that the fact that most of the jazz I listened to was played by Blacks intensified my night-oriented web of associations: the melody parts, even though I could understand them, somehow were less interesting than the in-between parts in which all sorts of things happened that I could not understand. I should add here that I had played the piano since I was six years old at my mother's insistence—I had had, I think, a typical "neighborhood piano teacher" musical upbringing, one lesson per week over the years, moving from *Teaching Little Fingers To Play* to "Rustle of Spring," some Bach Inventions, and several Chopin Etudes (by the time I was sixteen). Jazz was especially interesting, then, because you "made up" things that were not on the score.

Neither of my parents drank liquor or wine (my father once kept a jug of homemade dandelion wine in the refrigerator for a year without, to my knowledge, drinking any of it), and they more or less imposed on me a limited version of their own conservative social patterns. They always had to know where I was on the one or two nights per week that I was allowed out of the house after dark, and I was never, at fifteen, allowed to stay out after 9:30 P.M. I even had to tell my mother where I went (if I did not come home directly, as she preferred) after school in the afternoon. I was being set up to absolutely duplicate their daily/nightly lives. I think their "dream" was that I might go from fifteen to fifty-five (my father's age then) without dealing with sixteen to fifty-four. In fact, I think this is the secret life of the American Midwest: as the puberty vines begin to grow and rustle, they are bound up by the "system" and hurled forward, so that a growing boy or girl finds him or herself suddenly (and eternally) in a time

warp, passing over the present experience, rushing, in place, toward the ages of his or her parents and teachers. Sports are very effective in this witchcraft, as they intensify the "rules" grid at home, and focus the unsuspecting player on a life of winning vs. losing.

My mid-to-late teenage years were enormously complicated because while I was being bound up and mailed ahead of my years (the bindings being football, wrestling, track, and Boy Scouts), I was exchanging my childhood prayer pact for an obsession with Indiana Avenue, the "Negro tenderloin" of Indianapolis in the early 1950s, with its theaters, jazz clubs, booze, whores, its various initiations, as it were, into some of the shapes of the night. Most of my forays into the world of "The Orchid Club" or "The Surf Club" (the latter being on West Sixteenth Street and jazz oriented rather than blues oriented, as most of the Indiana Avenue clubs were) involved a plunge into sheer sensation. I mean that I was not a studious, reflective "student of jazz." I went down to Indiana Avenue like a demonized zombie intent on saving my "soul," whatever it was. Like a dead boy trying to find a connection, a jazz socket, into which I might stick one of my fingers and feel what then seemed to be the electricity of the night, forty-seven blocks south of 4705 Boulevard Place, a great raging interiority, with people dancing on tables, flashlights on our false ID cards, a black whore behind a candy store in the alley for eight of us whiteboys, in the back seat, one by one, fifty cents a head.

It seems remarkable to me today that I actually recall any of the people or the music, less because of being engulfed by the wildness and weirdness of Indiana Avenue than because of the schizophrenic dance I was trying to do between what seemed to be

Clayton with his parents, Indianapolis, 1953

two utterly incompatible worlds. For my parents had done a pretty thorough job on me. Unlike a few acquaintances who drifted out of the white middle-class world into the "floating world" of jazz, my anatomy belonged to Mom and Dad. Try as I might to look "cool," or to feel my way into bebop (in contrast to "White Christmas," which I had played every year for quietly assembled parents and relatives at the end of the holiday dinner), I felt like a salamander programmed into a color pattern that could not be altered at will. I was white and destined to very quickly become grey, and I didn't really want to be black, or a "white negro" either—for the world that blackness and jazz seemed to represent was a danger-ous half or quarter world from my viewpoint. I was willing to step off the land of 4705 at 9:00 P.M. (lying to my parents that I had gone to a late movie or that someone had had car trouble), and move about on the ice offshore for a few hours, but the idea of making the leap, fully, onto what seemed to be shifting ice in endless night, was unthinkable. I believe that if I had, such a move would have been disastrous. Since I lacked the kinetics of bop rhythm, I would undoubtedly have merely immersed myself in a "white negro" lifestyle and gone down the drain via booze or drugs.

Jazz, thus, over several years, became an image filled with potential liberation, but liberation into what? An image crisscrossed by lines I both could not and would not cross. On one level, it was an excuse to "get out of it," to drown in a blur of neon, beer, and noise for a few hours, to feel a senseless, perilous alternative to 4705, and in that way in my still very innocent mind it tied creativity into a destructive lifestyle which in a queasy way made being home with "White Christmas," the piano, the relatives, food, and a warm, comfortable bed, all the more difficult to break with. In one stroke, it made home predictable and bleak, *and* reinforced its connection to childhood needs. If I had been reading poetry and looking at paintings at this time—if I had had other examples of creativity that showed people like me could success-fully do it, I probably would not have milled around without direction for another five years—in certain ways, the worst years of my life—trying to fit into a middle-class, business-oriented world that played with my split personality in a new way. Once away from home, at eighteen, in my new "home," the Phi Delta Theta fraternity house in Bloomington, Indiana, my need for parental reassurances turned me into a needy seeker of friends among young men whom in my guts I detested.

Much more important than being merely an excuse to get out of it, jazz was a lifesaving, explosive

connection to virtually everything I have come to experience outside of what now seems to be that little island of northside Indianapolis, with its 4705 light-house casting its white, white beam across the dark waters, as if seeking to lead survivors in—who were of course supposed to look like my parents and me, and have lifeboats of the right model. The initial attrac-tion of Indiana Avenue was Faustian—as if I, as one who had never dreamed, was being offered a night-mare in exchange for continuing to not dream at all. The discovery that the night was not just a wide, soundless, rather eerie basin, but a multistoried dwelling, with pits and altars, apparitions, sensual terror, and thrilling sounds, was a necessary stage in ultimately leaving my background and taking the risk of becoming an artist.

"The Orchid Club," and all the other clubs and dives and backrooms that I found my way to, were like stepping out of Gainsborough's *Blue Boy* painting (a copy of which was prominently displayed in the waiting room of the baby doctor I was taken to) and entering the world of Max Beckmann. It was as if I had been crouched on middle C all my life and suddenly through some mysterious grace had discov-ered that octaves stretched forth like Arctic wastes and Amazon jungle on each side. I remember being in clubs that seemed as if they were literally being destroyed the night that we had somehow found out about them, and slipped in to a sanctuary of blasting horns, incredible odors, and swirls of bodies that almost seemed amoebic, pulsing as if to suggest that all of us could part from ourselves and roar into an unending tunnel of "earthly delights." And then, just

Eshleman (on piano) with a jazz quartet, Indianapolis, about 1952

as suddenly, to find oneself outside, in the trashy, drifting dark, hungry, half-looped, wanting more and more—and ending up with a dozen White Castle twelve-cent burgers (the White Castle diner being halfway between Indiana Avenue and home) or driving around in the back alleys, slouched down in the backseat with a warm Coke half-filled with Four Roses, regarding the back of Dick Foltz's head in the driver's seat as he haggled, from time to time, with the pimps who mysteriously materialized as our Buick stopped behind the grim silhouette of a building that "looked like" it might be a cat house. The next afternoon, again safely ensconced in our dens or bedrooms, we would be on the phone with buddies, filling each other in on what happened the night before and plotting the next "club-hopping" evening.

I suppose most North American artists have, in varying degrees, a period like this, a period that Allen Ginsberg dramatized in _Howl._ In fact, one reason that _Howl_ remains so memorable may have to do with its sojourn in that "purgatory" between not being an artist and being an artist that haunts so many sensitive people. Yet most of the unnamed figures in Ginsberg's saga seem damned forever—if they do not kill themselves in the course of the poem itself, one feels that they will a year later, or that they will fade back into a life-style based on their backgrounds and never be heard of again. I envision an innocent middle-class youth wandering into the library to take out _Tom Sawyer,_ and by chance getting plugged into the library's "brain," which is as frightening a brain as I can imagine. At the point the soft, passive mind is infiltrated, really infiltrated, by a Blake or van Gogh, it goes crazy, if not mentally, certainly in life-style, attempting to reconstellate, or better, constellate for the first time, what "everything" _means._

Fortunately at the same time that I was hitting "The Orchid Club," I was a night later dropping in at "The Surf Club," where musicians such as the Montgomery brothers could be heard working out the music that would later make them famous. Especially in the case of the three Montgomery brothers (with whom I once played a set, at a Saturday afternoon jam session), I got the feeling that the club was their workshop, and that they were really thinking while they were playing, and in ways that I could not then even hope to understand, expressing _their_ lives. Thus jazz, at one end of the spectrum, was sheer descent into the hives of Indiana Avenue and its back alleys, but at the other end, a chance to glimpse genuinely creative artists working in a way that I imagine someone my age might have watched a painter paint in another time and place. I recall to what extent Wes Montgomery, who at that time was

hardly known at all, looked _at home_ as he played his guitar—as if he had a child in his cradled guitar, as he kept drawing sweetness and power out of that "force" in his arms. For he was childlike, not only as an artist in relaxed but utterly serious concentration, but in demeanor when he would chat with me. I would tell him the names of a few records I had recently bought and try to say something hip about what I heard on them, or make a comment to show that I was following articles in _Down Beat._ Wes would smile and more or less have something good to say about anything I mentioned. He seemed to be at peace with the world as a man, and, as an artist, capable of lifting me out of my chair. I think he was the first great artist with whom I had personal contact.

By the time I was eighteen, I had figured out what bop musicians were doing between beginning and ending melody-run-throughs—they were improvising. They were using the tune's chord structure on which to base their own melody lines, so they were free and bound, or in a pattern that was enabling them to add their own ideas to what someone else had written. They were not just repeating "White Christmas" over and over before an audience of uncles and aunts staring, as if in prayer, at the remains of the turkey on their plates. Did this mean that _I_ could change _my_ life? I knew that I was "different" than my parents—did this jazz information also mean that I did not have to repeat their lives for the rest of my life? If so, what was my "chord structure"? For once such a question got into me, I was, in my own way, standing before Rilke's archaic torso of Apollo who told the young poet "there is no place that does not see you" (the real climax of that famous sonnet for me, not the final line). Jazz, as Wes Montgomery seemed to embody it, was a way of life—more than hands on an instrument, it seemed to be a way of being, of comportment. But how could I be (I fuzzily argued with myself) _like Wes Montgomery?_ I knew in my bones that I was not a jazz musician. Other than my fragile connection to the jazz world, I was like an aimless kite, being buffeted about a hundred feet above 4705, for all practical purposes still attached to an umbilical string.

For the next four or five years I wandered, a "white ghost," unable to realize that my dilemma itself was a place to begin, if I could find a means of expression. The Phi Delt midnight living room, bristling with paddles and fire, was a caricature of "The Orchid Room"—even to the extent that while the actives pummeled us, they played "Slaughter on Tenth Avenue" on the record player because the fraternity was at that time at the corner of Tenth Street—and _Indiana Avenue!_ I had moved sixty miles south to another "Indiana Avenue" where instead of serving you Cuba Libres and "Night Train" they beat the shit out of you!

> O father swing away!
>   O mother draw away!
> O father swing away!
>   O mother draw away!

—that is one of the prayers I repeated, as I pressed myself to the mattress in my bunk in the third-floor fraternity dorm. How I yearned to be back in that white "castle" as 4705, through whose dining-room porthole-window I could safely peer at a grey autumnal sky that threatened never to reveal its interior orgies unless the little viewer literally stepped out of his skin.

II

My first poem, written in 1957, was called "The Outsider," and it was a timid, versified re-enactment of feelings I had picked up reading Colin Wilson's *Outsider*, a book that introduced me to such visionary figures as Blake and van Gogh on the periphery of societal centers. However, my first engagement with *poesis* took place when I was a freshman at Indiana University, 1953, in Herbert Stern's Freshman Composition class. After having given several assignments (which I had done poorly on), he said: write anything you want to.

I wrote a kind of prose-poem, in the voice of an aging prostitute, standing at her hotel window, watching newspapers and rubbish blow down a deserted street at 4:00 A.M. Stern gave me an A— and under the grade wrote: *see me.* When I sat down in his office, he told me that the piece was excellent but that I was in trouble because I had not written it. I still recall his words: "the person who wrote this did not write your other themes." I protested, and in the end he believed me, and said: "if you can write like this, there are a couple books you should read." On a scrap of paper, which he handed me, he wrote: *The Metamorphosis*, and under it, *A Portrait of the Artist as a Young Man.* To what extent Stern himself was conscious of the significance of this particular juxtaposition, I will never know—but by citing the Kafka story (which I waited two years to read), he had identified what had happened to me in my "free theme," and by citing the Joyce (which took me nine years to read), had he slyly challenged me to become an artist?

In my theme, I had aged myself, changed my sex, and dressed up as a parody of my mother (which as a thirteen-year-old I often actually did). The figure was utterly fictional—I knew nothing about the lives of prostitutes, and that was probably part of the point too: I had entered imagination by speaking out of a place I had never personally experienced. I had left the confines of an "assignment"—my entire life to that time and continuing beyond it was framed by assignments—and wandered into an "other." "*Je est un autre,*" Rimbaud had written when he was seventeen. I is a metaphor. Clayton is a prostitute, Clayton is not merely Clayton. Clayton does not merely live in the Phi Delt fraternity house and take abuse daily as a "pledge." Clayton is a fifty-five-year-old woman looking out on a street that does not exist.

A move toward origin, toward our so-called "face before birth," toward that which we are but will never be, toward what we were but are not. The initial fascination with writing poetry is similar to a visit to an astrologer to request a horoscope. My aged whore pointed me at a past in the present, indicating (though I did not realize it then) continuity and depth. The street was empty except for blowing (unreadable) newspapers, yesterday's news. It was empty and I was to populate it with my own news—I was to learn how to read the street, and to get used to not being myself. I was like a tree still rooted in Indianapolis earth, learning how to twist within my own background and to observe "other" things around me.

*

I had nothing to moor my "free theme" to, as I was drifting in the superficial social-world of the Phi Delta Theta house which took over all my waking hours. If you looked at an "active" in the wrong way, you could be beaten on the spot. Whenever they felt the "pledges" had it too easy for a few days, there would be a midnight "line up," with the twenty-two of us WASPs driven out of bed, stripped, and beaten naked with long wood paddles in a bent-over circle, as the "actives" whooped and hollered drunk around us. I had slipped through high school with average grades only because of rigorous home discipline. Now without my parents to rein me in, I went with the "fraternal tide," which meant figuring out how to do the minimal amount of study to just get by, learning how to be "one of the guys," while being driven by the need for sexual conquest. The "frat house" itself was a kind of gym echoing with the stress of our lives, constant chores, racing here and there, with picnics and beer-blasts on the weekends. As we got closer to "Hell Week," after which we would be initiated, the hazing intensified. During Hell Week itself, we all slept in our suits on the floor in a basement room, and in the evenings were subjected to a disgusting array of torments such as wearing a bull penis from a local slaughterhouse around our necks or participating in "Fire Drills" (a tub of "punch" consisting of dishwater, beer, catsup, and urine, etc., was set up in the dormitory, and a fire built behind the house—one by one we took a mouthful of "punch" and crawled down three flights of stairs on our hands and knees and spit it into the fire, the "drill" ending when the fire was finally quenched). For the entire "Hell Week" I wore a piece of raw stinking liver taped to one armpit; one of the pledges who was suspected of being homosexual had a string tied around his penis which then led up into his shirt pocket and was tied to a little sign dangling out of his pocket that said: PULL ME.

I had enrolled in Music School out of a vague affinity with the arts. After all, I had studied the piano with several neighborhood piano teachers, I had taken cartoon lessons while in junior high school, had done well in high-school life-drawing classes (my mother framed a drawing I did of a hobo paid to model for us and hung it by the living-room door), and like many others had participated in Junior Vaudevilles and Family Frolics, dancing and playing the piano. But the possibility of a commitment to art went out the window when I was faced with being on my own in the fraternity world. The split I had felt between jazz and my middle-class home existence was now deepened *and* undermined at the same time. I could not identify with the serious, pale, and non-regular-guy music students, but I also did not know how to be accepted by my fraternity brothers. I think they felt that I was an oddball masquerading as one of them, and they loathed me for this.

As a freshman, I studied with a concert pianist on the Music School faculty named Ozan Marsh who was appalled at my presumption that a few hours practice each week would meet his standards. In the spring of 1954, he suggested that I do something else with my life. I went back to Indianapolis, took up residence in my home bedroom, and prepared for a long, lazy summer as lifeguard at the all-white middle-class private Riviera Club, a twenty-minute bicycle ride from our house. Within a few days, I was befriended by a plantinum-haired ex-paratrooper named John Fish who drove a new, black Lincoln convertible. He was looking for someone to drive to Los Angeles with and dig the new West Coast jazz scene. I convinced my mother that I would continue to study the piano while in Los Angeles, and off John and I went. It was my first summer on my own, and it set a precedent for the later journeys to Mexico and the extended visits to Japan and Peru in the 1960s.

I really did end up taking piano lessons in Los Angeles that summer: with Richie Powell, Bud Powell's younger brother, killed a year later in the tragic Pennsylvania Turnpike accident that also took Clifford Brown's life. I paid my way parking cars for the Systems Auto Park Company, working a downtown lot across from the still-standing Cecil Hotel. Fish, who worked as a repossessor for Household Finance, would come by around 9:00 P.M.; I would change from my tan uniform into regular clothes in the collection booth, and we would take off for the clubs. Outside the Tiffany Club one evening, two very good-looking black women asked Fish and me where they could park their car, and when they walked out of the lot we latched onto them—to find out, on entering the club, that they were the wives of Clifford Brown and Max Roach! The two of us kept getting thrown out of apartments whose managers would discover my rented piano a couple of weeks after we moved in. We ended up in Echo Park at the end of the busline. Suddenly it was late August and my father was on the phone insisting (in order to get me to come back to school, I think) that I would be drafted if I did not re-enroll. He sent me busfare, and I entered Business School that September.

By doing so I lost my few hours of piano practice each week which had in the past year given me a little distance from fraternity life. I vaguely recall sitting through two years of accounting and business management classes not having the slightest idea of what was being discussed; of spending more time figuring out how to cheat on a final exam than it would have taken to study for it; of dreading and worshipping each coming weekend. Would I get a hot date? A feel-up? Pussy on the first date? Occasionally one of the brothers got a blowjob on a blind date; the date's name was flashed through the fraternity network which kept her phone ringing off the hook for months. Robert Lowell's image, in the poem "Skunk Hour," of "love-cars" huddled together "hull to hull," was magnified a hundredfold every weekend in fraternity parking lots. Not that people were happily screwing in the backseat; no, couples were more often than not telling dirty jokes in double-date situations, or endlessly necking. The energy was all in labyrinthine repressions. The guys were, almost without exception, hung up on the whore/virgin duality, eager to fuck anything that "walked," but at the same time only wanting to be seen, on a regular basis, with a pretty WASP popular-sorority pin-up who, in order to maintain her status, had to be a "prick teaser." Beyond the university, as if in a murky ghetto, were the "town girls," who, like the nursing students at Saint Francis Hospital in Indianapolis, had "easy" reputations. But they were hard to find.

By spring 1956, my grades were so low that I was put on probation for a semester. At that time, I made a simple but, in the long run, crucial decision: I would not go back to Indianapolis to spend the summer and my probation-semester with my tail between my legs at home. I would stay in Bloomington, move out of the fraternity, and get a job. I think that if I had gone back to Indianapolis at that point, my life would have sunk into mediocrity for good.

I moved into a two-bedroom apartment off campus with a couple of Korean War vets, history majors, only haphazardly studious, but older and pretty worldly. They regarded fraternities as beneath discussion. For about a year, I sold men's clothing at the Block Department Store at the edge of campus, and associated with old fraternity buddies, playing a lot of all-night poker, but also meeting psychology and philosophy students, and reading books like Wilson's *Outsider,* and poetry by e.e. cummings and Dylan Thomas. I had initially been brought into the fraternity by a slightly older high-school friend, Lee Lacy, a jazz drummer who seemed to be headed for a career in the world of the big bands. By the spring of 1957, Lacy had also moved out of the Phi Delt house and was playing with the Wayne Luby band. More and more I began to hang out with bohemian art-oriented students, some of whom lived in a rooming house called "Wino Junction." On the weekends we drank and jammed at The Stardust off the square in downtown Bloomington, while during the week we ate pizza and drank beer in Nick's English Hut. One night at the end of a poker game, someone owed me ten dollars he didn't have, so he offered me two paintings instead. One of the paintings was of a man and a woman, and someone had punched a hole between the man's lips and stuck a cigarette in. To get the canvas repaired, I looked up its painter, a graduate student named Bill Paden, who more or less introduced me to the visual arts and left-wing politics.

When I enrolled again in school I became a philosophy major, which enabled me to take literature courses as electives. I took an Introduction to Twentieth-century American Poetry course (from E.A. Robinson to Karl Shapiro) with Sam Yellen, writing my term paper on Robinson Jeffers' "Tower beyond Tragedy," and several creative-writing workshops with Yellen and Josephine Piercy. Both were sweet, undemanding, and encouraging professors, exactly the kind of people I needed to be around as I slowly swam out of a massive life confusion. I stopped working at Blocks, and got a job two nights a week at the piano-bar in the Dandale, little more than a steak house, but in those days the classiest place in Bloomington. I met a manic Shakespeare-drenched graduate student named Gene Koretz who was looking for a roommate, and moved into his roomy, bohemian apartment, where we had parties every weekend. Philosophy was going in one ear and out the other, but poetry was sticking. In the fall of 1958 I met several people who were seriously involved with contemporary poetry, and who, overnight it seemed, introduced me to the poets who have become my friends and peers over several decades, as well as to the twentieth-century European-American avant-garde tradition.

Jack and Ruth Hirschman were a dashing, gregarious couple from New York City who, over the following year, seemed to pull a string which released from the sky itself, Rimbaud, Mayakovsky, Lorca, Rilke, Joyce, Henry Miller, and Djuna Barnes. They also put me in contact with Robert Kelly, Jerry Rothenberg, and David Antin, friends from their CCNY days, before Jack became a graduate student at Indiana University in comparative literature. The Hirschmans also invited me to read English versions of St. John Perse in their triannual bilingual poetry reading series, called Babel, and got across to me that if I wanted to write meaningful poetry I had to become aware of world poetry, not just the poets in Yellen's introductory course.

At about the same time, I met Mary Ellen Solt, the wife of history Professor Leo Solt, who had taken a course with R.P. Blackmur in the summer "School of Letters," and had written a paper on William Carlos Williams and the American Idiom. Blackmur suggested that she show it to Williams, and a week later Williams had called Mary Ellen and invited her to Rutherford, telling her that she was the first person to really understand what he had been doing for years. Through Williams, Mary Ellen was put in contact with Louis Zukofsky, Robert Creeley, and Cid Corman. By the fall of 1958, I had become an associate editor of *Folio,* a literary magazine published by the English Department; the following spring the editor quit, and I offered to take his place. When my offer was accepted, I immediately wrote to all of the Hirschmans' and Mary Ellen Solt's writer friends, as well as to Allen Ginsberg and Robert Duncan, and on the basis of what they contributed, along with translations of Pablo Neruda, Karl Krolow, Ingeborg Bachmann, César Vallejo, and Vladimir Mayakovsky, began to assemble what I called "the NEW *Folio.*"

At this time I also began to drive to New York City over vacations and holidays, and like countless aspiring artists before me, to "knock on doors." Allen Ginsberg came to the door of his Tenth Street flat and told me he would talk with me if I would buy him a hamburger. I did, downstairs in the luncheonette, and he talked nonstop for an hour about Shelley and Mayakovsky. Then he told me to go meet Herbert Huncke and tell him Allen had sent me. I knocked, and was met by a gentle face from the pit who invited me in to a living room in which several people were silently camped out on battered furniture. "We're cooking a poem, man," Huncke said, "com'ere." He led me into the kitchen and opened the oven door. There it was! a typed poem on a sheet of paper turning brown around the edges in a 350° oven. Huncke closed the door and shuffled back into the living room, me following. Still no one said anything. After hanging around for a few minutes, I decided that I was not hungry, and slipped out.

While I was enthusiastic for something to finally commit myself, I was terribly innocent and utterly unaware of how many English Department professors felt about the grey, academic *Folio* being turned into a vehicle for "Beat" and "Black Mountain" poetries. After the second issue came out in the winter of 1960, at the instigation of the faculty advisor, Robert G. Kelly, the Department removed the *Folio* funds from the following year's budget, ending the magazine after twenty-seven years of publication. My sin, odd as it may seem today, had been in trying to print Allen Ginsberg's poem "Paterson," which contained the words "shit" and "fart," and a long section from Zukofsky's work-in-progress on Shakespeare (published a few years later as *Bottom: On Shakespeare*). Kelly had passed the Zukofsky essay around and no one could understand any of it; they therefore decided that it was meaningless and should not appear in "their" magazine. In both cases, in order to save the magazine, I had compromised, explained the situation to the writers, and received other work from them, which Kelly allowed to be published. Regardless of my cooperation, the message had gotten around that the barbarians were at the gates. Ironically, the chair, James Work, was a Swift scholar, and Kelly considered himself an expert on Joyce. The fact that neither of these professors would allow *Folio* to print the Ginsberg and Zukofsky work indicates that although their backgrounds should have amply prepared them to be able to accept this material, they were irrationally against the "new" when it appeared unbacked by the critical establishment.

Hirschman said: "they hate metaphors," and I quickly began to realize that many of the English Department professors were even less sympathetic to the poetry that was exciting me than my fraternity brothers would have been! I was in a very delicate situation, because I had entered the English literature M.A. program with only a few courses in English and

American literature, and in less than a year would be facing the same professors across the table for M.A. "orals" who had killed *Folio*. One day Yellen called me into his office, and told me that there was no way that I could pass my orals. "They will be laying for you," he said, "and the thing for you to do is to take an M.A. degree that does not involve orals, and then get out of here." I decided to switch to an M.A.T. (Master of Arts in Teaching), which involved courses in educational philosophy and two months of student teaching. As my thesis advisor, Yellen arranged for me to submit a manuscript of poetry, and, with graduation in sight, helped me to land an instructorship with the University of Maryland's Far Eastern Division, where I would teach composition and literature courses to American military personnel stationed in Japan, Taiwan, and Korea.

I had initially contacted the University of Maryland in the hopes of being sent to their European division, in order to spend some time in Spain. I had started to study Spanish on my own, in 1958, upon discovering real discrepancies between different versions of the same Neruda poems. Tasting Spanish, as it were, made me aware that Mexico was only several hitchhiking days away. By this time, I had also, via Kelly and Rothenberg, met Paul Blackburn who was quite familiar with contemporary Latin-American literature, and had translated some Octavio Paz poems for *Evergreen Review* 8, the "*Ojo de Mexico*" issue. On a June morning, in 1959, my father dropped my trumpet-player friend, Don Eggert, and me off at the southern Indianapolis city limits, and as he turned around, we faced the oncoming traffic with held-out thumbs.

I suppose that everyone wants to conceive of their lives as having a somewhat conscious developmental pattern, in which various blocks are met and removed, with, for Americans, the sky being the limit. In my own case, I feel that I lived underwater until my early twenties at which time, via poetry, I broke the surface and began to teach myself how to swim. For me, such action was peristaltic for years; the tension that I experienced as a teenager between parental restrictions and the lure of an expressive freedom via jazz, was, until the late 1970s, replayed in countless variations on expansion and contraction—a fitful going out of myself, followed by a fitful drawing back in. What I would call my creative anguish during the late 1950s to the late 1970s was a simultaneous desire to be outside of myself via translation, and participation in transpersonal systems (Blakean archetypal figures, the I Ching, primitive mythologies, etc.), and a counterdesire to uncover and evaluate these "underwater" years that seems to have culminated in the sadomasochistic embrace of the fraternity complex. I did not want to give up the outward for the inward, or put another way, the "other" for the background-coagulated "self" (or vice versa), and I think my attempt to not allow either "side" a clear victory resulted in my relatively long apprenticeship to the art of poetry.

*

The two summer trips to Mexico, in 1959 and 1960, made me feel that for the most part I had spent my life heretofore in the lobby of a hospital, not knowing whether to present myself for some sort of miraculous surgery or to simply stand up and leave. Mexico was the international gate, and when I passed through, it was, indeed, like being reborn—I had no language, and hardly any preparation for the plethora of odors, sights, tastes, or the Amerindian-Spanish presence of death that seemed to seep and yawn from the natural as well as man-made world. Indiana seemed dead, finished, *over,* an empty porcelain receptacle; in contrast, Mexico was a ripe wound, in whose depth stirred a still-sensible continuity with the deep past, as well as with the visible wretchedness of the human condition. A piece of meat in a nonrefrigerated butcher shop, so covered with flies that it looked as if it was wearing a black fur bonnet, was ghastly *and* wonderful all at once, a revelation of the grotesque exuberance and decay of the planet that had been hidden in Indiana behind a facade of sterile and brutal masculine assertion.

The first summer I spent most of my time bumming around Mexico City, ending up broke in Acapulco (where I briefly worked as an assistant bartender in a third-rate hotel until one of the staff confided to me that what looked like chicken on one of our lunch plates was actually buzzard). After a few weeks, I had less than two dollars left, and I decided rather than trying to borrow money or telegram my parents, I would just spend it and forget about tomorrow. I recall sitting down with a large, grilled *huachinango,* and a bottle of Corona, in one of the beach-cabana restaurants on Caletilla Beach. As I finished my "last meal," I noticed that a pretty blonde woman was watching me across the room. She turned out to be an American coed from the Bronx; she was sick of hanging out with her girlfriends and proposed that she rent us a hotel room on a romantic cove down the beach. We spent several very enjoyable weeks together and then got a ride with some of her friends back to the States.

The second summer I rode down to Chapala, Mexico, in the back of a truck, and spent the rest of

the summer there, studying Spanish and working on translations of Neruda's poetry from his *Residencias en la Tierra I* and *II.* I was determined to eat "real" Mexican food, and so, in the middle of July, gave most of my remaining money to the woman who ran a kind of truck-stop diner, and asked her to feed me for the next month. The food was awful and I was a fool to force myself to eat it (I acutely recall reading Hart Crane's Mexican poems over plates of foul-smelling fish). In a few weeks I turned curb-yellow and could keep nothing on my stomach. A local doctor informed me that I had infectious hepatitis, and gave me some medicine that made me hallucinate. With my remaining money, I bought a third-class bus ticket to Tijuana. At the point we hit the desert sun, roaches swarmed out of the bus ceiling down into our seats. I made it to Pacific Palisades where friends from Bloomington, the painter James McGarrell and his wife, Ann, had rented a house for the summer. I rested there two weeks, then hitched back to Indiana via San Francisco and Chicago.

I returned with most of the poems that went into my first (privately published) collection, *Mexico & North* (Tokyo, 1962). The poems still to come centered upon my first marriage in the spring of 1961 to Barbara Novak, from Logansport, Indiana, who was receiving her B.A. in sociology that spring. At the end of the wedding party, at 3:00 A.M., drunk and exhausted, I wandered out into the Bloomington night and stood in a vacant lot for a long time, knowing that we had made a mistake. While we genuinely liked each other, we lacked a deep and vital connection, and in the back of my mind I glimpsed

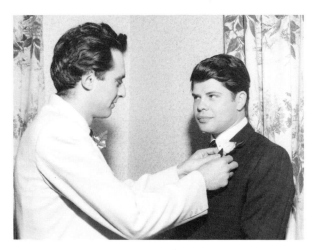

Jack Hirschman putting a carnation through Clayton Eshleman's buttonhole at the marriage of Clayton Eshleman and Barbara Novak, Logansport, Indiana, 1961

that by marrying Barbara I was refusing to let go of Indiana. Somehow I would take Indiana with me, everywhere, no matter where, for the rest of my life, as if it were a stinger broken off and embedded in me. How could I blame Barbara for this? I could not—but I sensed that she was much closer to my own parental background than she was to the life I was attempting to connect with—or had Barbara, as a "sister life," moved me to become aware of something I could not yet *see*—could sense only, unseeing. . . A month before the wedding, I had written, as Section 3 of "Prothalamion":

> as you move
> something ghostly
> moves beside
> me faint
> compassionate
> breath a
> child's breathing
> woman's mea-
> sure of bread
> depth, kneading
> meat & grain
> yellows &
> the reds, dust
> & the Mexican
> flower borne
> down to me
> root & vein
> a river you are
> in your slow &
> undersucking
> ways a shy
> girl of
> twenty-one, easily
> bruised &
> aching for the gamy
> love I'm
> burning with to
> make you
> list with children
> light as
> a reed bending to
> water, sails
> full you beau-
> tiful
> figure-head you
> soft
> horny woman o
> sing
> in a high
> voice o-
> riole

III

My move to Japan, in the fall of 1961, had under it an intuition that only in cultural isolation could I discover what kind of poetry I wanted to write. The temptation was to move to NYC and become part of an artistic "scene." There was a loosely knit circle of poets I felt I belonged with, and it included Kelly (then, with George Economou, editing *Trobar* magazine and books), Rothenberg (editing the Hawk's Well Press, and a tiny magazine, *Poems from the Floating World*), as well as Antin, Armand Schwerner, Diane Wakoski, and the slightly older Blackburn and Jackson Mac Low. What brought us together was an interest in experimental European and Latin-American poetries, surrealism (Neruda as well as Breton), occult systems (Jungian psychology, the I Ching, the goddess lore in Graves's *White Goddess*), and a sense that via certain North American predecessors, such as Whitman, Williams, Pound, Stein, Zukofsky, and Olson, the road was still an "open" one. We were not interested in irony, closed forms, or decorative art (the "*New Yorker* poem"). At the same time, we did not constitute a "movement" or a "group," and all of us have to this day remained peripheral to mainstream, textbook-anthology American poetry, dominated by the Lowell-Plath-Berryman "Confessionalism" of the 1960s and its academic imitators.

My first teaching assignment in the Far East was in Tainan, Taiwan; I arrived the night before the first classes, no textbooks were on hand, so I read to the GIs out of a Taiwanese pirated edition of Henry Miller's *Black Spring* for a week. While in Tainan, I tried to complete the "Mexico & North" manuscript that Kelly and Economou had offered to publish as a Trobar book that winter (they ultimately refused to do this, and I paid for the printing of five hundred copies myself in Tokyo that winter). The manuscript was in effect finished, but I was still involved with it, probably because of my initial reservations about our marriage, and an incident right after the marriage had made me aware of the manuscript's limitations. While on our honeymoon in Oaxaca, Barbara discovered that she was pregnant, and we had immediately returned to Mexico City where she had an abortion. Neither of us wanted a child right away, but we were both upset that our marriage had begun shadowed by this event. Walking down the road in Tainan one day, I spotted a kitten in the ditch, worm-infested and nearly dead. I brought it home, swabbed out its eyes, and tried to keep it alive by feeding it milk through a dropper. It died a week later, and in my mind became associated with the foetus aborted in Mexico. When I attempted to write about these two experiences, Barbara became very upset and insisted that I not publish such writing. The episode was a crucial one in several ways: it had raised the thorny matter of what was private, personal, and public; it indicated that Barbara and I had incompatible ideas regarding freedom and commitment in art; and it got me the first of a number of remarkable letters from Paul Blackburn, who turned out to be, by far, my most valuable correspondent over the next three years. After I had sent him a draft of the controversial poem, he wrote to Barbara, and explained at length why it was important that she support my working with anything that engaged me. While she respected Paul, she was not persuaded, and I never did publish the poem.

My second assignment was teaching composition courses at Tachikawa Air Base outside of Tokyo. We rented a small Western-style house in Musashi-Koganei, and in my spare time, I studied Suzuki's writing on art and Zen Buddhism, Whitman's 1855 edition of *Leaves of Grass,* and what had been published of Olson's *Maximus Poems.* I realized that if I wanted to experience Japan I had to disconnect from the University of Maryland, and when Gary Snyder and Joanne Kyger passed through on their way to India, they explained that if we wanted to move to Kyoto we could make a living teaching English as a foreign language. We visited Kyoto for the first time that December and were delighted with the city. It was snowing when we emerged from the train station, and the taxi ride, along the river through the old entertainment quarter, passing temple after temple, was so magical that we decided then and there to move the following summer. In contrast to Tokyo which had been 70 percent rebuilt after the war, Kyoto was intact, and still had an air of medieval charm.

I was first really hit by the extent of my confusion and unworked-out relationship with my background when I spent my last two-month assignment for Maryland alone in Seoul, Korea, the spring of 1962. I couldn't concentrate on reading poetry, but I couldn't justify not reading poetry. Part of me wanted to get involved with new women, and another part wanted to be faithful to the marriage as well as to what I was beginning to perceive were responsibilities for having committed myself to poetry. Given my "G-13," or Major status via Maryland's contract with the U.S. Army, I was housed in the Strategic Air Command compound in a building that the career-officer residents had turned into a combined gambling lodge, nightclub, and whorehouse. While I find it amusing today to see myself sitting in bed trying to understand Rilke's *Duino Elegies* while guys chased

their Korean girlfriends down the hall in their underwear, at the time it was sheer consternation, and after several weeks of it, I went out and picked up a middle-aged whore in old army clothing who stole my billfold while we grappled in a foul hotel room. I forced myself to complete an essay on discovering Neruda and Mexico which appeared as the postface to my Neruda translations, published the following year by George Hitchcock's Amber House Press in San Francisco but printed in Kyoto.

With the Snyders' help, Barbara found us an apartment in the Okumura house about a half-mile up the hill that partially rings the east side of Kyoto. We had two *tatami*-rooms (with an old-fashioned *kotatsu*— a table raised over the floor with leg room under the floor below it), a tiny kitchen, and a glassed-in back porch that I turned into a workroom. Outside was a small overgrown backyard with a persimmon tree and a teahouse reserved for use by the Japanese scholar/translator Donald Keene when he was in town. We lived there for a year, and then moved down the road to slightly larger and more reasonable quarters (fifteen dollars a month, in contrast to twenty-five dollars a month at the Okumuras) in the Ibuki house, across from Tsuruginomiya (a Shinto grounds with several shrines), where we lived until our departure for the States in the summer of 1964.

Kyoto was an ideal place to isolate oneself in. It had no American military bases or personnel, and very few foreigners. At the same time, it had been discovered by a few American writers in the 1950s— namely Gary Snyder and Cid Corman—and by the early 1960s there were a couple dozen foreign writers and artists—mainly potters—in residence there. It was possible to not see anyone during the week, and then go to a rambunctious Saturday night party at the Snyders (where Alan Watts or Allen Ginsberg might be visiting). In 1963 I helped my old painter friend Bill Paden move there from NYC, and the poet Frank Samperi and his wife arrived.

We became close friends with Will Petersen (who made stone prints in a shack by his house in Yase) and his wife, Ami, who was a potter. Petersen and Cid Corman both studied Noh dancing and singing with a local Noh family, and working together, or with Japanese friends, produced several splendid translations of Noh plays while I was there. Petersen introduced me to the word "apprenticeship," by describing a sixty-year-old bonsai gardener as an apprentice to a seventy-five-year-old one. Until then it had never dawned on me that one might learn an art from an older living artist. On another occasion, as he boarded a bus after we had been chatting on a street corner, Petersen shouted at me: "The caterpil-

*The author (right) with the painter William Paden
(second from left) and two Japanese students,
Shirahama, Japan, 1964*

lar on the leaf repeats to thee thy mother's grief!"
The statement amazed me, and upon discovering that
it was a couplet from Blake, I bought Blake's *Complete
Writings* at the Maruzen Bookstore in downtown
Kyoto and began to struggle through them. I tried to
read *Jerusalem* from scratch, and literally got headaches trying to penetrate its symbolism. So I also
bought a copy of Northrop Frye's book on Blake,
Fearful Symmetry, and read it slowly twice over the
following year. I once passed out while reading
Blake's *Book of Urizen,* and in an attempt to get at the
forces that seemed to be moving around in me, I
invented archetypal figures, such as Yorunomado and
Niemonjima, based on Blake's Los and Enitharmon. I
also brought caterpillars into the house, and tried to
raise them in a shoebox filled with mulberry leaves.
While I was in Kyoto, caterpillars and spiders became
totemic, numinous images of the creative process,
twin aspects of the artist's relationship to his body
and to his materials.

I had begun to correspond with Corman when
he was in Kyoto in 1959, and I was still in Bloomington. While aggressively pedagogical, he was also very
precise and awesomely dedicated to the art of poetry.
He returned to Kyoto at about the same time we
moved there. Cid would leave his room in the
afternoon, browse the bookstores and art galleries,
eat supper downtown, and then with books and
correspondence retire to the Muse coffee shop until
around 11:00 P.M. If you wanted to see Cid, you
called on him in his "office" booth there. Over the
next two years, I dropped in once or twice a week,
and learned the rudiments of translation and magazine editing. We translated a few of José Hierro's

poems together, and Cid went over the first two
drafts of my ongoing Vallejo translation. I watched
him assemble issues of *Origin* magazine, and would
often walk all the way home from the Muse (about
one hour), late at night, just to digest what Cid had
said.

At first in Kyoto, I tried to imitate the kind of
poetry Corman seemed to be publishing in *Origin,* but
doing so was like compressing my body into my eyes,
and my eyes into a few, mostly factual lines. After five
hours of evading what was actually on my mind, I
would end up with something that falsified my
situation and the blocked energy I had put into those
five hours. I began to feel that Corman was watching
me every minute in which I was writing. He was,
indeed, an unyielding advocate of what he practiced,
but I had set him like a Nevermore Alter Ego Raven
on my shoulder, and once I realized this, I was able to
start exploring the kind of poetry I felt that I had to
write, which went against Cid and *Origin.* It was closer
to what Cid called "the sick poetry of Ginsberg," in
that it began to unpack my impacted past and
confront my unresolved identity via some of the
"unmentionable" lower body areas that still today,
for many poets, fill the warehouses of repression.

My apprenticeship, at the beginning of 1964,
consisted of:

1. visits to Corman at the Muse, and
    correspondence with a wide range of
    poets, including Hirschman, Rothen-
    berg, Thomas Merton, W.S. Merwin,
    Blackburn, Hitchcock, and Solt.

2. working on my own poems every morn-
    ing, then after lunch motorcycling
    downtown to the Yorunomado coffee
    shop where I would translate Vallejo
    until going off to teach English at the
    Matsushita Electric Company, an hour
    south of Kyoto.

3. after supper, several hours of reading in
    a neighborhood coffee shop.

4. besides short poems, I was increasingly
    caught up in an interminable, unfo-
    cused long poem, "The Tsuruginomiya
    Regeneration," which had evolved out
    of my being unable to my satisfaction
    to complete a "Prothalamion" for
    Blackburn's marriage to Sara Golden.
    The only poem that I wrote in Kyoto
    that really pleased me, "The Book of
    Yorunomado," which I subsequently
    rewrote four times over the next twenty

years, was a section from this four-hundred-page work.

*

I also found a secret place to spend time in alone, an old bell shrine (missing its bell) off the road in the woods further up the hill. I went there about once a week the last year I was in Kyoto, and sitting on a crossbeam, leaning against a post, I would look out across the city into the western hills and try to recall scenes from my childhood and adolescence. One day I suddenly remembered that my father used to whip me with a beech branch in the basement behind the furnace, and I saw some of the ways that this punishment had set me up to accept beatings in the fraternity. I remembered how much I had wanted to have sex with the Woodring girl next door when I was about twelve, and how I would stand by the fence and hold onto the pickets so tightly I nearly cut open my hands. I was so desperate and confused, I once, in my bedroom, rolled over my pet dog and was considering penetrating her when my father suddenly opened the door (he pretended not to notice what was going on). I also recalled being in Sunday School and hearing a story about a heroic dog in the war, and then asking the teacher if the dog would go to heaven. No, I was told, there are no dogs in heaven. After this experience, I could not sleep at night, and became so frightened that I would cry out; my mother would awaken and come in to my bed and hold my hand until I fell asleep. Most of such memories seemed to just fall out of the sky and lie at my feet inert. I suppose that I should have been grateful to have them at hand at all, but I also felt that I had to assimilate them in my poetry. I was slowly getting through my head that the point was not to imitate other poets but to be inspired by what their poetry made possible, and to work with the nonpoetic, since what seemed to be poetic had been done by others and belonged to them.

In spite of my dissatisfaction with most of my writing, I was aware that I was in the process of changing my mental makeup. In the fall of 1962, I had a "visionary" experience while cycling home from the Snyders late one Sunday afternoon—everything began to transform itself before my eyes (the motorcycle became an ox, the handlebars, horns), and after parking and starting to circumambulate Nijo Castle, I saw about thirty feet over my head a huge (human-sized) red spider constructing a web. The Snyders had previously offered me LSD and I had refused it, and I have always suspected that Joanne put some LSD in my tea that afternoon; regardless,

the "vision" had a great deal of significance to me, and felt like a totemic offering at the time, confirming on one level at least that I was not simply wasting my time writing poetry. A year later, I began to have migraine headaches while working on poems, and after a couple of weeks the pain transformed itself in the following way: right before falling asleep, I would hear the sound of a bell between my eyes, and then the sound of a window being slammed shut. These peculiar events would then be followed by the same nightmare: I would be hurtling through a winding, smoking tunnel at breakneck speed, expecting to see my father's face at the end. I never did, as a matter of fact, and after several repetitions, I never had the dream again. But the important thing was that it was of a different order than regular dreams, and suggested to me that I had begun to activate a part of my unconsciousness that might provide metaphors for poetry.

*

We returned to the States in the summer of 1964, traveling on an immigrant boat to save money (I found a good spot at the stern and read Kafka's diaries over the eighteen-day journey). Jack Hirschman, then teaching at UCLA, met us in San Pedro. We spent several weeks with the Hirschmans, and I realized that things had changed between us. I was no longer a worshipful acolyte, and Jack, mesmerized by the life and writings of Antonin Artaud, was translating Artaud, smoking a lot of dope, and dictating hundreds of hours of monologue into a tape recorder on the floor of his workroom. He seemed to be searching for a deeper continuity than before but he also seemed lost.

I felt lost too, but in a different way; I wanted to live in NYC, but I had no idea of how to make a living. I was obsessed with doing accurate versions of Vallejo's ninty-five *Poemas Humanos,* and not only were they beyond my knowledge of Spanish, the editions I was working with were full of errors. The only way to resolve that situation seemed to be not only to find a Spanish-oriented cotranslator, but also to go to Lima, Peru, and arrange with Vallejo's widow to be allowed to inspect the poet's typescript as he left it when he died in 1938 (the book being posthumously edited and published by Georgette Vallejo). But I had no way of making a living in Peru either, and the people I had asked to help me either knew Spanish no better than I did, or if they were Spanish speakers misled me with interpretations of expressions they didn't really understand. In September, I succeeded, with Blackburn's help, in getting a small monthly grant from the Organization of American States Office in Washington, D.C. to translate selections from Latin-American authors that they would send me once a month for six months. We moved back to Bloomington, and Barbara got a job at the Indiana University bookstore.

After she went off to work in the morning, I would sit down in my workroom at the back of our little house on South Fess. In a way, I was still staring out the window at my childhood backyard, in a limbo between being a student poet and an accomplished one. I wrote a seventy-page prose-poem, "The Book of Eternal Death," and several more sections for "The Tsuruginomiya Regeneration," of which "The Book of Coatlicue" was the best, and appeared in Margaret Randall's bilingual magazine out of Mexico City, *El Corno Emplumado.* With several local poets, including Daphne Marlatt, I formed a talking/reading group, and several of us drove up to Detroit to visit the newly formed Artist's Workshop, directed by John Sinclair. That spring, I took LSD with Daphne and her husband in McCormick's Creek State Park. I saw Barbara's face spread out across the inside of the roof of an old barn, as I lay on the floor staring up. She had Chinese eyes, and her mouth leaked, then poured, blood out of which an infant twisted. In view of events that would take place in Lima the following year, the "vision" was oddly prophetic. We found out that Barbara was pregnant that spring, and I decided that I had to go to Lima and try to inspect Vallejo's papers.

Barbara flew to Cuzco, and spent a few weeks with one of our Latin-American friends, while I flew, bused, and hitchhiked from Indianapolis to Lima, arriving with three hundred dollars to my name, and knowing no one. In a pleasant neighborhood, we found a small apartment that was reasonable, as it was next to a noisy gradeschool playground. I went to the North American Peruvian Cultural Institute (NAPCI) looking for teaching, and ended up being asked by the Director to edit a bilingual literary magazine that NAPCI would publish. They would pay me two hundred fifty dollars a month, and loan me a typewriter for home use. My only restriction, I was informed, was that the magazine could not publish political material, as NAPCI was an "apolitical" organization. I called the magazine *Quena* (after a Quechuan word for a one-holed flute traditionally carved from a dead beloved's shinbone), and wrote a flock of letters to writers and translators. On my way to Peru, I had met the Costa Rican poet José Coronel Urtecho, at lunch with Pablo Antonio Cuadra and Ernesto Cardenal in Managua, and he agreed to translate Olson's "The Kingfishers" and "Projective

Verse." Within a few weeks I had what looked like a three-hundred-page first issue under way.

Quena #1 never appeared, for the following reason: the Peruvian poets I met in Lima urged me to print Javier Heraud, so I sent his book to Blackburn, who quickly translated fifteen pages. Heraud had been murdered by the Peruvian army in 1963 while involved in guerilla activity in the jungle. He had become a Communist while in Cuba the year before, but the poetry Blackburn had translated for *Quena* had been written when Heraud was an apolitical young man in Lima several years earlier. It was Machado-like nature poetry about trees and rivers. The Director asked to see the manuscript right before it went to the printer, and kept it mysteriously for a week; he then informed me that I had to pull the Heraud, because the poet had become a political figure. When I protested and investigated the matter, I found out that the manuscript had been sent to the American ambassador, and that NAPCI was really a USIS (United States Information Service) "front" organization, "apolitical" in appearance only. I refused to take the material out, and was fired on the spot. I then found out that by Peruvian law I was entitled to three months' severance pay, and we lived on that, and borrowed money from the Blackburns, to stay on a few more months in Lima, while I continued my work on Vallejo and Barbara prepared to give birth.

One of the people I met in Lima was the American Maureen Maurer (now Maureen Ahern), who had a Ph.D. from the local San Marcos University, and was eager to respond to my questions about translation problems with Vallejo. Were it not for Maureen's efforts on behalf of Vallejo in English, my 1968 translation of *Poemas Humanos* would not have been published. For not only had my *Quena* project ended in disaster, but my work on Vallejo had been thwarted at every stage by Georgette, the poet's French widow, who pretending to protect her husband's archive and name actually created endless complications that kept the poet's work either unavailable or in pirated, error-riddled editions. After denying me access to the worksheets, she decided that she would choose a handful of poems that I would be allowed to translate and publish. Since I had been working on the entire book for over four years, and now had a pretty good seventh draft, it was impossible to cooperate with her, and I began to go out to Maureen's chicken farm, thirty minutes outside of Lima, two evenings a week where we went over all my work to date. On February 26, Barbara gave birth to Matthew Craig Eshleman.

It seemed as if I was being tested by nether

On a mule in the Peruvian Andes, 1965

powers every time I turned around in Lima. One evening when I was to go out to the Maurers (and spend the night, so Maureen and I could work the next morning), her husband called and cancelled. An hour later, Barbara began to hemorrhage, and suddenly I thought I was watching her bleed to death (had I gone to the Maurers, I believe she would have died). I raced out into the street shouting for help, and then rushed into the facing apartment house, pounding on doors. One opened, a doctor appeared, and we bundled Barbara into the back of his VW and rushed her to a clinic, where they saved her life.

The eight months in Peru were extremely important for me. I had been exposed to the "third world" in a political context, and lost my own apolitical innocence. I had spent days wandering the hideous Lima slums, and had made two trips to the Andes (one with Barbara, to Huancayo, for a weekend, and one with Peace Corps workers on mules for two weeks in the Andes east of Ica). I had written a collection of poetry and prose pieces about all of this, called *Walks,* and kept a meticulous journal, *On the Mules Sent from Chavín,* while I was in the Andes. I had also translated a long attack on Neruda for Lawrence Ferlinghetti, and in the process of trying to write a defense of Neruda discovered his pathetic Stalinesque poetry of the late 1940s. And: I had become a father, though I did not feel very much like one. By

becoming a poet, I had resisted becoming an adult, or at least one in the image of my father. Yet at thirty-one, I still felt like a son, an old, tired son, performing what seemed to be an endless excavation.

IV

Upon returning to Bloomington, Barbara and Matthew stayed with our friends the Nystroms, and I slept on D. Alexander's couch. In 1964 Denis Kelly and I had translated together a small collection of the poetry of Aimé Césaire, and now, along with a long essay by Corman on Zukofsky (accepted for *Quena,* but still unpublished), I published my first two "Caterpillar" books, run-off on a mimeograph machine and then stapled and taped. This time I was determined to live in NYC, and the Blackburns offered me Paul's workroom in the back of their Seventh Street railroad flat to stay in while I looked for a job and our own apartment. Barbara and Matthew went back to Barbara's home in Logansport until it was possible for them to join me.

Once I got to NYC, I nervously began to seek out a new relationship. I was less interested in one-night stands than in meeting someone who excited me physically and soulfully. At Joel Oppenheimer's wedding party, upstairs at Max's Kansas City, I found myself dancing with an attractive woman a bit older than I was named Adrienne. As we jogged about, she

*With wife Barbara and newborn
Matthew Craig Eshleman, Indianapolis, 1966*

shouted through the blare, "What do you think the most important thing in life is?" I shot back, "Having a child," to which she responded: "No! It's an orgasm!" An hour later I was walking her down to the deep Lower East Side where, in a building that looked as if it were under siege, she lived with her two small children. She had left her husband, the photographer Garry Winograd, several years before, and had hid out to avoid an assault. During this time, she had gone into therapy with the Reichian-trained Alexander Lowen, and at the point I met her, she had finished therapy, and had the bristling aura of someone who had been through hell and come through into her own. We saw each other every evening for a week, and I knew that I had, in effect, left Barbara and Matthew.

I applied for an instructor's position at NYU's American Language Institute, to teach English as a foreign language, and was offered a one-year contract, at $5400. The Blackburns went on vacation, Barbara and Matthew arrived, and I broke my news to her. It was simply better than lying and prolonging a relationship that was dead. At the end of July, Adrienne and I went to Fire Island for a weekend. When we returned to NYC on June 26, I heard that Frank O'Hara had died, having been hit by a beach-buggy not far from the dune behind which we had been camping out.

In August, Adrienne and her kids went to Hydra, and I helped Barbara get settled on her own in the city. She was hired by the ALI at NYU, and through a new realtor friend, Barbara Beddoes, I found Barbara and Matthew a three-room apartment at Second Avenue and Eighteenth Street, and myself a room in the basement at 10 Banks Street. It was condemned for human habitation and filled to the ceiling with rubbish, but the landlord said I could have it for thirty-five dollars a month if I was willing to clean it out. I lived Japanese-style, on the floor, and showered at neighbors' as my bathtub drain had been filled up with concrete.

For the four years that Barbara, Matthew, and I were in NYC, I kept in contact with my son, spending an afternoon or two with him every week, and often taking him for the weekend. My leaving Barbara, however, had repercussions I had not counted on. The Zukofskys, who in their almost spectrally formal way had been friendly up to this point, cut me off when I informed them of what had happened. Other than for a few times that I dropped in unannounced, I was not invited for dinner at the Blackburns once during my first year in NYC. I found out later, at the point that Sara confided in me that she was going to leave Paul during their vacation at Aspen in the

summer of 1967, that my leaving Barbara had upset Sara because she unconsciously wanted to leave Paul.

I did make some new friends, however. I helped Jackson Mac Low, Michael Heller, and Robert Vas Dias get jobs at the ALI, and through Heller met Hugh Seidman. In reaction to a poem that she read at the Poetry Project at St. Marks, I wrote a letter to Diane Wakoski, which was the beginning of a strong friendship that has weathered all sorts of buffetings over the years. I had met the painters Leon Golub and Nancy Spero at Indiana University in the late 1950s, and we began to see each other again, generally through their gracious dinner invitations, in 1967. Through the Golub/Speros I met other painters, among whom Irving Petlin and Nora Jaffe have become dear friends. I also met and spent a lot of time with certain dancers and musicians, such as Elaine Summers, Jim Tenney, Carolee Schneemann, Malcom Goldstein, and Philip Corner. At that time, NYC was full of the heady atmosphere of experimentalism and collegial exchange that made all the arts feel like nodes in a forming/reforming constellation. The Vietnam War, which was beginning to infiltrate all of our lives and arts as an anti-imaginative pressure, rather than alienating us from each other became, in 1967 and 1968, an exasperating cohesive force: while it seemed to be a distraction from soul-making, it made us experience our own anger and gave us a rational public target to engage.

Most of the people mentioned above participated in an organization called "Angry Arts," which in 1968 must have had at least five hundred active artist-members. We attended mass meetings, as well as group sessions during which specific projects were mobilized. As one of the organizers of the poets, I was out on rented flatbed trucks, demonstrating in front of the Metropolitan Museum, as well as in Queens shopping malls. Our aim was to confront people with our outrage over the American aggression in the most potent ways we could imagine. In a 1967 issue of *Ramparts* magazine, we discovered horrifying photographs of napalm victims, and in New Rochelle I located the doctor who had taken them. He told me that he had photos that even *Ramparts* would not print, and I put two in my new magazine, *Caterpillar* 3/4, between poems by Allen Ginsberg and Aimé Césaire. We also had the doctor's photos blown up, and on our truck-bed "stage," we held them up high, and read poems and statements to, or *at*, unfriendly crowds who occasionally tried to pull us off the truck. One Sunday, twenty-three of us, dressed up, entered a High Mass at St. Patrick's Cathedral, with napalm-victim posters rolled up under our coats. One of us had apparently alerted the

*Newspaper photo of Eshleman (left) and an unidentified man (right) being escorted from
St. Patrick's Cathedral by a policeman for "disrupting Sunday mass. The group [of fifteen
men and eight women], arrested on charges of disturbing the peace, was protesting
statements made by Cardinal Spellman during his . . . Vietnam tour when he praised the
war effort and American soldiers."*

police, for as we stood up to unfurl the posters, we
were seized by two dozen plainclothes cops, and
hustled out to the waiting vans, and then locked up in
the "Tombs" for the night. Bailed out by sympathetic
supporters the next day, two of us saw our pictures
on the front page of the *New York Times.*

Of course the late 1960s was not only the period
of the Vietnam War (though I consider it to be the
most crucial formative force of the era)—it was also
the period of LSD, Aquarian astrology, student
revolution, feminism, black power, and encounter
groups. The realm many of us found ourselves
participating in, often with great intention, other
times willy-nilly, was electric with crossing positive
and negative poles. As if in defense against the
mayhem in the Far East, we found ourselves strolling
into Central Park for a Be-in, stoned and barefoot,
approaching a new Eden just around the corner. LSD
sucked one in to the irresolvable maelstrom of the
self, while encounter groups clawed one forth to toss
in the nets of interpersonal relations. It was a time of
terrible tearing, desperate attempts at healing, of
dropping emotional depth charges in one's own life
as well as in the lives of others (often whom one had

just met or would never see again!). Many were
simply eaten alive by the extent of the contradictions
in the field of force they found themselves in, while a
few others, such as Nancy Spero and Robert Duncan,
responded to the stress by creating major work.

Besides spending time with Matthew, to whom I
was extremely close in the late 1960s, and involving
myself in war protest, I was also in Reichian therapy,
starting *Caterpillar* magazine, completing the final
phase of my first Vallejo translation project, and
teaching at NYU. I got out of the Banks Street "hole"
in the fall of 1967, moving into a loft at the corner of
Grand and Greene Streets, partially fixed up by Jack
Boyce, the husband of Joanne Kyger at the time. My
rent went from thirty-five dollars to seventy-five
dollars a month, and I had a big, handsome, if
somewhat crude, space to live in. The Puerto Rican
"greasy spoon" below me is today the elegant
Chanterelle restaurant. Above me, on the third floor,
was a dapper glassblower, Ed Iglehart, who sold hash
pipes on Wall Street; above Ed was Jack Smith,
mainly known for his film *Flaming Creatures.*

After leaving Barbara, I realized that for the
second time in my life I had put myself through a

In New York City, 1968

prolonged period of anguish without doing anything about it for years (the first period being the fraternity years). Inspired by Adrienne's success with therapy, I read one of Alexander Lowen's books, *The Betrayal of the Body,* and had one session with him. Neither of us liked each other at all, so I wrote to Adrienne, on Hydra, and asked who was in back of Lowen. She responded by sending me her own copy of Reich's *Function of the Orgasm,* which I read in an afternoon, and followed up on by flying back to Indianapolis the next day and, for the first time, confronting my mother with the way I really felt about my life as *their son.* Upon returning to NYC, I called Dr. Sidney Handelman, the Reichian therapist Bill Paden had seen in the early 1960s, and went into therapy with him. As the therapy progressed, my hostility broke up into explosive anger, and I was able to recontact early painful events with bursts of emotion so that I knew how they felt. For most of 1968, I was involved in a sexually obsessive, emotionally destructive "romance" with Marie Benoit, a Macrobiotic, Scientologic actress, who at one point steered me into the

Martinique Hotel for several pointless and expensive months of Scientology. Once I saw that I had used Scientology to evade the very difficult last stages of Reichian therapy, I returned to therapy, and completed it in the spring of 1969.

The dynamic connecting of memory and emotion that Handelman encouraged had an effect on my poetry. My tendency in Japan had been to rewrite and rewrite, often sitting blocked before a line for hours. In the late 1960s, due to therapy, some remarks by Robert Duncan, and probably the volatile nature of the times, I stopped revising and started a new poem each time I sat down to write. I consciously worked on a more lively, shifting line, seeking a poetry that was responsible to self and world, a poetry in which there was a rapid, assimilative movement between the inside and the outside. On one hand, I was still working on a poetry of personal needs; on the other, I was picking up on something in the air that circulated in differing ways through the poetry of Vallejo, Artaud, Olson, Duncan, Kelly, and Rothenberg. It was as if, for all of us, the abyss had opened, revealing that it was, at once, the Pleroma, the deep and primitive past, Hell, and a pit in which world mythological bits glimmered. In August of 1969, I set myself the task of writing a long daily poem for one year based on a symbolic grid using the I Ching and zodiacal astrology. I also read Reich thoroughly at this time.

I followed up the first two "Caterpillar" books by bringing out eight more in 1966 and 1967, including small editions of Blackburn, Antin, Samperi, Mac Low, and myself, but I wasn't really set up to be a book publisher, so in the fall of 1967, I started *Caterpillar* magazine, which was to run twenty issues, over six years, averaging around two hundred pages per issue. Besides original and translated poetry, the magazine included an eclectic range of artists and thinkers, such as N.O. Brown, Leon Golub, James Tenney, Carolee Schneemann, and Stan Brakhage; there were special issues on Jack Spicer and Stephen Jonas, and the nineteenth issue printed Gary Snyder's ninety-nine-page letter to his sister on his 1962 trip to India. Robert Kelly was a contributing editor from the third to the twentieth issue. There was also a ten-part series, called "A Test of Translation," in which various poet-translators were asked to assemble differing versions of a single poem by such poets as Sappho, Catullus, Rilke, and Nerval, and to briefly comment on the merits/demerits of each version, focusing the reader on the translations and not on exegesis or extended evaluation. Over 250 artists and writers appeared in *Caterpillar,* which averaged a press run of 1500.

*

On New Year's Eve, 1968, Golub invited me to a party at the apartment of the art critic Max Kozloff. I spent most of the evening in the kitchen, talking with a gorgeous, imaginative woman named Caryl Reiter, and by the fall of that year, we had struck up a solid relationship that has continued and deepened over the years. Caryl moved in to the Greene Street loft, and I began to realize just how tired I was of living from month to month (I had quit my ALI job in the summer of 1968, and since then had met my expenses with a combination of little grants, selling parts of my literary archive, part-time teaching, and readings). Jim Tenney told me that a new art school, to be called the California Institute of the Arts, a kind of Black Mountain College with money, he said, was being formed outside of Los Angeles. I applied for teaching in the School of Critical Studies and partly through a misunderstanding was hired. The chair, Maurice Stein, thought I was not only a poet and editor, but an Abbie Hoffman-like radical.

When we met, Caryl was working in a design studio, doing commercial art work and free-lancing as a stylist for several photographers. She wanted to quit and study painting, and I encouraged her to. The opportunity for her to do this occurred at Cal Arts, where she studied with Alison Knowles in graphic design. She also studied for a year with R.B. Kitaj, then in residence at UCLA. Because we traveled a lot and her health was poor, she wasn't able to keep a fix on her work and decided to try her hand at jewelry making. She worked for several years as a designer for another jeweler and on her own at home.

Caryl and I moved to California the summer of 1970, renting a house in Sherman Oaks. The Disney family, which was sponsoring Cal Arts, also controlled the Board of Trustees, and they had refused to allow Stein to hire Herbert Marcuse. Stein, in reaction, lost interest in the school, and by the time we arrived we were greeted by a chaotic assembly of underpaid young faculty, drug-oriented students, and Stein in a Mickey Mouse T-shirt. Within two months, the Disneys fired him, and the school split down the middle between those of us who had to admit he had been a disaster as an administrator (and thus became unwilling supporters of Disney policy) and those who simply hated the Disneys and would defend Stein at any cost. By the spring of 1971, the president and provost had also been fired. I stayed on for the duration of my two-year contract, after which my school was more or less dismantled and most of us not rehired. While at Cal Arts I taught Blake, Reich, Eliot, and Crane seminars, along with creative-writing workshops. I also organized a visiting writer program, bringing to campus Kenneth Rexroth, Kelly, Corman, Theodore Enslin, and Joanne Kyger, among others.

Before the move to California, the health of both my parents deteriorated to such an extent that they sold the family house and moved into an old-age home north of the city. I helped them move, and during one visit had an extraordinary experience with my mother.

Soon after I started writing poetry in 1957, I met a slightly older couple, both painters, named George and Dolly Stewart, who lived in Indianapolis. I began to visit them, staying over for the weekend, without letting my parents, twenty minutes north of the Stewarts, know I was in town. They were warm, nourishing friends, and I only lost contact with them because I moved to Japan right before they moved to Chicago. While talking with my mother in the spring of 1969, I became curious as to where I had spent my second and third years. I knew where we were before and after this period. My mother's health and memory were failing, but she agreed: if we were going to find the place, it was now or never. We drove south to a neighborhood that had changed immensely in the

Caryl Reiter, 1965

Alan Breslaw

*Eshleman with wife Caryl and son, Matthew,
Logansport, Indiana, 1970*

past decade, and after driving around block after block, my mother said: stop. We were on Delaware Street, in front of a large, nondescript house. The place meant nothing to me, but since we were there, I thought I should at least go up and walk around it. My mother remained in the car. At the southeast corner, there was a public side-door, which I opened, to a staircase. Impulsively, I decided to climb, and as I ascended, I felt a strange, yet pleasant, kind of buoyancy. My god, I thought, she found it—and then, I nearly dropped in my tracks, for as my head came up to the level of the landing, I found myself staring at George and Dolly's door! A diagonal crack in the interior panel had been painted over, but it was still there.

My distressed mother could have been mistaken in regard to finding the house in which we lived when I was two—but regardless of that, she did lead me back to the place to which I had been magnetized, my chrysalis, as it were, at the point I broke free of college life in Bloomington and sought a new place in poetry. And if this was indeed the house we had moved to in 1936, where I would over the next two years learn the rudiments of speech, the overlay of chance and meaning elements involved suggested a pattern at work that I would probably never fully grasp.

My mother died in December 1970, and my father in June 1971. They left me a little unexpected money, so Caryl and I decided to go to Europe in the fall of 1973. *Caterpillar* had ended that spring (I had accomplished, I felt, what I set out to do, plus editing and typing up for the printer eight hundred pages of poetry and prose per year was too much work to do for more than five or six years); even more importantly, in terms of preparing for an extended trip, I had gone back to the mass of worksheets of the incomplete "Tsuruginomiya Regeneration" after my mother's death, and with massive cuts, honings, and additions, created a new, more focused, and shorter two-hundred-page "serial poem" called *Coils*, published by Black Sparrow Press in early 1973. It was my attempt to sieve Indiana through my life after leaving Indiana, and in an exhaustive self-portrait, both visionary and realistic, to work through the materials I had struggled with to gain a sense of imaginative manhood. It was on one level a brutal exposé of the much more brutal machismo engrained in my upbringing, and my journey through its venom toward a sense of reciprocity with woman; the book culminated in a "death and transfiguration," in which I set against the death of my mother the vision of the life I proposed to live with Caryl. I had been haunted for years by the fear that if I did not remember *and* reinvent my background, I would be doomed to circumambulate it for the rest of my life, and that if I allowed this to happen, all projects of a transpersonal nature would constantly be vexed by an imminent "return of Indiana."

I was also at a turning point with Vallejo. In 1968, after a bitter year of negotiations with Georgette Vallejo, Grove Press cleared the rights and published a bilingual edition of *Poemas Humanos/Human Poems*. I still had in worksheets a translation of the rest of Vallejo's European poetry, his sheaf of Spanish Civil War poems, completed shortly before his death. In 1971 I finally met someone I could work with and trust on a cotranslational basis, and over the next year, José Rubia Barcia, a Spaniard in the Spanish Department at UCLA, and I completed a translation of *Spain, Take This Cup From Me*, which Grove published in 1974. Barcia and I also decided to retranslate *Human Poems*, and we completed this work, based on accurate texts and new scholarship, in 1977, with the University of California Press publishing *César Vallejo: The Complete Posthumous Poetry*, in 1978. My work on Vallejo, thus, spanned nearly twenty years, and represents not only my apprenticeship period, but in terms of textual attention its greatest concentration. Vallejo taught me that only via the willingness to contradict myself could I create a poetic self and achieve an imaginative freedom, and offered me a complexity of viewpoint, made up of a triple Marxist-Christian-Indian crucifixion, that is more essential to twentieth-century world poetry than that of any North American poet.

*

We sublet the Montmartre apartment of the Brazilian film director Alberto Cavalcanti, and lived in Paris until the spring of 1974. While we met a number of European artists—most significantly the Syrian painter Marwan—we did not meet the contemporary French poet whose work has engaged me the most until he came to Los Angeles in 1976: Michel Deguy. With *Coils* behind me, I was faced with the perennial problem of breaking new ground, and in an attempt to get new material into my work, as well as get beyond a poetry dependent on personal life material, I began to do "portraits" of other artists, restricting myself to materials from their lives and work, somewhat in the same way that Browning developed his "dramatic monologues." I wrote "through" artists whose work had deeply moved me, and I worked on a tone, and imaginal registration that was both inspired and critical. I began my first portrait the second night we were in Paris, writing at a sidewalk cafe, through the painter Chaïm Soutine, with Caryl making editorial suggestions. From that point on, she has played an increasingly important

Caryl Eshleman

At Stonehenge, 1974

"Clay sculpture of Clayton Eshleman's head, by Caryl Eshleman," 1975

role as a reader/editor; she has helped me spot obscurity, nonsense, repetition, not as a supporter simply, but as an acutely responsive—I want to say—old-fashioned reader. She has made me aware of the subtle discrepancies between what I intend to say and what I do say. Her presence, in effect, brings home a memorable remark by Vincente Huidobro: "*inventa nuevo mundos pero cuida tu palabra*" ("invent new worlds but watch what you say").

Over the next year, I did portraits of Paul Celan, van Gogh, Charlie Parker, Hart Crane, Robert Duncan, and Artaud, with additional portraits of Francis Bacon, Wakoski, and Frida Kahlo, in subsequent years. In the winter of 1974, we had dinner with the Spanish translator Helen Lane, who was then living on a farm outside of Tursac, in the Dordogne region. She convinced us to take an apartment in her farm complex for the summer and spring of 1974.

I had been dimly aware of the Upper Paleolithic painted caves, the largest concentration of which are in the Dordogne, for many years, but it was not until we moved there and began to leaf through Helen's books on the subject that the awesome implications of what they represented dawned on me. Decorated throughout the last Ice Age, from roughly 30,000 to 10,000 B.C., the some two hundred deep cave "sanctuaries" and shelters, in the Dordogne, the Ariège, and the Spanish Cantabrian region, contain the origin of art as we know it today. They indicate that as early as 17,000 B.C. (the period in which Lascaux was painted), man had a vision of his place in the cosmos, and the paintings and engravings range from crude, "abstract" lines, to realistic and elegant depictions of the herbivores and carnivores that ranged the Ice Age tundra.

Virtually no one had made any use of the caves in imaginative writing, and no American poet had much more than mentioned them in his poetry. Since no one knows why the paintings exist, what they mean, or most importantly the mental processes involved in their conceptualization and creation, they are a bottomless source for the imagination—beyond Dante and Shakespeare, beyond even the early Greeks and the Neolithic agrarian settlements, the Cro-Magnon vista opens. Its black beam penetrates the recesses of human psyche when Hades was an animal, and man belonged to a fabric that meshed all things. I had spent the first fifteen years of my life as a poet staring at my personal Indiana past; it now struck me that by turning 180° I could begin scrutinizing the most impersonal and fundamental image-core we know of. My bridge between these two perspectives was the portraits of the early and mid 1970s. I had located a territory of my own to work as my long, long apprenticeship approached an end.

Since the summer of 1974, Caryl and I have made eight trips to the cave regions, and by now have visited around fifty caves. On two occasions I had Guggenheim and NEH (National Endowment for the Humanities) "Summer Stipend" funds that covered our expenses; on other occasions, we have written travel articles, or acted as guides for small groups. In such books as *What She Means* (1978), *Hades in Manganese* (1981), and *Fracture* (1983), I've attempted to not write descriptive poems "about" the caves or their images, but to draw on their presence to imagine the origin of art and how it still manifests itself in the belatedness and cruelty that frame the twentieth century.

From the fall of 1974 to the fall of 1986, we lived at 852 South Bedford Street, in west Los Angeles, a place that was neutrally effective to live and work in; that is, while L.A. lacks the intellectual concentration and artist network of NYC, it can be less frenetic and

Matthew Eshleman, age thirteen, 1979

depressing. In 1974, L.A. was also a good deal less violent, at least in our neighborhood (adjacent to southeast Beverly Hills)—but by the late 1970s there were break-ins and muggings on our block every week. We were burglarized twice in the early 1980s, and on the first occasion Caryl lost nearly three years of her handmade gold and silver rings and pendants. She had been making jewelry since the late 1970s and was just beginning to sell her work when the burglary occurred. Since then, she has divided her time between editing my poetry and prose, and acting as managing editor for *Sulfur* magazine.

While these years in Los Angeles were hardly inspired by the place itself, we enjoyed our life there very much. Our friends in Los Angeles, and near by, made all the difference. Joyce Vinje and Antonet O'Toole, whom I first met as poetry students, became close friends as did Martha Sattler, a book collector now completing my bibliography, the French poet Bernard Bador, the owner of Chatterton's Book Store, Koki Iwamoto, and his family, the translator

Michael Heim, an old friend from Indiana University Ron Gottesman, Ellen Gelula, who runs a film-dubbing studio, and Joanne Leedom-Ackerman, a novelist, and her husband, Peter, an investment banker. As the reader might notice from our friends' work, I had little close contact with Los Angeles poets and artists. True, we became close friends with the poets Jed Rasula and Leland Hickman, and the painters Arthur Secunda and Linda Jacobson, in the 1980s, but for reasons that have baffled me, I was treated like a pariah by the poets who identify themselves as "The Los Angeles Poets," and to discuss poetry I occasionally drove south to visit Bob Peters, Jerry Rothenberg, or Michael Davidson, or north to John and Barbara Martin, of Black Sparrow Press, who had moved to Santa Barbara in 1975.

The mid 1970s were lean years; I could not get a full-time teaching position, so Caryl supported us by secretarial work (while I learned to cook). Things began to look up in 1977 when I received an "Artists in the Community" grant from the California Art Council, to teach poetry to black students in a downtown L.A. high school; the following year I received a Guggenheim Fellowship, and the year after that, an NEA (National Endowment for the Arts) Fellowship. In 1977, Annette Smith (a professor at the California Institute of Technology) and I decided to translate all of Aimé Césaire's poetry, and when Caryl and I returned from Europe in 1979, Annette

Clayton and Caryl Eshleman, 1985

*Diane Wakoski, Caryl and Clayton Eshleman,
Mary Caponegro, and Robert Kelly,
New York City, 1980*

and her husband, David, also a professor at Cal Tech, helped me land a part-time position there, where I taught a creative-writing class each semester for the next five years. Between 1984, and the fall of 1986, when I became a Professor at Eastern Michigan University and we bought our first house in Ypsilanti, I taught as a visiting writer on various University of California campuses.

Translation-wise, since the completion of the Vallejo project, and the Césaire *Collected Poetry,* I have done a *Selected Poems* of Michel Deguy, and over the past few years involved myself with two Czech poets, Vladimir Holan, and a protégé of his, Milan Exner. With the help of Jan Benda, Frantisek Galan, and Michael Heim, I have done versions from a language I myself do not read—something I would never have done a decade ago. However, after years of translating difficult poets like Vallejo, Césaire, and Artaud, I feel it is possible to do responsible versions with astute cotranslators under such circumstances.

While living in Los Angeles I also began to review for the *Los Angeles Times Book Review;* between 1979 and 1986, I wrote around fifty reviews, mainly of books that editor Art Seidenbaum sent that I had not requested. Doing such reviews was, in the best sense, doing finger exercises in expository prose, and they led to my writing much more of my own prose in the 1980s than I ever had before: essays on Leon Golub, Vallejo, Artaud, Césaire, Jack Spicer, Allen

Nina Subin

Clayton Eshleman, 1985

Ginsberg, Upper Paleolithic Art, Translation, and the Grotesque, all carefully edited by Caryl. I also taped several hours of conversation with the psychologist James Hillman, some of which has been transcribed and published as a dialogue on poetry and psychology. This past winter, I wrote a short book called *Novices,* reflections on origins, poetic curricula, and the image of the labyrinth, as they might pertain to one who has just begun an apprenticeship to poetry.

While I was the Dreyfuss Writer in Residence and Lecturer in Creative Writing at Cal Tech, in 1980, I proposed to the chair of the humanities division, Roger Noll, that we start a new literary magazine there, to be called *Sulfur.* Noll agreed, and helped me launch a magazine that I still edit, now in its twentieth issue. *Sulfur,* among other things, means a bright yellow moth, and is, on that level, an

evolution of *Caterpillar.* As of this date, there are eleven editors and correspondents making up the masthead, and the magazine covers an interdisciplinary range of materials, sensing poetry as a force in a complex field of forces, that is a flowering of the responsibilities of poetry that Yellen, the Hirschmans, and Solt offered me thirty years ago. To their encouragement I should add three phrases that I discovered in the late 1950s that have been with me daily ever since: Hart Crane's "to loose yourself within a pattern's mastery which is your own from birth," Robert Duncan's "to exercise his faculties at large," and William Blake's "Never can the soul of sweet delight be defiled."

BIBLIOGRAPHY

Poetry:

Mexico and North. Privately printed, 1962.

The Chavín Illumination. Lima, Peru: Ediciones de la Rama Florida, 1965.

Lachrymae Mateo: 3 Poems for Christmas 1966. New York: Caterpillar, 1966.

The Crocus Bud. Reno, Nevada: Camels Hump, 1967.

Walks. New York: Caterpillar, 1967.

Brother Stones (illustrated with woodcuts by William Paden). New York: Caterpillar, 1968.

Cantaloups and Splendor. Los Angeles: Black Sparrow Press, 1968.

The House of Ibuki: A Poem. Fremont, Mich.: Sumac Press, 1969.

The House of Okumura. Toronto: Weed/Flower Press, 1969.

Indiana. Los Angeles: Black Sparrow Press, 1969.

A Pitchblende. San Francisco: Maya, 1969.

T'ai. Cambridge, Mass.: Sans Souci Press, 1969.

Yellow River Record. London: Big Venus, 1969.

Altars. Los Angeles: Black Sparrow Press, 1971.

Bearings. Santa Barbara, Calif.: Capricorn Press, 1971.

The Sanjo Bridge. Los Angeles: Black Sparrow Press, 1972.

Coils. Los Angeles: Black Sparrow Press, 1973.

Human Wedding. Los Angeles: Black Sparrow Press, 1973.

Aux Morts. Los Angeles: Black Sparrow Press, 1974.

Realignment (illustrated with drawings by Nora Jaffe). Providence, R.I.: Treacle Press, 1974.

The Gull Wall: Poems and Essays. Los Angeles: Black Sparrow Press, 1975.

Portrait of Francis Bacon. Sheffield, England: Rivelin Press, 1975.

Cogollo. Newton, Mass.: Roxbury, 1976.

The Woman Who Saw Through Paradise. Lawrence, Kan.: Tansy Press, 1976.

Core Meander. Santa Barbara, Calif.: Black Sparrow Press, 1977.

Grotesca. London: New London Pride, 1977.

On Mules Sent from Chavín: A Journal and Poems 1965–1966. Swansea, England: Galloping Dog Press, 1977.

The Gospel of Celine Arnauld. Willits, Calif.: Tuumba Press, 1977.

The Name Encanyoned River. New Paltz, N.Y.: Treacle Press, 1978.

What She Means. Santa Barbara, Calif.: Black Sparrow Press, 1978.

A Note on Apprenticeship. Chicago: Two Hands Press, 1979.

The Lich Gate. Barrytown, N.Y.: Station Hill Press, 1980.

Nights We Put the Rock Together. Santa Barbara, Calif.: Cadmus, 1980.

Our Lady of the Three-Pronged Devil. New York: Red Ozier Press, 1980.

Foetus Graffiti. East Haven, Conn.: Pharos Press, 1981.

Hades in Manganese. Santa Barbara, Calif.: Black Sparrow Press, 1981.

Fracture. Santa Barbara, Calif.: Black Sparrow Press, 1983.

Visions of the Fathers of Lascaux followed by *The Staked Women.* Los Angeles: Panjandrum, 1983.

The Name Encanyoned River: Selected Poems 1960–1985. Santa Barbara, Calif.: Black Sparrow Press, 1986.

Translator of:

Residence on Earth, by Pablo Neruda. San Francisco: Amber House, 1962.

State of the Union, by Aimé Césaire, translated with Denis Kelly. Bloomington, Ind.: Caterpillar, 1966.

Translations from the Spanish, by César Vallejo and José Hierro, translated with Cid Corman. Reno, Nev.: Quark, 1967.

Poemas Humanos/Human Poems, by César Vallejo. New York: Grove Press, 1968; London: Cape, 1969.

Letter to André Breton, by Antonin Artaud. Los Angeles: Black Sparrow Press, 1974.

Spain, Take This Cup from Me, by César Vallejo, translated with José Rubia Barcia. New York: Grove Press, 1974.

To Have Done with the Judgement of God, by Antonin Artaud, translated with Norman Glass. Los Angeles: Black Sparrow Press, 1975.

Artaud the Mômo, by Antonin Artaud, translated with Norman Glass. Santa Barbara, Calif.: Black Sparrow Press, 1976.

Battles in Spain, by César Vallejo, translated with José Rubia Barcia. Santa Barbara, Calif.: Black Sparrow Press, 1978.

César Vallejo: The Complete Posthumous Poetry, translated with José Rubia Barcia. Berkeley and Los Angeles: University of California Press, 1978.

Antonin Artaud: Four Texts, translated with Norman Glass. Los Angeles: Panjandrum, 1982.

Aimé Césaire: The Collected Poetry, translated with Annette Smith. Berkeley and Los Angeles: University of California Press, 1983.

Given Giving: Selected Poems of Michel Deguy. Berkeley and Los Angeles: University of California Press, 1984.

Chanson, by Antonin Artaud, translated with A. James Arnold. New York: Red Ozier Press, 1985.

Sea-Urchin Harakiri, by Bernard Bador. Los Angeles: Panjandrum, 1985.

Lost Body, by Aimé Césaire, translated with Annette Smith. New York: Braziller, 1986.

Editor of:

Folio magazine, three issues. Bloomington, Ind., Vol. XXV, #1-3, 1960.

Caterpillar magazine, twenty issues. New York and Los Angeles, 1967–73.

A Caterpillar Anthology: A Selection of Poetry and Prose from Caterpillar Magazine. New York: Doubleday, 1971.

Sulfur magazine, twenty issues. Pasadena, Calif., Los Angeles, and Ypsilanti, Mich., 1981—.

Nikki Giovanni

1943-

IN SYMPATHY WITH ANOTHER MOTHERLESS CHILD

(One View of the Profession of Writing)

Nikki Giovanni, Atlanta, Georgia, 1983

Writing is like any other profession—break-dancing, doctor of philosophy, surgeon—it's what I do to justify the air I breathe, the food I ingest, the time I take up on Earth. I'm ever and still amazed that any artist considers himself God or in close proximity thereof. It's not like a double-O number—it's no license to kill, no excuse to not exercise normal courtesy in human relations, no copyright on bigotry. I suppose there is, or at least there appears to be, some human need to cull from the general stock those who should be exalted. I don't trust that instinct at all. The more you are in public life the less likely it is that your life will be worth living; unless you exercise great care to be sure it's your life that you are living and not what someone wants your life to be. I feel as sorry for the modern politicians and rock stars as I do the Roman Claudius who was told by his Praetorian guards he had one of two choices: "You will be Emperor or we will kill you." Ass kissing is not a normal human posture for the kisser or the kissee.

I am not at all sure that forty is the proper age to look at a career. At forty, first of all, the body changes. No one in his right mind would ask a teenager to write or evaluate his life because those who have been through adolescence know that every day there is another major change, another crisis, another reason to feel life sucks and there is nothing that can be done about it. I'm not sure that at forty we know much more. At sixteen we can feel there will be another sixteen and another and another; at forty you pretty well know there will not be another forty; you are pleased to think there might be another ten and depending upon the rate of body deterioration you can hope for another twenty with the coda: If I'm healthy. Most Americans are medically indigent; I know I am. I have instructed my mother to sign nothing should I be struck with any disease more serious than cellulite. I'm probably going to die anyway and there's no point in her, my son, and my dogs going into bankruptcy to stave off the inevitable. Can we talk? It's not at all that I'm interested in dying. As a matter of fact, I think life is one of the more interesting propositions offered on Earth; it's just that I have lived through a terminal illness and have seen.

I like my profession. I hope the telephone operators, the hamburger turner at McDonald's, the pressure checker at Kentucky Fried who sees to it that those spices and herbs get really deep in the chicken are proud too. I know some degree of incentive is necessary to my profession. Writers are the world's biggest procrastinators and the second biggest paranoid group, being bested only by politicians. I know that we have to get some kind of seed in our craw to write, and then we only write after we have washed all the windows, cleaned the oven, weeded the garden, and are threatened with either bodily harm by our publishers or imminent bankruptcy by our creditors. I have a dear friend who invites me each summer to come to her home to write. "You'll have lots of privacy," she always points out, "and there are the swimming pool and the tennis courts when you need to take a break." What she has also figured out is that her closets will get both waxed and straightened out, her silver will get polished, all repairs will be made on the porch furniture, all door knobs will be tightened. I'm very handy. In fact, I'm a joy to have around. I paint, stain, rescreen, file crystal; the only thing I don't do well in a house is electrical work that requires the box to be turned off. I'm terribly handy with plumbing and have been known in my mother's house to repair roof shingles. Of course we seldom mention that the books don't get written . . . To tell the truth my secret desire is to open my own *Nikki's Best* handy-girl service. Hey! if this poetry doesn't work out I've got my second career all planned. As you may have guessed—I'm compulsive.

Ecclesiastes teaches us there is a season and a purpose for everything under the heavens; what is not mentioned is that there is a place. I really can stand dirt since in my mind there is a purpose for dirt; I cannot stand disorder. I am stupefied that people haven't alphabetized their books and records, that clothes in the closet don't hang on proper hangers in color and length categories. An unbalanced closet is the sign of a sick mind, much more indicative of the true personality than a cluttered desk for which there is at least *one* excuse. It used to be that you could tell all you needed to know about a woman by the way she kept house; the same is true of men these days. Chalk one up for the E.R.A.

Rage is to writers what water is to fish. A laid-back writer is like an orgasmic prostitute—an anomaly—something that doesn't quite fit. I have been considered a writer who writes from rage and it confuses me. What else do writers write from? A poem has to say something. It has to make some sort of sense; be lyrical; to the point; and still able to be read by whatever reader is kind enough to pick up the book. Certainly there are poets who deliberately use language to obscure the fact that they have nothing to either share or convey but we aren't discussing them. Those would be the academicians who write for each other and, let us not forget, to impress the department head. I have even gone so far as to think one of the duties of this profession is to be topical . . . to try to say something about the times in which we are living and how we both view and evaluate them. Relevance will lead to either critical ridicule or total dismissal. One of the most severe criticisms of Rod McKuen is that people read and enjoy him. Imagine!

What nerve! Poetry isn't to be read and enjoyed. It's to be difficult, dark, full of hidden meanings, allegorical, with strange images in even stranger words about some other poet no one ever heard of. If Black writers write about slavery we are told it's parochial, no one is interested in this stuff; but when Jewish writers write about their history, it's called the Old Testament. When women write about the reality of our lives it's called too dull; when white men write their lives it's called heroic. The ultimate literary confrontation will be The Old Testament Meets the New Holocaust vs. Deliverance of The Man in the Grey Flannel Suit. You the reader are invited to compare these two marvelous anthologies by some of our greatest writers. You can use the coupon at the bottom of the page to check your preference for the work of the millenium, and while you're at it, we're sure you will want to own these two black glove-leather-bound copies for your children. For only $5.95 down and $5.00 a week for the next two hundred and fifty weeks we will put these right on your bookshelf. And if you order now and mention Joe sent you, we will give you free of charge this marvelous bookmark blessed by three living rabbis and two popes. Don't miss this opportunity to help hubby get ahead and the kiddies do better in school! Phooey!

I think a lot of the Black poets because we honor the tradition of the grioes. We have traveled the length and breadth of the planet singing our song of the news of the day trying to bring people closer to the truth. As the written word became both possible and accessible, poets such as Dante, Milton, T.S. Eliot carried on the African tradition. Though some people were as unhappy with our "motherfuckers" as in other times some were shocked by Chaucer's eroticism; some people were simply born to be shocked.

On a scale of one to ten I have to admit literary excess is about 380. Whether it's done smoothly or crudely; whether it's the rantings of *Mein Kampf* or American Unionists in 1852 clutching *Uncle Tom's Cabin*. It's neither *The Klansman* nor *The Strawberry Statement* that causes action; it is action that gives life to literature. I do confess to being shocked. I am not nor do I recommend being blasé, accepting any and everything. But what is shocking to me will never come from the lips of Prince on a record but rather from the lips of the New Bedford men *for* the record who stated that the woman they raped on a pool table must have really wanted to be raped, or else why would she have come into the bar to buy a pack of cigarettes? I am totally shocked by the Cincinnati father who raped his five-month-old baby while his wife was out shopping. Guess that will teach his wife to ask him to baby-sit. I'm shocked that child molesters now simply open day care centers to which unwitting parents take innocent children. I'm shocked that people, estimated in the millions, will die of starvation on this earth; that people sleep in the crevices and corners on the streets in our major cities; that mass murderers and attempted presidential assassins get to plead mental anguish. Talk about a headache! I'm disappointed that Ronald Reagan thinks trees pollute and that the Democratic party nominated Walter Mondale. But hey! Who asked me? I'm sorry that every time I like a television program it goes off the air. That kind of thing makes you feel like you are a one-woman Nielsen ("What does Giovanni like this season? . . . Well get it off!")

How we as a world got into book censorship is well beyond my powers to understand. It's really funny in a way. We can get *Little Black Sambo* off library shelves because Black Americans may be offended and it isn't even about Black Americans but we support *Penthouse* and *Hustler* because of First Amendment protections. I'm not shocked at pornography but it's awful. And what makes it so awful isn't naked women in totally absurd positions, rather that somebody needs to make someone else submissive. But I attended a colored college so I may have missed something. Maybe some reader will be kind enough to explain it to me because all I see is a married man angry because his mistress was unfaithful.

The Miss America Pageant gathers together all the winners of the fifty Miss State contests. They come to Atlantic City, which used to be just a playground for the rich and others who liked salt water taffy and maybe an occasional Monopoly freak. They have never in their fifty-six-year history picked a girl of sturdy character, high intelligence, fluid articulateness who was ugly. They have never picked a girl who declined to participate in the swimsuit contest. They always say talent is important but if what I see on screen is what they call talent either I am crazy or they are deaf. But hey! I'm not going to intimate that perhaps the true talent contest takes place in another arena and that the inability to properly judge that contest is what really cost Bert Parks his position. No. I will stick to my question. What is the difference between porn publishers and the people who make up beauty pageants? What is the difference between how any of them are using women to earn their living? In every issue, in every contest, they all, like the butcher, look for fresh meat. What continues to make men think they have a right, first dibs actually, on the bodies of women? I like Vanessa Williams. Nobody would even ask me to pose naked or pay for

the photographs should I insist, though my doctor just informed me I am at my optimum weight and for a woman of my age in pretty good health. Oh, I'm sorry. We weren't discussing health, were we, but rather looks. I think it must be awful to be beautiful. No matter what anyone says I don't think people cheer for beautiful people; I think they are jealous. It's bad enough being intelligent or truly talented but at least you can hide that a lot by just not talking. But beauty is a walking billboard to every bimbo who has eyes. I was more than delighted when Vanessa Williams was chosen Miss America in 1984; it made my day. She is cute and seemed to have a lot of moxie. And, let's face it, it was damned boring to have all those little miss blondies paraded before us all the time. It was time for a radical change and the pageant had one of two choices: an ugly white girl or a beautiful Black one. They made the right choice. Of the two Black women in the running I was pulling for Vanessa because she had a glint in her eye. I love a risk taker; I liked her existential approach. Though she appeared to be happy she didn't look as if her whole damned life depended upon being chosen. She was cool. Even after her title was taken away, she was still the best choice because she was a thoroughbred all the way. Until the mess with *Penthouse* no one had anything other than praise for the way she handled herself and even while people around her crumbled, Williams faced the print press and the television cameras with style. She never backed down; and, as much as people don't like to deal with it, it's her body. If she would stand on the stage for the judges of the contest why wouldn't she have posed nude for her boss? She had no more an obligation to mention the photographs than they did to acknowledge she was their ticket to ride. But maybe there is something else that bothers me more than the shabby treatment panicking old men meted a young woman. They were all panic and no purpose. Call a press conference! Denounce Williams. Sort of Rumpelstiltskinish, flailing wildly about for an anchor ("It's all her fault!"). They were pitiful. What happened to that "Grace under pressure" of which Hemingway spoke so well? What happened to "Let's give her a chance to explain"? No. They looked like the first Lite Beer Camping Trip when Rodney joins the party: It's the creature! Which was not Vanessa Williams but their own veneer so neatly stripped. It's the mirror Bob Guccione held for them and they, like Dorian Grey, saw who they really are—old, grey-chested men with ten tons of gold around their necks from which hang 56 little skulls (55 ivory, 1 ebony), their prissy little mouths spouting prissy little platitudes while the Poligrip worked overtime. The Pageant men and

Guccione did what some would have thought impossible—they made a compassionate man of Hugh Hefner. They made a graceful, articulate, caring man of the grandaddy of them all. And let us not forget their first pronouncement after demanding the burning of Vanessa was that the first runner-up is busy with her own career and obligations so we will go to the second. In other words, "Let's get a real white woman in here swiftly. Louisa will save the day yet." In walks Little Miss Muffet, though, to save the spiders from the curds and whey.

I saw the photographs. I am one of those who rewarded Guccione as I had previously rewarded John Dean and Jeb Magruder. Tacky would be a good word for both occasions. Naive would be another. Having also viewed the work of David Hamilton (*Sisters; Country Cousins*) I found it highly credible that pornography passes as art; that someone who thinks her looks are the entree rather than the appetizer would easily be persuaded to expose herself. I simply won't buy the this-is-a-fantasy-of-hers bull. Chaipel didn't tippy-toe into his studio with his Kodak Instamatic and catch two girls off guard. These photographs are obviously posed. And frankly had they been properly cropped wouldn't have been too bad. What's wrong with naked women, as opposed to naked men, is that women don't pretend shock at the sight of a photo of a penis; men are always upset that another man will see what he "treasures." It's time for men to grow up. Sex isn't dirty-dirty or nasty-nasty. It's time men quit using the anatomy of a female against her; it's overdue that men quit using the penis as a weapon. But the most disgusting statement on the Williams situation that I read was in *USA Today*'s Opinion section in which a twenty-year-old Black woman from "hopeless" Georgia said Vanessa had "Let the race down." Little chipmunk-cheeked Bryant Gumbel leered the same question on the "Today Show." Then in his role as Mr. Compassion wanted to know, "When do the tears come?" A friend of mine said Vanessa should have said, "Nigger please!" There were too many people who wanted to pretend that the sight of that young woman without her clothes on had set the human race back to the stone age; the American people closer to nuclear confrontation with Russia; Black people back to head scratching and yessir boss. I mean, what did she really do other than mistakenly believe she could utilize her own self? While Little Miss Muffet Charles (was "Do Dah" her talent entry?) tells the world she has no secrets. That's admirable. One in every four girls and one in every ten boys have secrets by the age of twelve. Three out of four people have halitosis. Some have even known the heartbreak of psoriasis. I join

with Marvin Gaye in a salute: Right on. There is no reason to think Miss Charles understood she was chosen only to make sure Vanessa was not shot down by some crazy American. She thought the pageant had made a mistake in overlooking her in the first place. There is no reason to think she would accept the pageant's offer not to disrupt her schedule. ("But I have to follow the white rabbit," said Alice.) There was certainly no reason to think she would simply decline to participate in the humiliation of Vanessa. Oh no. She was the understudy whose moment had arrived. I alone raised the value of Excedrin stock that week. It all gave me a headache.

Actually I'm not in a rage frequently. For some reason, after all these years, meanness and stupidity still get to me. I work on it, honestly. I understand not everyone has had the advantages I have enjoyed of being able to both read and digest material and apply the lessons learned. I'm told by my young friends that experience is much more important than books. Of course Ben Franklin had something to say about experience and fools, but Franklin thought that even a fool would learn by his experience. That has proven false in the modern world. Some people are simply unwilling to learn under any circumstances, and even that wouldn't be so bad if they weren't so damned proud of it. Doesn't it just make your skin crawl to hear somebody spout off about what they don't do and how they're never going to do it? It makes you cheer against the human race. I'm sure to be a crotchety old lady, assuming I have not yet achieved that state, because things like people refusing to eat oysters will drive me up a wall. Stick one of the damned things in your mouth then you can say, "I don't care for oysters though I have tried them." This argument does not apply to cocaine or other hallucinogenic drugs since the experience of other people will do just fine. Isn't that the purpose of people living and sharing? So that others will at least not make the same mistake, since we seldom are able to recreate the positive things in life.

I guess one of life's experiences that I have always wanted to avoid was bitterness. Yes I know I wrote a poem on bitterness and I know that earlier in this career critics thought I was bitter but I am not, nor was I. Just sick and tired of the same song and dance. The bitter people are as bad as the drug people because they seem to descend to a place from which no light ever emerges. I had an experience with the Council on Interracial Books for Children that did push my bitter button though.

It started with a book, *Jake and Honeybunch Go to Heaven* which is illustrated by Margot Zemach, a white

Bill Moore

Giovanni, 1982

woman. She had taken the old Black folktale and placed it in the thirties. Jake and his mule, Honeybunch, are killed by a train because the mule wouldn't move out of the way. Jake gets to Heaven first and in his attempt to adjust runs into trouble. He picks up two left wings, he sees a jazz band, there is a big fish fry . . . all the usual things. He finally meets God who is a Black man with a white beard who tells him he'll have to leave because of the disturbance he is causing. Jake just misses Honeybunch who has finally arrived in Heaven. If Jake was a disaster, Honeybunch is a blind man with a pistol. No one can control the mule so God sends for Jake who promises to both control his mule and do better himself. God gives Jake the specific job of putting the stars and moon out, so if you look at the night sky and there is only darkness, just know that Jake and Honeybunch are probably off fishing and forgot to do their work. A really rather harmless story that has been around, for anyone who knows her folklore, for ages—from the rather modern day "People, Get Ready (There's a Train a'Coming)" to "Oh Pray My Wings Are Going to Fit Me Well." There were literary complaints that God was both male and Black though I had a difficult time picturing Jake being greeted by Sheena of the

Jungle or Marilyn Monroe. Some said one of the illustrations which showed a Black man sleeping in a pullman wasn't real but neither is the idea of L.C. Greenwood and Bert Jones exchanging letters in a commercial. Some didn't like the food Jake saw being cooked and consumed. I just had a difficult time trying to see Jake enjoying lox on an onion bagel. Some didn't like the jazz band in Heaven. Mostly what none of them liked was that a white woman illustrated a Black folktale. Why, they cried, couldn't a Black illustrator have done it? Because a Black illustrator didn't, that's why. It neither added to nor subtracted from the book that was before us to ask that kind of question.

Anyway, the Council decided to wage holy war against *Jake* and began lining up its Black pawns. My mother took a message for me to call the Council. I returned the call and was told that the *Jake* situation was racist and something should be said about it. Having been familiar with the Council, though not its tactics, I asked if they would send me the book. I recalled several years ago they had accused *Sounder* of being racist because the book was named after the dog and the characters weren't given names. Since I hadn't been offended by *Sounder*, I was at least cautious. The book arrived the next day. I read it and looked at it carefully. After dinner I read it again. Since my mother is a much better folklorist than I could hope to be and since she has a special interest in children's literature, I asked her to read it for me. I called a librarian at the Cincinnati Public Library and asked her for an opinion which she was unable to give because she had not seen the book, though she did supply me with additional material. I read the additional material. Neither my heart nor my mind could find any racist intent in *Jake and Honeybunch*. I could see why some people might not want to purchase a copy for their children but that's hardly the same as condemning the book. Many people don't want to purchase *Slaughterhouse Five, Catcher in the Rye*, all of my books, but that doesn't mean a full-scale literary war should be raised. Books are self-censoring agents. First they have to be written, then they have to be published, then they have to find their way into the homes or hands of readers, then they still have to go the extra mile of being interesting enough to be read. I figure books have a hard enough time without the added pressure of misleading information leaking out about them. I sat down and wrote the Council a letter that ended, "I do not find *Jake and Honeybunch* racist," which was a simple statement of how I thought about the book. I don't like *Charlie and the Chocolate Factory* because I didn't like the way the "Oompa Lumpas" were characterized; I really thought William Styron's *Nat Turner* was just a total waste; but Dahl and Styron probably don't read me either. I would not be disappointed to find that is so; I would be disappointed to find that they demand the removal of my books from the shelves.

I wrote the Council a long letter explaining my reasoning since it was more than obvious that *Jake* was going to get reamed by most writers. I thought it the honorable thing to do. When the Council's Newsletter came out that fall every response to *Jake* ranged from "Yes, it is racist and should be removed from the shelves," to "Yes, it is racist but should be left alone"—except for *one* response—mine. Maybe I wouldn't have burned so much if the Council had published my whole letter or at least given some of my reasoning. Since I was the only voice who spoke up for *Jake*, it seemed to me only fair that a fuller explanation was needed than "On the other hand," and then quoting me as saying I did not find *Jake and Honeybunch* racist. What was the great fear? That the reasoning would be so persuasive that all others would repent? No. The great fear, I think, is that one Black writer decided to say what she believed. This little soldier didn't join Nixon's army, neither would I start banning books.

About ten years ago James Earl Jones starred in an Off-Broadway production of a one-man show on Paul Robeson. Friends of mine and people who knew Robeson were very upset with the portrayal and decided to take out an ad or something in the *New York Times* to protest. A friend called me and asked if I would join them. He explained their point of view and I said, "Yes." I did say to him that if anyone asked if I had seen the production, I would be forced to tell them I signed out of friendship. The ad ran and I *was* asked about it by the CBS local. James Earl Jones then said in the *Times* the next day he was disappointed with me because he expected more of me. I was actually ashamed. I had not even thought about James Earl or his feelings. I had only thought that I was helping out a friend. I knew I never wanted to feel that way again in my life. Not like a fool, because I have been a fool enough to know that doesn't matter one way or the other, but insensitive. If you're going to hurt people's feelings it should definitely be because of something you believe in. In that way that people are when they learn something, I'm glad James Earl expressed disappointment, otherwise it would never have crossed my mind again and though I don't think my friend was exactly using me, I also know I seek no concurring opinions of my own beliefs.

When I saw what the Council said about *Jake* in its Newsletter, I felt compelled to write and tell them

I thought they abused my good offices. Their response was to send me a xeroxed copy of another book they didn't like. As fate would have it, the *Jake* controversy started with the refusal of Milwaukee librarians to purchase copies for general circulation. The *Jake* publisher had accused them of censorship; they retaliated with racism. It just goes to show how wars get started. I had a speaking engagement in Milwaukee that fall. At the reception that followed, I had the pleasure of meeting one of the librarians. She asked me if I had seen the Newsletter and I sort of went off on her. Then she said, "You know, I did additional research and the book is basically sound." "Are you going to write the author to let her know?" "Oh no. I still don't like the book," she said. "But you do see that not liking the book isn't the same as saying the book is racist." "Yes . . . well . . . but it's probably best to let things alone." I have an unshakable affection for librarians. I'm sure, because she was a charming lady who probably meant no harm, that there was some unstated reason like, "My job would be at stake"; "Nobody was really hurt"; "The devil made me do it." Aren't those the traditional excuses we seek? The lessons of Nuremberg have yet to be learned. But at least we are all trying. Each in her own way. I hope.

Mine, like most families of writers, lives in absolute terror that one day I shall tire of contemplating my own navel and turn to theirs. The most at risk in this situation are, of course, children because we, the writer, can sign a release for them, the minor. I look any day now for the family of Erma Bombeck to file a class action suit and take away her tennis court. I'm luckier than Ms. Bombeck because I don't have any tangible assets. They can only hope that I will one day peck into a mega-seller, then Bingo! they can pounce. Of course, this will never happen because I'm a poet. But then there are advantages to having a poet in the family. I write marvelous little thank you notes with just the right touch of both joy and humility at receiving a present. I do nifty invitations and Ma Bell or rather the new AT&T Regionals owe me one because I have raised the art of letter writing to the point that very few people in my family will write—they generally just reach out and touch.

The only one who has successfully escaped my poetic intrusion is my girl dog Wendy, though I did, of course, dedicate a book to her because I got tired of her bitching that she was left out. Dogs are funny. If you write about them they accuse you of exploitation. Look at the heartache Lassie and her family went through—always having to do a heroic number to keep the affection of her owners; look at poor Rin Tin Tin galloping across the plains leading the cavalry . . . then having to listen to Black Beauty and the others complain that *he* gets all the glory. What's even worse is that sexism is ever present. Lassie was played by a male though of course you can't get away with that with horses. So I have low-keyed it with Wendy. She's a really marvelous cairn terrier with a highly developed sense of self and duty. Truth is she would give her life for me. She's a great watchdog and will let you know when anything is awry. Her desire to protect me got her into trouble in the house because she would always bark at my father when he got up to go to the bathroom in the middle of the night. He would curse her and say clearly, mostly I think for my benefit, "Damned crazy dog!" I naturally had to support Wendy so I would get up and pet her and say, "Good girl." My mother would by that time have stumbled out of her room to see what the commotion was, which always woke up Bruno, my boy dog, who then had to go out himself which meant someone had to wait on him since he never, in rain nor snow nor dark of night, could just go out and pee; he always had to patrol the entire back yard. My son Tommy slept through it all which was just as well, as he usually had left his TV running and would have been reamed at two in the morning for the waste.

Bruno, by the way, is worthless. If I ever hit *Lotto!* and get a big house and new car and buy a lot of nifty things people would want to steal, I'll have to find a new home for him. Nothing on Earth should be as friendly as that dog. He sucks up to repairmen, telephone guys, the Orkin man, anyone who comes to the door no matter how menacing or strange looking. When we moved here my mother said two dogs were too much but every morning, while she worked her crossword puzzle, Bruno would climb over her feet to put his head in her lap. Bru has her convinced that he is actually of help with some of the words. My cousin Pat who lives in California, has Bruno out each summer and he's such a nerd that she reads fairy tales to him before he goes to bed. He ignores me completely. If I just needed something little like help with getting a twig out of the way he would pretend to be busy. The only thing I do that really delights him is make ice cream, but as I always tell him, I'm on to his tricks. He and Tommy like to wait until they hear me go "Uumph! Uumph!"—knowing those are the last couple of turns—then they both come bounding over. I always give the dasher to Wendy cause she'll stick with me through the whole thing—to hell with that sometimey dog and boy. Mommy says I ignore Bru but it's his own fault. I'm the one who bought him and his food; who takes him to be groomed; who sees

to it he has his shots. And who does he suck up to? Everybody else. Now as far as children go I have no special insight into teenagers save this: the fourteen-year-old personality was invented to give ulcers to otherwise calm mothers; to cause normally tranquil, proud, loving parents to snarl, growl, and threaten; the fourteen-year-old personality was created, in other words, to drive forty-year-old mothers to the nut house.

Everyone says babies are difficult; it's just not true. Changing diapers, wiping pabulum from chins, heating bottles in the middle of the night are a snap compared to picking up your own telephone that you pay for every month and never hearing a familiar voice of either friend or relative but rather a barbarian girl or boy demanding, "Tom home?" I was at first annoyed by the question and then by the tone but I've since trained myself to respond only to the question asked: "Why, yes, he is. How kind of you to call and inquire. I must go now." I then hang up. The barbarian response next was, "Can I speak to Tom?" to which I replied, again, as sweetly as possible: "It appears you are quite capable. I hear you very well. I must go now." Finally they reached the desired question: "May I speak to Tom?" which unfortunately elicits, "I'm sorry, dear, but Thomas may not use the telephone until his grades improve." And I don't add "or hell freezes over." Whichever comes first. Hell will surely win.

Why, sister Mothers, do children want to fail? Is it the new high? Is there some sexual charge experienced when our ninth graders come home with report cards full of F's and I's? What sado-psychological satisfaction is gained by them watching our hearts leap from our breasts, our eyes involuntarily tearing over, our breaths coming in short, unnatural spurts? What kick do they get standing over us watching our lives pass before our eyes? All my friends have marvelous children who clean their rooms, excel in extracurricular activities, pass their classes, get honors and awards. I've even taken, and I don't mind to admit it, to avoiding certain parents of perfect children, though I have not been a competitive parent. When little Billy Bob joined the Boy Scouts, climbed a twelve-story building and rescued the blind, paraplegic unwed mother from raging flames, I never said to my son: "How come you never do anything worthwhile?" No. I smiled at the parent, congratulated the child, and dutifully went back to pinning Tom's sox for the laundry and picking up the comic books that spread across the floor making his room a hazardous area. When little Sally Mae, in just the fifth grade, was invited to Athens to address the Senate in her fluent Greek on how stability could be obtained with Turkey, I said to her mother, my friend, "You must be very proud." I did not say to Tom, "Why is it that that little snotty-nose twerp is hailed the world over while you refuse to write a simple essay for English *in* English about the Alaskan cruise I had to mortgage the house to take you on?" I didn't even heap abuse when he replied, "Alaska wasn't so much." No. I calmly said, "Dear, I sincerely think you can improve this Incomplete by turning in your assignment." I am, however, about to be convinced that kindness, civility, and logic have no truck with teenagers. My son had a classmate last year who was spanked every time she brought home a B or less. Tom was appalled. "But dear," I pointed out, "look at your grades and look at hers. Surely I am the parent in the wrong." "Well," says Mister as he makes his way to the freezer to get a pizza and pop it in the oven, "she hates her mother and I love you." If this is love, folks . . .

My son, I do believe and have had demonstrated, has a lot of character. He has never lied to me. I'm told by friends with perfect children that that is because it's all the same to him. He doesn't lie because he knows I won't go off on him or stop him from doing anything he wants to do anyway. I like to think that's not true. I like to think he is truthful because 1) I *will* go crazy on him if he lied; but mostly because 2) somewhere, despite that pickled fourteen-year-old mass that commonly is called a brain, he has absorbed some of the values I've been trying by example to teach him. When I am hasty in my judgments or just plain wrong about something I don't mind apologizing. When I don't know something I don't mind admitting ignorance. When I don't want him to go somewhere or do something for no particular reason other than I think it's not right for him I explain, "Mother is making an arbitrary judgment that has no logic nor reason. You are right to be angry about this. I would feel the same way if the tables were turned." It may not be any easier to take but it's honest.

I've also seen Tom come through a situation that would be difficult for a stable adult. My father developed a bladder cancer following a stroke which is the reason we moved from New York back to Cincinnati. Those years could not have been easy; living with someone who was in fact dying. My father was brave in the face of his impending death and so was my son. Neither complained of the burden nor the pain. The night my father died Tom, my mother, and I were the only ones at home. My sister was coming in from San Francisco. My nephew from Seattle was not contacted until the day after. The

hospital called that Gus had died. I had to go out to pick up his personal property and sign for the autopsy. Tom, who was then twelve, said "I'll go with you." He went to the hospital, viewed the body, got his grandfather's walking cane, stayed while the other arrangements were made. That night he came into my room and curled next to Wendy, my dog, and slept on the floor. The next morning we had to pick a casket. "I'll go with you," he said to my mother, my sister, and me. He put on his tie and jacket and sat through the funeral arrangements. He stayed by my side as the family made calls, placed flower orders, took care of the kind of base-touching a funeral requires. For two days he looked after us as best he could. On the morning of the funeral he asked: "Mommy, when is Chris getting here?" Meaning, I think, that he had gone as far as he was capable. It was more than caring . . . it was character.

Last year we visited a boarding school of note in the East. He and I stayed three days and he loved it. My child would prep in the ninth grade. I too would have something to brag about over beer and barbecue. As the three of us, Tom, my mother, and I, talked over our fall plans I started outlining how he could have his own MasterCard, how to check his bank balance, the numbers to call to reach me wherever I might be, the numbers for Grandmother. Tom looked up and said: "Wait a minute! Where *are* you going to be?" "I'll be out working to pay for your tuition. That's why I'm going over these plans with you." "Well, where will Grandmother be?" "She'll be here a lot but she may want to travel, visit her sisters, or anything she wants to do." "You mean I'm going off BY MYSELF!" Eyes getting larger. "Well, yes, Tom. That's what it means to prep. You go off to school by yourself." In that let's-get-this-straight-manner he says: "You're not taking an apartment in Wallingford?" "No." "Well I sure didn't think you were kicking me out!" with just a touch of the indignant in his voice.

He went to public school. And turned fourteen. Since I know the school system is one of the best in the country; since I know he has ability; I can only blame it on fourteen. My grandmother, Louvenia Watson, used to baffle me when she said, "I'll be glad when you get off Fool's Hill." I never used to know what she meant. I certainly do now. He'll turn fifteen this year and I, who was supposed to turn forty-one, will turn one hundred and three. As they sing in the coffee commercial with all the winners sitting around smiling: Hold on tight to your dream. Actually, though, I am a very hip mother. I was into Prince and Michael Jackson before Thomas realized what he could be in life. Yeah, sure, you'd like a kid who could

The author with son, Tom, 1984

pronounce "perfect" and not "purrfect" but I think the way Michael says it is cute. I know *Thriller* is in the *Guiness Book of World Records* but there will always be a special place in my heart for "Rock with You." I haven't quite adjusted to parachute pants but I'm into ties and boots . . . what I call my Tina Turner look, though I have an Afro. We can't all do long hair. I tend to be a bit old-fashioned and nothing, absolutely nothing, will get me totally out of my elephant bells. I mean the big chill may have settled on the rest but I'm going forward. The sixties stood for something.

I shall always remember the joy on my grandmother's face when she came back from the mass meeting to tell me I *could* march and how proud she was. She and Grandpapa caught a cab to come see me. I actually figured I was on my way to meet my maker but one must have a sense of social responsibility. When I enrolled in Fisk University the following fall one of the things I most looked forward to was sitting-in. There was a sort of style to it. Assuming you weren't actually molested, it was cool. You sat on the stool and watched the white people panic. Dick Gregory has the best story. When he stopped at a diner the waitress said, "We don't serve niggers" —to which Gregory replied, "I don't eat them." You always hoped someone would say something to you to let you be cool. Mostly you were scared. I was home alone the Sunday the little girls were bombed in Birmingham. I remember the news flash saying they were dead. And it was enough to make you want to kill. Like all southern youngsters I went to Sunday school in a big church with a basement that could have hidden anything. It seemed so damned unfair. Our personal tragedy in Knoxville was the bombing of Clinton High School. It really made you wonder

about the people we lived among. Racism is at best boring. When I was younger it was frightening. You always felt someone was trying to kill you. Or hurt your feelings. Now it's just tiresome. Who really wants to be bothered with it anymore? It's dull to hate though I doubt that my generation will ever be able to graft new emotions to the scars. Emmett Till. Schwerner, Chaney, and Goodman. Nina Simone said it best: "Mississippi Goddamn!"

The summer of '64 was frightening. All else became a release and to many a relief. And when you look at Miami where the police are back to shooting black boys down or L.A. or New York, and anyone unfortunate enough to be arrested committing suicide in jail, you really have to wonder when will we learn. It's just so unworthy and spirit-sapping. I do think we have been deeply touched by the past decade. Even the little things. In Knoxville we couldn't go to the movie theatres downtown or to the amusement park. I do like movies but to this day I won't go to any amusement park. Cincinnati was no better. Coney Island, the local southern Ohio place to play for white kids, had to be sued before Blacks would be admitted. It's boring. Gwen Brooks and I shared a reading in New Jersey a few years ago and in the Q. and A. someone asked about racism in America. Gwen gave an intelligent response; I said it was boring. At lunch Gwen said, "Boring?" Well, what else do you call it? It can't be a sickness 'cause the cure is known. It's not a condition 'cause the times they did a-change. It doesn't make anybody happy. I mean I never ran into a hater who said, "You know, this hating business is really good . . . It makes my day to deny a job to some Black man or woman . . . I really love flunking the Black kids I have to teach . . . Yesterday I dumped my Black neighbor's garbage on his lawn and I just want you people to know how pleased I am with myself."

We used to laugh at the Klan that liked to think it was the sheets that frightened us. Hell, it was the men in the sheets and we knew that all along. One of the sure signs that Blacks and whites are coming closer together, which is not necessarily for the good of this Earth, is Black people have begun sneaking around doing murder for no reason, committing real suicide as opposed to the overdrinking/bad-driving/fight-picking way we used to and standing around making reasonable sounding excuses for our failure to live up to what we ourselves know to be our emotional potential and moral obligation. But hey, what does this have to do with autobiography?

I took a test recently in one of the popular magazines. I, not surprisingly, find myself quite an attractive personality though my test score indicated that people find me opinionated and perhaps pushy. Not bad traits for writers. I know this profession does not easily lend itself to friendships. Our friends are either deathly afraid we will write about them or terribly bored at hearing the same subject discussed from all possible points of view. It's what writers do—talk. I think I am pretty ordinary. I think if I was looking for somebody to hang out with I'd be the last person I'd choose. There is a mirthful side to my personality and I basically like to laugh but mostly I take things pretty seriously. A friend of my mother's was having dinner with us recently and we began discussing movies which, frankly I think of as a pretty safe topic. I kept saying, "What was the intent of that scene?" and she kept trying to tell me why she laughed. She finally said, "I know your problem! You're an intellectual!" Not really. I just think things should mean something and I get confused when there is no meaning to be found. We waste too much, we humans, because we refuse to recognize that there is a possibility of order and things making sense and us as a planet doing better. I really don't know what to say about myself. I like music. There is something very special about capping on my headphones and drowning in a vision of sound. Someone once asked me if I played an instrument and I replied, "My stereo."

It's not surprising that man's first musical instrument was a drum; the image of the heart had to be manifest. The African people made use of the ability of the drum to both inform and incite; for over two hundred years of the American experience drumming was outlawed. A people, though, are rarely stopped in their legitimate desire for either knowledge or pleasure. Whether the Eighteenth Amendment would outlaw alcohol, or the Miss America Pageant would desire the clothing of their Black Venus, a people—through individual risk or simply aesthetic innocence—will bring word of a new day.

It is sheer folly to assume the various African cultures were without stress, frustrations, discriminations. It is only our desire to escape the challenges of our own times that leads us to envision some African Eden with fruit dripping from every branch, fish jumping in clear cool ponds, women willing with no discernible persuasion, men strong, beautiful, and capable after undergoing some variation of initiation into "manhood." If the human species alone among the mammals is capable of dreaming, we are also alone in our capacity for fantasy. America did not invent the blues for Africans—it simply made us sing them in English.

All mammals, most insects and, as we have learned to listen to the ocean, not an inconsiderable number of fish make some sound. Among those on Earth the chirping of birds is universally considered pleasant; the howl of a single wolf on a mountain ridge the most mournful. We howl with the wolf not so much in imitation of his sound as in sympathy with another motherless child. The African slave bereft of his gods, his language, his drums, searched his heart for a new voice. Under sun and lash the African sought meaning in life on Earth and the possibility of life hereafter. They shuffled their feet, clapped their hands, gathered a collective audible breath to release the rhythms of the heart. We affirmed in those dark days of chattel through the White Knights of Emancipation that all we had was a human voice to guide us and human voice to answer the call.

Anthropologically speaking, humans were divided in the work force by gender. The men became the stalkers of prey; the women tended the fire, garden, and children at the home site. Men learned at a very early age the value of quiet; women learned the necessity of talk. Men learned to compete for the best spot, the biggest share; women learned to cooperate, to socialize. If there was a benefit of slavery to the slaves, it broke down gender barriers; men and women shared the work, learned the songs, began and ended the day together. If there was a benefit to white people during the Great Depression, men learned how to deal with enforced idleness; women learned having a "good marriage" would not protect them from the reality that everyone has a right, if not an obligation, to do productive work.

Historically considered, we are told there have been two American Revolutions: the one against the British for the right to tax ourselves; the one against the South to free chattel slaves. The revisionists consider there was perhaps a third revolution: the recovery from the Great Depression to meld compassion to free enterprise. Those of my generation know there has been a fourth: the American youth, not with fife and bugle, but with drums and boogie headed for the twenty-first century with the battle cry: "OO Whoop Baba Loo Boop OO Whop Bam Boom!"

The Coasters said they'd been "Searchin' " and once again an African-AfroAmerican ritual—the Stomp—was being practiced. Anytime that song hit the airwaves Black youngsters would pour from their cars to form a big boss line. James Brown begged "Please, Please, Please" and the Midnighters informed us "Annie Had a Baby." Sam Cooke intoned "You Send Me" but the Dominos were only a "Sixty Minute Man." Jesse Belvin said "Good Night My Love" but the Dells asked "Why Do You Have to Go?" The Brown Decision was rendered by the

*With sister, Gary, and
mother, Yolande, September 1984*

Supreme Court and Eisenhower had a heart attack. In the heart of Black America it finally was made clear that no matter what we did, no matter how much we abided by the rules and regulations, no matter how straight our hair, correct our speech, circumscribed our behavior, no matter what, we were, in the words of Moms Mabley, "still a Negro."

The advantage to a people who have clearly defined an issue is this: the individual is relieved of the burden of carrying his people forward. He can dance upon his own floor in his own style. Though white Americans would try to this very day to make Black Americans responsible for each other, Black people recognize that just as individual accomplishments open no doors, individual failures close off no avenues. The Right Reverend Ray Charles said it best: *Tell the Truth!* We no longer were ashamed of being Black; we no longer wished to hide our love of chitlins and hog maws; we no longer wished to pretend we cared. Rosa Parks in Montgomery said "No!" and Chuck Willis asked "What Am I Living For?" Johnny Ace, who allegedly shot himself backstage at Houston's City Auditorium, went number 1 in England the next day; with "Never Let Me Go" Jesse Belvin's car blew four tires, killing him after he played a dance in L.A.; Chuck Willis died; Sam Cooke was murdered in L.A.; Frankie Lymon left the Teen-Agers to begin his involvement with drugs; Little Willie John was arrested for murder and died in

prison; Otis Redding's plane crashed. Don't send me Murray the K as some kind of friend, let alone god to rhythm and blues. We paid for that music. Mr. K changed his Cleveland station format because Black and white kids were tuned into WCIN in Cincinnati, WDIA in Memphis, WDAS in Philadelphia and all-night-long WLAC in Nashville where "Randy" played and packaged the hits. Black people had some place to run! We, like Max Schmeling, lacked a place to hide. We went "Dancin' in the Streets" behind Martin Luther King, Jr., behind Malcolm X, behind mighty, mighty Sly and the Family Stone. If they snickered when Little Richard brought his painted lips, mascaraed eyes, hair piled high on his head out of his closet, they were silent when Cassius Clay echoed "I'm Black and I'm proud." Otis Redding cried for "Respect," a coda to Chuck Berry's anthem "Roll Over Beethoven." And in case the message was missed Aretha covered both Redding and Sam Cooke: "A Change Is Gonna Come." But Lady Soul, ever the lady, softened it with "A woman's only human." The Intruders replied "Gotta let a man be a man."

I'm an old unrepentant rocker who joins with Bob Seger in demanding "Old Time Rock and Roll." I've never been asked to do a commercial but even if I were, I couldn't demand "My MTV." No way. I like my music in my head and, when I was younger, my foot on the pedal. One of life's great thrills is putting Little Richard on the auto-reverse cassette in your car and heading from New York to Cincinnati. You don't even see the Jersey turnpike. You pull over in Pennsylvania just before the first tunnel and get an orange sherbet from Howard Johnson's and you don't tune down until you creep through West Virginia. I liked being young and I like being not young. At the risk of being very, very dull I agree that "to everything there is a season." I think I would classify myself as happy. Which in no way means I don't go off on people, myself, situations . . . but more, that given a choice there wouldn't be too much too different in my life. I'm finally old enough to know it would be nice to have money but not all that necessary. I think I'd be a good rich person. At least I know I would enjoy my money. Nothing galls me more than somebody who's come into some sort of fortune or been born to one bitching that life is hard. I'm sure life is, since the end of life for all of us is death. It just seems unfair when you keep hearing people who can call long distance and talk as long as they like, who don't worry how their children's tuition will be paid, who don't fear for their health since they are properly insured, going on and on about life's difficulties. It's tacky. The very least the rich can do for the rest of us is either enjoy or shut up. But what

Nikki Giovanni

does that have to do with what I have written? Nothing.

I can think of nothing less interesting to me than to walk slowly through my poetry and say " . . . and then I wrote." The books stand on their own. They will either live or die. I hate that pretentiousness of writers who think people are too dumb to understand what is being discussed. I lecture part of the year and it's a great joy to me. I like to meet people and I like to talk. I don't like to fly but there are few college campuses that will agree to come to Cincinnati so I grit my teeth and go. The one thing I'm very conscious of is not going over very old ground. I'm a space nut so I do talk about space a lot; I'm into the Global Village but mostly I try to bring the best of me to my audience. Even if it's not good, it's honest. I simply refuse to believe the public has nothing better to do than come out on a cold night to hear me read a paper that could have been slipped under their door when the morning milk was delivered. The whole point to being "Live and In Person!" is that you bring a live person. Academia is such a controlled situation that people like me cause prob-

lems. I think speeches and fruit should always be fresh. I know, sure I do, that there are those who will say, "Well, what about dried fruit? I like dried fruit." This is not against dried fruit. A little Stilton on dried apricots is one of the taste treats of the world. Maybe a bowl of hot garlic soup followed by a roasted lamb shank and hey, you've got something. Yet one should always consider that fresh has its charm. I'm just not a star. I think about it a lot. I say to myself: "Giovanni. Be demanding. Make them put Perrier on the platform. Refuse to sign autographs when Saturn is in the house of Mars. Be peculiar. Get your make-up together. Need to change several times during your appearance. Demand a better dressing room. Keep people away. Work on your sneer. Practice hurting their feelings. Need special foods. Do something so folks will know that you know that they should know that you are special." Yet I distrust in the human species the need to exalt. Writing is like any other endeavor.

I hope I am always able to bring the best to any audience that is kind enough to share an evening with me. I'm not humble. This is no Nikki Washington Carver. I believe in myself. I believe in what I do. Yet people need both gentleness and a challenge. Our college students especially need someone to talk to them as if they had sense. I would remind any program chairman that it's *your* program. While it is unreasonable to ask your speaker to go to bed with you, it is not a burden to ask your speaker to have dinner with the committee. Your speaker has a right to be picked up on time. You have a right to a press conference. If your speaker is a funny eater he should provide the food he needs. You provide what you can. And I'm not saying be sloppy. I don't care for McDonald's or Pizza Hut but if that's what you can offer, then my job is to help you feel good about it while refusing to eat. I'm only your speaker for a short while. I will not try to change your habits if you don't change mine. I smoke. Anyone who picks me up after an airplane ride will find themselves facing cigarette smoke. That's because I don't drink. If you hate smoke, do not pick up your speaker. But hey, Miss Manners covers all this so much better than I. Your speaker at her best is there to serve you. If you are positive, she will be. If you are clear, she will relax and trust you. Should you also happen to know what your speaker does for a living ("Are you going to sing tonight") you will win her affection ("No. I don't sing") and pretty please don't decide to be honest ("Frankly I was hoping they wouldn't invite you") because that will depress your speaker and she will become very closed instead of very open. Recognize that it is a human being whose dog may be sick, whose son has a science project due, who had water in the basement this morning when she left for the airport. Assume that she wants to be there and let her know you are pleased. Happiness is just such a nice thing to share. Try it. It may just make your day, too.

I date all my work because I think poetry, or any writing, is but a reflection of the moment. The universal comes from the particular. I like the nuts and bolts of life. I want to know everything. Sometimes, especially in the fall, if you're a morning person, you wake up around 5:30 A.M. and start your coffee. The dark is just beginning to lift and in my backyard the birds come to drink and bathe. They will soon not come so early because it will be too cold. But now they come and chirp. There's a big German shepherd that roams the neighborhood who is usually passing. You can sometimes hear him bark to other dogs. But mostly you hear nothing. The sun rises in my eastern window where I am growing African violets and I just like to watch the red break and wonder about all the world. There is an ad concerning space which asks "How long do we have to look at an organism before we recognize it?" How many little boys chunked the Rosetta Stone into the Red Sea before someone recognized that that was the key? And if there is never an answer, the quest is so worthwhile.

I like lace handkerchiefs. I like to look at those my Grandmother passed to my Mother; they are beautiful. Someone, perhaps Louvenia, perhaps my Great-grandmother Cornelia hand-embroidered them. They are as delicate as a spider's web, as strong as a silkworm's cocoon. I cry when I watch "Little House on the Prairie." I like to be happy. And other than an occasional response to an infrequent query, I don't contemplate my work. I do try to be a good writer. I believe that I bring my best when I try to share. It's an honorable profession. There are so many pieces to my puzzle I have no interest in trying to judge what I have done but only to try to do more. I like my awards and honors. I love it when people say they have read my poetry. I never make the mistake of asking if they understood what I was *really* talking about or if they *really* liked what I did. I just thank them because whether I disappointed or delighted them they took the time to be involved in my effort . . . to explore with me . . . to extend themselves to me as I have extended myself to them. It's lonely. Writing. But so is practicing tennis or football runs. So is studying. So is waxing the floor and changing the baby. So is life. We are less lonely when we connect. Art is a connection. I like being a link. I hope the chain will hold.

Nikki Giovanni

12 September 1984
CVG

BIBLIOGRAPHY

Poetry:

Black Feeling, Black Talk. Detroit: Broadside Press, 1968, revised edition, 1970.

Black Judgement. Detroit: Broadside Press, 1968.

Re: Creation. Detroit: Broadside Press, 1970.

Black Feeling, Black Talk, Black Judgement. New York: Morrow, 1970.

Poem of Angela Yvonne Davis. New York: Niktom, 1970.

Spin a Soft Black Song (juvenile). New York: Hill & Wang, 1971, revised edition, 1985.

My House. New York: Morrow, 1972.

Ego Tripping and Other Poems for Young Readers. Westport, Conn.: Lawrence Hill, 1973.

The Women and the Men. New York: Morrow, 1975.

Cotton Candy on a Rainy Day. New York: Morrow, 1978.

Vacation Time: Poems for Children. New York: Morrow, 1980.

Those Who Ride the Night Winds. New York: Morrow, 1983.

Other:

Night Comes Softly: An Anthology of Black Female Voices. Edited by Giovanni. New York: Niktom, 1970.

Gemini: An Extended Autobiographical Statement on My First Twenty-Five Years of Being a Black Poet. Indianapolis: Bobbs-Merrill, 1971; London: Penguin, 1976.

A Dialogue: James Baldwin and Nikki Giovanni, with James Baldwin. Philadelphia: Lippincott, 1973; London: M. Joseph, 1975.

A Poetic Equation: Conversations Between Nikki Giovanni and Margaret Walker, with Margaret Walker. Washington, D.C.: Howard University Press, 1974.

Sound Recordings:

Truth Is on Its Way, Right On Records, 1971.

Like a Ripple on a Pond, Atlantic Records, 1973.

The Way I Feel, Atlantic Records, 1974.

Legacies. Folkways Records, 1975.

The Poet Today, interviewed with Dan Masterson. New York: The Christophers, 1979.

The Reason I Like Chocolate, Folkways Records.

The American Arts Project: Nikki Giovanni Reading from Her Works. New York: Holmes Cassette Group, 1984.

Visual Recordings:

Spirit to Spirit: The Poetry of Nikki Giovanni, produced by Perrin Ireland, directed by Mirra Banks. New York: PBS, 1987.

Nat Hentoff

1925-

"My neighborhood as a boy." The junction of Blue Hill Avenue and Warren Street, Grove Hall, Boston.
Photograph from Picturesque Boston Highlands.
Published by the Mercantile Illustrating Company, 1895.

Not long ago, I was being interviewed by a reporter in Phoenix and she asked me to cite the key influences on my life. No one had ever asked me that before, but without a pause, I knew, and gave, the answer: Being Jewish. Jazz. The First Amendment.

I grew up in Roxbury, then a ghetto of Boston. It was in the 1930s and early 1940s, a time of righteous anti-Semitism around the country, but nowhere more fierce than in Boston. Indeed, one journalist, John Roy Carlson, having explored most of the major cities in the nation, concluded in a book that Boston was the capital of American anti-Semitism.

There were pamphlets, broadsides, newspapers that spread the inciteful word that Jews were simultaneously in the highest ranks of international communism while also being capitalist bloodsuckers who were draining the very life out of working people.

The printed assaults were scary in view of what the radio and the press told us of what was happening in Germany. But far more frightening were the raids—the squadrons of young hooligans descending on our neighborhood and acting as if they were imitating the newsreels: pushing Jews of whatever age into the gutters and punching out kids. Me included.

So, being Jewish under these circumstances had a considerable impact. I knew I was an outsider; I thought like an outsider; and therefore I learned to be continually skeptical of what insiders with power said they believed (like, "America the beautiful land of pluralism") by contrast with what they did. As I grew older, I wasn't in the least surprised that the most prestigious Yankee clubs—supposedly heirs in spirit to the goals of Emerson and Thoreau—had no places for Jews. And, of course, during those years, many colleges had Jewish quotas—a cutoff point on the number of Jewish applicants accepted, no matter how qualified they were.

The men's shop owned by Simon Hentoff, Nat's father

As I grew older, the knowledge of what it feels like to be an outcast led me to learn empathy with others of the excluded—blacks, women, homosexuals, and in time, Arab-Americans, Hispanics, Catholics (anti-Catholicism being "the anti-Semitism of liberals"). I lived on the margins of the mainstream, and over the years, I have written primarily about people on the margins.

Being Jewish shaped me in another way. From my father, from other elders in the ghetto—however much they disagreed among themselves politically—I constantly heard that to be just is to be Jewish, and to be unjust is to be un-Jewish. Where I lived, this came not so much out of a religious imperative but from the social and political ethos of the Enlightenment—when Jews in Europe freed themselves from the ghettos and the shetls in their minds as well as the geographic ones in which they lived. The sunlight turned many of these Jews into idealists. They believed in the perfectibility of man and therefore of society. Accordingly, they believed justice—economic, personal, national, Zionist—was a realistic possibility, let alone necessity, in any new world worth making. Justice not only for Jews.

Few of these contentious Jews among whom I grew up knew or cared anything about jazz. But from the age of eleven, I was obsessed with the music—and the musicians. The emotional openness, the deeply pulsing and contagious beat, the wondrous fact that each player had his own "sound" and was telling his own story. And the risks, the nightly risks each of

them took—improvising as if on a high wire (as one of my daughters, a circus performer, does now: a jazz performer though she doesn't know it).

When I was very young, I would slip into Sunday jam sessions and then into jazz clubs at night. At Boston Latin School, I hid *Down Beat* in my geography book; at Northeastern University, we talked of jazz, James Joyce, and Trotsky between classes; and at Harvard, I abandoned a scholarship in the graduate school because I realized one night, in Widener Library, that I was not going to be a professor. I was too much of an outsider, but no, that wasn't the real reason. There was a lot I liked in the academy—especially that library—but I didn't feel the academy had much joy in it or rage or intimate lyricism. It was all so well-mannered.

That night, I walked out of Widener Library and took a streetcar to Boston and the Savoy Café where Sidney Bechet, the moon-faced soprano saxophonist from New Orleans, was passionately, daringly, and so satisfyingly filling the air with memories, desires, and luminous fantasies. As always, I felt at home at the Savoy. Not only because nearly everybody there, certainly including the musicians, was an outsider but also because the freedom—in the music, in the conversations—was way beyond any I had known in school or at home. It was exhilarating, and it all originated from those sounds. The sounds—as jazz critic Whitney Balliett was later to write—of surprise.

The First Amendment was known to me only briefly and abstractly until I became the editor of the

Northeastern News. The staff was composed largely of muckrakers or, to use the more refined term, investigative reporters. We reported, without fear or favor, on what was wrong with the university—too much money going to the athletic department; too many elementary-school kinds of rules imposed by the autocratic president throughout the university; and, of course, cafeteria food that would have violated the Eighth Amendment, if we had known what that was.

But we didn't stay on campus. The *Northeastern News*—more thoroughly than any of the dailies in the city—covered anti-Semitism in Boston. Who provided the money for the hate sheets? Which "respectable" organizations were the cover for the ravening bigots?

The Administration became nervous as our paper grew more and more unpredictable. The tipping point occurred when we decided to do a series on the Board of Trustees. Who were these people? Did they know anything about education, or were they on the board only because they gave large contributions to the university?

As soon as the president of the university heard of our alarming project, a ukase came down. We were to pledge either to confine all newsgathering to uncontroversial matters on the campus, and only on campus, or we would be dismissed from the paper. All but one of us (who was to become the instant new editor) resigned forthwith, in sorrow and anger.

At that point, I became passionately interested in freedom of the press, and indeed years later, the page of acknowledgements in my book on the First Amendment, *The First Freedom: The Tumultuous History of Free Speech in America*, began:

"For my abiding concern with the First Amendment, I am particularly indebted to those officials at Northeastern University in Boston who tried to censor the writings of the staff when I was editor of the *Northeastern News* in the early 1940s . . . I never lost my sense of rage at those who would suppress speech, especially mine. Those administrators truly helped inspire this book."

In a fantasy come true, in the early 1970s, I was invited to return to Northeastern to receive a medal as a "distinguished alumnus." I devoted my acceptance speech to telling the students what had happened to me and the other staff members of the *Northeastern News* in the city that prided itself on its contribution to the Zeitgeist of freedom that created the American Revolution.

While still in college, I worked at a Boston radio station, WMEX, and continued working there during my brief stay at Harvard Graduate School.

Nat at age two

Being in radio was a most instructive postgraduate experience. I got to know such storied political figures as James Michael Curley (fictionalized in Edwin O'Connor's *Last Hurrah*) and most important, I had a chance to actually talk to such jazz heroes as Duke Ellington, Charlie Parker, Rex Stewart, and Frankie Newton on my own jazz program. That too was a fantasy come true.

For some years, I also programmed and announced a classical-music hour. What made it different was that I didn't give the name of the work or the performers until the recording was over. This greatly frustrated most listeners, but many eventually discovered that their tastes were a lot broader than they had realized. People, for example, who despised Tchaikovsky—who was not "in" during those years of the popularity of baroque music—were astonished and even pleased when they discovered that a piece they very much enjoyed was one of his. And listeners who couldn't abide certain pianists, for instance, were startled to find that one of those excluded musicians was the very pianist who had just performed so beautifully.

From this experiment, I learned a lot about what W.H. Auden called "rehearsed responses." And when I moved into journalism, I was able to recognize

A class photo at William Lloyd Garrison elementary school, Boston.
Nat is second from right in the back row.

"rehearsed responses" from all kinds of people who had made up their minds before they had actually examined the evidence. Including journalists.

While in radio, I parlayed my jazz series into work as a stringer for *Down Beat*, the nation's leading jazz magazine. I was sufficiently controversial in the articles I wrote to be invited in 1953 to become the New York editor of *Down Beat*. For several years, until I was fired, I was utterly immersed in the jazz world—reviewing musicians in clubs every night, writing during the day and all through the weekends.

For someone as jazz-struck as I was, and still am, it was a glorious period. The giants of jazz were still jousting and surprising their audiences and themselves. I heard and talked with Thelonious Monk, Charles Mingus, Miles Davis, Cecil Taylor, and many more. When I was a boy, I romanticized jazz creators. By the time I was working for *Down Beat*, I knew their flaws as well as their strengths, but I continued to admire the honesty and courage of their art.

As a journalist and author of books, I have come to know a wide spectrum of people—from members of Congress and schoolteachers to judges and bioethicists—and by and large, with exceptions, I still find jazzmen and jazzwomen in disproportionately high numbers among the nobility of the realm.

What has saddened me through the years is that most American schoolchildren know practically nothing of what drummer Max Roach has called "America's true classical music." For one example, Duke Ellington is the most original and far-ranging com-

poser in all of American history, but how many American youngsters know that? In how many schools is his music taught?

I was fired from *Down Beat* because I had been agitating for some time for someone black to be hired in the New York office. Here we were writing about and profiting from an essentially black American music, but no blacks were on staff. One day, a dark young woman applied for a job, and I insisted that headquarters in Chicago hire her. Weary of my hectoring, headquarters in Chicago hired her and told me to clear out my desk. The young woman stayed. She wasn't black, as it turned out. She was a dark Arab-American.

Trying to survive—with a first baby on the way—I quickly discovered that I was stereotyped. Editors knew me as a writer on jazz and they promised assignments whenever something of jazz interest to them came up. Maybe once or twice a year.

What saved me from penury or almost as bad, work in advertising or promotion, was a job that for a long time paid nothing. In 1956, a very small weekly had started in Greenwich Village, the *Village Voice*. Two years later, I was offered a column. The paper was so financially precarious that only a couple of staff people and the editor received a meager salary. For the rest of the writers, there was only psychic income.

I worked out a deal. In return for no money, I would never be asked to write a word about jazz. As time went on, I wrote in that column about civil liberties, education, politics, police Red Squads, school segregation in New York, corporal punishment in schools everywhere, and the Supreme Court. Not a word about jazz.

As the paper's circulation began to rise, I was able to escape from the stereotype of being capable of writing only about jazz. I free-lanced for a number of magazines, wrote books on subjects other than jazz, and was even asked to lecture on a fairly wide spectrum of subjects at colleges and before librarians' associations.

The lectures, which have continued, are very useful for me. I get a far more immediate sense of the diversity of the country—despite the ubiquitous shopping malls and fast-food insignia. I learn, for instance, that attempted censorship of books is combated differently in, let's say, a small town in downstate Illinois than in Phoenix. I get story leads—both for journalism and fiction—that I couldn't have learned about without being there.

Also, it is extremely valuable for a New York writer to get out of that city (which imagines itself America) frequently. There is a parochialism in New York—especially among some of its writers—that is far more narrow and self-congratulatory than exists in most very small towns. So, like Willie Nelson, I'm glad to be on the road.

A good many of the invitations to lecture come because of my books for young adults. I had never even remotely considered writing a book for young readers until Ursula Nordstrom called me in the early 1960s. She was head of Harper and Row's division of books for young readers. Among her many other accomplishments, she had discovered Maurice Sendak.

She asked me if I'd like to try writing a book for that audience. I told her that, first of all, it had seemed to me that if kids like to read, they go right to adult books on subjects in which they are interested. That's what children of my generation did. Second, I did not want to work with any kind of required vocabulary list, avoiding words "too difficult" for young readers.

Ursula Nordstrom said that there really were kids out there who were as devoted to reading as we were back then who also liked books written particularly for them. She also told me not to worry about any vocabulary list. Use the words you need to tell the story, she said.

The result was *Jazz Country*, which may be the most durable book I've written. I wanted to show something about the jazz life and how hard—though not impossible—it is for a white kid to break into it. I wanted to show all kids how rich and deep this music is. Because of the book, I received the highest compliment any work of mine has ever received. A librarian in New York told me it was the most stolen volume in her collection. White kids have told me that they'd never realized how much there is to jazz and that now they've started collecting records of the music. And black readers have written and even called to talk about the book.

I have since written a number of other books for young readers and I've found, as with *Jazz Country*, that kids write to authors far more often than adults do. Some of the letters come as obvious class projects, but many are decidedly and flavorfully individualistic. I often fall behind with my other correspondence, but letters from young readers always get answered. I have never forgotten the acute disappointment of one of my daughters when she wrote to an author whose book she'd liked very much. After several months, she finally received a glossy photograph of the author as the sole response to her questions.

That daughter, Jessica, now thirty-two, is a circus performer, traveling all over the United States doing an intricate trapeze act with her partner, Kathie

Nat at twelve in Roxbury

Fifteen years old

have longer pieces printed there than in almost any other publication in the country. And the payment is abundant. The editing is exceptionally respectful of the writer's intent—and his feelings. There is also the fabled checking department which assures a writer that by the time a piece is printed, he will not be embarrassed by whatever factual errors were in his manuscript. All will have been purged before publication.

As I came to write less about jazz—although I still cover the music, along with country sounds, fairly regularly—my obsessions encompassed the Bill of Rights (and not only the First Amendment); education (a continuing national scandal, with most poor children foredoomed by bad schooling to a life in the underclass); and what John Cardinal O'Connor of New York has called "the consistent ethic of death."

Euthanasia, from handicapped infants to the elderly in nursing homes, has become increasingly accepted in this country; and there are grim parallels between the Third Reich and the ways in which

Hoyer. Like jazz musicians, she makes her living by taking risks and does it with grace, wit, and élan.

Her younger sister, Miranda, twenty-nine, is a compelling jazz pianist as well as a singer and composer. She is also what they call a master teacher at New York City's Lincoln Center which sends her to schools throughout the state, and as far as Australia to teach teachers how to learn to open schoolchildren to the pleasures of music.

Nicholas, twenty-five, has been a journalist, a Congressional aide, a writer in the national press on Indian law and Indian civil rights, and is finishing his work for a law degree at the University of Arizona, after which he will clerk for a Federal judge in Phoenix.

Thomas, twenty-three, is a novelist who has been accepted at Columbia University Law School.

Nicholas, I should add, was the model for Sam in *This School Is Driving Me Crazy* and *Does This School Have Capital Punishment*? The title for the former book, probably the most popular title of any book I've done, came from Tom.

In the years after *Down Beat*, along with writing books for both young readers and adults, I became a staff writer for the *New Yorker*, doing primarily profiles. The *New Yorker* is an extraordinary place to write for. If you can justify the space, you can

As a nineteen-year-old student at Northeastern University, Boston

American courts are removing the barriers to killing human beings.

Accordingly, I've written a great deal about the killing of handicapped infants and in the years ahead, I intend to focus on the accelerating danger to the old and the chronically infirm from those who believe that their "quality of life" is not good enough for them to be allowed to keep on living.

I'm convinced that all these obsessions of mine—from euthanasia to the killing of the spirit and self-confidence of youngsters in classrooms—come originally from the contagious life-force of jazz. And that sense of justice which for me, growing up, was synonymous with Judaism.

There is also a basic orneriness of temperament that had its roots, in part, in both jazz and being Jewish. The kind of reporting, for example, for which I have no respect is "herd journalism." When I first came to New York, reporter and Pulitzer Prize columnist Murray Kempton gave me valuable advice: "If you see a bunch of reporters at a story, go find some other story."

When there's a herd of reporters, the skepticism that ought to be natural to a journalist tends to be rubbed smooth and the reader gets a bland, consensus report. My heroes and influences in journalism have been the "lonely pamphleteers," the rambunctious muckrakers—particularly George Seldes and I.F. Stone. When I was in my early teens, I began reading Seldes's broadside, "In Fact," and was astonished that this one man had the courage to go after the tobacco interests (he was the first to report the link between cancer and cigarettes), the manufacturers of other dangerous products, and the newspapers that kept back information from their readers so as not to lose their advertisers. "Izzy" Stone too refused to be intimidated by any pressures, and his regular newsletters were a continuing source of rare information—and inspiration—for young reporters around the country, including me.

Other enduring influences on my work, and not only journalism, have been editors: particularly William Shawn of the *New Yorker* and Dan Wolf, cofounder of the *Village Voice*. Mr. Shawn (as everyone calls him) was not only exceptionally skilful at detecting soft spots in a manuscript, but he also excelled at giving a writer confidence. I have never known a writer who did not need reassurance, constant reassurance. For Mr. Shawn, I worked on long profiles of complex people requiring formidable amounts of research, and then more research. Whenever I began to feel that this time, I had finally reached beyond my capacities, I could hear Mr. Shawn's soft voice from the last piece I had done: "That was a very hard thing

Interviewing Massachusetts governor Maurice Tobin at WMEX, Boston

Fay Foto Service, Inc., Boston

to do, and it worked out very, very well."

I mention this both because his confidence has been valuable to me in all areas of my work but also because this quality of Mr. Shawn has seldom been stressed in the many other accounts of this nonpareil editor.

Dan Wolf, who left editing to become the principal adviser to Ed Koch, mayor of New York, was and is the quintessential skeptic. The *Village Voice*, in its early years as now, was a place of true believers in various holy expeditions of the Left. Except for Dan. With just a look, he could skewer a writer's fervent, one-dimensional tribute to—or denunciation of—a person or a political movement. The look said: "Are you a writer or a propagandist?"

Growing up an outsider in Boston, I've always been a skeptic and distrustful of rhetoric, whether jingoistic or radical, but from Dan Wolf, I learned to be even more questioning—questioning what I was told and questioning myself.

No one I've ever met is quicker to discern and scornfully reject cant, newspeak, and lies (however unwitting) than my wife Margot. We disagree on a good many things (she is pro-choice, for instance, and I'm pro-life), but she is the most valuable editor I have. She seldom goes over copy as such, but as I talk out ideas for books and articles, I've learned to pay attention to her resounding signals when she hears the slightest trace of buncombe or just plain infirm grammar.

A continuing influence is what I learn from students in schools I visit in the course of any given year. My own schooling, particularly from the seventh to the twelfth grades, was vital to what eventually became of me. I went to Boston Latin School, the oldest public school in the country (founded in 1635). Among its alumni: Cotton Mather, Sam Adams, Ralph Waldo Emerson, George Santayana. Any boy in the city (it was later integrated with Girls Latin School) could get in if he could pass the entrance exam. But once you were in, there was no guarantee you would stay. As Theodore H. White, an alumnus, said in his memoir, *In Search of History*, Latin School "accepted students without discrimination, and it flunked them—Irish, Italian, Jewish, Protestant, black—with equal lack of discrimination."

The survivors learned a simple but very basic and lasting lesson: If you work hard enough, you can accomplish anything. Homework averaged three hours a night, all the courses were tough, as were the masters (the school's name for teachers). But the masters made it clear that they expected us to be able to do the work, and that if we failed, it wasn't because we came from poor families (as many of us did) or because we were not intelligent enough, but rather because we did not work hard enough.

It wasn't until years later that I realized that these stern, often flinty, masters had given me an extremely important boost for life: their confidence that I could do what I was supposed to do. Ever since, the often long, tedious work that goes into research has not seemed to be too dreary a burden because, from my Latin School years, I know that if I stick with it, it'll pay off.

In going around to schools throughout the country, I don't see nearly enough principals and teachers with high expectations of their students. But most of the kids themselves, from small schools in Wyoming to large high schools in the East, are just as open to learn and to stretch themselves as we were at Boston Latin School. Much of the time, we talk about the First Amendment and censorship and while it's clear that most of them have had far too little classwork in the most important subject that can be taught in this constitutional democracy, once they get the lay of the land, they become enthusiasts of freedom of expression.

One of my main regrets so far is that although I have occasionally taught college classes for an academic year, I have never spent more than two or three days in a junior high or high school. I'd much rather teach students of that age because, by and large, they have yet to be constricted in their minds and imaginations by careerism.

With son, Nicholas (top), and daughter Miranda

Fred W. McDarrah

What I do try to teach, in classrooms and in lectures, is the necessity of surprising yourself, of discovering that even your most cherished absolutes—including even freedom of expression—are not as one-sidedly unambivalent as you fondly believe.

For instance, some years ago, a junior-high-school librarian in downstate Illinois taught me a lesson. She is an active member of the American Civil Liberties Union, works with the Intellectual Freedom Division of the American Library Association, and in her town and county has worked hard to keep the First Amendment intact.

She told me that one of my books for young readers was being shunned by some of the parents. She felt I should understand why. The novel, *This School Is Driving Me Crazy*, has a couple of mild expletives, "damn" and "hell." The objections, the librarian went on, were from Christian fundamentalists who take "damn" and "hell" literally. They will not allow their children to be exposed to blasphemy.

"It's simple," the librarian said, "to just yell

censorship! But you have to know where these people are coming from."

The librarian would not, and did not, remove my book from the school library. But she respected the concerns of those parents and refused to categorize them as simple censors. They would have fallen into that category if they had insisted that no child in the school could read my book.

As for some of the more lasting satisfactions I get from my work, one is the fact that high-school school kids still read my book on the First Amendment, *The First Freedom.* I take very seriously what Abraham Lincoln said:

"All the armies of Europe and Asia . . . could not by force take a drink from the Ohio River. . . . As a nation of free men, we will live forever or die by suicide."

If kids do not get a strong sense that the Constitution, very much including the Bill of Rights, actually belongs to each of them, they will grow up indifferent to their own—and others'—liberties and rights. And if enough of the citizenry are careless in these matters, those liberties and rights will be suicidally lost.

Of all my obsessions, this is the strongest, and that's why in just about all the writing I do, fiction and nonfiction, freedom—how to get it, how to lose it—is a fundamental theme.

Nonetheless, I also like to tell stories because otherwise, my work would consist of tracts, and they're so boring they're not even remaindered. I intend to write more fiction, as time goes on, particularly a long multigenerational novel about New York, some of whose main characters will be intellectuals who never went to Elaine's, never won any prizes, and never appeared on television.

There will also be more books for young readers about Sam, a decent kid who gets into trouble from the moment he gets out of bed in the morning. After Sam is graduated from high school, I expect to follow him to college.

I keep thinking I will not do any more nonfiction books because I so enjoy writing fiction, but something always comes up. A *New Yorker* profile of John Cardinal O'Connor led me to write a book on the changing American Catholic Church with O'Connor at the center of both that change and the resistance to that change. And I know I will eventually have to write the sequel to my memoir, *Boston Boy.* It'll be about my years in New York and such tumultuous people I came to know well as Malcolm X, Dr. Kenneth Clark, Charles Mingus, Lenny Bruce, and Mario Cuomo.

"My office at the Village Voice," *New York City*

And some day, I would like to do a book for very, very young children, like *Goodnight Moon*. But that takes very special skills, particularly the ability to remember all the way back.

Meanwhile, from time to time, I receive signals from out there that one way or another, I'm reaching somebody. One afternoon, in the summer of 1987, a teacher from Mowat Middle School in Bay County, Florida, called to tell me that the principal had just banned a number of books. One of them was mine: *The Day They Came to Arrest the Book.*

BIBLIOGRAPHY

Fiction:

Call the Keeper. New York: Viking, 1966; London: Secker & Warburg, 1967.

Onwards! New York: Simon & Schuster, 1968.

Blues for Charlie Darwin. New York: Morrow, 1982; London: Constable, 1983.

The Man from Internal Affairs. New York: Mysterious Press, 1985.

Nonfiction:

Jazz Street (illustrated with photographs by Dennis Stouk). London: Deutsch, 1960.

The Jazz Life. New York: Dial, 1961; London: P. Davies, 1962.

Peace Agitator: The Story of A.J. Muste. New York: Macmillan, 1963.

The New Equality. New York: Viking, 1964.

Our Children Are Dying. New York: Viking, 1966.

A Doctor among the Addicts. Chicago: Rand McNally, 1968.

A Political Life: The Education of John V. Lindsay. New York: Knopf, 1969.

State Secrets: Police Surveillance in America, with Paul Cowan and Nick Egleson. New York: Holt, 1974.

Jazz Is. New York: Random House, 1976; London: W.H. Allen, 1978.

Does Anybody Give a Damn? On Education. New York: Knopf, 1977.

The First Freedom: A Tumultuous History of Free Speech in America. New York: Delacorte, 1980.

Boston Boy (memoir). New York: Knopf, 1986.

Juvenile:

Jazz Country. New York: Harper, 1965.

I'm Really Dragged But Nothing Gets Me Down. New York: Simon & Schuster, 1968.

Journey into Jazz (illustrated by David Stone Martin). New York: Coward McCann, 1968.

In the Country of Ourselves. New York: Simon & Schuster, 1971.

This School Is Driving Me Crazy. New York: Delacorte, 1976; London: Angus & Robertson, 1977.

Does This School Have Capital Punishment? New York: Delacorte, 1981; London: Angus & Robertson, 1982.

The Day They Came to Arrest the Book. New York: Delacorte, 1982.

American Heroes: In and Out of School. New York: Delacorte, 1987.

Editor of:

Hear Me Talkin' to Ya: The Story of Jazz by the Men Who Made It, with Nat Shapiro. New York: Rinehart, 1955; London: P. Davies, 1955.

The Jazz Makers, with Nat Shapiro. New York: Rinehart, 1957; London: P. Davies, 1958.

Jazz: New Perspectives on the History of Jazz, with Albert J. McCarthy. New York: Rinehart, 1959; London: Cassell, 1960.

The Essays of A.J. Muste. Indianapolis: Bobbs Merrill, 1967.

Other:

Journey into Jazz: For Narrator, Jazz Ensemble, and Small Orchestra. Narration by Nat Hentoff; music by Gunther Schuller. New York: Associated Music Publishers, 1967.

Clarence Major

1936-

LICKING STAMPS, TAKING CHANCES

Clarence Major with Pamela Jane Ritter, just before their marriage, 1980

I am sitting in my studio-study, gazing at the screen of the computer as I type these words on the pc. My wife, Pamela, and I still forget and call the studio the toolshed because seven years ago it was a trashed ex-tool shop larger than a garage but smaller than a barn. When I bought the house in 1979 this separate structure came with it. Since that time, when we were not living in France or Italy, or California or Massachusetts, we worked at fixing up the place. A fenceless lot filled with weeds surrounded the house. Now, I can gaze over the screen this very moment at a backyard fenced with beautiful cedar and see a ground covered with rich, green grass. If I sound proud or self-satisfied, it is because I am.

It is a warm sunny day, November 23, 1986. I am in love with my wife, who, I believe, saved my life with her love. I will be fifty years old at the end of next month. What better time to assemble a view of the past?

On my father's side I was able to trace the family history back as far as the early 1860s, around the time my great-grandfather, Ned Major, was born in Alabama. He was probably born a slave but grew up free. He wandered from camp to camp, did odd jobs to survive. One of his sons, George Major, was my grandfather. He was born at Smith Station in Lee County, Alabama, in 1883. George moved to Georgia as a young man and eventually married my grandmother Anna Jackson. An adopted child, she was born in 1882 in either Clark County or Oglethorpe County. Her foster mother's name was Edith Jackson. Her biological father, a black man, was Barry Jewel; her biological mother, a white woman, was named Rebecca (variant spelling, Rebekar).

A white-looking woman, Anna grew up black in a social system that kept rigid divisions between blacks and whites. Her presence among blacks often confused white folks and caused many embarrassing incidents. Once, while working as a servant for a white family, she was serving dinner to the family and one of their dinner guests advised her employer to hire a colored person because the colored servants were cheaper.

Anna was one of my favorite persons in the whole world. She was a generous-hearted woman. My sister, Serena, and I stayed with her from time to time. I remember once accompanying her to her bank to get some money. She wept when the clerk told her the bank was broke and she would never get her money. I don't think she trusted banks after that. I saw her cry many times, usually, though, it was out of empathy with someone else's misfortune.

Anna had nine children before she married my grandfather George. All during my own childhood this was a well-kept secret. Together she and George had six children: two boys and four girls. I had a mean aunt and a nice aunt, just like in the storybooks. My father, Clarence Major (a man of humor and grace), was born at noon on July 10, 1910, at Grady

Hospital in Atlanta, and died in Atlanta on August 17, 1963.

He learned to survive with his dignity intact a good deal of the time and this was an enormous accomplishment in a, then, rigidly racist and segregated city. He never rode the public buses, for example, because blacks were obliged to sit at the back. He walked unbelievable distances, when he had to, to avoid the insult of public transportation. He was hard but never reduced to meanness. Some of us close to him knew him as a loving and compassionate person.

My mother was born Inez Huff on April 23, 1919, in Lexington, Georgia, Oglethorpe County. At the time of her birth Woodrow Wilson was president, the Harlem Renaissance was beginning, there were racial riots in twenty-six American cities. When she was ten, the New York Stock Market collapsed and the world economic crisis began and the American Depression set in. She had two older brothers and three older sisters.

My mother's parents were Henry Huff and Ada Bronner. They had more material wealth than did my father's people. They owned their own land and home and livestock. They were relatively self-sufficient even during the lean years of the Depression. I remember going with my grandmother once to a store to buy the only thing they could not produce on their little farm: salt. My grandfather built the house he and Ada shared.

Henry Huff, descendant of Anglo-Saxons and Africans, was born sometime during the 1880s and died in 1944 after years spent in a wheelchair. He'd suffered a stroke at an abnormally young age. His room always smelled of camphor. Son of a white Lexington judge and a black mother, he grew up to be a successful architect (I say architect because he designed as well as constructed the buildings he built). Many of the buildings in Lexington during the thirties were built by him, including the white and black churches.

Ada Bronner, descended from Cherokees and Africans, was born in 1888 and died in the early 1980s. I remember her as silent and brooding when she wasn't humming some spiritual. She was a person of few words.

My mother and father married when my mother

Father, Clarence Major, Sr., and Grandmother Anna Jackson Major, with Father's best friend, Sanders, mid-1940s

Henry Huff on his farm in Lexington, Georgia, about 1915

was sixteen. She was a very pretty girl and he felt lucky to get her. My mother was seventeen when I was born on December 31, 1936, at 7:33 A.M. in the then-colored wing of Grady Hospital in Atlanta. I was underweight. At the time of my birth, Hitler had been in power for four years. Roosevelt was president. New cars were selling for $375. But nobody had any money. Movies featured Shirley Temple, Nelson Eddy, and Jeanette MacDonald. Blacks on screen were invariably clowns or mammies. The Lindberghs had just fled to England. Jesse Owens won four gold medals in Berlin. The Scottsboro Boys were brought to trial. Haile Selassie was dethroned. Howard Hughes flew a plane a fantastic 260 miles per hour across country. Charlie Chaplin, Margaret Sanger, and Marian Anderson were household names.

My sister, Serena, was born February 19, 1937, in the same hospital wing. She was a big baby and she was smart as a whip. Among my first memories, one is of pinching her in her crib. Serena was a more aggressive learner than I was. I followed her lead. She taught me how to tie my shoestrings, how to tell time.

I also remember my sister and I, with our parents, among neighbors during a World War Two blackout and all of us on Woodrow Place turning out our lights and huddling together watching the night skies and the searchlights moving across them like drugged spirits. It was more festive than fearful.

We lived, at first, in a wood frame house on McGruder Street, then later on Woodrow Place. My first memories are housed there. (When I returned to Atlanta in 1984 and walked through that area I recognized nothing except the physical shape of the cul-de-sac.)

My parents divorced in the late 1940s. My father remained in Atlanta and my mother moved to Chicago where her sister Luvenia helped her get established. In Atlanta my father carried on a number of business interests. At various times he owned a restaurant, a gas station, a trucking service. We grew up mainly with our mother in Chicago. There were a few visits to Atlanta to visit our father during the fifties.

In Chicago, my family lived on Oakwood Boulevard. Across the street was a popular nightclub in a famous South Side hotel. I'm ashamed to admit that I've forgotten the name of it but it was on the corner of South Parkway and Oakwood Boulevard. In those days, some of the best jazz was being performed there in the hotel lounge. I wasn't aware of it then but it is a fact.

The house was owned by a woman named Mrs. Elizabeth Williams. She was something of a *grande*

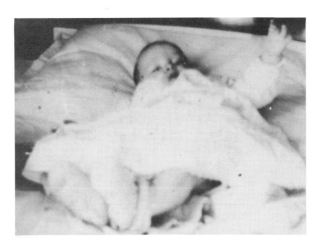

Inez Huff, one month old

dame with old New Orleans flair. Her apartment nearly always smelled of pies or cakes baking and she herself smelled of strong perfume and powder. There was a chattering parrot in her kitchen by the bar. Elizabeth Williams talked glowingly of the old days when Count Basie and Duke Ellington rented rooms from her while performing across the street. Lionel Hampton and many other musicians stayed there too. I grew up in this house with Johnny Otis's wife, Phyllis, walking around in a bathrobe and fussing with her infant, Janice. This was 1947. Otis himself was rarely there. I was in love with his wife, Phyllis. She never knew it but I was. I don't know whose vibraphones, Hampton's or some other musician's, were always there in the living room. We had the large apartment upstairs over Elizabeth Williams's.

I started writing seriously when I was twelve. I wrote novels, stories, and poems. I was also painting and drawing a lot. In elementary school, at Forestville, and later at Phillips and Dunbar, I won many prizes in art contests.

When my mother married Halbert Ming in 1949 we moved into a larger apartment in a building near a Catholic church and school. Having grown up Protestant, the Catholics, seen in passing, seemed so much saner in their faith. When Serena and I were small we were told we had to go to church. When given the choice, we went to Holy Angels, the Catholic church on Oakwood Boulevard, because there there were fewer moral appeals and demands on us generally.

Elementary school was as hectic as it could possibly be. Forestville was a gigantic school with a vast playground. After I got over earning my right to be there by fighting off the bullies, I found some time

Inez Major, Chicago, about 1947

was made redder with tomato juice. My job was emptying the cans beneath the meat counter. My coworkers, boys my own age, were into jazz. I first learned to respect classical jazz while listening to them.

My mother's foster parents, Mom and Pop, lived on South Parkway. They were simply "play" foster parents, the people who had taken my mother in when she was a young woman, and, along with Aunt Luvenia, had helped her get established in Chicago. For awhile, when I couldn't get along with my stepfather, I lived with Mom and Pop. I especially loved Mom. Pop I didn't know too well, but he was no problem. He was one of the head waiters at the Palmer House and had met many movie stars and came home telling us about them all the time. They tipped big. Pop also brought home Palmer House Worcester Sauce. I hated it as much as I hated Jell-O. Even today I can't stand the taste.

Meanwhile, I continued writing stories and novels. Crude things but there they were. My paintings were taking up so much room in my bedroom that we started storing them out in the hallway. Some of that work was good and I now wish the good things had

to concentrate on schoolwork. Boys were making zip guns but nobody, in those days, was smoking dope and street drugs generally were something we only vaguely knew about.

Some teachers singled me out for special treatment and I let it go to my head—but not for long. The United Nations was just beginning—and I was assigned to illustrate its workings for the class. Ralph Bunche was soon to win a Nobel Prize for his diplomatic work in Palestine. General MacArthur invaded the Philippines and Hitler had already committed suicide.

On the basis of several watercolors of figures and landscapes, I won a James Nelson Raymond Scholarship to the sketch and lecture classes in Fullerton Hall at the Art Institute and soon discovered that the city was literally full of gifted children like myself. I stayed with the art lessons till shortly before I joined the air force.

Because we were not well off, I had worked from an early age. One job I especially remember as a major failure was selling salve in tins. I'm sure I was not yet ten. This was on South Parkway. The grimness with which people walked by me was a profound lesson. I never forgot it. I think I went home, at the end of the day, with a quarter.

I worked in a grocery store where the hamburger

Clarence with sister Serena, Atlanta, about 1942

been saved. My mother has two works from that period, one in her bedroom, the other in her living room. Some of my teachers thought I was some sort of genius, others told me I was a misfit and that my laziness would cause me to fail in life. They thought it was a pity because I did have talent.

I was growing up in a time when not only was there much to lament but a time when new, positive things were happening. *Lady Chatterley's Lover* for the first time was being sold *over* the counter in the United States. A woman named Rosa Parks, a black woman in the South, one day would refuse to move to the back of a public bus. Something new was in the air. The Civil Rights Movement would soon begin.

In high school there were a whole bunch of us who had talent to burn. One example, the musician, Herbie Hancock. One year, we were both in Mr. Green's music class at the same time. Not having the sense to be afraid to try anything, I wrote a symphony, but had to ask Mr. Green to play it for me. I had this idea that, if Beethoven could write music while deaf, I could try to do it purely in visual terms. Mr. Green refused to play it but got Herbie to attempt it. Herbie managed to get through two or three pages of the twenty-five page symphony before he gave up. It made no sense to him. I considered it a Dadaist symphony influenced by Bud Powell. You can imagine how disorganized it was!

After high school and a brief time at the Art Institute on the Raymond Scholarship, sketching from moving models or listening to lectures from Addis Osborne or Synthia Bollingen and others, I joined the air force to seek new adventures. The recruiters had promised me the glory of new horizons!

In the air force I worked in an office after basic training. The office was on a base in Valdosta, Georgia, which depressed me. The training had been near San Antonio, Texas; that fact also had depressed me. Without my friends, black guys from the North, both experiences would have been unbearable. The towns and cities, then, were still extremely racist. There were endless restrictions on where a black person could go and on what he could do.

During these years I was reading extensively in philosophy, religion, anthropology, history, poetry, fiction, and biography. I was also writing and beginning to publish in the little magazines of the 1950s. Sometimes my friends went to dances but I couldn't dance. Sometimes they went to the roller-skating rink but I couldn't roller-skate (although as a child I had been a champion roller skater on the sidewalks back in the Chicago days when they called me Hopscotch-

Seven years old in Lexington, Georgia

Cowboy because I was equally at ease with the girls jumping rope and with the boys playing cowboy).

When I got out of the air force I started a little magazine of my own called *Coercion Review*. In it I published the works of people I was corresponding with, like D.V. Smith and Carl Larsen. I also published an original essay by Henry Miller called "Lime Twigs and Treachery." When it was reprinted in *Stand Still Like the Hummingbird*, he did not bother to credit my magazine for first appearance. There were things also by Ferlinghetti and Kenneth Patchen. The activity of publishing my own magazine threw me in direct contact with hundreds of other poets and fiction writers and editors all over the country and in Europe.

Meanwhile, there was the Chicago artistic life in general, which I found attractive. I used to go on weekends to the College of Complexes up on the North Side with friends who were interested in art and literature. I felt weird in my own community but up there on the North Side, among weirdos, I felt at home. Strange. There was something different being expressed. I ate it up. I recognized in it things I had read and dreamed about that had more to do with Paris of the 1920s and 1930s than with the present values of the South Side with its emphasis on big cars and fine clothes.

I also began a correspondence with painter Sheri Martinelli who had known Ezra Pound while he was at Saint Elizabeth's Hospital and who had earlier lived the good bohemian life in New York and knew Tennessee Williams and had been a close friend of Charlie Parker. She fascinated me and I wrote book reviews for her little magazine called *Anagogic and Paideumic Review.* At one point, she sent me a little book of her paintings Pound had published privately in Italy and to which he had written the introduction. I still have it and cherish it. Sheri was indeed one of my earliest mentors but also a friend, although we never met.

I also started corresponding with poet David Wang who was a guest editor of an issue of the *Galley Sail Review* where he published some of my poetry. I did not meet David till the early 1970s when he stopped in at my Waverly Place apartment in New York only a few months before he committed suicide. When he came to see me that one time I saw in his face that bewildering, almost apologetic look I later saw in the face of critic Arthur Oberg who came into my office at the University of Washington in Seattle and introduced himself only a few days before he killed himself. Oberg's office was next to mine and I was the new guy in the department and he was being a gentleman.

I sent some poems to William Carlos Williams on Sheri's advice and he wrote back a long bitter letter, leaving the impression that maybe writing was not worth the effort. I remember trying to understand the despair Williams was suffering but at my age and with my optimism it was difficult. This was during the time that LeRoi Jones was publishing *Yugen.* When the first issue of *Coercion Review* appeared Jones wrote and asked why "the campy photos." I had on the inside back page pictures of Henry Miller, Emilie Glen, somebody else, and myself. Jones was right: they were "campy."

Coercion Review has a history. Among the stories I could tell, is this one: I kept some of Charles Bukowski's poems too long, without accepting or rejecting them. He threatened to come and pick them up in person and he made it clear that I wouldn't like the encounter. That must have been around 1965. Meanwhile, I was publishing poems in Ron Padgett's magazine, *White Dove Review.* I think Ron was still a high-school kid at this point down in Tulsa, Oklahoma. I remember he wrote to me before he started *White Dove* and asked for advice on how to get started. Not long before, I had asked D.V. Smith, the publisher of my first published short story, the same question. He was still in the U.S. Army in Japan and about

Clarence Major, Chicago, about 1948

to bring out the issue of *Olivant* containing my story. The volume appeared in 1957, containing my story and works by Lawrence Lipton, Harry Hooton, Felix Anselm, George P. Elliott, Lawrence Ferlinghetti, Gil Orlovitz, James Schevill, Jon Silkin, and many others. So, my first published fiction was published in Japan.

Meanwhile, James Boyer May (yet another early mentor), editor of *Trace,* was encouraging me to read a wide variety of writers. He knew I was just a kid but he had taken an interest in my talent. At first, *Trace* was a writer's service magazine but later it also became a vehicle for fiction and poetry. May published some of my things in his pages then. Little-magazine writers wrote to *Trace* to bitch about various things. It was the only forum we had in those bleak Eisenhower years.

Another step I took when I got out of the air force was to get married right away to a cheerful young woman named J.S. and we had two sons, Aaron and Darrell, born in the 1950s. Hardly more than children ourselves, J.S.'s and my marriage inevitably ended by the early 1960s.

Later, still optimistic and eternally the romantic, I married again. Call her O.L. We had four children, born in the sixties: Serena Christine, Inger Lovette, Clarence Lambert, Angela Cassandra. When it became clear that divorce was the only sane solution to our problems, O.L. moved herself and the children to Los Angeles where the children grew up. I moved to New York where I grew up. But that's jumping far ahead. I was still in Chicago.

Poet Marvin Bell lived in Chicago at this time and was a student at the University of Chicago. He and I got together socially a number of times. He was publishing a magazine too, called *Statements.* When Marvin came to my apartment on Drexel and saw how many little magazines I had, he said, "Gee, you have a better collection than the University of Chicago." I had so many, they were crowding my wife and me and our two tiny sons out of living space.

Once I took Don Porter to meet Marvin, since Porter was mostly isolated as a writer and he liked knowing other writers. Don got drunk and at one point said to me, "What'd you know? You nigger like me." Marvin was embarrassed.

The publisher of *Big Table,* Paul Carroll, also dropped in at the Drexel place. It was a nervous meeting. He was hot at the time because the current issue of *Big Table* was under attack by the police for printing a chapter from William Burroughs's then unpublished novel *Naked Lunch.* Kerouac, Paul said, had named the magazine *Big Table* for him. It was the same week I received a copy of *East & West* from India: my poems side by side in a magazine with

Mother with Clarence's younger sister, Cassandra, about 1955

William Carlos Williams's. Confidence was growing.

Among the friends I was running around with was a young Afro-American singer who had lived and studied music in Paris for a number of years. He knew Lil Hardin Armstrong, who lived right there on Forty-fourth Street, the South Side. Lil had worked in King Oliver's Creole Jazz Band in the 1920s, with Baby Dodds, Johnny Dodds, Bill Johnson, Honore Dutrey, and Louis Armstrong, whom she married in 1924. She had also worked with other great jazz musicians such as Lawrence Dewey, Sidney Bechet, Sugar Johnny, Roy Palmer, Tubby Hall, Bab Frank, and Wellman Braud. She played the best ragtime piano I had ever heard.

My friend and Lil had met years before in Paris. We used to go by Lil's house and stay up late listening to her great old recordings and sipping wine and talking art and music and life and everything possible beyond life. I now know that Lil was fragile and tolerant, we were excited and needy. But I think our youth excited her and she warmed up to it.

Once my singer-friend gave a party at his own apartment and Lil, after much coaxing, agreed to play the piano and sing a little ditty. Her ex-husband's autobiography, *Satchmo,* had just appeared and was a best-seller. She lamented that militant blacks were dismissing it as representing the vision of an Uncle Tom. You could tell that some important part of her still loved Louis. She sang a tease number and then one about the infamous iceman as back-door man ready to take care of unfinished business. She must have sung three or four. Everybody loved her humor and the scattiness. It was wonderful.

As a child, hardly a man, I had met history by way of Lil. Lil's cousin was Chicago writer Frank London Brown. I heard Frank read from his work at a community center not long before his death. I remember the negative response the reactionary element in Chicago had to Brown's first novel, *Trumbull Park.* Frank died at an early age from cancer.

Another Chicago writer, Willard Motley, was not as friendly as Frank to young, beginning writers like myself. Young, new writers need to be able to see established writers in person, just to see for themselves that those books came from human beings. This goes a long way toward suggesting the possibility of themselves as creators of books. I met Motley through his brother, the painter Archibald Motley. Archibald had paintings in Gayle's Gallery on Sixty-third. I met Gayle through my childhood friend Jimmy Greer after I came out of the air force. Eventually she hung a few of my own paintings in her shop. But the meeting with Willard was brief and tense. Although he had written to me from Mexico and asked me to meet him at his mother's, I must have arrived at a bad time. He asked me to come back the next day. It seemed to me he had a very serious hangover. I never went back.

Omaha, Nebraska, 1962–1966. I went to Omaha never intending to stay longer than a couple or three months but I ended up staying much longer. My friend Don Porter had moved there and kept after me to come out and visit, so I originally went there to visit him. He was in a writers' group and they met every Saturday afternoon. Then there were musicians around and a few actors associated with the Omaha Playhouse.

Long before the editor of a slick Negro middle-class magazine that used to be published in Omaha asked me to write an article on Eddie Cleanhead Vinson, I used to see and talk with him in Paul Allen's bar, back when that place was called a dive. It later became a sophisticated jazz haunt. I used to go into Allen's when it was a rundown dive, because even then it was the only place in town that presented high quality jazz on the box and world famous musicians stopped there to perform from time to time.

When Eddie worked the weekends singing and

The author, Chicago, 1957

blowing his sax on the bandstand at Allen's he demonstrated for those too often unresponding people in the audience a very dramatic and important kind of improvisation. I doubt if more than two or three people falling in and out of Allen's in those pre-renovation days realized how permanently significant Eddie was to a blues-jazz context. Mr. Cleanhead had already worked with Cootie Williams in the early forties and in 1945 had formed his own sixteen-piece orchestra. He had worked in Chicago and New York in the fifties. In Allen's he'd sing in his powerful voice, belting out, "Cherry Red," or "Somebody's Got To Go," or "Kidney Stew Blues," then he'd pick up his alto sax and blow a rough, powerful blues-jazz solo.

It was especially painful, once in Allen's, watching a drunk laughing at Eddie in a derisive manner and calling him a has-been. I bought Eddie a few drinks from time to time and he told me about the great old days with Miles and with Bud Powell. I ate it up. At home I had the Riverside recording of him with Julian Cannonball Adderley. I would play that record and it was like living inside of history and culture.

Eddie told me about a time when he was backstage or in some apartment, I don't remember which, when cops busted in and started beating heads. For some reason they laid into Bud Powell harder than into anybody else ". . .and Bud was never the same after that beating."

Another Omaha friend was actor William Marshall, not the film actor, but the stage actor who went on to New York and worked for years with the Negro Ensemble, then famous for its production of Genet's *Blacks.* Bill was elusive and bright, sensitive and, at times, moody. Don Porter had introduced us. I later saw Bill in a 1969 production of a Negro Ensemble play and that was the first time I ever saw him on stage. I also saw him once play a supporting role in a TV series; but aside from getting together one time, talking over old times, I don't know what happened to Bill.

The political activist Ernest Chambers was my barber. (Ernie later became a state senator.) I remember weekend heated discussions about politics and race relations in that barbershop. In a way, it was a good "classroom" for raising consciousness.

Riots and so-called riots were sprinkling cities across America and Omaha was on the bandwagon too. I could no longer be the precious artist refusing to take part in attempting to shape the political destiny of my country. When you are born in a country that is torn over whether or not you belong, you either belong at great expense or you withdraw. In my early years, and in my later ones too, I alternated. One is torn between survival and principles.

Once I looked out of my second-story Omaha window and was almost shot by a nervous white cop who had come to investigate a complaint downstairs. Omaha was a segregated town. It was difficult to get through even one week without being verbally abused. I held a number of unskilled jobs before teaching myself welding. I became a welder and learned to drive a crane. But there was no future for me in Omaha, Nebraska.

I finally left Omaha because it became clear to me that it was not a place where artistic nourishment was endlessly available. For years, since my first visit to New York for a few days when I first got out of the air force, I knew that I would eventually try to live in Manhattan. Greenwich Village was the only place I would consider. As it turned out, when I finally did make the move in 1966, I first moved in with a friend from Omaha and his apartment was on the Lower East Side, on Twelfth Street between avenues A and B.

One of the first things I did was to go with another friend to Radio City Music Hall to see the Rockettes dance. There were many free things to do in New York: poetry readings, political rallies, concerts, dances, exhibitions.

Later, I'll talk about mentors, but for the moment, let me mention that among them, poet and activist Walter Lowenfels, who had been an expatriate in Paris for many years but was now back and living in Peekskill, New York, was delighted with my move to New York. Walter had been encouraging me by way of letters for about four years and had assisted in placing some of my poems in little magazines.

Shortly after I arrived in New York, Walter invited me to a memorial reading at Saint Mark's Church for the late Alan Swallow. Anaïs Nin was there and spoke of her late publisher. Looking at her was like seeing a transparent human being, so frail and white was she. And her voice was like that too. That night I walked Walter back to the subway which he would take to the train station.

Those were lonely days and nights for me in New York and especially since my friendship with my friend from Omaha had become strained. He needed his privacy which meant I needed to find a job and get the hell out of his apartment. I dreaded having to go back there and usually stayed up late with new friends in Jimmy's Tavern till I figured my friend was asleep. He was a social worker and always had to get up early.

I could sit in Jimmy's with one beer and make it last four hours.

When I landed a job as a teacher of creative writing at the New Lincoln School in Harlem and one as a research analyst for the Simulmatics Corporation, I was able to afford my own apartment and I moved into one in the building next door. The research job was interesting. We were analyzing how people responded to the news coverage of racial violence. John Lindsay was mayor at the time and was an outspoken supporter of the findings of those studies, which concluded that almost without exception the many hundreds of incidents of racial violence and death were either provoked by the police or resulted from the police's mishandling of the initial incident.

I also travelled to Milwaukee and Detroit to interview people who had lived through riots and so-called riots. I was the head of a three-man team. The other two guys were sociology students in Ph.D. programs. This was early in 1967. It was part of a program of research directed by well-known sociologist Dr. Sol Chaneles, who interviewed us for the job on the third floor of a building on West Ninety-fourth and Broadway. Looking back at the report I handed in to him I find this observation: "I would discover for myself how deeply trapped in a nightmare of socially produced violence, morally rationalized racism, and economically maintained exploitation black and poor people in this country are only to see, later, Mayor John V. Lindsay mad on T.V. because Congress hadn't implemented any of the proposals." Although the Johnson Administration paid for the study the results were not what that administration wanted to hear.

But the people I talked with in both Milwaukee and Detroit were interesting if not always intelligent. The three of us divided up the cities. I took the ghetto each time. One of my assistants was black, the other white. The black boy had grown up in a white neighborhood, if memory serves me well. He seemed more comfortable interviewing white people, so I sent him to department stores and other kinds of businesses. We hit Detroit just after the infamous Algiers Motel incident where three young black men were gunned down by white cops for being in a room, or rooms, with white girls. The city was still steaming. People had been packed like cattle into a truck since the jails were filled. A barber in his shop, as he cut my hair, told me horror stories that stirred my anger and gave me a sense of despair. I went into the greasy spoons for breakfast and talked with the waitresses and the garbagemen catching a cup of coffee before going to work. There was anger everywhere, some of

*With two of his children, Aaron and Darrell,
about 1974*

it directed at whites, much of it directed at white cops and at blacks who capitalized (in the form of theft, usually) off the disorder.

In Milwaukee one of the newspapers had done much to inflame the situation. If a group of black kids started singing in the streets, they called it a riot and the city government sent out the troops. Some people got killed. I went to Father Groppi's church which seemed to be just about the only place in Milwaukee that was integrated and where people were trying to work against violence and racism at the same time. An old black man who didn't know what was going on came out onto his porch one night to try to find out and was shot dead, framed by the light behind him.

I took off from work in Milwaukee to go to Chicago to see my sons Aaron and Darrell and my mother and other relatives. I took the boys to see a karate movie. It was their speed. We kicked around together for a few days. I played pool with them in my mother's basement. Already Aaron was thinking of buying a car (and in two years I would find myself sending him money to help in that effort). I wanted to take them to fancy restaurants but they twisted my arm and we ended up at McDonald's.

But the other important thing about Simulmatics was that I met there, in 1967, a young woman I was to live with for two years. I am here changing her name to protect her privacy. Rebecca was Jewish and had grown up in Brooklyn. I remember how touched she was when for our first Christmas my mother sent us a chocolate cake she had baked for the two of us. Rebecca had just finished earning her B.A., and

seemed somewhat at a loss. What next? She was a moody young woman who was intellectually gifted. I liked her ability to be quiet and to read books for hours but I disliked her smoking, especially since I had recently broken myself of the habit. I had also stopped drinking because of stomach problems. When I got my advance for the forthcoming *All-Night Visitors,* with nothing better to do, since our jobs at Simulmatics had ended, we decided to go to Mexico.

On arriving in Mexico City, we visited Margaret Randall at her home and spent the evening there having dinner with her and Robert Cohen and Robert Sward.

I wasn't to see Margaret again till 1984 in San Diego and 1986 in Boulder. This was during a time when she was waging an important legal battle to regain her American citizenship and thereby to test and change reactionary laws established during the McCarthy years.

Within a few days Rebecca and I moved on to Puerto Vallarta. It was here that Rebecca and I had our first crisis. In cultural shock, neither one of us were in any shape to survive our first fight with any great degree of dignity. I thought of Richard Wright leaving his first wife in Mexico and returning alone to New York. I thought of doing the same thing but I didn't. Instead, we rented an apartment on the top floor of a house. Our place had a wraparound balcony and four massive rooms and a bathroom larger than most living rooms I had seen in New York. The kitchen had a hand-laid marble-topped bar. The furniture was deep, rich mahogany and so was the woodwork. Some rather dense Mexican paintings insulted the walls. We were not offended enough to take them down and hide them behind the couches and chairs. The building containing the apartment had just been purchased by an American woman from Los Angeles. Later, she tried to convince me to stay and work as her manager. She didn't like Mexicans, so I didn't even consider it.

Meanwhile, back in the States, the riots were still going on, and the Democratic Convention was in Chicago. Before long Abbie Hoffman and Jerry Rubin, whom I had met through my friend Lennox Raphael on Saint Mark's Street one day, would be on trial with Bobby Seale and the others.

I don't remember how long we stayed in Puerto Vallarta but I do know that we spent the last two weeks up north in San Miguel de Allende. Before we left Puerto Vallarta, Rebecca became ill after we ate in a restaurant; she fell unconscious and I went racing through the night in search of a doctor. The first two turned me down. Finally, in a taxi, I was driven into the hills where I found a country doctor, an old man eating his supper, who agreed to come at once. She had a high fever and the runs. Then she passed out. When I got back to her with the doctor she was beginning to come to consciousness. He gave her a shot, careful not to look at her hip, which is the custom there. Once I went with Rebecca to a Mexican doctor's office for a routine checkup and was surprised when he insisted that I come into the examination room too. He covered her with a sheet and, as I watched, he examined her for yeast, while looking at the ceiling.

Before going to San Miguel, we did a little travelling through Mexico and stopped in Guadalajara. We saw *Zorba the Greek* with Spanish captions there. Because of my interest in D.H. Lawrence we also spent a day or two in Chapala, but it was a big disappointment because there were so many Americans from Texas who looked at us with contempt. They were retirees and the city was filled with them.

In Mexico, I saw my first bullfights and learned to dislike bullfights and saw for the first time the horrors of a type of poverty worse than any I had ever seen before.

I finished writing *All-Night Visitors* in Mexico. A book described later by Greg Tate in the *Village Voice* as " 'black letters' answer to *Tropic of Cancer*," it (in cut form) was published by Maurice Girodias's Olympia Press after being rejected everywhere. At that time, Grove Press was distributing Olympia Press's hardback line. But apparently not very well. *All-Night Visitors* remained underground and became the object of much scholarly concern during the nineteen years that followed.

The fact that I allowed *All-Night Visitors* to be published in an altered form was one of the things that came between Rebecca and myself. She thought I had sold out. I knew I hadn't but there was no way to convince her. I told her that Richard Wright had been forced to cut *Black Boy* in half, leaving out the adult, communist sections. She didn't care. Our relationship ended at the beginning of the summer of 1969 and the book had come out during the winter.

I spent the summer living in a house on a lake in the woods of Massachusetts near Lee. I felt very wounded. I kept my apartment in the city but went back there only twice during the summer. I was working on *NO*.

Nineteen seventy-one, 1972, 1973. These were years of literary parties. When I try to think of party highlights I come up with faces, verbal tidbits, digs, compliments, and the starkness of shallow moments. I also remember a lot of celebrities and near-celebrities.

For example, once at a very crowded party, during one of her last trips to the United States, Josephine Baker reached through a crowd and squeezed my hand. She didn't know me, of course. But the reason that is important to me has to do with the fact that when I was about twelve, in Chicago, she performed at the Regal Theatre, the place where South Side parents sent their kids on Saturday morning, often just to have some free time. I was so overwhelmed by her elegance and extravagance, the way I had been while seeing Cab Calloway, Peg-leg Bates, Illinois Jacquet, and many other great musicians at the Regal. (Gwendolyn Brooks remembers the Regal Theatre!)

Also I was beginning to gain some confidence in my ability to find publishers for the books I was writing. For years it had seemed impossible and it still wasn't easy. Wesleyan University Press had already brought out my first commercially available collection of poems, *Swallow the Lake*, in 1970. Later, when I talk about mentors, I will tell the story of its road to publication because it's interesting. Meanwhile, that same year, after the Philosophical Library declined to publish my *Dictionary of Afro-American Slang*, International Publishers brought it out. In 1969 they had published my anthology *The New Black Poetry*.

In 1971, Ted Wilentz, who had started the famous Eighth Street Bookstore, publisher of Corinth Books, published another collection of my poems, *Symptoms & Madness;* and in London, Paul Breman, an antiquarian book dealer, brought out a slim volume of newer poems under the title *Private Line*. The following year, Broadside Press in Detroit published my *Cotton Club,* poems about various moments in black history.

In the meantime, I met a young woman, S.J.S., at a book party in 1971. She seemed intelligent and pleasant. I had not met many black women who were interested in literature. She was also poetry editor for a woman's magazine. We started living together shortly after that, at first in my Saint Mark's Street apartment between Avenue A and First Avenue. Later we moved into an apartment at 11 Waverly Place where we stayed till we moved to Stamford, Connecticut, in 1974, but again I'm getting ahead of my story. As I said, these were the party years.

Meanwhile, Ishmael Reed had moved from Chelsea to Saint Mark's Place, one block up from my place. We saw more of each other socially during this period than before or after. W.H. Auden lived in the building next-door to Ish's. I used to see the great poet in the neighborhood in his house-slippers. The

At the Park Lane in New York City: standing, from left, Clarence Major, Ishmael Reed,
Joe Johnson, Quincy Troupe; seated, Lesley and Chester Himes, 1973

only person I knew who had gotten to know him was poet Norman Loftis (the one painted by Philip Pearlstein in 1974).

At one party I ran into the actor Robert Hooks whom I had just seen in a movie based on a Tennessee Williams story. When I told Hooks how much I enjoyed the part he played in the film, he was not particularly pleased because, in his words, he wanted to "make Black movies." Christopher Lehmann-Haupt was also at this party and he had just given *All-Night Visitors* a bad review. I think this was the party for Cecil Brown's *Life and Loves of Mister Jiveass Nigger.*

One of my closest and lasting friends from this period was the poet Art Berger, whom I had met in 1966. Art, in fact, got me my first teaching job, the one in Harlem at the New Lincoln School. Later on, we team-taught one or two courses at Queens College, CUNY. There were times when I would go to Queens to conduct workshops in community centers he was involved in.

Then, I met Chester Himes and his wife Lesley through Ishmael Reed and we had a party in Chester's hotel room, at the Park Lane in New York in 1973. Ishmael Reed, Steve Cannon, Quincy Troupe, and Joe Johnson were also there. It was then that I

understood Chester's bitterness. He was drinking scotch. He talked a long time about his relationship with Richard Wright, since somebody, Joe or Steve, I guess, had laid the question on him. Wright had dismissed Chester's relationship with an American woman he, Chester, cared a lot about, as frivolous. This was during Chester's first year in Paris, at the age of forty-five. After that, Chester did not read any more of Wright's books.

John A. Williams, who was also a friend of Chester's, and I became friends. We would both soon be teaching at Sarah Lawrence College. (Other writers who taught there while I was there were Ed Doctorow, Grace Paley, Jane Cooper, Cynthia Macdonald, Galway Kinnell, Joe Papaleo. I guess I got to know Cynthia, Jane, and Joe better than the others.) I didn't have a car at the time and I rode up with John. He called me his shotgun. Later, it made more sense for me to ride with Grace Paley who also lived in the Village. Grace had a dependable Bug.

Ralph Ellison and I were introduced to each other at a reception party when my friend Ronald Fair won a prize given by the American Academy of Arts and Letters. Ellison walked away quickly after we shook hands. I was a bit stunned.

Kurt Vonnegut, Jr., who had, during the formal

ceremony, delivered a very funny speech, was now standing alone, at the far end of the open area. In almost no time at all, well-wishers approached him. I watched from a distance with interest. I was studying the politics of literary parties without even knowing it!

In an elevator once, going up to yet another party, James Jones, author of *From Here to Eternity*, lamented over novelist Charles Wright's lack of commercial success. He and Wright had been at the same writers' colony in Illinois years before. (Some years later I would meet Charles Wright when I invited him to Boulder to read from his work-in-progress. I liked him a lot. I gave him one of my paintings because he fell in love with it. He was on his way to Paris.)

Parties usually brought you in contact with mentors you had never met but with whom you had corresponded. Even while I was living in Omaha, Nebraska, I was in touch, by letter, with many people I now think of as mentors—Walter Lowenfels, Wil-

With novelist Charles Wright, Boulder, Colorado, 1978

liam Meredith, Bern Porter, Norman Holmes Pearson.

I guess one of my first mentors, Walter Lowenfels, invited me to my first New York literary party. It was in a fancy but small hotel in midtown and it was for one of Walter's books. As I mentioned, he had for a number of years before I moved to New York encouraged editors to read my work. It was Walter who, in the end, got Wesleyan University Press to take my poetry seriously. The editorial process was clearly a shambles and his success is therefore all the more remarkable.

But far more importantly, I discovered that I liked Walter's zest and poetry for life itself. Lillian, his wife (whose dream was to have a grand piano on which she could keep all of her stuff), was less zestful but just as wonderful to be around. I visited them in Peekskill two or three times, spending weekends, being overwhelmed by Walter's excitement over whatever project excited him at that moment and listening to his critical responses to my own projects.

Bern Porter, publisher of Henry Miller. Bern had sent me checks from time to time and collected some of my "papers" in his collection at the University of California at Los Angeles. The checks were in compensation for my "papers." Porter had encouraged me as early as the late fifties. Later, he had many personal problems he only alluded to. He had been one of the physicists who worked on the atomic bomb at Los Alamos and apparently wanted to counterbalance the obvious outcome of that experience by doing constructive work for humanity. The last time I heard from him, over twenty years later, he urged me to not give up. That meant a lot at a time when I was in despair resulting from the feeling that both commercial and noncommercial publishing worlds were totally indifferent to my efforts.

William Meredith. Bill took it upon himself to drive from his home in New London, Connecticut, to Middletown, to make the final selection of the poems that went into *Swallow the Lake*. Originally, Walter had sent Wesleyan a big bundle of my poems, far too many for the size books they were bringing out. For over a year the various poets associated with Wesleyan as readers had scratched their heads over the bundle and refused to be decisive. Bill got mad and burst into the office that day he drove up there and said enough was enough. He went through the bundle and came away with the poems that make the book. He handed it to the editor and, finally, after a long, long delay, the book was on its way toward production.

Norman Holmes Pearson, a professor at Yale University, had taken an early interest in my efforts. I think I met him through Sheri Martinelli. He was collecting her papers at Yale and seemed very interested in her relationship with Pound during the Saint Elizabeth's years. Pearson, like Porter, got the impression I was poor. Both were right. Pearson sent me several checks in exchange for collecting my "papers." I now understand what that was all about. If one has money, why not spend it this way, on something one believes in?

I also got to know a few of the musicians and painters on the Lower East Side. Ishmael Reed probably introduced me to more painters and musicians than did anybody else. He was living on the West Side, in Chelsea, if I remember correctly. When I first met him he was as encouraging as a busy young writer who was trying to get his own career going could be.

Adrienne Rich was teaching poetry at the Society for Ethical Culture and invited me to speak to her class. I met Adrienne for a drink before going up to do the class. We talked about suicide and its causes. That's what I remember of our conversation.

Amiri Baraka had been beaten by cops and arrested over in Newark so a whole bunch of us poets

Reading to an audience at the William Carlos Williams Library, New Jersey, about 1974

got together and gave a benefit reading for him at Judson Memorial Church on Washington Square Park South. I remember the audience booing Fielding Dawson for some reason. Baraka later performed with his associates at Saint Mark's Church. He staged a revolutionary attack on the largely white audience, using—I think—cap guns. One girl almost knocked her own brains out trying to escape from the room the moment the lights went out and the firing started.

Meanwhile, there were the Black Nationalist writers up in Harlem who had been friendly enough till I showed up once with a white date. Nobody spoke to me after that. Among that group were Ed Spriggs and other Afro-American poets associated with *Soulbook, Black Dialogue,* and the *Journal of Black Poetry.* Many of these poets had recently migrated from the West Coast and were also newcomers in the city. Spriggs soon after this incident led a boycott against my forthcoming anthology. The conditions of his boycott were spelled out in one of the black magazines. If I remember correctly, he had two objections: he said the publisher was communist and white. His boycott wasn't taken very seriously, however, because many of the black nationalists he asked not to contribute, contributed anyway, including LeRoi Jones, who was just beginning to become Baraka. After the anthology *The New Black Poetry* appeared in 1969, Kenneth Rexroth said it was the least sectarian of any of the new collections; and the most nationalistic of the then-Black Nationalist critics, Addison Gayle, Jr., said in the *New York Times Book Review,* that it contained "The best work by black American poets."

In 1971, before Erica Jong published her first Novel, *Fear of Flying,* her book of poems *Fruits & Vegetables* had attracted a considerable amount of attention. She and I were awarded a Creative Artists Public Service grant by the New York Cultural Foundation that year. I think I already knew Erica from PEN parties but I'm not sure. Anyway, the "public service" we were to perform for the one thousand dollars the Foundation paid us was to give a reading together in Sunset Park on June 12 in the heart of the heart of Brooklyn. We got to the park accompanied by a representative from the city and discovered there was no audience nor were there the promised loudspeakers. So Erica and I sat down on the grass and read our poems to each other. (Erica and I were later on another program together with other poets arranged by Louis Simpson at Stony Brook. It was outside and on a sunny day but a windy one. You couldn't hear the poets because the wind took their words away as fast as they came out of their mouths.)

S.J.S. and I spent a pleasant weekend with June Jordan at her home out on Long Island when the weather got warm.

Poet Leopold Senghor came to New York to speak to a PEN gathering and it was one of the few PEN gatherings I bothered to attend.

Meanwhile, my friend Burt Britton, who at that time was a clerk at Strand Bookstore, was keeping me stocked with the latest and the most interesting books by poets and fiction writers.

I flew with S.J.S. to Europe in August. We arrived in England first, where we stayed a few days in the apartment of the publisher of *Private Line,* Paul Breman. Paul, at that time, had a good relationship with an editor, Jill Norman, at Penguin. We liked them both and they later—or was it earlier?—visited us in New York.

After England we flew to Paris. Norman Loftis, who was already there, had rented a room for us on the Left Bank but it was not the one we ended up with. Norman and his new bride were staying in the plush, old apartment of a famous art critic. We had dinner with them there at that great place. I remember thinking that Norman was also from Chicago's South Side. I admired Norman's knowledge of art and his sensitivity to poetry.

We spent a very brief time in Paris. We took a train down from Paris to Milan and met a wonderful West Indian woman on the way whose sister, I think, was married to an Italian. In any case, in our compartment there was a heartbroken Italian girl who was leaving her French lover in Paris. We had witnessed their tearful parting. The girl closed her eyes and attempted to blot us out but the West Indian woman wouldn't stand for it. She made the girl take off her shoes because, during the long train ride, her feet would swell otherwise. On second thought, said the West Indian woman, sister to a high official in Paris, everybody in the compartment should take off their shoes. We all did and we all survived the night without swollen feet. Arriving in Milan, the West Indian woman and I made hollow promises to stay in touch. She reminded me of the strong women in my own family.

S.J.S.'s Italian was good. That helped. She had majored in Italian and one or two other languages. But this did not mean that we had a handle on Milan. As it turned out, we didn't stay here long, mainly because I was eager to get on to Florence but before we left, we took the train over to Venice and spent a

day there mostly in and around San Marco.

Florence. It was August. The heat was unbearable and the mosquitoes worse. We stayed in a room on the top floor of a "family" hotel right on the river. The couple that ran the place was very old. They had no help. The woman was stingy with towels and even with breakfast rolls. They were on their way out. (Many years later, I looked for that hotel and discovered that it was no longer a hotel but a hostel for backpackers willing to sleep on the floor.)

We went next to Rome. I did not feel as comfortable in Rome as I had in Florence and, many years later, after I got to know Rome fairly well, I still disliked what seemed to me to be its confusion, noise, and aggressive personality. Venice, by contrast, was nonaggressive, even friendly. We did climb the Spanish steps and I guess we did all the other obvious touristy things tourists do such as taking tours of the city. I remember the hotel room and the ancient elevator and the street where the hotel was. I looked at it again in 1984, just before flying from Rome to Algiers. It hadn't changed.

We went on from Rome to Barcelona where we spent a few days. Saw a bullfight. Climbed the hills of Gaudí's park; ate lunch up there with the Sunday families. Explored the city.

Madrid, next. We stayed in a huge, nearly empty hotel, outside the main area of the city. We took the bus or walked every day. Saw the wonderful Goyas at the Prado. Goya had been a favorite since I discovered him while a student at the Art Institute of Chicago. Finally, we flew back to the States from Madrid. The whole trip had taken something like forty-five days.

The visit to Quebec City was brief in July of 1972. One was able to feel a sense of history there along the Saint Lawrence, in the shadow of the Château Frontenac. It was like somebody had lifted this huge thing up from the earth of France and moved it here, so strong was the older spirit of France in its presence. (I was not unaware of the fact that Richard Wright had some years earlier sought refuge in Quebec from the blistering effects of racism in the States.) We stayed at the Clarendon and did a lot of sightseeing. Before returning to New York, we spent a few days in Montreal. Unfortunately, we did not eat clam fritters or visit the whaleboats. Such a pity.

The next summer we went to the Caribbean. First, Dominican Republic, where I was searched like a common thief at the airport on entry. I disliked Santo Domingo from that point on.

In Haiti the children never begged without dignity. They always had something to offer you in exchange for money, even if it was only a twig they had picked up from the ground.

We took a taxi tour of the countryside and stopped at a mountain market, visited some mountain art galleries, bought a few paintings. The poverty was unbelievable. In the mornings at the hotel we listened to an American reporter, who knew Haiti well, talk about the place. He didn't bite his tongue in telling us that the government was a tyrant and a wasteful one at that. But we already knew.

I have a patchwork memory of Haiti. We visited that old famous hotel where famous movie stars had stayed. On the porch the owner, a huge woman, sat playing cards with friends. Going upstairs, we found lazy fans turned in the rooms, perhaps once occupied by Rita Hayworth or Humphrey Bogart. We sipped rums in the Jane Barbancourt tasting room. We visited all the famous galleries up in Pétionville. We saw the dying and the hungry. And we saw the differences between the tourist booklets and the reality.

I felt nothing of the spirit of Toussaint

Major in Stamford, Connecticut, 1975

L'Ouverture or that of Alexandre Dumas's father, General de la Pailleterie, or that of the great Henri Christophe. We did not visit the famous Citadel. Alas. We did see a silly parade paid for by the government. It consisted of floats filled with young women in swimming suits. This was obviously Baby Doc's idea of how to spend government money. A few fights broke out but were quickly contained by the strong arm of the police. We did meet one young man who was consciously working against the government by writing militant poetry. When we took him back to the hotel's lobby, where we talked with him, it became clear to us from the owner's reaction to the young man that he was an undesirable.

On Friday nights our hotel sponsored a dance outside by the pool. The model for one of the Tontons Macoutes in Graham Greene's novel about Haiti was there dancing with all of the tourist ladies. He was thin and handsome and full of himself. I was fascinated by how fascinated the women were by him. Everybody knew who he was. They were dancing with a fictional character.

Our next move was to the Washington, D.C., area. Living in a high rise in Maryland, I was teaching mainly at Howard University. S.J.S. and I were suffering the pains of a crumbling relationship. We stayed in the Maryland-Washington, D.C., area from the fall of 1974 till the fall of 1976. The Howard job came about due to the kind interest the scholar Charles H. Nilon held for my work. (He was tenured at the University of Colorado and later was instrumental in bringing me there.) Charles was a visiting chairman of the English Department at the time and as such hired me for the two-year period. I had no idea where I would go after that. It had been like that since 1968.

It was during the time that I taught at Howard that I was invited to read at the Folger Shakespeare Library. Doris Grumbach introduced me. It was on a cold, dreary winter night. My relationship with S.J.S., as I've said, was going down the drain at this time, and Washington, D.C., perhaps because of my pain and confusion, was not a rewarding city. But while there, the State Department decided to sponsor my trip to Yugoslavia to participate in the International Poetry Festival at Struga. Galway Kinnell had recommended me to the selection committee and William Jay Smith told me, when I went to Columbia University to visit a graduate class of poetry writing students (taught by Richard Eberhart), that the Yugoslavians were very anxious to have me come and participate. So I decided to go. Leopold Senghor of Senegal was to receive the highest literary award given to foreign-

*Attending the International Poetry Festival with poets from around the world,
Struga, Yugoslavia, 1975*

ers in Yugoslavia.

On arriving, I spent the night in a hotel in Belgrade. The people of Belgrade seemed grim, especially in contrast to the cheerfulness and friendliness of the people of Struga. Almost instantly I was aware of the great ethnic and religious and cultural diversity. Often ox carts got in the way of limousines.

They'd built a hotel especially for us poets—who'd come from all over the world, by the way. Metropol Hotel in Ohrid on Lake Ohrid was in sharp contrast to its modest, rural surroundings.

Many of the poets I met in Yugoslavia I stayed in touch with for years. My best friends were unforgettable. There was Melo C. Castro from Portugal; Ayyappa Paniker from India; Kjell Erik Vindtorn from Oslo; Eddy van Vliet and Frank de Crits from Belgium; Homero Aridjis from Mexico; Fathī Sa'īd from Egypt; Sergio Macias from Chile; Waldo Leyva Portal from Cuba; Lassi Nummi from Finland; Hans van de Waarsenburg from the Netherlands; and there were the Yugoslavs: Save Cvetanovski (translator of Faulkner), Jovan Strezovski, and Mateja Matevski. One very young Montenegrin poet, Stanoevski Bozo, proclaimed himself my little brother. We did actually look alike!

The whole week all of us danced, sang, played, talked theory, read our poetry to and translated it for each other. But there were many, many poets I never met, only saw in passing, people like the famous French poet Guillevic and the Russian poets and many of the poets from all over Eastern Europe. But those of us who became close stayed in touch and exchanged books over the following years, even met again at later conferences.

Nineteen seventy-five was also the year the Fiction Collective published my third novel, *Reflex and Bone Structure*. It was hot off the press when I went to Yugoslavia. I got interested in the Fiction Collective while teaching at Brooklyn College, where I met two of its founders, Jonathan Baumbach and Peter Spielberg. Painters had formed collectives for years and I was attracted to the idea of writers of fiction doing the same thing. It might prove to be an alternative to the dim prospects of commercial publishing. I submitted my novel and it earned the necessary four votes for acceptance. I had written the novel the year before, in my Waverly Place apartment, in a state of mind close to that of child's play. That is to say, I made up the rules as I went along. Writing that book at that time was a way of staying sane.

With Leopold Sedar Senghor (center) in
Struga, Yugoslavia, 1975

That same year, 1975, the Library of Congress held a conference on small press distribution at the Center for the Book. This was simply yet another example of business related get-togethers. It was beginning to seem to me that the only way I saw my old friends was at such gatherings and the parties they generated. But I did meet a man I admired there: James Laughlin, founder of New Directions. He and Clare Boothe Luce were both introduced to me at the same time. I couldn't find a way to talk with him without also talking with her so I never got the chance to say thanks for Kenneth Patchen and Henry Miller, for Pound and Williams, and most of the books I grew up on and loved.

I had been an academic gypsy for years, so it was especially important to me to get my first tenure-bound job at the University of Washington at Seattle. It came about, in part, due to Charles Nilon's recommendation. I went out to Seattle for the interview, met the committee members considering me, had lunch with them, then went back to Washington, D.C. In a very short time, I received a letter offering me an appointment.

In Seattle, in 1976, Chuck Johnson and Colleen McElroy were close friends. Other people I socialized with there were novelist Victor Kolpacoff and some of the academics. A small group of us started a wine-tasting party on a regular basis and that was fun for awhile.

I liked Seattle very much. The drizzle was well suited to my temperament. (When I went back there later to give a lecture, I still felt close to it. It was one of my cherished homes.)

While living in Seattle, I accepted an invitation to participate in the International Poetry Festival at Rotterdam, Holland. It was June 1977. My friend Eddy van Vliet had recommended me to the selection committee. This week-long experience was in every way as memorable as the Struga experience; and, in some ways, it was far more pleasant. Eddy and Frank were there so we had a reunion.

At these affairs, one tends to gravitate toward certain people and I am sure the people one begins to feel closest to are pretty much selected at random. Very often friendships might start because one happens to be standing or sitting near the potential friend. There were many people there I thought interesting and I wanted to know but didn't get the chance.

An American professor, Talat S. Halman, conducted a workshop for those poets among us who wanted to try their hand at translating the work of the famous Turkish poet Fazil Husnu Daglarca who was there. These sessions were wonderful in that they brought the participants in closer touch in a shared experience than did the readings and, in some ways, than did the many nightly parties.

On the second night, the fourteenth of June, I read with Belgian poet Paul Snoek; Stanisław Barańczak, from Poland; Sitor Situmorang, from Indonesia; Sonja Prins of the Netherlands; Daglarca himself; the young British poet Hugo Williams; and the Brazilian poet Marcia Theophilo, who was living in Italy, married to an Italian. Dutch novelist Remco Campert was master of ceremonies.

Remco made the presentations each of the following nights. Among the poets present were Renate Rasp, Seamus Heaney, Sándor Csoóri, Salab Abdul Saboer, Bogomil Guzel, Maurizio Cucchi, Wing Kardjo, Hans Verhagen, Andrée Chedid, André Du Bouchet, Hans Faverey, Shuntaro Tanikawa, Bernd Jentzsch, Hugo Williams, Robert de Hortogh, Erich Arendt, Dahlia Ravikovitch, and two other Americans, Stanley Kunitz and John Ashbery. Ashbery and I had shared an office at Brooklyn College with Jonathan Baumbach, Peter Spielberg, and Jack Gelber in the mid-seventies.

We were on an outing once, going to an ancient village, and Renate Rasp was sitting next to me on the bus. That is how we got to know each other. Later, she wrote a couple of poems dedicated to me in her book *Junges Deutschland.*

Boulder, in some surprising ways, turned out to be a rather unique community in that, at least at first, it seemed friendly toward eccentrics and artists and the university naturally generated an intellectual and,

A conversation with painter Jacob Laurence at the University of Washington, 1976

generally speaking, a liberal community. This is not to say that racism had not made its presence felt on campus and in the community from time to time. But I was especially impressed by the lack of economic or racial ghettoes. There seemed to be a good level of tolerance for differences among people.

The writers Steve Katz, Ron Sukenick, Sidney Goldfarb, Robert Steiner, Ed Dorn, Marilyn Kyrsl, Peter Michelson, and later, Joy Harjo, were interesting people to work with. We also had interesting visitors I got to know a bit, such as Bobbie Hawkins and Ron Tavel. At first there were lots of parties. I even gave some myself. Plus there were the writers down at Naropa Institute: Allen Ginsberg, Anne Waldman, William Burroughs, Michael Brownstein, and many others.

I remember going to one party Allen Ginsberg (to whom I always have to reintroduce myself) gave for visiting poet Amiri Baraka. Burroughs and I sat together on the couch. He was a very quiet and seemingly frail man with a sour face. He was complaining, as I remember, about having so little money to live on. The myth has it that Burroughs inherited a fortune from the adding machine business. I wondered if Burroughs was busy trying to counteract that myth.

Baraka and I spoke together for the first time at that party although we had read together in Harlem at the Apollo years before. He wanted to know what the Fiction Collective was and I felt a little foolish trying to explain how it worked. I guess I was also surprised that he knew so little about a publishing co-

op that had been around since the early seventies. He said he and his wife, wished I "would come on it." Not sure of what he meant, I did not respond.

Around this same time, Allen and I were sitting together in an audience on the CU campus listening to Robert Creeley introduce a film series. I knew Creeley from early fifties correspondence and a bit from my summer teaching at the State University of New York at Buffalo. Now, Allen wrote in my copy of *Planet News:* "For Clarence Major. Happy to be in his company, Robert Creeley talking into cinema microphone at the University, bunches of poets & students listening to the sybillant syllables—Creeley had on big cream colored straw hat in lecture hall pit." In my copy of *Kaddish,* he wrote this: "For Clarence Major, several decades after our first poetic correspondence mid-U.S. to New York now both of us poets in the same Boulder."

My first two years in Boulder were frantic. One always feels crazy after so many vast and quick changes but I went to Boulder with the hope for a new life. I wanted to be reborn and to find some degree of peace and a chance of sustaining it. Although I felt lonely and alone, I trusted that I was about to break through into a whole new area of personal hope. In 1978 S.J.S. and I separated and it began to happen.

Pamela Jane Ritter and I met at a dinner party in Boulder, Colorado, in September 1979. I fell in love with her right away and almost immediately we began to plan a life together. Call it love at first sight or whatever, it was the real thing.

Emergency Exit had just come off the press and the pub date was set for November, the worst time to publish a book. I went to New York for the book party, held at Carol Sturm Smith's apartment on Second Avenue. A lot of Fiction Collective writers were there, naturally, since the Fiction Collective was publishing the book. In addition to these writers there were Ntozake Shange and literary agent Charles Neighbors, who was first to tell me about the death of Clarence L. Cooper, Jr., America's most neglected, brilliant realistic writer of the 1960s. Cooper apparently had died alone in some dingy New York room. (We could make a long, long list of American writers, great and near-great, who have died alone in small, uncared-for-places.) Although I had never met Cooper, I corresponded with him briefly and admired his work. He was a good writer.

But this was the first day Sake and I met, although she and I had also corresponded while she lived on the West Coast. She had a play in production at the Public Theatre. Before Carol's party, Sake and

I met for lunch in a restaurant across the street from the theatre on Lafayette. I liked her immediately. She was smart and witty and could speak many languages, not all of them made with words.

Pamela and I started living together on December 22, 1979. Right after our first Christmas together I had to fly to San Francisco to appear on a Fiction Collective panel Joe Weixlmann had organized courtesy of the Modern Language Association's annual meeting. There was a letter from Pamela waiting for me at the hotel desk. I was truly surprised and deeply pleased. I called home right away.

Pamela was working on her dissertation, a study of the fiction of Robert Coover, and our next move was in the interest of her getting this thing finished. We settled into a kitchenette apartment in Bernardston, Massachusetts, which was a half hour's drive to Amherst. And stayed there till December 1980. I wrote poetry and she got a lot of reading done and occasionally met with members of her committee at the university. The heavy snow came and we spent much time in bed reading and talking and doing the other wonderful things that are so pleasant to do in bed while the whole world outside is frozen and static. We were suspended in time. At the local post office we picked up our mail daily and cashed checks, when we needed money, at the nearby drive-in bank. The town was dead. Teenage drunks, rednecks from the hills, silent, suspicious farmers were the people we saw. I can imagine how puzzled they were over our presence. They never spoke but they couldn't take their eyes off us.

While living there, I took time off from writing and drove to Albany to read poetry at the State University. Judith Johnson Sherwin (later Judith Emlyn Johnson) had invited me. I had known Judy from New York days and liked and respected her work. She gave a reception for me in her apartment afterward. At one point one elderly lady wanted to know if I had children. Yes. How many? I told her I had about fifty-seven children in and out of wedlock. She looked horrified and walked away. You get sick of people trying to find a way to tell you about their own children.

I went up to Boston by car. We stayed with Fanny Howe in her big old house. I gave a reading one evening at MIT. After Boston we drove up the Eastern Coast. It was winter and the drive was fabulous. All the resorts were closed but when we needed to stop we were able to find motels. At one I encountered the usual blatant racism but refused to feel bitter about it. We were happy. We stopped at a little cafe that made the best deep-fried oysters in the world.

Pamela finished her dissertation in Boulder and went back to Amherst to defend it before we left for France in September 1981. I had won a Fulbright exchange fellowship to teach for a year at the University of Nice. Normally, I taught modern and contemporary American fiction and poetry, but at the University of Nice, I also taught the history of literary magazines from Emerson's *Dial* up to the pre- and post-war *New Directions*. The University of Nice also made arrangements for Pamela to teach a couple of courses in composition. She and I both felt a sense of maturity, turning, growing, emerging: I was forty-four and she was thirty-four.

A French professor and his family moved into our house in Boulder and we took theirs in the mountains above Nice with a view of all of Nice and the vast sea stretching to the shores of Africa. I can think of nothing material I would trade for that wonderful year up there, waking to the view.

Maurice Couturier, a Nabokov scholar and the French translator of my novel *Reflex and Bone Structure* was teaching at Nice. Pamela and I became friendly with Maurice and his wife, Yvonne, and their chil-

Clarence Major, Rotterdam, Netherlands, 1977

Renate Rasp

dren. We also made friends with a number of other faculty members there. James Baldwin, who lived twenty minutes away, at Saint Paul de Vence, came once. We met Jimmy originally at a dinner party at Ann Samyn's, who, later, I think, translated one of Jimmy's books into French. I went to pick up Jimmy, who did not own a car and cared nothing for driving, and got to see his wonderful collection of Beauford Delaney's paintings, to which a whole room is devoted. The teaching load was manageable which allowed me to begin and finish my novel *My Amputations,* published in 1986.

I also agreed to lecture at universities in England, West Germany, and Italy. I had met Eric Mottram years before in the Village at the home of Ted Wilentz. Mottram was one of my hosts in London when I spoke on Afro-American literature at King's College, but the British-American Commission for Educational and Cultural Exchange paid the bill.

Pamela and I got into London on November 24. 1981. BACECE also arranged for me to read from my fiction to a group of graduate students and teachers at the University of East Anglia. On the way out there on the train, I managed to lose my ticket twice— before it was punched by the conductor. The habit on those trains is to stick the ticket under a clamp on the back of the seat in front of you. We did this then decided to change seats for better seats since the train was not full. I forgot my ticket and when I tried to retrace my steps, I couldn't be sure which car we had been in. But in the end I found the wayward ticket. Then, still in search of even better seats, we moved again, and, again, I forgot my ticket and had to repeat the crazy search all over again.

An old friend from the Lower East Side, David Henderson, was in London at the time and we both read, with a group of British poets, at the Young Vic. David had an Italian woman belly dancing while he read his poetry. The audience loved him. The next day a newspaper said he was the real stuff of Afro-America and that I was too academic.

Pamela and I stayed in a hotel where we had a room as big as the kind of room you might play basketball in. Every morning when we went down for breakfast, there was the daughter of the owner— herself the mother of two or three kids—lonely and ready to spill her guts. She had gone to America just the year before, after a divorce, and had meant to stay. All she had was a temporary visa and was now back here, living in her mother's hotel with her children. America fascinated her: hence her interest in us. As we ate our very English bacon and eggs, she would pick up from where she left off the previous morning.

Pamela and I hit Germany on January 10, 1982, landing in Nürnberg. The next day I gave a talk on the problems of literary publishing in America at the University of Erlangen, not far from Nürnberg. Our host, a mellow fellow with the American Consulate, took us around Nürnberg, in the snow. He pointed out the building where Hitler had held his headquarters, just two blocks from our hotel. When I was not busy with lecture work, Pamela and I walked the city and discovered its mall, which was a charm, even in winter.

The Germany trip was too quick and Pamela was not at peace with it. It was no way to experience a country; that is, while on a lecture tour. But at least it was the cheapest way to do it, since most of the expenses were covered. Too much an ego trip for me and not enough a mutual trip for us. Yet we could not have gone at our own expense.

We were swept to Berlin on the twelfth, where I again talked about black American literature to smart German students at the John Kennedy Institute, American Studies, Free University. Pamela and I took a tour of the city by regular tourist bus and visited the infamous Wall. Took pictures.

The next day I read at Berlin's Amerika House. The reading had been announced widely. A black American opera singer, Vera Little, who lived in Germany, came. During the reception that followed she gave me some pointers on performance-audience relationship. I thought she was wonderful. Yet another mentor. I also spoke, and read, on the American Forces Radio in Berlin with two radio hosts who were so up-beat they threw me off, and as Renate, my escort, drove me back to the hotel where Pamela waited, we heard the lively disc jockeys talking about my poetry and me. It had been fun but, as they said, I was different from David Henderson, who had been on their show just weeks before.

Next stops were Frankfurt, Mainz, Aachen, Bonn, Tübingen, and Munich. I like the city of Tübingen because it seemed to have been put together with some sort of idea in mind and it had a great cultural history which I knew about. Bonn went fast but the students there were good and alert. At Mainz I made friends among the professors, friends who are still friends. But it all went far too fast.

In Nice, Christmas was coming and schoolwork would soon end. I couldn't wait. We had met a couple next door, Richard and Claudie. We began making short trips with them into the Alps. We also spent a lot of time with a young woman, Muriel Lacotte, who was writing her dissertation on my work. We got in with Muriel and friends and went to jazz joints in various port cities. We talked art and literature

Clarence and Pamela, Nice, France, 1982

frequently in her or our apartment. Sometimes Pamela and Muriel would go out together on Muriel's motorcycle.

During Carnival in February we went to a small village in the Alps with Richard and Claudie and got a taste of the way Carnival had been for hundreds of years, as opposed to the gaudy commercialism of it in Nice where they had giant Donald Ducks and John Waynes floating in the plaza near Galeries Lafayette.

In March we drove up to Chambéry. The drive was wonderful, the countryside enchanting. I spoke a couple of times at the University of Chambéry.

In the meantime, another lecture tour had been set up and we found it hard to say no. This one was arranged in Rome and involved starting out in Catania, Sicily. Professor Maria Vittorie D'Amico, who later became a friend, had initiated the tour by inviting me to speak at the University of Catania. We loved Italy best of all the countries in Europe! We drove down to Genoa and drove our French car up onto a ship and sailed to Sicily. I got sick a couple of times from motion and was unable to eat. It was a blessing to disembark.

Next, driving north, through the countryside bright with oranges and the dark green leaf of the orange tree, we arrived again in one of our favorite cities, Florence, and stayed at Hotel Argentina. I gave a lecture at the University of Florence on postmodernism, on the twenty-ninth. My host, Professor Gaetano Prampolini, took us to lunch and invited a few of his graduate students.

After a lecture at the University of Milan on the thirty-first, we drove up to Genoa and reached the city from which we had set out by ship. The next day, on April 1, I gave the postmodern talk again at the University of Genoa.

The next big event happened in April. April 22, 23, 24. We were back in Nice. Maurice had worked long and hard to organize Nice's first international conference on postmodern fiction. It was called "Representation and Performance in Postmodern Literature." Not all were happy with the speakers he had selected but mainly the conference was a success. Guest speakers, aside from myself, were William Gass, Stanley Elkin, Regis Durand, Malcolm Bradbury, Marc Chenetier, Johan Thielemans, Ihab Hassan, Jerome Klinkowitz, Tony Tanner, André Le Vot, others. The scholar William Boelhower was also there.

Next, was my African tour. Pamela and I had decided that it was too expensive for us to go together so I went alone. My own expenses were being covered. I lectured in Ghana and Liberia, with a stop in the Ivory Coast.

In Ghana I saw my old friend Kofi Awoonor. Together we did a TV thing comparing Afro-American literature to African literature. (Earlier, in 1975, while Kofi was in prison in his own country for associating with "undesirable" people, I went on a noontime Washington, D.C., talk show called "Panarama" and talked about his plight.)

But in Ghana, I also met a number of other African writers, poet Vincent Opaku; Ghanaian playwright Bill Marshall; many others. The American ambassador invited them to a luncheon in my so-called "honor" at his mansion.

I spent the night in the Ivory Coast before going on to Liberia. Monrovia was a mixed treat. There, I helped to form a Liberian writers' association. The people's relative poverty, social and cultural, distressed me. One writer told me that there was no support from the United States, in the manner that ex-British and ex-French colonies get publishing support from England and France.

The flight back to Europe, on Thursday, June 10, 1982, was one of the most overwhelming experiences I have ever had. The Great Desert of Libya was the most incredible terrain I had ever seen: it was another planet.

Meanwhile, back in France, with friends, we were enjoying the beaches. I especially remember one near Monte Carlo, a nude beach Muriel introduced us to. No Puritanism here—except for my presence!

In Greece, 1982

In the meantime, we took a vacation—in Greece. Arriving in Athens on September 17, we picked up our rented car and got started. Setting out from Athens, we made the typical touristy stops at the Acropolis, Plaka, Volos, Kalambaka, Delphi, Clovino, Olympia, and Tolon, and came back to Athens (to a room where the air-conditioning circulated the worst cigar smoke I have ever had to spend the night with).

Being back in the United States was hard at first, especially for Pamela. We returned on February 10. In some ways, for me it was better. I had more direct contact with editors and my studio was filled with hundreds of reference books I always needed. In France, I had often experienced difficulty locating information I needed about something relevant to American culture or American experiences.

My Amputations, started in 1981, when we first arrived in France, was finished on March 12. I see that I marked it on my calendar. The next day, I started work on my novel *Painted Turtle: Woman with Guitar.*

It was clear long before the first of the year that we would be moving to San Diego and would be there for about six months, because Jerry Rothenberg and Shirley Anne Williams had taken the necessary steps to secure the invitation.

But first, I had to go to Georgia. Albany State College had invited me to serve as writer-in-residence from January 22 till the twenty-seventh. They had federal money. It was also a splendid opportunity for me to visit my relatives in Atlanta!

Returning to the South at this time inspired me later to write my novel *Such Was the Season.* But the novel also had been coming for a long time, especially out of the voices I grew up listening to in the South and in the North. Rereading *Huckleberry Finn* showed me what I could do with a regionally flavored voice such as that of my narrator, Annie Eliza.

I spent a week in Albany, talking with Pamela by phone whenever I could. I conducted workshops, gave readings, and got to spend some time rediscovering what black life was like in a small town like the one—Lexington, Georgia—I had known as a small child. The times were different, certainly, but the pace, mood, and spirit were not so different from what I remembered. I went around with my host, the chairman of the English Department. We checked out the blues and jazz joints. It was a true place. We ate in the red-beans-and-rice cafes and the neckbones and hamhocks were delicious.

Then Pamela and I were off to San Diego by car. It was a liberating trip! The night before we left, we had dinner with novelist Rhoda Lerman, who was in town briefly. She had just finished writing her wonderful novel *The Book of the Night.* On our way to San Diego, we visited Mesa Verde, saw the cliff-dwellings, stayed at Cortez. The Anasazi fascinated me. I was already writing *Painted Turtle,* mentioned earlier. We drove through the Navajo and Apache reservations.

On March 4 we arrived at Zuni for the first time. We were staying in a motel in Gallup which meant we could go back and forth to Zuni in a brief time. We got to know a Zuni family, the Sheykas, and were invited to their home. One night Arlin Sheykas took us up on the rooftop of one of the houses surrounding Sacred Plaza and we saw one of the social dances.

We were in San Diego by March 9 but it took us a few days before we located an apartment. When we did, it was in the Claremont area. I had already won a faculty fellowship from the University of Colorado, which would give me a year off with full pay, and we had already planned to spend the year in Venice, Italy. The only person we knew there was William Boelhower, who had been at the Nice postmodern conference. I had already written to Bill about our plans. After San Diego we planned to go almost directly to Venice.

Meanwhile, we celebrated Pamela's thirty-seventh birthday, March 17, by driving down into Mexico, stopping at Tijuana and Ensenada and San Quintin. It was ugly countryside. We drove and drove without finding a motel. This was hard, bitter land. We ended up, out of desperation, staying in a country motel near Mission Bautista on a marshy shore. The door wouldn't lock and the toilet didn't work. The family that ran the place served us a very fine lobster dinner with cheap but good wine. The next morning we got out of Mexico as soon as we could, and did not go back till our friend Jerry Rothenberg returned from Europe early in April.

Jerry knew how to do Baja. We started going down with him and his wife, Diane, to eat the great lobster and the baked birds and to shop for masks. We also were getting to meet a lot of the people in the Art Department, where Jerry taught. A friend of Jerry's, Michael Davidson, poet, and director of the Poetry Collection at the university, one night threw a beach party at Street Beach in Del Mar, which was great! Pamela and I had already spent much time walking the beach together but this was our first experience of it at night. We also drove up to L.A. once and explored other surrounding areas. We were by no means left to find our way on our own as so often happens in such circumstances. Novelist and critic Shirley Anne Williams, who taught there was in Ghana on a Fulbright. But we did see David and

Eleanor Antin a number of times. Friends from France also turned up and we met some of the local writers and critics. And we discovered a great Soul Food restaurant run by a very religious woman who made the best biscuits and gravy I have ever tasted.

We left on August 5. It was the worst possible time to have to drive through the Mojave Desert. The plastic in our car melted or warped. We drove for hundreds of miles without seeing another car. We were on our way back to Boulder where we would simply finalize a few domestic matters in two or three days then be on our way to Venice. Meanwhile, we stopped again in the Southwest and spent time around Gallup and Zuni.

We arrived in Rome on September 1 and checked into Hotel Sitea and arrived in Venice on the third. The friend of a woman who was translating my novel *Reflex and Bone Structure* into Italian as a student at the University of Venice, met us at the airport bus stop and escorted us to Hotel Tivoli in Venice. We already had an apartment lined up, on Fondamenta Tolentini, number 170, but it had just been painted and was still drying. So we stayed two or three miserable nights at the Tivoli.

Once we moved into our apartment our life in Venice became stable and comfortable. Pete Peters, an American Embassy man we had met in Germany, was now head of the Trieste office and he called right away, wanting to get together. I was intrigued by thoughts of Trieste because of the time James Joyce spent there but as it turned out, we never went. Muriel Lacotte, in the meantime, came to visit from France. We went with Bill, while Muriel was there, to the Feast of the Young Wine on one of the islands in the pouring rain. It was fun giggling and watching the shy Italian kids and their fascination with American rock music and eating corn mush and fried fish. That must have been Sunday, October 7.

Meanwhile, I was readying *My Amputations* for publication by the Fiction Collective. Fanny Howe was my editor. Communicating at this distance was not easy. The Fiction Collective editors decided that since I was out of the country it was best to delay the production process till I returned. I was not happy with that decision but had no choice. Meanwhile, I was hard at work on the Zuni novel and was developing ideas for a novel about Venice.

As fall turned into winter, we were happy, very happy in Venice. We learned to deal with the flooding and to do our shopping on a daily basis. Pete Peters, who also had an apartment in Venice, organized an election party for Americans (and their friends) in the area. We were supposed to be able to watch the election results by closed-circuit at the Cipriani Hotel on the Giudecca. But the circuits were not being very friendly that night. We did meet Kenneth Silverman, whose book on Cotton Mather not long after won a Pulitzer Prize, and Joan Fitzgerald, the sculptor who had been one of Ezra Pound's last friends.

I remember Pamela and me walking back through the winding narrow streets of Venice, since the vaporetto was so slow that late at night, and thinking, how quiet and wonderful the catacomb-city could be, how magical, how self-contained, how like the city of the idyllic future!

In this winter I was using a cane because of a knee injury earned from playing tennis in San Diego. I was in a very crowded *calle* one day approaching a bridge. Whom did I see coming down the steps of the bridge? The American actor, George C. Scott. As we approached each other, the mood of Scott's eyes was obvious. They said, I recognize you, you are American and don't you dare ask for my autograph. He was also walking with a cane. Later, I learned that Scott was in Italy for the filming of the story of Mussolini, which Pamela and I watched on television a year-and-a-half later. But Scott's warning-look reminded me of my encounter with the actor Dustin Hoffman in New York. I was with a friend in a little restaurant on Lexington Avenue, eating lunch. My friend and I had

Pamela and Clarence (center) with Bill and Franca Boelhower in front of a restaurant somewhere in the Veneto, 1984

a window table. Dustin Hoffman, accompanied by two women, came up to the window, just at the point where we were sitting. Except for the glass he might have touched us. He cupped his eyes and squinted, obviously searching for somebody he hoped or imagined might be inside. He was looking over my head. I, and my friend, were looking up at his face. When he had given up his search, he glanced down at me—saw my star-struck gaze and reacted with hostility.

In Venice we led a very routine life, which, for me, gave comfort. We went often, with Bill and Franca, to the mainland, and dined in countryside restaurants. Their little dog was always with us. Monte Grappa was not so amazing after the mountains of Seattle and Boulder but I loved the fresh mountain air anyway, and more than the air, I loved the comfort of being with our new friends.

I remember Pamela and me staying up after dinner to work in our little study up front, where we could still hear the boats going by down below. We did a lot of research on the history of Venice in that little room. Those nighttime times were among our best times, and we have had many and varied wonderful ones.

At Carnival time, in February, we made the rounds from *campo* to *campo* to catch the performances, to see the costumes, and photograph the masks. It was not particularly organized but it was fun. Pamela dressed in a black costume with a mask. At first she was a bit shy about it but everybody else was dressed up. I refused on the grounds that I already had a mask.

Slowly the severe winter was replaced by the good weather of spring and everybody seemed happier. Mothers pushed babies in strollers, which amazed me, given the fact that you can't walk five minutes in any direction in Venice and not encounter the steps of bridges. Pamela and I kept up our morning ritual. We'd go for coffee, usually to the same cafe in Campo Santa Margherita. The family that ran the place made their own ice cream and it was the best in all of Venice. Across the *campo* was a building which became one of the main settings for my Venice novel. Many of the people we saw daily became models for its minor characters. When I needed a face to go on a character, I often found one in the newspaper. I'd cut it out and pin it to the sheet with the character's history.

In April we went on a tour of the south of Italy in a rented car. We drove down from Venice to Monte Cassino and stopped there for the night. In the morning we set out for Salerno. This was a research trip. Once we were settled in a hotel above Salerno (a very human, if dirty and hectic city), overlooking the sea, we made a series of short day trips. First we went to Paestum to see the ruins, then to Amalfi, to Ravello (where we met a young Italian who bragged about being a close friend of Gore Vidal as if that really would impress us). We spent a whole day in the ruins at Pompeii.

In the meantime, I was making a series of watercolors of landscapes wherever we stopped. It became a kind of diary of the journey. These were later shown in a 1986 exhibition in Boulder.

In Naples, at the museum, we almost got taken for a ride—the very thing Franca had warned us against. A slick dude in a slick suit tried to con us into going with him to his brother's jewelry shop somewhere across the city. He really wasn't too determined, probably figured we were small fish. And we were. He claimed to be officially attached to the museum and this was his day off, and you know the rest of the story.

After leaving Salerno, we drove across to Melfi, then on to Venosa and Canosa di Puglia and to Trani. From Monte Sant'Angelo, where we saw the shrine, we began our upward swing north on the other side of Italy. Stopping at Urbino, we visited Raphael's home, high up the road. I could imagine the sensitive and gifted little boy in these rooms with his family. I looked at the backyard where the family pumped its water. This was city life in the fourteenth century; and not much had changed.

On the way back up, we stopped at Ravenna. I have no memory of what we did there. I could ask, couldn't I? I have chosen not to. So that's that.

On April 21 I flew to Algeria at the invitation of officials at the University of Algiers to serve on a *doctorat de troisième cycle* committee. It had taken a long, confusing time to obtain the visa in Rome. The nightmare of it is too much for an autobiography; it needs a whole novel. In any case, there I was in North Africa for the first time. My official duties were few so I had time to see the city and the people. They were the grimmest people I have ever seen. I could not help thinking that the weight of their religion and government and colonial past were heavy loads to carry. The cry of the muezzin in the mosque at four in the morning was awesome. I was there only a couple of days.

After our trip south and to Algeria I felt somewhat in limbo. I was ready to leave Venice. I had finished the Zuni novel and a group of Zuni poems, later collected as *Some Observations of a Stranger at Zuni in the Latter Part of the Century;* had also a fairly finished draft of my Venice novel, *The Boatman's Tenure,* and a

With friends Jerzy Kutnik (left) and Jerzy Durczak (right), Lublin, Poland, 1984

long poem about Venice, *Surfaces and Masks.* Plus I had painted more than fifty watercolors while there and while travelling in the south. When I think back on the time spent in Venice, it seems to me incredible that I was able to produce so much in such a short time, especially the writing, which was done on a small, user-unfriendly manual typewriter.

So, at the beginning of June we turned the apartment over to friends from Paris and moved to their apartment in Paris. Paris, this time, worked for me. I learned to like Paris. We were living in the Eleventh District, an area where few tourists are seen. We were near Père Lachaise where we spent a lot of time searching for the graves of famous people. But that was not our main activity. We saw old friends, Michel and Genevieve Fabre, Marc Chenetier, and Francine Ben-Susan. We'd met Michel and Genevieve in 1981 while staying briefly in Paris and we first met Marc in Nice at the postmodern conference. Francine had visited us in Nice and we had people over and gave a terrace party for her. Muriel was there and for the first time tasted Soul Food. I cooked hamhocks and beans. Everybody loved the food. Francine was still writing her dissertation at the University of Paris. It was on the relationship between Jews and blacks. She, a Jew, born in North Africa, was a natural for the subject.

Plus Bill and Franca came to Paris for a brief vacation. They brought their little dog. At one point, when we were trying to enter a museum, and Bill had the dog tucked under his coat, the dog stuck its little black head out from Bill's chest and nearly scared the ticket woman to death. She screamed. I imagine she thought she saw a little devil emerging from a man's ribcage. Bill wanted to see the monastery near Château Chantilly so the four of us spent a day out there. We had a picnic and toured the area.

Later, Pamela and I went out to Auvers-sur-Oise. We had a wonderful lunch in the restaurant which had once been a hotel-restaurant where Vincent van Gogh spent his last days. While lunch was being prepared, we went upstairs to see the room van Gogh died in. We also walked around the town and saw the church he made famous. We walked near the area where he shot himself. We went up the farmer's road and into the cemetery and saw his grave right alongside that of his brother, Theo. The headstones were barely readable.

In Paris, we also checked out the apartment building where Theo once lived at the end of the nineteenth century. I compared it with earlier photographs of Montmartre and realized that back then the whole area had been rather rural.

In Paris, of course, we did the Louvre and all the other museums. We saw Monet's water lillies, van Gogh's church at Auvers, Doctor Gachet, the "Bedroom" at Arles. In order to get some selfish time in front of the van Goghs and the Gauguins, Pamela devised a splendid plan. We got up early and stood in line for an hour. Once the doors of Jeu de Paume opened we filed in with the others but rather than following the crowd like sheep, we shot upstairs where the van Goghs and Gauguins were. Nobody up there but us and the guards! Downstairs, the tourists were packed and pushing in front of every picture on display. People start, naturally, from the ground up. By the time we got downstairs, the mob was just beginning to come up.

For a long time, a Polish critic of American literature, Jerzy Kutnik, had been trying to get me to visit him in Lublin, Poland. I felt close to the spirit of Jerzy. Even before we left San Diego, I knew Pamela and I would go to Poland because I had already won an IREX grant to cover the expenses for such a visit. When, was the question. While staying in Paris it became clear that this was the best time to make the trip.

Flying on Air France flight 280, we landed at Warsaw Airport at mid-afternoon, Wednesday, July 3. Jerzy Kutnik was there to meet us. The American official who was also there quickly left. Jurek, which was his nickname, drove us to the apartment of his friends, Tomasz Mirkowiez and Julita Wroniak, both translators of American fiction. They were away. (Jurek and his family lived at least three hours away in Lublin.)

The next day Jurek and I went to the offices of the national literary magazine, *Literatura na Świecie.* One or two of my poems had appeared in this magazine back in 1975. There, I met two of the editors, Piotr Sommer and Anna Kolyszko. Piotr handled poetry; Anna, fiction. Piotr knew American poetry and had a special love for Frank O'Hara, whose work he was then busy translating. Anna was especially interested in experimental American fiction. Her smile was sad. I liked her a lot. (Anna visited us for about a week in Boulder later that year.)

The next day Jurek, Pamela, and I had lunch with Professor Zbigniew Lewicki (who was arrested a few months later in Tomasz and Julita's apartment). A mild-mannered man, Lewicki had been in Buffalo some time before, teaching at SUNY there. He had a special interest in contemporary American fiction and had already translated many interesting American writers in his *Gabinet Luster* (1980).

After the luncheon, Jurek drove us to Lublin and we got to see something of the beautiful Polish countryside. Jurek was fun to be with. His wife, Barbara, was busy with their baby, a boy shy of us at first but later this two year old took it upon himself to teach us how to speak Polish. When we spoke he knew something was wrong.

The next morning, Saturday the sixth, Jurek had final oral examinations to conduct so his close friend and fellow Americanist Professor Jerzy Durczak took charge of showing us around. He escorted us to the university and then to the cathedral, the museum of art, the castle, the historical museum, and we walked through the restored old town.

At first I wasn't aware of it. Pamela noticed it first. People were staring at me. Almost everyone we passed. True, black people are rarely seen in Poland. But there were African students there. I saw at least three or four. But what was this look? I told Pamela it was only curiosity. She said it was hostility. I now think it was suspicion and curiosity and hostility. They knew I could not have been in their country without the government's consent. Therefore I was in league with the enemy. At first sight the people of Warsaw and Lublin seemed very sad. There had been something of that unhappiness in the faces in Belgrade.

Durczak was also fun to be with. That night he gave a dinner party for us at his home. His wife Joanna, also a professor of American literature, cooked a delicious dinner. Jurek came later. By the time he got there we were merry with drink and filled bellies. On the turntable was the music of Michal Urbaniak and later that of Zbigniew Seifert, Polish jazz musicians. But both Jurek and Durczak loved best of all American rock music, and at that moment, Bruce Springsteen was some sort of god passing himself off as a human being.

Sunday we spent the afternoon at the lake with Jurek, Barbara, and the boy. All the while Pamela and I were learning an incredible amount about the plight of contemporary Polish literature. But the thing that kept amazing me was what I was reading in Jurek's personality: a grim acceptance of the condition of his life in his country. Then suddenly he could be gay and playful, teasing and pinching his son or Barbara.

That night we watched a Russian movie on TV that was supposed to be set somewhere in the American West. It was a gangster movie. It had cobras in one setting and the same two American cars passed through every street scene. The story in the end had the two main characters, lovers, commit suicide by holding hands and jumping into something that looked like the Grand Canyon. We laughed all the way through.

On Monday morning Jurek drove us back to Warsaw. We had grown very fond of him and were sad at our parting (but he was to visit us in Boulder early the next year while in America on a fellowship).

After Jurek left the airport the trouble started. We were in the long line with the other passengers slowly being processed and let onto the aircraft. Pamela was in front of me. At the last check point, her passport was checked and she was allowed to board the plane. On the pretext that my passport had been incorrectly stamped, I was sent to a bench and made to wait with two Arabs. They too had been told that their passports were incorrectly stamped. Funny, the only passports incorrectly stamped in that long line were those of the three dark ones.

Pamela had not noticed that I was not behind her. When she came back off the plane to see what had happened to me, there I sat with the Arabs. Meanwhile, the Polish officials were doing nothing about the problem they said we represented. Pamela asked what was wrong and I said, "Isn't it obvious?" and she knew. It was obvious to anyone looking on and quite a few people in the waiting room were watching us the way people watch an accident or a dog fight. Once the entire line had been processed, the Polish officials took the three passports back to check-point-one and pretended to do something to them but it was clear to me that my passport had been stamped the same way Pamela's had been all the way through. I think it was fear of Pamela's wrath that got them moving. When she came back off the plane she looked pretty fierce!

We stayed on in Paris till August 11, then flew back to the States. Much was routine for us at first then word came that my forthcoming novel, *My Amputations,* had won the 1986 Western States Book Award for fiction. That news came in November 1985.

To receive the award, I had to be in New Orleans where it would be presented in an official ceremony on May 23, 1986, at the home of Congresswoman Lindy Boggs. New Orleans had been chosen because the American Booksellers Association convention was being held there that year. Boggs's place was a grand old French mansion. The ceremony was posh and well-catered in this elegant French Quarter home. The place was packed.

Editor Jonathan Galassi presented the award to me and to the other three winners, Mary Bernard, Anita Sullivan, and Kim Stafford, in the courtyard by the fountain. Later, courtesy of the Xerox Foundation, one of the sponsors of the prize, we were wined and dined at the New Orleans landmark restaurant Dooky Chase's.

There were too many parties and celebrations surrounding the ABA events. One couldn't and wouldn't go to them all. We were staying at a French Quarter hotel called Place d'Armes and our room opened onto a courtyard with a swimming pool and sitting places. It was very pleasant.

Pamela and I spent some time walking around the French Quarter catching snatches of jazz from the various places but a large part of the time we spent at the convention center. Because of the prize, the Western States Foundation people wanted me to be available for professional reasons. Still, there was plenty of time left over to wander around and to go to other events.

So, here we are back at the present moment in the studio. My radio is on the window ledge of one of the three windows behind me. A Denver station is playing classical music. If I turn around and look west, I can see the foothills and beyond them, the mountains. Here in Boulder, and especially out here in north Boulder, one easily forgets the hectic pace of say, Denver, a thirty-minute drive from here. The slowness has become a sort of haven for me. In it, I find it much easier to write and to carry on with my painting.

It seems to me at this moment that I am surrounded with the facts and artifacts of my whole life. To my left is my studio easel, bought some years ago in Washington, D.C., while I was teaching at Howard and Maryland Universities. The north wall and the south one are lined with library shelving and contain almost all the books—novels, criticism, poet-

Clarence and Pamela in Lublin, Poland, 1984

ry, history, art books—I have collected, kept, read, reread since that tremendous turning point in my life when I left Omaha, Nebraska, in 1966 and moved to New York's Lower East Side. To my right is the old desk, made in Yugoslavia, I bought in New York around 1971 from a used furniture store in my block on Waverly Place, two blocks east of New York University. Slightly behind me, in the north-west corner of the studio is the adjustable drawing table Pamela bought me one Christmas not long ago. I did a number of watercolors on it last December, just before my watercolor show at the First National Bank Gallery, here, in January of this year. By the desk, my old IBM Selectric on which I wrote *Emergency Exit*. I remember the fear I felt when first approaching my first electric typewriter. Last year I went through the same thing, learning the ways of this computer and the Diablo printer that came with it. At my left, within reach, my old *Random House Dictionary* is perched on the music stand. Both were picked up somewhere along the way about fifteen years ago. Sometimes I wonder about my ability to keep things. I still have a knitted sweater bought in Mexico in 1968.

Copyright © Clarence Major, 1988

BIBLIOGRAPHY

Poetry:

The Fires That Burn in Heaven. Privately printed, 1954.

Love Poems of a Black Man. Omaha, Neb.: Coercion Press, 1965.

Human Juices. Omaha, Neb.: Coercion Press, 1966.

Swallow the Lake. Middletown, Conn.: Wesleyan University Press, 1970.

Private Line. London: Paul Breman, 1971.

Symptoms & Madness. New York: Corinth, 1971.

The Cotton Club: New Poems. Detroit: Broadside Press, 1972.

The Syncopated Cakewalk. New York: Barlenmir House, 1974.

Inside Diameter: The France Poems. London: Permanent Press, 1985.

Some Observations of a Stranger at Zuni in the Latter Part of the Century. Los Angeles: Sun and Moon Press, 1987.

Surfaces and Masks. Minneapolis: Coffee House Press, 1988.

Fiction:

All-Night Visitors. New York: Olympia Press, 1969.

NO. New York: Emerson Hall, 1973.

Reflex and Bone Structure. New York: Fiction Collective, 1975.

Emergency Exit. New York: Fiction Collective, 1979.

My Amputations. New York: Fiction Collective, 1986.

Painted Turtle: Woman with Guitar. Los Angeles: Sun and Moon Press, 1987.

Such Was the Season. San Francisco: Mercury House, 1987.

Fun and Games (short stories). Stevens Point, Wis.: Holy Cow!, 1988.

Nonfiction:

Dictionary of Afro-American Slang. New York: International Publishers, 1970; also published as *Black Slang: A Dictionary of Afro-American Talk.* London: Routledge & Kegan Paul, 1971.

The Dark and Feeling: Black American Writers and Their Work. New York: Third Press, 1974.

Editor of:

Writers Workshop Anthology. New York: New Lincoln School/Harlem Education Project, 1967.

Man Is Like a Child: An Anthology of Creative Writing by Students. New York: Macombs Junior High School, 1968.

The New Black Poetry. New York: International Publishers, 1969; London: Central Books, 1969.

Sound recordings:

Tough Poems for Tough People. New York: Caedmon.

Black Spirits. Los Angeles: Motown.

The Voice of the Poet. Washington, D.C.: National Public Radio.

Clarence Major Reads the Cotton Club. Detroit: Broadside Press.

D. Keith Mano

1942-

INTRODUCTION TO ME

D. Keith Mano at the New York World's Fair, about 1965

Arthur T. Stephen

Truth is, I never have been at ease with Mano. It reminds me, I think, of some word I've seen on a foreign men's-room door. Or the acronym for your latest, defunct treaty organization. When I was poor and scholarshipped at Trinity High School—with Whitney on one side and Whitlock on another—I felt like an *au pair* boy. So, when dating a Chapin or a Spence girl, I stressed my maternal heritage: Minor. On that side we go back to 1360, when a Somerset tin miner was baroneted by Edward the Black Prince. Mother said she'd never gone without employment—1929 crash, no matter—be-

cause of her WASP last name. In any coming devaluation, I thought, Mano could put the wreath on his door. And I was *persona non* with Buffy Vandermost's father: he kept her hidden from me more thoroughly than a government witness before some Mafia trial.

By 1968, however, ethnic was in. I featured Mano not Minor: hell, back then, Edward the Black Prince would've worn an Afro. Only I couldn't be sure what eth I was. Italian, no (though I wasn't above pretending, so they'd dump extra clam sauce on my linguine). Grandpa Mano, you understand, said that his mother and father had been murdered in a silk caravan heist somewhere between Constantinople and Vienna. Brought up by a noble band of Gypsies the infant Mano was. But then Grandpa also claimed to have taken Lillian Russell's virtue. The birth certificate said, "Salonika, Catholic." Aha, Greek, I thought. But then an immigration paper said, "Salonika, Turkish, Muslim." Meanwhile every Greek who heard "Salonika" said, "You must be Jewish"—90 percent of that town apparently having been settled by Sephardic Jews from Spain. Aha, I thought, Jewish and Sephardic no less. With this maybe they'll let me write for the *NYTBR*. I am a one man ecumenical movement. Yet another paper said, "Born Cavadartsi, Turkey." I don't have roots, I have damn strawberry runners. No wonder Lillian Russell got so turned on.

Whatever. I was born on February 12, 1942, in New York City. For the first ten years of my life, we resided at 45 Thayer Street on Manhattan's Upper West Side. The Inwood area is still charming: art moderne facades, Fort Tryon Park. Bess Myerson had an apartment across the street from us. I was a typical New York sewer rat. Ma Bell had this thuggish-looking, calzone squat substation on Thayer. (We made our fall and spring collections of belts and watch bands from stolen umpteen-colored switchboard wire.) With two people you could play Telephone Ball. Across from the substation someone had painted several square strike zones on the Wigwam Tavern wall. These, unfortunately, were for taller children: belt high came around my part line. The substation sat four stories tall. Anything above floor one was a single. Above two was a double. Above three was a triple. Above four was the roof, of course—what did you expect? A ground rule snafu.

Say goodnight, Gracie, and go watch Buffalo Bob on your four-inch Dumont.

Typical. Except that, by Inwood standards, I was a child prodigy. A prodigiousness measured and chronicled and, Lord knows, half-created by my mother. For my first birthday she wrote the following doggerel, "And someday you'll hear people say that Abe was born on D's Day." I've taken my revenge by dropping the name she gave me. She was (and is) remarkably nurturing and bright. Even at seventy-seven she reads a book a day. Her tales of my precocity (which I parodied in *The Proselytizer*) have driven my own children around the bend. Apparently I spoke my first words at nine months, and had such a large vocabulary by a year and a half that the Gesell Institute at Yale wanted to give me a scholarship. On top of that I was on the cover of some astrology periodical, as having the most spectacular configuration of stars since, I dunno, Orion. I was hot stuff at age two—it has been downhill ever since.

At any rate I got into Hunter College Elementary School, where the cutoff IQ was 160 or better. The school had one virtue: because we all had such great numbers, none of us felt freakish. The disadvantages, however, were much more telling. To start with, the staff was terrified of us. We were treated the way African violets are. Second, we were constantly being used as lab animals for every variation of Stanford Binet that might come along. (We were so good at testing that I got my IQ up to 183 at one point.) Third and most damaging—we were taught just about *nada.* Homework was limited to one day a week in my last year. We were expected to *express* ourselves a whole lot and that was about it. When I graduated from sixth grade I didn't even know long division. We were a bunch of brilliant ignoramuses.

So dull-witted, in fact, that I spelled my middle name Kieth on an entrance exam for Fieldston. We were poor. My father worked as a peon at X-Pando Corporation, the cement factory owned by that above-named Mr. Mano, who, when he wasn't seducing Lillian Russell, liked to humiliate everyone around him. There was no money to put me through a quality private school—and a scholarship, considering my ghastly preparation at Hunter, seemed unlikely. But Trinity, to my eternal gratitude, read the IQ figures and said, "There has to be something there." I think they had their doubts through my seventh and eighth grades. I struggled desperately—but, in that struggle, through the strangest of mischances, I became a writer.

I tell this story, not because I'm particularly proud of it, but because it says something about the importance of confidence in any endeavor. My first

"Starting nose guard—probably eighth grade"

assignment at Trinity was a 500 word essay on the month of October. So staggering was the prospect of 500 words, so incapable did I feel, that I developed my first and last writer's block. And so (what else?) my mother wrote the entire paper. And got an *A,* with the notation "superb" scrawled next to it. My mother then proceeded to write *every single* English composition and exam essay (the tests were open book) for an entire year. I got a straight A and won the English prize.

Now two very important influences in my life derive from this bit of piracy. One: I became a sacramental Christian. That may seem a ridiculous connection, but the Lord can be an absurdist. In order to win this English prize (which my mother had earned) one had to be a confirmed Christian. I was baptized, but my head was innocent of episcopal hands. I came to God, in other words, to perpetuate a fraud.

The second influence was even stranger. I *believed* I had won the award on my own. I have that sort of dreamer's mind. I took credit for it. I began tutoring other students in writing. And, at the start of eight grade, I told my mother that her first composition wasn't good enough. She would have to rewrite so that the paper would reflect my new status. But she had shot her wad. And so I rewrote it for her, and from then on won English prizes on my own. Had I been left to write 500 words on October by myself, I would certainly have been crippled—and would now be earning much more as a computer consultant, I'm sure.

At just this time—that is, when I was making the transition from Hunter to Trinity—we moved to Whitestone in Queens. My mother decided that—for the sake of my sister and myself—she would set up housekeeping for Grandpa Mano (swallowing cruel abuse in the process) so we could have a more suburban upbringing. I lived in and around Whitestone for the next eleven years until, in 1970, with one child made (Roderick) and another (Christopher) in first draft, I moved upstate to Rock Tavern and then Blooming Grove, New York. That was my one infidelity to New York City and I regret it even now. I am a New York urban person. I tolerate nature fairly well in small doses but, travel I have no patience for whatever. If the Pyramids are worth seeing, I figure, they'll come to New York on an Exxon grant and you'll be able to get front row seats at Ticketron.

I was loyal to New York (and to my family) when it came to college. I don't think I applied anywhere else but Columbia. This may have been a mistake—

especially in view of the 150 consecutive Columbia football games, home and away, that I've attended in my maddest obsession. In no way was Columbia as critical to my developing personality as Trinity was. Trinity taught me everything essential: Spartan work habits, lust for reading, self-confidence. In fact, after Trinity, Columbia was not very challenging. I graduated tenth in a class of forty or so at Trinity—and was hard-pressed to manage that. At Columbia I was routinely in the top five or so (out of seven hundred) and graduated summa cum laude.

But Columbia did crystallize two of my most central instincts. First: it made me a worshipping Christian. I had been confirmed for the most cynical of motives. Yet, I suspect, the sacrament had done some work on me. In any case there is a survey course at Columbia called Contemporary Civilization. The second year of this course (which deals largely with materialistic Western thought in the twentieth century) was meant to be the faith-breaker. Columbia is quite proud of this sort of thing. My instructor told the class that if anyone had brought religious baggage along, he would dump it before the year was over. In time, I saw that he might very well be right. What a dreary prospect atheism suddenly seemed to me. And so, whenever I left class, I went to Saint Paul's Chapel and took Communion. An antidote, you might say. I kept my strangely acquired baggage. And from that

Mano (right) as Richard III, at Columbia University, 1963

moment forward I became a traditional, churchgoing Christian.

I had also been developing instincts that might have been called politically conservative. In those days—1959, 1960—no one really knew what conservative thought was. *National Review* had been founded hardly five years before. Today, one of the senior editors at *NR* is Jeffrey Hart. In 1961–63 he was one of my English professors (I specialized in eighteenth-century English literature). By 1963 Jeff had been denied tenure for his conservatism. If you were halfway prescient, you could predict the outcome— 1968 and riots. Jeff introduced me to conservative thought as a coherent body of sociological, historical, and economic thought. I became closely associated with him (I still am) and, when I won the Kellett Fellowship to Cambridge, liberal members of the English faculty threatened to have it rescinded if I didn't separate myself from Jeff Hart. They didn't prevail, but they did give me sweaty moments. And I learned for the first time what academic liberalism was.

Acting and theatre (and radio work at WKCR) were a determinative influence on my life—and later on my writing technique. In the seventh or eighth grade I won a scholarship to the Henry Street Playhouse. I handled language, especially the Shakespearean, unusually well for an American. By my senior year of high school I had memorized over 8,000 lines of Shakespeare. I performed in college plays, but found them unprofessional. So, throughout my career at Columbia, I did a considerable amount of off-Broadway work: showcases, productions in tiny churches, the usual. Truth is: I didn't want to be a writer. It wasn't fun then. It is less fun now. True, each adolescent summer I wrote at least half a novel as apprentice work. But writing was for the future: my mature forties, say, when I had some *experience.* I wanted to act. I still would rather act. But force of circumstance compelled me to become a writer. If I'd known in seventh grade that I'd be writing 500, 1,000, 10,000 word articles all my life, I would've found some piano wire and garotted myself.

In 1963 I sailed for Cambridge, a Kellett Fellow on elevator shoes. Phi Beta and Summa Cum Footgear. They were lubberly things: you could've buried a mature raccoon in the box: I think Peter Boyle wore them later when he did *Young Frankenstein.* I didn't much favor it, but we were poor, and this was my mother's loveful, expensive present—giving me what her genes had left off the checklist. I'm not *that* short, not sideshow short: five-four maybe. But I do have a marvelous aptitude for appearing two, three inches shorter than I really am. Dense is the right word. At

An early stage photo of "the young actor"

180 pounds (170 of muscle) I could pass for the chief caryatid on a small, neoclassical toolshed. Believe it or not, height/weight ratio almost got me unmatriculated at Columbia. Back then one of the B.A. requirements, don't ask my why, was an ability to swim. And, worse, to float. I float real fine. Real fine three feet under water. It took a note from my swimming instructor and particular dispensations: I graduated with honor, also with the highest specific gravity on record. But shortness had its compensations. If I were six-foot-three, I would've written only one novel not seven.

Cambridge was—and still is—the most beautiful university in all of academic creation. Bosch-painted flowers (each an allergen to me) sprang up even on Christmas Day. Who could concentrate? I was at Clare College doing graduate research on something—How Dr. Johnson's scrofula influenced his metrical style, I think. And taking informal instruction from F.R. Leavis. Leavis, by then, was a baroque, half-mad figure. Downing College had lent him cloakroom space to lecture at random in—he wore a bathrobe, one carpet slipper and many toast crumbs. Leavis would read Johnson or Addison or Swift aloud with interpretation—and you'd notice, after a while, that he had stopped turning the page. It was from pure memory. A world figure, yet all he cared for was his precarious (he made trouble) standing at Cambridge. "C.S. Lewis is dead," he announced to us one morning. "They said in the *Times* that we will miss him. We will *not.* We will *not.*"

I realize now that Cambridge had almost no effect on me. (Unlike the terrific influence it exerted over other Kelletts—Norman Podhoretz, for one.) Until this moment I have never written about my time there. True, Cambridge killed my passion for scholarly criticism (but Lionel Trilling had begun that process). True, I wed a Girton girl (Jo McArthur)—but something similar might have come to pass in New York. I began my first novel (*Bishop's Progress*) on the Cam banks—but I would've begun it beside another river and it was about Manhattan not England. I don't quite understand why such a severe cultural adjustment made so little lasting impression. It seems strange. I got on well enough. More than sport or intellect, drama was prime in Cambridge. I could act: for my age I had wide theatre experience. I was much courted: a small celebrity, in fact. But when my tutor suggested I learn Italian for the second-year final exam, I got uncomfortable. "Oh," he said, "you don't learn it. You just memorize passages from Dante and Petrarch that've appeared on previous exams." "Hmmm," I said. I finished a summer tour through sixteen German cities with the Marlowe Society (playing Bottom as if he were Peter Falk) and then took passage home.

That was the autumn of 1964. My father was dying of lung cancer that had metastasized to the bone. I expected my pregnant wife to meet me in New York at Christmas. For two months, while working on *Bishop's Progress* and making the rounds as an actor, I returned to Columbia to pick up a Woodrow Wilson Fellowship that I had won—and rejected in favor of the Kellett. Soon though, I was hired by the National Shakespeare Company, got my Equity card, and left to tour America with *Macbeth* and *As You Like It.* I was playing Touchstone in the Forest of Arden-in-Tampa when my father died. I had worked summers at the family cement factory—there was no one else who even knew where the filing cabinets were. The factory supported my mother and my sister. So there I was a young father, with half-a-novel written and a theatre career that had just capsized. I quit acting and took up cement. And reluctantly I became a writer.

I ran X-Pando Corporation for twenty years (we lost our lease in 1986). Nine of us, to the fourth Mano generation, gathered dust and sold it at the same 5,000 square-foot plant in Long Island City. Even now I miss the genial comradery of cement. There is great civil exchange in manufacture. Americans express affection best by making things for each other. Writing, by contrast, is an isolate, self-conscious transaction. Through X-Pando I have participated in buildings: elevator and glass wall and pipeline, from Meadowlands Stadium to the A1 Jubail refinery in Saudi Arabia. People have enjoyed my writing. But no one has ever needed it.

I finished *Bishop's Progress* in 1967—and began writing *Horn* the next day. I published six novels in six years (from 1968 to 1973). An athletic performance to say the least. As a novelist I am a conservative, committed to Western traditions. I consider myself a Christian writer, though some reviewers have called me a Christian pornographer.

My conservatism derives from my Christianity

"Lifetime batting average of .439": the author, about 1970

directly. I don't immanentize the eschaton. That is: I don't limit the ends, the hopes, the purposes of man to this life. I believe in an afterlife. And the devil. In my novels I have tried to relate traditional Christianity to the concerns of the modern world.

Bishop's Progress dealt with progress and the Christian and with death. *Horn* with civil rights and the Christian and death. *War Is Heaven!* with the Christian and war and death (just about the only non-antiwar novel written about a Vietnam-like situation). *The Death and Life of Harry Goth* with the Christian and death. *The Proselytizer* with the Christian and sex and death. *The Bridge,* a novel in favor of pollution, dealt with the Christian and ecology and death. And *Take Five* presents a man who loses his five senses one after another, until he is left a shimmering spot in absolute nothingness—at which point one either finds God or goes mad. Or both.

My novels are realistic, in one sense. They deal very explicitly with sex, drugs, bodily functions. I've even written the one great proctoscope scene in Western fiction. In any case, my reality is a subterfuge—as I think, probably, all reality is a subterfuge. For me, all real things are one term of a metaphor. The minor term—and they imply something greater. I haven't given up the medieval world view and the three-tiered universe.

I've never tried to write the Great American Novel. For a simple reason: Americans don't write novels. I refer you to *The American Novel and Its Tradition* by Richard Chase. I quote:

> The English novel, one might say, has been a kind of imperial enterprise, an appropriation of reality with the high purpose of bringing order to disorder. By contrast . . . the American novel has usually seemed content to explore, rather than to appropriate and civilize, the remarkable and in some ways unexampled territories of life in the New World and to reflect its anomalies and dilemmas. . . . The American novel is more profound and clairvoyant than the English novel, but by the same token it is narrower and more arbitrary, and it tends to carve out of experience brilliant, highly wrought fragments rather than massive unities.[1]

True. And yet American novelists feel an inferiority, a lack of seriousness in their work. It's what drove Henry James and his crew of expatriate Ameri-

cans to Europe. At the turn of the nineteenth century, American painters of great talent, returning from European art schools, found themselves suddenly stagnant on native soil: without tradition or sophistication. Cultureless. E.B. Morse gave it up and invented the telegraph. John Trumbull went into business. Washington Allston, a brilliant success in Europe, brought back an almost finished *Belshazzar's Feast* so celebrated that Bostonians subscribed $10,000 to purchase it. Allston worked the rest of his life and could never finish it. John Vanderlyn, another exceptional artist, said, "No one but an artistic quack could paint in America."

Ironic, isn't it? American artists and intellectuals of the nineteenth century felt a crippling inferiority before the mature, subtle European tradition. Yet, less than a hundred and fifty years later, American artists and intellectuals feel a crippling inferiority before the primitive nations. We collect African art. We praise ethnic primitivism. We yearn for naturalness. Such a dramatic *volte-face* is cruel. It speaks, of course, for the changing times. But it speaks, too, of an endless capacity in Americans for self-denigration.

And we still think of the Great American Novel, when in fact the novel is an English affair. We are, in Chase's terms, romancers. It's an unfortunate word. The English novel had to do with society, its levels and split levels. With the interaction of groups and sub-groups. The English novel was the first effort of a then unborn discipline: sociology. But there have been in America—with marginal exceptions—no classes, no sense of cultural placing. American writers were thrown back on the paradigmatic one-on-one situation, man against nature. Natty Bumppo against the forest. Ahab against the whale.

Hawthorne knew this. In his preface to *The House of the Seven Gables,* he wrote:

> When a writer calls his work a Romance, it need hardly be observed that he wishes to claim a certain latitude, both as to its fashion and material, which he would not have felt himself entitled to assume, had he professed to be writing a Novel.[2]

Yet we belittle and ignore our romancers. We tend to take more seriously the novelist who gives chapter, verse, and number: who describes his small social niche minutely. We haven't a culture, so we are reduced to making culture internal. In fact, the only legal tender we have is the glossary of terms Freud bandied around. But our interior landscapes tend to

---

[1] *The American Novel and Its Tradition,* by Richard Chase. Garden City, N.Y.: Doubleday, 1957, p. 4–5.

[2] *The House of the Seven Gables,* by Nathaniel Hawthorne. New York: Norton, 1967, p. 1.

Book jacket photo for War Is Heaven!

be particular and forced. They do not visualize well. We reject the evidence of Hawthorne and Melville and penalize our fiction writers for living in a classless, traditionless society.

If you asked me to define the characteristics of my fiction, I could do not better than to quote Chase on romance.

> By contrast [with the novel] the romance, following distantly the medieval example, feels free to render reality in less volume and detail. It tends to prefer action to character, and action will be freer in a romance than in a novel, encountering, as it were, less resistance from reality. . . . The romance can flourish without providing much intricacy of relation. The characters, probably rather two-dimensional types, will not be complexely related to each other or to society or to the past. Human beings will on the whole be shown in ideal relation— that is, they will share emotions only after these have become abstract or symbolic. To be sure, characters may become profoundly involved in some way, as in Hawthorne and Melville, but it will be a deep and narrow, an obsessive, involvement. In American romances it will not matter much what class

people come from, and where the novelist would arouse our interest in a character by exploring his origin, the romancer will probably do so by enveloping it in mystery. Character itself becomes, then, somewhat abstract and ideal, so much so in some romances that it seems to be merely a function of plot. The plot we may expect to be highly colored. Astonishing events may occur, and these are likely to have a symbolical or ideological, rather than a realistic, plausibility. Being less committed to the immediate rendition of reality than the novel, the romance will more freely veer toward mythic, allegorical, and symbolistic forms.[3]

After seven idiosyncratic, modestly fantastic novels, this paragraph—which I read only recently— came as a revelation. An outcast, I suddenly found myself in the mainstream of American fiction. It was like discovering, abruptly, that your unknown father is king of the land.

Certainly my Christian orientation has helped to

---

[3] Chase, *The American Novel and Its Tradition,* p. 13.

shift my fictional practice from novel to romance. It has also, though this may sound oxymoronic, caused my writing to become both more grotesque and more obscene. For any serious Christian writer the obscene, the grotesque, the violent seem almost prerequisite. After all, he or she is trafficking with an ineffable theme: the transcendent God. A subject matter that has no matter to it. How am I to describe the Living God: to see Whom is death? It's an exasperating business. Particularly so when writing for a readership which—more likely than not—doesn't share the powerful sign language by which Christians communicate in shorthand with one another: the Cross, the Trinity, sacraments, Grace. And that enormous paradox: death into life.

Give me a simile for God. An image, a locution that can do justice to the omnipresent, all-lovely, and very active Being. You might as well try to draw Leviathan out with a hook. The best that writers can do is rough out a vague equivalent for certain of his qualities: strength and rapture and ruthlessness. His power to abrogate rules: the way Paul in *Romans* understood God-the-Law-Breaker. This isn't easy. But I sense that the obscene (and its subheadings, the grotesque and the violent) though they do not pierce to his goodness—do at least approximate his energy, as far as humans can comprehend it. These are the only images vivid enough to move an atheist or a fallen-away Christian to some crepuscular feeling for the benevolent savagery of Grace. A sexual act enraptures the average attention, in some small and transient measure, as the sacred enraptured Saint Anthony in the desert. The Incarnation was God's compassionate and, well, artistic attempt to capture the fickle human imagination in an event. The agony of Golgotha was grotesque and violent: expressly so. I don't mean to equate my creative and propagandistic works to these of the Supreme. But we—if that pronoun is possible—we have the same problem: an inattentive audience. And we each—to plug the title of my fifth novel—we are each a proselytizer.

Ah, you say, he's talking about shock value. And I suppose I am. The burning bush had shock value. Blindness on the road to Damascus, too. God comes from the realistic school of spiritual fiction: real snakes in imaginary gardens of Eden, to pervert Marianne Moore. Theologians have made religion abstract and eristic: God has always been considerate enough to plot and act out his revelation in physical, historical moments. It's hard to get through to men: a human mind needs distraction from the continual, vulgar input of its five senses.

Though there are passages in my fiction that might well be considered obscene, I feel pretty sure

that my motives have not been mercenary: my book sales tend to confirm that. As Bob Gottlieb, who edited my fourth and fifth novels once told me—sex as a cashable commodity in serious fiction went out in 1959 or so. It's too available now: other media supply it better. In the time of Miller and Lawrence and Joyce scenes of explicit sexual contact were, willy-nilly, a philosophical or political statement: the-artist-is-exempt-from-strictures-of-bourgeois-morality. I'm certain there were those in 1928 who read *Lady Chatterley's Lover* for the wrong reason. Then an inordinately sensual moment would stop the action—no matter how well that moment was integrated into the tone and purpose of the writing. It is not so today. Explicit sex, four-letter words, do not distort the relationship of writer and reader: do not make it suddenly personal, an assault on the reader. Obscenity is now just another aspect of life: something that a conscientious writer can draw on for effect and point, without clogging the metabolism of his book.

If there are nonartistic considerations, they derive from the Christian novelist's feeling of loss, of separateness. We are only a few centuries away from an era when all things—public, household, natural—were thought to be metaphors for (or at least in and of) the Christian world view. What joy Dante must have known: writing for such a prodigious consensus of emotions and shared symbolism. There has been a terrific dropping away: not only for the priest, for the artist as well. Emblems and words that have a mighty resonance are precious: there are many fewer now. And the Christian writer is made defensive: even paranoid: I sense it in myself. Flannery O'Connor has explained this special alienation best. I quote from an essay in her marvelous collection *Mystery and Manners*:

> When I write a novel in which the central action is a baptism, I am very well aware that for a majority of my readers, baptism is a meaningless rite, and so in my novel I have to see that this baptism carries enough awe and mystery to jar the reader into some kind of emotional recognition of its significance. To this end I have to bend the whole novel—its language, its structure, its action. I have to make the reader feel, in his bones if nowhere else, that something is going on here that counts. Distortion in this case is an instrument; exaggeration has a purpose, and the whole structure of the story or novel has been made what it is because of belief. This is not the kind of distortion that destroys; it is the kind that reveals, or should reveal. . . .

Our salvation is a drama played out with the devil, a devil who is not simply generalized evil, but an evil intelligence determined on its own supremacy. I think that if writers with a religious view of the world excel these days in the depiction of evil, it is because they have to make its nature unmistakable to their particular audience.

The novelist and the believer, when they are not the same man, yet have many traits in common—a distrust of the abstract, a respect for boundaries, a desire to penetrate the surface of reality and to find in each thing the spirit which makes it itself and holds the world together. But I don't believe that we shall have great religious fiction until we again have that happy combination of believing artist and believing society. Until that time, the novelist will have to do the best he can in travail with the world he has. He may find in the end that instead of reflecting the image at the heart of things, he has only reflected our broken condition and, through it, the face of the devil we are possessed by. This is a modest achievement, but perhaps a necessary one.[4]

I can hear the tumblers of your mind as they click and align themselves. You wonder: Can art be an efficient tool of the spirit? Of conversion? Probably not. I doubt—after seven novels—if I ever have been the first cause, or even the least cause of any single person's headlong sprint to piety. Perhaps, you suggest, I write too little as a missionary and too much in the missionary position. That might be so: I neither apologize for my style nor inculcate it. But I suspect that no art can be a substitute for—or even a reasonable record of—the mystical experience. Great Christian writers—Lewis, Williams, Buechner—have witnessed, too: and in somewhat less sensational ways. They certainly reinforce the Spirit. But authentic mysticism presupposes a relationship of excruciating intimacy between a Higher Being and the human soul. Usually that latter—the human—makes itself both blank and vulnerable so that it may better be filled. As in the ancient Taoist maxim: "It is the emptiness which makes the cup useful." And in that intimate colloquy, at a certain level, there can be no middleman: not artist, not guru, not priest.

---

[4] *Mystery and Manners*, by Flannery O'Connor, ed. Sally Fitzgerald and Robert Fitzgerald. New York: Farrar, Straus, 1969, pp. 162, 168.

I've been interviewed now and again about my *oeuvre*. (I cotton to that overdone French word, *oeuvre*. No matter how you say it, it comes out like you're laying an egg. Painfully. Which makes it pretty much onomatopoeic.) Anyhow, these writer interviews are all of a dull sameness. First they ask you if you use a pencil or a typewriter. Then they ask if you write before porridge or after. Third: they inevitably want to know what author or authors have had the most influence on your French egg-laying. I've never been able to give an intelligent answer. "None," is probably honest. By the time I had written my third novel, at twenty-eight, I could recognize affiliations and shared intentions—but the tenor and mode of my fiction had long been spaceshot to its permanent orbit. Yet, if there is anyone with whom I feel a blood brotherhood, whose purposes and tactics are mine, it is—not a fiction writer—but the poet, John Donne.

Batter my heart, three person'd God; for, you
As yet but knocke, breathe, shine, and seeke to mend;
That I may rise, and stand, o'erthrow mee,' and bend
Your force, to breake, blowe, burn and make me new.
I, like an usurpt towne, to'another due,
Labour to'admit you, but Oh, to no end,
Reason your viceroy in mee, mee should defend,
But is captiv'd, and proves weake or untrue.
Yet dearly'I love you,' and would be loved faine,
But am betroth'd unto your enemie:
Divorce mee,' untie, or breake that knot againe,
Take mee to you, imprison mee, for I
Except you'enthrall mee, never shall be free,
Nor ever chast, except you ravish mee.[5]

But you say, this is erotic, not obscene. And I answer that John Donne wrote in a time when Christianity was strong medicine. When bells stunned the air of an urban Sunday. In a profane age, the profane must be taken unawares and in their own tongue. Today, a Christian writer—one who is outside the huge, inbred evangelical world—has two choices: either to give up his apostolate to the secular population (which is despair, the greatest sin) or to strike home: pummel with body blows. You might say that the end, doubtful as it is, cannot justify the means. But the Flood was a means. Saint Paul's blindness. And the Crucifixion. God does not go gently into our self-imposed night.

Be sure, there are perils. Pride of art. Egotism. In any contact between sacred and obscene, the quality of veneration will make the difference between a Holy

---

[5] *Holy Sonnets*, XIV, by John Donne.

Sonnet and a self-indulgent blasphemy. There were perils enough in God's reaching out. We've all come across good humanists who read the New Testament as literature: who see Christ as the Great good man, and nothing more than that. When modes of experience are mixed, there is always room for catastrophic misunderstanding. Works—charitable or artistic—cannot alone jumpstart a dead soul. And often the shock, placed on the wrong nodes, will burn the cell out. The reader's cell. The writer's also. The obscene as a metaphor for the holy implies a riskful spiritual leap. But such risks must be taken. And I must hope that Grace—the thief of God, the prison cracker—will break in.

On the first day of April 1979 I was baptized and chrismated as a member of the Orthodox Church. That statement is bald enough. It doesn't sound the wretchedness of separation: nor the jubilee time of coming home. After all I had been much more than a Sunday Episcopalian for eighteen years. I was diligent and loyal: the parish knew my work: the region, too: and the diocese. My decision (conceived *in vitro* over three years) was lacerating. It meant, first, that I would no longer share the Eucharist with my wife and children. It disjoined me from a hundred friends: devout folk, who—when the Episcopal Church dies of its terrible fever—will, by their grace and presence alone, touch it with an absolving unction. Several partook of my anguish. In those latter years, watching the Episcopal Church has been like watching a father kill himself with strange debauchery.

For me the dusk had come. My spiritual constitution was breaking down. I entered every parish church in New York Diocese with the skin white and drawn across my knuckles. What would it be this week? A woman or a media-consecrated lesbian administering the chalice? A vapid-chic modernization of liturgy? A sermon on Marxist-Christian dialogue? I had more than sufficient experience with Episcopal pork-barreling. (I was then, ironically, Bishop Paul Moore's representative on the Mid-Hudson Regional Council.) I knew that a bishop, like a determined rapist, will have his way. I knew, moreover, that the Episcopal house of bishops would never—or never in my lifetime—renounce its titillating common-law marriage with the Zeitgeist. Oh, I could set up as a gadfly: I could (and did) unrepresent Paul Moore. I could (and did) articulate my dissent. Which is to say: I could, at my pleasure, be bitter, defensive, furious, forlorn. But such an attitude, aside from being quite useless, does not prepare one well for the sacrament of Holy Communion. I had sins enough without that.

For years—it must have been at least fifteen (my father knew him)—an American Orthodox priest, now bishop, would visit X-Pando Corporation. John Schneyder is urbane yet bashful: a devotee of Victorian fiction and the New York Rangers. We were a "contact"—that is, we gave. His small church was sustained almost entirely by un-Orthodox contributions. He would gather them on foot, day by day, weather by weather. A dollar, two, sometimes ten, sometimes nothing as the Paraclete saw fit. I can recall once asking him (1969?) if he would show me how a clerical collar attached itself (the description was useful to a scene in *Horn*). We became semiannual friends. Yet somehow it never traversed my mind to ask him what Orthodoxy was.

Once or twice each year "The Gimlet Eye" (my column in *National Review*) would squint at Episcopalianism: rather as you might squint at a serious accident. And readers, out of empathic compassion, had started mailing me literature on Orthodoxy. They were all either ex-Episcopalian or ex-Catholic. I began to read. With the uncoiling of time my dead father's face has recapitulated itself in me: brow and hairline and nose. And that has been so with Orthodoxy: the religious features were there: I am its natural child. In reading I learned that Orthodoxy was the most ancient and least-tampered-with Christian communion. Priests could marry. Women did not agitate for ordination. The Catholic bishop of Rome is recognized, but just as one bishop among equals. The Orthodox liturgy—of Saint Basil and Saint Crysostom—has not been altered in, oh, fifteen hundred years. Moreover, for an Episcopalian there was no momentous adjustment—creedal or ceremonial—that I would be subjected to. One complication did obtain: but it was not theological. Though Orthodoxy is a worldwide communion (with about 80,000,000 members) each jurisdiction has autonomy. Language and national custom—whether Greek, Russian, Syrian, Ukrainian—make it somewhat difficult at first for an American to assimilate himself.

So I called Bishop Schneyder. His Orthodox American Church had been sanctioned by the Synod of Bishops Outside of Russia in 1951 as an English-speaking outreach toward Americans like myself. But the Bishop didn't think I would be comfortable with the facilities. In actual fact his congregation numbered three. Mind you, this did not make the church seem empty: the church was an apartment on West Fifty-seventh Street.

In that tenement room (and later in a private home in Jackson Heights, Queens) Christ has raged through me. If peace can be said to rage. There is no sermon. There is no collection plate. But with the Orthodox liturgy, in a majestic translation by Archimandrite Lazarus Moore, my power of devotion has stoked itself bright. After eight years I have found both spiritual rest and spiritual confidence again. In a church, part of an immense and ancient international communion, that isn't afraid not to change.

In 1980, soon after I left the Episcopal Church, Bishop Schneyder officiated at my wedding to Laurie Kennedy. I had left Blooming Grove in 1978. Laurie and I settled into an apartment on Central Park West. Soon after our wedding I overheard my new wife saying, "He's a writer," on the telephone. Uh-oh, I thought: time for a little marriage counseling here. "Listen, Laurie," I explained, "this may not sound important t'you—but t'me it's razor wire and gravel stew. I'm not a writer, I'm a *novelist.* I mean, people who hack out ad copy for Lubriderm can call themselves writers. People who string filler for the Kankakee *Daily Notion* think they write. Scratch any housewife with one sonnet and a recipe printed in the parish bulletin, she's a writer, too. Your friends might know me from *Playboy* or *Esquire,* but I'm a *novelist.* The way you're not just an actress—like every other hatcheck girl and cuticle pusher in New York—you're a *Broadway* actress. I'm a maker of worlds. A peopler of the human imagination, you know—and all that

"Our one wedding photo together": D. Keith Mano and Laurie Kennedy, 1980

good, highminded stuff. So *novelist,* huh? It matters a whole lot to me."

"Okay, sure. Fine."

"After all, I've written seven of them. It may sound like much ado about—"

"No, I understand. Novelist it is."

You can guess what comes next, right? Some very short time later a friend called Laurie to congratulate her.

"And I hear your new husband is D. Keith Mano, the writer."

"Uh, well, no. . . Actually he's a novelist."

"Oh, I'm so sorry," the friend said. "Everyone told me he was a writer."

Hoist on my own dumbwaiter rope. I suppose the friend thought "novelist" meant a starting-wage corporate trainee. Or maybe I was some postulant at the Mendicant Order of Crutched and Plethoric Friars.

So, yeah, I am a *writer.* Since about 1971 I've published 1,000,000 or more words of nonfiction: column and review and magazine feature piece. Not only does that just about match, word count for word count, my fictional output—in large part it made the fiction possible. Moreover, if *Take Five* (which took almost one full decade) is different from, say, *Horn* or *The Proselytizer,* in style and POV and syntactical intensity, the step-up transformation can be put down to those hard-nose, compressed magazine jobs I was hustling. Oh, I did begrudge now and then. On average three months of nonfiction bought one month of *Take Five* (fiction being as economically irresponsible today as cocaine use or go-go investment in linotype stock). I might groan when, say, *Sports Illustrated* sent me to cover a dog show in Atlantic City. But it all fed back. Some small part of *Take Five* probably barks.

On occasion a tenderfoot college journalist will ask me how he or she can safecrack the magazine business. I'm not much use. Far as I know, you do it by writing four or five novels first. I never solicited nonfiction work. And, up to 1972, I had done just some book reviews for the *NYTBR,* plus one feature piece each for *New York, National Review,* and *Esquire* ("Portrait of the Artist as a Cement Manufacturer" in fact). Then William F. Buckley, Jr., rang up and offered me $150 per issue to do a regular column on American manners for *NR:* "Whatever subject you choose, we won't change one word." (They haven't yet.) Soon after *Playboy* commissioned a container cargo-size piece on the Disney Organization and my long relationship with 919 N. Michigan Avenue, Chicago, had begun. By 1977 I was film critic for *OUI* (a *Playboy* organ then), "The Gimlet Eye" for *NR,* and

With William F. Buckley, Jr., 1973

up-front book columnist at *Esquire* under Lee Eisenberg.

Take Five suffered, but it could only blame itself. I will never essay such a mad, ambitious project again. Until that time—with one novel a year for six years—I had managed to pay mortgage and obstetrician and the odd poker debt out of advances. Now I no longer could. I was, well, a writer for good. And today I'm the only person ever to appear on the masthead of both *NR* and *Playboy* simultaneously (as contributing editor). Hefner and Buckley: one could develop groin pulls from straddling, you might think. It is either a tribute to my shameless opportunism or to the generosity and open-mindedness of those writer-aware gentlemen. Somehow I prefer the latter tribute, thanks.

NR is a journal of conservative opinion. I didn't have any trouble with the political magnetic north, but its contributors—men like James Burnham and Frank Meyer and Hugh Kenner, WFB, Jr. himself—intimidated that 1972 me. Hell, you can be marvelously ignorant and a good novelist, too. Happens all the time. One thing *NR* did lack, though, was live coverage. I felt more confident if "The Gimlet Eye" had actually been there, wherever: I'd be authentic at least. And fictional techniques were useful to the forward observer position (besides, someone had just invented Tom Wolfe). My first paragraph usually began, "I am at or in or with." At a Gay Mr. America Pageant, in the squad car, with migrant laborers. And

at, in, with just about every radical demonstration from 1972 until 1979 or so, when that cultural phenomenon went dry as halvah. New York was the beat I could afford: I began to read curbstone stencilling and my corner lamp post for leads. A POST NO BILLS sign would worry me. I bought lunch (often liquid) for marginal or seditious or just plain barmy folk: paranoids who advertised in *Village Voice*, bookies, cigarette smugglers, topless dancers, Nobel sperm bankers. And, for a first time, I conjugated myself regularly to the present tense. My previous novels had been written in perfect past. But present, I found, was more shapeable than rockwool: you can regress into perfect and pluperfect or anticipate with a startling use of future time. Simon Lynxx, my *Take Five* protagonist, originally was. Now, because of *NR*, he is.

In *Playboy* and *OUI* I assumed a side-of-the-mouth, attention-hooking voice. Pssst, hey pal. Or, *A-hem*, over here. Or even: all right, Buster, hands on the car hood and spread 'em. When your prose is in direct visual competition with soft, nubile young women all set for some antic hay, you better talk *loud*, brother. This tone I call my Klutsy Macho style. I'm the kinda tough customer, pulls his switchblade on you. Only, like, he has it backward and—whick!—when he presses the button, it'll cut his own jacket lapel off. My Klutsy Macho style is pure second person. (Hey, you reader, you with the gel bed for a brain.) I liked it: I like to establish the relationship between you and me. No other writer was doing quite that (they were all better brung up, I guess). The aggressive intimacy is offset, I trust, by an equal lump sum of humorous self-deprecation. Though I had known the prototype for Simon Lynxx since 1959 at Columbia, his peculiar noise—ravage and rant and read-you-your-rights—my fluency in it, came from *OUI* and *Playboy*.

From all three comes my violent-ward passion for colloquial language. I have here, I think, a verb or two that'd stop your excursion train. Yet—like English itself—my style is top-laded with hard nouns. Fictional prose we expect to be timeless, deathless, and royalty-less. But magazine nonfiction should derive from the same clutch purse as ad copy and news. "Static cling" and "stone washed" and "fuzz-buster" and "hair food" and "combination skin," each is a phrase that, through TV, will reach full circulation faster than intravenous Methedrine. When set, for example, in some abstract context—intellect or love or sexual desire—they form gang tool combinations that are tonally oxymoronic. I began to interview my patient children (when they weren't being quiet because HE was writing). They spoke of

Sports Illustrated/Lane Stewart

At Baker Field, Columbia University, about 1974

"bloach" (fat idiot) and BOCE (dumb person: taken from the acronym for a local remedial program) and "no durr" (no kidding). I wanted to scoop idioms: her fratch and your woobie and my hypostem. This drove copy editors, who, by definition, live by definition, into virtual azfraxia and felf. "Mr. Mano, hem, that word doesn't appear in my unabridged." At which point I would paraphrase an answer once given (with more authority) by WFB, Jr. "Ah, but after this it will, it will."

Yet, more than anything, I began to hear a meter running. After six open-ended, write-it-until-you're-done novels, I became sensitive about arithmetic. Six hundred, 800, 1,000—tick, tick, tick—words at a time. I treat any magazine assignment as though it were negotiable paper. If they want 1,000 words, they'll get not less than 995, not more than 1,005. I'm either a literalist or coward: when my junk mail has Dated Material Open At Once on it, I ask the postman to countersign. As a result I began resenting certain filler language. The apostrophe economized: "don't" was one word, not two. "Whatcha doon tonight?"

rang up five for the price of three. This reinforced my samurai devotion to colloquial speech parts. But it wasn't enough. A, an, the, for instance, seemed unthrifty. When your piece rate is 75¢ per word, you—okay, I—feel dishonest charging six bits for "the." I hadda find a way to budget diction and that meant *not starting so many sentences.* The phrase would be my unit of measurement, not subject-verb-object. One picture, some motor-minded idiot said, is worth 1,000 words. Uh-uh, I say, not *my* 1,000 words. Which of us can afford to be replaced by an illiterate staff photographer?

Around 1976 I began calling it Solid State English. I was particularly intrigued by the "equal sign" effect of a colon. $E=mc^2$. It was connective tissue in syntax; it stuck unlike ideas together better than that goo on a movie-theatre floor: it made the terms of any metaphor, well, static cling. You can date my work, more or less, by a colon-per-paragraph count. About that time, also, I met two elegant writers—Harold Brodkey and Hugh Kenner—who had made the same run at "transistorized prose." They, though, could explain what was happening. Me, I wrote this modular English because nothing else sounded quite right.

Look, Keith, they said: Henry James is dead, we all grant that. But Hemingway can't run up a decent bar tab in 1978 either. Dead, dead, boring as well. You don't have to write, "Nick put the worm on the hook. The worm squirmed. Nick liked the worm. The worm hated Nick," or whatever any more. His style was clear (God knows): it purged the language of baroque ornateness. Yet that same simplicity was often pretentious and fake-naive. Worse, it was predictable. The declarative sentence can declare too much, too insistently: with a repetitious verbal metabolism. So much for the importance of writing Ernest.

In contrast I give you a Brodkey sentence. "My father's face, full of noises, is there: it looms: his hidden face: is that you, old money-maker?" The changes in voice, POV, and syntax play pepper with your head. It has magic and yolky richness. And I had been writing that sort of sentence all along. In no time it led to a greenstick fracture between me and the copy editor at *OUI.* He got (or planted) this letter from some "name-withheld" reader. "Dear *OUI:* Does: Mano: need: a: laxative? He sees more: colons: than a proctologist." I was flown, believe it or not, to Chicago for punctuative rehabilitation. My worm was on the hook: I didn't like it: I almost quit. But then editor Nat Lehrnman decided in my favor. I was the only person at *OUI* who didn't have to write complete sentences.

In 1977 I wrote an extensive interview piece on

Harold for *Esquire*. He said then: "Most American style is based on French grammar; my style is highly Teutonic. In the first place, our grammar didn't grow up naturally. It was invented in the eighteenth and nineteenth centuries as a class distinction. It has religious overtones: I want to root all traces of God out of the language." And while our program and approach might be different (I'm essentially a Christian writer, after all: I root God into my subtext, if not my language), Harold and I have the same feel for English. I went on: "Grammar is arithmetic: colons expose that arithmetic to its algebraic potential. They signal a descending or ascending (or lateral) tendency in clause modification and connection. . . . Periods, semicolons stop action: a colon is always open, kinetic. Best, though: more colons, fewer sentences started. And the fewer you start, the less frequently you're caught up in a syntactical mechanism with its small-change flunky words: a, the, that, which, have been, had been, -ed, -ing. And all the formal language history that their use implies." *Take Five* would become my showcase for Solid State prose.

D. Keith Mano, on assignment, 1971 or so

William Chu

Beyond exposure to Harold and Hugh (Kenner once said that a semicolon was the ugliest punctuation mark conceivable), magazine work opened my spiral-bound world. Given inertia and perfectionist crochets, I would have sat at home writing, rewriting, re-rewriting in Scripto pencil that one 250 word fictional paragraph per day all life long. (My style has been called "gnomic." I now realize that doesn't refer to my height.) Except as it is unavoidable, novel-writing for me has seldom been drawn from personal experience. I've never visited Central America (Guatemala, I mean, not Kansas) nor was I in the army. Yet I wrote a convincing (so they told me) novel about Central American guerilla warfare. The only fun for a writer is, well, *lying*. But each magazine assignment widened my limit of resolution. Moreover, editors at *NR*, *Playboy*, *OUI*, and *Esquire* knew that Mano wrote best, funniest, when he was in physical or social pain. Trust me, it is hard to be even Klutsy Macho if you have panty hose or lipstick on, for instance. Or are locked in a mental home. They were all, I felt, competing to see who could make me suffer most exquisitely.

For *Playboy* and *OUI* I lived as a transvestite: had my skeleton bent by Rolfers: sank, glub, underwater in a rebirthing tank. I met incestuous fathers and people who knew all about cannibalism. I gave blood: pretended I was a wino: went under hypnosis: had myself put away in a goofy garage. With my ex-wife, Jo, I tested $5,000 worth of sex equipment. I met my present wife on a NY-LA plane trip heading out to examine a dildo factory. I interviewed men and women as different as Wilma Rudolph and Roman Polanski, Norman Vincent Peale and Mr. T., Stevie Cauthen and Andre the Giant. I got to see at least 500 films. For "The Gimlet Eye" I watched Krishna children, Evel Knievel, Norman Mailer, Reverend Moon, and a breast implant: I gave live coverage on the whole state of Colorado, Muhammed Ali, sense deprivation tanks, one Inaugural Ball and everything Jane Fonda did around New York from anti-Vietnam to anti-cellulite. Of course, I also documented each ultra-chic twist in the Episcopal Church. Until, having read myself and found it right, I became Eastern Orthodox. Converted by prose, you might say.

And, of late, I have begun yet another period in my writing. My second wedding vows, you see, were somewhat irregular. By implication, anyway, they went, "I promise to love, honor, and write you at least one momentous dramatic role." Laurie is sheer thermite on stage: she has Tony and Drama Desk nominations, not to mention her Clarence Derwent Award for Best Broadway Performance. But here we

Laurie Kennedy

were, wed since 1980, and I hadn't yet consummated the relationship with a pencil. My wife was, I thought, ready to sue for divorce on grounds of theatrical abandonment.

So, rather peevishly—what would a novelist know about drama?—I began first drafting *Resistance*. It was drawn from old fiction themes strewn here and there on the gob pile of my mind. You have this Solzhenitsyn-size writer imprisoned for his Christianity and anticommunism. And a KGB colonel who must reeducate him. Two very different priests. Give me credit, I didn't write about ARC syndrome or the Holocaust.

In one sense, I found, playwriting is easier than a digital readout. After all it took me nearly one decade for *Take Five* and just three weeks for *Resistance*. Quicker, but more intense: intense as calf cramps. You can call time-out at a paragraph end in narrative discourse and go have some Raisin Bran. But dialogue between three characters, say, is seamless and organic. You jeopardize the creative mechanism by so much as a hesitation to rephrase and polish. And you can't conveniently evict these interlopers from your head. I entertained my garrulous dramatis personae, bourbon or Placidyl notwithstanding, through half a night.

And, predictably enough, there are genre differences. When writing fiction I fight toward precision in language. Even ambiguity should be exact ambiguity. Yet plays came to our house that seemed careless, dead flat in their diction. Most, of course, were. But playwriting by nature is more potentiality than definitive art. Yes or no dialogue, flaccid and repetitive speech, can give actor or director crucial latitude. There are moments when hand gesture and double take become part of syntax. When the pause will be not a lapse, but an essential opening, when dullness is instrumental. My own discipline—a novelist must act as performer-director-lighting man—often led me to finish what should have been mere preparation and cue. Play creation is always fluid: that, I discovered, was the most alien, exasperating thing about it. I didn't easily trust.

Much of *Resistance* was (and still is) absolute first draft. Why rewrite, I thought, if you don't know what you've written to start with? By then *Resistance* had become my wife's chore. And we learned that playwriting is expensive. Artistic directors don't return your manuscript. They pour coffee on it and scrawl indelible cuneiform marginalia. For every cut I made (the first reading ran over three hours) a clean copy had to be produced. But, to my bewilderment, Linda and David Laundra, who head Writers Theatre and, later, Nikos Psacharopoulos at Williamstown each put on staged readings. No novel of mine has gotten that much exposure. Then again, my wife isn't in publishing.

Mind now, I had always considered collaborative art to be a contradiction in terms. And writing, I soon understood, had been the easy part. In fiction your characters speak as you want them to speak: not the way some *actor* would like them to speak. How can any playwright (let alone any first playwright) defend his text and yet be flexible with a cast that is both brilliant and far more experienced than he. I've had some marvelous performers for *Resistance:* Austin Pendleton, Brian Clark, Dwight Schultz, Jo Somer, Beatrice Straight, my wife, all of whom worked more or less gratis. The page-to-stage transition is like a dreadful teething. Only once did I feel certain of myself. A walk-on actor, playing The Guard took me aside one afternoon. "You know," he said, "this man's attitude is central. He represents the people. I suggest you add a few lines. . ." He thought my play should be called *Resistance; or, The Guard's Dilemma*.

The creative process, I believe, should retain mystery. Or some decent privateness at least. I never explain, for instance, what a symbol or a structural element means in fiction I've written: danged if I'll provide gossipy New Criticism of my own work. Art should stand (or not stand) without autobiographical reference or crib sheet. Nonetheless, when your actors ask for clarification, you must attempt to clarify. I loathed the constant prying interrogation. And, worse, I often had to fake outright. After all it is embarrassing when you say, Well, actually, I wrote those lines because they sounded nice. Try to motivate emotional speech on that frail evidence.

Yet there were sharp glories, and such as I have never felt in authorship before. At dress rehearsal, for the first full time, my wife uncoiled magic. *Resistance* became fire and unanimous show of hands. Her great scene, I know, worked. This was my woman, those were my lines, and there is no more exquisite intimacy in marriage. She had given me a love gift so dynamic and joyous that I was left powder-burned with adoring.

But *Resistance* does represent a watershed in my life. Having devoted half my life to a definition of New American prose, I'm now interested in writing for performance. The cement factory closed in May of 1986. I find now that I have more time and certainly more flexibility than ever I had before. Last autumn I wrote my first episode of "St. Elsewhere." I hope to be a regular contributor this year. Be it noted that I received for that first episode (which took a week's writing) *twice as much money as I received for the entire nine year plus effort on Take Five.* Let that tell you something about publishing. I'm too depressed to go into it.

Since 1963, when I first started writing, I have been the benevolent dictator of an imaginary island called St. Malherbe. It isn't easy: to remain autocratic and petulant Monday through Sunday, for twenty-four years: never overthrown. Each writing day, you see, is one day in the life of my people: syntax and drought, deadline and dengue, semicolon and machine-made archeological finds for our American tourist trade. Understand: after every paragraph draft (I average fifteen) Papa Short has to shelf mark at least one aspect of Malherbian history: weather, elbow-capping terrorism, new wife, damn Mojo and his Perdue chicken cult, whatever. Estimate one half minute on St. Malherbe for fifteen or so at the desk. Events are chosen, are set in random sequence, by an electronic dice throw system more complex than five-handed contract bridge. And I, Papa Short, must then make some hard decisions. Now and then I am compelled to execute a Tall One: this is regrettable. Dilettantes from Amnesty International monitor St. Malherbe. They suspect torture. Yes, I admit it, there is torture: the writing is torture. By comparison any Tall One with no fingernails or a tattooed cornea can consider himself well off.

Wrong, amigo: my mind hasn't been collecting

empties in a dark sandlot. St. Malherbe *is.* I live there and quite sensibly, too. What are novels, after all, but a long archipelago: separate, authoritarian, make-believe? The nature of creativity—fictional creativity in particular—is the nature of play. I have, moreover, caught on to this: an associative brain does not function well directly: as in say, $7 \times 8 = 56$. The splendid metaphor must be driven by dream and shout from a subconscious place. One way or other, any good artist will learn to poach in that rank game preserve. I outline a paragraph and the problem has been set: "Her hair was the color of. . ." Time now to become Papa Short. I face the sand table map of St. Malherbe and spin dice. Will the garbanzo weevil put me in receivership this season? I am involved: often I am even bitter or afraid: I cry out: they'll need an act of extradition for my head. But after, when I return to that paragraph, the synapses will have done their unconscious matrix algebra. And her hair was the color of. . .grand pianos.

Yet, to be honest, these are matters perceived in an after-time. I first took sail for St. Malherbe because, as you must know by now, I loathe the act of writing. Ah, if writing were an animal and knew pain: I would gut it: I would flense the live fat off. Since I began writing I haven't had a natural night of sleep. My stomach has eaten its own ulcered blood: a self-protein diet. St. Malherbe was, back then, just my reward contraption: one paragraph would endow me with sovereign aggressive power: play, release. By

Sons, Roderick and Christopher

"Still playing softball": the author and his wife

now, though, I am the victim of my own colonialism. I can't even indulge in a writer's block. Too many people depend on Papa Short. It would be, well, uncivic.

Nonetheless, I stopped writing for a month after I had finished *Take Five*. I dreamed of pencils that bent: of last draft writing that would vanish—zip up, gone—from a Magic Slate. Oh, predictable enough: but there were more disquieting revelations. I realized this: that I petted our cats, gave out neighborly elevator talk, hit handballs with my children—to avoid, for a moment, St. Malherbe and the desk. These small affectionate acts had once been stolen: been exciting for that. But now there was no reason to pet or talk or play with the children. I became sullen, nervous: I lost spontaneity. Writing, life built with most savage intent around ten or fifteen dreadful work hours per day, writing had made an invert of my native passion. I was loving people, dammit, in order not to write. Pathological thieves released from Attica must understand similarly: that they will never

again fit within the social textile. As I, as recidivist writer, never will. This doesn't please me: this sure reckoning that I have been disabled emotionally by a trade for which I cherish the most elegant distaste.

BIBLIOGRAPHY

Fiction:

Bishop's Progress. Boston: Houghton, 1968.

Horn. Boston: Houghton, 1969; London: Barrie & Jenkins, 1969.

War is Heaven! Garden City, N.Y.: Doubleday, 1970; London: Barrie & Jenkins, 1970.

The Death and Life of Harry Goth. New York: Knopf, 1971; London: Barrie & Jenkins, 1972.

The Proselytizer. New York: Knopf, 1972.

The Bridge. Garden City, N.Y.: Doubleday, 1973.

Take Five. Garden City, N.Y.: Doubleday, 1982.

Harry Mathews

1930-

Harry Mathews, Paris, 1986

Appearances

Here is an outline of my life:

I was born in New York on the Upper East Side at 2:40 A.M. on February 14, 1930. I was educated in private schools, first in the city, then at Groton School in eastern Massachusetts. I entered Princeton College in the fall of 1947. At the end of my third term I enlisted in the Navy for a year, in the course of which I married French-born, New York-raised Niki de Saint Phalle. I completed my college studies at Harvard, graduating with a B.A. in music in June 1952. A daughter, Laura, was born during our stay in Cambridge. I and my family moved to France in July 1952, and lived there—in Paris, Menton, and Nice—for over two years. (I studied piano and conducting for a few months before deciding to make a career of writing.) In the fall of 1954 we moved to Deyá,

Mallorca, for two years; a son, Philip, was born in 1955. We returned to France in the summer of 1956, living first in Paris, then in Lans-en-Vercors in the French pre-Alps. Separated from my wife at the end of 1960, I came back to Paris with my children soon afterwards. My daughter left school and home in 1969, after which I settled in Lans with my son, who in turn ran away to America in 1972. I again lived in Paris until mid-1974, then in Venice for two years. While there, I met the French writer Marie Chaix, and I came back to France to live with her and her two daughters, from 1976 to 1986 in Lans, for the past year in Paris. During this period I began spending almost half of each year in America, where in 1978 I began teaching, first at Bennington College, later at Columbia. Since 1962 I have published four novels and six collections of poetry.

223

Family

I was born in Manhattan, on Saint Valentine's Day, 1930, of parents who had married on May 29 the year before. The interval of 261 days—just over thirty-seven weeks or eight and a half months—later made me suspect that my conception had precipitated my parents' marriage. (I believe that I once asked my mother if this were so and that she calmly replied that it wasn't and explained why. I have meticulously erased from my memory the details of this conversation, if it ever took place.) It has always struck me as odd that my parents, both of whom were respectful of customs and devoted to *their* parents, chose to be married after the briefest of engagements in a summary, private ceremony. Nor did they ever consider having another child; indeed my mother, while extraordinarily fond of me, often expressed a dislike of children in general and wondered why anyone would voluntarily choose to have them. (Family planning was her favorite charity.) Events following my own marriage confirmed my suspicion that I came into the world by no means unloved, but probably unwished for.

Both my parents had been born into, and had remained dues-paying members of, the world of Upper-East Side WASP respectability. Although neither was entirely happy in this world—my father had to curb a "difficult" character that might have felt easier in less polite surroundings; my mother longed for the styles and pleasures of Mediterranean Europe—neither questioned their adherence to it. In both their cases the source of this social loyalty is, I believe, to be found in filial devotion. My father adored and passionately admired his mother; my mother felt no less love for her father.

Edward Mathews's family on his father's side came from Philadelphia and Valley Forge, although he himself was born and raised in New York. My paternal grandfather, who died when my father was nine, was rarely spoken of by his children. His name evoked ghosts of irresponsibility. He had squandered his money and his privileges with the result that, when he died, his family was left in poverty—the genteel poverty of boarding houses, admittedly, but a painful come-down all the same for people used to an easier life. My grandmother evidently reacted to these straitened circumstances wisely and courageously, making sure that my father and his sister got the best possible upbringing as well as the best education her disciplined thrift could provide.

Currie Duke, my father's mother, came from a respected Louisville family. She was the daughter of Basil Duke, second in command of Morgan's Raiders,

Parents, Edward and Mary Mathews, about 1930

descended from the Marshalls and Jeffersons of Virginia. She was an exceptionally gifted violinist who studied with Joachim and made her debut at seventeen with the New York Philharmonic. After her husband's death, her musical skills enabled her to provide for herself and her family; but arthritis brought her musical career to a premature end. I first knew her as a kind, firm lady in her sixties, fearfully curbed in her activities by double cataracts, at that time a crippling affliction.

I was always astonished by my father's reverence and affection for this "poor old lady," as I childishly thought of her. For him she embodied the perfect mixture of adamantine character and gentleness. I think he would have endured any kind of pain to avoid seeing her in pain, or even offended. He paid a price for this, I'm afraid. He had once disappointed her by not going to college; he did his utmost never to disappoint her again. He had refused college because he was so eager to become an architect that he did not want to wait three or four years before

Grandfather Henry Burchell holding infant Harry, about 1933

starting work, and so he went straight into Yale Architectural School, paying his way by teaching drawing (he was an immensely gifted draftsman) at the art school of the university. The price I think my father paid for his filial respect was that of accepting architecture as a profession rather than pursuing it as an art. He had a successful career (when he retired, he was a partner in Skidmore, Owings, and Merrill); he did excellent work for public and private clients; but he never relinquished the conventional ambitions of his profession to explore idiosyncratic, pioneer realms in the manner of Wright or Le Corbusier. To do that, he would have had to turn his back on the world of his upbringing, that is, on his mother's world.

I must admit to a bias in this matter. At the age of twenty I broke with my parents, deeply offending them, causing myself considerable suffering, spending years in an uneasy, ambiguous, indeed dishonest relationship with them. I am no longer so sure that I had to do this in order to write my novels and poems;

but for years I was convinced that I would never have been able to write at all if I had not made this violent break. It is clearly tempting for me to tell myself that, no matter how modest my achievements, I did my father one better by pursuing the course I did.

My mother was the only child of Henry Burchell, son of an Anglo-Irish immigrant who made a fortune in cold-water flats, and Candida Paleari, a native of Monza in Lombardy.

My grandmother's background has remained a mystery to me. I presume that my mother once knew more about it than she was able to tell me. Judging from photographs of them together, I feel certain that my mother and grandmother were devoted to one another during my mother's early years. By the time I was born, that devotion had withered. As I grew up, my grandmother became increasingly deaf, solitary, cantankerous; my mother's daughterly love was increasingly directed to her father.

My grandfather and my mother had adored one another from the start. In his eyes she could do no wrong; and if she recognized his shortcomings, she was always more than ready to acknowledge his seemingly fathomless store of good nature and good will.

His chief shortcoming was his peculiar weakness. Intelligent, urbane, an amateur of all the arts, endowed with a fine gift for languages (he was a master of classical Greek and Latin, and he could speak and write Italian, French, and German), competent in business matters, he suffered domestically and professionally from chronic timidity. He was frightened of his wife, who could scold him for spending fifty dollars on a new overcoat. He did not dare disturb strangers on whom his comfort might depend (I can still see him docilely waiting in line when his admission was already paid for); worst of all, at a crucial moment in his life he declined to defy his family when, after several gloriously happy years teaching Greek and Latin at Columbia, he was asked to give up his career. As the only brother not actively engaged in business, he was the obvious choice to "look after the family fortunes"—the reinvested wealth of the cold-water flats. My grandfather dutifully brought his life as scholar and teacher to an end.

For well-to-do men of my grandfather's generation, not working was no disgrace; but my mother could hardly accept such a life as exemplary, especially after her marriage, when she had committed herself wholeheartedly to my father's professional career (not an easy one in the Depression years). She certainly deplored my grandfather's weakness towards her mother, who she felt cruelly deprived him of many pleasures in his later years, and she regretted his timidity towards the world at large, even if she could chuckle over its consequences. But I do not believe she would have wanted him different from what he was. She had an unqualified respect for the values he incarnated. He was quintessentially American in his honesty, forthrightness, and generosity; at the same time his knowledge and love of European culture—manners and attitudes as well as the arts, but most importantly the arts, of which the greatest was literature—distinguished him from the majority of his compatriots. He was the perfect gentleman; one furthermore whose loving attention had followed her from the day of her birth, something that may have left her a little spoiled but that understandably secured her lifelong devotion and loyalty.

Now my grandfather knew Europe well, and he had helped my mother know and love it in turn. He was, however, definitely settled in New York and entertained no serious thoughts of ever leaving the city. My mother, in spite of the strong attractions Europe had for her, one of them being perhaps the most intense love story of her life, followed her father's example and settled in the city where they both had been born. She did not attribute the responsibility of her choice to him; and I do not mean to suggest that without him she would necessarily or even probably have chosen otherwise. But her father's choice encouraged her own. It allowed her to live happily enough in America and at the same time to keep intensely alive the idea of Europe as a haven of pleasure, romance, and elegance—a view she staunchly maintained and sometimes vehemently expressed throughout her life.

If I have spoken at length about my grandfather, it is because of the influence he exercised not only on my mother but on me. During my first eighteen years he was a constant and considerable presence in my life, one I took great delight in. He was just over sixty when I was born, young for his years. From the first he unstintingly expended on me that attentive sweetness for which so many loved him. In my early childhood he often drove me to Central Park or to distant playgrounds he thought I might enjoy, patiently waiting for me to accumulate my afternoon's ration of bloodied elbows and knees. As soon as I could follow stories, he introduced me to the best of them he knew, reading aloud to me in the early evening from Grimm and Perrault and, a little later, book-length versions for children of the *Iliad* and the *Odyssey.* My interest in classical mythology having thus been awakened, he brought me other books drawn from it (and perhaps from classical history as well) for me to read myself. By the time I had reached fourth

grade, ancient Greece and Rome formed a natural part of my imaginary world: so that it would have been inconceivable for me not to begin the study of Latin. My grandfather of course encouraged me in this, countering the dismays of the endless grammar lessons of the first years with promises of future delights—Catullus, Ovid, Horace. Later, when I growled with impatience at Cicero's orations, he would tell me, Wait till you read the letters; or when I struggled with the first book of the *Aeneid,* Wait till the fourth. And his encouragements extended far beyond the study of Latin, to reading in general (he lent me many volumes of Mark Twain after I discovered *Tom Sawyer*) and to listening to classical music. I believe it was my grandfather who gave me, at the age of nine or ten, the two 78-rpm records of leitmotifs in *The Ring of the Nibelungen* that opened up to me the world of Wagnerian opera, my first great esthetic passion.

Or perhaps my mother gave me the records. Where matters of high culture were concerned, she and my grandfather acted as members of a team, with a clear, consistent purpose: I was to be exposed as often and as thoroughly as possible to the best composers, the best painters, the best writers of the West, in the last category especially to Shakespeare. Their purpose was not fueled by class or cultural snobbery but by the intense, at times almost ecstatic pleasure they themselves found in high art (and in much low art, too). Because they were motivated by this spontaneous experience of pleasure, which was essentially the pleasure of knowledge in its sensuous forms, their efforts to share their experience with me attained their goal (even if, in the case of painting, that goal was attained only many years later, when I made my first trip alone to Europe: and even then their influence was manifest, since over the years they had nourished in me a longing to visit Europe, and especially Italy, where they had so often and so happily traveled together).

Of course the sensuous pleasure my mother took in art made art attractive to me for less obvious or at least less avowable reasons. She was a passionate, sensual woman, devoted to her only son. His upbringing, not to mention *her* upbringing (that is, her feelings about her father), prohibited expressing her sensuality and her passion to me overtly. Art and literature provided a vehicle for their less direct expression, and I quickly showed myself willing to play her game, one that no doubt I still am playing.

My mother claimed to dislike children, which meant the children of others, particularly girls. I was her own, and male. A place was cut out for me as the third of an exceptional series that had begun with my grandfather and continued with my father, a series of men committed to her happiness. Her designation of me for this role was not less evident for being unconscious; by which I mean that she lavished on me as a child and as an adolescent the same consideration, support, and patience (and her capacity for impatience was as large as her generosity) that she showed her father and husband. She was stern—reliably stern—in teaching me the techniques of politeness and cleanliness, as well as the necessary ethical hypocrisies of the class to which she belonged (ultimately no more hypocritical or less necessary than those of any class); she properly backed my father in his usually futile efforts to direct my energies to the world around me; but she never failed to forgive my shortcomings, to sympathize with my sufferings, or to share my sometimes wildly confused enthusiasms.

Here are some examples, trivial but relevant. When I had soiled my bed in my sleep around the age of five (an age well beyond any approvable limit), she dogmatically excused the accident as due to my having eaten unpeeled baked potatoes. She treated the horrendous juvenile acne with which I was afflicted between the ages of thirteen and eighteen with an awareness and reassurance that were more gratifying than any saintly commiseration. She read every author and listened to every composer that I discovered and by making my delight in my discoveries her own gave me a recognition that in my ornery solitariness I was hard put to find elsewhere. Her loyalty to me gave me the possibility of accomplishing one of the most deceptive, destructive schemes of my life: that of becoming an element of discord between her and my father, of winning her as an ally in my utterly unnecessary combat with him.

As I have said, my father was a man of great talent, both as an architect and as a graphic artist. He was also a prodigious reader. He may have preferred Melville, Prescott, and Kipling to my mother's favorite James, Wharton, and Proust, but his sensitivity in literary matters was hardly inferior to hers. His sensitivity, indeed, was his weakness, and most of all in his own eyes. He looked for success in the approval of the well-to-do and preferably well-born businessmen and professional men among whom he had to make his career. There, his abilities as a fisherman and shot, combined with his charm and even his irrascibility, could only serve him well. How could sensitivity, esthetic scrupulousness, and doubt seem anything but unnecessary and useless to him, especially when he saw them magnified in his only son? He wanted me to be happy in the world—to be a good fisherman, to be manually and practically com-

petent, to be sociable, to be successful. I caught the line of my rod in the nearest tree; I could not drive a nail home before I was eighteen; the notion of worldly success made me feel like a weasel on a rock pursued by a lunchless hawk. He loved me no less than my mother, but he wanted, or at least felt obliged, to make me into someone I had no chance of being. He sent me to summer camps when I longed to stay home. He took me fishing when I wanted to read, gave me kits for making model boats that paralyzed me with bored incompetence (he finally made the boats himself), oversympathized with my love of baseball which on the playing field could not make up for my dismaying clumsiness. I didn't have the sense to discern his love in all this. I preferred to make him my enemy.

I engineered our opposition one evening when I was nine, perhaps a little older. I stole a set of disposable cigarette holders from my mother's bureau drawers and hid them in my room. The place I chose to hide them was so conspicuous that I could count on their being found. My mother missed them and indeed found them. When she asked me about them, I responded with patent lies. Not unreasonably offended, she told my father what had happened. The facts being as plain as my future pimples, he eventually forced me to admit them, whereupon he scolded me with exceptional sternness, at exceptional length, concluding with a homily on the virtues of honesty that hurt and humiliated me. For the first time in our relationship a moral absolute had been invoked, to my entire disadvantage. Since the insignificance of my fault clearly did not deserve such an anathema, I "learned" that my father totally disapproved of me and probably hated me. I told myself that I must never trust him again.

A few months later, a replay of the event—the conspicuous theft of five dollars, this time perpetrated while my father was away—enabled me again to provoke my mother and this time to secure through pitiful imploration the assurance of her silence in the matter. Through her silence she became my accomplice. Thereafter she remained my thoroughly bribed court of appeal in family disputes. My father was relegated to the inimical "outside world." It took me more than thirty years to realize that the enmity of that world was almost entirely my own creation, and that not only did my father love me but that I myself bore him so grateful and gratifying a love that when, at last, I allowed it to emerge into the light of consciousness, all my efforts to deny and pervert it had proved incapable of lessening its power.

In the meantime we waged our war. It had some happy truces: trips to the Florida Keys and the

Bahamas on school vacations (after his return from the Pacific and the war), where I at last learned the joys of fishing; much later, working on the Long Island property he created, where he revealed unsuspected genius as gardener and landscape designer; and, later still, numerous summer evenings spent walking and talking together. These moments were few and brief. Our estrangement had been reinforced when I was nineteen years old by a more radical alienation that I had instigated: my marriage, which brought to an end my privileged relationship with my mother. From that time on, *both* my parents were excluded from what was central to my life. So at least I thought; so at least I wished.

In June 1949, a few months into my mid-college enlistment in the Navy, I eloped with Niki de Saint Phalle, the daughter of a French banker and businessman who had emigrated to the United States when she was two. I shall go into the whys of this event later on; whatever our reasons, they bore no weight with my parents, any more than did the ulterior series of justifications Niki and I spent much time inventing. Niki's parents, who had four other children, were offended but not bitterly so. My mother, however, faced with the abrupt removal of the son on whom she had lavished so much time and passion, behaved as though *her* daughter had been kidnapped and raped. My parents tried energetically to undo what had been done—a waste of their time, since both Niki and I were of age. (My father's distinguished record

Laura, Philip, and Harry Mathews, 1962

as a Naval Reserve officer gave him enough influence to keep me stuck in the Norfolk Receiving Station through one steamy Virginian summer.) Eventually they resigned themselves to the inevitable, and Niki and I were publicly (re)married after my discharge from the Navy the following winter.

My relations with my parents, however, were to get worse. I had decided to finish college because I did not have the courage to disappoint my father on this score, and also probably because I was not sure what else to do. While I was at Harvard, the possibility arose of Niki's having a child. My mother, convinced that our marriage would fall apart, and the sooner the better, had a durable fit at this prospect. The violence of her opposition to Niki's pregnancy ensured its happening, and it also incited me (whether rightly or merely righteously some dispassionate witness alone can say) into breaking with my mother completely—that is, into refusing to see her or speak to her for a period of several months.

On April 23, 1951, our daughter, Laura, was born. From then on there was no question in my mind what the word "family" signified to me: it meant the one I had helped make, not the one into which I had been born. The latter now became part of the past, part of a difficult, hostile world, part of

Niki de Saint Phalle, daughter Laura, and Mathews, in Mallorca, about 1954

everything that I was eager to leave behind. Niki, Laura, and I embarked for Europe in the early summer of 1952, a month after my graduation. It could hardly be said that we were leaving America. Neither of us knew what America, or even New York, really was.

My parents proved patient. They were conscientious in trying to keep up their role as helpful family guardians. I'm afraid I was incapable of giving them any credit for that, interpreting their most helpful actions (such as providing Niki with the best available medical care in New York, when her thyroid trouble was at its dangerous worst) as attempts to meddle in our lives. The only reconciliatory gestures I approved of were those I could claim as my own. In 1959, for instance, when my beloved grandfather died, I insisted, over my mother's objections, on flying to New York to be with her, and, once there, I efficiently took charge of the disagreeable details of cremation and burial.

It was almost ten years later that, in order to restore the long-shattered relationship with my mother, I concocted a stratagem of unwitting brilliance, one that still delights me, all the more so for my obliviousness of what I was doing. I had bought two tickets for the *Ring* cycle at Bayreuth. Since I knew that my mother had a busy schedule that summer, I told myself that it would do no harm, and certainly entail no risk of her accepting, if I offered her my second ticket for the four performances. When a telegram arrived shortly afterwards announcing her arrival in Frankfurt on the eve of *Das Rheingold*, I was, nevertheless, anything but amazed. I would have been amazed, I realized, if she had declined to join me; I saw that I had never intended her not to be at my side when I visited the shrine of my "first passion."

And so, without a word of reference to our violent disagreements or our years of estrangement, we effected a reconciliation that was to prove lasting. We spent a happy week together, not only attending the operas that were its pretext but jubilantly fleeing the pompous horror of the Bayreuth opera crowd to investigate the various attractions of Lower Bavaria, of which Bamberg and the church of Dreizehnheiligen would alone have made the trip worthwhile—on this we agreed, and the agreement perhaps gave her the satisfaction of finding me properly aligned with the two other men in her life, with her two other favorite traveling companions.

Several years later, after participating in the course of a seminar I was taking in a demanding exercise called the "Truth Process," I discovered, tearfully and happily, that for much of my life I had been painstakingly transforming my parents into monsters, and that I had furthermore done this for no better reason than my own convenience. The ploy of the stolen cigarette holders, the eagerness with which I'd seized the chance to belabor my mother with her wrongs during Niki's first pregnancy, and all the self-justifications consequent to those events were revealed to me as ruses to blame others for my displeasure at being in the world. This revelation brought me great relief. It also brought an annoying problem: how could I possibly tell my mother and father what I had just learned? The problem turned out to be imaginary. Paying them a visit the next day, I found, on entering the room where they were waiting for me, two people I had never seen before: in place of the redoubtable pair I was familiar with, an elderly man and woman overjoyed to see me, full as they were of a love that I suppose had never once failed them since my birth. I had nothing to tell them. I had nothing to do except look and listen.

I have written at length about my parents because I know that next to them most of the people who have figured in my life can only assume the roles of substitutes, replicas, replacements of this original man and woman. Most of the time, other people can only set an "objective" and partial reality against the imagined and absolute reality with which, out of the limbo of my first years, I invested the actual couple who engendered me. I have learned more from my own children (and from the children of my present companion) than I did from my mother and father; and I can say as much of the men and women to whom I have been closest. But these few, dearest others can never replace, only enlarge, the primordial family in which I discovered life in our world.

From the age of nineteen I did my best to deny the importance of this family, to pretend that whatever mattered in my life was of my own choosing and making. I tried to evince the notion of family from my dealings with the world and from my thinking about my life. I was painfully taught how deluded I was. Between the ages of thirty and forty-three, I "endured" the departure of my wife, my daughter, and my son (Philip, born in 1955). During my years of living with them, in addition to many palpable joys and upsets, I had had an advantage, a continuing font of well-being, of which I had remained almost entirely unaware: I had lived among others who were plainly "inside" my life, plainly demarcated from the rest of the world. In them I had found, if not replacements for my parents, beings who could satisfactorily conceal from me the void I had created in my life by rejecting my parents. After Niki, Laura, and at last Philip had left, I found myself an orphan. Even though I had claimed to despise it, the idea of family turned out to have been my mainstay, or perhaps my crutch—in any event, the unadmitted assumption about my life that had allowed me to advance with a sense of security across the years, not to mention the Atlantic Ocean; so that, finding myself "alone," I sank into a despondency of utter helplessness. Needless to say, this experience of "abandonment" made my reconciliation with my mother and father at a later time all the happier. I trust as well that it allowed me to attend them in their last years aware of the curiously parental role a child assumes in its parents' eyes.

Teachers and Masters

My best teachers were also friends: teachers who became friends, friends from whom I was willing to learn. Ten years ago I first started teaching, and I found that being a teacher disposed me to accepting a role not superior but equal to the students I had to teach. Teaching implies a devotion to possibility for the tandem of teacher and taught in one and the same event. I hope that my own teachers shared the joy they gave me.

In grade school I had Captain Fry, whom I came to address as Humphrey after several years of savoring his distinguished South-English discourse. Tall and lean, a little sallow from having been gassed in the First World War, he presented himself to us as a figure of lanky, intense, somewhat otherworldly (or at least Old Worldly) elegance. He taught Latin and English, in the first subject relaying my grandfather's enthusiasm by nudging me through the hard grammatical years with hints and occasional samples of satisfactions to come; in the second, opening wide the doors of poetry through his eloquent advocacy of the romantics and post-romantics. I think he had almost no use for any poetry after Shakespeare and before Wordsworth, and this did me no harm, since my mother had exposed me to Milton with her incantatory recitations of "Lycidas," and her love of Marvell prepared my way for discovering the metaphysical poets.

Humphrey Fry not only confirmed my hedonistic addiction to Keats and Shelley, he converted me, purely through a crafty exposition of his own rather superannuated taste, to the fascinations of Robert Browning. Indeed for several years I was a Browningite; neither a good thing nor a bad in itself, but in shifting my interest in poetry from its sensuous to its riddling, difficult, "intellectual" side, he prepared me for my later fascination with T.S. Eliot, through whom I would discover the domain of modernist writing. Humphrey Fry disliked Eliot and would surely have denied any connection between him and the affirmative Victorian whose work he revered.

One connection I later made had to do with Humphrey himself. He was imbued not only with Shakespeare but with the King James translation of the Bible. (I remember once, when a few of his students were summering with him in New England, his returning after a day's absence to find that we had left all the household chores undone, upon which he declaimed as we scurried for our hoes and brooms, "O generation of vipers, who hath warned thee to flee from the wrath to come?" I have done my chores conscientiously ever since.) The abundance of Biblical reference in Humphrey's speech made "Ash Wednesday," for instance, reassuringly familiar when I later came to it.

It was in one of Humphrey's English courses that I wrote my first poem, which began:

> It was a sad autumnal morn,
>   The earth was but a mass of clay;
> Of foliage the trees were shorn,
>   Leaving their branches dull and gray.

I remember covertly staring at him over my assignment book as he read my verses. When he finished, he gazed into the distance with a look that economically expressed two views: "What must happen will happen" and "My God, what have I done?" Masters at expensive schools are supposed to teach their wards the pleasures of reading poetry, but not perhaps the exhilaration of writing it.

After Pearl Harbor, my family moved to Washington, where my father, commissioned in the Naval Reserve, served in the intelligence department. As a result I was sent to boarding school a year sooner than expected; and so I found myself at Groton School in eastern Massachusetts, a place where I had no desire to go or, during the five years I spent there, to stay. After I had graduated, John Pick, a teacher who had left Groton to teach at Marquette University, wrote me this comment about the school: " . . . The mass conformity there is horrible and stupefying: possibly this is because everyone there lives so communally: and no one can be so tyrannical as the young: the refined and yet athletic bourgeois spirit is a terrifying combination." Theodor Mommsen, another mentor, who went on to teach at Princeton and Cornell, used to say that he had never seen a place where Christian charity was so much preached and so little practised.

If my life at Groton was often unhappy, it was by

no means wholly so. In the first place, my class was a rather un-Grotonian one, full of brilliant, irreverent individualists. In the second place, the war had removed many members of the faculty to perform their patriotic duty, and the shortage of qualified teachers often led the school to hire in their place men very distant in background and temperament from the ideals of WASP Episcopalianism the school embodied. Among these replacements were Ernst Loewenberg, a Jew from Hamburg; Mommsen, another German, whose specialty was Petrarch and the Italian Renaissance; and Pick, a Roman Catholic, the author of the first book-length study of Gerard Manley Hopkins. These men brought to the cloistered and narrow-minded place a most welcome atmosphere of European culture, with its respect for art and intellectual distinction. To my regret I was never close to the extraordinary Ernst Loewenberg; but Pick and Mommsen both befriended me, and by the time they left, two or three years after I had come to the school, they had (with the considerable support, I should in fairness add, of such school regulars as Malcolm Strachan and Ned Gammons) radically expanded the frontiers of my mental life, and indeed kindled the curiosities that still sustain me during my working hours.

To John Pick I owe my discovery of modern poetry—not only Hopkins but Eliot, whose haunting musical lines bewitched and bewildered my melancholy adolescent reveries. (It was my passion for Eliot that later led me to other contemporary poets and also to Joyce and an extensive reading of Henry James.) John Pick, however, became far more to me than a literary counselor. His almost impudent worldly urbanity put Groton's provincial gravity very stylishly in its place—a respectable place, but clearly not the only one where the good life could be led. He also proved to be a man of truly Christian kindness: I say this not in praise of Christianity, only as an indication of how obstreperous, demanding, and impatient I was. He dealt with my shortcomings firmly and attentively; the rest of the time he was all encouragement and useful entertainment—by which I mean a regaling fountain of information and even gossip, which was never just that, rather gossip disguising a parable from which I could not fail to learn because I could not fail to be amused. John Pick was witty and jovial and ruthlessly serious in his concern for me; and if at the time I didn't have the sense to recognize the seriousness through the delightful sparkle of its embellishments, I must have known it was there, because I never let go of him. After he left Groton, we at once began corresponding. I visited him in Milwaukee when I was at boot

camp in Great Lakes; he visited us (with his late-wed, Maltese-Florentine-Catholic aristocratic wonder of a wife) in Mallorca in the mid-fifties. During the latter visit I showed him my scanty but hard-worked-over work, and it was John, by sending my poems to William Alfred, who was responsible for my first publication—a poem called "The Pines at Son Beltran" that appeared in *Hudson Review* in 1956.

During my second year at Groton, while I was submitting to John Pick's rewarding influence, I contracted an even more remarkable debt to Ted Mommsen. Because I was his student, Ted was able to intervene in my life more directly than John. He was able to observe not only my general attitude towards school but how I actually worked. Because he too treated me with ruthless seriousness, he refused to accept me as he found me: someone who never consented or dared to do his best but was satisfied with getting slightly above-average, essentially mediocre grades. At the end of two months, Ted told me that he would no longer put up with my "laziness." Henceforth he would take ten points off any grade under 85, which was the lowest honors grade; furthermore, he intended to inform the faculty that I was for all intents and purposes a slacker and that he recommended pressuring me mercilessly until I did much better. I was outraged by this treatment; but outrage was of no use. (I should point out that I felt honestly victimized: I was truly unaware of being capable of more than I was doing.) My other teachers delightedly followed Ted's prescriptions, and escape quickly became impossible. I had no choice but to work harder. By the end of the year I was an honors student, one of the best in my class.

Ted did more than badger me into these results. As soon as he saw that I had begun working seriously, he supplied me with the tools I most needed. He taught me how to read schoolbook if not scholarly texts; he taught me how to write papers and (blessed man) exams. What he showed me was simple, obvious, necessary: how to organize the subject at hand. In reading, this meant abstracting what one read and then realigning the skeleton of the text so that it was readily available (for writing exams, for instance). In writing, organizing meant marshalling all one's knowledge of a subject and then giving it the same analytic and available form. I thus learned that in writing conceptual structure can lend incomplete, even inadequate material a convincing weight. After that, I never needed to pretend that I knew more than I did: whatever I did know usually proved more than sufficient for my needs. This has sometimes made of me an infuriating and slightly stupid conversationalist.

Outside of the classroom, Ted Mommsen talked to me about music, art, architecture, the literatures of Italy, Austria, Germany, and France, his life as a scholar. Ted to me exemplified the European humanist intellectual: cultivated, undogmatic, universally curious, gifted with a power of synthesis as great as his meticulousness in matters of detail. He left Groton a year or two before my graduation to teach at Princeton, where his presence was one of the main reasons I attended that college. Although we remained good friends, in time I lost touch with him, something I bitterly regret in view of his untimely death a few years later. Three decades have passed since then, and I still miss him, wishing he could read my stories and poems, wishing I could be sitting with him on some Renaissance piazza, learning where I was and who I was, wishing I knew someone able to reveal to me Petrarch, Stefan Georg, *The Abduction from the Seraglio*, and the painting of Sassetta.

After school, those I learned from were friends rather than teachers, although I had the privilege of studying under some prodigious intelligences: at Princeton, Blackmur, Rowley, and Gordon Craig; Cam, Piston, and Gombosi at Harvard. Emerging from the sheltered regime of Groton, however, did more than free me from certain Puritanical fetters: it cost me the intellectual passion that at school had provided me not only with a defense but with a way of distinguishing myself. The relief of escaping from a small, staring world allowed my curiosity to turn towards more ordinary social satisfactions. And in college my somewhat fierce schoolboy stances in cultural matters looked feeble: dozens at Princeton knew T.S. Eliot as well as I did and, furthermore, considered him old hat. I did have the luck (I cannot call it wisdom or even cleverness) to choose music as my major, so that throughout my college years I had to keep working hard to stay abreast of my courses in that most practical of the arts. Both at Princeton and at Harvard I learned harmony and counterpoint from young composers and scholars such as Elliott Forbes, Allan Sapp, and Robert Middleton, who transformed theory into a discipline of esthetic discovery.

My choice of music was primarily founded on this crazy reasoning: since my overwhelming passion was for literature—for reading and writing it—I must take care to preserve that passion from the contamination of the academic mind. So I took no courses in English literature. Luckily my precautions proved insufficient, because I did continue my grandpaternally-blessed study of Greek, and so found myself (with only two other students) spending a semester reading Greek tragedy with Eugene O'Neill, Jr., a powerfully imaginative explicator of texts so in

advance of his time that I discovered no one comparable to him before the French post-structuralist critics of the following generation. If I remember correctly, his first class was entirely spent deducing the totality of *Oedipus Rex* from its first two lines, and doing this in so convincing a manner that the scope of reading was definitively transformed.

I did not become friends with O'Neill. I don't think I would have dared pursue that grand, capacious man, whose booming bass voice, more Russian than Irish, invested the antique lines he read with a solemnity both spellbinding and intelligent. Elsewhere the teachers who mattered most to me were those I saw mainly outside of the classroom. Randall Thompson (he would later oversee my transfer to Harvard, where he himself had moved, "to be nearer," as Paul Henry Lang said, "the souls of his ancestors") not only helped me through my first courses in music but invited me from time to time to his house, where I became friends with his daughter Varney. With the other ladies present, she did much to wean me from my adolescent gaucheness. Even more helpful in ridding me of my old apprehensiveness was the poet William Meredith, with whom I studied writing for a year. He was a sympathetic and perceptive teacher, but our views of poetry were too far apart for me to learn what I might have from him: much a post-Audenite, he pursued a poetic "magic" compounded of charm and reasonable discourse, while I was still attached to the Eliotic mysteries of initiation and propitiation. Socially, however, Bill had everything to teach me, and if I did not learn everything, I developed an ability to survive cocktail parties lasting well past midnight, drinking martinis of ever increasing dryness with practically nothing to eat, in the company of men and women somewhat or more than somewhat my elders, and so far surpassing in wit anyone I had theretofore known that for once in my life I was satisfied to observe, pleased if I managed not to make a fool of myself before crossing the one or two courtyards that separated me from my spinning bed in Henry Hall. Thanks to Bill, I met my first young writers: Frederick Buechner, James Merrill, W.S. Merwin (to whose off-campus porch I sometimes repaired to listen to him converse with his GI-Bill, un-Princetonian fellow students about writing, art, and politics). Bill's gatherings, and Bill himself, brought me the blessing of reassurance about traits that at Groton (and in the WASPish New York that was the only one I knew) seemed peculiar. There was absolutely nothing wrong with having a passionate interest in Guillaume de Machaut, Henry James, late Beethoven quartets, or the woodcuts of Hokusai. My problem was no longer knowing more than my peers about such things, but so much less.

Friendships

Before the age of six, I found the world an easy, happy place to be. If it was mainly peopled by my parents and maternal grandparents (for whom I was an only grandson as well as an only son), I had no trouble including in it the boys and girls of my age with whom I played. When I reached six, this comfortable period ended. I have told myself that the reason for the change lay in in my reaction to school (that crowd of others) or to the arduous process of becoming literate (when my mother tongue was taken away from me) or to some real or imagined event that I have suppressed. The only thing I am sure of is that at that age I and the world became two.

Until then I had been good-humored and agreeable; I now became, at least in my own eyes, disagreeable, moody, and mistrustful. Although it would be overdramatizing my life to say that between the ages of six and fourteen I had no friends at all (my older cousin Frank Cabot, with whom I have so happily renewed an affectionate relationship in recent years, was one constant if intermittent companion), I think back to that time as a systematically friendless one; and what was systematic about it was my determination to let no one close to me. I entertained an inconsistent attitude: no one should be allowed to see how basically vile I was, and no one could be trusted to appreciate me at my true value. The early and soon obsessive awakening of my sexuality (to use a vague term covering a multitude of urges and acts) strongly reinforced this attitude. By the time I was thirteen I felt that I had been condemned to prurient solitude, from which I prayed to be rescued some unforeseeable day by an incarnate goddess both sublimely romantic and unspeakably crude.

Patricia Ripley was beautiful, and perhaps with others romantic, but certainly not crude; rather, generous, perceptive, and full of mischievous wit. I met her during summer vacation in Maine in 1944. I trusted her because she too read and wrote poetry and liked to sing the poignantly remote music of the late Renaissance. I suppose she liked me because I made her laugh and because she could see in me not unappealing qualities of which I was desperately unaware. We never "dated," but we managed to see each other often, and in the course of that vacation Patricia allowed me to start realizing that friendship could be something other than a trap to catch, possess, and eventually humiliate me. I liked her lively company so much that with her I forgot all my

Young Mathews with Patricia Ripley, Maine, 1944

obsessive precautions. Thanks to her, I took my first steps in the direction of the men and women who would become the new stuff and substance of my life.

My social education was continued during the ensuing months by a classmate at school, a genial, intense, soft-spoken Philadelphian named Bobby Scott, who even more mysteriously than Patricia chose to make me his friend. We had no particular tastes in common; indeed an element of his fascination for me was the competence he showed in domains I had never explored. He had a startling ability to sense what actually was going on in situations and relationships, so that through him I began to understand that there exists an active, practical intelligence distinct from that found in books and no less impressive. Almost alone in our class, he was well informed and acutely concerned about national and international politics, and through his example I discovered (by reading the *Nation* and the *New Republic*, for instance) that wartime patriotism did not supply answers to all public questions. Lastly, Bobby paid the most serious attention imaginable to the theoretical issues that arose in and out of the classroom—ethical, religious, philosophical—again providing me with an incentive to divert my attention from my dream-soaked head to the world around me.

But Bobby's chief effect on me lay elsewhere. By readily accepting me as his friend, not only keeping me company at school but, during vacations, traveling with me or inviting me to stay with his delightfully stylish parents, he encouraged me to wonder whether my character might not be the irremediable mess I had thought: his liking me encouraged me to like myself. Furthermore, the quality of his behavior towards me gave me a first and best lesson in human relationships: from the start he relegated the "question" of our being friends to the category of assumed facts, thereby clearing the time we spent together for the fun of observation and improvisation. I wish I had been a better disciple; but I was too touched at having been singled out by this exceptional boy, and too grateful for his patience, to be able to accept myself as his equal—something I inevitably came to resent, so that in time I felt justified in turning to less demanding (and less entertaining) friends.

Another boy with whom I was close at school and during my college years as well was Paul Bator. He was gifted with passionate charm and one of the most impressive intelligences I have ever encountered. He was also a fine musician; his enthusiastic advocacy of the classical and romantic repertories, as well as that of Italian opera, did much to expand my severe taste, which tended to scorn everything between Palestrina and Stravinsky.

Paul had come to America from Hungary with his family in the late thirties. Through him I had my first inkling of the huge intellectual and cultural resources of that country, so small on maps, so large in its influence on the world. Much later, Paul was to introduce me to two other Hungarians, Ivan and Suzanne Waldbauer, professional musicians of great distinction (Ivan a genius of analysis and interpretation, Suzanne a superb performer). They revealed to me the world of music in its nonacademic, practical guise, in addition to offering a kind of friendship I had not yet met with: pessimistic, frank, witty, open, and warm.

Paul Bator, the Waldbauers, and I shared a friend in Cliff Baum, whom I had known at Princeton through William Meredith. He had then brought into my life such quantities of fresh air that I was almost blown down by them. Through him I had my first glimpse of what at the time might have been described as Greenwich Villagedom: a world where social theorizing, left-wing politics, psychoanalysis, and radical artistic enterprises mixed in a giddyingly glamorous and scary sexual/cultural free-for-all. The glimpse was useful in weaning me from my tiny gentility, but I hardly dared do more than watch.

At Harvard I had excellent companions; but it was not until I moved to Europe after my graduation that I found a friend who intimately affected my life. I had already met Anthony Bonner in 1944 and since then seen him occasionally. I knew him first as the son of family friends, then as a jazz musician, then as a classical composer. In 1951 he had come to Paris to study composition. When I looked him up, in the autumn of 1952, he and his wife Eve were living on Rue Lincoln, off the Champs-Elysées. My wife, Niki, and I saw them more and more frequently. They came to visit us during the months we spent in the south of France, and after our return to Paris we rented a house with them. In the late summer of 1954 the four of us moved for an indeterminate stay to Mallorca, then tourist-free and thrillingly cheap. Tony and Eve are still living there. (Tony, after trying his hand at many trades, has become a world-respected authority on the greatest Mallorcan of all, the medieval philosopher and theologian Ramon Llull.)

Because of distance—Mallorca practically speaking is much farther from Paris than Los Angeles—I have seen little of Tony since the mid-fifties, but for four crucial years he was the friend with whom I made my way. He is perhaps the only friend of whom it can be said that I learned not only from him but with him: experimenting together life in France, life in Spain, methods of musicianship, the works of Ezra Pound (whom we spent a year reading, collating by mail our interpretations of the *Cantos* between Palma de Mallorca and Deyá, ten miles away).

Tony intervened to extraordinary effect on certain occasions in my life: notably in giving Niki, at a critical moment, decisive support in her ambition to become an artist; soon after that in encouraging my own efforts when I started writing again. But essentially I think of Tony as someone with whom I was able to explore possibilities. When we became friends we were in our mid-twenties. I was riddled with doubts as to what I could or should do with my life. Tony's skepticism towards received ideas, towards everything the world and especially our parents' milieu felt entitled to expect of us, was of incalculable help to me. So was his patience, most strikingly his patience with himself. On the road to his present distinction he was willing not only to try out different ways of supporting his family but to devote exhaustive attention to whatever new subject attracted his interest—Villon, the Troubadours, higher mathematics—as though he had a truckful of lifetimes ahead of him. Whatever doubts he himself may have felt were never allowed to spoil these sustained exercises in learning. From his example I myself learned to take my time; and where writing is concerned, never to settle for results that are merely reassuring.

During my two years on Mallorca I made a number of friends: Robert Graves (when we found a house to rent in Deyá, he turned out to be our neighbor), a difficult, demanding, restless man who proved more than kind to us—he and his wife Beryl accompanied the premature birth and early precarious months of our son, Philip, with not only sympathy but considerable practical help; the poet Alastair Reid, who with an abundance of good humor both encouraged my ambitions as a writer and kept them from making me (I had not yet published a line) altogether obnoxious; and finally Walter Auerbach, whom I met in Barcelona and persuaded to move to Deyá, where he spent the rest of his life.

In his late forties when I met him, Walter was a German Jew from Darmstadt who had left Germany in the early thirties and worked at many trades, among them filming newsreels in Palestine and photographing works of art in the United States. He had always worked as little as possible, his priorities being survival and pleasure. When I found him in Barcelona, he was surviving not only pleasurably but almost grandly on a U.S. Army pension of fifty dollars a month. There and in Deyá he never failed to be well housed, well supplied in food and drink, and neatly dressed. He was rather tall and stocky; he had been bald from late adolescence, as a result of a nutritional malady during World War I; he had big eyes that he turned on people in an unscrupulously dramatic stare that produced an immediate reaction, whether of sympathy or mistrust.

After he moved to Mallorca, Niki and I adopted him, and he us. We gave him a family, in which he played a discreetly avuncular role. To us he brought a world of new culture: of Germany in the twenties—Brecht and Marxism, to simplify matters—and also of New York in the late forties and early fifties, distinguished by unheard-of painters such as Robert Rauschenberg and Jane Freilicher and remarkable young poets of whom the most remarked was someone named John Ashbery. Walter and I also used to share a passion for walking, spending many hours in the hills or on the little-motored roads of Mallorca's spectacular northern coast.

In the spring of 1956, Niki, Laura, and I visited Paris to start looking for a place to live when we moved back there. Walter joined us in May or June. In the course of his visit he arranged a meeting that would greatly affect my life. Walter had gotten in touch with John Ashbery, then a Fulbright scholar in Montpellier; and on a gray, warm afternoon, in a café on the Jardin du Luxembourg, I first spoke with an affable, apparently diffident, conventionally suited and cravatted man in his late twenties whose first collection had just been published in the Yale Series of Younger Poets.

I find myself hesitant, although hardly "at a loss," to describe my friendship with Ashbery. The friendship has been uninterrupted since our meeting, and throughout it John has shown himself (as with his numerous other friends) utterly tolerant and encouraging: an attitude that has allowed me to evolve in my relationship to literature and to the world in general in progressions that only become apparent to me after they have occurred. The spur to my development has never come from injunctions on John's part, or even advice. (He is notoriously reluctant to make anything resembling a pronouncement on general issues, at least not in a serious vein.) If his witty discourse serves as a delightful, indirect medium for defining his preferences, it is above all his example as a masterly and, more impressively, as a dedicated artist that he exerts his influence on those around him; although even this statement too grossly ennobles the manner in which that influence works. Soon after we met I asked John what contemporary French poets he recommended I read. He mentioned several familiar names, such as Reverdy and Michaux. A week or two later, when I showed him a new poem I'd written ("The Battle"), he commented, "Oh, I see you've been reading those poets we were talking about." But I hadn't. Somehow the words he had said about them had given me a perception of their approach to poetry, and I had at once been able to incorporate this in my writing. A simple conversation with John had let me emerge from my conservative, provincial, and precious attraction to the kind of lyric poetry then being written in America and discover the possibility of "modernism"—a world where I was allowed and in some sense obliged to invent what I wrote.

John found me a provincial, very much on the defensive, reluctant to trust my own powers and tastes. Over the years he has greatly enlarged my views. In the domain of literature—especially by introducing me to the works of Raymond Roussel and by suggesting an unacademic and thoroughly exhilarating approach to Kafka—he started me on the way at last to writing fiction. (His detailed critique of *The Conversions,* after he read the first draft, provided me with the encouragement I needed then and during subsequent years of frequent incomprehension.) His

With John Ashbery, 1973

then unlikely enthusiasms in film (the silent works of Feuillade and Lang; musical comedies; schlock horror movies), in painting (Ad Reinhardt), and in music (post-romantic composers like the still under-appreciated Busoni, as well as all that is most innovative in more recent music) saved me again and again from the most deadly of esthetic fates: making final choices. And in exercising this liberating influence, John never for a day ceased being his generous and funny (and difficult and anxious) self. His unstinting readiness to be my companion in the early sixties, when the breakup of my marriage had left me depressed and lonely, still warms me with the memory of our evenings, our travels together.

One of our trips together brought us in (I think) November 1961 to Mallorca, where Walter Auerbach had arranged with a local printer to produce the first issue of *Locus Solus*, a magazine we were starting. John and Kenneth Koch had long wanted to create a vehicle for their work and that of friends they admired; for my part, I was discouraged by my initial failure to find a publisher for *The Conversions*. (Kenneth Koch would successfully propose it to Random House soon afterwards.) When I inherited a small legacy from my grandfather, John suggested I use part of it to pay for *Locus Solus*, where we could *all* be published. John and Kenneth asked James Schuyler

to be a fourth editor. Over the next two years we brought out four issues of the review (one a double issue), the first printed in Palma, the others in Geneva.

John also opened up new social horizons to me. Through him I met around 1960 an incandescent galaxy of New Yorkers, thanks to whom my native city became a place where I felt at home: the painters Jane Freilicher, Larry Rivers, Alex Katz, Joe Brainard, and Ellen Adler (then married to David Oppenheim); writers, in addition to Koch and Schuyler, like Kenward Elmslie, Arnold Weinstein, and Bill Berkson; John's colleagues at *Art News*, Tom Hess and Betsy Baker. I have remained friends with most of them to this day. Later, it was through John that I came to know David Kalstone, Tomasz and Julita Mirkowicz, Joseph McElroy, and John Ash, all of whom much affected my life.

In the year following the end of my marriage I became friends with a young Englishwoman named Tina Packer, whom Niki and I had met on our return from Mallorca. In the spring of 1961, in a state of catastrophic disarray, I instinctively turned to her as someone of sufficient strength, compassion, and a wisdom beyond her years (she was almost a decade younger than I) to help me emerge from my despondency. Tina, then an ill-paid novice journalist, responded to my appeal with great tough-mindedness; and in doing so she established what has been one of the strangest as well as the most exuberant relationships I have known. For the next fifteen years Tina and I considered ourselves good friends, yet we scarcely ever saw each other. When we did, it was "only" because one of us was experiencing a gigantic crisis in his or her life. When Tina decided to leave her husband, for example, she drove straight from London all the way across France to Grenoble, where, half an hour from the village where I lived, she announced her urgent and imminent arrival with her infant son. A few years later, after my son, Philip, had run away from home, and two weeks of thinking and drinking had not reconciled me to the fact, I knew that my only hope lay in a visit to Tina. (She condemned me to a macrobiotic diet for a week, then sent me off to New York to raise money for her new theatrical enterprise, thereby replacing a set of impossible worries with another, more productive one.) I am happy to say that Tina and I now meet frequently and in calmer circumstances, since she is settled in Massachusetts, where she is the artistic director of Shakespeare and Company (in Lenox) as well as of the Boston Shakespeare Company. Still, when the bottom falls out of the boat, both of us know where we can and probably must turn.

I have never had many friends in France, where friendliness or at least polite and discreet acquaintance rather than friendship is the rule. John Ashbery introduced me to a number of Parisians, some of them American artists (most notably Joan Mitchell and James Bishop), poets such as Denis Roche and Marcelin Pleynet, and his great companion Pierre Martory. After John returned to New York, I sought out and frequented a number of French writers, André du Bouchet and Maurice Roche in particular. It was indirectly through Maurice that I one day in 1970 received a letter from the thirty-four-year-old novelist Georges Perec.

Georges had written me to express his enthusiasm for *The Conversions*, which he had just read in proof in its French translation. I answered his letter, and we soon arranged a meeting, which took place at the Bar du Pont-Royal, an agreeable place much frequented by writers and publishers. We drank together, and went on to have dinner, and I thus entered into the most exhilarating, hilarious, intense, and satisfying relationship I have ever known with a man, and doubtless will ever know.

I find it increasingly hard to write about Georges, who died five years ago of lung cancer at the age of forty-six. Two years after his death, when a Paris newspaper asked me to contribute an article

Georges Perec and Harry Mathews, 1975

about our friendship, this is what I wrote:

Georges Perec wore a comic goatee that made him look like a silly scientist in the comics. His complexion was rough and peppered with warts. When I first met him he used to speak with one hand in front of his mouth to hide his disreputable teeth. Wiry hair swelled about his head like a disintegrating bird's nest. I often used Alcibiades' words about Socrates to describe him: a grotesque without, the golden image of a god within.

I was wrong. I thought Georges looked funny; he *was* funny. He wore himself as his own mask. The mask revealed his unquestionable beauty, through eyes that were green, large, tender. It took me a while to realize that he was not someone to be liked but loved. After that, I loved him passionately.

Literature can hardly explain such a passion. In our case it supplied a pretext for friendship and, later, the means of doing things on each other's behalf. What mattered to me in having Georges as a translator was not his talent or even (for one of my novels) his undertaking the work without any guarantee of publication, but his willingness to translate works that he had not even read, simply because I had written them. More than of literary sympathy, his collaboration was an assertion of loyalty. Whatever his motives in encouraging my election to the OuLiPo, I know that he was happy that among its brilliant and tolerant members I at last felt at home in the country of my adoption. For his friends, Georges turned every opportunity that presented itself into an act of efficient generosity.

When we met, in 1970, our lives were at an ebb, professionally and privately. Georges was more obviously depressed; I maintained an air of confidence as though my life depended on it. In admitting his suffering, Georges was the wiser; and he admitted his friendship for me, too, while I dared not acknowledge how much I liked him. After all, I mistrusted no one as much as myself. Georges soon knew me better than I knew myself and taught me what friendship could be. With tact: knowing how Queneau's death would affect me, he made

sure I learned of it from him, telling me the news coolly over the phone, even though the event was much harder for him to bear. With intelligence: through the years of intellectual "terrorism" he eloquently explained everything from Althusser to *S/Z*, never taking sides as he lured me out of dogmatic hypotheses.

He was famous for his wit, which was a defense against those he mistrusted and a spontaneous expression of gaiety among those he liked. His wonderful puns (*le phalle et la memelle*) were nourished by a boyish playfulness. There was childish enthusiasm, too, in his taste for American films, which I particularly liked seeing with him since he teased and scolded me mercilessly for my Americanness. I remember the summer before he died seeing *Raiders of the Lost Ark* with him (in the afternoon—it was obviously a movie for hookey players): we enjoyed it like reading a new *Tintin*. Later, at a revival of *A Foreign Affair*, our pleasures were not altogether shared ones. Georges was thrilled by the efficacy of Wilder's situations. I was touched more by the story itself: that of a moralistic American who learns in Europe the unsimple truths of history and passion, especially love. I was glad to see the film at Georges's side.

What can his friendship be called if not love? He attended with fierce intensity to those close to him (of whom I was only one: I said of him what Larry Rivers declared after Frank O'Hara's death, that he was my best friend, and forty others could say the same). Friendship with Georges was passionate love, and if ours because of our natures lacked the seal of physical involvement, I almost regret it, if only to know that nothing between us was missing. We did sometimes manage to "consummate our passion" in (again) a childish way: after dinner together, we would go home, lie on the living-room floor with a drink or a joint, and listen to somewhat "monstrous" works of music—*Tristan*, the Verdi *Requiem, Tommy*. Georges then reminded me of a faun or a bear cub, one that I would have longed to cuddle; but it was left to the music to supply our fleshly apotheosis. Afterwards we would give each other a hug and go our ways to bed.

Harry Mathews and David Kalstone, Venice, 1984

Georges is dead. Of course his work in all its greatness remains. Unfortunately, it doesn't help.

(From "Mon Ami." Published in *Le Monde,* July 27, 1984.)

The article on Georges was written in the Venetian apartment (if so ordinary a word can apply to so ducal a dwelling) of David Kalstone, benefiting from his critical attention as well as from his hospitality; and different though David and Georges may have been in many ways, there is a certain appropriateness in speaking of one after the other. I met David in New York through John Ashbery, who had the good sense to introduce us on the eve of my moving to Venice. David had for years spent his summers there, and it was in Venice that we came to know each other. David was nonetheless a thoroughgoing New Yorker, of the sort only those born elsewhere seem capable of becoming; and just as Georges articulated the mysteries of Paris literary and intellectual life in terms that I could grasp, so David generously came to be my interpreter of what was taking place in the world of American writing and publishing.

David Kalstone taught English literature, first at Harvard, later at Rutgers; he was an extraordinary critic, author of the best book I know on the poetry of Sir Philip Sidney as well as of a perceptive series of essays on modern poets. Good as his written work undoubtedly is, it hardly expresses the greatness of the man himself, even if it clearly illustrates one of his rarest qualities, one virtually extinct in our day: that

of never allowing his penetrating intellect to outshine his even more penetrating sensibility. David's writings never draw the reader's attention to him, always to his subject, with an acuity that does not fear hiding beneath a harvest of bushels because it is so clear, confident, and perfectly focussed; and as his innumerable friends will testify, this ready and concentrated attentiveness was marvelously available to them in all of their encounters with David, whether gossiping on the phone or evaluating a performance at the ballet or discussing a work of poetry, fiction, or criticism.

David combined absolute compassion with absolute independence of judgment; and lest that sound all too serious, he had a capacity for gaiety that was positively lowdown. He was constantly in touch with almost everything that seemed to matter to me—what was good or bad in my most recent work, how and where to get it published, how and where to get seats to a performance at the Met, or on Broadway, or off-off-Broadway, why Roland Barthes might usefully contribute to the cultural brew of 1983, why such-and-such a poet mattered, what poetry was, what art was, who had just gone to bed with *that* friend (and was he a real friend?), the delicious nuttiness of current political events.

What I chiefly learned from David was perhaps this: to relish everything that happens as the best possible entertainment and at the same time to take it with the utmost seriousness, for what else do we have? I'm afraid that he also, like Georges, taught me not to count on friends forever. Like Georges, he died before his time, a victim of AIDS. This is something to which I have not been able to reconcile myself in any coherent way.

An account of my friendships cannot be complete without at least mentioning a man who has had no connection with my activity as a writer (but he was the first to supply a "correct" explanation of the third riddle in *The Conversions*): Fred Warner, a British diplomat whom I met traveling in Egypt in 1963, when he was on leave from the Foreign Office. If I have left Fred to the end of this section, it is no accident. While I have enjoyed in the course of our visits and travels the many facets of his High-Renaissance character (adventurousness, enthusiasm, worldly wiseness, melancholy, intellectual sophistication, fervent intelligence), I have also over the years acquired from him something I might have been more comfortable without: a notion of how the world really works. Such knowledge leaves no room for preconceived ideas, either of the left or of the right; so that now, almost equally dismayed by the dogmatic arrogance of the left and the unprincipled accommodations of the right, I have come to occupy an awkward political position, one consolingly close to Queneau's: that of not knowing the answers, remembering that this is no excuse for not asking the questions.

When I think of Fred, however, I don't think primarily of politics: rather of sitting with him in the shade of the Parthenon listening to him expound its magnificence down to the last shadow of a gilded shield; of hacking exorbitant brambles out of a stand of conifers on his Dorset farm; of striding hard after him as with Simone, Valentine, and Orlando I tramp through a primrose-studded wood overlooking England's once pirate-ridden southern shore.

Les femmes, les femmes, il n'y a qu'ça . . .

If I learned much from my teachers and more from my friends, I learned most from the women in my life: Niki de Saint Phalle, Anne Hollander, Elyette Héliès, Maxine Groffsky, Loredana Balboni, Marie Chaix.

I met Niki de Saint Phalle on summer vacation in the Berkshires when I was twelve. I saw her from time to time during the following years, usually at a distance, or at least distantly. One Saturday afternoon in the fall of my first year at college, I was addressed in the dining car of the New York–Princeton train by a dazzlingly beautiful young woman whom I did not recognize, whom I at once pursued, and with whom several months later I eloped while AWOL from the Navy, whose disapproval was nothing compared to that of Niki's parents and above all my own. The step I thus took was not only rash but truly blind, and altogether salutary: I cannot imagine finding another way of breaking so emphatically and effectively with the world I had been brought up in, a world (whatever its virtues) that in 1949 offered me little hope of doing what I imagined I wanted to do. I hardly knew what the results of our initiative might be, and Niki knew no better than I; but where I had intermittent misgivings, Niki held doubts to be not only useless but irrelevant. What mattered was making the break, not what we would do after it. She supplied the determination to carry out our enterprise, rescuing me repeatedly from my quaint fear that if I turned my back on my family I would simply cease to exist. She showed me repeatedly that our life—which meant my life—was ours to create.

This determination of Niki's sustained me in many ways during our eleven years together. She was unwaveringly committed to life, to moving on, to discovering what lay around the next bend in the road. She manifested this determination in her hammer-and-tongs battle with my mother over having a child; in her ardent insistence on saving our marriage during the difficult summer of 1953; in her fidelity to her particular "primitive" gifts as an artist; in the tenacity with which she clung to her identity (and her life) after her health was ruined by hyperthyroidism, and in the tenacity no less great with which, sick herself, she cared for our son, Philip, during his frightening childhood illnesses; in her witty, aristocratic confidence in my work as well as her own, a confidence all the more credible for the rare critical eye she turned on what I wrote; and finally, painfully, positively, in her willingness to end our marriage once she saw that the life had gone out of it and that preserving it so as to avoid suffering would mean betraying both of us.

She was right. We had married when I was nineteen and she eighteen: our marriage had given us a context in which to finish growing up, and now that we were at least potential adults, new contexts for new kinds of growth were in order. At the time, I was far too attached to our marriage to see this. Marriage had become the sheltering family without which I secretly believed I could not survive. Niki's departure left me in a state of recurrent gloom whose surface symptoms would require almost two years to be cured and whose less obvious, more pernicious effect—a paralysing reluctance to risk loving or being loved—would stay with me for well over a decade.

I know now that this condition was nobody's responsibility but my own. Niki may have left, but even then, and for all but a few months of the ensuing time, I was provided with good reasons *not* to feel abandoned. During the breakup itself I had met Anne Hollander, an American who was warm, generous, bright, elegant, charming, and pretty enough to have consoled Orestes bereft and enraged. Unfortunately, except for occasional transatlantic visits, our romance had to be consummated in letters. She was married, by no means unhappily, and there was no question, in spite of our passion, of our devoting ourselves to one another. (If there had been such a prospect, I myself would have probably thought it a kind of sacrilege, after eleven years of strenuous conjugality.) Yet the time we managed to spend together was uniquely precious to me. Anne taught me that my adolescent yearnings for a relationship uniting tenderness and intense sexuality (here, too, Niki and I had had to do too much of our learning together) could exist outside of my reveries. Furthermore her epistolary genius showed how powerful the written word could become when animated by love. Her letters mattered to me more than any book, but they surely mothered *The Sinking of the Odradek Stadium.*

I was then spending almost all my time in Paris, where I had moved back with my children from Lans-en-Vercors, the mountain village where we had lived as a family for the previous two years. I was without Niki, without Anne, brooding compulsively over my less-than-unique fate, looking after Laura and Philip with distracted inconsistency. It was in these circumstances that I had a year-and-a-half-long affair with a Frenchwoman slightly older than I named Elyette Héliès. She was tough, sharp, experienced, no respector of persons or of anything else, except for her friends and, fortunately, her lovers. Insofar as it was possible, she weaned me from my well-meaning wishful thinking about the ways of the world, and she did so with a kind of merciless geniality that was inspired more by what she saw as a waste of my energies than by a desire to score points. Her teachings were grounded in her fidelity to the present, to what was actually happening at any given time; there was not a day I knew her when she was not willing to hazard our relationship, her possessions, her job, her comfort, anything apparently worth saving, if it conflicted with her intensely felt sense of what was fitting for the moment. She lived uninterruptedly at risk and clearly did so not out of a taste for recklessness or conspicuous individuality but with a confident, perhaps bitter wisdom that I willingly trusted, even if I could not begin to understand it. With Elyette, I felt that I was being driven by a nonchalant, expert driver at exhilarating speeds over unmapped roads. The landscape going past would never look the same again.

My time with her (and with Anne, too) came to an end when I made a trip to New York in May 1962. I rented an apartment on West Thirteenth Street for an entire month, the longest I had ever stayed in the city on my own. The publication of *The Conversions* was the occasion for my visit, and I had been looking forward to it, having not yet learned what disappointments such an event can bring. Although the novel made scarcely a public ripple, friends like Jane Freilicher and her husband Joe Hazan responded so enthusiastically to it that disappointments were forestalled; and I had meanwhile been given satisfaction of an altogether different sort. The editing of *The Conversions* had been done at Random House, with a skill and a tact I appreciate to this day, by Berenice Hofmann and Maxine Groffsky. I corresponded with these editors at length, so that by the time I arrived in New York I felt on friendly, almost intimate terms with them. Where Maxine was concerned, the intimacy soon became fact.

Maxine was a woman of Olympic and no doubt Olympian prowess in looks, charm, energy, intelligence, and wit, imbued with a sexual candor that might have made her a winning fourth in the contest for Paris's apple. (It is foolish to say "was"; she is still capable of precipitating a four-lane pile-up.) Endowed with irreverent frankness balanced by good nature, with a caustic, rather cynical sense of realities that only makes her affections more convincing, capable of sustained anger and devotion, Maxine brought into my life a presence that was entire, powerful, and demanding. Maxine was challenging in many domains. She was as inspiring a dancer as she was an editor, she had incredible artistic flair, with a phenomenally perceptive eye and ear and a capacity for zeroing in on the critical heart of whatever was at issue whose only possible drawback was its speed—I sometimes felt like taking at least one breath before having to confront such superbly definitive judgments. As a result, during the eleven years we spent together, I learned to love dancing (and to watch it, too, especially Merce Cunningham and Ballanchine, those last great twentieth-century masters); I learned how to edit my own writing and came to read the work of others, such as James Salter, Dallas Wiebe, and Keith Cohen, that I might otherwise have regret-

With Maxine Groffsky, Paris, 1967

J.P. Bonnotte

tably missed; I discovered at least some of the lively things that were happening in American painting and sculpture; and, in general, I was cheerfully obliged to recognize the world around me as a place for discovery and communication, rather than the realm of a vaguely hostile otherness that I kept stubbornly conceiving it to be. Maxine brought openness, possibility, and generosity into my life. I was, foolishly, not ready for so much.

I made two mistakes, or what now look to me like mistakes, even if at the time I felt I could not act otherwise: I should have married Maxine, or I should have not taken her away from New York. If Maxine had stayed in New York, where she led a brilliant social and professional life, we would have had a very different kind of relationship, one that probably would not have left me with my present sense of opportunities squandered. Since Maxine came back to France with me, to live for eleven years in a country whose language and ways were as yet largely unknown to her, I should have committed myself definitively to her well-being. Fifteen years later I would not have hesitated to do so; but I was then pathetically enthralled by the dread of what my first marriage had ultimately brought me: the "unbearable" pain of its ending. I had been totally committed to Niki, and I had suffered for it. I wouldn't be caught in that trap again. Thanks to such reasoning, I stifled my capacity for love and denied myself what would have made me happiest. Maxine patiently put up with me as long as she could, and no doubt longer than she should have. I knew periods of great happiness with her; and at the end of each one of them I insisted perversely on turning back to a condition of what I had the presumption to call independence. Because both she and I have since dealt more justly with ourselves, the consequence of my attitude was less than disastrous—waste, not ruin; but what a waste!

Maxine went back at last to New York late in the winter of 1974. A few months later I moved to Venice, where I was to live for a little more than two years. Soon after my arrival, I met and at once fell under the spell of a Venetian unlike any woman I had known: Loredana Balboni, a paragon of loveliness, elegance, sweetness, hospitableness, and cultivation. Lest these words make her sound too good to be interesting, I can say that she is also a tough and agile art dealer and, in her personal life, capable of quite irresistible gaiety.

I was quickly enchanted by Loredana, and I found myself drawn as well to the social pleasures of life under her roof. I became an almost disreputably constant guest at her table and in her drawing room. I underwent a fascinating apprenticeship in the life of a certain stratum of Italian society that is hard to identify, since it included, as well as writers and artists, professional men and businessmen and an occasional politician. Loredana watched over my successes and my gaffes among her guests with a reassuring, fond serenity. And when the cold and darkness of winter emptied the city of visitors, she filled up her salon with her own genial radiance: so that the evenings spent alone with her came to be those I by far preferred—they came to seem my special rewards for having not too disgracefully survived the more arduous social occasions. In the course of those evenings *à deux* I learned to benefit from my friend's knowledge and experience, listening raptly to her accounts of her extraordinary and not too happy life.

I know that explaining relationships is a dubious if tempting enterprise. Loredana's feelings about me were subdued by what I thought of, perhaps egotistically, as an essential dread of happiness. As a young woman she had been married twice, to two exceptional men; both had died. Did these experiences lead her to recoil from yet another serious attachment? For the first time since Niki's departure I was beginning, in Loredana's presence, to feel capable of making such a commitment myself. She herself spoke of the possibility warmly enough. At the same time I felt that I never was allowed into the most intimate circle of her thoughts and choices, no matter how much openness and kindness she showed me.

Then, during a visit to New York in the fall of 1975, I was offered the job of translating a recent French novel, a book unknown to me, although it had, during my Venetian absence, been a best-seller in France: *The Laurels of Lake Constance*, written by a woman in her early thirties named Marie Chaix. The novel was thoroughly autobiographical, describing the life of Marie Chaix's father during his politically appalling career as a high-ranking member of the Fascist *Parti populaire français*.

I agreed to translate the book because at first glance I assumed that it would be easier than the avant-garde work which had provided me with my previous experience of translation. *The Laurels* proved much harder and also much more affecting than I expected; in fact it overwhelmed me. Having read it through twice and started on the work of translation, I wrote the author (her discreetly alluring photograph adorned the book's cover) a letter that I hoped would lead to a more than ordinary acquaintance. I used every writer's trick I knew to make myself interesting; and when I had finished the letter, I tore it up. I realized that the author of a book so intensely felt and so compassionate deserved better than a disguised

Mark Lyon

Harry Mathews with Marie Chaix,
Bennington, Vermont, 1978

come-on. I composed a new, short letter, courteous and respectful, sent it off to Marie Chaix, and relegated my fantasies to the Venetian fog.

On receiving this second, respectable letter, Ms. Chaix, mother of two and until then a resolutely devoted spouse, almost left her family to pay me a visit in Venice. It was as though my first letter had been encrypted in the second one—an interesting lesson in the workings of language. Six weeks later I had my first conversation with her, by phone, mostly about her book; but much else happened during that hour-long talk, and not entirely in my imagination, because when we finally met two weeks after that, neither I nor Marie could long entertain any doubt that something new, challenging, "impossible" had come into our lives; and, except for necessary separations, we have never left each other since.

It is hard to sum up what I have learned from Marie, with whom I have lived through the most trying and most productive time of my life, and from whom I am still constantly learning. When we met, she offered me that opportunity of making myself wholly available to a woman towards which I had been slowly moving since the collapse of my first marriage; and available not only to herself but to her two daughters, then aged two and seven, who with their mother have given me a second-family that has filled my days with new life. There is no greater

satisfaction than that of being useful to others, except that of being useful to others one already loves: Marie, Emilie, Léonore.

Marie is also a writer (I had sworn never to live with a writer), and a French writer, and a writer whose practice in no way resembles mine. Showing perfect respect for my own concerns, she has revealed to me possibilities in writing that I might never have discovered; and what is true of writing applies to the rest of my life. Through her I have been able to see that my parents, my children, my cousins and my cousins' cousins, and friends long unseen and those freshly made, are the substance of my life: that my life is what I have and what I can make of that, not some wishful hope of what may (and doesn't) happen. She has demonstrated what happiness is without ever telling me what it should be.

It is now close to eleven years that Marie and I have lived together. Knowing her has not changed me: I am no less distracted, dilatory, self-indulgent, or confused than I was before. But there is not an hour in which, aware of and I trust responsible for my failings, I cannot subsume them in the intention of my continuing to live with her to the end of my counted days.

Listening, Then Reading, Then Writing

One of two recollectable beginnings:

During several years of my childhood, I would go into my father's room most mornings and sit on a stool on the threshold of his bathroom while he shaved. Shaving for my father was a long, carefully executed rite, one that provided ample time for story-telling; and every morning my father, between prudent swipes at his chin, would slowly enunciate a new episode of whatever fabulous tale he was in the process of telling me. (In the evenings he would draw masterly illustrations of the stories.) I can't remember the first tale—perhaps one that involved crossing the isthmus of Panama, as a hilarious drawing of the world's greatest seaworm suggests. I know that when I was around six or seven we took trips to the moon and to Madagascar (where tribal rivalry set the lanky N'Gombos against the pudgy Bambos).

Perhaps my father derived his narrative skill from his Kentucky grandfather, Basil Duke, on whose knee he had sat and listened to accounts of the Civil War. In any case, the only talent I feel I possess is that of telling stories, and clearly those fifteen-minute morning sessions with my father taught me what story-telling is about: beyond provoking the question

"And then what happened?" digging the Procrustean bed from which that question can be reborn new every time.

The other beginning:

Aged eight or nine, I am walking with my mother westwards across Seventy-second Street, climbing the hill between Second and Third Avenues. Near the top of the hill, responding no doubt to some remark or question or impertinence I have just uttered, my mother stops, turns to me, and says

"O for a beaker full of the warm South,
  Full of the true, the blushful Hippocrene,
    With beaded bubbles winking at the brim,
      And purple-stainèd mouth;
  That I might drink, and leave the world unseen,
    And with thee fade away into the forest dim. "

My mother and father had read poetry to me—Stevenson's *Child's Garden of Verses,* some delicious poems of Kipling ("And the steward falls into the soup tureen . . ."), and Tennyson, who had given me my first moment of poetic wonder: "The splendor falls / On Castle walls / And snowy summits old in story . . ." But not until my mother recited those lines from Keats did I know that poetry was a life-and-death matter, capable of arresting in her busy stride one of the two central divinities of my world, of bringing tears to her eyes, of evoking a vastness of longing and regret and desire altogether surpassing the words she was so deliriously letting fall from her so-strangely-lipsticked original mouth.

A couple of years later, at the bottom of the same hill, on the opposite side of the street, I saw in the window of (perhaps) a stationery store a book attractive enough to draw me inside, where I spent a respectable portion of hoarded allowance in buying it. The book was *Tom Sawyer.* It had an intriguing cover that showed Tom painting the fence in front of his envious friends. I had never heard of Tom or Huck or Mark Twain. I might have read and liked the book anyway, but having bought it gave reading a special relish.

(This event is confused in my memory with the purchase of another book at the same store: a Pocket Book, then the only paperback available. When I proudly announced that I had bought myself a pocket book, glimmers of is-my-son-gay anxiety visibly troubled my mother's gaze until I made clear what I was talking about. The book wasn't *The Constant Nymph,* although I particularly remember reading that in the Pocket Book edition, but certainly later, during early adolescence.)

Meanwhile I was exposed to more poetry at school and duly swooned at some of it, Shelley's "Invitation," for instance—no: I discovered that for myself, in a slightly trashy book about Trelawny that wasn't trashy enough, since I expected romantic sex from it. Humphrey Fry began expounding his enthusiasm for Browning, turning me curiously into a century-late Browningite snob. There are worse fates for inexperienced proto-proto-writers, who are at least led to ask such questions as: is poetry a simple vehicle for complicated thoughts, or is it a complicated vehicle for simple thoughts?

I read lots of prose as well, although without, I think, the hope for the transformational, redemptive power I attributed to poetry. After *Tom Sawyer* I devoured all its sequels. Some time after that I binged on Noel Coward and Bernard Shaw. In between I regularly bought *Action Comics, Detective Comics,* and others whose names I've forgotten, although I shall never, ever forget Submariner, The Human Torch, or The Flash. The book that most affected me in the last years of grade school was *Out of the Night,* by a former German communist who took the name Jan Valtin: in it I learned about Hitler's concentration camps and their anti-Semitic horrors.

In adolescence reading took on a new virtue. I was in the midst of my "friendless" stage; books became my friends, and better than friends because my communion with them wholly depended on my willingness to lose myself in them, to take them seriously, to think and dream about them. They were my link with humanity, and with my own humanity, in which I hardly dared otherwise believe.

Not only reading offered me this refuge, but my own poetry. From the age of thirteen to seventeen I deemed myself happiest when I could be alone in the mudbath of language. I can't claim it was much more than that for me, although I was bright and soon well trained enough to appreciate and appropriate certain elements of abstract thought. The glory of language, however, for me had to include not only the mind but the rest of the nervous system as well, which it fed and consoled for its foolish but intense anxieties.

Just as a glutton desires more food than he needs, and eats more food than he desires, I heaped my life with books. Not only books to read but to own. Each new volume on my shelves added a brick to my defense works, the culture castle in which some day I hoped to live safely and alone (except perhaps for my sexpot goddess). I read as much as I could, well over a hundred books a year, but my craving for new acquisitions outstripped my reading. Eventually I came to realize that the prospect I was creating for my future (a lifetime of reading or of *not* reading, since one lifetime would hardly suffice) was more depressing than reassuring, and I gave up buying books systematically. To this day, however, the sight of a book catalogue can give me an almost pornographic twitch.

During those teen-age years I read a great deal of modern poetry: after Eliot came Marianne Moore, Frost, E.A. Robinson (I voluntarily concocted a forty-page analysis of *Tristram*), and others to whom I was led by Louis Untermeyer's anthology. Eliot also pointed towards Donne and Marvell; in school I read Shakespeare and Milton. I have forgotten most of the fiction I read—I couldn't now identify a single situation in *The Rise of Silas Lapham* or *Giants in the Earth.* I read most of Hawthorne and Melville, *The Red Badge of Courage,* the incomparable *Walden* (still to me an exemplar of writing as a complete art), and such books left me with a lasting sense of their particular worlds, Hawthorne perhaps most of all: his bleaker moments may have appealed to me (as *Ethan Frome* certainly did) as reflections of my own little midwinter–New England melancholy, which I sought to express in the poems I wrote during my long months away from home.

I arrived at Princeton aspiring to become a poet. For the first year I continued to write, although less than before, and after that even less, and at the end of a year and a half not at all. This absence of not only the ability but the desire to write lasted until after my graduation from Harvard, from which I concluded that American college life was to blame for it. I may not have been wrong, but it no longer matters, and even then I never took what I imagined to be a permanent loss as tragedy. The Navy, marriage, fatherhood (the enthralling presence of Laura), the study of music, the prospect of Europe provided a full enough life. The loss also felt like what it was: an unwished-for renunciation that had left me stranded in a desert of unformulated questions.

In Paris, in 1952, Niki studied acting, to which she brought her beauty, dramatic instinct, and determination, and I conducting, to which I brought knowledge, enthusiasm, and an insurmountable lack of ear training. The following summer our still very young marriage endured a crisis. Niki had a pseudo-suicidal nervous breakdown that allowed her, while she was being treated in a clinic in Nice, to rediscover her passion for art, and to discover her gift for it. When she then renounced the seductive, real prospects of an acting career to embark on her ultimately spectacular but then pathetically uncertain life as a painter, I watched her transformation with growing jealousy. And not only jealousy: with a sense that she had begun an existence that was all possibility, something like the possibility that I had guessed at in

my poetry-making days at school. I started writing again.

I had the best imaginable partner in my undertaking, because Niki had once again no doubts about the life she had chosen. She welcomed me fervently into my belated resumption of an activity commonly called "creative," in any case one that depended wholly on its solitary practitioner. I picked up, I suppose, where I had left off years before; several more years would be necessary before I wrote a poem that I would keep, and it was not until my meeting with John Ashbery that I became conscious of what I might do, which is to say anything I wanted. Until then I remained conscientiously and not unrewardingly stuck in a kind of respectable neo-imagist exploration. I learned during this time the habit of relentless rewriting, something I came to rely on when I began working in prose.

Niki was also an acute reader. She insisted that I not miss what she recognized as great: Proust, Dostoevsky, Ford Maddox Ford, *Oblomov,* Walter de La Mare's *Memoirs of a Midget.* (She also saved me the trouble of reading works like Roger Martin du Gard's *Les Thibauts.*) Niki was the first person I relied on to fill the gaps in my own reading; the others were Ashbery, Perec, and Marie Chaix. To Ashbery I owe my acquaintance with Roussel and Firbank and, as I've said, Kafka freshly read; to Perec, Flaubert; to Marie Chaix, Bruno Schulz, Colette, Marcel Schwob, and (perhaps the best of these four) Marcel Blecher.

In 1956 I began a novel, not knowing what to do. I tried to somehow elevate events in my life to the self-contained intensity of fiction. I still admired Albert Camus and half-heartedly half-took him for a model, managing one chapter that was at least readable, a second chapter that was at least finished, then a few aimless pages. It was like going to college all over again. The crises in Poland, Hungary, and the Middle East interrupted my efforts. Meanwhile I had begun reading Roussel: a hard task, one that at first amused me, then convinced me that Roussel was a thoroughly nutty eccentric, until I at last emerged on the vast, coldly illuminated plateau of his sovereign genius.

Reading Roussel brought me several revelations. He demonstrated to me that psychology was a dispensable fashion, that the moral responsibilities of writing did not lie in a respect of subject matter, and that the writing of prose fiction could be as scrupulously organized as Sir Philip Sidney's double sestina. Roussel taught me that I did not have to write out of my "experience" (the quotation marks indicate: what one thinks one has been unable to avoid); that I had the universe to play with, not merely the pieties of a

The author, in 1959

late-capitalist society; that writing could provide me with the means of so radically outwitting myself that I could bring my hidden experiences, my unadmitted self into view. I have sometimes felt that the aim of Roussel's imperturbable and arbitrary procedures was to supply the truths of paradox (such as "life after death") with the unchallengeable evidence of tautology (make a machine to revive the dead and they will "by definition" show signs of life). Such a project suggested that his methods were powerful and original enough to accommodate my own, as yet undiscovered ambiguities. That Roussel's procedures were based on word play did not surprise me unduly. Who in my own country wrote more cunningly than S.J. Perelman, representing James Joyce on a package tour through supermarketed America? With Roussel I found myself in a familiar, wholly man-made landscape, where linen-and-thread baby's-breath smelled of real babies: the landscape of our re-inventable, startling world. And if Perelman shrugged off his sometimes nightmarish fantasies with a public smile, Roussel stared at them with the unpainted gaze of a sea-washed statue of antiquity—one whose nakedness had been distractingly reclothed in strict turn-of-the-century costume.

In 1958, after we had moved to Lans-en-Vercors in the French pre-Alps, I began another novel, at first called *Invitation to a Sabbath,* later *The Conversions.* To the writing of this book I brought my Roussellian enthusiasm for freely and puzzlingly inventing new things to write about, as well as an ear entranced by Roussel's frighteningly, provocatively, movingly neutral voice. For my central subject matter I turned to my experience of Robert Graves's life and work,

especially *The White Goddess* (almost as liberatingly strange as Roussel himself). The time I had spent with Robert had produced mixed feelings about him, if unmixed agreement with Eric Linklater's dictum that wanting to meet a writer because one admires his work is like wanting to meet a goose because one likes *foie gras.* (The dictum rings unfairly in my ears, because of Robert's kindness to me, for which I remember him affectionately. I remember too his admirable fund of knowledge: he was the first European I knew at all well who put my exaggerated intellectual assurance in its proper place. For some time to come, graduates of Oxford and the Ecole supérieure des lettres are going to continue to make most of us look like promising freshmen.)

The White Goddess and Robert's ancillary writings on the subject, together with his rather goofy applications to life of his doctrine of the nine-fold Muse, provided me with material for a story, which I reoriented to the history of witchcraft as I reimagined it after readings in Baissac, Michelet, Lea, and of course Margaret Murray. All these preparations, Roussellian, Gravesian, and witchy, provided fuel to the hypnotic passion with which I wrote the book: a passion that resembled less that of a romantic poet oozing inspiration through the tip of his pen than that of a shoemaker making boots for a queen. Because of certain reactions to my novels, I would like to add that the bootmaker's passion excluded indifference and ridicule. I and the "I"s telling my stories are never free of the stresses of emotion; but the "I"s and I know we are bootmakers, or only sandalmakers, throttled (not inexpressively for an attentive reader) by a restraint producing a kind of anguish-ridden understatement. We leave it to described events, to told stories, to do our speaking for us.

When I wrote *The Conversions* I was leading a happy life; a precariously happy one, it turned out. By the time I began *Tlooth* Niki had left, my life felt blackened. My second novel taught me that writing one book never makes the next one easier. Everything I set down had to be rewritten, not merely revised, and after that there was more rewriting to do. Maxine Groffsky patiently showed me ways that helped bring the intricate work to completion. Intricate, because so much of the religious underpinning of the book, recognizably close to the surface in *The Conversions,* was here mostly shoved out of sight. Combining the imperatives of this hidden subject matter with those of an adventure story whose main characters had to be kept sexually ambiguous, and inscribing the result in acceptable English sentences, often proved discouragingly difficult.

This is not the place to explore at length the

reasons for the indirect, elaborate, and apparently frustrating approach to experience to which I resorted in my first three novels. In my opinion, which is no more than that, I was preoccupied with the problem of knowledge: what it is, how it can be communicated, and also what it is not and how it is often belied. Certainly the three books' cargo of cultural junk—historical, theological, and so forth—confirms this opinion; in that all the cultural constructs eventually go up in smoke, are shown to be misleading, or meaningless, or to mean things other than what they claim. In *The Sinking of the Odradek Stadium* I pushed this approach to what I hope is its limit. The religious substructure—in the narrative it appears in the wedded opposition of a decadent Roman Catholic and an efficient Buddhist—was complicated by projections of a future society, by painstaking accounts of economic and political life in medieval Florence, by a slightly loony application of the rules of the Big Con to a scholarly treasure hunt, to name only the more visible constraints. The problems I set myself were so daunting that I sometimes resigned myself to setting them down without finding their solutions—a recourse that hardly makes for easy reading. I was almost surprised when the book was finally published (thanks to Maxine and Fran McCullough) and gratified that it was so well received critically, at least in some pleasantly conspicuous places. I had become in the course of writing the book much attached to my two odd-ball spouses, and I was happy to have secured their love story a niche in the public world.

Waiting to find a publisher—*The Sinking* survived twenty-five rejections—I hesitated to begin another novel. If the best I had been able to do provoked such reluctance, why undertake another lengthy project? I wrote shorter fiction, poetry (*Trial Impressions*), and a book including both poetry and prose, *Selected Declarations of Dependence*. This last work was based entirely on a set of forty-four proverbs, which I exploited in terms of vocabulary, structure, and subject matter. This curious and demanding project was the result of my membership in the Paris-based group of writers and intellectuals known as the OuLiPo.

The OuLiPo—the *Ou*vroir de *litt*érature *pot*entielle, or Workshop of Potential Literature—was founded in 1961 by Raymond Queneau and his friend François LeLionnais. Queneau was not only an outstanding novelist and poet but a practicing mathematician; LeLionnais was a chess expert and a mathematical historian; and at the outset the OuLiPo's declared purpose was to apply mathematical structures to writing. The notion of mathematical structure was later expanded into that of constrictive form, a "constrictive form" being one that makes inescapa-

In Lans-en-Vercors, 1969

Elizabeth C. Baker

bly hard demands on the ingenuity of its user: a form arduous enough to oblige anyone who uses it to say what he might never otherwise have said, and certainly not in the way he has to say it. A constrictive form can be as rudimentary as a snowball or as complex as Queneau's *100,000 Billion Poems* (a set of ten sonnets that through permutations can produce that astronomical figure). What all constrictive forms have in common is the satisfaction they offer: that of difficulties overcome.

Cursory descriptions of Oulipian activities and attitudes almost invariably lead to reactions such as: it sounds interesting and amusing but you're really just playing games. If Queneau, Calvino, and Perec like playing such games, who could help wanting to join the team? However, that is not how the OuLiPo works. Writing in the sense of producing works is not its true concern. Meeting once a month for a working lunch or dinner of great and irreverent liveliness, the OuLiPo supplies its members with a forum in which to explore the *potentialities* of the novel and the poem, or the paragraph and sentence, in terms of constrictive form and its consequences. It is a kind of laboratory of structural studies (it has nothing to do with structuralism, by the way). Later, or elsewhere,

Mathews, 1971

Laurie Asprey

its members may choose to avail themselves of Oulipian methods in their work. That is their business, not the OuLiPo's, which only formulates procedures and at most supplies minimal examples to clarify them.

My own near-Oulipian tendencies were well established before I even heard of the group, to which Perec introduced me in 1972. I have ever since rejoiced at having been co-opted into that unique body; but it is hard to say how much it has influenced what I subsequently wrote. The support of its members is certainly influence of a kind. I would prefer to say that the OuLiPo has empowered me to reach what I was already struggling towards; by clarifying and expanding my awareness of what I was doing, it has enabled me to move towards what I had not yet done.

A description of the first section of *Selected Declarations of Dependence* may illustrate what I mean. I there set myself the task of writing a story using only the vocabulary of the forty-four proverbs on which the book as a whole is based. The task proved hard: the number of words at my disposal was less than two hundred. I had no idea of what to say, of what I might say. I found myself during my writing hours literally obliged to start living inside a world circumscribed by

my chosen vocabulary. I began by saying possible things, writing them down, and comparing them. Little by little, possibilities of events appeared, and then links between the events. In time situations were created, although hardly by me. At least that is how I felt: I was becoming the medium for some unsuspected and strangely inevitable whole—as though in the course of a long walk I had stumbled into a valley full of dreamed trees, fissures, and dancers. The story in the end "told itself." It was perhaps not the only story that could have evolved from that material, but it was certainly the only story I could then write in those circumstances. It was a story furthermore that I would never otherwise have written. The apparently arbitrary constraint that I had agreed to comply with turned out to be the means of unlocking an unsuspected cupboard of knowledge, so that I was able to make pages altogether fresh out of some of the most worked-over words in the language: as though I had constructed, like some genial castaway, a pleasure pavilion out of the worn pebbles edging the deserted beach where I had been stranded.

Many writers will recognize in this account a most familiar experience. From this I would conclude that Oulipian practice, seemingly extremist, provides a useful way into the central domains of writing or, more accurately, of the act of writing.

It may be all too easy for me to see the work I did in the years before starting *Cigarettes*, my much-postponed last novel, as preparation for it: *Selected Declarations* as an Oulipian workout; *Trial Impressions* (perhaps my favorite among my books) as an experiment in discovering how formal pretexts lead into intimate experiences; the translation of three autobiographical books—one by Perec, two by Marie Chaix—as an apprenticeship in applying the imagination to past personal events; the subsequent translation of Jeanne Cordelier's devastating memoir of her life as a prostitute (*La Dérobade*) as a lesson in writing colloquial, intensely felt dialogue. If at the time I could not have foreseen how these projects would contribute to a new novel, it is undeniable that they gave me an excellent training for writing it. I knew, long before *Cigarettes* was conceived of, that my next book would have to realize my desire to express in fictional transformations particular experiences of childhood, parenthood, friendship, and love. The stories the book tells have little enough to do with the events of my life. At the same time, those stories could not have been told if I had not looked for material, rather than in imagination giving substance to the ambiguities of language, in imagination giving substance to the ambiguities of remembrance. The distinction may be only an illusion, but the illusion ultimately provided a constraint absorbing enough to produce a book.

Leaving and Returning, Living and Dying

During the writing of *Cigarettes,* my life underwent a number of changes, some apparently superficial, some less so, that now strike me as corresponding to a shift in my attitude towards myself and towards the world. I would say that in general the focus of my life shifted from what I could learn by experiment to what I could learn by commitment, although I hasten to add that the first demand of commitment is to make the most frightening experiment of all: that of giving up what one already has. I surrendered my mistrust of others and accepted my relationships with the men and women I loved. I agreed to work with others in questioning the nature of life, of my life. I returned to my family: I reclaimed my mother and father as my mother and father. Each year I spent more time in the country and city of my birth. I started to teach. I started to write about myself. Out of these changes new relationships were born, and in the midst of the changes familiar relationships ended in death. So circumstances confirmed my impression that I was moving out of one realm of learning into another.

My work with Werner Erhard, to whose activities Tina Packer introduced me (screaming and kicking) in 1975, involved several of these changes, especially my new relationships with friends and family and my becoming a teacher. Erhard's work deserves a lengthier appreciation than I can give it here. Leaving out its more substantial aspects, I can say that from the start it appealed to me as the wittiest, most intellectually sophisticated example of social drama created in our versatile age (perhaps the instigators of the May 1968 events in Paris came close, in a quite different arena); and that Erhard and those he trained supplied me with so appealing a model for teaching that when in the spring of 1978, at the invitation of Georges Guy, I was invited to teach French literature at Bennington College, I was able to begin a new career.

I approached teaching with contradictory feelings. The work attracted me because I was eager to share with others the knowledge I had accumulated over many years of writing and reading. On the other hand, I was appalled by my lack of training in the disciplines of intellectual synthesis that I considered indispensable to a decent academic presentation of that knowledge. Werner Erhard's teaching method was anything but decent. He taught Heidegger and Wittgenstein in the language of a drill sergeant. He stripped philosophy (and culture in general) of its forbidding and also reassuring pretensions and made it relevant, even linguistically, to the concerns of the present moment. This method demanded great attentiveness and a willingness to take risks—challenging qualities, no doubt, but ones that to me still seemed more attainable than academic authority.

When I at last made the plunge, I found myself swimming in a new sea of discovery; and since the sense of discovery is what best holds the interests of students, the venture was not the failure I had so long dreaded and postponed. The guarantee of not failing, I later concluded, lay essentially in the promise I repeatedly made to myself always to be sure I learned more in a given class than anyone else in the room. My satisfactions, however, surpassed the new education I received. I discovered the unsuspected joy of working with others, with my students most conspicuously, but also with my colleagues, several of whom immediately became my friends, and whom I shall count as friends until the end of our lives: Georges Guy, Reinhardt Mayer, Nicholas Delbanco, Phebe Chao, Stephen Sandy, Leroy Logan, Vivian Fine, John Lydenberg, Martin Horwitz—a cluster of people so brilliant, kind, and loyal it seems nothing less than miraculous to have found them gathered in a little college in southern Vermont in the space of three years.

I believe that it was soon after my first semester at Bennington that I started work on *Cigarettes.* A year later, in the autumn of 1979, I began another process of discovery: a much admired (if not intimate) friend in Paris died of cancer. At the beginning of the new year two other men who were close to me died, and at the end of March my father suffered a grievous heart attack which he survived for only a week. I spent all but one day of that week with my father and mother, experiencing intervals (and no space of time was not an interval) of grief, fear, hope, and reassurance that I plumbed with (to me) bewildering clarity. The most bewildering interval of all was the fearful one. I found myself driving along the shore towards Southampton Hospital, certain that my father was dying there, with my teeth chattering and my hands firm on the wheel only by dint of desperate pressure (reinforced by the presence of my mother in the "death seat" next to me). I quickly identified my fear: I saw that, even if I had in recent years come to the warmest and most confident of understandings with my father, he was still a conveniently available enemy; that, once he was lost to me, I would have to find other enemies to take his place—something (someone) that I looked hopelessly for in the darkness that extended over the Atlantic to the distant left of the car I was hurriedly driving through the midnight March darkness.

With son, Philip, daughter, Laura, and her husband, Laurent Condominas, holding their daughter Bloum, Lans-en-Vercors, 1972

Two Marches later I discovered something else about my father's death: that I had been able to endure it so faithfully, so clearly, so comprehensively because I knew that in my life I had the friend of friends, a second father who was also the older brother I had never had, and the younger brother, too, since (even if my ready deference to him suggested otherwise) he was my junior by six years: Georges Perec.

In the fall of 1981 Georges was invited to Australia, where in his letters he first mentioned a nagging pain in his hip. On his return to Europe, he went on a lecture tour through Italy, where the pain became worse. In November, back in Paris, he consulted doctors fleetingly, tried different painkillers, saw an acupuncturist, who didn't help either, until a friend made him take tests that showed he had lung cancer.

In the light of such a revelation, it should have been obvious to the most indifferent observer that the pain in the hip was a metastasis of the cancer; but I wasn't indifferent. I could not bear any such obvious explanation. I took my leave of Georges while he was still determined to fight his illness with every resource he could summon. That was in mid-January 1982; I was on my way to New York and Columbia. I spoke to him by phone a month later. In the

beginning of March, on a date that I do not remember and that I haven't the courage to look up, he died in a hospital outside Paris, among others who loved him, spared the last gasping failure of his lungs by a timely administration of morphine.

After Georges's death I might well have fallen back into a convenient and familiar syndrome of isolation and abandonment if it had not been for Marie's presence, and if the "wake" of this death had not cast up on my needy passage two incorruptibly determined friends. The first was Joseph McElroy, who had for mysterious reasons come to live in Paris appropriately at the very moment Georges's illness was first manifesting itself. Joe was not like Georges, except in two things: he was confident of his genius as a creator of fiction, and he was committed to the celebration of present possibilities. We became friends without even trying, but I can scarcely scrutinize my own impulses at the time we came to know each other. It was as though I had been crying out for help when I did not have the least awareness that help was needed. Joe responded to that silent cry, and in the ensuing blinded months became a rock.

My second new friend showed up a year later, thanks to the recommendation of Werner Erhard. In the course of a seminar that I taught in San Francisco, I had lunch with Elizabeth Cowan, later to become Elizabeth Neeld. At the time she was best known for an extraordinary book on writing that she had coauthored with her late husband. We would have become friends whatever the circumstances; that we had each experienced painful loss only made our sympathy more immediate, and made it on my part a source of undying gratitude. Elizabeth had explored the consequences of death in a way that I was incapable of, or in any case unwilling to follow. She gave me clues as to how to move on, as to how to move out; she made available to me the lessons she had learned without ever suggesting that I believe in them. She gave me the opportunity to give up grief for a new world from which grief need not be excluded. Since then, like Tina Packer, like Marie Chaix, she has been someone to whom I turn when events are more than I can handle alone, and who, with a reliability that never fails to amaze me, decisively demonstrates that I can indeed handle them alone, because nobody else is going to do it for me.

In the spring of 1985, in another March, David Kalstone was hospitalized with pneumonia. Its cause was diagnosed as AIDS. David began a fearful process of accepting and combatting and being terrified (he kept that to himself). He lived another fourteen months, during which he returned a last time to his beloved Venice, where Marie and I spent a happy fortnight with him in early summer.

Later that summer, the summer of 1985, my mother began complaining of recurrent pains in her lower back. I told her that, on the eve of her eighty-second birthday, she should consider herself lucky that in a society decimated by aching backs she should have been spared this long. She was worried, but she put off serious examination of her trouble so as to be able to make one more September trip to Italy with Marie and me. She had hardly ever been sick; she was a woman of hearty appetites. In Italy her appetites failed her, she felt less and less well. On her return to New York, tests revealed an inoperable, untreatable cancer of the colon. Cancer was thus revealed, except to her: Mary Mathews, more herself than ever, carefully and deviously refused to recognize what was happening to her. At first I thought that she was wrong in this, that she would find her well-being in acknowledging the truth, in coming to terms with it, in accepting her end with some kind of serenity that was entirely my concern and not hers. What she did was exactly what she should have done, although I regret that I shall never know exactly how she interpreted the words "malignant tumor"—whatever the interpretation, she found a place for the words spacious enough to let her live with them, and with the tumors, too, for many more months than she was supposed to.

During that time, I commuted transatlantically every month to stay with her. I was her only child, she was her father's only child, and I no longer knew who the child in question might be. She had a nurse, and a housekeeper, and me. Every evening we spent together she would tell me stories of her past that I had never heard before, and she told the stories with an exquisite clarity that laid before me the splendid hopes and disappointments (and the gossip, too) of her intensely lived younger years. On the first of July 1986, two weeks after David Kalstone, at the end of a death agony that lasted eight days and confounded the predictions of doctors and nurses, she died, having lived her life out to the last unjustified, pressureless heartbeat. As long as her heart kept beating, she remained my eternal shelter, so that I told myself, in some unspoken part of my being, that she could go on dying until the end of time, until the end of my time anyway, and I would still be protected by her. Such matters may be incomprehensible to those who have not experienced them.

In time the shelter I had lost dissolved into a stuporous haze. One afternoon, walking up Madison Avenue, I looked up, looked around. The haze had withdrawn. I saw my new shelter, now no lower than

Harry Mathews, Venice, 1976

the sky itself. I looked in astonishment at the messengers, businessmen, businesswomen, shoppers, idlers on the sidewalk where I was standing. If they noticed me, they must have thought there was a crazy man in their midst, such was the love with which I stared at them.

BIBLIOGRAPHY

Fiction:

The Conversions. New York: Random House, 1962; London: Weidenfeld & Nicolson, 1962.

Tlooth. New York: Paris Review Editions/Doubleday, 1966.

The Sinking of the Odradek Stadium and Other Novels (includes *The Conversions* and *Tlooth*). New York: Harper, 1975; also published as *The Sinking of the Odradek Stadium.* Manchester, England and New York: Carcanet, 1985.

Country Cooking and Other Stories. Providence: Burning Deck, 1977.

Plaisirs singuliers (sketches). Paris: P.O.L., 1983.

Cigarettes. New York: Weidenfeld & Nicolson, 1987.

Nonfiction:

Le Verger (memoir of Georges Perec). Paris: P.O.L., 1984.

Poetry:

The Ring: Poems 1956–59. Leeds, England: Julliard Editions, 1970.

The Planisphere. Providence: Burning Deck, 1974.

Selected Declarations of Dependence (poetry and prose). Calais, Vt.: Z Press, 1977.

Trial Impressions. Providence: Burning Deck, 1977.

Le savoir des rois: poèmes à perverbes. Paris: Bibliothèque oulipienne, 1976.

Armenian Papers: Poems 1954–1984. Princeton: Princeton University Press, 1987.

Translator of:

The Laurels of Lake Constance, by Marie Chaix. New York: Viking, 1977.

Blue of Noon, by Georges Bataille. New York: Urizen Books, 1978; London: Boyars, 1979.

'The Life,' by Jeanne Cordelier and Martine Laroche. London: Secker & Warburg, 1978; New York: Viking Press, 1978.

Ann Petry

1908-

Mother, Bertha James, with her brothers and sisters: (rear, from left) Helen Lou, Fritz Morris, Willis, Bertha; (front, from left) Harry and Harriet

Having been born black and female, I regard myself as a survivor and a gambler, writing in a tradition that dates back to 1859 when *Our Nig*, the first novel written by a black woman in this country, was published in Boston, Massachusetts.

I write about the relationship between black people and white people in the United States: novels, short stories, poetry, books for children and young people.

When I write for children I write about survivors: Tituba of Salem Village, indicted for witchcraft in the seventeenth century; Harriet Tubman who helped runaway slaves escape from the South before the Civil War.

When I write for adults I write about the walking wounded: Lutie Johnson in *The Street*; Abigail Crunch and Link Williams in *The Narrows*; Charles Woodruff

in the short story "The Witness."

Like all writers, black or white, I work against odds, real or imaginary, against hostility, against indifference. I keep seeking uninterrupted time in which to write and so I wage war against interruptions. I am usually defeated by my archenemy the telephone or by people who do not regard writing as work and drop in to visit.

I regard myself as a survivor because I have written eight books and had them published.

I regard myself as a gambler because each one of these books was written against odds that it would ever be finished, enormous odds that only a gambler would have accepted.

I am by birth a New Englander, a Connecticut Yankee. Four generations of my family have been born in Connecticut. My maternal grandmother was born in New Haven, my mother was born in Hartford, I was born in Old Saybrook, my daughter was born in Middletown.

To borrow a phrase from the Society of Friends, from the Quakers, I am a birthright New Englander, specifically a Connecticut Yankee.

But, of course, I am not. I am by birth an outsider, a maverick. I am not a member of the club. I am not a part of the establishment. I have a tenuous, unsubstantial connection with New England.

Old Saybrook, Connecticut, is a very old town—it celebrated its 350th birthday in 1935. It is located at the mouth of the Connecticut River, where the river goes into Long Island Sound. The town barely escaped being an island, for it is connected to the rest of the area by a narrow neck of land. It is almost surrounded by water—a picture-postcard kind of town.

I have always felt that I had a special understanding of Mrs. Susan Fosdick in a book called *The Country of the Pointed Firs*. When she heard a story about a minister who suddenly stood up in a small sailboat and nearly capsized it, she said, "I do think they ought not to settle any more of them landlocked folks in parishes where they're liable to be on the water."

Old Saybrook was a very small town when I was growing up. A relatively quiet place filled with the salt smell of the sea and with the yammering sound of gulls. At certain seasons of the year the sky over the town is enlivened by the comings and goings of water birds, for the coves and inlets and creeks offer a perfect resting-place for migratory birds.

I was familiar with the smell of the marshes at low tide. I knew the difference in the smell of the air when the tide was going out, and I knew how it freshened when the tide was coming in.

As for the town itself, I said it was a picture-postcard kind of town. There is a town green, a large open space in the center of the town, where cows and sheep once grazed. A drugstore is housed in a building that faces the green. The Congregational Church is directly across the way from it on the other side of the green.

The winters were long and cold and dark set in early. My mother used to read aloud to us—usually *Grimms' Fairy Tales* and Andersen's. Her voice transported us out of that bleak environment into a world of magic, filled with animals who talked, wicked stepmothers, enchanted princesses, dwarves, lost children. Of all these stories my favorite was "The Ugly Duckling"—the story of the drab, rejected misfit who discovers that she is a swan, "the most beautiful of all beautiful birds."

Maternal grandmother, Anna Houston James

I became a full-fledged reader when someone gave me *Little Women* and I discovered Jo March, the tomboy, the misfit, the impatient quick-tempered would-be writer. I felt as though she were part of me and I was part of her despite the fact that she was white and I was black. Occasionally she "felt rumpled up in her mind" and so did I. Sometimes she said things like "I wish I was a horse. Then I could run for miles in this splendid air, and not lose my breath." And so did I.

I was eleven years old when I read Wilkie Collins's *Moonstone*—that intricately plotted story about the theft of an enormous yellow diamond (the moonstone) from the head of an idol known as the moon-god. This occurred in India in 1799. The search for the stolen diamond takes place in England in the mid-nineteenth century. It involves faithful servants, inept aristocrats, a clairvoyant child, Indian jugglers and, of course, the great Sergeant Cuff: "When it comes to unravelling a mystery there isn't the equal in England of Sergeant Cuff." There still isn't.

The Moonstone served as my introduction to the world of books written for adults and it turned me into an omnivorous reader.

My writing has, of course, been influenced by the books I've read but it has been much more influenced

Maternal grandfather, Willis Samuel James
(rare photograph)

That is not what my grandfather Willis Samuel James sang to his children as he dandled them on his knee. He came out of Virginia as a runaway slave, just ahead of the white men who patrolled the road leading north. The slaves called them Patterrollers. This is what he sang:

> Run, little baby, run
> or patterrollers
> goin' come,
> run, little baby, run.

My grandfather's little nursery song is the first bit of evidence of my tenuous, unsubstantial connection with New England.

And next is the town in which I was born. The Congregational Church is still diagonally across the street from the building that houses the drugstore, a picture-postcard of a church, painted white, New England architecture in its purest and most elegant form.

My father opened a drugstore in this picture-postcard of a town in 1902, just beyond the turn of the century. Two days later a small white man came

by the circumstances of my birth and my growing up, by my family.

My maternal grandfather, Willis Samuel James, was a runaway slave. He escaped from a plantation in Virginia shortly before the Civil War. He came north via the Underground Railroad and settled in Hartford.

The difference between me and most third and fourth generation New Englanders can best be illustrated, most vividly illustrated, by the recitation of two very different nursery rhymes.

If your grandfather was descended from people who came from Great Britain, the chances are good that he sang "Ride a Cockhorse" to his children as he dandled them on his knee (dictionary definition of the word dandle is: "to move a small child up and down on the knee or foot").

Your grandfather probably sang:

> Ride a cockhorse to Banbury Cross
> to see a fine lady
> upon a white horse
> rings on her fingers and
> bells on her toes
> She shall have music
> wherever she goes.

Father, Peter Clark Lane, Jr.: "I'll be back"

into his store and said, "I come in here to bring you a message. They don't want no black druggist in this town. If you ain't gone by to-morrow night they're going to run you out of town, run you right out of here."

My father said, "What?"

And the little man repeated the message.

My father grabbed the little man by the throat and shook him and shouted at him, talking faster and faster, saying,

"You brought a message? You take a message back. You tell *them* that I close my store every night at nine o'clock and I walk down this street alone to the house where I live at the corner of Maple Avenue. And as soon as my wife gets here I'm going to be living in this building. Meantime any night *they* think *they* can run me out of town tell 'em to try. Mebbe they can run me out of here. But you tell *them* that I come from Madagascar and we slit throats. We're stranglers. If I have to leave here I'll be back. And I'm going to bring my great-grandfather, and my grandfather, and my father, and my ten brothers with me. And this damn town will never look the same again."

Almost all old buildings in New England have what are known as coffin doors—they are extraordinarily wide in order to permit the passage of a coffin being carried by pallbearers. There is a door like that in the house where I live at the present time. There is a door like that in the building that houses the drugstore that belonged first to my father and then to one of my aunts.

My father threw the little man out through the coffin door of the drugstore, tossing him back and forth and up and down before he threw him outside to the street. The little man must have delivered my father's message because nobody ever threatened him again.

I was four years old when I entered the first grade in the elementary school in Old Saybrook. There wasn't a kindergarten, and my sister, who was six, was going to school, and I insisted on going, too. And my father said, "Oh, let her go, they'll send her home when they find out how old she is." But they didn't. Nobody ever asked for our birth certificates.

My mother took us to school on that first day. We wore our hair in pigtails, and there were new bows tied on the pigtails, and we had new dresses and new shoes.

On our way home from school ten- and twelve-year-old boys threw stones at us and called us names, using the kind of profanity that their parents used when angry. This was the vocabulary of the barnyard and the stables and the docks and the wharves, for these young attackers were the offspring of farmers

and fishermen. We ran and ran and ran. They followed us, pausing now and then to arm themselves with more small stones, stones that they picked up from the side of the road.

When we arrived home disheveled, crying, we said we were never going to school again. But my mother and father said yes, we were. And that we would be fine, no one would ever attack us again.

And so—the next morning my mother walked to school with us. Nothing happened. She assured us that we could come home alone safely. We didn't quite believe her.

Sure enough, as soon as we were out of sight of the school the same boys started to stone us. Two of our uncles appeared, quite suddenly, and started knocking the attackers down—some of them they held and knocked their heads together, as they threatened them with sudden and violent death. After that we walked home from school without incident.

Years and years afterwards, I wrote a short story, "Doby's Gone" (*Miss Muriel and Other Stories*, 1971), in which a small black girl is attacked by her white classmates. The action takes place in a small town in New England, and it begins on the first day of school.

This story is in a way another expression of the outrage that has stayed with me all these years. To paraphrase a sentence from one of James Baldwin's great essays, this sense of outrage stayed with me, "indivisible from me forever, part of the passion that drives me."

When I began this piece I referred to this town in which I was born as a picture-postcard kind of town, the typical New England town that shows up on calendars. The reality is something different. There is an ancient burying ground in the town, said to be the oldest cemetery in the state of Connecticut. Way in the back of the cemetery, so far back it is almost in a swamp, there is a gravestone erected to the memory of Rose Jackson, "a colored woman." There was no other gravestone anywhere near this one. It is the nineteenth-century equivalent of the back of the bus. And it is not only segregated but the stone is standing, so to speak, the wrong way round. The other stones face towards the front of the cemetery; Sister Rose Jackson's gravestone faces towards the rear.

Every time I have looked at this stone I think about that spiritual "On That Great Gittin' Up Mornin' I'll Be There." Well, come the Day of Judgement I am certain that Sister Rose Jackson will be there with all the other risen souls. But Sister Rose Jackson, "a colored woman," will be standing alone and she will be facing the swamp. The other folk will be facing the main street of the town.

Obviously the small New England village in which I was born provided an essentially hostile environment for a black family. How did my family manage to survive intact in this largely all-white community? How did my parents manage to transmit to their children a feeling of self-confidence, of self-worth? And—how did I manage to become a writer?

I once figured out that black writers (authors of fiction and poetry) constitute about .000000005 percent of the American population—and that's a generous figure. There isn't a book maker or an odds taker who would have been willing to bet on my ever becoming a published writer.

But first, my family.

I don't know whether my parents stumbled on the strategy they used or whether they devised it deliberately, thoughtfully. In any event they created a warm, rich, life-sustaining environment. All birthdays were a cause for celebration, holidays were great occasions and every meal was special.

The building that housed my father's drugstore was fairly large. We lived in back of the store and on one side of it and upstairs over it. We always had relatives visiting us. They added excitement to our lives. They brought with them the aura and the customs of a very different world. They were all storytellers, spinners of yarns. So were my mother and my father.

Some of these stories had been handed down from one generation to the next, improved, embellished, embroidered. Usually there was a message in the story, a message for the young, a message that would help a young black child survive, help convince a young black child that black is truly beautiful.

I had these extraordinary uncles. They were my mother's brothers. They were, for the most part, footloose and fancy free. They had quite literally lived all over the world—in Africa, in Asia, in Europe. They had been roustabouts with circuses, seamen, pullman-car porters, longshoremen, butchers, barbers, waiters, bartenders. They had worked in factories. One of them had helped smuggle Chinese over the border between the United States and Canada.

One of them was a veteran of the Spanish-American War. I have his discharge papers: from Company E, Forty-eighth Regiment, United States Volunteer Infantry. He enlisted September 26, 1899, and he was discharged on June 20, 1901. He was made a sergeant in the U.S. Army at La Loma, Manila, Philippine Islands, March 14, 1900.

It was Uncle Bill who taught me how to drink water out of my cupped hands, and how to whistle through my teeth—a skill I lost a long time ago.

He had spent time on a chain gang in Georgia,

Uncle Fritz Morris James

sentenced to five years for being caught in a small town in Georgia after sundown.

My family received word that he was ill, seriously ill, and that it would take two thousand dollars to get him released from prison. All the members of the family contributed this money. It came from small savings accounts, out of sugar bowls, from under mattresses, out of the toes of shoes, small private hoards, sometimes hidden in the pages of books. Two thousand dollars was an enormous sum for a poor black family to raise at the turn of the century. They sent the money south by an old black preacher, who had it sewed into the lining of his coat. He paid it to the sheriff of the county where my uncle was imprisoned. I have the letter that my uncle wrote to my mother when he was finally released.

Another uncle, always referred to as an uncle by marriage, having married one of my mother's sisters, was a juggler. Not professionally. It was a hobby. He could juggle oranges and plates. He could make plates spin around on his nose. He could make cups

Uncle Bill—Willis S. James (center), sole owner of the L.J. St. Clair Tonsorial Parlor

appear and disappear, he could do the same thing with cards and coins.

He had an absolute passion for Bert Williams, the Williams of Williams and Walker, a famous black vaudevillian team. They were the authors of a memorable song called "Has Anybody Here Seen Miss Dora Dean?" and they made the cakewalk (a dance) famous and fashionable. Bert Williams was starred in the Ziegfeld Follies from 1910 until 1920. He made a great many records. I think my uncle must have owned all of them. He memorized many of the stories on these records. He used to tell them to my sister and me, reproducing the exact intonation of Bert Williams's voice. I heard these stories all during my growing up.

This uncle, the juggler, the admirer of Bert Williams, was also an expert card player. He taught me how to play whist and then bridge. He said I was his best pupil and he turned me into what is known these days in Atlantic City and Las Vegas as a card counter. He also taught me how to play those great gambling games blackjack and poker. In some other place and at some other time, he might have been a riverboat gambler. He was that good. And so was I. But I stopped playing cards when I was in my early twenties.

Almost all of the stories I heard were about survival, one way or another. The uncle who had been on the Georgia chain gang, Uncle Bill, had countless stories to tell about Ma Jones, an old black woman who ran a rooming house in Chicago. During the 1919 race riots, a mob of white men broke down the door of her house. Ma Jones stood at the top of the stairs with a shotgun in her hand pointing it down at them, and saying quietly, not shouting, "I'm goin' to kill the first one of you who puts his white feet on my stairs!"

And Uncle Bill said nobody moved. Nobody.

My father told stories about his family, too, especially about his grandfather. The old man had been a farmer in New Jersey, only they always said Jersey. He decided to sell his farm and move his family and most of his belongings to Connecticut, specifically to Hartford. So they went from New Jersey to New York, and then they boarded a boat that would take them up the Connecticut River to Hartford. He had his wife and six children with him, one of them an infant. He brought along his most-valued possessions, including six painted rush-bottomed parlor chairs, a mirror, most of their household goods, a couple of crates of ducks, and a vicious black dog. When the boat reached Hartford it went in towards the dock and then started back out again in order to straighten out and dock properly.

My great-grandfather Peter Clark Lane jumped off the boat, landed on the dock. He yelled up at his family, "Jump. All of you, jump. Grab as much as you can and you jump." He started walking up and down on the dock in an absolute fury, shouting, "Throw the baby down to me."

To the horror of the other passengers, someone threw the baby down to the old man, who caught it. And then others grabbed what they could, took these long running leaps, carrying chairs, and pots and pans, and somebody even jumped carrying the vicious dog in his arms.

The old man kept thumping the dock with his cane, walking up and down, yelling, "We paid to get here, we paid to get here, they ain't takin' us back now. We paid to get here."

My father said that the old man had the baby by the leg, swinging it back and forth as he shouted, "We paid to get here. They ain't takin' us back now."

Great-uncle Charles T. Hudson, a Civil War veteran, and his wife, Tillie

I worked this adventure into a short story, "The New Mirror," almost as my father told it. It is included in *Miss Muriel and Other Stories*.

My father told us many wonderful stories about his family: his great-aunt Hal, my great-great-aunt, was a conjure woman who sold roots and herbs in Hartford. She worked for a doctor, a perfectly legitimate doctor of medicine, but it was Great-great-aunt Hal who did most of the prescribing, and what she called "the doctoring."

And there was my great-great-great-uncle Zeke, named after Ezekiel the Old Testament Prophet—immortalized for me in that great spiritual: "Zekiel saw the wheel way up in the middle of the air, little wheel run by faith, big wheel run by the grace of God."

Great-great-great-uncle Zeke had red eyes, or so they said, and I assume that means his eyes were bloodshot. He always carried a toad in his pocket—and in certain parts of the world a toad is regarded as a symbol of witchcraft. According to my father, Uncle Zeke had mastered the art of levitation, could rise about four feet above his bed, moving in wide circles and shouting, "Watch those coattails flying."

These stories transmitted knowledge, knowledge on how to surive in a hostile environment. They were a part of my education.

As a writer, I am really the endproduct of what Reynolds Price (*A Palpable God*) calls a "powerful oral-narrative tradition. . . . A need to hear and tell stories is essential to the species—second in necessity after nourishment and before love and shelter. Millions survive without love or home, almost none in silence—the sound of story is the dominant sound of our lives."

Before I became a writer I had to grow up. Here are some of the highlights:

My father was Peter Clark Lane, Jr. (1872–1949), licensed pharmacist (1895), storyteller, tenor in the choir of the Congregational Church, fancy figure skater, expert swimmer, collector of old drug bottles, occasional gardener; he wore the highly polished shoes of a city dude. In the summer he wore bow ties and stiff straw hats, known as boaters. He had an extraordinary sense of humour. Though he was a truly accomplished swimmer he refused to swim in the waters of Long Island Sound or in the Connecticut River on the grounds that they were totally polluted, and this was at the turn of the century. He cited as proof of his theory the extraordinary number of eye, ear, nose, and throat infections that swimmers had all summer long.

Mother, Bertha James Lane

My mother was Bertha James Lane (1875–1956), chiropodist, hairdresser, licensed barber, manufacturer of hair tonic, creator of a liquid cleaner for use in the bathroom, owner and creator of a thriving business in the creation of elegant embroidered and hemstitched linens: guest towels, banquet cloths, napkins, place mats. This thriving business was called "Beautiful Linens for Beautiful Homes."

She was an expert needlewoman and hired other women to help her create this exquisite handwork. I still have some of the letters written by the women she employed. They lived on isolated farms, and often there was illness in the family. The letters almost invariably said the same thing:

"Dear Mrs. Lane: If it wasn't for you and the money you pay me for my work and I love doing it we wouldn't be alive. My husband has been sick for months now. Please send more work. . . ."

My mother was a dedicated gardener and a collector of antiques. Years before other people began to buy some of the old and rare things in the world she was buying them.

I was born October 12, 1908, in Old Saybrook, Connecticut—literally born upstairs over my father's drugstore.

My mother thought I was about to arrive on September 3 and so went up to Middlesex Hospital, which is located about twenty miles up the river in Middletown, Connecticut. She spent the day in the hospital, and was finally told that it would be four or five weeks before I would arrive. So she returned to Old Saybrook. The hospital charged her two dollars for the day. She wrote on the bill "thought Ann was coming. B.J. Lane."

She said she was so embarrassed at having misjudged the imminence of my arrival that on the morning of the twelfth of October she delayed her departure for the hospital lest she make the same mistake and arrive too early. By the time she decided that she really should get started, it was too late and I was born upstairs over the drugstore. And my father greeted my arrival into the world by saying, "Oh, good Lord! It's another girl!"

We lived in that building that housed the drugstore until I was twelve years old. Then my mother decided that she wanted a house of her own, one that had no relationship, no connection to a drugstore.

She bought a piece of land in another part of the town and had a house built on it, a house with a fireplace. I still remember vividly the day we gathered around this brand-new fireplace, my father and my mother and my sister and I, and burned the mortgage, well, symbolically of course. It was a copy of the receipted bill for the final payment on the mortgage. A cause for celebration. The house was ours, free and clear.

I have a sister, two years older than I am, Helen Lane Bush. We began school at the same time. When we reached the third grade the school tested all the youngsters. As a result of the tests my sister skipped two grades. My family told me that I didn't pass the test. As a result, I was convinced that my sister was infinitely smarter than I was.

When my father was in his late seventies I asked him about this. I said that I had never been able to understand why Helen was able to skip two grades and I couldn't. Was she really that much smarter than I was?

It was quite a few minutes before he answered. Finally he said, "Your mother told me I was never to tell you this. I don't think it matters any more. It was a long time ago. Yes, you passed the test and the school wanted to put you two grades ahead with your sister. But your mother said, No. She made quite a fuss about it. She said you were too young, that you'd probably be out of high school by the time you were twelve years old and ready to enter college at that age. And that she simply wouldn't allow."

I remember thinking, well, I suppose she was

right. But it would have been nice to have had a little more self-confidence about my mental ability all those years.

During those early years my aunt Anna Louise James (born January 19, 1886; died December 12, 1977) lived with us. She graduated from the Brooklyn College of Pharmacy in 1908, the same year that I was born, the only woman in the class, probably the first woman licensed as a pharmacist in the state of Connecticut. She opened a drugstore in Hartford, and then later came to live with us in Old Saybrook, acquiring the pharmacy that had belonged to my father. In the meantime he went to work for a wholesale druggist in Hartford.

When my aunt applied for membership in the Connecticut Pharmaceutical Association, her application was rejected because the Association did not accept females as members. I still have the letter that the Association sent saying that she was welcome to join the Auxiliary, made up of the wives of pharmacists.

She was a most remarkable woman—beautiful,

Aunt Anna Louise James, when she graduated from the Brooklyn College of Pharmacy, 1908

brilliant, compassionate. She never married. She died just a few weeks short of her ninety-second birthday. She retained her mental ability, and her physical agility all those years.

My mother and her sisters (Anna Louise James, Helen James Chisholm), were extraordinary women. They abandoned the role of housewife in the early part of the twentieth century. All three of them became successful businesswomen, financially independent.

My mother and my aunt Lou (Helen James Chisholm) handled the finances in their families. They seemed to have been born with a high degree of business acumen. Aunt Lou had been a schoolteacher, had taught in the Hawaiian Islands, lived in Boston, moved to Old Saybrook with her family, and lived next door to us. She created a highly successful correspondence course in reading and literature.

It was Aunt Lou who taught me how to sew. She was my first sewing teacher. I was determined to make my own clothes. By the time I was twelve I was terribly overweight. The only clothes sold for young fat girls in those days were navy blue surplice dresses, designed for old ladies. These dresses had a diagonal line down the front, supposed to fool the eye into believing that the person wearing this hideous garment was, well, if not thin, then really not too fat.

There was an ancient Singer sewing machine, a foot-treadle machine, in the cellar of our brand-new house and Aunt Lou showed me how to use it.

The cellar had an absolutely flawless cement floor. In the area where the sewing machine stood there was a small rug, a fairly large table, and there were brilliant overhead lights. This was where I learned to sew, to make all of my own clothes.

By the time I was fifteen I had become sufficiently expert to take on some fairly complicated jobs. I made all the draperies for the living room of a huge summer cottage. For days I was enveloped in yards and yards and yards of chintz. I became skilled enough to tailor a pair of jodhpurs for a woman who was going salmon fishing in Canada.

When I was about twelve I began to develop another skill. I taught myself to cook. My mother was never really interested in cooking. She made wonderful pies, inferior cakes. She was what is known as a good *plain* cook. But I—well I liked to eat.

So I haunted other people's kitchens, preferably the kitchens where there was an honest-to-goodness cook, who cooked for a living. I learned how to make baking-powder biscuits, fancy cakes, fancy breads, great soups and chowders and stews, wonderful salads, and salad dressings.

The author at age three with sister, Helen Lane (later Bush), Old Saybrook, Connecticut, 1911

I became a first-class cook and something of an entrepreneur. I used to make pound cakes and sell them. I had a standing order for six pound cakes every week.

I was also the family laundress. I can remember following the instructions on how to iron and fold men's shirts, instructions that I found in a U.S. Department of Agriculture government bulletin.

I kept a diary, largely a report on the weather: it was cold, it was hot, it rained, it snowed. Each entry began with the same two words: "Rose early."

My parents truly believed that early to bed, early to rise would make *any person* healthy, wealthy, and wise. They had two daughters, so they did not say this would make a *man* healthy, wealthy, and wise but that it would have this effect on *any person*. So we rose at 6:00 A.M., went to bed promptly at 10:00 P.M. as regularly as clockwork.

All during this period I was, of course, going to school. For the most part I enjoyed it. I had some interesting teachers. One of them was Miss Chloe Whittlesey. She taught the third grade. She was eighty years old—and would not be permitted to teach in a public school these days at that age. The school systems are the poorer for the lack of the Miss Whittleseys of the world.

It was Miss Whittlesey who taught me how to tell time. She was shocked when she discovered that I couldn't tell time. Even now I can hear her voice when she said, "Child, you are now in the third grade. And you can't tell time? You sit right down here."

I sat down by her desk and tried to explain that I'd never found it necessary to learn how to tell time. There was always someone around who could tell me what time it was.

Her response was, "One of these days there might not be someone around—"

She took out of a desk drawer a huge gold watch, the kind generally referred to as a turnip. It was the kind of watch that a man carried in his vest pocket; it even had a heavy gold chain attached. It had probably belonged to Miss Whittlesey's father. She taught me to tell time in about three minutes or less. She said, "It is better to learn to do things for yourself, and that way you will never be dependent on other people to do things for you."

There was Miss Whittlesey in the third grade. And then there was Harold White, one of my English teachers, in high school. To this day when I pass a

Ann at age eight, standing on the steps of her father's drugstore, Old Saybrook, Connecticut, 1920

birch tree I think of Robert Frost's poem and wonder if "Some boy's been swinging it."

It was Harold White who made me love poetry. If the weather was foul (heavy rain or a snowstorm) or we finished class a few minutes early, he read poetry to us. He didn't discuss the poems. He read them out loud and he read beautifully. This happened once or twice a week. Most of the students in his classes grew to love and appreciate poetry because of him; they came to admire Robert Frost.

Another interesting teacher was a woman named Gertrude Avery. I did not like Miss Avery. Miss Avery did not like me. I was the kind of student who read the whole book in one evening, when we were supposed to read one chapter at a time. I usually twiddled my thumbs in class or thought up ways in which I could disrupt the class.

The day came, finally, when we were to have an end-of-the-term examination in English. Miss Avery included in the exam the kind of question that makes students groan and rack their brains and sometimes just give up in despair. It is known usually as an "unfair" question because there is no *right* answer and there is no *wrong* answer.

Her class was held on the top floor of an old wooden school building. It was the smallest, darkest, dingiest room in the building. Only one window.

Miss Avery pointed out that there were five questions on the exam but one of the questions counted for more than any of the others. If you failed it you wouldn't pass the exam.

We had been reading *A Tale of Two Cities*. The important part of the exam was to write an imaginary scene between Jerry Cruncher, the grave digger, and his wife. It had to be at least two pages long.

The answer required an act of the imagination. Something stimulated mine—perhaps because it was such a dark dreadful little room, perhaps it was the lack of rapport between me and Miss Avery, perhaps it was the weather—it was a cold rainy day, wind from the northeast—anyway I let my imagination take over and I made up a scene between Jerry Cruncher and his poor wife. I called on them when they weren't expecting me—it was a very realistic scene.

I handed in my paper on a Friday afternoon, and then forgot all about it until the following Monday when it was time for the English class. I thought, well, she doesn't like me anyway, and I can't imagine what she's going to say when she reads that stuff I wrote. To my very great surprise she read it to the class and she said, with I can not tell you what astonishment in her voice, "I never make predictions, but I honestly believe that you could be a writer if you wanted to."

My life did not change—I did not then and there decide that I wanted to be a writer. Life went on as usual. I worked in the drugstore after school and on weekends. I sewed and I cooked and when I was sixteen I learned how to drive a car.

My sister graduated from high school and was accepted at Pembroke, the women's college at Brown University. My mother accompanied her to Providence. They went by train.

It was truly a great event. The whole family celebrated the acceptance of a member of this family by one of the East's prestigious colleges. My mother said that when they arrived at the office of the Registrar, there seemed to be a great deal of scurrying around, movement, whispers. They were told to wait. And after about a half hour they were ushered into the office of the Dean of Women. She told my mother that Pembroke did not accept young black women in its dormitories, that my sister could live with a "nice colored family" that took in students as roomers.

My mother called my father and asked him what she should do. She said there was a pause, a silence, and then finally he said, "We've come a long way. We're not going to turn back now. If the people who run this rooming house seem like respectable people, well then she stays. You'll have to go and see for yourself."

I thought he sounded much like my great-grandfather: "They ain't takin' us back now. We paid to get here."

My father had said the same thing to the little man who had told him "they" didn't want a black druggist in the town: "Sure. Mebbe they'll be able to run me out of town. But I'll be back."

My sister lived with a "nice colored family" in Providence. She graduated from Brown University in 1928.

I was still in high school when she entered Brown. It was during that period that my writing career really started. I was paid five dollars for a slogan that I created for a perfume company. This came as a revelation—I could actually be paid for putting words on paper.

And so I began writing stories and plays. A couple of years after I finished high school I entered pharmacy school. No one pushed me towards a career in pharmacy. In fact my family seemed surprised.

After I graduated from the Connecticut College of Pharmacy (now the School of Pharmacy at the University of Connecticut) in New Haven, I worked in the family drugstores, for by then we had two stores—one in Old Saybrook and one in Old Lyme.

My sister and I used to drive up to Hartford to

visit friends of the family. And it was on one of those visits that I met George Petry, who came from New Iberia, Louisiana. A couple of years later we were married in my mother's house, standing in front of that fireplace where the family had symbolically burned the mortgage all those years ago. We were married on February 28, 1938.

During the ceremony and for awhile afterwards all the gentlemen and some of the ladies cried. Later, on the train heading for New York, George said, "Tell me what went wrong? What was the trouble? Why were they all crying? Was it something that I did?"

I said, "No, no, no. They were crying for the loss of all those hot muffins, blackberry turnovers, pound cakes, frayed shirt collars turned, buttonholes reinforced, trousers shortened, shirts beautifully laundered—all those items were going right out the front door with you—and they were mourning their loss."

We lived in New York City for about nine years. I decided that I did not want to work as a pharmacist, that I would seek and find jobs that were somehow related to writing. Here's the time table:

1938–41—worked for the *Amsterdam News*—a Harlem weekly—sold space for the advertising department

1941–44—worked for the *People's Voice*—a weekly published by Adam Clayton Powell, Jr.—edited the women's pages, covered general news

While I lived in Old Saybrook, I had kept writing short stories and receiving rejection slips. I can remember my aunt (the drugstore aunt) saying as she handed me two bulky envelopes of material that were being returned, "Oh! here are more chickens come home to roost. And all that postage—wasted, simply wasted."

I did finally sell a short story. The *Afro-American*, a weekly newspaper published in Baltimore, sent me a check for five dollars for a story entitled "Marie of the Cabin Club." The story was published August 19, 1939. I was tempted to frame the check but I didn't.

I kept on writing and collecting rejection slips. I began reading the autobiographies of writers. One of them was Arthur Train's *My Day in Court*. He said that if he were a young unpublished writer he would enroll in Mabel Louise Robinson's Workshop Course at Columbia University. And I did. It was a great experience. She made me believe in myself. She said, "You have all the necessary qualifications: imagina-

Ann Petry in the garden of Mr. and Mrs. J. Louis von der Mehden, Old Saybrook, Connecticut, 1939

tion, command of the language. Whether or not you become a writer is entirely up to you. Plough to the end of the furrow."

The *Crisis* (official organ of the National Association for the Advancement of Colored People— NAACP) paid twenty dollars for a short story of mine: "On Saturday the Siren Sounds at Noon."

An editor at Houghton Mifflin Company in Boston saw the story and wrote to me, asking if I was working on a novel, and if I was would I be interested in applying for one of their Literary Fellowships. I said no, I wasn't, but perhaps by the following year I would be.

In the meantime my husband was drafted, I lost my job, the *People's Voice* was about to fold up. I decided that I would spend a year working on a novel and other things and during that year I would work only for myself or at jobs that didn't require too much intellectual effort.

So—I took a part-time job as a typist for which I received thirty-five dollars a week. I received a fifty-dollar allotment check every month from my husband. I knew I had to have a nest egg—an emergency fund.

I spent three weeks working practically day and night creating the advertising copy for a catalogue for a manufacturer of hair pieces: wigs, beards, moustaches, eyebrows, toupees. The manufacturer was so pleased (I made all of his hair pieces sound highly desirable) that he wanted me to work for him exclusively. He paid a huge sum for the work on his catalogue—it was a *big* catalogue. Whenever I see anyone wearing a wig I have to suppress an impulse to lift my hand in salute—because wigs helped subsidize my writing career. I had my nest egg.

I decided that if I lived as frugally as possible I would be able to pay the rent and buy food. I would have to develop a life-style that was simple, inexpensive.

I began my first novel, writing every day from 9:00 A.M. to noon, and then stopping for an hour for lunch and writing from 1:00 P.M. to 2:30 or 3:00 P.M. Every day.

As to the actual writing of the book *The Street*—I had finished it and the first chapter still consisted of one page—and that was all. When I originally wrote that first chapter I wrote it directly on the typewriter and I did not change anything in it. That was unusual because I always make a first draft in longhand and then type the second draft on manila and then make a final draft. This method of composition gives me an opportunity to revise each one of these versions.

In the first chapter, Lutie Johnson, the protagonist, encounters right then and there, from the word go, the people who will affect her destiny: the Super, Min, and Mrs. Hedges. It contains a kind of warning, a hint of disaster: "Even with the wind twisting the sign away from her, she could see that it had been there for a long time because its original coat of white paint was streaked with rust where years of rain and snow had finally eaten the paint away—down to the metal and the metal had slowly rusted making a dark red stain like blood."

That first chapter is about as good as a first chapter can be. I went over the book, not that chapter, but the rest of it, over and over and over again, simplifying it, testing the dialogue, the descriptions of people and places. I put all of my feelings, my sense of outrage into the book. I tried to include the sounds and the smells and the sights of Harlem. I wanted a book that was like an explosion inside the head of the reader, a book that you couldn't put down once you'd started reading it. I tried to create a vivid sense of place.

I tried to do the same thing in a long short story called "In Darkness and Confusion." It is based on the Harlem riots. I can remember walking through 125th Street when the street was filled with the shattered glass from store windows. It made a scrunching sound. I can still hear it.

In December 1944, I entered *The Street* in the Houghton Mifflin Fellowship Contest. I submitted five chapters of the novel, a complete synopsis, and two letters of recommendation. I won. To my absolute astonishment, I won.

The Street was published in 1946. In those days a 436 page book, hardcover, sold for $2.50. It sold over 1,500,000 copies in hardcover and paperback. It received great reviews. I became famous, a celebrity, almost over night.

The sad and terrible truth about *The Street* is that now forty-one years later I could write that same book about Harlem or any other ghetto. Because life hasn't changed that much for black people.

Here are some statistics:

New York Times (Connecticut Weekly section), August 18, 1985: " . . . black children are three times more likely to be poor than whites. Most are the children of single mothers. They live in the cities and in the countryside."

New York Times, September 7, 1985:

Bertha J. Lane holding her first granddaughter, Anna Bush

" . . . half the black children [in the United States] under six are poor."

New York Times (editorial), June 30, 1985: " . . . black children now twice as likely as white children to die before their first birthday, three times as likely to be poor, four times as likely to be living in a foster home, and five times as likely to live on welfare. . . ." (Based on a study by the Children's Defense Fund).

After the publication of *The Street* I began to feel as though I were public property. I was beleaguered by all the hoopla, the interviews, the invitations to speak. I decided that as soon as my husband was discharged from the Army we would start looking for another place to live, a place where we would once again have some measure of privacy. We finally bought a house in Old Saybrook, Connecticut—an old house built about 1790, a house with great "vibes."

I have been writing ever since *The Street* was published.

Like most writers I intermingle fact and fiction. I have used a drugstore as the locale in the novel *Country Place.* The druggist could have been based on

Father in front of the drugstore, Old Saybrook, Connecticut

my father, except that my father was not white, and he was an infinitely kinder man than "Doc." Some of the short stories and novels are laid in small New England towns. *The Narrows* is laid in a medium-sized city, supposedly in New York state, but somehow its flavour is New England. Sometimes I have used Harlem as the background.

I have occasionally used an incident that actually happened as the germ, the starting point, or the climax of a short story. "The Witness" is based on the fact that I did once know a Congregational minister who wore his hair in a crewcut, that very short, almost brushlike cut, when most males, young and old, were wearing their hair quite long.

He told me about his experience with a group of sixteen-year-old boys. There were six of them. They came to his office once a week for religious instruction—as an alternative to reform school. He said these were the children of middle-class parents and that he seemed utterly unable to reach them. Furthermore they made him feel uncomfortable for they simply sat and stared at him. They refused to respond in any way. He said it was a most unpleasant ordeal. Then one night as they were leaving his office, one of them patted him on the head and said, "Don't sweat it, Doc."

I felt impelled to use this situation in a story—it took me about six months to work it out.

Miss Doris in *The Narrows* is based on a friend of mine. She did really look as though she had been hewn out of rock or as though she had been created out of iron. The stories that Miss Doris tells in the novel are hers, with a little editing here and there from me. She used to call her husband "Sugar."

The love story in *The Narrows,* between Link Williams who is black and Camilo Treadway who is white, troubles many people. The reason that some readers refuse to accept the idea that this was truly a love affair is simply that racism, especially as it manifests itself in reactions to miscegenation, is "so deeply imbedded in American society, in its laws, in its social structures" (James Baldwin) that it is impossible for most readers, reviewers, critics to look at Link Williams squarely, forthrightly, head on, and recognize him for the three-dimensional, fully-realized, compelling figure that he is and to recognize the reality and the validity of his love affair with Camilo.

I have an absolute passion for motion pictures— I'm addicted to them—good ones, bad ones, indifferent ones. I still remember how I felt about the first movie that I saw. We lived in a small town and once a week there was a movie shown in the Town Hall. When Link Williams sees his first movie at the age of eight I endowed him with my reaction to the sight of an exciting new world:

> I went in the Emporium and it was daylight when I went in. When I came out it was dark. It confused me because I thought time should have come to a stop while the movie was being shown. I kept thinking that somehow I had been leading a double life, my own life . . . and another far more exciting life. The fact that it got dark while I was in the world that was the movie made the whole thing very strange. . . . I never quite got over it.

I still haven't.

I don't think that New England had any particular influence on my writing. Though I was born in this area I am not a New Englander. I have been influenced by Thoreau. His account of his life on Walden Pond made me realize how superficial and unimportant most of the trappings were with which I had surrounded myself. Before I began writing *The Street* I studied *Walden* and made notes: " . . . Beware of all enterprizes that require new clothes . . . water is the only drink for a wise

person . . . the swiftest traveller goes on foot . . . a taste for the beautiful is most cultivated out of doors, where there is no house and no housekeeper. . . ."

And finally and most beautifully: "The true harvest of my daily life is somewhat as intangible and indescribable as the tints of morning or evening. It is a little star-dust caught, a segment of the rainbow which I have clutched."

We were all of us, in my family, influenced by that old New England dictum: use it up, wear it out, make it do, or do without. And I still am. In that sense, I suppose I am a New Englander though there must be other parts of the United States where being thrifty and frugal are regarded as virtues.

While I lived in New York I did many other things besides writing for newspapers and writing short stories that were always being rejected. I studied painting and drawing at the Harlem Art Center. I joined the American Negro Theatre which was housed in the 135th Street branch of the New York Public Library. I acted in a comedy, *Striver's Row*, by Abe Hill.

The courses at the Harlem Art Center taught me to look at objects—people, landscapes, everything—

Daughter, Liz—Elisabeth Ann Petry

Stan Gilbert, the groom, 1984

with great care. Acting didn't really interest me—but what did interest me was to experience firsthand the way in which the dialogue in a play furthered the action.

Dollie Lowther Robinson, a great friend of mine, and I created a consumer's group in Harlem, composed of women; its object: help women get their money's worth for everything from hats to groceries to furniture. It was called Negro Women Incorporated—a name that someone once said is arrogantly all-encompassing.

And there was more. I took piano lessons. I took an advanced course in tailoring. I taught an elementary course in writing business letters at the Harlem branch of the YWCA.

In between all of this activity I kept writing. I still am. My most recently published short story is "The Moses Project." It was published in the *Harbor Review* #5/6, 1986—published by the English Department, University of Massachusetts/Boston.

Along the way I've had various honors bestowed upon me: two that I cherish: an honorary Doctor of Letters from Suffolk University in 1983; and a Citation from the City of Philadelphia signed by the Mayor—W. Wilson Goode—on April 9, 1985.

Quite often people ask me when I began to write. I don't know. I'll quote Isaac Singer, the writer. When someone asked him when he began to write he said: "When I was born my mother asked the midwife, 'Is it a boy or a girl?' And the midwife said, 'Neither. It's a writer.' "

Perhaps that was true of me. On the other hand all those great teachers that I had influenced me: Chloe Whittlesey, who said learn to do things for yourself; and Harold White, who introduced poetry into my life; and Gertrude Avery, who said I think you could be a writer if you wanted to. And Mabel Louise Robinson in 1941: "You are bound to make a success of fiction. Your experience, your wisdom about people, your judgement in the use of the English language, are a combination which amounts to a gift."

Speaking of gifts—probably the greatest gift that my husband and I have had bestowed upon us was the birth of a child, a daughter, our only child—Elisabeth Petry Gilbert. She is an attorney practising in Philadelphia—she is beautiful in body, mind, and spirit—our greatest, most important creation.

When I began writing this I said that I was an outsider, a maverick, not a member of the club. The reason is that I am my grandfather, a runaway slave heading north, running away from a plantation in Virginia. I am my father, a young man, opening a

Liz and George Petry: the bride and the father of the bride, 1984

drugstore in a New England village, being told, "We'll run you out of town, don't want no black druggist in this town." I am my sister, brilliant, beautiful, graduating from high school at the top of her class, accepted at Brown University in 1928, arriving in Providence with my mother only to be told that Brown, that great New England college, does not permit black students, male or female, to stay in its dormitories. I am a conjure woman. I am my great-grandfather, "You can't take us back now, we paid to get here." I am Rose Jackson, "a colored woman," buried the wrong way round near the swamp at the back of that ancient burying ground in Old Saybrook.

I am old Ma Jones, armed with a shotgun, standing at the head of her stairs, South Side of Chicago, looking down at a mob of white men who have broken down her front door, saying quietly, "I am going to shoot to kill the first one of you who sets his white feet on my stairs."

I am my great-uncle Charles Hudson of the New York Cavalry. I have been on a chain gang in Georgia,

"Liz and I at the airport," 1975

caught in one of those towns where it was a crime for a black man to linger after sunset. My family used their small savings to buy me out.

A New Englander? No. I am all of those people. And I am a writer.

Above all I am a survivor "born in the U.S.A."

BIBLIOGRAPHY

Fiction:

The Street. Boston: Houghton, 1946; London: M. Joseph, 1947.

Country Place. Boston: Houghton, 1947; London: M. Joseph, 1948.

The Narrows. Boston: Houghton, 1953; London: Gollancz, 1954.

Miss Muriel and Other Stories. Boston: Houghton, 1971.

Juvenile:

The Drugstore Cat (illustrated by Susanne Suba). New York: Crowell, 1949.

Harriet Tubman: Conductor on the Underground Railroad. New York: Crowell, 1955; also published as *The Girl Called Moses: The Story of Harriet Tubman* (illustrated by Judith Valentine). London: Methuen, 1960.

Tituba of Salem Village. New York: Crowell, 1964.

Legends of the Saints (illustrated by Anne Rockwell). New York: Crowell, 1970.

M. L. Rosenthal

1917-

NOTES TOWARD AN UNAUTHORIZED AUTOBIOGRAPHY

M.L. Rosenthal, 1978

I

14 March 1987

I'm seventy today! The Biblical prophecy's half right! From now on it's sheer gravy! I'm in position to bet against the odds.

As for the past, I agree: One ought to have learned *something*—not just that things do change and people do die. But what? How am I to sort things out when everything that comes to mind at once becomes, by that very token, important? (I.e., "important.")

Everything. My father bought me (age 3 ½–4 ½) a marvelous tricycle. Later, after my mother had borne me off elsewhere, I would spend my holidays with him; but the tricycle had disappeared, never again to be seen. Why?—seeing that he was a most indulgent father?

Everything: the first conscious sight and touch of snow; the smell of earth and grass when one's scarcely more than a few inches above the ground; finding a prize in a Crackerjack box for the first time, while watching an amateur production of *The Drunkard* (what a vile brute he was to his wife and children!) with my parents in Brentwood, Maryland, whence my mother and I departed, one strange and fatal day, not long afterward.

Was that departure a "good thing" for me? I'll confess I didn't think so then. Yet I had a happy childhood, or so it now seems despite what Hart Crane called "the curse of sundered parentage"; for indeed the separation remained a constant aching reality. I was five. I thought to persuade my parents it was only logical to come together again. And when my mother remarried, I tried to persuade my new stepfather that there was no reason why all four of us couldn't be loving inmates of the same household.

We were now in Woodbridge, Connecticut, just outside New Haven. Those were long country days after interminable travels and visits with friends, in one city after another. I entered first grade in a small, friendly school. I must have seemed strange: a curious little Jewish newcomer (the only non-Christian child there) who had been reading since the age of four and who loved games and running races and the tiny bottles of milk served at recess and the Eskimo Pies sometimes given us as well. Aching heart or not, how ready I was to be happy!

I'm curious (is it too self-indulgent?) about that little newcomer. Devoted to both parents as he was, and for good reason, he early grew accustomed to "seeing both sides" of things, not without guilt at "betraying" both at the same time. Did he have any sort of Yiddish accent in those days? I'm sure he must have done. His parents were left-wing (*Poale-*) Zionists, and saturated with a religious background both undogmatic and morally powerful; all decisions and relationships were deeply considered, however carefree and spontaneous they might seem. The father retreated into orthodoxy as he aged, especially after his late second marriage. The mother held to her vulnerable moral independence, shaken by her own daring, full of self-reproach and doubts yet staunchly her own person, anyone's equal, self-educating, too much given to sacrifice, with a genius for friendship and love.

271

Those two immigrants, with relatively little formal education, yet were possessed of knowledge and much-pondered memory and enlightened concern. The father, gentle, a bit passive, stubborn, fond, could not at last cope with the mother's more turbulent energy. But he retained, without insistence, his little son's loyalty despite the extroverted confidence, and kindness, of the stepfather. So of course the outsider, the stepfather anxious to show and receive affection, was only guardedly accepted. His keen mind and fiery hatred of oppression were striking and endearing but bordered on ideological intolerance. The boy, more like his own parents, learned much from this man and from the experiences of a company of sad dreamers unknown to most Americans.

To what avail? A child of loving parents divorced from one another—a boy, that is, with a natural father and a good stepfather who is nonetheless alien to him—is an exiled prince, honored within his generously large confinement. His circumstances are to him baffling, irrational. But he is a child, running, playing, falling asleep sometimes in his stepfather's arms, impressed by the man's certainties and bohemian flair yet holding himself apart. He learns the humanity of the unacceptable, if mainly to justify his beautiful mother. Later, whenever he hears any vehement dogmatic assertion, he is seized with annoyance. Sorrow seems natural; anger, merely chaotic.

Surely, on one's seventieth birthday, complacency is in order? Well—on one count perhaps. There was, after all, freedom from the ordinary tyranny of family, from the sense that there is only one way of life. And that freedom, despite necessary sorrow, has been a perpetual emotional gyroscope for me.

II

The drama of ordinary life: I was born in Washington, D.C., and taken fairly quickly to nearby Mount Rainier and Brentwood, Maryland. In Brentwood I entered kindergarten and—to quote Hart Crane again—I "quickly fled." That is, I walked home at recess-time the same morning, satisfied I had experienced "school" for what it was worth and that was that. Some thirty-two years later, my younger son, Alan, was to go through the same thwarted realization, stopping on his midmorning return homeward to join a funeral throng outside a Catholic church. A good neighbor recognized him and led him home, whence his mother forthwith—amidst kisses and admonitions—drew him back to "shades of the prison house" to resume his education. So it was with

The author as a young boy, 1923

me. Guided back to kindergarten by my mother, and carrying the congratulatory orange-tinted marshmallow bunny she had been saving to greet me with after my triumphant return at the end of the school day, I was then and there initiated into the larger madness of things. I couldn't even divide the bunny with my classmates. It simply disappeared into the world's storehouse of lost childhood possessions and hopes, like the tricycle, and the trip to the circus that never happened, and the restoration of the Eden I had shared with my parents.

A flurry of sorts in New York City, about which I remember nothing save a day (hour? minute?) in Washington Square Park, a scene held with such photographic brilliance and precision in memory that when I next saw it after more than a score of years I reentered that eternally fixed and prolonged childhood moment. The memory has the vividness of the powerful images or visions that have always appeared to me, intensely real and "recognized" in color, form, and detail, but that I can rarely trace to actual experience.

And then—the tranquility of Woodbridge: a pet turtle; fishing with a bent pin from the aforesaid small "wood bridge"; the dirt road rising into the hillside;

West Rock, where "Judges' Cave" (hiding place of regicide judges protected and fed by local farmers) is still, I should hope, commemorated; the marsh at the foot of the hill where I first found water lilies; the small, hospitable, tomato-fragrant farms all along the road; the Italian farmers scattered here and there with their scrappy little sons who taught me that "Jew" was an insult and that the price of friendship was an obligatory fight. Thither we were brought after the long blurred interval by my stepfather. And there my half-brother Danny came into being, at first sickly but thereafter a sturdy, clever, endearing child.

Woodbridge I remember as an idyll, a time of special contentment. My stepfather, a house painter, worked in New Haven. Very early on, he began bringing me books (among them the entrancing one I knew simply as "the King Arthur stories"—probably Howard Pyle's version) from a library near the trolley line he rode to and from the city. Our grown-up friends were a volatile crew of laborers and their wives, intellectually and politically vivacious people and avid readers. Among them were Yiddish poets and an occasional artist. They were skilled workmen of one sort or another, and I would listen, enthralled by their passionate speech, to their discussions during their improvised "banquets." A group would suddenly arrive, laden with bags filled with corned beef, pickles, rye bread, and so on. There would be a noisy downing of tiny glasses of *schnapps* (one drink for each), accompanied by an exuberant "*l'chaim!*" and, perhaps, some woman's laughing shout: "Look! I'm getting drunk!" But for the rest of the evening it was simply tea and sandwiches and ardent talk. Often the visitors would bring their children, and we would alternate playing games with listening to our elders, sometimes asking questions or even offering a squeaky opinion that was invariably greeted with fond laughter and congratulations.

In the winter, if there was a sudden snow, I would trudge the half mile or so to the end of the trolley line to meet my stepfather and give him his galoshes. When we returned home, I would warm my feet in the huge wood-stove provided by our land-lord, Mr. Laudano, who dwelt downstairs. The house we'd lived in previously belonged to Mr. Pipi, whose name gave us a certain innocent pleasure. Like many other small landowners in that part of Woodbridge, he was a truck farmer who worked his land in the manner of the *Mezzogiorno*. But the dairy farmers thereabouts were of New England stock. For all I know, they didn't particularly care for immigrant newcomers; but when I carried a small milk-can to the Warners' house for fresh warm milk straight from the source, they were exceedingly welcoming.

Two or three years ago I revisited Woodbridge after doing some work at the Yale library—not unlike my stepfather, who was once employed painting some Yale buildings. Mr. Laudano's house, and the little wooden bridge, and the small farms along the road, and the dirt road itself were all gone: a world of organic soil for human continuities obliterated by an "industrial park." Only my childhood body-sense of the earth's contours there under the concrete made the little necropolis of memories at all familiar.

All over the country America's forgotten history lies buried in eternal anonymity under concrete resurfacings and the official memoirs and documents of important persons.

I could return in memory to Woodbridge and live there forever. It seems to me the matrix both of my dream-life and my education in the world's larger realities. My first fight, for example: over a difference of opinion. I had told some boys I was playing with that I'd been born in Washington, D. C., and that it was the capital of the United States. I was called a liar. *Hartford* was the capital. I admit that at the time I didn't yet know that Hartford existed, let alone that it was the capital of Connecticut. An infuriated little demon punched me on the ear—very painful; and as he seemed about to repeat the punch I imitated what he had done and gave him pause long enough for an older boy to step between us. From another playmate I learned that I was a dirty Jew, and that the Jews had killed Christ. I relayed the news to my mother, who seemed to have heard it already. She explained who Christ was supposed to have been and that he had been crucified, if we were to believe the New Testament, by Roman soldiers: the ancestors, as it were, of the modern Italians.

With the natural gracious impulse that has always been with me to clarify things I do not quite understand to people who probably know even less, I hastened to explain all this to the child who had first instructed me. The result was my second fight, which lasted longer and ended just as inconclusively. We then shook hands and more or less forgot the terms of the quarrel. That never happened in the Polish neighborhood we lived in later on for a while, in Passaic, New Jersey, where being Jewish was unalterably wicked and there were no handshakes after the almost daily fights thrust upon me. But in Wood-bridge things were different. Italian children seemed less principled in their observance of anti-Semitic dogma.

Jobs became scarce in the New Haven area, and so we moved on after the fourth grade to Passaic, and thence to Newark, and thence to Boston, and thence to Cleveland, and thence to Chicago. We were

Mother Ethel Rosenthal, née Brown (seated), with paternal aunt, 1916

barest furnishings; Van Gogh's paintings of peasant interiors will give you the idea, except that the flat had bookcases and piles of newspapers in strategic places. And we had neither telephone nor radio anywhere we lived (strange even to imagine now) but never seemed to miss them. We didn't feel deprived, though. Maxie's house seemed to me a cluttered palace; and the meals his father and mother, who addressed me as "Einstein," forced upon me seemed wantonly sumptuous.

Summers and at Christmas break I would be put on a train to visit my father in Washington. *He* was hardly wealthy either, but he was neither bohemian nor proletarian. He boarded with friends in a middle-class home, with sturdy furnishings, a dining room, regular mealtimes, a radio *and* a telephone (of course), sets of *The Book of Knowledge* and *The Harvard Classics,* and separate rooms for their children. They went to bed at decent times, dressed nicely, and owned, respectively, a successful tailor shop and a successful beauty parlor. They never bought groceries on credit from a poor devil almost as strapped as his customers. They had *meat* whenever they wished. And suddenly I would be dropped into their midst from a world in which cream, or pot roast, or going to

certainly extremely poor. My mother occasionally took menial jobs; and I earned some money as a newsboy, and by hauling blocks of ice in my small wagon for the neighbors and delivering suits and dresses that had been cleaned and pressed or re-paired by a tailor, or tutoring other children. Yet we never considered ourselves *needy,* or even insecure, but rather as persons of privilege in transit.

Like a tiny Tolstoy, I moved among varied social levels, observing and thinking all the time. No Russian aristocrats were among our acquaintances, but I did, for instance, get to know the family of a prosperous bootlegger whose son, Maxie, I tutored from time to time. They owned a huge house on the other side of town (though distances in Passaic were not great). It was full of shiny furniture, rich rugs, and gaudy lamps—and doubtless much else I was hardly equipped to notice. Our tenement flat had only the

Father, Jacob Rosenthal, 1939

a movie was a very special treat. And they were generous folk, old family friends with the simple hospitality of another age. I was treated as a loved child along with their son and daughter, and lived in guilty "luxury" during these precious intervals with my father, a talented salesman with undeveloped musical gifts. He dreamt of setting up his own business and occasionally, in a small way, did so. He was made for high talk and good song, not the loneliness and hard, unrewarding work in which he was trapped.

It was the same when I'd spend a week or two with the families of my mother's sisters and brothers in Baltimore, or with those of my father's sister in nearby Maryland and brother in nearby Virginia. Affection was rampant, and with it pocket money and utterly unwonted lazy ease if I so chose. Then back to the freer, more astringent, intellectually more strenuous life of poverty-ridden *noblesse*. I grew used to the nomadic life, to meeting entirely new people every year or two as we moved along, and became restless if we lingered in any one city. In Passaic, great textile center wracked by the strikes of the twenties and befouled by the stench of the Botany woolen mills, I learned in school, alongside the transplanted peasant children destined to become millhands, how to work hand and machine looms. A smell like burning rubber often filled the air along the river; had I been just a little less sturdy, my life would have been full of terror because of the daily fights I have mentioned. Even so, I often had dreams of being in a jungle at the mercy of wild beasts. At the same time, I somehow relished being able to see how forms of life that touched me intimately, sometimes bitterly, and yet were not, ultimately, *my* life were nevertheless ineradicably real. Gaunt figures with hardened faces were everywhere in the slums of Passaic, of the same kind we can see in the neighborhood of the abandoned old Black Church in Dublin today.

And there were special joys. The bliss of roller-skating on city streets more or less free of heavy traffic, moving from comparatively rough surfaces that caused a thrilling, half painful vibration in one's feet and legs to the smoother ones that made skating seem a form of flying, pre-sexual ecstasy, like Willie Wordsworth's sensation in his stolen boat. The aroma of newly baked Polish rye bread, still hot and silkily doughy when you bought it in the bakery. The divine charlotte russes sold in the streets: a sort of shortcake topped with generously piled-up whipped cream, doubtless sufficiently bacteria-laden (though no one ever thought of it) to lay the city low overnight. The Yiddish school I attended two late afternoons a week, whose teachers, far superior to

those in the public schools, were genuinely literate: writers and scholars and thinkers eking out a minimal income from their knowledge of the Yiddish of Sholem Aleichem and the poets. And of course it was in Passaic, too, that I became a friend to the beautiful and gifted Eva E., my first little innocent love. She was to die of tuberculosis at the age of seventeen or eighteen, when we were already out of touch because of my family's peregrinations—we had long since left New Jersey for Boston and then the Midwest. The charm of our walking and talking and reading together lingers, disappears, returns recurrently like a cherished yet elusive state of mind.

I had no other friend "like" Eva until I entered the world of more conscious love (if "conscious" ever fits the case). But in Newark, where I began high school, I discovered adolescent boon companions and had my first taste of Latin and of French, sweet studies that opened unsuspected worlds at the same time that reading ancient history was doing so as well. In early spring, though, we moved to Boston, where I went first to Dorchester High School for Boys, famous then for food-battles in the lunchroom and, with a few exceptions, a reciprocally bored faculty and student body. Hearing that Boys' Public Latin School was a superb and demanding place, I rode the trolley there one day and asked the headmaster if I might enroll. He quizzed me orally, then and there, on Latin and mathematics, and forthwith invited me to enter.

Boston Latin School stirred me awake in a new way. It was a brief sojourn, just one year, yet confirmed my interests mightily and made whatever difference a school can make. It was a wrench, despite my never-failing pleasure in discovering new cities, to have to leave the delights of having a reasonable number of truly bright and thoughtful friends, the prospect of a scholarship to Harvard, and the chastely warm exuberance of Irene L., who attended Girls' Public Latin School, a paradise just a short way off. Nevertheless, autumn found me beginning my senior year in Cleveland, then a beautiful and tranquil, tree-lined city. There, at the suggestion of teachers, I took a scholarship examination for the University of Chicago. This was a happy coincidence, for Chicago was the family's next place to alight in its migrations—and thus it came to pass that I went to the University of Chicago near the start of its much-publicized New Plan, for better or for worse.

And thus, too, endeth my account of earliest years, much condensed as may well be imagined. All the experiences I've been describing have in one way or another entered my poems or shaped (or distorted, or eroded, or reoriented) my thinking. It is that fact alone, it seems to me, that could conceivably justify the public sharing of private memory. That consideration aside, it strikes me that my somewhat chaotic life proves nothing much psychologically—that too much depends on the luck of the draw, on one's inner gyroscope, and on the unpredictable benefits of adversity ("and the like, and their opposites," as my old Latin grammar put it concerning verbs and compound-formations taking the dative of the indirect object).

III

Concerning the *Sturm und Drang* of college years and after, there are films and novels aplenty to fill in all possible details. For our purposes here, it's enough to offer just a very few details. The most important is that I met my future wife, Victoria, when we were students at the university, where she took a degree in sociology and then went on, after three or four years, to become a psychiatric social worker. I, meanwhile, studied English and American literature, earning B.A. and M.A. degrees at the same university and, after the war, my doctorate at New York University. The war years themselves I spent at Michigan State College (later Michigan State University), where I taught Army Air Force cadets and Army Specialized Training Program engineers, as well as the usual civilian classes. (I had volunteered for air combat intelligence service in the Navy, but my physical examination showed I would need some minor surgery before being accepted. The surgery took place, but the surgical wound did not heal in time for me to serve either as a naval officer or as an enlisted man in the Army.)

I have jumped ahead a bit. My prewar university years were of course in the time of the Depression. I had felt the vocation of a writer—a poet especially—since childhood. The vocation itself was my special secret privilege, for it made me sure of myself in some strange way, persisting independently of whatever circumstances I found myself in. Thornton Wilder encouraged me, during the brief time he taught creative writing in Chicago. But I didn't have the turn of ego or, I suppose, the confidence of social status and family money, that enabled my exact contemporary (and later, my friend) Robert Lowell to present himself to Allen Tate as an insistent disciple. The starting points, the life-involvements, the clarity about one's place and rights within the culture were simply very different. All this reveals itself to me in retrospect only, for it never occurred to me to think in terms of literary self-advancement. In truth, I had no inkling of such things but simply drifted. I was always absorbed in literature, and scholarships and fellowships came my way, and so I became a graduate student while writing my poetry. Unemployed except for tutoring, I applied to the Federal Writers Project and was accepted on the basis of a sheaf of poems. I hitchhiked to Michigan one day to visit a friend teaching at Michigan State College and shortly thereafter was offered an instructorship there by the chairman, whom we had visited and who engaged us in what seemed to me an unpleasantly abrasive conversation. (It turned out he "liked challenging young people.")

So it was that I floated into the worlds of scholarship and teaching. I found it easy to publish prose and found myself writing essays and reviews in *Poetry* and elsewhere but in the main kept my poems to myself during the war years and for a few years thereafter. I cannot quite understand why this should have been so. I should like to think that something like modesty was involved; for a long time I cherished the notion, without quite formulating it to myself, that I would publish poems only when they seemed to me to "make it new," in Pound's famous phrase. Meanwhile, sending them to magazines to "get published" seemed too much like the world's ordinary business, like taking time to get a haircut or to check a bank statement. It was only later, after we left the comparative isolation of East Lansing, Michigan, that I realized the subjective usefulness of publishing one's poems: namely, that doing so frees one's psyche of the particular pressures they embody—frees it for more such pressures, it's true, but yet is a disengagement from previous fixations of style and form and literal subject. In any event, I escaped both the advantages and the disadvantages of developing "in public."

Everyone's life had special complexities during the war years. The victims of the Nazis had the worst of it, suffering the unspeakable. And there were the innocents of all countries, the children and others, whose "incidental" killing and maiming and terror are so taken for granted that the word "atrocities" is rarely used for what happened to them. Nor is it used for what happens to men and women in combat: the "normal" casualties of "honorable" warfare. For the rest of us, in this country at least, our discomforts were negligible. And yet the war distorted our lives, and often made us mark time, too. Deprived of the "opportunity" for adventure abroad, even if in olive drab, I pursued my solitary writing like an addiction, and was also immersed in a merry-go-round teaching program as new groups of soldiers kept arriving on campus. As we had anticipated my going into the Navy or Army, Victoria had accepted a fellowship in social work at the University of Chicago and therefore lived in the city through much of 1943–44. We contrived to be with each other as often as possible. It was a long, slow train-ride from Lansing to Chicago, or vice versa, in those days, with the trains full of service men and women and war-brides and people who, like us, had become inter-urban commuters because of the war's contingencies. Life on the rail lines had a restless, nomadic flavor. Conversation sprang up easily; people told all; it was a kind of street-life on wheels. I was on my way to Chicago the day the news broke of Roosevelt's death. A conductor went through the cars making the mournful announcement. A sleeping woman just ahead of me woke with a start and cried to her seat-mate:

"Whuddee say?"

"The President died."

"Whuh President?"

"Roosevelt."

"Who's President now?"

"Truman."

"Is he a Democrat?"

Writing, teaching, commuting, I laid waste the hours. My one writer-companion in East Lansing was Art Smith—i.e., A. J. M. Smith, a Canadian poet of distinction who had studied seventeenth-century literature with the formidable Herbert Grierson in Edinburgh and was the first influential advocate of the new poetry in Canada. He affected a "classical" stance as perceived by Eliot, Tate, and others while in reality he took delight in anything, however anarchic or romantic, that had the spark of life in it. He had perfect pitch in poetry; that is, he caught the rhythmic life and basic sense of a poem as quickly as anyone I've ever known, picking up its tonalities at once. We concocted a plan for a wonderful anthology of international avant-garde literature so dazzling and original that only we and a few other radiantly anointed spirits could possibly teach from it, and sent it to the college textbook department at Macmillan. It was the mad autumn of 1944, when the war still had its final agonies to go through, and when nothing and anything seemed possible. Art and I planned to attend the Modern Language Association meeting in New York that December, and wrote Macmillan we'd be happy to discuss the book during our visit.

Macmillan's college advisor in literature then was Professor Oscar Cargill of New York University, a pioneer in American literature study (then still only a very small part of the scholarly scene). He was enthusiastic about the book—or so he said—but knew it could not hope for more than a very few adoptions. At the same time, though, he persuaded me that I should leave the Midwest and come to New York

A.J.M. Smith, 1940

University as a teaching fellow to complete my doctorate. I could work with him and write my dissertation on living poets, and in general could be in my natural literary milieu.

Ergo, the end of the summer of 1945 saw us bidding farewell to our little patch of uneaten corn and tomatoes in the countryside a few miles from East Lansing and setting off in our 1937 Dodge with our books and records and not-yet-born first son, David. Life really does change. The war was over, and I had the old gay feeling of moving into the unknown again.

Yeats, in another context, used the phrase "Gratitude to Unknown Instructors" as the title of a poem. With any luck, one's life is brushed by the wings of good angels from time to time. Often we do not know who the good angel, making a decision or recommendation or inquiry somewhere away from us, may be. But there are the known ones, like Oscar, who flew overhead as we drove along the Pennsylvania Turnpike, making sure that our good old Dodge didn't break down and that we'd actually reach New York. Art Smith was another such, exchanging poems with me, recommending my work to a magazine or two, and—in particular—considering me a peer despite his greater age and established reputation. And a writer must feel fortunately indebted—as I do toward Sheldon Meyer of Oxford University Press and the late J.G. Chase of Macmillan—to editors who have shown confidence and given good counsel over the years. There are other men and women whom I should name, as well, simply because, sometimes quite unwittingly, they reinforced my self-regard when some confirmation was devoutly to be wished. God forbid, though, that I should give public credit for benign acts my benefactors may perhaps have grown to regret! Yet such people are there—offstage or on it—in the theater of every life that has known some gratification.

Human indebtedness, in any case, presses constantly, and mostly unconsciously, on all our souls. I am aware, in writing these pages, that as I do so I am accompanied by shadowy presences, seen in another dimension as with night-vision, many of whom I would not even recognize. But there are also many I *would* recognize, figures associated with pleasure or grief or humiliation the psyche can hardly cope with, some deeply involved with my life and others known only for a few passing moments. And there are scattered instances when one suddenly *saw* a hidden reality, had a fleeting insight, grasped the glory or horror lurking in existence, either through personal engagement or just as a casual observer. I do believe we are tremendously indebted to all that we experience, happy or sad. The revelatory moment, objectifying the subjective, is what makes us human; and art, especially the art of poetry, enables us to grasp and hold the moment and explore its resonances.

I am not speaking abstractly. The accidental death of my friend Thomas Riggs, Jr., over thirty years ago, a young man close to our whole family and with a promising literary career just opening for him, makes him no less vivid a figure in my psyche than he was the summer we spent together, with our two young wives and tiny David, writing our dissertations. We read poems aloud, talked, swam, drank, played tennis and poker, in the Riggses' country home. Our conversations, those rich days, Tom's face—all still here.

I was on leave from Michigan State when we went off to New York, but we never returned except as visitors. Life there had been limiting and isolated, as it must be in any setting removed from the many dimensions and challenges of a metropolis. And yet Victoria and I had been given a blessed opportunity to grow up together in a quieter world than Chicago's and to experience the kindly friendship of my new colleagues and their families, who showed extraordinary tolerance toward our naïve young ways and radical attitudes. We were, after all, children of the

thirties as a later generation was of the sixties, although we didn't dramatize the fact through the way we dressed or through taking street-language for our very own. The Depression, the still-lingering disillusionment of intelligent elders with World War I, and the grimness of what the Axis was already doing made for a considerably different atmosphere from the one that produced hippies, flower-children, the Beats, and the demonstrations against the Vietnam War, although a tortuous psychological bond links the two eras.

Of course, the thought wouldn't have occurred to you that the Third Reich had anything to do with your own life had you been a boy or girl from, say, Holland, Michigan, scuffing the autumn leaves on your first day as a freshman at MSC the year we arrived (1939) as the youngest faculty couple in town. The "other world" of vicious history receded a little even for us. We assimilated a bit of what it was to be a Midwesterner in the rural sense, and found it pleasant, and learned a good deal from our faculty elders. When the war crashed in on Michigan with a vengeance—altering the character of the auto plants, bringing floods of black workers from the South and of women from their homes into the factories, and

M.L. Rosenthal, 1950

superimposing the map of the world on isolationist minds, a certain innocence disappeared pretty rapidly. And yet, for all that, the cultural isolationism remained fairly intact. I think it was reflected in a heartwarming experience I had when I returned to the campus to take part in a conference on modern literature a few years after leaving. To my amazement, the entire English Department came to meet me at the airport in Lansing; it was a community, a family, held together by alienation from surrounding indifference to the life of art and ideas, and I was a son who had gone forth into the much-mocked dream-world of New York and was returning to tell about his adventures. (And in fact the title of my paper was "Alienation of Sensibility and 'Modernity' in Literature.")

After two years in the city, I was offered an instructorship at New York University, and so the break became final. I was indeed writing my dissertation on contemporary poets. It was called "Chief Poets of the American Depression," and served me primarily as an extended exercise in exploring and evaluating poetry, and drawing relevant conclusions from the study inductively—"with my bare hands"—concerning work by living, uncanonized poets of substance. In the course of writing the dissertation, I came to develop fairly close friendships with the three poets on whom it centered, all of whom lived in or very near the city: Horace Gregory, Kenneth Fearing, and Muriel Rukeyser. They were all survivors of the literary and political battles of the thirties, increasingly neglected—though at the height of their productivity—in the postwar repressive backwash already well under way in the late forties. They were all hospitable, and very unalike: Gregory increasingly conservative, with an air of distinction well-earned but vulnerable; Fearing boisterously witty, alcoholic, and mordant in his dead-accurate, Flaubertian hostility to cruelty and cant; and Rukeyser a most generous-spirited and affectionate woman, half-mystic, half-scientist in her pursuit of correlations (as in her study of Willard Gibbs) of historical, literary, and scientific tendencies in America.

As in my earlier relations with my parents, I experienced a certain natural conflict between my affection for these people and my need to think quite independently about what I saw in their poetry. They were all the real thing, yet they—especially Gregory and Rukeyser—had certain weaknesses as well. Clearly, I had to avoid compromising, and therefore corrupting, my inner seismograph critically: a felony that might also, somehow, warp my own poetry in the process. What happens in this circumstance (as in personal relationships that demand choices) is a

curious inner click of detachment, enhancing affection because it becomes more free but also clearing one's mind for greater objectivity.

We had come to New York on the strength of my fellowship, our savings from Victoria's work in a child guidance clinic in Lansing, and the royalties from a textbook I had helped write. We found a small, inexpensive apartment not far from Manhattan, in a corner of Brooklyn that soon became our son David's first address. It was a working-class neighborhood, largely Italian, close to Prospect Park in one direction and the East River in the other. At that time the *New York Herald-Tribune* was still flourishing, and its Sunday book-review section was edited by Irita Van Doren. I liked the tone of her section and one day, thinking of ways to make ends meet a bit more handily, telephoned her and asked about reviewing. She invited me to visit her office, gave me a sample review to write, and in short order I became, for a time—almost until the demise of the paper—her chief poetry reviewer. I then, luckily, had a similar experience with Robert Hatch, literary editor of the *New Republic*. Openness to young free-lancers in tough New York was something I hadn't really anticipated. But the result, for me, of these fine editors' accessibility was that I had my choice of the most interesting new books of poetry to read and think about and review for a number of years. My *New Republic* reviews, actually, were often essays. When the *New Republic* moved to Washington, Hatch did not go with it, nor did my columns. A couple of years later, however, he became literary editor of the *Nation* and asked me to be its poetry editor, and so we worked together for another five years or so, until the end of my first Guggenheim Fellowship year in London, in 1961.

IV

Thus it was that various life-contingencies gave me a reputation as critic and editor before my first book of poems, *Blue Boy on Skates*, appeared in 1964, and even before my poems began appearing from time to time in various magazines. In the early 1950s, too, Macmillan (at the indefatigable Oscar's suggestion) invited Art Smith and me to write a poetry textbook, with a format somewhat similar to that of the famous *Understanding Poetry* of Cleanth Brooks and Robert Penn Warren: that is, combining our own commentary with a suitable anthology. I had, naturally, been immersed in modern and contemporary poetry in my teaching as well as my reviewing, and before that in the reading for my dissertation. So I was happy to turn my august attention again to the nature and varieties of poetry in general.

Arthur and I were thoroughly familiar with the approach embodied and popularized in the Brooks and Warren text. "New Criticism," often ignorantly dismissed nowadays, was more a tendency than a united movement with shared principles. People as different in all sorts of ways as I. A. Richards, John Crowe Ransom, Allen Tate, Kenneth Burke, William Empson, T. S. Eliot, and a host of others were simply carrying their thought to levels free of the kinds of facile impressionism and academic historicism that were dominant at the turn of the century. Of course, sensitive response to what one reads—too easily dismissed as "impressionism"—is necessary if criticism is to be of any use. And scholarly knowledge, when not trivialized by pedantry, is indispensable for obvious reasons. However, twentieth-century poetic criticism could hardly help venturing on new paths— partly under the influence of scientific method, partly out of curiosity about the light that modern developments in psychology, anthropology, politics, and art itself might shed on poetry, and mainly because of interest in objectifying poetic process and structure. Whatever its limitations, "New Criticism" was a reflex of all this.

We called our book *Exploring Poetry.* We wanted to humanize poetic analysis, using a "poet's poetics" (a phrase that occurred to me much later, however) to emphasize the elusive, living stuff of actual poems. The book took us only so far toward the liberation of criticism and teaching from classroom formulas of interpretation, especially the habit of seeing poems as subtle discourse rather than volatile expression. We ourselves were not entirely free of the spell of such terms as "irony," "ambiguity," and "voice": terms useful enough at times but too readily picked up by minds impervious to the evocative elements that constitute a poem. One can hardly say that the liberation we sought has finally been achieved in most discussion of poetry today—but that is quite another subject.

Written over thirty years ago, *Exploring Poetry* was for me just a start. Most of my teaching and criticism has had to do with actual poems: how they take on their specific organic life and what they teach us about themselves, not only as works of art but as expression responding to life-pressures. From these concerns came my books *Poetry and the Common Life* and *The Poet's Art* and also my efforts to understand the leading directions of twentieth-century poetry in four other books: *The Modern Poets: A Critical Introduction; The New Poets: American and British Poetry since World War II; Sailing into the Unknown: Yeats, Pound, and Eliot;* and *The Modern Poetic Sequence: The Genius of*

Modern Poetry (a collaboration with Sally M. Gall). These are all forays in self-education, whatever else they may be—for, despite the mountains of critical and scholarly tomes in our libraries, the ones engaging individual works with both human companionability and artistic empathy are few and far between.

What I've just done, in the preceding paragraph, is to describe my contribution to inductive critical theory without going into the detail that would show the revolutionary implications of such exploratory engagement. We have ancient enough precedent, at least as far back as Longinus' wonderful insights into Sappho's most famous poem. But Longinus only started the job.

Self-education has always been my instinctive critical purpose. It is inseparable from an almost helpless participation in any poem I read, as though I had merged with its author and were in some sense thinking my way into it once more. From one perspective, every poem is a draft that might have gone beyond its present point and might have been altered in some interesting way or other; and so we cannot respond fully to its quality, or respect its elastic integrity, without understanding the tentative nature of even the most accomplished writing. It's for this reason, I think, that I've never felt a conflict, except of time, between my vocations as poet and critic or teacher: that is, between writing poems and thinking, or talking, about them.

V

As I write this account, my sixth book of verse, *As for Love: Poems and Translations,* waits at the

With wife, Victoria, and daughter, Laura, 1953

The Rosenthal children: Laura, Alan, and David, 1975

publisher's, proofread and ready to appear fairly soon. These six books are my only "authorized autobiography"—if any phrase so long and heavy can do for what, Paul Verlaine wrote, verse should be:

Let your verse be a winged living thing
Fleeing, we feel, from a soul in flight
Towards other skies, to other loves.

Let your verse be sheer good luck
Scattered in the crisp gusts of morning wind
That arrive breathing mint or thyme . . .
                                                    ("Art Poétique")

These lines, in my translation from the lovely original, may at first appear merely intangible romantic fantasy, but in fact they suggest an empirical reality. The essential, internal drift of our lives in action—no matter what wise characterizations of ourselves we may propose in sober prose—reveals itself only glancingly, in quick flashes of reverie or in the way insights and phrases emerge from the subconscious while a poem is in the making.

I had meant to quote passages from certain poems here as illustrations, poems somehow related to my wife and children and others, living and dead, close to my heart. But now, when I come to the point, I see that many of these poems are too intimate and elusive—too much already "fleeing from a soul in flight"—to be commented on readily once they intrude their intractable selves within this hitherto orderly account. They will not serve to show the external facts, for instance, about our children: David, Alan, and Laura, now grown up—a writer, a composer and pianist, and a doctor respectively, and two of them parents themselves. Rather, they "tell" of other things: a cold night in London when I thought one son was lost and I went searching for him through deserted streets and "met" an image of irrevocable loss, the sudden memory of my dead father, instead; a moment of intense love after reproaching another child; a dream in which "one of us" was about to die and I learned with elation that it was myself rather than anyone close to me; a remembered scene in which adult family-members and friends stood in silent wonder for a minute around a newborn grandchild:

A sleeping infant, babe of the stars,
holds a roomful of men and women in thrall:

the distance, untouchable distance,
and delicate persistence
light years away, in the sway
of the streaming hours.

The passage is part of a poem which begins with memories from my Woodbridge days and ends with the later discovery of the obliteration of my little world there and with images widening the scope beyond my own personal memory. The lines on the "sleeping infant" do not name our little grandchild who occasioned them, nor do they offer any other *fact*. They tell much, especially in the context of the poem, and yet I shall have to let them—and other passages in many other poems that "tell all" about me and my world—speak for themselves.

It is interesting, at any rate to me in my present mood, to think how everything in a life flows together, no matter how disparate one's experiences and activities. My career as a teacher, which began as an accident, is an instance. I never felt "academic," in the nasty sense in which many poets use the word, although there is hardly an American poet now alive who has not taught in the academy and very likely found a home in it. But still, I've had a full-fledged, very professional and devoted teaching career. I have "taught poetry" almost from the start, from undergraduate literary and creative-writing courses to advanced doctoral and post-doctoral seminars in every aspect of poetic theory; and I sometimes think that I've directed more dissertations on modern poetry than anyone else. The strange thing, to my mind, is that while the teaching has been so varied and has involved so many different subjects and such a wide variety of works, my plain orientation has always been the same: thinking about what happens in poems, from a poet's point of view.

That word "thinking" I mean literally, not just in the sense that someone in love "thinks" about the beloved—although that certainly (all ye shallowly "anti-romantic" poseurs take note) is very much part of the process. One must think about poetry both in relation to one's own practice and in response to the practice of others very unlike oneself. If the labor is one of love—and it is—perhaps we should use the word "passion" to get at what that means; for sweetness and bliss are not the only feelings involved. Rather, conflict, endurance, self-doubt, and fear or despair have also played their parts.

Put another way, the critic's labor is an effort to strengthen one's understanding of poetry as an art—but as an art with tremendous human bearing: one to be apprehended as simply and directly as possible, through a poem's movement of feeling, to start with;

and always so to be apprehended despite the most sophisticated ramifications. As a teacher I have tried—for my own sake quite as much as theirs—to encourage a group of students at any given time with whom I would be able to discuss poems beyond the most elementary levels. This was my larger motive in founding the Poetics Concentration and Poetics Institute at New York University just as, more tangentially, it has been in my criticism as well.

For all this, I cannot say how much I've "finally" learned. But at least I know something about living within poetry as a natural human element and about surfacing to look at that life objectively from time to time. The poets I've loved being with most have taken their art seriously in a manner unfamiliar even to most knowledgeable readers. They have had something like mystical faith in the revelatory power of language, at whatever cost of dire recognitions. W. H. Auden—who would utter almost any half-truth that came into his mind at a given moment—said, notoriously, that "poetry makes nothing happen." But he went on, in the very same poem ("In Memory of W. B. Yeats"), to instruct Yeats's poetry in what, after all, it must make happen:

> In the prison of his days
> Teach the free man how to praise.

—Safe enough advice to give a body of poetry as sure to outlive its creator into the distant future as any

With Victoria, in Italy, 1980

body of poetry can be—and whose "praise" is often in the elegiac mode, or consists of defiant or "giddy" assertions in the teeth of dark knowledge. But one of the chief forms of affirmation, in a very special sense of that word, achieved in poetry is its implicit belief in the organic coherence of one's life: that the bits and fragments and accidents of relationship and situation scattered through the years constitute a whole that means something of great import. Wordsworth's *Prelude* is perhaps our most obvious example.

If I try to summon up representative instances from my own life, in addition to those in the earlier sections of this account, I turn most naturally (in part as a way of avoiding the overly confessional) to periods when I have lived or traveled abroad. In the 1960s, on Guggenheim fellowships and at other times as well, we spent two full years and parts of other years in London, and briefer periods in Paris, and I sometimes returned to both cities on my own for a month or so each time. During the same decade, I also found myself invited to Pakistan to organize a conference on the uses of criticism in a developing country. (I discovered this only on arrival. I had been under the impression that I was simply going to give a few lectures on Western poetry and criticism at the University of Karachi.) A couple of years later, I had a period of lecturing in Poland, Bulgaria, and Rumania, and more recently have had similar missions in

France, Switzerland, and, most often, in Italy. Our son David lived for some years in Barcelona, absorbing Catalan life and literature, and we have visited him there. The most exotic single sojourn abroad, I suppose, was a period of some five weeks in China, where the Distinguished Scholar Exchange Program brought me in 1982, and where I lectured in various cities, talked with poets and other writers, and walked the streets as much as possible.

The subjective side of these and other such periods is crowded with disparate memories that yet "connect" with one another and compel my imagination. For one thing, the shock of British hospitality in the sixties was overwhelming in its geniality, so that I was almost an immediate participant in the world of the poets shortly after arrival. London seemed bent on depositing new friendships on our doorstep every other day, including lifelong ones like those with the Welsh-Jewish-English poet Dannie Abse and his scholar-wife, Joan, and Al Alvarez, advocate of a new style of English poetry that would have some bite to it (and who took me tearing about in his hair-raisingly fast sports cars as though we were acting out in the flesh the kind of daring we both called for in verse). People seemed to have plenty of time for conversation, from the cheerfully if vehemently argumentative Eric Mottram to poets like gently intense Jon Stallworthy or the highkeyed couple Sylvia Plath and Ted

In Pisa with Professor Rolando Anzilotti, and Dr. Laura Coltelli, 1980

Hughes, who came walking across Hampstead Heath to visit. Neither resembled their later reputations, on short acquaintance at any rate. Sylvia Plath seemed a typical gifted young woman of her American generation, eager to excel in everything quickly, at once confiding and proud, perhaps somewhat angry. I never spoke to her alone, and had no warning of her problems or the drastic choice she constantly considered.

Other new friends or close acquaintances crowded into those years: the ebullient, irritable Peter Redgrove; the stubbornly rural Charles Tomlinson (of Brook Cottage, Ozleworth Bottom, Wotton-under-Edge, Gloucestershire) who was cultivating one of the most sophisticated, symbolism-&-American-experimentalist-influenced styles in Britain; the ex-South African deaf poet David Wright and his wife, Philippa Reid, an actress whom I met while coaching actors in reading Pound aloud for a program George Fraser and I prepared for the Mermaid Poetry Festival—where, in turn, I met Louis MacNeice, John Montague, and other Irish poets, etc., etc. Those years, too, brought me to Christopher Grieve (Hugh MacDiarmid), the great Scottish poet, whose *Collected Poems* I had edited as virtually my first act upon becoming Macmillan's poetry advisor in New York—a

mild-mannered, gently agreeable man who apparently reserved his wrath for printed diatribes against chosen literary or political enemies—and with him Norman MacCaig and other poet friends of his in Edinburgh. There too lived one of the anathematized, the Concretist Ian Hamilton Finlay. In Ireland, we had been warmly received by the novelist Francis MacManus and his wife Joan (one of those immediately lifelong friendships that take us by utter surprise) and were soon introduced to the group that included the composer Seán Ó Riada, the publisher and theatrical producer Liam Miller, and the poets Thomas Kinsella and Austin Clarke. Suddenly I was "discovering" the new Irish poetry!

Along with this little flood of names and circumstances, came certain jolts of private observation: our children's school experiences (as, for instance Alan's being taunted by classmates with a song about some British victory during the American Revolution); a visit with Robert Lowell during his sad time with his new family in Kent, when he precariously served us each an artichoke and we shared a sort of chummy, gossipy misery for some hours; conversations with Clarke in his crumbling house that he neglected because his mother's will stipulated that it go to the Church after his death (and also because, despite the

The Rosenthal home in Suffern, New York

fact that he was then Ireland's most distinguished poet, he eked out only the barest living from radio broadcasts and newspaper columns); a visit with Grieve and his wife Valda in their damp cottage in Lanarkshire, during which he amazed our American children by his unselfconscious avowal that he was a Communist (and amazed me by seeing no contradiction between that and his being a Scottish Nationalist—although I shouldn't have been amazed, since I knew his work and also something of modern history); a strange meeting, in his favorite pub on Harry Street in Dublin, with Patrick Kavanagh, who in some way became the conscience of literary Ireland: a reminder of working-class and poor-farmer origins, of elitist pretensions, and of the humiliations of poverty and alcoholism and other seedier realities of Ireland.

I must stop myself before launching into a description of life in a whore-infested hotel where I'd often stay, near the Luxembourg Gardens in Paris—a place recommended by Ramon Guthrie for its cheapness and its relative cleanliness. There my friend Serge Fauchereau, the dynamic lover of everything experimental, exciting, or genuine in art, or the Irish poet Montague, who lived in Paris for many years with his first wife, would seek me out for boisterous discussions and forays. I shall head myself off from all that by recurring to our Chinese adventure and memories of Chinese poets weeping as they read me poems about humiliation and worse during the Cultural Revolution; of tiny dwellings open to the street in which so many people lived their stricter-than-Spartan lives; of dauntless survivors of more than one anti-intellectual campaign, in the wake of Japanese and Nationalist atrocities; of workers in their thousands cycling to work in the morning and home again in the evening, impassive multitudes whose masked expressions gave an oddly nightmarish impression (like the packed-in masses of New York subway riders during rush hours). And there was one poet—I am not at all sure what his whole oeuvre amounts to—who showed me a single poem recalling youthful days in Souzhow that magically, with painful nostalgia, opened his living sense of the past to me in such a way that it became mine too.

I have plucked this and that from here and there, have not mentioned the gaudily exotic wild birds flying freely in the great marketplace in Karachi, or the deliberately mutilated beggar-children in the same place, or the great scholar of classical Chinese poetry who showed such exquisite courtesy to me while excoriating with sharp wit certain local philistinisms in his country, or the long evening with poets and thinkers in Jerusalem that went on and on

M.L. Rosenthal, 1987

because, after our very grave discussion, as we were all leaving, I asked if there were any good Israeli jokes. What a foolish question—but what a glorious result! (*Do you know the story of . . . ?*) I have not mentioned my quixotic intellectual comrade-in-arms, Emile Capouya, critic, editor, and nonconforming thinker, who shared with me the launching of the Macmillan Paperback Poets: a score or so of new volumes before we were stopped. Nor have I mentioned other close friends or, certainly, any of my more ludicrous mistakes. Stay tuned, if you're still with me, for more news on some other station, at some other time.

SELECTED BIBLIOGRAPHY

Poetry:

Blue Boy on Skates: Poems. New York: Oxford University Press, 1964.

Beyond Power: More Poems. New York: Oxford University Press, 1969.

The View from the Peacock's Tail: Poems. New York: Oxford

University Press, 1972.

She: A Sequence of Poems. Brockport, New York: BOA Editions, 1977.

Poems 1964–1980. New York: Oxford University Press, 1981.

As for Love: Poems and Translations. New York: Oxford University Press, 1987.

Criticism:

Exploring Poetry, with A.J.M. Smith. New York: Macmillan, 1955. New edition. New York: Macmillan, 1973.

The Modern Poets: A Critical Introduction. New York: Oxford University Press, 1960.

A Primer of Ezra Pound. New York: Macmillan, 1960.

The New Poets: American and British Poetry since World War II. New York: Oxford University Press, 1967.

Randall Jarrell. Minneapolis: University of Minnesota Press, 1972.

Poetry and the Common Life. New York: Oxford University Press, 1974. Revised edition. New York: Schocken, 1983; New York: Persea Books, 1986.

Sailing into the Unknown: Yeats, Pound, and Eliot. New York: Oxford University Press, 1978.

The Modern Poetic Sequence: The Genius of Modern Poetry, with Sally M. Gall. New York and Oxford, England: Oxford University Press, 1983. New edition. New York: Galaxy Books, 1986.

The Poet's Art. New York: Norton, 1987.

Translator of:

The Adventures of Pinocchio: Tale of a Puppet, by Carlo Collodi. New York: Lothrop, 1983.

Editor of:

Chief Modern Poets of Britain and America, with Gerald DeWitt Sanders and John Herbert Nelson. New York: Macmillan, 1962. Revised edition. New York: Macmillan, 1973.

The William Carlos Williams Reader. New York: New Directions, 1966; London: MacGibbon & Kee, 1967.

The New Modern Poetry: An Anthology British and American Poetry since World War II. New York: Macmillan, 1967. New edition. New York: Galaxy Books, 1969.

100 Postwar Poems: British and American. New York: Macmillan, 1968.

Selected Poems of William Butler Yeats. Franklin Center, Pa.: Franklin Library, 1979.

Selected Poems and Three Plays of William Butler Yeats. New York: Macmillan, 1986.

Poetry in English: An Anthology (General Editor). New York: Oxford University Press, 1987.

Karl Shapiro

1913-

Karl Shapiro (left) with Mother, Sarah; sister, Margery; and brother, Irvin;
Norfolk, Virginia, about 1918

The B & O Railroad station sat below ground on a large and seemingly elegant brick pavement and ornamented with a high clock tower. It was never crowded, it was spotlessly clean and quiet as a library. This was the elegant station in Baltimore. Though classless like all American vehicles, the B & O trains were first class. Everybody knew that. They floated almost noiselessly through the beautiful rolling countryside of Maryland and Pennsylvania, slowly it seemed, without the roar and flash and melodrama of the Pennsylvania Railroad trains, which went an entirely different route, straight through the city.

The Pennsylvania station was just a few blocks away, also below or rather underground. To be sure, the steel and glass depot sat above the street and its tile mosaic floors, like bathroom floors, were always crowded and in a hurry and excited with coming and going. Wire-laced glass doors led down to the tracks when they opened and the pungent and delicious reek of locomotives rose up the stairs and the travelers poured below. Porters and hawkers and gate keepers were everywhere among the throngs, and there were always throngs in Pennsylvania Station. At the B & O station there were never throngs. One might set up a meeting for a quiet talk at the B & O; hardly at the Pennsylvania.

The young poet sat on the immense scrolled wood bench alone. There could not have been a half-dozen other people in the station. His concern was to spot Professor Hazel, whom he had never seen and to whom he had sent his book of poems. He was shy, tremulous, and bold at the same time. So, it turned out, was Professor Hazel, with his great bulk and bald head and English tweeds. The poet was dressed approximately like a college student of the Middle Atlantic States of the thirties, or so he hoped. It was all very satisfactory, more than that.

When the professor strolled to his chair car with his shabby briefcase, and they shook hands in a kind of glow, the young poet knew he would have the scholarship. He would be a university student again, among gentlemen, and even ladies. He walked home mantled in his new superiority and supercilious glee, up Eutaw Place, past the mansions built in the Civil War, past the nineteenth-century solid stone rock-faced apartments which he described as Assyrian, to his own modest car-lined street where the almost-rich Jews lived.

*

The young poet's brother, a year the elder, had been exemplary almost from birth. As an infant he had won a baby prize in a kind of photo beauty contest, a photo taken by the father himself. One of the young poet's earliest recollections was this picture, the beautiful baby naked and sitting on a white blanket in the backyard. Thereafter and ever after the brother's picture was in the papers. "Ten years old and in the seventh grade" read one caption. He was gentle, kind, brilliant at everything, won the State of Virginia prizes for poetry and short story while still in high school, and matriculated at the university at sixteen.

The young poet had no such career, was coaxed and cajoled through grade after grade after grade and in fact attended three different high schools, occasioned in part by family moves, but not entirely. When he entered the university he stayed only one semester and dropped out before they could drop him. The father was more than solicitous. He asked what the young poet wanted to do and was answered, to study French and piano and Latin—sounding somewhat like an English governess of the last century. The father agreed. True, bills were not frequently paid, or not at all, and these effete activities, two of which the young poet could have done on his own, eventually faded away. Sincerely worried about the boy, the father even took him to a psychiatrist, an unheard-of move in those days. The psychiatrist recommended eyeglasses. The father took him for eyeglasses and the world doubled in clarity. There were few jobs to be had during these depressing years and the young poet became exactly that, writing and reading and dreaming, laughing and

crying. He cried a lot, especially over his poems and letters to distant girls he had or had not met.

*

Poe had been struck down in the streets of Baltimore in October, the month of all months he would have chosen to die.

October, we will walk your windy paths
Brisk into the lumined night.
And we will smell of iron winter's wrath
And we will taste of love's twilight.
We will walk pavements to the park
With cigarettes to light us through the dark.

It was part of a long poem he had written to his sweetheart when he was drunk on Eliot, who had certainly been drunk on Poe. In October one fell out of love. It was a dark tarn and ghoul-haunted season when the very streets and sidewalks were stained with the wet blood of oak leaves, a time for delicious self-pity. April and October were his favorite months—in Baltimore. Very proudly he would say throughout the years that he, the young poet, had been born in the hospital where Poe died when they dragged him around from Lombard Street to Broadway. Broadway where his first sweetheart lived, lower Broadway, where the poorer people lived, only three blocks above the piers for the oceangoing freighters. Ocean-going passenger ships did not come to Baltimore, only the beautiful white Chesapeake Bay overnighters to Norfolk. Still, he never thought of his city as a kingdom by the sea, and hardly ever of the ships. His thoughts faced inland, far into the city and into his room.

*

There was a cultivated ignorance about his knowledge. He knew nothing really, in the way educated people do. One knows Latin or doesn't, it's as simple as that. He "once" knew Latin, very well in fact and had translated a few poems of Catullus. He had known French but only as an American college student does, which is not enough. But he did know what he didn't know, enough to blunder only rarely. He passed for a well-educated man, and this reputation ate at his heart. He could have been that and had had every opportunity, but passed it up. Perhaps he entertained some secret peasant-like superstition that a true education would spoil his simplicity, his poetry. His poetry was both simple and "educated." He liked it that way.

*

The poet wanted to be seduced in German! Or in Japanese! He had once been seduced in French by an Australian woman without understanding a word. He was as twangy, he thought to himself, as Des Esseintes, and in fact equated language with sex. But he also considered himself a voyeur, a spectator. Americans were divided into participants and spectators. He was of the latter party, outside or in his secret room. Was there a bridge between these characteristics?

Languages notwithstanding, he was amazed how he "passed" for a native in foreign countries. On a bus in Rome he had made heads turn when he said, Excuse me, to get off at his stop. He had stood among the Romans and passengers had said casual things to him in Italian. He would smile and nod. The same happened in Paris. In Berlin he was constantly accosted on the street with questions, he presumed about directions. He had heard that American shoes gave one away—and was he trying to hide with no reason?—but it didn't seem to work in his case. Even in London—well, he wasn't that sure. He and his wife and another U.S. professor and his wife had lunch in a pub near the Keats house. At a nearby table sat two English gents dressed to the nines, cuffs, pocket handkerchiefs, every hair well-cut and in place, who simultaneously turned their gazes on the Yankees and stared for a full two minutes while the poet and his companion rattled on about Hart Crane and Keats. No question about who was American here. Still, in England an American always felt at home, like a sheep dog that has run off for a few days and comes home for a bath.

*

His invisibility acted sometimes in curious public displays of himself in the act of feeling superior. For instance, he might select a book from the public library as much for its appearance as for its content and then stroll with it down crowded streets or toward a park bench which faced a stream of traffic. He would open the book and actually read in it. He was never without a book any more than a woman was without a purse. Or if the book were of convenient size he would read it while walking, being careful of curbstones and cross-traffic. One tome he lugged for a while was a fat quarto of a popularized life of Goethe. More often it was the green and already battered copy of *Leaves of Grass,* great chunks of which he was committing to memory. Nor did it bother him

to switch from Whitman to, say, Herrick and murmur to the passing of streetcars

> Her Eyes the Glow-worme lend thee,
> The shooting Starres attend thee;

This would not be an apostrophe to the trolley but more perhaps of an exorcism of it, yet not quite that either. He loved his own world and city but could move backwards or forwards in poetic time like a rook on a chessboard.

He gibbered to his friends and they expected him to; he was already a poet and had the liberty, as the Japanese put it, of behavior other than expected. But the point of introducing gibberish was something else; he was trying out his *sui generis* language like a baby saying Da. On an April night in Baltimore at Mount Vernon Place, the most beautiful spot in the city, where the Trajan-like column to George Washington rose up over the fountains and the mansions below, he leapt from the car and yelled, *Stetson!* Who is Stetson, said a serious friend. (They were all on their way to a poker game which they played for pennies and nickels.) "You who were with me in the ships at Mylae. . . ." the poet went on. It didn't matter who Stetson was. He was a word in the sexy April air of Baltimore. It was everything that rang true and that nobody understood, except him of course. But they did understand—with a little translation.

*

The poet battened on rejections, deflections, aborted journeys, broken trysts and ran, as a great poet had it, howling to his Muse. Action was compressed into imagery, anguish into long vowels. He wrote a sonnet to the obliging but unrequited girl of Central Park West:

> O roseate tremolo
> Of lips I have not lain with nights

as a form of assuagement and an unintentional travesty of Swinburne's "O mystic and somber Dolores" not even knowing at the time of the actual whips laid on the flesh of Swinburnian lovers and their pleasure of blood. Baudelaire was already enough with his dark talk of intercourse as a surgical operation. And yet he was not so delirious with lust as he was with imagery and suggestion. When he walked past Poe's door at the University of Virginia, now a little shrine, not a student room, he would always pause and touch the door with the flat of his hand, like a mezuzah, and if no one was looking, would kiss his hand. Soon he would quit school and go home to his Baltimore study. Suffering, such as it was, would be more productive there.

And yet, by the time he had gotten to his third high school, what with the father's moves to other cities, his young poet reputation had followed him. One teacher made him act (and he hated acting ever after) in *As You Like It* with tights on his skinny legs, but pinned a sonnet on the hall bulletin board which he had written about Gandhi.

> Dim adumbration of a dim intent

said the young poet in a time when Gandhi was a culture hero. And in the Baltimore high school which was his last he would play hookey on those viscid spring days and walk seven or eight miles to Fort McHenry and sit there on Federal Hill and look out to the place in the water where Francis Scott Key, imprisoned on a British war vessel, wrote the "Star-Spangled Banner," and write another sonnet, for he was bombarding the sonnet:

> These black and slumbrous cannon once held
>   fire,
> Where now the spider holds demesne in rust,
> And men who rule these ramparts now are dust,
> And dust those things to which they did aspire

and so on. He was busy learning not only technique but how to dissent from dissent. It was the secret within the secret and it would mean battle dress.

*

He dreamed of an omnium-gatherum, the clown-word itself, to draw his dimensions in like kites. But he wasn't sure and started leafing through notebooks, those blackboards of the automatic hand which are constantly erasing themselves. He looked or rather listened for recurrence, the reprise, in those scratchings which he wrote down sometimes half-wined-up or in anger or tears. They must have some messages, dreams of a torn fabric in execrable script. Notebooks were mutterings like an old man talking to himself on the street, which he feared he did from time to time. Volubility will out. Still, he could overhear himself, his almost better self, in these musings.

Poets—the unfinished people, he read.

Creative Writing is for goyim.

"Adulterer I may be, fornicator I may be, murderer I may be, suicide not yet! Tennyson." Poor Tennyson also had been accused of committing

suicide.

He walked into the onrushing streetcar at night in a snowstorm.

The bridge over the campus, Berryman's fate.

Autobiog and versets a la Vita Nuova more or less. *The Prelude.*

How one becomes a poet, "psychic wounds and scars," distraction, interiority, tunneling (into language), symbolic speaking and acting, lack of seriousness, inadequacy as superiority, homosexual art, romantic dualism, architecture old and mod, brother & family.

The war against the poets: religious, societal.

But poets are hard to kill.

Word-fooling, killing for the word, tulgey wood, fable, dream, bleeding, beach-humor & acclaim, school humor & acclaim.

Violating the Codes. Humanities protocols. Embracing babbitry.

I didn't fit into their theory, he said.

Learning not to read books all the way through.

Burial at crossroads to confuse direction of the ghost.

O.T. and N.T. suicide not sin—Samson, Saul, Judas.

John Donne's defense of suicide (3-page list) in *Biathanatos.*

Montaigne's defense and list. Masada.

The nobility of being a Jew. The peril of it.

The Untermeyer caper.

egotistic, altruistic, anomic, alienated, idealistic.

Durkheim—lawlessness, anomie, trees of blood, hanging harpies.

Chatterton, Goethe (Werther) suicide as fashion. war poets—Homer, Vergil, Shakespeare, Milton, Whitman the poet himself—the poet distorted, his embarrassment, tempters.

the temptations, the diseases, drink, drugs, suicide, insanity catalog: the ones that strut and fret.

the ones that hide and spy.

the ones that mince, the ones who push.

(there are terrible bullies in this circle).

levels of taste in: Agitprop, Advertising, Pop poetry, "upper taste."

homo po, The Code, Hebrew prosody.

start with disclaimer.

great was the day I sat on a green park bench reading a bad

biography of Goethe

blue buicks whispered past on lake shore drive.

in Baltimore of Sidney Lanier, Lizette Woodworth Reese and Edgar

Poe.

the book was heavy and the bench was hard.

censorship at Nebraska, ostracism.
Green dance, crepe paper and rags.
Autobiographers—
Augustine, Bunyan, Fox, Wesley, Saint Theresa,
Juliana, Rolle, Saint John of, Rousseau, Casanova,
Gibbon, Vita Nuova, William Ellery Leonard, Berlioz,
Franklin, Scott, Tolstoy, Dostoevsky, J. S. Mill, H.
Spencer, Ruskin, Newman, Kropotkin, Henry
Adams—really their lives? Especially the lives of great
men are unwritable. Lesser lives do better on paper;
they have less to explain. "I knew the barber who cut
Thomas Hardy's hair," some anonymous person
once said. (How and why this touching imbecility was
recorded is unknown.)

*

When the good Professor Hazel had gotten him
a scholarship to Johns Hopkins the poet had felt
rightly that his little book of poems had forced the
lock to higher education for him, and he entered with
a high heart and would achieve at least a cosmetic
education, reserve himself for Latin and Greek and
history and read the English geniuses and lesser
lights. Pure snobbishness, he frequently thought, to
separate him from the business life and the blind
pettiness of the world outside his books. He plunged
into study with a powerful will and did perfectly. He
had to; one slip or even a fraction of a slip and he was
out. In a small tight competitive academy he had to
be within one point of perfect in grades to be on the
safe side—he who had had to be coached in algebra
and then barely scraped by, had to be perfect in
French, Latin, Greek, European history and (no
problem) English literature. The first year, three days
of final exams and all, he did it, knowing he would in
spite of an off-and-on night job at Sears, Roebuck in
the work clothes department and all day Saturday.
The second year the same, receiving his *H*s—H stood
for Honor, or 95-100 on the Richter scale—in all
subjects, with gleaming remarks on papers, including
history of philosophy which he had added. Here his
term paper was on the deism of Jefferson and Lord
Herbert of Cherbury—Virginia was never far away—
and the brilliant professor, not given to praise, wrote
compliments under his *H.* But there was an unseen
hidden flaw in the second year's work which was to
change his direction, his career, even his life, a single
comment on the final history exam on one question,
which x'd the poet out of student life forever.

The question was about the Fashoda Crisis and
colonial expansionism. And the answer the professor
wrote in the margin of the poet's essay was *Too bitter
against big business.*

In the poet's mind it was a headline that would
haunt him for the rest of his life, for the exam as a
whole was marked *B* and the *B* would cost him his
scholarship and mean the end of school unless he
could raise tuition, which was impossible. Student
loans had not been invented; such an idea was
laughable.

He went to see the history professor, a famous
history professor at that, one who was to be put in
charge of the official history of the Second World
War when it came, as it was about to do, engulfing
poet and professor in separate ways. The professor
was kindly at the interview, this fatal interview, and
even paid the poet the compliment of seeming
warmed-up or heated for a decent number of minutes, about the poet's interpretation of Fashoda, but
the verdict would stand. Guilty! The poet said
nothing about the consequences to him—he would
rather die than plead. In this he was consistent, for
not long after he could have said, I would rather die
than go before a draft board, had there been such a
thing, as there probably was.

The poet had a faculty for seeing ahead and
knew with an almost occult canniness the consequences of the single act. Sometimes he stood in
front of a mailbox for long minutes before he
dropped a letter in and in these minutes he was
reading the unborn reply and even thinking of the
strangers who would also learn of this stone dropped
in a pond that rippled in their direction. It was a kind
of wide-angle vision or prescience which prepared

*The Shapiro family, about 1952: from left, Irvin;
Margery; Father, Joseph; Karl*

him for a choice of consequences, so that whatever happened he would not be taken by surprise. The future, as it were, unveiled itself, and he was not much impressed when one of the possibilities materialized. That sort of thing didn't take much imagination—nearly all human responses are predictable, and only those that aren't are interesting. That is what fiction is all about, he thought, and continued to prefer poetry to plots.

He was both sad and relieved at his fall. No shame or humiliation entered into the matter—there was nobody who cared really. The father had disappeared, the brother had dropped out of graduate school in mathematics and was working in advertising and was about to marry his secretary. The sister was about to marry. Mother was home alone with him, suffering the hells of desertion and fears of penury or at least dependency. So he too was alone with his poems, where he wanted to be. He had done his best, better than he was capable of really, for he was not a born student, and besides, he had no academic ambitions beyond putting himself out of reach of the business world. Little did he suspect that in a few years he with his smattering of education, a sophomore undergraduate, would be brought back to the same university an an associate professor *with tenure,* the magical synonym for sinecure, a great almost unprecedented honor with a capital *H,* and which he would blithely abandon after three years for a chancy and ill-paying job as editor of the poetry journal which had accepted his first good poems.

Through the summer he wrote his first characteristic poems that would see print in a renowned poetry magazine and continued his part-time job selling work clothes and leather jackets at Sears. One day in August—the library school didn't start until the fall—as he was about to board the streetcar for the long ride to the job he opened a letter he had carried from the mailbox in the vestibule to look at on the trolley. He could see the yellow trolley floating toward him several blocks away as he tore open the small envelope printed simply *Poetry* and which he assumed was an ad. Inside was a blue slip with a letterhead, a rather pre-Raphaelite Pegasus, and the name and address of the Chicago magazine. His eye lighted on the words, "We are pleased to accept for publication" and listed four of his poems. The streetcar stopped for him and opened its door with a welcoming sigh but the poet waved to the conductor and turned and ran back to his apartment. He called the store and said he could not come in that day. Then he sat back and read holes in the blue notice and went and got the poems they had accepted and studied them with new eyes.

*

The Pratt Library, like many another notable landmark, was built during the Depression, occupying an entire block across from the important and undistinguished cathedral of the Roman Catholics, for Baltimore was an archdiocese of the universal church. The original library, gray and crepuscular, still stood around the corner and would soon be leveled and put to rest. The new building gleamed with near-white Indiana limestone, and the new librarian, also from Indiana, gleamed in the newspaper interviews and photographs. This was not just another library—this was a revolutionary concept, as the reporters were told and as they happily reported. Instead of the old passive book depository of reverence and whispers, this was a place of conviviality and happiness, of talk and cigarette smoke, for armchairs and ashtrays were everywhere in the vast hotel-like lobby flooded with actual daylight from enormous plateglass windows and skylights, and the book borrowers were customers, guests. Where were the books? Everywhere, but not immediately under the eye. For part of the revolutionary concept was the new open-shelf system (no stacks) in which every volume was accessible to the hands of the visitor. Patron was the new word used for borrower.

It was the end of March when his summons came. He must report to the Fifth Regiment Armory to be examined for induction into the army. It was only a matter of weeks before the final exams and he informed the instructor and the librarian himself, who expressed great surprise and regrets for the library. No one even dreamed of an alternative; there was no such thing. Like thousands, soon to be millions of other young men, he was saddened, bewildered, and excited. His name had been in the lottery system. What was there to do? Was he glad to be leaving the library school for something else? That couldn't be. For the army, the unthinkable. Soldiers had always been in his growing-up the least common denominator of society, sailors only slightly better. They were people who lurked in shady neighborhoods at night and beat each other up and never smiled and were stationed in places like Panama where they contracted malaria and syphilis. No one he knew had ever even known a soldier, and had there ever been one in a family he knew *entre-deux-guerres* his name would not have been mentioned. They were the really declassed. And now he was slated to be one of them. Still, he told himself, it's only a physical examination, and even if they want me it will be a long time . . . but he didn't believe that.

*

It was a Baltimore outfit by and large, with sprinklings from Philadelphia, Newark, New York (Staten Island for some reason), but strongly Baltimore, a hospital town from which to extract orderlies and other hospital workers. He was assigned to the Medical Corps, maybe because his vita, or whatever data they had, said Baltimore and then Hopkins. That would equal "medical" in the quick and simple mind of the clerk or officer who made such decisions by the thousand every day. The army, like all armies everywhere, operated within the governance of its last war, if it had won that war, as we certainly had. The defeated country's military, on the other hand, would be operating in the future, like Hitler, and would be inventing methods which would be a constant surprise to the old victors who would watch them sweep across old boundaries as if they didn't exist, and lay down their obsolete weapons in despair. The poet would notice that on the hospital forms they studied there was a place to report on the number of horse-drawn ambulances. This was 1940; what war were they thinking of? What horses? But the forms had to be filled out daily and sent on to some headquarters in Washington.

*

There began the first rankings and the poet received a stripe and he was Private First Class and carefully sewed on his stripe on each sleeve and in spite of himself felt proud when he hitchhiked home to Baltimore on weekends and could joke about his rank. By now he had been marked for office work because of his superior education and spent time at a typewriter in company headquarters, even though he would never learn to type with more than four fingers, but that somehow did not seem inappropriate to the military way. The messages were always brief and in a set stilted style, totally objective, reminding him of certain kinds of poems. His poems that had been published in a couple of little magazines were always nearby and, marvelous to say, he could show them discreetly to some of the others, for they were hospital personnel and were somehow softened by their occupation and open to such things as poetry and were at least not hostile to his interest. With the typewriter and his stripe and his poems he felt that the choice part of his life had not been interrupted too drastically, as had the lives of everyone else around him. Lucky for him he wasn't an artist who needed paints and canvases impossible to keep in a barracks, or a dramatist who needed a stage and

actors to put on it, or even a novelist with weighty drafts of books and probably a library or two nearby, or a composer who probably would quit without his piano, his vocalists, his fellow performers. In the army one could be a poet without anybody knowing it really, unless you told them, as the poet must. Writing was not suspect; everybody wrote—letters of course—many for the first time in their lives; writing is a part of soldiering, unless one was regular army. One suspected that the regular-army man never wrote anyone but transacted his business with the outside world in other ways, more directly, by deeds not words, as the saying goes. And with a number of his fellows, as he came to know them, writing poetry, though very unusual, was not alien to their tastes. One Baltimorean was a classical singer who was snatched from the conservatory to sing under the army showers; another was a violinist from Philly who volunteered to become the company bugler and was excused from drill to take his GI bugle into the pine woods to practice the calls. The poet loved the late night tattoo of the bugler with its strange wistfulness and note of farewell, a lullaby to this large lonely family whose heart ached.

*

The most highbrow literary magazine of all, and one that was printing his poems, asked him to write a monthly letter about army life and he said he would. He wrote one, about the treatment of the army to its new conscripts, how the army acted like a parent to its children, how the new not-yet soldiers were cajoled and punished like children and they put a bright orange in front of each place setting at breakfast—a huge room full of oranges! This would never do for the highbrow ultra-radical review which obviously wanted something deeper and darker. The poet knew he could not do himself or the magazine any good with this kind of orangerie and tush-tush. Should he write about the greasy cutlery, never wiped but tossed in a sheet at four o'clock in the morning, fried eggs that had petrified for six hours, bread that was gray, made from the coarsest potato flour and inedible, coffee that was not coffee? The drilling? The poison ivy? The endless scrubbing of crude floors, the open toilets, the homosexuals? He decided against it and stuck to his poems. The oranges stuck in his mind. It was all a bad kindergarten that everyone had to go to. And it would be over soon and the next bunch would have their turn.

*

A captain called the poet to his office and said, Corporal—he had two stripes by then, toward the end of his year—Corporal, I want you to go to officer training school. No, Sir, said the poet.

In nine weeks one could become an officer, with all rights and privileges appertaining thereto. One could walk into and through the best hotels in the world and be bowed to, as it were, with the fine twill uniform and good leather and a certain American sloppy hauteur which is irresistible to practically everybody. One could be highly paid, and be driven by enlisted men wherever you wanted to go. One could jump from bus driver to aristocrat in one fell swoop—in nine weeks.

No, Sir, said the poet.

Why, said the captain.

The captain was a regular-army doctor, a bad recommendation for anything in the days of the peacetime army. A doctor in the army? Unthinkable. He was a big, sallow, pockmarked, soft-looking man who shambled. He had big swimming bluish eyes. He was Jewish, the poet knew. "Because, Captain Honig," the poet answered politely, "I am getting out in a couple of months." It was early winter and the poet's year of soldiering was three quarters over. He like others in the outfit had toyed with the idea of becoming an officer, for the honor and the pay, and a couple of the men actually had disappeared into officers candidate school.

"What makes you think you are getting out?" said the captain, and the poet had no reply. All his life he would remember this mysterious question and ponder it. It was three months before Pearl Harbor.

*

The poet was sitting on his porch on that mild Sunday afternoon, working on a poem in his notebook. He could hear the radio in the living room playing *Till Eulenspiegel*, his favorite funny-sad music which he would frequently whistle in the barracks and at the typewriter. He would see his girl for a couple of hours before Delgado picked him up on the way back to camp. They would usually leave late on a Sunday night and get into camp stomach-tired. When short of sleep fatigue would manifest itself in the poet's stomach, or somewhere down there and he would feel stomach-fatigue all day. A funny place to get tired.

The lyrical wistful composition finished and Till Eulenspiegel's soul danced off into the sunset, as it were. Then there was a long silence and the poet went to adjust the dial of the radio. And then he heard news of a bombing of American ships somewhere, the announcer was not sure where; it was not a

newsy station and he switched to an ordinary number and heard excited voices breaking in on one another and such declarations as "the American navy in flames," "total confusion," "sneak attack," and such alarms. He settled down to listen as it dawned on him for the first time that he was in uniform and that the uniform meant war. Delgado called and said he was rounding up the others and that he had heard the order for all men in uniform to return to their bases immediately. It was already dark when the Ford rolled up. The poet had said goodbye to his girl on the phone; the mother was not yet home and he left her a note on the kitchen table.

*

And before long the summons came, the last roster, alphabetical with name, rank, and serial number all typed to perfection and stamped in large print POST. The sergeant went himself to post the orders and the lists. It was his privilege.

The poet himself for his own reasons felt sick at heart. He was on the verge of falling in love with New York where the poets were, the important magazines that had accepted him now, the editors that he had

Shapiro as a young soldier in Sydney, Australia, 1942

begun to contact to print his new poems in a book. And now he was to be banished from his beginning triumph, to disappear into the bowels of the leviathan and spewed up God knows where, forgotten. He never thought about being killed or drowned, even in those days when every other ship that left an East Coast harbor was sent to the bottom by the wolf packs of the Nazis. He didn't believe in his death; it was simply unthinkable. It was neither bravery nor cowardice; it was disdain. But the depression, the sorrow were almost unbearable, and he knew it was for each and every man and officer stuffing their barracks bags for the embarkation. Each GI had to have two fat bags by regulation, with all the regulation clothing, gas mask, boots, toilet articles, and whatever personal belongings he would fit in, books in the poet's case, and the requisite photo of "his girl" which seemed almost an army requirement. He was heavy with books, for a hundred-and-four-pound man, and would many times be shouted at by an officer for dragging one of the two barracks bags on the ground instead of shouldering one and gripping the other in his fist. His *Les Fleurs du Mal* he had, his Rilke *Neue Gedichte*, his own *Five Young American Poets* with his own part, his debut, taking a fifth of the book, his Untermeyer anthology, his Bible, and a few other assorted items. It was before the birth of the American paperback and the books were heavy, especially when added to in the bookshops down under where he was going.

*

The poet had few duties for the time being and went into the city by day to look for bookshops. He found a couple that reminded him of the Victorian Baltimore stores that stocked old libraries or their remains and whiled away a few hours leafing through tooled editions of minor poets but didn't want to add to the weight of his barracks bags which he knew he would be lugging for many a day. The proprietor was surprised and pleased to find a Yank soldier in his shop and gave him directions to a place that carried European highbrow journals, as he called them. The poet went there and was thrilled to find *Horizon* and *Athenaeum* and even a *Partisan Review* that had a poem of his! and several Aussie journals, one called *Angry Penguins* and another called *A Comment*, which was printed in Melbourne. He bought them all and hurried back to his camp in the beautiful park. Maybe he would find writers here, even a poet. The females in the parks and under the arches of banks could wait.

He read his own poem first, proud and homesick for New York, where the writers were and the lucky

poets walking around free. He would show the poem to some poets here, if there were any. Then he looked at the little Melbourne publication in its brown paper and staples and paste-in photographs, a labor of love for somebody. He studied one of the photos minutely, a woman dancer, naked but not lasciviously so, in accordance with the delicacies of police and church wardens, so that "in case," anyone could see that the picture was art not life. The woman dancer had tiny breasts and downturned eyes, the opposite of oriental eyes, and long blond hair. That was as much as he could discern; her private parts were hidden in a turn. He looked at the poems impassively and saw nothing exciting, read a story and a couple of reviews and a statement of purpose by the editor and the usual plea for support. He looked at the address of the publication and decided to call the editor in a couple of days or write him a note, to announce his presence, to meet other writers.

He found the editor's name in the phonebook, Quorn, Bonamy Quorn. Having never seen the Christian name before the poet thought it belonged to a man, and asked for Mr. Quorn when the lady answered. Mr. Quorn, he was told in a British accent, not an Australian, which the poet could distinguish, was in Bizerte with the artillery, and might she know who was calling. The poet announced that he was looking for the editor of *A Comment*, that he was an American, a writer. There was a pause and the lady said that she was the editor of *A Comment*. The poet fumbled for apologies and a date of meeting was arranged, her place, Malvern, one of the flowery suburbs, and she would be pleased if he would stay for dinner. He would be pleased.

*

He decided to write a book of poems and prose, snatches of prose to bridge the poems about Melbourne and love and war. She would publish it herself after he had sent enough pages and they had decided what to use. It gave him purpose and took some of the sting out of the coming separation. Even so, he was not bitter although a heavy sense of loneliness began to invade him. A soldier should know better than to fall in love but that is precisely what most of them do in time of war. He let his anguish flower as his form of bitching against circumstances; it helped "inform" his lust, his imagery, which was already sufficiently Baudelairean and Frenchified and now, he believed, antipodal. He told himself arrogantly that he would put Australia on the map. Had there ever been an Australian poet? He would show them how to be one by providing an amerigo-antipodal example. Bonamy laughed delightedly; she suffered from her own expulsion from her Mediterranean world and from Paris.

She had given him a silver ring with an ancient Greek coin and the profile of Alexander the Great and he began a prose poem about it. The ring inflicted a wound on the hand, he said, and compared it with a nail used in a crucifixion, but he avoided the word blood and there was no blood in the poem. Blood was a superfluity in time of war, in a hospital unit, though he had not yet seen a dead man. The poem "worked," as painters say about a detail or a corner of canvas, and curiously, the poem summed up as a kind of rejection of the ring. He was fascinated. No one ever knows how a poem is going to come out; it speaks for itself like a dream. The poem barely escaped being a reproof but he liked it, she liked it, and it would be the first poem in the book, *The Place of Love,* published in Australia.

Now for the first time a really portentous rumor started to circulate, like a report of cholera. Individuals were to be drawn from the roster to form tiny portable hospital units and to perform surgery on beaches and in jungles for the marines and infantry in landings. It was the beginning of the famous island-hopping strategy that MacArthur invented to shorten the war and save lives, except for those who did the actual hopping, like the portable surgical teams whose lives wouldn't be worth a nickel, with or without guns, and medical soldiers had no guns.

One day the sergeant told the poet that he was putting him on switchboard duty and that the GI going on emergency furlough would show him how the thing worked. He was given an hour of instruction in front of the old-fashioned hotel switchboard with a hundred or so red and black rubber plugs and small contact switches that moved back and forth and a multitude of red lights and earphones and he thought he could manage it. It was the beginning of the weekend and the officers were making dates in Sydney and non-coms were placing orders for supplies and truck drivers and chauffeurs were calling in and at headquarters a warrant officer wanted to place calls to Melbourne, Brisbane, and Darwin, and Naval Intelligence. It all went well for a while until the poet began to make a few mistakes. A few mistakes on a switchboard can lead to disaster; each mistake means a delay and a consequent speedup, leading to more mistakes. Red lights began to flower on the board, voices started to yell at him in his earphones, curses replaced yells, chaos reigned, and the poet took off his earphones and sat back blankly. Suddenly he had

an idea, he would pull all the plugs and start over. He gathered the snakes in his hands and let them be sucked back into their nests.

Officers began to burst into his cubicle, "Mother" Sergeant—a nickname—glared at him through the window, GIs crowded around at the commotion.

"Get that soldier out of there!" a red-faced major bellowed at everybody. Mother Sergeant beckoned to the poet who slithered out and disappeared down a long corridor. Later the poet would wonder if this fiasco had something to do with his selection for the death list, as the soldiers were already calling the beach-landing roster. An army is a structure of incompetencies but a public mistake involving the discomfiture of others is swiftly punished, as when a cook drops a bar of soap in the soup pot. There could be a bad consequence to his telephone action and he was shaken.

He was on the list.

*

Simultaneously with his letters to his girl in America, New York now, not Baltimore, and the occasional ones to his mother he was also writing Bonamy and working up their book, mostly by excerpting her purple lines and setting them off by space. The book was to have the purple tone of the fin de siècle, they agreed, of *les lauriers sont coupées,* not of the murex, the imperial dye fished up by John Keats who was not allowed to display it in life, but the soiled purple of Verlaine's erotica, not the official blue of Grecian urns. *Un peu de merde et de fromage,* as the Frenchman said. That kind of book. When a year later in New Guinea he finally got a copy he showed it around proudly, even to the officers, especially to the officers, the gentle Southern commanding officer handed it back to him with a single comment and a smile. "Too much kissing of thighs." But after all, the poet thought, he is a surgeon and he didn't imagine that surgeons went in for the kissing of thighs.

*

The poet wrote what was to be his most anthologized poem in afteryears, an elegy for a soldier who was killed, who died while he was watching, whose funeral he took part in. He was not a battle casualty, but the poet left that up in the air; he was an accidental death, maybe even a suicide. The soldier was cleaning his M-1 and it fired and struck him in the chest. Accident, suicide, battle casualty, it was neither here nor there; the poet saw his first dying, first death, first funeral—at the age of thirty. The infantryman had been carried to the palm grove on a stretcher and it was too late to operate and he was given blood and plasma and oxygen in the open tent. He expired. An officer took his dog tags and left in a recon car. For some reason the funeral was held in the palm grove next day and the poet got it all down like a reporter in the poem. He liked the poem, which used a kind of sonnet stanza which he invented. It set up the time and place. It led into a kind of funeral oration about the unknown man and his sense of history, or lack of it, and led out again into the scene itself. And it ended with an epitaph with religious benediction tones, ironic he hoped, but he was never sure. There was no message after all except inevitability, even a kind of fatalistic acceptance of the death, a consequence of one's American-ness which the poet accepted in himself and all the others. It was not a flag-waving poem and it was not an anti-flag-waving poem, a hard balance which the poet always tried for, slipping from one side to the other while his balancing pole wavered.

*

In the early morning they followed a line of ships and entered into the bay where some of them had already perched on the beach and the soldiers were moving toward the jungle with vehicles beside them. There was no firing, no noise to speak of when a marine landing barge drew alongside and a solitary marine stood up and waved a Japanese flag at them in a gesture of triumph. Simultaneously the Japanese planes came down from the mountains with their guns wide open. Most of the men didn't even have their helmets on and they all fell on the iron deck seeking whatever protection they could get, while the Bofors started their thumping firing straight up. One of the gray wooden patrol boats churned in a curve to turn back out of the bay when it exploded into a million bits. The poet's boat continued toward the beach with bombs exploding on both sides of the ship and men and bullets screaming and the Bofors grunting and pumping. The poet heard the CO yell at him, "The galley!" and he turned and followed him into the cramped cooking area where the men were already setting up an operating area and laying out the gleaming instruments in their cloths. The ship struck the sand and the ramp came down and the men raced to the trees, all except the poet's outfit who were told to stay aboard and get ready for wounded. The poet could see the stretchers coming to the little boat which was now flying the red cross as a signal and in the vain hope the Japs wouldn't strafe them. They were bombed through the night but not

hit. Everything else was. The dead and wounded were carried into the little galley and sometimes carried out again after a word from one of the doctors, all four of whom were operating elbow to elbow. After an operation, even an amputation, the patient was carried out on deck to make room. A few times the just-operated-on man would be struck again by flying shrapnel or a bullet and would be brought back in. The poet was kept busy opening wooden cases of blood plasma with a prying tool. He knelt on the floor in the din and felt hypnotized. Now and then he was called to help with the stretchers and then would go back to the cases of plasma. He tried to think of words and thought of *triage,* which was what the doctors were doing now, winnowing, winnowing the living from the dead, deciding in a split second whether a man might have a better chance than the next man and never pausing after the decision was made. He shuddered at their responsibility and was thankful to be opening crates.

The poet could never write a poem about the night of death, a night which people were experiencing all over the world. Instead he wrote a prose-poem about the next morning on the beach, a bitter and hopeless poem about a dying GI with a Spanish name.

*

It was a model hospital. Generals came to visit it and sometimes checked in for a rest if they couldn't get to Australia. The poet was assigned to write the history of the outfit, a routine journal which supposedly every outfit had to submit to the War Archives in Washington but he took great care over his entries, trying unsuccessfully to elevate the language a notch above army officialese. He knew that real historians had been assigned to battle zones on land and sea and that a poet had been made Librarian of Congress; he felt a tie to these writers. He himself had just won his first poetry prize, his mail said, and he was electrified.

His first literary admirer came to visit him, there, in New Guinea, the farthest place in the world from anywhere, and he almost felt he had expected it. He was even to have a visit from a reporter and a photographer from the army newspaper *Stars and Stripes.* The poet was delighted but not as surprised as he felt he should be. The soldier who came to see the poet was a Ph.D. student at Columbia who had been writing on modern poetry when he was drafted. He had the magazine with the announcement of the prize but how had he found the poet in that jungly place with thousands, hundreds of thousands of scattered

The poet in New Guinea during World War II, 1943

Dr. Samuel Berg

soldiers? He had taken an educated guess and called the various hospitals in the area and found him. He was attached to Special Services himself and helped serve out what entertainment and enlightenment were available in New Guinea, magazines, recordings, visiting comedians and singers, beer.

To talk with someone of his knowledge and interest was a miracle to the poet, who had only himself for dialogue. They visited back and forth and exchanged the few books they had between them. He was a Roman Catholic who bitterly resented the Church and flew into a rage when he talked about it. The poet on the other hand was fascinated by the Church and read whatever he could find about it, spurred on by the letters of his library friend who was now barraging him with beautiful letters of indoctrination and love, not exactly declarations of love for the poet but something in that neighborhood, something personal quivering under the dogma and the argumentation.

The reporter-soldier called and made an appointment and the poet sat down and typed out what journalists call a prepared statement, though it was merely a list of the magazines that had printed his poems and where he had gone to school. But the reporter looked at him archly and said, "A handout,"

and asked him a few questions while the photographer clicked off some pictures. Nevertheless the poet felt proud, and he got copies of the little article and sent them to all three women, the librarian, the dancer, and the bride-to-be. News of the interview spread around the hospital camp and the poet was ribbed and slapped on the back. He was a kind of camp mascot, a kangaroo that typed poems, and the officers talked to him with a kind of deference. One of the nurses spoke to him at some length about poetry and he longed for her, but the taboo was in force and though one might dare, one didn't know how to cross the chasm. She was good-looking too, shortly to be smuggled home for pregnancy.

*

The tremendous sense of relief which he felt, the peace of this new orderly world, sick and wounded, vulture and suicide subsumed under the name of order, an unconscious acceptance of the military way of life which he would have denied hotly if it came to discussion, that and his first recognition as poet in this the most unlikely of places in the whole world threw the poet into a religious frame of mind and created a need in him to converse with something, somebody on a higher plane. His new friend's anti-Roman diatribes only intensified his wish to get closer to *Her,* he found himself thinking, that religion that was a woman. In his own religion, insofar as he knew anything about it, there was no woman except for a few heroines like Ruth and Deborah, but they were not divine. In his religion there was only one Divinity, the angry, the impatient, the Father. The poet knew this God and felt he was on good terms with Him but he wanted something more, as David wanted Bath-Sheba. The poet had written a jazzy poem for the Australian book which was laudatory of David's lust for the adulterous woman. His new piety, if it could be called any such thing, was lustful and atavistic, the old whoring after strange gods, and not gods but goddesses. Later he would write a poem about his "conversion" in which he said, "When I say the Hail Mary I get an erection. Doesn't that prove the existence of God?"

*

But the orders gave a paragraph of what the poet thought good news: they were to be deactivated for ninety days after moving out of the hospital and were to stay in a staging area down the hill until ready. Three months and no duty, thought the poet, and started to plan a book.

He would write a verse essay on poetry, loose iambs like Wordsworth, about thirty lines a day. He started to block it out in sections. There would be three "chapters," on prosody, on language, on belief, and each chapter would have five subsections. There would be marginal glosses. He loved marginal glosses. He loved the whole idea.

They moved from the high hill down the slope to a flat area near the beach and ran a dispensary instead of a full-blown hospital. They treated base hospitals' cases, mostly nuisance cases. A marine who liked fishing went out in the bay in a rowboat and tossed hand grenades in the water to kill fish, and blew himself up. Two drunken soldiers had a drag race on a mud road and smashed themselves and the trucks in the mud. Sprained ankles were plentiful. It was generally a time for goofing off and the poet goofed off on his poem.

It was this essay on poetry—on Rime he called it ambiguously, rime as white frost, on the waves, and the old spelling of rhyme, or poetry—that really put him on the front pages before the poetry community. It would be reviewed as a book by a Harvard scholar–critic of American literature on the front page of the *New York Times* book section, and everybody would take the cue. The friendly Harvard professor exclaimed that this little work might be the foremost work of literature to come out of the war. The poet was exalted and horrified: his book was no such thing, but who was he to argue. He had the same feeling of recoil when a novelist had one of her characters say that he was reading the poems of Karl Shapiro. *In a novel!* He wasn't ready to be memorialized; he was only experimenting, he hadn't even started; to be put on a pedestal before your clay was dry was to invite disaster. He wanted to be more unknown than known. The notoriety, the glorification redeemed the years but they were premature, he hadn't earned what is called a permanent place and didn't want one. He was almost relieved when the sniping and brickbats started, and simultaneously wounded that the attacks came from his contemporaries, the poets he felt he belonged to as blood brothers. He wouldn't have minded attacks from his elders, but they were the ones who chose to praise him out of all proportion.

He wrote the book on schedule, about thirty lines a day, suave, opinionated, ex cathedra, this soldier-poet who never for a second believed that anybody would print a line of it. He sent it to his Intended, as he did all his verses, knowing she was having success in placing his poems in good magazines, and suddenly he knew that his verse tour de force would be printed also, because he had become a

In New Guinea, 1943-44

kind of phenomenon, a poet in the battle zone, which he had seen almost nothing of, who was serenely writing good poetry. The reviewers were especially impressed that this faraway poet, supposedly dodging Jap bayonets every five minutes, had no books, no access to any civilized tools. Some other soldier-poets said this was a lie, that there were plenty of books, even libraries in New Guinea. One of these critics was a poet who had moved in with the Sydney girl, who had also attacked a poem called "The Intellectual," which he misread. But then, the poet thought, everybody misreads my poems, and he wished they wouldn't. The poem wasn't about intellectuals at all—he wasn't sure what an intellectual was—but about the unfairness of the age in which some went free to stroll through corridors of paintings while others who wanted it as much or even more were consigned to the life of mud and filth and death.

*

The new book made its way quickly, even in New Guinea, and this time a Signal Corps photographer came to take his picture, one that would be his "image" for decades, a bare-chested soldier with cropped hair, sitting on the wood steps of a tent staring into his book of poems. It must have looked exotic to people back home, even more than that, had he known, like some kind of Lawrence of Arabia or Richard Halliburton. To him it looked like a photo of a common soldier sitting on the steps above the mud and the stench of the mud, unaccountably reading a book.

*

The rumor spread through the troops like a flash of lightning: they were to be quarantined! There was no way off the island, called with a bitter irony, Angel Island. What had they done, were they contaminated? Were they cursed for serving overseas while other soldiers and sailors in neatly pressed uniforms were strutting around San Francisco with their bright-eyed women and floating from bar to bar and bed to bed? An insurrectionary rage swept over the boat as they prepared to land. They had been at sea for twenty days, they had been overseas for two to three years, they had had the worst of it, and now the purgatory was not going to let up. Look, said one of the soldiers, pointing to the next island up the bay, that's Alcatraz, and they all turned and stared, for they were on their own Alcatraz now and a chant started up among the men: Alcatraz, Alcatraz, Alcatraz, intermixed with Al Capone, Al Capone, who was the most famous guest on the Rock, as the movies called it.

They were home and they were not home; they were prisoners with wounds and medals—the poet had four Bronze Stars which people in the know about military heraldry would stare at as if he were some kind of Goliath, though he had barely earned them and had only happened to be there in those four landings which merited such decorations. In later times he always meant to send to the War Department for the medals themselves and not just the ribbons and the little bronze stars, but never did. They were prisoners with wounds and medals and crack-ups and sicknesses that would never be cured and organs blighted with tropical this and tropical that, and they were incarcerated on Angel Island to stare at San Francisco across the bay, and Alcatraz, their neighbor. And to cap it all, someone said they would be allowed one phone call. The poet began to think in his fashion, the Japs have won the war; the Yanks in charge of us are traitors, we are going to be paraded in Tokyo. He looked up, half expecting to see a Japanese Rising Sun flag over the island, but no, there was the American flag. And here they were in quarantine.

The poet would get married, astrologically on the same day he was drafted, and his mother's birthday. It would be at a fashionable temple, not a synagogue; it would be a small wedding.

He wrote a poem about the wedding, a chilly T. S. Eliot kind of satire in rhymed quatrains, and printed it. It could have not sat well with anybody. He referred to the bride as an atheist and himself as a heretic. Two days before, he had gone to see the librarian who had tried to convert him. She told him where to meet her, at the handsome lounge at the top of the building at an hour when the lounge would be empty. He knew where it was. She flung herself into his arms and kissed him wildly, more wildly he thought than anyone had ever kissed him in his life, as if begging him not to get married perhaps, at least not right away, and wanted him to cross the street to the cathedral once more while she said a prayer for his marriage, but he felt he should decline, and after a while they parted in confusion.

The wedding was short and serious, with a not very rabbinical rabbi expressing his pleasure in this union of the poet and his erstwhile literary agent, for he would now do the agenting himself. There had been many articles in the Baltimore papers about the poet as soldier or the soldier as poet and his prizes and fellowships and the marriage was something of a feather in the cap of the Jewish community and it was reported in the papers with emphasis which the poet had almost already begun to expect as his due, for he was feeling his somebodyness and was finding it a little difficult not to be deferential all around.

*

All the poems in the winning book had been written while he was overseas except one, a satire on himself written in the style of Andrew Marvell, and there were as many love poems to the Melbourne girl as to the Baltimore girl and the book was well-titled *V-Letter,* or victory-letter as the photostats of mail from overseas were called, and the book would be reprinted in England on bad butcher-paper at the dead end of the war and copies of the American edition would be put into ship libraries of the U.S. Navy which he would not know about until years later when ships were decommissioned and people would send him copies from the USS *This* and the USS *That,* and that to him, though it wouldn't be to the other poets, was the major achievement, so maybe he deserved to win the Prize that he felt so ambivalent about. After a while he began to call it the Golden Albatross because he knew fairly well that he would always be able to get lectures, even jobs, even good

At the house of Robert Coates,
Gaylordsville, Connecticut, about 1945

jobs, doing what he wanted in and around poetry and he wouldn't have to sit behind a librarian's desk answering silly questions about how to address a duchess or which zoos keep unicorns, and that people who had never read a book, much less a book of poetry, much less Rimbaud or Hart Crane, would know that he had won the Prize, it didn't matter whether for cartooning or "covering" a battle or writing poems, he had won the Prize and that made him special with all rights and privileges appertaining thereto and he was hands off to ordinary occupations and preoccupations and could go his own way and do practically whatever he liked, even to not paying his bills. He would have to fight to keep the Golden Albatross from owning him.

*

There was a Southern poet of a more practical turn of mind who was visiting one of the nearby twenties people for the weekend and who asked the young poet about next year. Where was he going next year? Would he be interested in becoming the poetry consultant at the Library of Congress? It could be arranged. Of course it would mean a move to Washington, D.C., not exactly the cultural capital of the world or even the U.S.A. Without thinking or in a sense caring the young poet said yes. Simple as that. It was done, he found out later, not without literary bloodshed, for a woman poet who had already been asked to fill this post had to be postponed. What disappointment and fury this shift entailed the young poet never really found out. It was his first introduction to cultural politicking and he didn't know the rules of the game and never would though he would see enough to learn that power has a shining nakedness like electricity and can turn lives off and on with a touch of the finger.

*

The consultantship was only for a year, which didn't bother the poet who couldn't see a year ahead and saw no reason to, but one day he was invited to give a lecture at his old school, Johns Hopkins in fact, for a few faculty of the English department "on a subject of his own choice." He had an unlikely choice, prosody, a secret love the very name of which had been forgotten except among the old philologists who still had the upper hand in their corner of the small famous university. The poet had always had a penchant for this crotchety disestablished subject whose tomes had gathered dust for a century in vast libraries which coveted such things. He had done the whole bibliography on the qt for his personal predilection; he knew that most prosodists were batty Brits, eccentrics from the eighteenth century mostly, who sat in country houses trying to figure out the versification of metrical feet in Elizabethan soliloquies and because they couldn't succeed invented a Theory and then decorated the Theory with a Notational System; the poet found this not only charming but satisfying, he could have talked for days with these nuts, he was such a nut himself and he loved the people who devised these screens to keep themselves from milking cows or beating servants for stealing the silver.

He wrote his lecture, contrasting the stress and foot system of Saintsbury with the "temporal" system of the American poet and musician Lanier, also a Baltimorean of sorts and a Southern Gentleman of high repute from the Civil War days. "The obscurities of recent versification," he said, "are explained as an attempt to introduce prose structures into regularly metrical lines," and he explained the reunification of

Professor of English at Johns Hopkins University, about 1948

the two systems as a fusion of two older systems, a fusion of the North and the South, as it were.

The Johns Hopkins English department offered him a job. He took it.

*

It was all new and had a name which the poet would try to make opprobrious and never succeed, creative writing, for the university was dabbling in blueprints for writing factories and they were the blueprint. There had been one such experiment, way out on the plains of Iowa, and it was already a monumental success and a model for other English departments which had fallen into acedia and ennui and backbiting boredom and had in fact run out of gas, as the poet put it, and had become narcissistic and bitter and brittle and were ready to fly apart at the first brickbat from an administrator. Greek and Latin had long since been abolished or at least relegated, even at Oxbridge, and Literature with a capital *L* was on the proscribed list. Creative writing appealed to the psychologists as a playground for them, the sociologists, all the social sciences loved the idea, making monkeys out of writers, though they

didn't put it quite that way, and the administrators seized the opportunity to justify their seriousness as the business end of the establishment and to get bigger salaries and blacker silk suits, but so far the writers were left alone and hadn't yet been organized.

*

He already felt both wanted and out-of-place, somehow fraudulent and peaceless like an animal tortured by boys. If there was a chance to leave he would leave, to go where?

He got the chance. A letter came from Chicago asking him if he would be interested in editing the famous *Poetry* magazine because the present editor, a good poet, was not working out as an editor and would be leaving before long, and would he come to Chicago, at their expense, and talk things over. He could stay with one of the board members on the North Side or one of the board members on the South Side, the Blue and the Gray again, the poet thought, elated at the idea of leaving the East Coast behind. Something told him that the choice of where to stay, North or South, was very important, maybe even crucial. Where there was poetry there would be fights, there were always people, rich people, bored people, people on the make one way or another who wanted to stick in their thumb and pull out the plum called poetry, art, culture.

*

It was as if the poet's little absence caused him and the magazine to fall. It wasn't simply his trip to Salzburg, it was his departure from the scene, the physical absence of the one for whom the little palace of art had been built. And it was not only that he had absconded, leaving his volunteer as well as his actual family to float on their own, not simply that he had failed at the bankers' party in New York, that he had asserted his neutrality toward his patroness. There was more. He had been met with rumors of scheming, plots to take over the magazine by the patroness's business manager, now the purser of the art center and her close adviser and confidant. The magazine had not paid its bills, the manager said, and could be thrown into receivership and turned over to some executor, perhaps to be made the personal property of the owner of the mansion. The poet spoke to a couple of the Board, lawyers who watched the city from office towers, lawyers with eagle vision, who weren't about to let their pet Pegasus be led off by a horse thief.

Karl Shapiro, editor of Poetry, *meeting with Dylan Thomas, Chicago, about 1950*

*

The poet said yes to California and decided to buy a car to drive his little tribe to the Promised Land. A friend of his wife's from childhood, a kindly tough Southern meatpacker, found a beautiful secondhand Ford station wagon, all wood, a "woodie," and the poet drove it around and bought it, on time from the friend, for there was never any money at hand.

The visit was only for a semester and the wandering would start up soon again. Roethke was leaving Washington for a year and asked the poet to

Karl Shapiro with T.S. Eliot at a party in Eliot's honor at the Poetry *office, Chicago, about 1951*

"Moving from Poetry," *with Joan Farwell, about 1952*

from Beirut to Karachi, a fine way to treat a Jew, he thought, and he would never see the land of his ancestors.

*

Answers came to his self-advertisement for a full professorship (with tenure). He had not written any schools east of the Missouri, wanting to stay as far west as possible. The university at Boulder offered him an associate professorship with tenure and he carefully declined. The University of Nebraska offered him what he wanted and he took it. Interviews were not necessary. He had lectured there for a week while he was editor at *Poetry* in Chicago and they wanted him and needed him. The editor of their regionally famous literary magazine was retiring and the poet was exactly their man. It was West enough but, oh God, two thousand miles from the oranges and the sun-dusted girls and boys.

He had picked the prose poem up from Baudelaire during the war and wrote several, one of them, his best of the genre, called "The Dirty Word," and satisfied with the experiment dropped it and

take his job, and a little campus in the Sacramento Valley also asked him for a year and the poet decided that he couldn't leave the Promised Land so soon, even for Seattle which has its own kind of beauty, and he decided on the campus in Davis, even for less salary.

He was finishing his semester teaching at Berkeley when the invitation came from the State Department. He was still the editor of *Poetry* in Chicago and they wanted a poet to carry the message of Walt Whitman around the world. It was 1955, the hundredth birthday of Whitman's *Leaves of Grass* and though he would have preferred to stay in California, which he had fallen for, he agreed to go, not just to India but to several other countries beginning with *I*—Ireland, Italy, Israel. He wondered what kind of bureaucratic idiocy this could be. Why were they working on the letter *I* at the State Department? Why not Belgium, Brazil, Bolivia and Borneo? He was boning up on Absurdism at the time and getting a new appreciation of the nonsensical. And of course he wouldn't be able to land in Israel at all, because his itinerary would land him in Beirut and planes from Israel were not allowed to land there. He didn't interfere or even ask questions. His plane would go

Karl in Chicago, about 1954

Conducting a poetry seminar, about 1958

returned to his more settled ways of writing. He was not ready to commit himself to the prose thing as a method, he hadn't enough life experience under his belt in spite of the war, war is not exactly life experience but a parody of it, he would have to wait twenty years before he sat down in his study and wrote, almost at a sitting, so to speak, the whole of *The Bourgeois Poet,* you needed a stationary vantage point to do that, to pick up the kaleidoscope and start turning the bits of imagery in the mind's eye. He could see plainly that he had a start with clear sailing ahead and he could now concentrate on the form, first the typographic form, paragraph form but with the indentation reversed, the margins justified but the first line or any further paragraphing of a first line jutting to the left and the rest of the paragraph indented, roughly in the shape of the state of Oklahoma with its panhandle sticking out on the left and the body hanging from this stem. That was a simple problem solved, length was something else, what are the limits of the poem, of the book itself, and when the manuscript was completed and he had sent it to the editor, who had never seen such a thing as

this peculiar book of "poems," said drily that the only limit to the manuscript seemed to be physiological, he was right in a sense that he didn't know, that the size and shape of the poem depended on the size and shape of the piece of paper in the typewriter! A discovery, he believed, a secret, a key to prosody, the proportions 9×11, the ever-mysterious rectangle that painters had always used without saying why, the shape of books, in varying sizes but always with the same ratio. He had never before written poems on a typewriter and abhorred the idea while admiring that Williams and Cummings did, they used the typewriter as a painter uses a palette, there was something in it after all.

*

He had started scraps of his novel, hesitating to think of it as a novel, it was in the third person and he would write the whole thing in the third person when he would see that that was a mistake, his new wife would translate the whole thing back into the first person making it surprisingly less rather than more

Proofreading The Bourgeois Poet, *1964*

personal or confessional, a word he loathed, when he began to write in earnest. The book started in an airplane flying home from his European trip and began with a sentence he cherished—*Seven miles over Labrador the ice had melted in my martini,* it wanted to break into a kind of poem. He told the story of his trip abroad, of his new bachelorhood, of the woman he snuffled after, of the creative-writing madness at the university, the visit of the country's foremost guru, he called him Akiba Mem, made him a cross between Ginsberg and Robert Lowell, poets who exploited political events partly for self-aggrandizement and partly because they believed what their followers wanted them to, about his alienation from the revolutions and thus his alienation from his colleagues, about his meeting with the woman who was to become his second wife, the burning of his office by radicals, a good invention he thought, a wishful idea perhaps, his banishment to a campus greenhouse, ending with heterosexual intercourse in a snowstorm. Some of the book he wrote on the beach off Tampa, Florida, with a portable typewriter on his lap, there was no effort to this writing, he was highly suspicious of this but kept going, it flowed out, it was fun, he had no plans for publication, he seldom did, but when it

was done he had copies made and sent it off. His own publisher rejected it, large parts were obscene if not porn, he wanted to try his hand at that, most porn was so wooden and lusterless, barely even exciting, an avant-garde publisher rejected it with a slur, the millionaire avant-gardist saying he was a publisher not a grocer, this for some reason sounded anti-Semitic to the poet, he gave up sending it out and forgot it until one day someone suggested a New York publisher who had made his fortune publishing a dope-and-sex novel but who also had what are called serious writers, he sent the manuscript with a xerox of his career from *Who's Who in America* and got a prompt phone call, the publisher had read two chapters and was sending a contract, would you and your wife meet me in Las Vegas, I will be your host, he said. They went, he put them up in a huge brothel-style room with a canopied bed on a dais, and more or less Roman statues lifesize, a bathroom fit for a harem, Caesar's Palace in fact, and the publisher gave the poet's wife chips to play roulette and she won.

The book appeared in orange, magenta, and yellow stripes like a beach awning on the Riviera, a photo of the author on the inside jacket looking like a highly successful banker, there were some reviews, not many, a couple of good ones but no blockbusters, it wasn't on the front page of the *Times* like his poetry, he wasn't too concerned, he could hardly see his mixture of sex and antiradicalism as a dish for them and apparently it wasn't important enough to attack. In Lincoln, Nebraska, it caused a furor, there were attempts to ban this insult to the city which he had

Talking to Irving Howe (far right) at a party for Howe in Davis, California, 1975

Karl Shapiro with William Stafford, 1980s

called Milo, wonderful choice of names he thought, milo is a sorghum, Nebraska was sorghum country, maybe also Venus of Milo, a full page review appeared in the local paper trying to match the book characters with actual people, risky proposition for the reviewer and the poet, the publisher was arranging for him to go on a nationwide tour to be on talk shows and news segments, he had called the poet to Las Vegas to look him over for the part, the poet loathed that kind of huckstering but said yes, he always said yes first and no later, one of the publisher's staff, a very expert woman publicist would accompany the poet on his trips, all this for the paperback which was coming out shortly, they were talking to movie people about rights, who knows where this book is headed said the publisher, there was an advance of fifty thousand dollars for the paperback, not much, but the biggest money for a book that the poet had been near, until one day he received a registered letter stating in legalese that the publisher's company was in bankruptcy and that no advances or future royalties could be paid, the poet had a curious reaction, or so his friends thought, he laughed, he was not even angry except for a slight feeling of indignation about publishers in general. How can you laugh, asked one horrified English professor and the poet only looked at him, it was funny, that's why he laughed, authors weren't even

allowed at the bankruptcy hearing, they were not "preferred creditors" and the poet thought, the Muse did it.

He knelt at Auden's grave, not to pray certainly, but to twist off a sprig of what he thought was rosemary. Do people plant herbs on graves he wondered and pocketed the sprig before his third wife noticed, perhaps she would have minded, she was an Austrian herself and he had come to Vienna with her to see the city she had grown up in and to visit with Auden, as he would put it. The grave was crowded to suffocation, the poet thought, with low plantings and small flowering creepers, squeezed between a family plot on one side, a family plot on the other. Auden was at home now among the villagers he had chosen, a Roman Catholic churchyard in Austria for the great English poet who called himself a New Yorker not an American.

Auden had felt more at home in the twentieth century than any other poet, in Iceland, Italy, China, Manhattan, though always with an Edwardian nostalgia for the steam engine and the hydraulic pump, he cursed the diesel engine and mourned in horror the decay and violence of cities, robbed and assaulted even at Oxford where he was the honored guest, it would be different in Austria, safety was the order of the day, tourists back from Vienna said you can eat off the sidewalk and stroll the streets at midnight.

He wrote his tribute and elegy to Auden and liked it. The heuristic line that he prized most was one which he thought the best tribute to Auden ever made and he wanted it engraved in marble and bronze *aere perennius* to read

I come to bless this plot where you are lain,
Poet who made poetry whole again.

For Auden had ended the era of fragmentation, no more heaps of broken images, no more hoards of destruction, no more slogans saying that the fragment is king, he had miraculously healed the poem and given it back to the world.

At Auden's Grave

From Vienna it's picture-postcard all the way,
Tell me, was ever such a land at ease!
The fat farms glistening, the polished pigs,
Each carven windowbox disgorging red
Geraniums, pencil pines and chestnut trees,
The gaily painted tractor rigs,
Steeples with onion domes that seem to say
Grüss Gott, come lie here in our flowerbed.

How many times did Auden take this train
Till that bright autumn day when he was borne
Back in a baggage car after his last
Recital, back to his Horatian house,
His cave of making, now the mask outworn,
The geographical visage consummated,
Back to the village, home to the country man
Without a country, home to the urban bard
Without a city he could call his own.

But suddenly a startling word
Leaps from the signpost of the country lane,
It's AUDENSTRASSE—
The poet becomes a street, the street a poet,
English with German music mated.

Here will arrive no pilgrim mob
As in Westminster Abbey, where his name
Is chiseled next to Eliot's. The sole cab
Has never heard of Auden, has to ask
Gasthaus directions, but we find him there
Ten yards away and settled with his slab,
The bracketed dates, the modest designation,
His plot planted to suffocation
In the country style of *horror vacui.*

Close by, a granite soldier stands
Bareheaded, bowed, without a gun,
Wearing his empty cartridge belt,
A blunt reminder of the First World War,
Signed *Unseren Helden* for those villagers
Who never returned and lay somewhere in
    France
Entre deux guerres before the next
World War should be begun
By the ultimate twentieth century hun.

Far from his foggy isle
The poet rests in self-exile.
Earth of the great composers of the wordless art
Enshrouds this master of the English tune
Not many miles from where Beethoven
    scrawled his will
When he could no longer hear the trill
Of the little yellow-hammer, nor the titanic
    storm.
In such a place Dame Kind
Released the intellectual minstrel's form.

Across the *Audenstrasse* from the grave
A bee drops from the chestnut, sips my beer,
Brings back his image to me, on a day
I bought him a tin collapsible cup to sip
His whiskey from on some Iowa train,
Knowing his dread of that vertiginous plain.
Now all is comfy in his delectable cave
I scatter the bee and greet him with my lip.

Whatever commentators come to say—
That life was not your bag—Edwardian—
Misogynist—Greenwich Villager—
Drifter—coward—traitorous clerk—or you,
In your own language, genteel anti-Jew—
I come to bless this plot where you are lain,
Poet who made poetry whole again.

Sandwiched between two families Auden lies,
At last one of the locals, over his grave
A cross, a battle monument, and a name
History will polish to a shine.
Down in the valley hums the Autobahn,
Up here the poet lies sleeping in a vale
That has no exits. All the same,
Right on target and just in time
A NATO fighter rips open the skies
Straight over Auden's domus and is gone.

The poet in retirement

BIBLIOGRAPHY

Poetry:

Poems. Privately printed, 1935.

Five Young American Poets, with others. New York: New Directions, 1941.

Person, Place and Thing. New York: Reynal, 1942; London: Secker & Warburg, 1944.

The Place of Love. Melbourne: Comment Press, 1942.

V-Letter and Other Poems. New York: Reynal, 1944; London: Secker & Warburg, 1945.

Essay on Rime. New York: Reynal, 1945; London: Secker & Warburg, 1947.

Trial of a Poet and Other Poems. New York: Reynal, 1947.

The Thin Bell-Ringer. Privately printed, 1948.

Poems 1940-1953. New York: Random House, 1953.

The House. Privately printed, 1957.

Poems of a Jew. New York: Random House, 1958.

The Bourgeois Poet. New York: Random House, 1964.

Ligature 68, with others. Chicago: Madison Park Press, 1968.

Selected Poems. New York: Random House, 1968.

White-Haired Lover. New York: Random House, 1968.

Auden (1907-1973). Davis: University of California Library Associates, 1974.

Adult Bookstore. New York: Random House, 1976.

Collected Poems 1940-1978. New York: Random House, 1978.

Love and War, Art and God. Winston-Salem, N.C.: Stuart Wright, 1984.

Adam and Eve. Lewisburg, Pa.: Press Alley, 1986.

New and Selected Poems 1940–1986. Chicago: University of Chicago Press, 1987.

Fiction:

Edsel. New York: Geis, 1971.

Nonfiction:

English Prosody and Modern Poetry. Baltimore: Johns Hopkins Univ. Press, 1947.

A Bibliography of Modern Prosody. Baltimore: Johns Hopkins Univ. Press, 1948.

Poets at Work, with others, edited by Charles D. Abbott, New York: Harcourt, 1948.

Beyond Criticism. Lincoln: University of Nebraska Press, 1953; as *A Primer for Poets*, 1965.

In Defense of Ignorance (essays). New York: Random House, 1960.

Start with the Sun: Studies in Cosmic Poetry, with James E. Miller, Jr., and Bernice Slote. Lincoln: University of Nebraska Press, 1960.

The Writer's Experience, with Ralph Ellison. Washington, D.C.: Library of Congress, 1964.

A Prosody Handbook, with Robert Beum. New York: Harper, 1965.

Randall Jarrell. Washington, D.C.: Library of Congress, 1967.

To Abolish Children and Other Essays. Chicago: Quadrangle, 1968.

The Poetry Wreck: Selected Essays 1950-1970. New York: Random House, 1975.

Plays:

The Tenor: Opera in One Act, with Ernst Lert, adaptation of a work by Frank Wedekind, music by Hugo Weisgall, produced 1952. Bryn Mawr, Pa.: Merion Music, 1957.

The Soldier's Tale, adaptation of libretto by C.F. Ramuz, music by Igor Stravinsky, produced in Chicago, 1968. Chicago: University of Chicago Department of Music, 1968.

Editor of:

Modern American and Modern British Poetry, with Louis Untermeyer and Richard Wilbur. New York: Harcourt, 1955.

American Poetry. New York: Crowell, 1960.

Prose Keys to Modern Poetry. New York: Harper, 1962.

Tyrne, by Cynthia Bates, Steve Ellzey, and Bill Lynch. Privately printed, 1976.

George Woodcock

1912-

Father, Samuel Arthur Woodcock

Mother, Margaret Gertrude Woodcock, née Lewis

Now that I grow old I find myself following Voltaire's injunction and cultivating my garden in the time I have to spare from cultivating my thoughts in writing. And as I gain both a physical and an emotional pleasure from this plunging of my hands in earth, I realize that however far I may live from my ancestral lands, I am in my own way carrying on family traditions. For until my father's generation my forebears as far as I have troubled to trace them, which is back to the eighteenth century, were all workers on the land; even my father and I were involved in farming at certain times in our lives, as if we could not escape the soil.

My parents, Arthur Woodcock and Margaret

Lewis, both came from the northeastern corner of Shropshire, where their little home town of Market Drayton lay close to the borders of Cheshire and Staffordshire. It was the country of the Welsh Marches, where King Offa of Mercia had built his great dike to keep out raiders from Wales, and the population was a mixture of races, marked at their extremes by a brawny, blue-eyed, red-cheeked Saxon type with hair the colour of pale wheat, and a dark, slight Celtic type.

I know my more remote ancestors through documentary fragments and local legends. My great-great-grandfather William Woodcock had been a prosperous yeoman farmer who lived to a great age.

Once my father took me to the village church of Norton-in-Hales, and there in the vestry he showed me William's photograph as a frail nonagenarian; I later found his tottering tombstone in the yard of another church. My great-grandfather Thomas was one of a generation of farmers for whom life was made difficult by the repeal of the Corn Laws, which allowed cheap Canadian and American grain into Britain, and finally he killed himself in what his age regarded as a gentlemanly kind of suicide. I celebrated this unmet ancestor in my poem "Victorian Custom":

> Grasping the barrel,
> within season of course,
> you pulled a shotgun,
> loaded and cocked,
> through a quick hedge,
> across a stone fence.
> A thorn
> or a rock edge
> tipped the trigger,
> blew your side in.
> It was almost a
> Victorian custom.
> Speke of the Nile
> did it
> to avoid facing Burton,
> and my great-grandfather,
> Thomas Woodcock,
> to avoid facing
> a roomful of daughters
> without dowries.
> Juries of sportsmen
> returned appropriate verdicts.
> They knew
> in those days
> that life also
> is mainly accidental.

Thomas Woodcock's roomful of daughters were by his first marriage; he left a young second wife as his widow and my grandfather as his and her only son. The creditors foreclosed, the farm was sold over my great-grandmother's head, and to avoid the shame and terror of the workhouse, which in those days before widows' pensions was her only alternative, she retired to a cottage in the village and took in washing, while my grandfather left school at the age of twelve to "starve" crows, which meant chasing them from the freshly sown wheatfields with rattles and stones. Sam Woodcock worked later as a footman, and then on the Great Western Railway, and

eventually married a prim, fat little ladies' maid—Shropshire Welsh, ten years his senior and as dowdy as Queen Victoria—and with her nestegg he set himself up as a coal merchant in Market Drayton. He became a town councillor, a churchwarden, a pillar of the Tory Primrose League, but the soil was still in his nature, and he bought himself four acres of orchard and meadow, with a big brick house on it, which became one of the generative loci of my childhood. He and his Hannah had four sons; preserving a good Victorian average, two died in childhood, and my father was the elder of the survivors.

On my mother's side there was the same pattern of rural origins. My grandfather Harry Lewis was the temperamental opposite to Tory Sam Woodcock. He was a dour rebel, elder of a Baptist church and a political radical after the manner of Lloyd George. He was the illegitimate son of a rich farmer by one of his dairymaids, and although his father had endowed him with enough to buy a smallholding, he regarded the rich and the powerful with a mixture of hatred and disdain. He worked as a signalman on the Great Western, and his cabin with its brightly painted levers and its jangling bells was one of the magic places of my childhood. It was a job that gave him time to cultivate his four acres—curiously enough, the same area as Sam Woodcock's—and to rear pigs and chickens. His sandstone cottage facing out from its orchard on to the village green of Little Drayton became the other generative locus of my childhood.

My mother, his third daughter, was a tall, good-looking but delicate girl who had suffered from rheumatic fever in childhood and never, to the end of her life, enjoyed very good health, though she inherited Harry Lewis's pride and refused to surrender to pain or self-pity. By the time she met my father, she had left the village school at Little Drayton and had become an apprentice milliner, going, like the characters in *Kipps,* to work in the large women's wear stores of cities like Hereford and Worcester and to live in the dormitories over the premises. She had a taste for music from her Welsh forebears, and sang Handel more than once in the Three Choirs Festivals, which were the great musical gatherings of the Welsh border country.

Meanwhile my father had attended the old grammar school at Market Drayton where Robert Clive was once a student, and had done various clerical jobs, though his real interest was music, which perhaps first drew them together. He became a pianist and a tympanist good enough to attract the attention of the Shropshire musician, Edward German. He organized a band that played at the balls the local gentry organized at the turn of the century in the big country mansions of northern Shropshire. Finally, he was offered a position in a theatre orchestra; he seemed on the verge of a professional career as a musician.

His parents reacted with the impassioned prejudice of Victorian evangelical puritanism. The arts were permissible only as unimportant amateur pastimes. Professional artists were regarded at best as irresponsible Bohemians and at worst as dedicated immoralists, and people connected with the stage were seen as lost to Babylon. My grandmother protested hysterically at this defection of her most beloved son to the forces of Satan; my grandfather offered him a partnership in the coal business if he would give up the theatre. With a characteristic combination of weakness and obstinacy which I recognize that I inherited, my father chose a third alternative. He left for Canada in 1907.

He worked as a stableman for a Shropshire landowner who had established a ranch on the prairies. He worked as hired man for a young Englishman who was homesteading. But he had no taste for the combination of pioneering hardships and climatic extremes, and soon he drifted into Winnipeg, where he frequented such Bohemian haunts as existed there, met Charlie Chaplin when he went through western Canada with Fred Karno's troupe, and struck up a friendship with Victor McLaglen, then a hard up prize fighter; the two of them went to Cobalt at the end of the silver boom, and came back penniless. Then my father got a job on the Canadian Northern Railway and afterwards as a bookkeeper for Imperial Oil. When he was appointed accountant in 1911 he sent for my mother, to whom he was already engaged when he left England.

She in the meantime had already experienced North America; she had lived a while at Brookline, Massachusetts, where her uncle was Amy Lowell's head gardener. This was the first literary connection, to my knowledge, in the family, but given the circumstances, a peripheral one. My mother's sharpest memory of that interlude was the great fire when the Lowell stables burnt down, the horses all died, and Amy wandered the grounds like a madwoman, wailing, "My poor Gazebo! My poor Gazebo!" in grief over her favourite mastiff that had shared the horses' fate. And later, when I knew of Amy as a poet, my mother refused to take her seriously in this role, for all she could remember was a ridiculous, overbearing woman, with a hysterical disposition and, of course, the Boston saying that "The Lowells speak only to the Cabots, and the Cabots speak only to God."

My mother sailed in the spring of 1911. In May she and my father were married in Winnipeg; long afterwards, remembering the difficulties of her wedded life, she would wryly repeat the Shropshire saying, "Marry in May, you'll rue the day." I was born a year afterwards, on 8 May 1912, in the old Grace Hospital, and spent the first months of my life in the wooden building on Portage Avenue where my parents had an apartment. I have no memories of the Canadian part of my infancy, since by the autumn my mother decided she could not endure a second prairie winter. She and I sailed in October 1912, and settled provisionally with her parents in their Little Drayton cottage. Anxious to rejoin her, and tempted by my grandfather's renewed offer of a partnership in the coal business, my father followed her on the first liner to leave Montreal after the spring breakup of 1913.

Neither of them would ever go back to Canada. Yet my father longed to resume his life there and as the years went by his memories of the country grew softer, and through my boyhood, when he was trapped in the long illness from which he would die young, he talked constantly of plans to return and to go far over the prairies to the Peace River country where the white mountains would rise up on the horizon and we would build ourselves a house of poplar logs and walk in autumn through our fields of wheat billowing in the sun.

It was I who in the end returned to Canada, going beyond even the Peace River and settling far to the west within hearing of the Pacific tides. And if in these first pages I have written at length of the time before I was born, it is because I have often wondered how far my life has been shaped to give a different and less pathetic end to my father's.

My memories begin to establish themselves in the ancestral setting of Shropshire, where we lived after my father returned in a semidetached house in Frogmoor Road, Market Drayton. The other half of the building was inhabited by my father's boyhood friend Kent Godwin, another frustrated musician who lived by selling insurance. But my first recollection—an extraordinarily vivid and concrete one—is not of the sonatas they played together, or of the tin drums which in those belligerent early years of the Great War the Godwin boys and I would beat in the echoing little arched passage that ran between the two houses, but of the wedding of my aunt Jessie, my mother's youngest sister, when I was three years old. So much that characterized the belated Victorian world in which I spent my first conscious years is encapsulated in that memory.

The wedding took place in the Baptist chapel

George Woodcock, aged three, with Grandmother Hannah Woodcock, née *Rodgers*

where Harry Lewis was an elder and his daughters sang in the choir. I remember the biblical texts glittering in gold lettering as the sun shone through the windows on to the green walls, and the loud and sonorous singing. Singing, flowers, the smell of polished pews, and then, clear as a photograph, the scene as we left the chapel: the older men in frogged and braided frockcoats; the women corsetted in hourglass dresses, topped by hats like great extravagant mushrooms, and enveloped in ostrich-feather boas that were still having a last flicker of fashion in that backwater of social change; and me, among them, a lumpy infant in a brown-velvet suit and a large and detested lace collar. I remember the excitement of jumping and shouting among a crowd of adults who had lost their customary gravity, wildly hurling confetti at my aunt, and then the swaying clatter of the horse cab as we rode away, the mouth-drying smell of dust and straw in its upholstery, and the grinding sound of its iron-tired wheels clattering over the cobblestones towards my grandfather's cottage. There the wedding breakfast took place, in the great kitchen where hams and flitches of smoked

bacon from Harry Lewis's pigs hung from the smoke-black beams. Here the territory to which my stature entitled me was the floor of worn bricks which I shared with Jack, my grandfather's mongrel dog, the dearest friend of my infancy. I was observant of what happened at the table, standing tiptoe with my chin on the edge, fascinated by the little silver balls on the wedding cake that was served to me in homeopathic mouthfuls. But the most exciting incident of all, which perhaps imprinted the wedding so sharply on my mind, was Jack's feat of catching a mouse that had incautiously emerged to share in the feast. He ate it in front of the assembled guests, and I remember the guts of the mouse spurting out around his teeth like grey spaghetti in tomato sauce as he bit the poor beast in two.

It was still a premechanical world in which I lived my Shropshire infancy. Hardy's "man harrowing clods / In a slow silent walk" was a regular sight on the farms that prided themselves on their heavy, hairy-footed shire horses. A drive in an automobile was a rare and exciting treat in a world where everyone drove around in pony traps. People ran out of the houses to look at the training planes that occasionally flew over the town from the nearby military aerodrome.

Otherwise, to my family at least, the war seemed remote. My mother's brother, drunken Uncle Harry, had enlisted in the Coldstream Guards to get out of worse trouble, had been sent immediately to the front in the British Expeditionary Force, and had managed to get himself taken prisoner and out of the conflict in the first week of the war. My father, already beginning to suffer from Bright's disease, was rejected for military service. Even the shortages of wartime affected us little, for we lived in a semisubsistence economy, growing our vegetables and fruit, and benefitting from Grandfather Lewis's pigs and Grandmother Woodcock's eggs and the other produce such as milk and butter that filtered through the barter system to anyone who had surplus food to offer. Even the shops in Market Drayton seemed generous in what they had to sell if my olfactory memory serves me well, for, in among the whiffs of horse dung from the streets and of hot metal and burning hooves from the black-smiths' forges and of leather from the saddler's shop, I scent the intriguing mélange of smells from the era before packaged foods that assaulted an infant's nostrils entering Billington's grocery store, smells emanating from its bags and bins and barrels, from its spice boxes and red-and-gold tea caddies, from the coffee prepared in a grinder operated by a great iron handwheel, from the hanging hams and flitches of bacon, from the great wheels of Cheshire cheese (the best of it made in northern Shropshire as we would contend with local patriotism), and the aromatic piles of crusty and pungent gingerbread, which was a local speciality.

In this secure, abundant little backwater, change came slowly. Ladies of my grandmother's age still went to market veiled and gloved, with skirts that almost licked the dust. People had doubtless heard of socialism but there were no socialists among them, and only the railwaymen belonged to a labour union. The Russian revolution in 1917 created a mild stir and "God the All Terrible" would sometimes be sung in church on a Sunday instead of "For Those in Peril on the Sea," since it was felt that the Tsar perhaps needed divine help more than the British navy. Otherwise religion, whether it was Sam Woodcock's Low Church Anglicanism or Harry Lewis's Baptistism, was evangelical and dogmatic. We had no truck with ritualism, and we sang hymns with loud enthusiasm because they were the only liturgy we knew. Darwin's name was not even mentioned, and Bishop Ussher's argument that the world began in 4004 B.C. was accepted without question. Every word of the Bible was literally true, and most Sundays, the dour Scottish parson of Emmanuel Church, where Sam Woodcock was warden, contrived to remind us of hellfire.

It was Mr. Thompson's preaching that led me into my first antireligious experience. According to him, an unfailing cause of damnation and hence of punishment by hellfire was the lack of love for Jesus. A dawning sense of logic told me, at five years old, that I could only love a person I knew, like my grandfather Sam or Jack the dog, but that I did not know Jesus and obviously could not love him. While I troubled myself with this question I began to have a strange recurrent dream, in which the road outside our house in Frogmoor Road would open beneath me, and I would go falling down (never reaching the bottom) in a chasm among rocks that were burning with blue and purple incandescent flames. The dream recurred at intervals for several years. Curiously, I never had the sensation of being burnt by the flames, and this, I decided, was a sign the Devil had indeed claimed me for his own. I accepted this conclusion with equanimity, and from that time onwards, though I observed the forms of religion until my adolescence, I had no faith. In later years, though I have tried to live according to the ideals of human brotherhood that I believe inspire all great religions at their best, I have been drawn towards those currents, like Buddhism and Taoism, that demand no belief in the supernatural.

Round about 1917 my father's health declined so

much that he could not carry on the often heavy work involved in running a coalyard, so he left the business of S. Woodcock and Son, and we moved away to Altrincham in Cheshire, where he worked as bookkeeper in a flour mill. There the war seemed nearer, since there were a number of military camps in the area, and columns of troops would often march down the street past our house, with bands playing; I detested the noise of them, and would run to hide in the damp earthy quietness of the cellar. But it was a silent march that lingered most insistently in my mind. A long column of German prisoners of war was routed through our street on their way to a special camp a few miles out in the country; the authorities seem to have thought a Caesar's triumph would boost local morale. British soldiers in their familiar khaki uniforms marched as escorts. But it was the prisoners in their field-grey or sometimes navy-blue uniforms who drew everyone's attention. Their desperate melancholy, their sense of helpless defeat impressed itself even on my child's mind, as I think it did on the minds of all the women and old men who came out of the houses to stand and silently stare.

I was a very fair little boy, with corn-coloured Saxon hair that in later years, perhaps as my Celtic ancestry asserted itself, turned darkish brown until, in my early twenties, I became prematurely white like most of my mother's family. On that day in the spring of 1917, as we watched the prisoners march by, my mother held me in her arms and one of the Germans looked at me with his tired eyes and suddenly smiled. He said a word to the man marching beside him and looked again and smiled a second time with a great sadness. By an immediate intuition I knew that I reminded him of his own child. I remember the incident as one of life's few epiphanies.

My father's job at the flour mill was only temporary. He knew that if its previous occupant returned from the wars he would have to abandon it. So, to find some more lasting employment, he used what we called "pull" with some old friends in high positions in our family's customary haven in time of trouble—the Great Western Railway. And in 1918 he went south to Marlow, on the Thames, about thirty miles outside London, where there was a vacancy for a goods clerk at the station. It was a temporary job, miserably paid, and because of his chronic ill health it would never become permanent, but it lasted him for the rest of his short life. He searched for a house, but the town was filled with prosperous Londoners fleeing the Zeppelin raids, and the only home he could afford was a wretched little hovel in an early Victorian brick terrace, so primitive that we relied on a pump to bring us water populated by visible creatures and on a paraffin lamp for our light. My mother wept when she first saw its four cramped rooms, two up and two down, but we never climbed far enough out of poverty and discouragement to find anything better, and it remained our home until my father's death in 1927 and my mother's in 1940, by which time we had at least the amenities of piped water and electricity.

The discomfort and inconvenience of our new home were bad enough, though my child's eye found in it all a novelty and adventure my parents did not perceive. Worse was the social stigma of which, as members of a shabby, genteel lower middle class detached from its peasant roots, my parents were perpetually conscious. We were certainly as poor as many of the people among whom we lived, and poorer than some, but we were still conscious of being too good for the working-class area to which want had condemned us. I was not allowed, I quickly learnt, to become too intimate with the children of our neighbours, lest I acquire their bad habits and—even worse—their frightful accents, in England the unerring index of class. My mother was so ashamed of her home that she could not invite people she regarded as her social equals. This meant that she could not accept invitations she might have to repay, and so, as a family, we had many acquaintances in Marlow and few friends. Yet I cannot recall that this made me especially unhappy. One can find ways of making almost any condition liveable, and, more instinctively than deliberately, during my life in Marlow, I picked the kind of friends who, like me and my parents, had no real place in the social structure of the town, and to whom our genteel poverty could be safely exposed and our meagre hospitality offered: the son of an Italian chef at a local hotel and the son of a French mystery woman who tantalized the town for a few seasons; the dyslectic son of a local builder whom I befriended and helped at school, and a Roman Catholic boy (an ardent entomologist and an excellent Latinist) in a town where Protestantism was militant and the old religion was regarded as a kind of treason to be ritually and uproariously rejected every fifth of November when we danced around the bonfire where we burnt the effigy of Guy Fawkes.

I am running ahead of my narrative, and here I should turn back to admit that our primitive little house did not become for me the prison it might have been. Sam Woodcock, as a good Shropshireman living north of the River Trent, which was always regarded as dividing the English into North Country people and Southerners, regarded with apprehension the possibility that his only grandson might be brought up entirely in the wicked South. I would forget the Shropshire way of speaking, I would forget the blunt straightforward manner of Salopians, and grow up an effete and shifty Cockney. So—as soon as I started at school, which happened not long after we reached Marlow—he invited my parents to send me to Market Drayton for every school holiday, and this continued through my childhood until I left school at the age of seventeen.

My life became, as it turned out, fruitfully divided. By the time I entered grammar school, I was spending three-and-a-half months a year in Market Drayton and the rest in Marlow. But the equation was more complicated than that, since in Marlow I lived in a time-obsessed world and in Market Drayton in a subjectively timeless one. Though I turned out to have a naturally scholarly bent, and learnt quickly and easily, I never liked schools, where I first realized how much more frightful people encountered in the mass are than people met as individuals. So I regarded each school term as a kind of limited purgatory, and on calendars and inside my classroom desk I would keep the tally of days until my mother and I could go on our day-long train journey through the English Midlands—through the Chiltern chalk hills and the Oxfordshire meadows and past the dark satanic mills of the Black Country and into the rich sandstone lands around the Wrekin—until we reached my grandfather's great house and the fields and orchards around it, where the tensions relaxed and I lived almost without consciousness of time until that evening when my mother would arrive to stay the night and take me back to another round of purgatory.

It was out of this personal dialectic that my being as a writer emerged. Marlow developed my mind and Market Drayton nurtured my imagination. In Marlow I went to a dame school and then to a village school (to preserve me from the ill-spoken toughs of the elementary schools in town), and finally to Marlow's ancient grammar school, Sir William Borlase's, which was founded in 1624 and masqueraded as a minor public school. This meant that our first eight rowed against Eton's third eight at Henley Regatta a few miles upriver, and our first cricket team played against Harrow's fourth, while we had a few boarders who had been expelled from better schools and were marched *en crocodile* to church every Sunday, dressed in Eton bum-freezer jackets and top hats and jeered at by the dayboys, who were in the majority. Still, Borlase's standards were high, it had a handful of fine and dedicated teachers, and by the time I reached the Upper Sixth I was learning the kind of things I later taught students at sophomore level in American and

Canadian universities. I did not like the cult of sportsmanship nor was I impressed by Borlase's imperial pretensions (it specialized in preparing boys for minor posts in India and the colonies), but I soon learnt the devices of evasion.

But school learning, even at its best, in England then, was tightly related to the requirements of standard examinations like the Oxford School Certificate and the London Matriculation. Only occasionally did the more adventurous masters venture into literature beyond Wordsworth or history beyond Waterloo. It may have been a liberal education, but it was hardly an adventurous one, and the gaps were filled at home. For, as well as being a failed musician, my father was also a writer manqué, and his frustrated love for literature had found a substitute in bibliophily. He loved handsome books and old books, first editions and facsimile editions, and, despite his poverty, he had such an eye for bargains at sales and on bookstalls that he accumulated a fine library that astonished everyone who entered our hovel and saw the packed shelves around the walls of our front room. Back from Shaw and Wells and Wilde and the decadent poets, it ranged to Blake and Keats, to Sir Thomas Browne and Izaak Walton, to Sir Kenelm Digby and Henry King, to Captain John Smith's account of the settlement of Virginia and William Lithgow's *Rare Adventures and Painful Peregrinations,* and to the splendid reprint volumes of the Tudor Translations, in which I read with growing interest the old Greek romances like Heliodorus's and the essays of Montaigne, Machiavelli's *Florentine Wars* and Bandello's Renaissance tales, and dipped surreptitiously and with growing delight into Boccaccio and into Rabelais in the vigorously scatological version of Sir Thomas Urquhart; splendid training texts for an aspiring prose writer.

In this way, during my school terms, I began to acquire not merely an unorganized knowledge of literature, but also a taste for it. At the same time I began to develop a passion for natural history, which my father encouraged by buying me the travel narratives of the great Victorian naturalists, like Darwin's *Voyage of the "Beagle"* and H.W. Bates's *Naturalist on the River Amazon.* And there those long summer holidays at Market Drayton took their place, and I spent them day after day in close contact with the world of living beings, first in the four acres of Sam Woodcock's orchards and meadows, and then, year by year, in a widening circle of hills and woodlands and mosses (as we called our boglands) and ancient villages and the Jacobean town itself with its great colourful weekly markets. It seemed to offer an unspoilt rural ambience, to which I became so

devoted that for a while my only ambition was to withdraw there for good, and when circumstances took me away from that idyllic setting I felt for long a sense of deprivation that I have found adequately described, curiously enough, only in one of the less celebrated pieces of A.E. Housman's *Shropshire Lad:*

> Into my heart an air that kills
>   From yon far country blows:
> What are those blue remembered hills,
>   What spires, what farms are those?
>
> This is the land of lost content,
>   I see it shining plain,
> The happy highways where I went,
>   And cannot come again.

I gradually developed friendships there as well, and one of them was with a young poet (one of the tin-drumming Godwins of my early childhood) with whom I competed in celebrating the girls glimpsed in the gaslight of Saturday night *paseos* who became the objects of our romantic infatuations.

I read the nineteenth-century scientists and the Elizabethan poets. I wrote at sixteen a natural history of Market Drayton based on my observation of birds and beasts and flowers (following on my father's exhortations "to watch and see—to keep your eyes at work") and I also wrote what I still feel were creditable pastiches of sixteenth-century poets. One of them, a neat derivative exercise entitled "My Lady's Eyes," survived the destruction of most of my juvenilia:

> The diamond shineth like a star
>   When held up to the light,
> And e'en when taken in the dark
>   It still doth glitter bright;
> But O, no gem of any size
> Can glitter like my lady's eyes.
>
>   The violet demure and coy,
>   The springtime's azure flower,
> Is fit to grace some wood nymph's fane,
>   Or great Diana's bower,
> But Flora can no flower devize
> As pretty as my lady's eyes.

I wrote those verses six years after *The Waste Land* was published, and the fact that I could have done so shows how isolated much of even relatively sophisticated English society outside London itself was from the contemporary currents of literary modernism. Yet as soon as I became aware of modernist trends, there was a magnetism that drew me forward from derivation to derivation into originality. I wrote Georgian poems and imagist poems, and with three of my schoolfellows put together a magazine reproduced by some jelly process which we would rent out for a penny a read to our classmates and thus make a little money to buy ourselves books of poetry. But it was not until I was well into my twenties that I began to find my own voice, and then immediately my work was accepted by the characteristic English magazines of the late 1930s, like Geoffrey Grigson's *New Verse* and Julian Symons's *Twentieth Century Verse* and shortly afterwards by Dwight Macdonald at the *Partisan Review.*

In the meantime a great deal had happened to change my life and make it more desperate. When I was fourteen my father eventually died of his kidney sickness. Somehow or another, by vast sacrifices, my mother kept me at school. I had been undecided whether I should become a biologist or a writer, but I found that biology in the 1920s was a much more technically oriented discipline than it had been for the great nineteenth-century naturalists; in any case, I recognized that I had been drawn to them mainly by their clear and vigorous prose, and I chose to imitate the prose rather than the science. But having decided my destiny was to become a writer, I was faced with the double problem of getting entry into the literary world and of taking my father's place and keeping the household going until I began to earn money with my writing. A university education might have given me access to the right literary circles, and this was the course my teachers urged me to follow, particularly after I was placed in the top 3 percent in the London Matriculation examinations of 1928. But there was no universal access to higher education in Britain in those days. Universities were regarded as the domain of the privileged classes, and one needed money to enter them. I might have won a scholarship, but that would not have been enough without extra funds.

At this point Grandfather Sam Woodcock intervened. He had always wanted a clergyman among his descendants to rival the Archdeacon of Stoke who belonged to another branch of our family. If I would agree to become an Anglican priest, he would support me at Cambridge. On such issues I had already made up my mind in childhood, when I decided that I could not love a Jesus I did not know; in the interval Jesus had not sought my acquaintance, and I felt that to accept my grandfather's offer would be shamelessly hypocritical. Besides, I was so shy a young man that I could not imagine myself standing in a pulpit to interpret the intentions of the Lord.

So I turned down my grandfather's offer, left my

school, and followed a family tradition, now three generations old, by taking a job on the Great Western Railway. It was 1929, the economy was collapsing around our ears, unemployment was growing apace, and I only got the job because we were an old railway family with "pull." And for eleven years, before my mother's death in 1940 finally liberated me from obligation, I worked as a clerk and a bookkeeper for railway engineers.

The Great Western Railway by this time was an old, venerable Victorian institution, and in the interstices of its crumbling structure a parasitic population of eccentrics and dilettantes found a refuge. Discipline was lax, and wandering from office to office in the long corridors of the general office under Brunel's great metal arches at Paddington Station, I found encouragement for all my artistic or intellectual inclinations and all my rebellions. There were always people who knew a little more than I in particular areas and who were willing to share with me their knowledge and discoveries, so that my introduction to the very vital/world of the arts in London between the wars was often eased by these chance acquaintances. And I myself grabbed voraciously everything the city had to offer, spending what pence I had on gallery seats for plays at the Old Vic (fivepence to hear Laughton in *Cherry Orchard*) and for ballet and opera at Sadler's Wells (sixpence for *La Bohème* or *The Marriage of Figaro*) and becoming converted to instant balletomania when Colonel de Basil's company arrived at Covent Garden with such great dancers, immortal in the memory, as Massine and Danilova. The Ballets Russes, with their splendid scores by Stravinsky and de Falla and their visual echoes of the cubist and Fauvist traditions, were veritable schools in the contemporary arts. I also haunted the museums and art galleries, and just as I worked my way in poetry from the nineties to the thirties, so I worked my way in painting from the Pre-Raphaelites to the *dernier cri* of the surrealists.

Politically I responded to the fluidity of ideas at that period, and read widely without any immediate sense of the need to commit myself in that forest of exciting alternatives until one summer's evening, when I was going home from my daily drudgery and reading a volume of William Morris's socialist writings in an empty railway carriage, I suddenly had a kind of conversion, relating my present lot to the general condition of the world, and knew that from this time on I would be dedicated to rebellion, which on the whole turned out to be an accurate premonition.

I began to look for causes. Convinced of the enormity of war, I became a supporter to the No

Broadcasting "Voice" at the BBC, September 1942: standing, from left, George Woodcock,
Mulk Raj Anand, George Orwell, and William Empson; sitting, from left,
Herbert Read and Edmund Blunden

More War Movement and then of the Peace Pledge Union. I dabbled with socialism, joining the Labour Party and then the Independent Labour Party for short periods. I came into contact with communists, but I had a temperamentally libertarian inclination that made me suspect any authoritarian politics, of the left as much as of the right, and so I avoided the disillusioning kind of involvement with Stalinism into which so many English writers of the 1930s were drawn. I had heard rather vaguely of anarchism, and when the Spanish Civil War began in 1936, I realized for the first time that it was not merely a romantic doctrine of the nineteenth century, long since superseded by Marxism, but a political way of life still followed by millions of Spaniards. Nevertheless, when I did decide that I myself was an anarchist, I came to it by a very different way from the Spanish anarchists, who were fighting physically against their enemies. I came to it through my pacifism, which led me to refusing the authority of the state on a vital issue like war, and so by ultimate implication to denying its authority on any issue.

I reached all these conclusions through my own thought, supported by conversations with schoolmates and workmates and friends as far from the centres of intellectual life as I myself still was. In my childhood and youth I knew only those writers who happened to live in or near Marlow, like Jerome K. Jerome, Rebecca West, and L.H. Myers, and with them I had no more than acquaintance; I was far too diffident to force myself on them as an aspiring colleague. The first editor to take me up was A.R. Orage, who printed some of my poems in the *New English Weekly* when I was twenty-one, but Orage died and it was another five years before I began writing the poems that attracted editors interested in contemporary trends, and then I began to form friendships with other poets of my late 1930s generation, notably Roy Fuller, Julian Symons, Dylan Thomas, Derek Savage, and Kathleen Raine.

Nineteen forty was a year of crucial changes. My mother died, and I gave up the cottage at Marlow where my formative years were spent and moved to London, beginning a rather nomadic period. In the same year my first book, a volume of poems called *The White Island,* was published by an eccentric pornographer named Caton, whose Fortune Press combined the printing of under-the-counter novels with the publication of young poets; Cecil Day Lewis, Dylan Thomas, Roy Fuller, and I were all first published by Caton, who had never been given due credit for his encouragement of young poets in the late 1930s and early 1940s. I also started in 1940 my literary magazine, *NOW.* Many magazines, including *New Verse, Twentieth Century Verse,* and T.S. Eliot's *Criterion,* had closed down when the war began. To fill the gap Cyril Connolly and Stephen Spender had founded *Horizon,* but that tended to cater to establishment writers, and I felt a journal was needed for young writers and for writers who went against the grain of the times: pacifists, anarchists, dissident socialists. *NOW* ran intermittently until 1947, and if *The White Island* drew attention to me as a poet, the magazine gave me a position in the literary world, and many of the writers who appeared in its columns, such as George Orwell and Herbert Read, Alex Comfort and Roy Campbell, Mulk Raj Anand and Henry Miller and Kenneth Rexroth, became my friends.

Nineteen forty brought another moment of decision. Long before I registered for military service I had made up my mind to become a conscientious objector. I went before the tribunal and was granted exemption provided I carried on agricultural work, so I gladly gave up my job with the Great Western Railway. My mother's death had released a legacy from old Sam Woodcock that relieved me of the immediate need to earn a living, so I went first to live and work for a while in a pacifist community founded by John Middleton Murry at Langham in Essex. I quickly realized that I did not have the humility or the self-discipline needed to fit into a community, and went off to do work clearing the land on old derelict farms near Cambridge. There the editing of *NOW* gave me entry into literary circles and so in the end, despite Sam Woodcock, I had my experience of Cambridge intellectual life without needing to succumb to academic drudgery. In 1942 I moved back into London and for a time worked a small suburban truck garden.

Now, through Herbert Read, I came into contact with the group of young anarchist intellectuals who ran Freedom Press. For a few years, working with them, I became a kind of political activist, writing for their paper, *War Commentary,* which at the end of the war became *Freedom,* and eventually becoming its editor, in collaboration with Marie Louise Berneri, a

With Marie Louise Berneri, 1947

brilliant and beautiful Italian who died young in 1949 and while she lived became my closest friend. With Herbert Read and George Orwell I also ran a small civil liberties group called the Freedom Defence Committee, which got out of jail a few people arbitrarily imprisoned under wartime regulations and generally acted as a watchdog group for infringements of civil liberties; I saw a great deal of Orwell at this time and his influence came at a crucial time in my development as a writer.

It was now that I began to take prose seriously for the first time. I began with pamphlets on various aspects of anarchism which Freedom Press published, ephemerae that occasionally crop up in antiquarian book catalogues at startling prices (thirty dollars for a threepenny brochure!). Eventually, out of my libertarian studies, I wrote my first major book. This was *William Godwin* (1946), the first modern biography of that pre-anarchist thinker. It was unexpectedly successful, getting praise from literary mandarins like Harold Nicholson, Charles Morgan, and H.N. Brailsford, and so, in a modest way, my career was launched and I entered seriously into the process of becoming a professional writer.

I did all the things young London writers then did to maintain a necessary cash flow. I wrote reviews for magazines like the *New Statesman and Nation* and *Time and Tide.* I wrote London Letters for Dwight Macdonald to publish in *Politics* in New York. I gave occasional radio talks for the BBC. I did free-lance editing and reading for publishers. I compiled an anthology to celebrate the centenary of the year of Revolutions, 1848. And I found the time and energy to write three more books that hovered between biography and literary criticism, on Aphra Behn, Oscar Wilde, and Peter Kropotkin, as well as putting together a book of essays, *The Writer and Politics,* which reflected my experience as a poet engaged in radical journalism. These books aroused the same kind of interest as *William Godwin,* were reviewed favourably and intelligently by leading critics. *The Paradox of Oscar Wilde* became my first book accepted by an American publisher, and a French publisher undertook a translation of *The Anarchist Prince,* the book on Kropotkin.

Clearly I had made a good and rapid start on a literary career in England. But I was perversely restless, and the urge to wander began to afflict me. I had already been to France before the war—to Paris and Provence, and after six years cooped up there during the war, England had begun to seem a very small island, even with Wales and Scotland. Inge Linzer had become my companion in 1943—we would marry in 1949 at the same Kensington registry office as D.H. Lawrence and Frieda—and as soon as the frontiers began to open we went to the continent of Europe: to Switzerland in 1946, to Holland in 1947, to France several times. Far from being satisfied, our desire for travel grew; even in comparison with continental countries that had been ravaged by the war but were quickly recovering their spirit and their ways of life, England in the later 1940s still seemed deprived and dismal, kept in a needless austerity by an unimaginative Labour government from which, when it was elected in 1945, people expected everything.

How could we escape? Having been born in Canada, I had always carried a Canadian passport, so that I could enter the country of my birth at will, and in the spring of 1949 we sold most of our books and set off on one of the Furness Line cargo-passenger boats that plied the route from Liverpool via St. John's to Halifax and Boston. Our friends thought we were crazy, except for George Orwell, who laconically remarked: "The sort of country that could be fun for a bit, especially if you like fishing." (He did.) A sad finality was given to our departure by the death of my dear friend and fellow anarchist, Marie Louise Berneri, unexpectedly, at the time our boat lay overnight in the harbour of Halifax. I dreamt of her death in the hour it happened, and when I received the cable confirming it, I knew that my links with the past were being severed. Orwell died eight months later.

For a long time it seemed as though the friends who thought us mad were right. We went with a kind of Tolstoy-Thoreau idea of combining writing with farm work, and bought ourselves a piece of land on Vancouver Island within sound of the Pacific breakers. The place was idyllic visually, the change of pace was exhilarating, the new ways of life among loggers and fishermen were intriguing. But we had been deceived over the land, which was worked out. Our money ran short on building a house even though we sawed every plank and knocked in every nail ourselves. There were almost no ways in which a writer in western Canada at that time could earn much locally, and, out of sight being out of mind, my agent did little to further my interests in Britain. To top it all, the pound was heavily devalued, and my income from Britain, on which I had relied, fell sharply. But even if there had been great demands for my work, farming and carpentry left me too tired for months on end for serious writing. A Guggenheim grant that took us to France and California was a lucky break in that period, but by the time we extricated ourselves from the rural life in 1953 and went to Vancouver, I had nothing except experience to show for my four years, since I had destroyed the novel I began while I was there, having learnt enough in the agonizing process to make me a good critic if not a good writer of fiction.

There followed a period lasting from 1954 to 1963, when I taught at universities—Washington and British Columbia—and alternated my teaching with long travels. I had never taught before, and on the first day I entered a classroom I was certainly the most frightened person there, my hands trembling visibly as I handed out reading schedules to my students, but I discovered an unexpected histrionic streak in myself and became a popular and, I think, a good teacher, constructing a course on continental European fiction and drama that fitted my interests and enabled me to talk with love and understanding on the books I offered. I found that my lack of a degree told in my favour with the students; they admired and envied someone who had made it from outside the system and competed with the professional scholars on their own ground.

The travels took us first to Mexico in 1954, then to Peru in 1956, and on several returns to Europe, until in 1961 we went to India for the first time and acquired a liking for the country that would lead us back for five long trips in later years. My return to writing was largely connected with these travels, and also with my renewed study of anarchism, this time from a less committed and partisan viewpoint. Out of the travels appeared books like *To the City of the Dead* (about Mexico, 1956), *Incas and Other Men* (about Peru, 1959), and *Faces of India* (1964). India also led

*George and Ingeborg Woodcock, née Linzer,
with Harold Orlans at the
Pyramid of the Sun, Teotihuacan, Mexico*

me to write some historical books—*The Greeks in India* (1966) and *Kerala* (1967)—and a study of its greatest leader, *Mohandas Gandhi* (1971). These travels and the studies arising from them certainly widened my view of life and the world, and they forced me to adopt a broader and less partisan stance towards anarchism in the books I wrote at this time, which I consider my best in that field. In *Pierre-Joseph Proudhon* (1956), researched on my Guggenheim trip to France, I found myself so deeply moved as I told the life of the great French libertarian that I began not only to think like him but even to share his physical states, so that by the time I finished the book I was suffering from the asthma of which he died. Once the book was finished and the biographical identification died away, I never had asthma again. *Anarchism* (1962) was the first complete history of libertarian ideas and movements ever written, and it confirmed my belief

in the essential truth of the natural sociality of man that underlies anarchist doctrine, while it freed me from the need to sustain my loyalty to the passing manifestations of that great doctrine of personal and collective liberation. It turned out to be the most enduringly successful of all my books. I have revised it again and again for new editions, and now, twenty-five years later, it is still selling as broadly as ever it did.

The late 1950s brought me into two other new fields of creation. I had been giving talks and preparing documentaries for the Canadian Broadcasting Corporation ever since reaching Canada in 1949, but in 1959 one of the drama producers induced me to write radio plays for him, and for the next decade and a half I wrote a steady flow of original plays and adaptations of stage dramas, including a series of burlesqued crime dramas out of writing which Inge and I got a great deal of fun and quite a lot of money. I found writing drama satisfying in two ways; for various reasons I had virtually ceased writing poetry when we left England for Canada, and verse plays were a way of luring the muse out of reclusion, while in drama I found a way of presenting the fictional situations I had not been able to handle satisfactorily in the novel form. The radio play is an odd, ephemeral genre that rarely lends itself to print, but a few of mine were eventually published, and one of them, *The Island of Demons,* was performed on the stage. But for me drama was really a divertissement, a way of releasing flights of fancy, and my successful *jeux d'esprit* were holidays of the mind, outside the general flow of my interests, which took a serious change in direction at the end of the 1950s when at last, after a decade living in Canada, I finally began to feel that I was committed to this new country that was also, by chance of birth, my native land.

In 1958 we returned from a year's sabbatical, which I had mostly spent writing in France, supported by blocked funds which the Canadian government was spending on grants to writers and artists who wanted to work in Europe. As soon as I got back to the University of British Columbia, a group of my colleagues approached me with the suggestion that I might become the editor of a new quarterly the University planned to initiate. I enjoyed editing, and since the cessation of *NOW* I had been hoping that I would have the opportunity to operate or even create a magazine. But the field proposed for UBC's new magazine made me hesitate; it was to be a critical journal dealing with Canadian literature, and since our arrival in 1949 I had acquired only a rather superficial knowledge of Canadian writers and what they had written. My colleagues refused to accept this as an answer. They rightly felt that the prime need was for an experienced and imaginative editor; my books suggested to them that I had an unusual power of mastering a subject when I set my mind to it, and that as soon as I began to deal with Canadian literature as an editor I would quickly learn. And if I became editor, my teaching load would be halved. That offer perhaps convinced me more than their arguments, and I accepted and set to work, so that in 1959 the first issue of *Canadian Literature* appeared. Dismal prophets gave it only a few issues to live. There were so few books by Canadians to write about. And where would I find people to discuss them? Critics were even scarcer in Canada than poets or novelists.

The nay-sayers were proven wrong, and to this day *Canadian Literature* flourishes as a senior review, though I gave up editing it in 1977. It appearance coincided with the beginning of a great upsurge in Canadian writing on whose crest the journal rode. There was never any lack of new books or new authors to write about, and the magazine served as a kind of focus for what critical trends existed in Canada at the time. Not only did the few established critics gather round, but I set about persuading poets and novelists to discuss their own and each others' works, and I also found a whole generation of younger critics emerging in the universities, where the study of Canadian writing was at last being taken seriously. *Canadian Literature* lay at the centre of this development, and while I would not claim that it had much influence on creative writers (except in so far as being taken seriously sustains a writer's confidence) the magazine certainly was the beginning of a serious critical tradition in Canada. And the emergence of a critical tradition is one of the signs that a literature is gaining maturity, which that of Canada did during the 1960s and 1970s.

As I carried on with my writing I found myself more and more drawn into the Canadian literary world, and slowly began to cease thinking of myself as a kind of English writer living abroad. Canadian writers accepted me and became my friends; I entered into their problems and read their books, and very soon I was not merely editing a magazine devoted to Canadian writing but was taking an active part in the critical process. In the end my contribution was so generally acknowledged that it gained me not only the Molson Award, the highest cultural prize in Canada, but also five honorary doctorates; after the fifth I felt that I should operate the Apollonian maxim—moderation in all things—and I declined the four that were offered afterwards. I also declined the

Order of Canada because this was a state honour, and my anarchism remained too strongly implanted for me to accept.

Among the lasting results of my immersion in Canadian writing were books on Mordecai Richler and Hugh MacLennan, and three volumes of essays on Canadian writing which discussed most of the important writers—*Odysseus Ever Returning*, *The World of Canadian Writing*, and *Northern Spring*, the first appearing in 1970 and the third in 1987. Parallel with my interest in Canadian writing, my interest in other aspects of Canadian life and history developed. My wife and I travelled over the whole country, twenty-five thousand miles of inter-looping journeys, including the Arctic, and I wrote a number of books that ranged over the broad terrain from cultural to political history.

One of these books was the first complete history of that strange Russian sect, the Doukhobors, who fled with Leo Tolstoy's help from Tsarist Russia to Canada in the 1890s and then found themselves persecuted by Canadian democratic governments as well. I wrote *The Doukhobors* with my friend Ivan Avakumovic, with whom I had collaborated during the 1940s on *The Anarchist Prince*, and my studies in connection with this book, and later with films and radio programmes that sprang out of it, led me into a close acquaintance with these incredibly hospitable religious rebels who offer the world's only superb vegetarian cuisine. I made many friends among them, and they appreciated my interest so much that sometimes they would refer to me as "the Canadian Tolstoy." Inge and I at one time thought of settling among them, for we shared their pacifism and were fascinated by their music, but I realized in good time that if I accepted their offer of building a house and remained with them I would condemn myself to becoming a kind of pet wise man. I had lived in a close-knit community once in my life, in the early years of World War II, and I realized it offered no place and no way of life for a person of my critical temperament.

I also wrote some general books on Canada—impressionist social histories like *Canada and the Canadians* (1970) and *The Canadians* (1979), and balanced them with more polemical works like *Confederation Betrayed* (a protest against Pierre Trudeau's attempt to centralize Canada's essentially confederal society) in 1981, and *Strange Bedfellows*, a discussion of the relationship between the state and the arts in Canada, in 1985. I wrote biographies of Canadians who fascinated me for their sharp individuality, like Amor de Cosmos, the eccentric British Columbian journalist-politician named Smith who rechristened

The house the Woodcocks built with their own hands at Sooke on Vancouver Island

himself Lover of the World, and Gabriel Dumont, the generous-hearted guerilla warrior of the Métis rebellion in 1885; both books appeared in 1975. *Amor de Cosmos* was one manifestation of the intense regional loyalty I developed over the years to British Columbia, a local patriotism so strong that eventually I defined my position as that of a Canadian by birth and a British Columbian by choice, with the implication that choice made the greater bond. I celebrated this loyalty with other books, including first a pictorial history of the province, then an anthology of West Coast writers illustrated by the splendid landscape photographs of Janis Kraulis, which we called *British Columbia: A Celebration,* and finally a book reflecting the deep interest in the great artistic and ceremonial culture of the West Coast Indians which began in my first years in Canada when I found their splendid artifacts crammed in a little troglodytic museum in the basement of the Parliament Buildings in Victoria, British Columbia. That book was called *Peoples of the Coast,* and its appearance greatly angered the local ethnologists who refused to accept that a non-professional might write with understanding about matters in the field. Curiously, American, French, and eastern Canadian ethnologists, who either reviewed the book or discussed it with me, were much more appreciative. It was an interesting experience of the insecurity

of narrow specialists faced by a creatively generalizing mind, and I learnt from it.

But this immersion in things Canadian did not diminish my interest in the world beyond; I have always found that cultural regionalists are far more cosmopolitan in their sympathies than political nationalists. Inge and I still travelled to Europe and India, particularly after 1963 when I gave up teaching and merely edited *Canadian Literature* for the University of British Columbia, with freedom to depart when and where I wanted. Our involvement in India had already been complicated on our first visit there by a series of coincidences that led to our meeting the Dalai Lama in his refuge in the Himalayan foothills and seeing the distress among the hundred thousand Tibetans who had followed him into exile in 1959. We promised to help, and when we returned to Canada in 1962 set up a Tibetan Refugee Aid Society which worked with similar groups in other countries and eventually did solve the problems of the refugee Tibetans by establishing agricultural settlements for them around Mysore in southern India. Out of that work emerged a warm personal friendship with the Dalai Lama that still continues.

But our work with the Tibetans, which led us into the remote jungle areas where we settled them, also taught us how deep was the poverty among marginal groups of the Indians who were the Tibetans' willing or unwilling hosts. When India became independent Gandhi declared that the first aim should be to solve the problems of the villages where 80 percent of the people lived; until the existence of the villagers was made acceptable, the problems of the cities would be endless, since they would be constantly invaded by villagers who had lost their land or had never owned any. Gandhi's views were disregarded; India set out to become a modern, militarized nation-state and the villages where most Indians lived were quickly forgotten. Now, as a result, India has become a classic example of the former colonial country where the rich are getting richer and the poor poorer, and a heartless and flamboyant middle class grows in wealth, influence, and corruption while an estimated three hundred million people, more than a third the country's present population of eight hundred million, live without land, or regular employment, or adequate shelter. It is these people, often thrust from their land by ruthless moneylenders, who swell the population of the frightful slums around cities like Bombay and Calcutta. It is easy to push the problem aside as too large to be soluble, but one can always do a good deal in an apparently hopeless situation if one makes a start on even a small scale, as we had found with the Tibetans. So, adopting Gandhi's motto, "One step enough for me," we and a handful of Canadian friends started Canada India Village Aid in 1981, devoted to modifying one of the most glaring of Indian inequalities—that 75 percent of the people still live in the villages while 75 percent of the medical facilities are in the towns. We are all volunteers, but even without professional fund raisers we have collected money enough to set up clinics, training schemes for village health workers, and build small dams in villages where there is a threat of drought, in five different states of India, from the Himalayan foothills down to the poorer parts of Tamilnad in the far south.

With a writer, whatever he does tends to be grist for the mill. Thanks to my involvement with the Tibetans, I developed an interest in past European connections with them, and wrote a book, *Into Tibet* (1971), on early British travellers to that country; to help raise funds for Canada India Village Aid I went to India in 1982–3 with a Canadian painter, Toni Onley, and together we prepared a travel book, prose and paintings, which we called *Walls of India*, since Toni painted mostly buildings or mountains (the great wall of the Himalayas) while I wrote of walls of a different kind, the social walls of caste and language and religions that still divide India, as they did in the days of the Raj.

My wanderings over the earth had already, by the early 1970s, covered much of the former British Empire. They were rounded out in 1972 by a trip to the islands of the South Pacific, followed by trips in later years to Australia and New Zealand. In 1972 we went with a Canadian Broadcasting film crew for five months through the islands from Tonga and Samoa to the Gilberts, the New Hebrides, the Solomons, and eventually New Guinea, with Fiji as our pivotal centre, making a series of nine films—called "In the South Seas"—on primitive cultures subjected to the long impact of white intrusion. We were amazed how much of these fragile lifestyles had in fact survived and what strange and sometimes pristine images of human community we were able to create. Inevitably, a book emerged, *South Sea Journey* (1976).

I had started on my great travels a determined anti-imperialist, and I do not think that in any real way my attitude changed. But I did find myself forced into admiration by the sheer effrontery and capability with which the British maintained their rule over such vast areas with small armies and even smaller squads of civil servants. And I also developed an interest in some, at least, of the administrators, who genuinely improved conditions, or who showed a special interest in the cultures of the colonized people, or who merely carried out with fairness and without corruption, and often in depressing circumstances, the duties they had accepted. It was all very well, I found, to sneer about "the white man's burden," but for many their work was indeed burdensome and carried out with some real hope that they were preparing the way for Indians and Africans and South Sea Islanders to become European-style democrats.

This interest led me to agree when Peter Quennel invited me to write *The British in the Far East* (1969), a kind of social history of the British of all kinds who had ruled the scattered colonies from Malaya eastward and had populated the trading concessions in China and even for a while in Japan. And a few years later I wrote a kind of inquest on imperial decline, *Who Killed the British Empire?* (1974).

But for all my involvement in Canadian affairs and my excursions into history, literary criticism with a social flavour remained at the centre of my preoccupations, and the interest I developed in Canadian writers did not diminish my consciousness of being part of the larger tradition of English writing; this consciousness, and also a certain friendly piety, led me to write a series of what I called "intellectual biographies," less than full Lives but more than critical studies, of English writers, two of whom had been close friends and all of whom had influenced me greatly in my formative years. They were *The Crystal*

Spirit: A Study of George Orwell (1966), *Dawn and the Darkest Hour: A Study of Aldous Huxley* (1972), and *Herbert Read: The Stream and the Source* (1972). *The Crystal Spirit* was perhaps the best and certainly the most successful of these; it won the Governor-General's Award for Literature and it is still in print. In 1984 I supplemented it with a more polemical book, *Orwell's Message: 1984 and the Present.* At the same time I sang my swan song as a writer for radio by preparing and narrating the five-hour radio biography of Orwell which the Canadian Broadcasting Corporation aired on New Year's Day, 1984, and which was carried also over the NPR network in the United States.

My cycle of critical books was completed in rather curious circumstances, for one day I had a visit from two priests, one Anglican and one Catholic, who were preparing a celebration of Thomas Merton and invited me to write a brochure for them. I took it on as a kind of whimsical challenge, for it seemed to me that not two writers could have been less alike than Merton and I; I found we had an extraordinary amount in common, and the brochure grew into a book, *Thomas Merton, Monk and Poet* (1978), which to my further surprise was hailed by Merton's associates and friends as one of the best studies ever written of him.

I have left to the end the more personal aspects of my writing in recent years, the poetry and the autobiography. Since I first began writing as a poet, I have always regarded this as my original and most precious vocation, yet for the middle third of my life, from 1949 to 1974, I wrote no more than six lyric pieces. By 1949 I had published three volumes, and when I left England for Canada in 1949 I had no doubt that a continuous poetic career lay ahead. But when I reached Canada the inspiration withdrew. This may have been partly due to the disturbance of my life by the changeover to an unfamiliar and temporarily poverty-stricken way of life. But I showed myself resilient and adaptable in other ways, and changes in one's creative patterns usually have deeper causes than economic anxiety or physical discomfort. And indeed I have always been convinced that my failure of voice as a lyric poet at the beginning of the 1950's was mostly due to my inability to find a way of expressing adequately in verse the deep grief I felt over the death of my friend Marie Louise Berneri in 1949. I felt I had failed in some unforgiveable way, and this sense of failure was what made me fall silent.

Certainly it was the deep feelings arising from witnessing two people close to me dying in the early 1970s that released my inspiration and set me writing poetry again. I had published a volume of *Selected Poems* in 1967 in a mood of resigned acceptance that my career as a lyric poet—though I was at the time writing dramatic poetry—was in the past; I saw the book as a kind of monument. But by 1976 I had enough new poems to add them to a new selection from the past and publish them as *Notes on Visitations;* they were poems, as I said then, that sang:

> . . . .of death
> and the dark love
> that grows in
> death's dark shadow
> like the purple blossom
> of soldanella
> thawing its way
> up through the radiant
> snow.

Through the rest of the 1970s and the early 1980s the impulse continued, and I thought that, now my muse was liberated, I would probably continue as a poet for the rest of my life. I published three small collections of new poems, of which *The Mountain Road* (1981) was the most memorable, and then, in 1983, gathered the lyrical and elegiac pieces of a lifetime and published them as a *Collected Poems.* The result of this hubristic act was that my muse again took her departure; since the *Collected* appeared I have written a mere handful of occasional poems. I have no idea whether I will write lyric verse again. Certainly the intermittencies of my poetic career have led to my being regarded as a prose writer rather than as a poet, which I often regret.

I have written two volumes of autobiography. The first of them, *Letter to the Past* (1982), covered the first half of my life, from 1912 to 1949, when I left England to return to Canada. The writing of the book was an experience in itself, for as I wrote day by day my memory opened out in the most extraordinary way, with forgotten incidents constantly fighting their way to the surface of my mind, yet at the same time I was aware that in the very process of emergence these recollections were undergoing a kind of Proustian shaping, and that what flowed from my mind as I sat at my typewriter was a selective arrangement of the past that in its own way was as fictional as a novel. The facts were there indeed, but the mind interpreted them and transformed them so that they ceased to be merely literal. And so, without lying, my two volumes of autobiography are the most imaginative books I have ever written. The second volume, *Beyond the Blue Mountains,* carried my life through the Canadian years and the great foreign travels to the end of the 1970s;

George Woodcock, about 1980

as I write this essay, that book is going through the process of publication.

With my seventy-fifth birthday just a month away as I complete this essay, I find that my need to write, my desire to experience anew, have not diminished. I am about to make my first journey to China, and shall travel on its remoter frontiers. I have two more books in the process of final revision for publication; one a cultural history of nineteenth-century Canada and the other a history of the known world in the amazing sixth century B.C. I have other books planned for the years ahead. I still write for many magazines and work daily at my typewriter. And I cultivate my fruit trees and flower beds and leave it to others to change the world, though at times I offer them advice across the garden wall.

BIBLIOGRAPHY

Poetry:

The White Island. London: Fortune Press, 1940.

The Centre Cannot Hold. London: Routledge & Kegan Paul, 1943.

Imagine the South. Pasadena, Calif.: Untide Press, 1947.

Selected Poems. Toronto: Clarke Irwin, 1967.

Notes on Visitations: Poems 1936-1975. Toronto: Anansi, 1975.

Anima; or, Swann Grown Old: A Cycle of Poems. Coatsworth, Ontario: Black Moss Press, 1977.

The Kestrel and Other Poems of Past and Present. Sunderland, England: Ceolfrith Press, 1978.

The Mountain Road. Fredericton, N.B.: Fiddlehead, 1980.

Collected Poems. Victoria, B.C.: Sono Nis Press, 1983.

Nonfiction:

William Godwin: A Biographical Study. London: Porcupine Press, 1946; New York: Irving Ravin, 1946.

The Incomparable Aphra: A Life of Mrs. Aphra Behn. London and New York: Boardman, 1948.

The Writer and Politics: Essays. London: Porcupine Press, 1948; Folcroft, Pa.: Folcroft Press, 1970.

The Paradox of Oscar Wilde. London: Boardman, 1949; New York: Macmillan, 1950.

The Anarchist Prince: A Biographical Study of Peter Kropotkin, with Ivan Avakumovic. London and New York: Boardman, 1950.

Ravens and Prophets: An Account of Journeys in British Columbia, Alberta, and Southern Alasksa. London: Wingate, 1952.

Pierre-Joseph Proudhon: A Biography. London: Routledge & Kegan Paul, 1956; New York: Macmillan, 1956.

To the City of the Dead: An Account of Travels in Mexico. London: Faber, 1957; Westport, Conn.: Greenwood Press, 1975.

Incas and Other Men: Travels in the Andes. London: Faber, 1959.

Anarchism: A History of Libertarian Ideas and Movements. Cleveland: Meridian, 1962; Harmondsworth, England: Penguin, 1963.

Faces of India: A Travel Narrative. London: Faber, 1964.

Asia, Gods and Cities: Aden to Tokyo. London: Faber, 1966.

The Crystal Spirit: A Study of George Orwell. Boston: Little, Brown, 1966; London: J. Cape, 1967.

The Greeks in India. London: Faber, 1966.

Kerala: A Portrait of the Malabar Coast. London: Faber, 1967.

The Doukhobors, with I. Avakumovic. London: Faber, 1968; Toronto and New York: Oxford University Press, 1968.

The British in the Far East. London: Weidenfeld & Nicolson, 1969; New York: Atheneum, 1969.

Henry Walter Bates: Naturalist of the Amazons. London: Faber, 1969; New York: Barnes & Noble, 1969.

Hugh MacLennan. Toronto: Copp Clark, 1969.

Canada and the Canadians. Toronto: Oxford University

Press, 1970; London: Faber, 1970; Harrisburg, Pa.: Stackpole, 1970.

The Hudson's Bay Company (for children). New York: Crowell-Collier, 1970.

Mordecai Richler. Toronto: McClelland & Stewart, 1970.

Odysseus Ever Returning: Essays on Canadian Writers and Writing. Toronto: McClelland & Stewart, 1970.

Mohandas Gandhi. New York: Viking Press, 1971; also published as *Gandhi.* London: Fontana, 1972.

Into Tibet: The Early British Explorers. London: Faber, 1971; New York: Barnes & Noble, 1971.

Dawn and the Darkest Hour: A Study of Aldous Huxley. London: Faber, 1972; New York: Viking Press, 1972.

Herbert Read: The Stream and the Source. London: Faber, 1972.

The Rejection of Politics and Other Essays. Toronto: New Press, 1972.

Who Killed the British Empire? An Inquest. London: J. Cape, 1974; New York: Quadrangle, 1974; Toronto: Fitzhenry & Whiteside, 1974.

Amor de Cosmos: Journalist and Reformer. Toronto: Oxford University Press, 1975.

Gabriel Dumont: The Métis Chief and His Lost World. Edmonton: Hurtig, 1975.

South Sea Journey. Toronto: Fitzhenry & Whiteside, 1976; London: Faber, 1976.

Peoples of the Coast: The Indians of the Pacific Northwest. Edmonton: Hurtig, 1977; Bloomington, Ind.: Indiana University Press, 1977.

Faces from History: Canadian Profiles and Portraits. Edmonton: Hurtig, 1978.

Gabriel Dumont (for children). Don Mills, Ont.: Fitzhenry & Whiteside, 1978.

Thomas Merton, Monk and Poet: A Critical Study. Vancouver: Douglas & McIntyre, 1978; Edinburgh: Canongate, 1978; New York: Farrar, Straus, 1978.

The Canadians. Don Mills, Ont.: Fitzhenry & Whiteside, 1979; Cambridge, Mass.: Harvard University Press, 1979; London: Athlone Press, 1980.

100 Great Canadians. Edmonton: Hurtig, 1980.

A Picture History of British Columbia. Edmonton: Hurtig, 1980; Seattle: University of Washington Press, 1982.

The World of Canadian Writing: Critiques and Recollections. Vancouver: Douglas & McIntyre, 1980; Seattle: University of Washington Press, 1980.

Confederation Betrayed: The Case against Trudeau's Canada. Madeira Park, B.C. Harbour, 1981.

Ivan Eyre. Don Mills, Ont.: Fitzhenry & Whiteside, 1981.

Taking It to the Letter. Montreal: Quadrant, 1981.

Letter to the Past (autobiography). Toronto: Fitzhenry & Whiteside, 1982.

Orwell's Message: 1984 and the Present. Madeira Park, B.C.: Harbour, 1984.

Patrick Lane and His Works. Dover, N.H.: Longwood, 1985.

Strange Bedfellows: The State and the Arts in Canada. Vancouver: Douglas & McIntyre, 1985.

The Walls of India. Toronto: Lester & Orpen Dennys, 1985.

Northern Spring. Vancouver: Douglas & McIntyre, 1987.

Beyond the Blue Mountains (autobiography). Toronto: Fitzhenry & Whiteside, 1987.

Plays:

The Benefactor. Lantzville, Ontario: Oolichan, 1982.

Gabriel Dumont and the Northwest Rebellion (broadcast as *Six Dry Cakes for the Hunted*, 1975). Toronto: Playwrights Co-op, 1976.

Two Plays (includes *The Island of Demons* and *Six Dry Cakes for the Hunted*). Vancouver: Talonbooks, 1977.

Translator of:

The Métis in the Canadian West, by Marcel Giraud. Edmonton: University of Alberta Press, 1986; Lincoln, Neb.: University of Nebraska Press, 1986.

Editor of:

A Hundred Years of Revolution: 1848 and After. London: Porcupine Press, 1948; New York: Haskell House, 1974.

The Letters of Charles Lamb. London: Grey Walls Press, 1950.

Rural Rides, by William Cobbett. Harmondsworth, England: Penguin, 1963.

A Choice of Critics: Selections from "Canadian Literature." Toronto: Oxford University Press, 1966.

Variations on the Human Theme. Toronto: Ryerson Press, 1966.

The Egoist, by George Meredith. Harmondsworth, England: Penguin, 1968.

The Sixties: Writers and Writing of the Decade. Vancouver: University of British Columbia Press, 1969.

A Tale of Two Cities, by Charles Dickens. Harmondsworth, England: Penguin, 1970; New York: Greenwich House, 1982.

Malcolm Lowry: The Man and His Work. Vancouver, University of British Columbia Press, 1971.

Wyndham Lewis in Canada. Vancouver: University of British Columbia Press, 1971.

Typee: A Peep at Polynesian Life, by Herman Melville. Harmondsworth, England: Penguin, 1972.

Colony and Confederation: Early Canadian Poets and Their Background. Vancouver: University of British Columbia Press, 1974.

Poets and Critics: Essays from "Canadian Literature" 1966-1974. Toronto: Oxford University Press, 1974.

The Canadian Novel in the Twentieth Century: Essays from "Canadian Literature." Toronto: McClelland & Stewart, 1975.

The Anarchist Reader. London: Fontana, 1977; Atlantic Highlands, N.J.: Humanities Press, 1977.

The Return of the Native, by Thomas Hardy. Harmondsworth, England: Penguin, 1978.

British Columbia: A Celebration, edited with J.A. Kraulis.

Edmonton: Hurtig, 1983.

A Place to Stand On: Essays by and about Margaret Laurence. Edmonton: NeWest Press, 1983.

Twentieth-Century Fiction. London: Macmillan, 1983.

Sound recordings:

Utopias: Pro and Con. Toronto: Canadian Broadcasting Corp., 1972.

Cumulative Index

CUMULATIVE INDEX

For every reference that appears *in more than one essay*,
the name of the essayist is given before the volume and page number(s).

INDEX

INDEX

INDEX